ANGLO-NORMAN STUDIES XIV

PROCEEDINGS OF THE BATTLE CONFERENCE

1991

The present volume includes papers which embody important new research on a very wide range of topics in the fields of history, archaeology, literature and palaeography. The second Allen Brown Memorial Lecture on 'Belrem' offers a new interpretation of some of the castles in the Bayeux Tapestry; and other military themes are considered in studies of the fortification of Rouen in the ducal period and horse-armour in England before the Conquest. Historical papers range in time from the Anglo-Saxon period, with new investigations of bookland, folkland and fiefs and the early endowment of the see of London, to the reign of Stephen, where topics include finance, *conventiones* and the activities of Ranulf II earl of Chester. Three papers, on the charters of King David I, the counts of Boulogne, and Adela of Blois, concern the frontiers of the Anglo-Norman realm. Other papers investigate the work of the scribe of the Margam Annals, French literature in twelfth-century England, the size and structure of the Anglo-Norman family, and the fraternity of Rochester cathedral priory about 1100.

ANGLO-NORMAN STUDIES

XIV

PROCEEDINGS OF THE BATTLE CONFERENCE

1991

Edited by Marjorie Chibnall

THE BOYDELL PRESS

First published 1992 by The Boydell Press, Woodbridge

The Boydell Press is an imprint of Boydell & Brewer Ltd
PO Box 9, Woodbridge, Suffolk IP12 3DF, UK
and of Boydell & Brewer Inc.
PO Box 41026, Rochester, NY 14604, USA

ISBN 0 85115 316 X

ISSN 0954–9927
Anglo-Norman Studies
(Formerly ISSN 0261–9857: Proceedings of the Battle Conference
on Anglo-Norman Studies)

British Library Cataloguing-in-Publication Data
A catalogue record for this series is available
from the British Library

Library of Congress Catalog Card Number: 89–646512

This publication is printed on acid-free paper

Printed in Great Britain by
St Edmundsbury Press Ltd, Bury St Edmunds, Suffolk

CONTENTS

ILLUSTRATIONS

Anglo-Scandinavian Equestrian Equipment in Eleventh-Century England

Figures

The Author of the Margam Annals

Plates

The Endowment and Military Obligations of the See of London

Figure

EDITOR'S PREFACE

This volume includes all the papers read at the fourteenth Battle Conference, held in Pyke House, Battle, in July 1991. It is a particular pleasure to be able to include the second Allen Brown Memorial Lecture, delivered by Dr Arnold J. Taylor to a packed audience on 'Belrem' – a subject which most appropriately concerns both castles and the Bayeux Tapestry.

Once again the Conference was full to capacity; its success was due to the kind sponsorship of the East Sussex County Council Education Committee and the help of Mrs Gillian Murton, Mr Ian Peirce, and Mr Peter Birch with his wonderful staff at Pyke House. The Outing was to Canterbury; Mr Tim Tatton-Brown generously gave his time to escort us round the city, from the Castle to St Martin's Church and from the Cathedral precincts to the Hospital of St Gregory, and to bring to life from his intimate knowledge the history, topography and archaeology of Canterbury. We thank him most warmly.

Some of the papers in this volume have involved complicated setting, and we are indebted to Dr Richard Barber and the highly-skilled editorial staff at the Boydell Press for their help in producing the *Proceedings*. The reproduction of the 'long strip' of the Bayeux Tapestry was made possible by the kindness of Mrs Elly Miller, who lent the original plates used for the Phaidon edition of the Tapestry and gave her permission for their use in this volume. We are very grateful to the British Academy for a subvention that enabled us to meet the heavy expenses involved in making this special illustration. The photographs illustrating Professor Patterson's paper are reproduced by courtesy of the Master and Fellows of Trinity College Cambridge and of the National Library of Wales.

Clare Hall, Cambridge *Marjorie Chibnall*

ABBREVIATIONS

Antiqs Journ.	*The Antiquaries Journal* (Society of Antiquaries of London)
Arch. Journ.	*Archaeological Journal* (Royal Archaeological Institute)
ASC	*Anglo-Saxon Chronicle*, ed. D. Whitelock *et al.*, London 1969
Battle Chronicle	*The Chronicle of Battle Abbey*, ed. Eleanor Searle, Oxford Medieval Texts, 1980
BIHR	*Bulletin of the Institute of Historical Research*
BL	British Library
BN	Bibliothèque Nationale
Cal.Docs France	*Calendar of Documents preserved in France* . . . i, 918–1206, ed. J. H. Round, HMSO, 1899
Carmen	*The Carmen de Hastingae Proelio of Guy bishop of Amiens*, ed. Catherine Morton and Hope Muntz, Oxford Medieval Texts, 1972
De gestis pontificum	William of Malmesbury, *De gestis pontificum Anglorum*, ed. N. E. S. A. Hamilton, RS 1870
De gestis regum	William of Malmesbury, *De gestis regum Anglorum*, ed. W. Stubbs, RS 1887
Domesday Book	*Domesday Book, seu liber censualis* . . ., Vols. 1, 2, ed. A. Farley; Vols. 3, 4 ed. Henry Ellis, 'Record Commission', 1783–1816
Dudo	*De moribus et actis primorum Normanniae Ducum auctore Dudone Sancti Quintini Decano*, ed. J. Lair, Société des Antiquaires de Normandie, 1865
Eadmer	*Historia novorum in Anglia*, ed. M. Rule, RS 1884
EHD	*English Historical Documents*, 2nd edn. i, ed. D. Whitelock, London 1979; ii, ed. D. C. Douglas, London 1981
EHR	*English Historical Review*
Fauroux	*Recueil des actes des ducs de Normandie (911–1066)*, ed. M. Fauroux, Mémoires de la Société des Antiquaires de Normandie xxxvi, 1961
GEC	*Complete Peerage of England, Scotland, Ireland, Great Britain and the United Kingdom*, 13 vols in 14, London 1910–59
Gesta Guillelmi	William of Poitiers, *Gesta Guillelmi* . . ., ed. R. Foreville, Paris 1952
Historia Novella	William of Malmesbury, *Historia Novella*, ed. K. R. Potter, Nelson's Medieval Texts, London 1955
HMSO	Her Majesty's Stationery Office, London
Huntingdon	Henry of Huntingdon, *Historia Anglorum*, ed. T. Arnold, RS 1879

Journ. BAA	*Journal of the British Archaeological Association*
Jumièges	William of Jumièges, *Gesta Normannorum Ducum*, ed. J. Marx, Société de l'histoire de Normandie, 1914
Lanfranc's Letters	*The Letters of Lanfranc Archbishop of Canterbury*, ed. H. Clover and M. Gibson, Oxford Medieval Texts, 1979
Med. Arch.	*Medieval Archaeology*
MGHSS	*Monumenta Germaniae Historica, Scriptores*
Monasticon	William Dugdale, *Monasticon Anglicanum*, ed. J. Caley, H. Ellis and B. Bandinel, 6 vols in 8, London 1817–30
ns	New Series
Orderic	Ordericus Vitalis, *Historia Ecclesiastica*, ed. M. Chibnall, Oxford Medieval Texts, 1969–80
PRO	Public Record Office
Procs BA	*Proceedings of the British Academy*
Regesta	*Regesta Regum Anglo-Normannorum*, i, ed. H. W. C. Davis, Oxford 1913; ii, ed. C. Johnson, H. A. Cronne, Oxford 1956; iii, ed. H. A. Cronne, R. H. C. Davis, Oxford 1968
RS	Rolls Series, London
ser.	series
Trans.	Transactions
TRHS	*Transactions of the Royal Historical Society*
VCH	*Victoria County History*
Vita Eadwardi	*The Life of Edward the Confessor*, ed. F. Barlow, Nelson's Medieval Texts, London 1962
Wace	Wace, *Le Roman de Rou*, ed. A. J. Holden, 3 vols, Société des anciens textes français, Paris 1970–3
Worcester	Florence of Worcester, *Chronicon ex Chronicis*, ed. B. Thorpe, English Historical Society, London 1848–9

Allen Brown Memorial Lecture

'BELREM'

Arnold Taylor

Everyone here this afternoon will, I am sure, have seen through the simple title I
have chosen to give this Allen Brown Memorial Lecture, and recognised it as
belonging to the laconic caption which the Bayeux Tapestry accords to its pictures
of earl Harold's arrest by count Guy on the coast of Ponthieu and subsequent
detention at Beaurain-sur-Canche:[1]

HIC : APPREHENDIT : VVIDO : HAROLDVM :
ET DVXIT : EVM AD BELREM :
ET IBI EVM : TENVIT

As David Douglas reminds us, almost every detail of these pictures of Harold's
adventures after setting sail from Bosham on his mission to duke William in 1064
has been made the subject of controversy; and here, at the very outset of what I
want to try to say to you, I would stress Douglas's *dictum* (for such it should be
seen to be) that no finality can be claimed for any single interpretation which may
be put upon them.[2] Let me say at once that any interpretation that I myself may
suggest certainly makes no claim to be the only right or possible one. I wish
simply to set before you what my own scrutiny of this part of the Tapestry
suggests to me is the way in which one has to look at the pictures and their
captions, remembering that these had to ring true, in as authentic detail as was
possible with the medium of embroidery, in their purpose of bringing graphically
to mind facts and places and incidents that would still be within the recollection
of eye-witnesses who would themselves have participated in the events described.

Perhaps I should first explain how it comes about that I am here and presuming
to speak on this particular subject, for, whatever century I might like to regard as
particularly my own, it could certainly not be the eleventh. But the castles of the
Tapestry have always fascinated me; and, given the distinctive differences of
treatment accorded to Rennes and Dinan, Dol and Bayeux and Hastings, I have
never felt able to accept the assertion that they are merely – in the words of one
recent commentator – 'the artist's convention for a fortification of any form'.[3] By
that token, would not the pictures of the Confessor's church at Westminster or
Harold's church at Bosham have to be seen as the artist's convention for an

---

[1] See illustration inside back cover.
[2] David C. Douglas, *William the Conqueror* (London 1964; paperback reprint, London 1969),
175.
[3] *The Bayeux Tapestry*, with introduction, description and commentary by David Wilson (London, Thames & Hudson, 1985; hereafter cited as Wilson), 214.

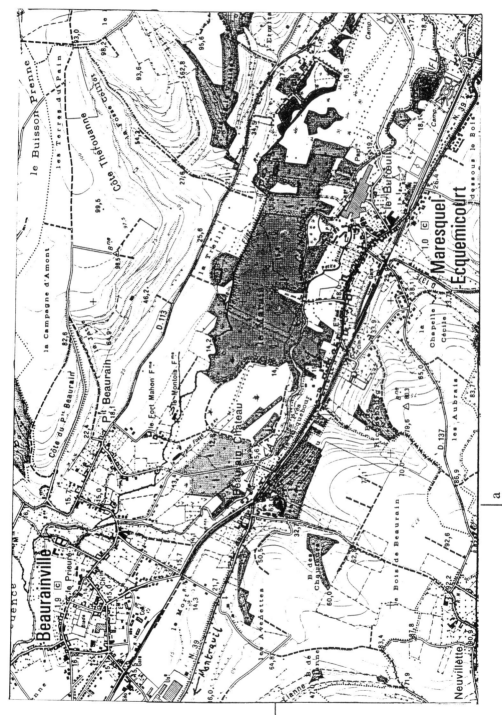

ecclesiastical building of any form, which there is good reason for believing they are not? (Plate 1a)[4]

In 1958, the year after its publication, I was given a copy of Stenton's Phaidon Press edition of the Tapestry, and it was then that I first remember noticing marked on its map a place called Beaurain,[5] and wondering if sometime it might be worth a visit to see if there was any kind of identifiable castle site there; if there were, then Hastings would no longer be, as one had thought, the only Tapestry castle of which recognisable remains still existed on the ground. So I underlined Beaurainville on my Michelin to remind me to visit when opportunity offered. I was always meaning to fit it in, but somehow it was not until I was en route to the Château-Gaillard conference at Najac in 1988 that I finally contrived to pass that way. And there, sure enough, on high ground beside the road that follows the left bank of the Canche from Montreuil to Hesdin, quite unmistakeably to anyone familiar with motte sites on the Welsh marches (I think particularly of the wooded silhouette of Trecastell, the motte of Llywel, beside the A40 between Brecon and Llandovery, a site remarked on by John Leland in the 1530s), there was the rounded tree-covered outline of a large motte-and-bailey (Fig. 1).

It was late on a dull afternoon, and with another hundred-odd miles to go to our first night's stop at Noyon it was no time for exploration or photography. A proper visit had therefore to be deferred till 1989, followed by others in 1990 and May of this present year. After the 1989 visit I felt I had to look afresh at the whole sequence of the Tapestry's story of Harold's mission to duke William. Having done so, I hoped I had perhaps found the makings of a paper, but with no thought of where, if ever, it might one day see the light; certainly the possibility of presenting it at a Battle Conference, still less of its becoming a way of honouring, as I hope however unworthily it may, the memory of Allen Brown, never entered my head. For that quite unexpected outcome I have to thank Henry Loyn and Marjorie Chibnall.

I referred a moment ago to the view that the Tapestry's representations of mottes are merely 'the artist's convention for a fortification of any form, . . . a

---

[4] Despite reservations that have been expressed (Richard Gem, 'Holy Trinity Church, Bosham', *Arch. Journ.* 142 (1985)), it seems hard not to believe that the insertion, in an older structure, of the noble chancel arch in Harold's church of Bosham must antedate, by however little, the making of the Tapestry; that its existence was known to the artist's mentor(s); and that they would have known there could be no more telling way of giving the church recognisable identity than by including the arch as an 'inset'. This was accomplished by using a thin outline to indicate its *internal* position in an otherwise stylised *external* view. In endorsing Pevsner's judgment (*Buildings of England, Sussex*, Harmondsworth 1965, 111) that 'very few arches built since have the architectural presence of this one', it is worth recalling that, whether before or after 1066, its erection can hardly be dissociated from the aegis of the Confessor's clerk Osbern, William fitzOsbern's brother, who held the church of Bosham from King Edward, and as bishop of Exeter from 1072 continued to hold it under King William (*Domesday Book* i, 17; Douglas, *William the Conqueror*, 166–7; Stenton, *Anglo-Saxon England*, 669; A. W. Clapham, *English Romanesque Architecture before the Conquest* (Oxford 1930), 111; H. M. and Joan Taylor, *Anglo-Saxon Architecture* (Cambridge 1965–78), i, 81–4).
[5] Sir Frank Stenton, ed., *The Bayeux Tapestry* (London, Phaidon Press, 1st edn 1957), 8; henceforward cited as Stenton.

Fig. 1 (opposite)   Map of Beaurainville and Beaurain-Château, reproduced from Institut géographique national, Carte Topographique 1:25,000 (4cm = 1km), 2205 ouest, Beaurainville. Château de Beaurain at intersection of 'A' and 'a'

walled town, an encampment, a hill fort or any other major military work'; the propounder of that view further argues that the artist, though able to picture mottes, could not depict baileys; finally he denies the representation of the fortresses as being 'in any way indicative of the appearance of the actual sites or towns' the artist is recording.[6] One wonders, perhaps, why a mere 'convention' should take a form so markedly different in detail for each of the places it purports to indicate. Putting it another way, why, if this view is correct, should the Hastings picture accord so closely with the independently supported fact of a motte under construction there at exactly that point in the narrative? However, it is not my present purpose to examine site by site the five familiar motte pictures, but rather to consider what I want to suggest is a sixth, namely 'Belrem', Beaurain, hitherto largely neglected by English scholars.[7] That the word 'Beaurain' may not previously have been heard in this room is indeed suggested by its absence from the index to the first ten years' proceedings of the Battle Conference.

'Belrem' (Beaurain-sur-Canche) is the place to which, as the narrative of the

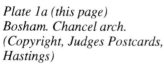

Plate 1a (this page)
Bosham. Chancel arch.
(Copyright, Judges Postcards,
Hastings)

Plate 1b (opposite page)
Bayeux Tapestry:
'Bosham: ecclesia'

---

[6]   Wilson, 214.
[7]   With the one exception of J. Pelham Maitland, FSA, who in 1924–5 conducted the 'Balliol Earthworks Survey' of motte-and-bailey sites in Ponthieu and Vimeu, undertaken to identify and study the ancestral lands and castles of John de Balliol, king of Scotland 1292–6, and his parents the founders of Balliol College Oxford in the 1260s. See Chanoine Le Sueur, *Les châteaux-à-motte dans le Vimeu et le Ponthieu* (Abbeville 1927), 7–8; J. Pelham Maitland, 'The early homes of the Balliols', *Transactions of the Dumfriesshire and Galloway Natural History & Antiquarian Society*, 3rd ser., xviii (1934), 235–42.

Tapestry tells us, count Guy of Ponthieu took Harold Godwinson earl of Wessex when he and his company were driven ashore on Guy's territory in 1064.[8] I propose to re-examine the sequence of incidents which the Tapestry depicts as happening between Harold's landing and his eventual arrival at duke William's *palatium* at, presumably, Rouen; next, to look at what is to be seen at Beaurain-château today and outline what is known of its past; and, finally, to suggest a number of inferences which would seem to me to follow, in regard to the interpretation of the Tapestry's more familiar motte pictures, from this bringing together of Beaurain's eleventh-century record and twentieth-century actuality.

It has more than once been pointed out, notably in the *Proceedings* of previous Battle conferences, how the arbitrary chopping up of photographic reproduction of the Tapestry to fit the pages of a book often breaks the sequence and flow of scenes where visual continuity is crucial for their elucidation.[9] In their effect on our present study, the breaks between plates 14 and 15 of the Stenton edition, and 9 and 10 and 11 and 12 of the Wilson edition, are particularly insensitve and indeed, as will here be argued, liable to be actually misleading. An unbroken presentation of the original is a *sine qua non* in weighing the claim that certain scenes are 'misplaced'.[10] Only the visible and uninterrupted continuity of groups of related scenes conveys the remarkable artistic balance and rhythm of the composition, achieved by the near-symmetrical spacing of horses and riders, trees and buildings. This running balance is dominant; the captions are secondary, fitting in as best they can. Ideally, I should be demonstrating this point with an undivided strip covering the whole seashore/Beaurain/Rouen sequence, but on the screen I am afraid this is not possible.[11]

We begin our investigation with the scene of earl Harold, minus shoes and stockings, being apprehended by count Guy, with mounted bodyguard, in the very act of wading ashore – HIC APPREHENDIT WIDO HAROLDVM. The scene continues with Harold, bodyguard following, being conducted by Guy to Beaurain – ET DVXIT EVM AD BELREM, where Guy detained him – ET IBI EVM TENVIT. The next picture is captioned 'Harold and Guy in conversation' – VBI HAROLD & WIDO PARABOLANT. Harold, brought in by a guard, is apparently being harangued by the count, who is seated on a chair of state, with footstool, and sword held aloft. It is what today would be called a 'cutaway', showing the meeting taking place inside a roofed building or apartment. And look how the colour facsmile edition slices it in two! Whether or not this indication of a covered structure is intended to be in any way representational can be asserted or denied at will; for what it may be worth, however, and in view of what we shall find in the pictures that follow, we should take particular note of the effect of curvature conveyed by the treat-

[8]   For Beaurainville and Beaurain-Château, see R. Rodière, *Le Pays de Montreuil* (Amiens 1933), 155–9; Paul Billaudaz, 'Le château de Beaurain sur Canche', *Bulletin des Amis du Passé*, 1970; 'Les premiers siècles de Beaurainville', *Dossiers archéologiques, historiques et culturels du Nord et du Pas-de-Calais* (Berck-sur-Mer 1982), 11–15.
[9]   N. P. Brooks and H. E. Walker, 'The Authority and Interpretation of the Bayeux Tapestry', *ante* i, 1–2; Shirley Ann Brown, 'The Bayeux Tapestry: why Eustace, Odo and William?', *ante* xii, 15, n.33.
[10]   As made by C. H. Gibbs-Smith in Stenton, 165, in regard to scenes therein numbered 12–14.
[11]   Such a strip, covering the sequence in question, will be found in the pocket at the end of the volume. I am greatly indebted to Mrs Elly Miller for the loan of the photographs 10–14 and 16–21, taken for the Phaidon Edition of the Bayeux Tapestry, and for permission to reproduce them.

ment of its roof. This may, of course, be accidental, meaningless, an instance of the embroiderer's inventiveness, a mere 'convention' perhaps; yet on the other hand it may not. In either case its purpose seems at least to be to convey the impression of some form of *round* building (Plate 2a).

The caption of the next section says 'This is where duke William's emissaries came to Guy' – VBI NVNTII WILLELMI DVCIS VENERVNT AD WIDONEM. The scene must again be at Beaurain. The count, with an impressive battle-axe, and with his household officer beside him, stands facing William's two envoys; one of them, 'Turold', is a personage of sufficient consequence to be indicated by name; they have dismounted to deliver William's orders, of which they appear to be leaving Guy in no doubt; a diminutive jockey-like groom holds their horses. Who, then, is this 'Turold', to be so marked out from among the rest? He has been identified with, and may indeed be, the father of the Ralf *filius Turoldi* who afterwards held a considerable estate in England of bishop Odo, but Stenton cautions that the name Thorald was so common in pre-Conquest Normandy that the identification cannot be regarded as certain.[12] However, he is the only individual figure in the Tapestry whose name is not merely set apart from the main line of captions but is also given the distinction of an enclosing frame.[13] Indeed he and his fellow knight are shown twice, dismounted to the left, mounted and galloping to the right, of the central illustration of Guy's tower. Was he someone contemporaries would be sure to be on the look-out for when they looked at the Tapestry, and was he thus emphasised for their benefit? Self-evidently he had seen Beaurain and was an eye-witness of events that had happened there, and could thus have given a first-hand account to the artist. Could it perhaps even be that he was in some way the originator, or under Odo the director, of the whole Tapestry project, and thus given this special form of identification when the work came to be executed?

The next scene, with the terse caption 'William's messengers' (Plate 2b) – NVNTII WILLELMI, is what nowadays would be called an 'inset', supplementing the main narrative with an action picture of Turold and his companion galloping towards a prominently portrayed building, again split into two unequal segments in the facsimile edition.[14] This seems likely on two grounds to be another version of the building of the Harold/Guy conversation piece: first, the riders are hasten-ing *towards* it, not away from it, and secondly the curving roof recalls, and may be meant to repeat, the curving roof in the preceding picture. The treatment of the arches, with the outer sides slightly bowed and the centre arch higher than the others, gives the impression that this may be an attempt to represent a round building in perspective.

The wall above the arches is ashlar-faced. Might the intention be to indicate a shell keep? C. H. Gibbs-Smith, in the Stenton edition, claimed that this section and those on either side of it are 'misplaced', but this seems to me to cast uncalled-for doubt on the competence of the narrator or embroiderer or both.[15] One supposes the patron or commissioner of the work would have provided a note of incidents that were within his knowledge, indeed probably within his personal memory, which he wished the pictorial record to perpetuate. As to the

---

[12] Stenton, 24, n.2.
[13] A contributor to the discussion mentioned the possibility that the 'frame' might be a later repair; this has to be noted as a matter for investigation.
[14] Wilson, Plates 11 and 12.
[15] See note 10.

alleged 'misplacing' of these Beaurain scenes, it seems to me to be illusory and need only result from the impracticability of picturing happenings that were concurrent rather than successive except side by side, and therefore apparently in sequence when in fact they would have been taking place simultaneously.

After the two pictures of William's messengers to count Guy, yet another facet of the story is recorded, its separateness perhaps signalled by the cross-sign introducing its caption – + HIC VENIT NVNTIVS AD WILGELMUM DVCEM. The duke is threatening or remonstrating with a cringing-looking individual pushed forward by two knights, perhaps a messenger from Guy, perhaps an Englishman bringing a message from Harold. This is an isolated scene, presumably significant to contemporaries, but of which the precise explanation must to us remain unknown.

Where was it enacted? We do not and cannot *know*. The Tapestry's showing of it suggests it took place in the open: there is no attempt to indicate a roof, or pillars, or arches; nor would there be anything unusual about a messenger tracking the duke down while he was in the field or on progress; that this was the case is perhaps meant to be shown by the posting of a look-out in the nearby tree. Gibbs-Smith and Allen Brown thought that this scene took place at Rouen, both commentators linking it directly to the picture that follows, both, subconsciously perhaps, predisposed so to do by the unfortunately positioned 'cut' between sections 14 and 15 of the Stenton edition, which *ipso facto* seems to me to create an overemphasised juxtaposition between on the one hand the picture of the duke attending to business 'somewhere in the country' and on the other the elaborately detailed building-picture which comes immediately after it, and which Allen thought very probably represented the ducal tower of Rouen.[16] But I suggest nothing is 'misplaced': in the picture to the left of the building the frightened messenger is being told to get back to Beaurain as fast as his legs will carry him; in the picture to the right we see what followed. We are still a long way from Rouen; there is no 'reversal of events'.[17]

HIC WIDO ADDVXIT HAROLDVM AD WILGELMVM NORMANNORVM DVCEM: this is the illustration of count Guy conducting his prisoner to his lord, a solemn and significant act of feudal submission, and therefore recorded with some degree of formality. The party are shown in the act of riding *away* from count Guy's castle, i.e. from Beaurain, much as in a later picture we see the knights riding out from Hastings. Beaurain, I suggest, is the true identity of the remarkably portrayed structure which as I see it provides the commencement of this new scene, not the conclusion of the scene preceding it (Plate 2c). The horses of the escort are trotting out from the open-gated building, the bottom right-hand corner of which is actually indented to link it to the last of the departing hooves, the wall above flicked by the last of the departing tails. The building they are leaving cannot, as I see it, in any sense represent Rouen, as hitherto so generally supposed, for surely Rouen was the direction in which the party were heading, not the point from

[16] R. Allen Brown in Stenton, 2nd edn (1965), 81, and in *Château Gaillard, European Castle Studies, III* (Chichester 1969), 13.
[17] Gibbs-Smith in Stenton, 165.

Plate 2 (opposite)
a *(top)* Bayeux Tapestry: *'Harold et Wido parabolant'*
b *(middle)* Bayeux Tapestry: *William's messengers gallop towards Guy's castle*
c *(bottom)* Bayeux Tapestry: *Guy's castle, from which he brought Harold to duke William*

which they were starting. Nor, surely, can it be one of the artist's alleged 'conventions for a fortress in any form', to quote again the phrase of Sir David Wilson. On the contrary, it is, I would argue, a very clever representation of a motte *and bailey*, and as such the only example of its kind in the Tapestry. This, I think, is incontrovertible, even though there may always be conflicting views as to its most likely identity.

What has the picture to tell us? The detailing merits the closest attention. First, it is the picture of a castle, raised above the average ground level (generally identical with the top of the Tapestry's lower border); the elevated position is here depicted by bands of red and green wool placed horizontally one above the other, but with the wool worked so as to make them appear to slope downwards and curve round at either end. On the upper band there stands what appears to be a formidable stone-built gatehouse, drawn larger than life in relation to what lies behind and beyond it, so as to form the forefront of a perspective view of the whole castle. Its stonework is composed of ashlar blocks, their bizarre radial coursing an ingenious way of indicating the curvature of the enclosure in which it is set. A battlemented parapet curves off at either end towards the rear of the picture; the way in which this parapet merges into two prominent towers suggests that these may perhaps be intended to be standing further back on either side of the bailey, rather than attached to the gatehouse itself; their vertical treatment could be a way of conveying the idea of strip pilasters, such as those we see on the eleventh-century towers of, for example, Loches, or Chepstow. The whole composition culminates in yet another version of a round-roofed building such as we have already twice seen illustrated at Beaurain (Plate 3).

This round-roofed structure is shown standing on a motte, whose flat top and steeply sloping sides appear as it were at a distance – across the bailey, but high enough to peep over the battlements of the gatehouse; they are tricked out in the same green and red wools as those used to set off the high ground on which the whole ensemble is sited. The motte's relative isolation is cleverly brought out by the position of the two watchmen, who from the observer's viewpoint stand half hidden behind the mound's rounded profile, a little way down the slope but where they will still be able to see over the top of the bailey ramparts. I, for one, find it difficult to believe that the makers of the Tapestry would have devoted such a wealth of circumstantial elaboration to the design, not to mention the needleworking, of a mere symbol, of a wholly imaginary idea. How far it may rather correspond to a known extant reality will be considered in a moment.

Meanwhile we have to move on with Guy and Harold from Beaurain towards Rouen, a distance of eighty to a hundred miles. The river Bresle, Ponthieu's boundary with Normandy, was probably crossed at Eu, where there is good authority for believing the handing over of Harold by count Guy to his lord was effected;[18] on the Tapestry it appears to be shown as taking place in open country. The next scenes conclude the first chapter of the story, with duke William riding ahead of Harold up to the outer gate of his *palatium* – HIC DVX WILGELM CVM HAROLDO VENIT AD PALATIVM SVVM. As with the exit from Beaurain, so with the entrance to Rouen: the gate stands open. A high gate-tower rises above it. The palace is illustrated by a conversation-piece reminiscent of the picture of Harold

---

[18] Douglas, *William the Conqueror* 176; Douglas explains how Guy 'may be regarded in some sense as a vassal of William'.

Plate 3   Detail of Plate 2c

and Guy's tête-a-tête at Beaurain; the spaciousness of the 'cutaway' points to a major apartment, surely the duke's hall, with the blind arcading perhaps introduced to recall to the memory of those familiar with it a prominent feature of the actual building (Plate 4a). Do we not have here an attempt to portray a form of architectural embellishment similar to that of which hidden portions are still preserved along the wall-tops of the great hall of the *palatium* of the king-dukes at Westminster (Plate 4b)? Do the Tapestry arches not also resemble the arcaded recesses still to be seen in William fitzOsbern's hall-keep at Chepstow (Plate 4c)? Surely this, and not the motte-and-bailey of the preceding picture, is the Tapestry's thumb-nail sketch of Rouen, represented by the principal chamber *in turre Rothomagensi* (as it is called in Henry I's charter of 1113 to St Evroul), the chamber where on 30 November 1074, *apud Rothomagum in aula Turris*, in the presence of king William, queen Matilda, Roger of Montgomery, the king's sons Robert and William and fifteen other named witnesses, Odo bishop of Bayeux notified his acquisition of the land of Cheffreville in Calvados for possession by St Mary of Bayeux?[19]

The unexplained (and, to all but those who were there, unexplainable) incident of the clerk and Aelfgyva, another 'inset' like the earlier 'nuntii Willelmi', one can only suppose will have been introduced to recall a bit of gossip, or some celebrated scandal, that everybody who was anybody would know about; whatever it was it evidently occurred at Rouen. I am, though, always a little unhappy about its caption: why 'unus' clericus, not 'quidam' clericus? I do sometimes wonder whether 'VNVS' may not have been the *name* of the clerk concerned? Several of us will remember Decima Douie; other like names that come to mind are T. Tertius Noble, the organist; the poet Horace, Quintus Horatius Flaccus; the Monmouthshire antiquary, Octavius Morgan; Nonus, the tenth-century physician; I personally know a 'Una' today. I only make bold to voice this thought as an aside, knowing that wiser heads than mine will probably reject it out of hand.

When we are able to look at the Tapestry as a continuing, not a broken and divided picture, we cannot but be struck by the spacing of what I have suggested are the three Beaurain figures, both in relation one to another and also as a central to the whole saga of Harold's interrupted journey to the Norman capital. The centre picture is of the heart of count Guy's castle, a stylised round tower which if it followed the outline of the motte would probably have been a shell keep; to the left, the 'cutaway', taking the observer to the encounter in progress within; lastly, to the right, a 'general view' of the fortress in its entirety, a kind of needlework *multum in parvo*. Not only are these three pictures set roughly the same distance apart, but the one in the centre comes almost exactly midway between Harold's arrest on the coast of Ponthieu and his eventual arrival with duke William at Rouen.

By way of diversion, a capital in the choir of the Abbaye aux Dames at Caen illustrates a rather different approach to the problem of depicting castles in

---

[19] *Cal. Docs France*, 219, 529 (nos. 624, 1432).

Plate 4 (opposite)
a (top)   Bayeux Tapestry: William in conversation with Harold in the hall of the duke's palace
b (middle)   Plan and elevation of the king's/dukes' hall in their palace of Westminster. (History of the King's Works, *i, 45, based on* RCHM)
c (bottom)   Wall arcading in William fitzOsbern's hall in Chepstow castle

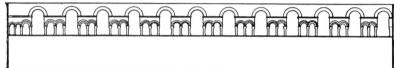

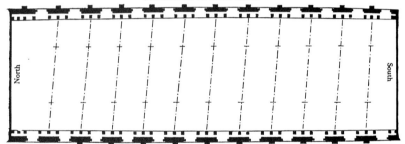

ELEVATION OF EAST WALL

North   South

PLAN AT WINDOW LEVEL

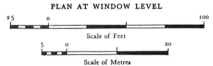

25   0   100

Scale of Feet

5   0   20

Scale of Metres

*Plate 5   Caen. Elephant and Castle on capital in choir of Abbaye aux Dames.
(Editions Gaud, Moisenay-le-Petit)*

perspective (Plate 5); not very different in date from the Tapestry, it represents, in
the guise of an elephant-and-castle, a crenellated stone-built tower, perched, one
may imagine, on a concealed motte, and rising above a similarly crenellated
bailey wall, in this case a curtain in more senses than one.

Let us now turn from the puzzles and problems of the Tapestry to the actualities
on the ground. Beaurain is in Artois, the district which looked to Arras as its
centre. At some later date Beaurain passed out of the direct lordship of the counts
of Ponthieu to become a detached castellany of the comté of St Pol-sur-Ternoise,
a river which flows into the Canche at Hesdin. I think this may be why, in an
admittedly hasty scanning, I have been unable to find any reference to Beaurain
in the many Ponthieu accounts that survive from 1279 onwards in the E101 and
C47 classes in PRO. On the other hand it is for this same reason, its connection
with St Pol, that we do have, as will be explained in a moment, an authentic
picture of how the castle looked, albeit from a distance, before it entered on its
final decline in the seventeenth and eighteenth centuries.

As it survives today, Beaurain-château bears a near resemblance to Ewyas
Harold, the best preserved of those few identifiable castles known to have been
founded in England before 1066, probably during the tenure of the earldom of
Hereford by the Confessor's nephew Ralf son of Drogo, i.e. between 1053 and
1057 (Plate 6b): Ewyas was *re*-fortified by William fitzOsbern between 1066 and
1071, a refortification which judging by what fitzOsbern did at Chepstow must
surely have been in stone; G. T. Clark records evidence for there having been a

Plate 6 (opposite)
a (top)   Beaurain. Castle from north-west. (Photo Roger Agache, Abbeville)
*b (bottom)   Ewyas Harold. Castle from north-east. (Cambridge University
Collection of Air Photographs)*

shell keep on the motte at Ewyas.[20] Both mottes have oval tops, Ewyas about 30 by 40 yards (Clark's figures), Beaurain about 25 by 30 yards (as paced by the writer). In neither case does there appear to have been a ditch between the mound and the bailey.

Beaurain's present appearance and condition can perhaps best be judged from the accompanying air photograph (Plate 6a), for permission to reproduce which I am indebted to M. Roger Agache of Abbeville. This brings out the nearness of the castle to the Canche and shows most of what survives of the medieval borough that lay between them; a little chapel and graveyard seen at the bottom left-hand corner may occupy the site of medieval predecessors. The castle was entered from within the borough, the gateway's position in relation to the motte at the opposite end of the bailey corresponding to that represented on the Tapestry. The site is bounded on the north by the RN39 Montreuil-Hesdin road which here formed the main street of the borough, on the west by the lane to Neuvillette (Fig. 1). The track into the bailey passes between two hummocks which rise to a height of 142½ feet, compared with 131 feet for the pathway between them; the motte rises to 206½ feet, a difference of over 70 feet. The hummocks look like the debris of fallen towers; to that extent they might approximate to the towers that appear to flank the gatehouse on the Tapestry, but only insofar as tenth-to-eleventh century work might have been retained in later rebuilding. The stated heights are derived from an unpublished survey carried out in 1989 by students of the *Section Géo-topo du Lycée Technique d'Armentières* under the direction of Professeur-ingénieur G. Lefranc, through whose kindness I am able to reproduce it here (Fig. 2).

Today from across the Canche one can hardly pick out the top of the motte from the dense surrounding woodland. But if we could have gone to the same viewpoint in the year 1610, as did Adrien de Montigny of Valenciennes, who was employed as a topographical artist by the Duc Charles de Croÿ (1560–1612), we should not have had the same difficulty, for there was then much more to be seen. His sketch of 'Beaurains Castel' (Plate 7), distant though it is, shows that by the sixteenth century, and probably much earlier, the bailey was enclosed with a curtain and flanking towers of stone, while the motte, whatever may have surmounted it originally, was by then crowned by a two-storey building of brick, perhaps embellished with corner turrets.[21] Now there is not to be seen one stone or brick standing on another, the last remaining masonry having been removed in

[20] *Domesday Book* i, 186; G. T. Clark, *Mediaeval Military Architecture in England* (London 1884), ii, 40; Stenton, *Anglo-Saxon England*, 561. For plan and description see *RCHM Herefs.* iii, 64.
[21] *Albums de Croÿ* xx, Comté d'Artois IV (Crédit Communale de Belgique, Bruxelles 1989), 86 and Planche 27. Froissart records how on Monday 28 August 1345, two days after the battle at Crécy, only eight miles away to the south, the English fired the town of Beaurain but found the castle too strong and too well defended to attack: '. . . ses Mareschaux coururent devers Hedin: & ardirent Vamban & Seram: mais au chastel ils ne peurent rien faire: car il estoit trop fort & bien gardé . . .' (*Histoire et Chronique memorable de Messire Iehan Froissart*, 4 vols, Paris 1574, i, 141); John Bourchier, Lord Berners (1525) reads this as ' . . . and brent Waben and Serain . . .' (Globe Edition, ed. G. C. Macaulay, London 1895, repr. 1913, 107); 'Serain' is also the reading of Thomas Johnes (Hafod Press 1803–05, i, 331) and Siméon Luce (Paris, 11 vols, 1869-99, iii, 191). The more recent English editions (Oxford, Basil Blackwell for Shakespeare Head Press, limited edn, 1927-8, I, i, 272; II, iv, 1286, 1447, 1476; Penguin Classics, ed. Geoffrey Brereton 1968, 95) are almost certainly right to read 'Beaurain' for 'Serain'.

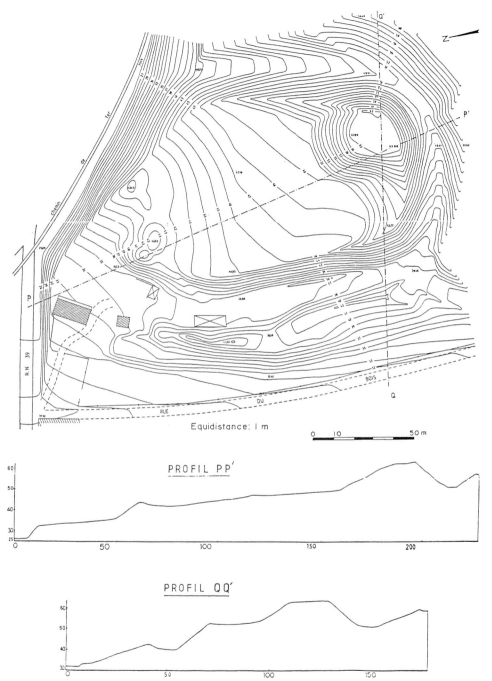

Equidistance: 1 m

PROFIL PP'

PROFIL QQ'

Fig. 2   Beaurain. Contoured survey of castle (1989) by
Section Géo-topo of Armentières school of technology.
(By courtesy of Professeur-ingéniéur G. Lefranc)

*Plate 7　Beaurain. Castle and borough in 1610, drawn by Adrien de Montigny for Duc Charles de Croÿ (1560–1612). (*Albums de Croÿ *XX,* Comté d'Artois *iv (Crédit communal de Belgique, Bruxelles 1989), plate 27)*

1822 to construct a channel for a new water mill.[22] Very recently the whole area of the bailey has been planted with young trees, thus ensuring a still greater abundance of Allen's detested *verdure* in years to come, as well as administering an archaeological *coup-de-grâce* to a site of unique potential interest (Plate 8). As to the motte, one would guess that in a castle of the standing of Beaurain it would be likely to have carried a *donjon* of stone from the first; that it is this that the Tapestry seeks to portray; and, though the interval between 1060 and 1610 is a long one, with time for many changes, that this is the story to which the picture in the Album de Croÿ lends support.

The buildings of the Tapestry will always present problems of interpretation to which there can be no certain solution. The argument of this lecture is that the interpretation of the five more usually recognised examples of castles, three in Brittany (Rennes, Dinan, Dol), one in Normandy (Bayeux) and one in England (Hastings), must be influenced by the recognition of a sixth, namely Beaurain in Ponthieu. Hitherto Hastings has generally been assumed to be the only survivor, leaving the question of the validity of the Tapestry's representation of the four continental mottes open to every kind of speculation. If our reading of the picture of the building from which count Guy conducted Harold to duke William is right, then Beaurain's importance is that it provides the Tapestry's one unquestionable instance of a complete motte-and-bailey that was not only in existence in 1064 but still remains open to inspection *in situ* today.

If this be accepted, what inferences can we draw to guide our attitude to the authenticity or otherwise of the other five castle pictures? First, Hastings. If the Tapestry's illustration of Beaurain can be identified with the motte-and-bailey that still exists there, this must surely strengthen the case, were there to be any real doubt about it, for accepting that the motte that survives in much mutilated condition on Hastings cliff today is indeed the motte seen under construction in the Tapestry. A limited excavation carried out in 1968 on behalf of the Royal Archaeological Institute's 'research project into the origins and development of the castle in England' had, as one of its objectives, 'to show whether the Hastings castle mound could be related to the Bayeux Tapestry'.[23] In other words, the archaeologists *did* have doubts which they supposed the spade might resolve, doubts implicit in such a phrase as 'the Bayeux Tapestry *appears to record* the throwing up of a motte-and-bailey castle at Hastings',[24] when 'the Tapestry *records*' would be no more than a statement of fact. Hastings thus occupies a crucial place in our story, and a number of points in the 1968 excavation report seem to call for particular comment:[25]

i. *Report*: The lower levels of the mound were not examined . . . the original mound was found to have lost *many feet* (author's italics) of its top in later times.
   Comment: Any assessment of the composition of the motte on the evidence of archaeology can thus only be regarded as incomplete.

[22] P. Billaudaz, 'Le château de Beaurain-sur-Canche', 1970 (unpaged).
[23] *Arch. Journ.* 134 (1977), 80.
[24] *Arch. Journ.* cxxiv (1967), 210.
[25] P. A. Barker in *Arch. Journ.* cxxv (1968), 303–05; 134 (1977), 81–90.

ii. *Report*: The original mound was found to be composed of sand mixed with clay.

Comment: Sand, because of its density and weight, is still generally handled in bags and probably always has been. May not this be the explanation of the little bags, tied at the neck like puddings, seen being thrown up by one of the Norman diggers, and included to indicate sand as a component in forming the mound?

iii. *Report*: The mound produced a large sherd of Conquest period pottery, which 'suggests that the mound was constructed at some time very close to the Norman conquest'.

Comment: No evidence is known for supposing there were *two* castles of the Conquest period at Hastings; therefore the significance of this find is that it effectively disposes of the idea of William having built his castle on the beach 'to protect his shipping'.

iv. *Report*: 'The layering depicted in the Tapestry is purely theoretical', no sign of such layered construction having been identified.

Comment: Having regard to the limited nature of the excavation and the original mound's loss of many feet in height (i above), the evidence of the Tapestry cannot be dismissed so lightly. John Pelham Maitland, who carried out the 'Balliol Earthworks Survey' in Ponthieu and Vimeu in 1924–25, recorded that the motte at Maisnières-en-Vimeu, eleven miles south-west of Abbeville, was constructed *en couches de craie dure et de terre, pareille à un gâteau russe*.[26] Similarly Mrs Armitage records that when the motte at Carisbrooke was opened in 1893 it was 'found to be composed of alternate layers of large and small chalk rubble'.[27] The Carisbrooke motte may be presumed to be the work of William fitzOsbern and therefore not later than 1071.

v. *Report*: 'How this first of many seaside sand-castles supported a timber tower remains a mystery.'

Comment: Ignoring the flippancy about seaside sand-castles, we have to remember that there is no suggestion in the Tapestry picture that the Hastings motte *did* support a tower; what it appears to show is a close-set ring palisade of double thickness whose timbers, if linked below the surface, would have exerted a binding force down to whatever depth they were taken. We may also recall the possibility that the immediately adjacent chapel of St Mary, with its own tower, may have antedated the motte and been considered sufficiently commanding for this cliff-top site, with its coastal panorama from Dungeness to Beachy Head, without the need to construct a tower on the motte at all.[28]

[26] Le Sueur, *Châteaux-à-motte dans Le Vimeu et Le Ponthieu*, 9.
[27] Ella S. Armitage, *The Early Norman Castles of the British Isles* (London 1912), 112.
[28] L. F. Salzman in *VCH Sussex* ii, 122; A. J. Taylor, 'Evidence for a pre-Conquest origin for the Chapels in Hastings and Pevensey Castles', *Château Gaillard III* (Chichester 1969), 144–51; H. M. Taylor, *Anglo-Saxon Architecture* iii (Cambridge 1978), 1073.

Plate 8 (opposite)   Château de Beaurain, 27 March 1990
a (top)   Motte from bailey
b (middle)   Bailey from motte; in centre, village of Beaurain-Château; in background, village of Beaurainville
c (bottom)   West slope of motte with bailey below

As was said at the outset, site-by-site examination of the Tapestry's other motte pictures, Rennes, Dol, Dinan and Bayeux, is not part of the purpose of this lecture. If disproportionate attention seems to have been given to Hastings, this is because Hastings alone has, albeit in very partial fashion, been investigated archaeologically, and it has seemed important to challenge a tendency of the excavation report to disparage the Tapestry and to give its evidence less than its due. Having attempted to redress that particular balance and to look as objectively as possible at what seem to be the lessons to be learned from Beaurain, whether as depicted in the Tapestry or as visible on the ground, I believe we may be in a better position for assessing the likely validity of these other four representations. All four castles had mottes, of this we may be sure; it is inconceivable that in 1064 lords of the standing of Odo of Bayeux, Conan of Brittany, Riwallon of Dol or Ralf de Gael would not have had mottes as the crowns of their *capita*.[29] As to the constructions shown surmounting them, with Hastings and now Beaurain in mind it seems even more unlikely than before that the differences in their portrayal would not have been intentional, making sense to knights who would have known them at first hand and perhaps themselves have participated in the events of 1064–65. It would be surprising indeed if so much circumstantial detail, involving so much intricate and painstaking needlework, were no more than the 'artist's convention' for 'fortifications of every sort and kind'. The essence of a 'convention' is uniformity, not diversity.'[30]

May I end with a brief postscript? Sometimes I think that I may in an indirect sort of way have been an instigator of the Battle Conferences. At this time twenty-five years ago I was settling the programme for the 'Third Château-Gaillard Conference on European Castle Studies'. Allen and I had attended the first of the Château-Gaillard *colloques* at Les Andelys together in 1962. At the second meeting, at Büderich in the Rhineland in 1964, I said to our French and German friends, 'Why not come to England in 1966 and help us celebrate the novocentenary of Hastings at Battle?' And so it came about that on the evening of

---

[29] Wilson, 215, asserts that there is no evidence for the existence of mottes at Dinan, Dol or Rennes, and that 'in these cases it is clear that the mottes on the Tapestry represent fortified towns'. See, however, for Dinan, M. -E. Monnier, *Dinan, Mille ans d'Histoire* (1968), 18-21, with town plan of 1701. For Rennes, see town plans of 1685 and 1720 in Paul Banéat, *Le Vieux Rennes* (J. Larcher, Rennes, 1925); Rennes had two mottes, (i) the 'Emplacement de la Motte du Château' within the northernmost curve of the wall of the Vieille-Ville or *Cité* (so named in 1455), and (ii) the Motte à Madame (levelled in 1664) outside the Porte St. Georges in the walls (begun 1422) of the Ville Neuve, 'Madame' standing for 'Madame l'Abbesse' of the adjacent abbey of St George; the Fougères road, leading from the Porte St Georges and named 'rue de la Motte' in 1720, is today named 'Contour de la Motte'. Dol is less well documented and the castle site at the higher end of the town almost obliterated; this would have been the natural position for an earlier motte, perhaps levelled when new fortifications were erected in 1371. A 1780 street plan of Bayeux marks the castle as occupying the rising ground in the south-west angle of the cathedral precinct wall; this could well have been the successor of a levelled motte. Demolition of the later medieval towers and curtains of the castle, said to have been founded by duke Richard in about 960, was begun in 1775 and continued at intervals until 1804, the ditch on the side towards the rue de la Poterie being the last to be filled in (Frédéric Pluquet, *Essai Historique sur la Ville de Bayeux* (Caen 1829), 90–96.

[30] *Acknowledgements.* The author wishes to thank the following for their assistance: M. Roger Agache, Abbeville; Dr David Bates, Cardiff; MM. G. Dilly, Berck-sur-Mer; Bernard Gauthiez, Lyon; Loïc Langouët, St Malo; Guy Lefranc, Armentières; Pierre Leman, Villeneuve d'Ascq; Mlle Annie Renoux, Le Mans; Dr J. K. St Joseph, Cambridge; Mme Elisabeth Zadora-Rio, Paris; and, especially, Prof. Henry Loyn and Dr Marjorie Chibnall.

Monday 19 September 1966, after a wonderful candlelight reception given by the Lady of the Manor, Mrs Evelyn Harbord, in the then unrestored Abbey Gatehouse, we gathered in the Memorial Hall under the chairmanship of Michel de Boüard for the opening paper on the theme of *The Norman Conquest and the genesis of English Castles*, given at my special request by Allen Brown. I like to think that that occasion, and the week that followed it here in Battle, may have been at least in Allen's subconscious when he came to plan the Battle Conferences, as it is certainly in my own mind and memory this afternoon.

THE CHARTERS OF DAVID I

G. W. S. Barrow

The acts of David I, king of Scots 1124–53, survive in 153 exemplars, of which twenty-six are originals.[1] Only three items in this admittedly modest total may safely be classified as spurious,[2] and of these one at least may possibly be based on a genuine lost act. It seems odd that only two items exist both as originals and as early copies,[3] and that with three exceptions the surviving originals belong to the years 1124–44, thus leaving the last decade of the reign to be represented by fifty-three copies and only three originals. In addition to these texts of charters, diplomas, letters and brieves (*anglicé*, writs) issued in the name of David as king of Scots, presumably always bearing his seal, we have four original documents and nine copies (none of them coincident) of acts issued by David as earl,[4] none of which can be proved to be earlier in date than Christmas 1113, when it is probable that David received Maud, daughter and heir of Earl Waltheof and the Countess Judith, and widow of Simon I de Senlis, as his bride, and with her the vast complex of estates in Huntingdonshire, Northants and elsewhere which were to form his chief English honour.

It is convenient to think of this *corpus* of documents as the sum total of full-text charters of David, but to be more precise one is a true letter, in fully epistolary style;[5] one is a hybrid between a letter and a writ-charter;[6] one is a declaration of a public act of peace-making;[7] one is a declaration that the bishop of St Andrews has been consecrated by the archbishop of York without any profession of obedience;[8] five are diplomas of Anglo-Norman type[9] – although of these one is an amplified re-issue,[10] while two others are hybrids of diploma and writ-charter;[11] leaving twenty-four brieves in the strictest sense and one hundred and twelve documents composed in writ-charter form, of which no fewer than forty-six embody commands and prohibitions which could well have formed (and perhaps

---

[1] The texts may be found in A. C. Lawrie, *Early Scottish Charters* (Glasgow, 1905) [= *ESC*] and G. W. S. Barrow, *The Acts of Malcolm IV king of Scots, 1153–1165. Regesta Regum Scottorum* I (Edinburgh, 1960) [= *RRS* I]. Lawrie's roman numerals have been converted to arabic in my frequent citations, to save space and reduce the possibility of error.
[2] *ESC*, nos. 116, 242; *RRS* I, no. 19 (which might be derived ultimately from a genuine original charter for the burgesses of Salorch, i.e. Montrose).
[3] *ESC*, nos. 71, 134.
[4] *ESC*, nos. 29, 30, 32, 34, 35, 46, 51, 52, 53; *RRS* I, nos. 1, 3, 5, 6.
[5] *RRS* I, no. 8.
[6] *ESC*, no. 161.
[7] *RRS* I, no. 5.
[8] *ESC*, no. 75.
[9] *ESC*, nos. 74, 153, 179, 189, 209. No. 35 (David's 'foundation charter' for Selkirk (= Kelso) issued before his accession) may have had some of the features of a diploma.
[10] *ESC*, no. 209.
[11] *ESC*, nos. 153, 179.

did in fact form) the subject of separate brieves. In addition to these surviving texts we have good evidence of some fifty transactions in the name of David I,[12] fifteen of which were certainly,[13] and most of which were probably, the subject of written acts. It is not worth attempting to analyse this half century of lost acts by surmising which were letters, which charters, which brieves etc., although in a few instances – for example the 'friendly letter' to Abbot Suger of St Denys which accompanied King David's gift of narwhal tusks of wonderful size[14] – we may be quite sure what kind of document has been lost.

At first sight, 153 royal charters (I use the word here in the popular sense) must appear to be a disappointingly meagre corpus to illustrate the government of a king who reigned for nearly thirty years and attained, as few kings of Scotland have succeeded in doing, to a genuinely European reputation. A closer acquaintance, however, with the documents will lead us to a more positive and optimistic conclusion. The sheer quantity of information about the reign of David I which can be obtained from his surviving charters, the richness and variety of that information, the degree to which by the last decade of the reign certain fundamental, long-term features of the official written acts of the Scottish crown were firmly established – all these considerations emerge as a heartening element of profit to offset the more immediately obvious entries on the loss side of the account.

For one thing, the geographical reference of the surviving charters is appreciably wider than the conventional picture of David I's reign usually seems to allow. Our corpus includes a brieve addressed to the earls of Orkney and Caithness relating to monastic operations – possibly trading operations – at Dornoch in Sutherland.[15] Three charters mention the king's revenues from Moray, Argyll and Kintyre,[16] and another shows the king holding judicial sessions at Banff and Aberdeen.[17] The area of the Scottish realm within which the king's governmental activity is most intensively revealed by surviving record stretches from Brechin and Forfar in the east to Cunningham, Kyle and Carrick in the south west and thence across to Berwick upon Tweed in the south east. It is unnecessary to remind this audience that the western isles, from Man to Lewis, formed no part of David I's kingdom, but it seems likely enough that David did see Cumberland and Westmorland as falling within his realm. For this reason we find the religious houses of Wetheral, Holm Cultram and St Bees figuring among the beneficiaries of David's charters,[18] and the silver mines of Alston laid under tribute to implement the king's goodwill towards Nostell Priory in the West Riding.[19] If the 'new castle of Culchet', the place-date of two of the king's charters, was Culgaith in Cumberland then the Scots' lordship of Cumbria is enough to account for the reference.[20] But a preferable alternative identification points to Tulketh in Lancashire, and if King David was issuing charters there it would be explained by his

---

[12] *RRS* I, nos. 54–73, 76–101, 103–4.

[13] *RRS* I, nos. 55, 57, 62, 63, 66, 70, 72, 76, 78, 79, 81, 86, 90, 93, 103.

[14] M. Bouquet, *Recueil des historiens des Gaulés et de la France* (Paris, 1738–1904), xii, 105.

[15] *ESC*, no. 132.

[16] *ESC*, pp. 118, 171, 205.

[17] *ESC*, no. 223.

[18] *ESC*, nos. 52, 123, 140 (Wetheral); 245 (Holm Cultram); 187 (St Bees).

[19] *RRS* I, no. 39.

[20] *ESC*, nos. 138, 139 (both from the Shrewsbury Abbey cartulary, now edited by U. Rees (1975); see next note). Culgaith, Cumberland, appears as Culchet in 1204 (*Pipe Roll 5 John*, 256), but no

brief possession of the Honour of Lancaster in the earlier 1140s.[21] His much lengthier tenure of the Honour of Huntingdon is surprisingly reflected in only two place-dates, Huntingdon itself and Yardley Hastings, unless we include London where David's presence was due at least in part to his position as lord of an English estate of the front rank. Comparably, David's very real interest in the earldom of Northumberland is illustrated by two occurrences of Newcastle upon Tyne as a place-date,[22] and at least indirectly by a solitary charter issued during the siege of Norham on Tweed in June 1138.[23]

The largest geographical gaps, naturally enough, relate to those political subdivisions of the kingdom of the Scots where delegated power was at its strongest and royal interference correspondingly slight – the lordships of Galloway and Nithsdale in the south west, and the earldoms of Scotia; especially Lennox, Menteith, Strathearn, Atholl, Mar and Buchan. Even allowing for the fact that no new religious houses were founded in these earldoms before King David's death it is rather remarkable that not a single royal act survives relating to Lennox, Menteith, Strathearn, Atholl or Mar, while Buchan is represented solely by the slightly odd brieve in favour of the clerical community at Old Deer.[24] The most intensive coverage is provided by the Merse, lower Teviotdale and Tweeddale, East and Midlothian, east Stirlingshire, Glasgow and its immediate hinterland, Fife and the lower basin of the River Tay. Here, of course, royal demesne was most abundant and pervasive, here were founded most of the religious houses closely associated with David I from whose records so many of our surviving charters take their provenance. All the circumstances favourable to a nice circular argument seem to be present here. Does the concentration of royal documents on the area from Tay to Clyde and Tweed mean that the king's writ ran only – or at best most effectively – in this region? Or does it merely reflect the fact that this region contained most of the earliest religious houses which were likely to generate and preserve record? But then is not that very fact to be explained by the strength and influence of the monarchy in south-eastern and central Scotland? To some extent we are at the mercy of the chances of survival and loss. For example, the well-endowed Augustinian abbey of Jedburgh must once have possessed a large archive, but practically all of it has perished, doubtless because Jedburgh was only a few miles from the English border. The earliest Jedburgh charters would surely have enhanced our picture of a well-documented south east. But against that we may set Dundrennan, to which Cistercian monks were brought by Fergus, David I's contemporary, and Whithorn cathedral established, probably before King David's death, as a Premonstratensian priory. All Dundrennan's records are lost, and so too are the earliest records of Whithorn. If we add to this

---

traces of a twelfth-century castle are to be found there. Tulketh near Preston (where there was a castle) seems a rather more probable identification.

[21] See G. W. S. Barrow, 'King David I and the Honour of Lancaster', *EHR*, 69 (1955), 85–9; *ESC*, nos. 138, 139. The MS reading of the place-date, as given in *The Cartulary of Shrewsbury Abbey*, ed. U. Rees (Aberystwyth, 1975), nos. 87, 322, is Thulchet(h). Dr Rees suggests that King David repaired a castle at Tulketh originally built by Stephen of Blois, but allowed to fall into ruin when Stephen established a colony of monks from Savigny at Tulketh who later transferred to Furness.

[22] *RRS* I, nos. 30, 31.

[23] *ESC*, no. 119, a protection for Tynemouth Priory.

[24] *ESC*, no. 223.

the absence of any early documents connected with the abbey of Soulseat (near Stranraer), we can appreciate that our lack of knowledge of David I's acts of government in Galloway may be due to archival loss rather than to the absence of any royal interference. This must surely be true for Moray, where although the Cistercian abbey of Kinloss was founded by David I himself its surviving records are exceedingly meagre and especially so before c.1200. We know that the burghs of Elgin, Forres and Inverness had been established in King David's time, but none has preserved royal record before the time of William the Lion.

A rather more reliable argument may be founded upon the surviving record of place-dates of royal acts, although here too we must proceed with caution. The table for David I[25] is as follows: Scone and Perth together, 16; Edinburgh, 14; Stirling, 13; Dunfermline, 12; Roxburgh, 9; Kinross, 5; Berwick, 4; Cadzow, 3. Two sojourns each are recorded for Clackmannan, Eldbotle,[26] Haddington, Irvine and Peebles; one each for Aberdeen, Abernethy, Banff, Clunie, Coldingham, Earlston, Forfar, Glasgow, Kinghorn, St Andrews, Staplegordon and Traquair. This omits places which are now unequivocally in England, but Cumberland gives us Carlisle (2), Lamplugh (1), and doubtfully Culgaith (2),[27] while Northumberland yields one for Norham and two for Newcastle upon Tyne. Assuming that the unidentified Abernethy is the old royal centre on the Tay and not the probably equally royal estate or thanedom of Abernethy on the Spey,[28] the table seems to show the king and court straying only very seldom from the Tay-Clyde-Tweed zone. But once again we must beware of circularity. There was certainly a tendency for beneficiaries to obtain royal acts when the king was sojourning with them or at least in their vicinity. Thus the preponderance of surviving record from south-eastern Scotland might be expected to produce a bias in favour of south-eastern place-dates. Of course there were exceptions: we may never know why Alexander of St Martin's charter of Athelstaneford (E. Lothian) passed at Forfar,[29] or why two of Dunfermline Abbey's charters had to be issued at 'Strathirewin in Galloway', that is Irvine in Ayrshire.[30] Foreign beneficiaries or seekers after favours would have to pursue the king wherever they could find him. The monks of Whitby found King David at Edinburgh,[31] the monks of St Andrew's, Northampton found him at Berwick and Dunfermline (and his son at Kinghorn),[32] while the monks of Thiron-le-Gardais, north west of Chartres, tracked the king down to the pleasant hunting-lodge of Clunie near Dunkeld[33] –

---

[25] Based upon the texts as published in *ESC* and *RRS* I. It does not seem necessary to cite the individual documents, but spurious items are ignored.

[26] In Gullane. Its importance in the twelfth century (for which see, incidentally, *RRS*, I, no. 194 and G. W. S. Barrow, *The Anglo-Norman Era in Scottish History* (Oxford, 1980), 169–70) is explained by the fact that it was at or close to the southern terminus of the 'Earl's Ferry' joining East Lothian to Fife.

[27] But see n. 20 above.

[28] *ESC*, no. 132, 'Abernithi'. On general grounds Abernethy on Tay is likely, but the document is a brieve addressed to the earls of Orkney and Caithness, which might point to a sojourn in northern Scotland.

[29] *ESC*, no. 186.

[30] *ESC*, nos. 84, 85.

[31] *ESC*, no. 254.

[32] *ESC*, nos. 56, 60, 114.

[33] *ESC*, no. 136.

deceiving the French scholar, Lucien Merlet, into supposing that the king of Scots journeyed to Burgundy.[34]

It is not only in the geographical field that the surviving written acts of David I give us an abundance of important leads. They are equally rich in information regarding the higher echelons of government personnel, the extent of imitation of Anglo-Norman practices, the need to choose formulae which adequately expressed indigenous practices, and in general the formulation and hardening of the conventions of written government. The language, of course, was invariably Latin, the phraseology and style adhering closely, for the most part, to models derived from the England of Henry I. Occasionally the Frenchness of a particular clerk's mental processes shows through, as in a charter for the king's knight Arnulf, who is to hold the rich Berwickshire estate of Swinton as freely as Udard son of Liulf son of Eadwulf, and sometime sheriff of Bamburgh, had possessed it.[35] Here Earl Madeth or Madad of Atholl is called Maduc the consul, Manasser Marmion appears as Marsel, Herbert is not *camerarius* but Chamberlein, while Ralph Lovel of Castle Cary makes his début in Scottish record as Ralph 'Nuuel'.[36] The king's declaration in support of the claims of the *clerici* of Old Deer to immunity from secular exactions poses a trickier linguistic problem.[37] As far as royal style, address and main text are concerned, the document – it exists only in a mid-twelfth century copy – appears entirely authentic, although the place-name Banff has a Gaelic spelling form.[38] It is the witness-list and place-date which raise questions. Each of three bishops is introduced by a separate 'Teste' – instead of the usual 'Testibus' – and then a further single 'Teste' introduces eight lay witnesses. One, perhaps two, of the bishops' dioceses are given in a Gaelic form,[39] while all the secular witnesses' names appear in Gaelic spelling, although (as was common enough in Old and Middle Irish scribal practice) linked by Latin 'et'. The place-date appears as Abberdeon instead of Aberdon. We can be absolutely certain that if the royal seal was applied to an authentic brieve of immunity the document would have been written in Latin. Has this then been translated into Gaelic, to be partially retranslated into Latin? Has the original Latin text been copied by a learned scribe of Deer who has, almost unconsciously as it were, gaelicized the place-names and personal names? Or is the document as we have it a subtle and ingenious forgery designed to underpin the little cache of *notitiae* and charters, all written in Gaelic, copied into the gospel book, the truth of whose statements we are in no position to deny or corroborate? At present there seems no way of resolving a pleasingly tantalizing problem of diplomatic.

---

[34] *Cartulaire de l'Abbaye de la Ste-Trinité de Tiron*, ed. L. Merlet (*Société Archéologique d'Eure-et-Loir*, 2 vols, Chartres, 1883), i 80–1.

[35] *ESC*, no. 100.

[36] If this suggestion is correct, 1136 or even 1137 seem more probable years for its issue than Lawrie's 'c.1135'. For Ralph Lovel's activities at this period see *Gesta Stephani*, ed. and translated by K. R. Potter, with new introduction and notes by R. H. C. Davis (Oxford, 1976), 66–9 and pp. xxvii–xxviii.

[37] *ESC*, no. 223. Also edited and translated by K. H. Jackson, *The Gaelic Notes in the Book of Deer* (1972), 22–3, 32, 36. The form of the greeting *salutes* (instead of *salutem*) hardly tells against authenticity in a copy evidently made by the beneficiary's scribe.

[38] Banb, literally 'sucking pig'. But it may also mean land unploughed for a year, fallow. A Latin-trained clerk would have written Banef or Banf.

[39] Duncallden for Dunkeld, perhaps Cat' for Caithness, although the name might represent Catanesia.

Three of the lay witnesses to the Deer charter are earls; or at least two are earls (Fife and Angus) and one (Atholl) was perhaps tutor of the earldom for the child earl Malcolm.[40] In general, the relative autonomy of the earldoms is reflected in the fact that most earls witnessed only solemn documents or at least on solemn occasions. Once, in a solemn charter for Dunfermline Abbey issued by Malcolm IV before 1159, this exclusivity of the earls is recognised by the provision of a separate witnessing-clause introduced by the words *et de comitibus*, followed by the names of the earls of Dunbar, Strathearn, Fife, Mar, Atholl and (unnamed) Angus.[41] (So much, incidentally, for the alleged primacy of the earldom of Fife.) But one way or another all the earldoms save Menteith and Lennox are represented in King David's charters by the attestation of their holders. While the majority of earls occur only rarely the earls of Fife and Dunbar are frequent witnesses, and clearly formed part of the inner circle of courtiers and household notables by whom the king was regularly accompanied.[42] The royal clerks imitated the practice of Henry I's chancery in producing short and apparently ephemeral brieves to which one or two individuals (often office-holders) were witness. They did not, however, take matters to the extreme of Henry I's terse writs to so many of which the chancellor or some other royal familiar is sole witness.[43] Much more commonly, David I's brieves and charters were witnessed by anything from half a dozen to a dozen individuals, two or three of whom may have had household offices such as chancellor, chamberlain and steward while others may have held the position of justiciar or sheriff yet will not usually be so styled. In fact, although the address of David I's brieves and charters in the second half of his reign commonly included *justicie* or *justiciarii* not a single individual figuring in royal acts before 1153 is actually identified as a justiciar, and comparatively few are explicitly styled sheriff. Now and again we have evidence from the witness-lists that a notable outsider was visiting the Scottish court. Such, I believe, was Robert 'de Paintona' who witnessed David's foundation charter of Selkirk Abbey, which seems to have been issued round about 1120.[44] This witness was surely Robert lord of Bampton in Devon, son of Walter of Douai, and an important opponent of Stephen in 1136.[45] According to the author of the *Gesta Stephani* Robert's son and kinsmen took refuge from Stephen's forces at the court of the king of Scots and incited him to invade northern England in 1138.[46] One of Robert of Bampton's followers (perhaps his kinsman) was the lord of Castle Cary in Somerset, Ralph Lovel, and we have seen that, disguised not too heavily as Ralph 'Nuuel', he is named as witness to a charter which Lawrie dated c.1135 but which should perhaps be placed in 1136 or 1137. A further visitor from the same

[40] Duncan earl of Fife, Gillebrigte earl of Angus, Maelmuire 'of Atholl'. See Jackson, *Gaelic Notes*, 81–3.
[41] *RRS* I, no. 118 (p. 185).
[42] G. W. S. Barrow, *David I of Scotland (1124–1153). The Balance of New and Old* (Stenton Lecture for 1984, University of Reading, 1985), 15–16 (where 'nine' in line 2 should read 'ten') and nn. 97–99.
[43] E.g., *RRAN*, ii, nos. 511, 519, 520, 522, 523, 528, 597 and many others.
[44] *ESC*, no. 35 (p. 28). Compare the spelling form Paintona with Baentona, Badentona for Bampton, Devon, appearing in *Pipe Roll 31 Henry I*, 153–4; *RRAN*, ii, no. 1391; iii, no. 276 (p. 103).
[45] For Walter or Walscin of Douai as a Devon and Somerset landowner in Domesday see *VCH Devon*, i, 485b–489a, 563–4; *VCH Somerset*, i, 497a–501a.
[46] *Gesta Stephani*, ed. Potter and Davis (1976), 54–5; cf. pp. 30–1.

part of England was Robert of Montacute (Montagu), presumably a younger son of Drogo de Montagu who in 1086 was a Somerset landowner. Robert of Montacute witnessed the earlier of David I's two solemn charters for Dunfermline and the king's comparable charter for Holyrood Abbey, both documents perhaps belonging to the same period in or not much later than 1128.[47] No member of the Montague family is known to have settled in Scotland, in contrast with the Lovels who were established at Hawick around the middle of the twelfth century.

The most interesting visitor from England, to my mind, was Robert *de sigillo*, who had served for a number of years in the chancery of Henry I, appearing as early as 1121 as keeper of the king's seal.[48] John of Hexham tells us that after Stephen had made himself king of England in 1135 Robert *de sigillo* became a monk at Reading.[49] In June 1141 the Empress Maud secured his appointment as bishop of London, and Robert was present in the empress's court that summer when she was at Oxford. Among the company there were David I of Scotland, William the chancellor, Edward abbot of Reading and Brian FitzCount lord of Wallingford.[50] The editors of *RRAN*, iii would see William the chancellor as William brother of John FitzGilbert and were inclined to dismiss a somewhat fleetingly recorded William Giffard as a copyist's misreading.[51] But we should perhaps take William Giffard more seriously. He occurs (once as 'Brother William Giffard') as a witness to three acts of King David in Scotland,[52] in a remarkably high position – e.g. preceding two abbots and King David's chancellor, or immediately following a brace of bishops. With the king and his long-serving chamberlain Herbert, William Giffard helped to perambulate a parish-sized estate, Rindalgros (now the Rhynd), east of Perth.[53] This estate was evidently intended to provide the site and the resources for a powerful Benedictine house, filled with monks drawn from Reading Abbey, following the Cluniac observances, which would exert a considerable influence on the hinterland of one of King David's favourite royal castles and burghs. Is it far-fetched to imagine that if the mother house got into difficulties under Stephen it could count on a sympathetically Angevin 'safe haven' in Scotland?[54] Is it far-fetched to surmise that Brother William Giffard was indeed chancellor to the Empress, that he was, like Robert *de sigillo*, a monk of Reading, or even that had King David's original plan been put into effect William Giffard might have become the first head, as prior or abbot, of the grandest Scottish abbey that never was?[55] I hope we are back

[47] *ESC*, nos. 74 (p. 63: Robertus de Monte Acuto) and 153 (p. 119). Cf. Barrow, *Anglo-Norman Era*, 100 and n. 48; *VCH Somerset*, i, 410–411.
[48] J. A. Green, *The Government of England under Henry I* (1986), 270–1.
[49] *Symeonis Monachi Opera Omnia*, ed. T. Arnold (Rolls Series, 1882–5) ii, 309.
[50] *RRAN*, iii, nos. 68, 275, 316a, 328, 377, 393, 629, 630, 634, 647, 651, 899.
[51] *RRAN*, iii, p. xxx. The charters of the empress to which 'William Giffard chancellor' was a witness are *RRAN*, iii, nos. 792 and 793, given at Devizes. Both come from the Vetus Registrum of Salisbury. The editors date them '1141–7'.
[52] *ESC*, nos. 161, 207; *RRS* I, no. 44, this last also witnessed by the prior of Reading. Within the date-limits of this charter, 1147 x 51, the known priors of Reading were Robert, Hugh and possibly Reginald: B. R. Kemp, *Reading Abbey Cartularies* (Royal Historical Society, Camden Fourth Series 31, 1986), i, 26.
[53] *ESC*, no. 161. Rindalgros means 'point of thorny promontory', referring to the land between Tay and Earn at their confluence.
[54] It must be allowed that the twenty-two surviving acts of Stephen in favour of Reading Abbey (*RRAN*, iii, nos. 675–694, 695–6) do not suggest any hostility on the king's part.
[55] Dr Marjorie Chibnall makes no mention of William Giffard as chancellor of the empress (or in

from speculation to certainty when we observe that Robert *de sigillo*, the pro-Angevin monk of Reading, was in Scotland long enough to be named as witness to seven royal acts, five of King David and two of his son Earl Henry.[56] All these documents, to which Lawrie assigned dates ranging from c.1136 to c.1144, could belong to 1140. Scottish visits by Robert *de sigillo* are not to be multiplied beyond necessity, but even if he paid more than one his sojourns must have been earlier than June 1141 when he was promoted to the see of London, and are not likely to belong to the time of war and turbulence in 1138 and 1139.

It seems probable that Robert *de sigillo* was employed by the Empress and her supporters as a go-between to communicate with the Scottish court. But further than that, and bearing in mind his membership of the Benedictine community, are we not on fairly strong ground in assuming that Robert was carrying on negotiations between Edward, abbot of Reading since 1136, and the king of Scotland which were designed to lead to the creation of a Scottish daughter house of Reading? In this connexion we may notice that while two of Robert's Scottish appearances were at Roxburgh, others were at Perth, Scone and Clunie[57] a few miles to the north, suggesting a visit to prospect the site King David had clearly marked out for the new foundation. It is interesting to note that the Scottish royal clerks accorded the same respect to Robert *de sigillo* as to William Giffard: in witness lists he is placed once immediately after the chamberlain, once immediately after bishops and heads of religious houses and before earls and barons, once between a bishop and a mixed bunch of lay notables, once between the constable and a major baron, twice after the constable, an earl and the chamberlain but before four other lay notables, and once between an earl and the chamberlain on the one hand and three lay notables on the other.

These royal clerks, the majority of whom we probably know by name, made substantial progress towards establishing verbal conventions which remained the hallmark of Scottish royal charters down to the eighteenth century. Already in the 1120s, in a charter for Daventry Priory which passed at Yardley Hastings on the day its church of St Andrew was dedicated, David 'by God's grace king of Scots' addresses 'all his responsible men (*omnibus probis hominibus suis*)', although with 'friends' (*amicis*) added.[58] Thereafter – or therewith – the address to *omnes probi homines* of all his land (or kingdom), contrasting conspicuously with the English address *omnibus fidelibus suis*, steadily overtook the various alternatives with which King David's earlier charters were sprinkled – 'all his lieges', 'all his liege men and friends', 'all his barons and lieges', 'all those, Scots and English, established throughout his realm in Scotia and Lothian', etc. etc.[59] Despite the occasional use of variants of the brief general address as late as the reign of Malcolm IV it had clearly become unusual from the 1140s to depart from the norm of *omnibus probis hominibus totius terre sue* [*regni sui*], the formula still employed for Queen Anne, or for that matter for George III.[60]

any other capacity) in her study of *The Empress Matilda. Queen Consort, Queen Mother and Lady of the English* (1991).

[56] *ESC*, nos. 114 (reading *de Sigillo* for *de Nigell'*), 134, 136, 168, 170, 171, 175.

[57] *ESC*, nos. 168, 175 (Roxburgh); 134 (Perth), 136 (Clunie), 170, 171 (Scone).

[58] *ESC*, no. 59.

[59] *ESC*, nos. 57, 62, 65, 66, 70 etc.

[60] See David I's acts in *ESC* from no. 118 onwards, *passim*, and in *RRS* I, nos. 31, 44, 46. Cf. *RRS* I, 73; G. W. S. Barrow with the collaboration of W. W. Scott, *The Acts of William I king of Scots,*

The royal style *rex Scottorum*, with or without *dei gratia*, can be taken back before David I, certainly to the reign of his elder brother Edgar (d.1107)[61] and to the intervening reign of Alexander I.[62] It seems impossible, on available evidence, to state whether this style, which was carefully preserved until 1603, derived from the way native kings of Picts and of Scots had been designated either in Latin or in some vernacular, or from imitation of the style employed for William I and William II of England, or from a common west European tradition of royal *intitulatio*. By the fifteenth and sixteenth centuries the Scottish royal style had come to appear distinctive and reinforced populist theories of sovereignty,[63] but in the period before 1300 it can hardly have seemed significantly out of line among the familiar designations of European rulers.

King David's clerks were obviously aware that the chancery of Henry I normally styled the king *rex Anglorum* without *dei gratia*, and there are instances of this austerely simple style from quite early in the reign.[64] The lack of originals from its last decade makes it difficult, if not impossible, to be sure whether the simple *rex Scottorum* had by then become standard, as it certainly was throughout the reign of David's eldest grandson and successor Malcolm IV and for the first eight and a half years of the reign of William the Lion (December 1165 to May 1174).[65] Probably documents drafted in the king's chapel or writing office usually omitted *dei gratia* while those produced by beneficiaries, as well as exceptionally solemn or old-fashioned documents, tended to include it.[66] Three examples of David I's short brieves and charters may give something of the style and flavour of productions of the *capella regis*.

David by God's grace king of Scots to all his responsible men, greeting. Know that I have quitclaimed the abbot of Dunfermline's ship and everything contained within it of all custom belonging to me. Witness Bishop John, at Perth.[67]

David king of Scots to all the responsible men of his whole land, greetings. Know that I have given and granted to God and the brethren of Newbattle (Abbey) in perpetual alms one saltpan in Callendar as free and quit as any alms in my land may be given and granted most freely. Witness Earl Duncan.[68]

David king of Scots to all his men, greeting. Know that I have given and granted in alms to the church of the Holy Trinity of Dunfermline Crefbarrin

---

1165–1214, Regesta Regum Scottorum II (1971) [= *RRS* II], 76. For Anne, I have based my statement on a charter anent the barony of Marchmont, 31 January 1704, which I was able to inspect recently. For George III, see the original charter for the Society of Antiquaries of Scotland, 1783, of which a photograph is given in *The Scottish Antiquarian Tradition. Essays to mark the bicentenary of the Society of Antiquaries of Scotland, 1780–1980*, ed. A. S. Bell (Edinburgh, 1981), plate 1 facing p. 6.

[61] *ESC*, nos. 18–22.
[62] *ESC*, nos. 26–28, 31, 37, 39, 47–9.
[63] G. W. S. Barrow, 'Das mittelalterliche englische und schottische Königtum: ein Vergleich', *Historisches Jahrbuch* 102 (1982), 388–9.
[64] *ESC*, nos. 61, 67, 72.
[65] *RRS* I, 69–73; *RRS* II, 75–6.
[66] Examples of inclusion from late in the reign include *ESC*, nos. 179, 189, 194, 209.
[67] *ESC*, no. 88.
[68] *ESC*, no. 149.

[Carberry, Midlothian]. Witness Bishop John, Edward the chancellor, Hugh de Morville, at Eldbottle.[69]

Such, by 1153, was the well-established medium by which the king's will was conveyed and recorded in permanent form.

Thus far I have considered the reign and written acts of David I, already in his forties when his reign began and an old man when it ended some twenty-nine years later. What is commonly overlooked is that from as early as the 1130s David's was a dual reign, shared with his only son and apparent heir Henry, commonly styled earl from his holding one or both of the honours of Northumberland and Huntingdon. The precise nature of the relationship between David's rule and his son's is not easily understood, but there can, I believe, be no doubt that we have to deal with joint or at least coadjutorial royal government.

No fewer than nine examples survive in full texts of pairs of acts referring to the same transaction and issued simultaneously or almost simultaneously, by King David and his son.[70] In addition, we have record of five lost pairs of acts.[71] These fourteen paired acts were for beneficiaries as diverse as the parish kirk of Haddington, the abbey of Thiron-le-Gardais, the Scottish religious houses at Jedburgh, Melrose, Newbattle and St Andrews, and the northern English priories of Hexham, Nostell and Tynemouth, as well as Huntingdon Priory and Richard Cumin and his wife. Moreover, when Earl Henry issued a charter for Holm Cultram a confirmation from David I followed very soon afterwards,[72] while the king's initial grant of revenues at Stirling to the rather obscure northern French Augustinian community at Arrouaise – the record of which is now lost – was confirmed, again quite quickly it seems, by Earl Henry.[73] The geographical spread of the properties involved in these dual acts is comparably wide, taking in Perth, Fife, Stirling, Lothian, Tweeddale, Teviotdale, Cumberland and Northumberland and the Honour of Huntingdon. This spread rules out any suggestion that Earl Henry's responsibilities were confined to Lothian or south-eastern Scotland, still less merely to the earldom of Northumberland. Attention has often been focused upon the charters issued by David and Henry for the cathedral priory of St Andrews in 1144,[74] the conventional date at which the Augustinian house was formally established. The occasion was clearly invested with special solemnity. In addition to charters from the king and his son there was a dignified document from the bishop of St Andrews with an A.D. date of 1144,[75] and a solemn privilege issued by Lucius II at the Lateran on 14 May 1144.[76] The bull was said

[69] *ESC*, no. 157.
[70] *ESC*, nos. 134/135; 136/137; 141/142 (= *RRS* I, no. 41); 146/147; 163/164; 189/190; *RRS* I, nos. 24/30; 37/38; 39/40. In the case of the pair for Thiron it is clear from the edition of L. Merlet that the documents were copied into the cartulary together (*Cartulaire de Tiron*, i, no. LX, ii, no. CCXLI). The original charter of Earl Henry survives in the Archives départementales de l'Eure-et-Loir at Chartres.
[71] *RRS* I, nos. 70, 72, 83, 103 and *Registrum Sancte Marie de Neubotle* (Bannatyne Club, 1849), no. 263.
[72] *ESC*, nos. 244, 245.
[73] *RRS* I, no. 35.
[74] *ESC*, nos. 163, 164.
[75] *ESC*, no. 162.
[76] *ESC*, no. 165. Cf. R. Somerville, *Scotia Pontificia. Papal Letters to Scotland before the Pontificate of Innocent III* (1982), no. 25.

to have been prompted by the request of Bernard bishop of St Davids, for whose see another bull was issued on the same date.[77] (Bishop Bernard, incidentally, was among the Empress Maud's supporters who gathered about her in the Thames valley in the summer of 1141.)[78] What has attracted the interest of scholars is that in all three Scottish documents, those issued by Bishop Robert, King David and Earl Henry, the king's son and heir is styled *rex designatus* – most elaborately in the two royal charters, *Henricus filius et Deo donante heres meus et rex designatus* and *ego Henricus gloriosi et illustris Regis David filius et Deo propitio heres et rex designatus*. The title also appears in the mid-twelfth century 'Legend of St Andrew', hardly independently since the author seems to have made use of the 1144 charters, to which as a canon of the cathedral he would naturally have had access.[79]

Although the Capetian title *rex designatus* occurs only in texts of St Andrews provenance, there seems no reason to doubt that Henry son of the king of Scots did indeed enjoy this status, possibly conferred as early as 1136 when he attended King Stephen's Easter court and sat at the table on the king's right hand.[80] The very close association between Henry and his father in the government of Scotland and northern England is by no means incompatible with Henry's having been a 'designated king'. Henry's position as his father's son and heir apparent would of course be enough to explain why eleven of David's charters speak of gifts for the salvation of Henry's soul,[81] why Henry occurs as witness to sixteen of David's acts,[82] and why some fourteen of David's acts speak of his son's assent or agreement to what the king had done.[83] But a rather more formal status as 'designated king' would more readily account for charters actually issued jointly: D[avid] rex Scot[orum] et H[enricus] suus filius – with verbs in the singular(!);[84] 'Know that I and Earl Henry my son . . .';[85] 'Know that I have granted and have given, simultaneously with my father, . . .'.[86]

Altogether, some fifty-two acts of Henry of Scotland have survived, fifteen of them originals and thirty-nine copies.[87] His style in these acts varies considerably, but the common thread running through almost all the variants is *filius regis Scotie (Scottorum)*. *Dei gratia* is used twice,[88] *comes* by itself twenty-five times, and *comes* along with a word for Northumberland or the Northumbrians in five acts,[89] two of them originals. We should hardly expect Earl Henry's documents to show the same degree of standardization in their *formulae* as King David's, but

[77] Somerville, *Scotia Pontificia*, 35. The bull for St David's is no. 8607 in the calendar of Jaffé-Löwenfeld.
[78] *RRAN* iii, nos. 68, 393, 629.
[79] *Chronicles of the Picts: Chronicles of the Scots*, ed. W. F. Skene (1867), 192–3.
[80] *RRS* I, 4, n.3.
[81] *ESC*, nos. 109, 122, 171, 189, 209, 224, 225, 237, 242; *RRS* I, no. 39.
[82] *ESC*, nos. 72, 83, 104, 108, 134, 141, 145, 146, 155, 172, 176, 179, 189, 194, 229; *RRS* I, no. 37.
[83] *ESC*, nos. 65, 74, 99, 104, 108, 119, 134, 141, 144, 153, 179, 189, 209, 220; *RRS* I, no. 37.
[84] *ESC*, no. 100.
[85] *ESC*, no. 224.
[86] *RRS* I, no. 29.
[87] As with those of David I, the acts of Henry of Scotland are to be found in *ESC*, from no. 112 onward, and in *RRS* I, from no. 11.
[88] *ESC*, no. 133 (c.1141), *RRS* I, no. 32 (1141x52).
[89] *ESC*, nos. 137, 190, 217; *RRS* I, nos. 23, 32.

nevertheless the overlaps are very numerous: imitation and borrowing were clearly commonplace. The earl had his own chancellor and *clerici*, possibly implying his own writing office, and it is surely significant that clerical and cancellarial personnel moved from Earl Henry's household to that of the king. In particular Ingram or Enguerrand, who was bishop of Glasgow from 1164 to 1174, had served as clerk and chancellor to Earl Henry, clerk of the king after his master's death, and then chancellor to Malcolm IV from 1162 to 1164.[90] But Jordan, the elusive and obviously short-lived chancellor of David I c.1141, may have served as one of Earl Henry's chaplains,[91] and some other overlaps may be discerned. Earl Henry, in any case, maintained – or was maintained by – his own household, obviously totally distinct from – and for most of the time at some distance from – that of his father. Moreover, although the earl was not restricted politically to Lothian or Northumberland, it must be recognised that his surviving acts seldom show him to have been present north of the Forth. But no account of the government of King David I can be sufficient which fails to give due weight to the fact that it was directed by a team of father and son.

It remains to consider how best to make this corpus of evidence relating to twelfth-century Scotland and England available to scholars. The 1905 edition by Sir Archibald Lawrie is now manifestly inadequate. Not only did Lawrie omit some forty documents which have since been edited in *Regesta Regum Scottorum* 1, he produced texts which were designed to be read and understood perfectly by persons – one might, not unfairly, say gentlemen – who had received a sound classical education. Lawrie was a highly intelligent, historically sensitive man of a somewhat sceptical disposition who had been thoroughly trained in Scots Law, had assisted Cosmo Innes with the Record Commission's edition of the *Acts of the Parliaments of Scotland* (especially in compiling the splendid index), and had spent by far the greater part of his working life serving as a judge in Ceylon.[92] Passionately and patriotically devoted to the history of his native land, Lawrie's aim was 'to collect the charters and other documents written in Scotland, or by or to Scotsmen, prior to the death of David I in 1153'.[93] In fact, as the large volumes of papers in his sprawlingly illegible handwriting amply demonstrate, his ambition was to extend the task to the end of William the Lion's reign in 1214.[94] Although he had studied the work of Giry, he was not a trained diplomatist. He was not interested in the minutiae of spelling or phrase or formula, or even whether a text came from an original document or from a copy, although he does take care to label an original as such. He revised the spelling of his texts to conform to classical conventions, and extended initials and abbreviations, so that (for example) it is impossible to tell from Lawrie's edition that the

---

[90] *RRS* I, 28–9.

[91] *ESC*, nos. 123, 131, 141; *RRS* I, nos. 21, 22, 41.

[92] A brief but sympathetic notice of Sir Archibald Campbell Lawrie (1837–1914) appeared in *Scottish Historical Review*, xii (1915), 113–14. He was the son of James Adair Lawrie, professor of surgery in the university of Glasgow. He retired in 1901 from the post of Acting Chief Justice of the Supreme Court of Ceylon.

[93] *ESC*, p. v.

[94] Twenty-six volumes of Scottish historical documents collected by Lawrie, largely in his hand but some in typescript, are in the National Library of Scotland, catalogued as Chart. 74, 36.3.1–15, 37.4.1–11.

preferred style of the twelfth-century clerks was *D. rex Scot'* (or *Scot(t)orum*), or occasionally *D. dei gratia rex Scot(torum)*, not *David rex Scotiae*, or some such.[95]

I would therefore propose to prepare a simple diplomatic edition of David I's acts, along with those of his son. This edition would broadly follow the conventions established by the *Ecole des Chartes*, although the idiosyncrasies of scribal usage in surviving originals would be treated with respect. It must be hoped that the publishers of the volume, whoever they might be, would agree to the generous provision of facsimiles to illustrate the handwriting of the scribes employed by beneficiaries or by the king himself, and to show generally the physical make-up of charters and brieves and the application of the king's seal. As a mere historian, I am utterly persuaded of the importance of presenting the documents in chronological order, even although the majority of our texts do not bear any date of time. In my judgement, the advantage of perceiving the development of a king's reign, of being able to set the sequence of documents against an unfolding of political or other events, above all of studying the changing composition of household and court in the order in which offices were filled and vacated and refilled, far outweighs the opportunity of assessing royal impact upon or interest in this or that monastery or baronial family. The resulting volume, which would not contain any equivalent of the many pages (almost 250) of informative and often amusing notes with which Lawrie still holds the interest of his readers,[96] would be modest in size, perhaps twice the length of the late Hilary Offler's edition of *Durham Episcopal Charters*.[97] It would, I hope, be a useful tool for anyone who may wish to study kingship in twelfth-century Europe.

---

[95] This is especially noticeable in the case of the Durham originals, e.g. *ESC*, nos. 65 (correct), 99, 100, 101 (extended without notice), 111, 121 (incorrect).

[96] Lawrie excelled at discouraging mere surmise. Having cited five authorities four of whom ventured to guess at the identity of a witness to Alexander I's solemn charter for Scone Priory, Lawrie concludes: 'In short, nothing is known of Beth comes' (*ESC*, pp. 283–4).

[97] *Durham Episcopal Charters, 1071–1152*, ed. H. S. Offler (Surtees Society 179, 1968).

IN NEUTRO LATERE: THE ARMED NEUTRALITY OF RANULF II EARL OF CHESTER IN KING STEPHEN'S REIGN [1]

Paul Dalton

The political behaviour of the magnate community during the troubled years of King Stephen's reign has attracted the attention of many historians over the last century or more. The barons have commonly been portrayed as men who, either out of greed, a desire for independence or necessity, were regularly prepared to change sides in the succession crisis; so helping to reduce England to the terrible state of anarchy described by contemporary chroniclers.[2] It is a portrayal based largely upon the careers of a few great men, and among the greatest of them Ranulf II earl of Chester.[3] It is one which is made, however, from the perspective of the leaders of the rival factions rather than that of the magnates themselves. The purpose of this paper is to re-examine the conflicting historical interpretations of Ranulf's career and the sources on which they are based, to introduce relevant new evidence, and ultimately to offer a more balanced assessment of the earl's political policy in Stephen's reign; one which may help us achieve a better understanding of the behaviour of many other magnates during the anarchy.

The earliest general interpretation of Earl Ranulf's career was made by William Stubbs in 1880: 'The earl of Chester, although, whenever he prevailed on himself to act, he took part against Stephen, fought rather on his own account than on Matilda's.'[4] Commenting on this view John Horace Round declared that Ranulf's policy, 'could not be expressed more tersely or more accurately', but added that the magnates were prepared to sell their loyalty to the highest bidder and that in this respect the earl of Chester was very much a man of the same

[1] My thanks are due to Dr David Bates, Dr Marjorie Chibnall, Dr David Crouch, Prof. Edmund King, and Mrs Kathleen Thompson for their help in preparing this paper for publication, and to the other participants of the conference for their stimulating comments and suggestions. Research for this paper was undertaken with the support of a British Academy Post Doctoral Fellowship.
[2] Most notably by J. H. Round, *Geoffrey de Mandeville*, London 1892; F. M. Stenton, *The First Century of English Feudalism*, 2nd edn Oxford 1961, chap. VII; R. H. C. Davis, *King Stephen*, 3rd edn London 1990; R. H. C. Davis, 'Geoffrey de Mandeville Reconsidered' *EHR* lxxix, 1964, 299–307; J. O. Prestwich, 'The Treason of Geoffrey de Mandeville' *EHR* ciii, 1988, 283–312, and his subsequent debate with R. H. C. Davis: *EHR* ciii, 1988, 313–17, 960–68; *EHR* cv, 1990, 670–2. For a rather different view of baronial policy, see Edmund King, 'King Stephen and the Anglo-Norman Aristocracy' *History* lix, 1974, 180–94.
[3] In addition to considerable possessions in Normandy Ranulf held land in nearly twenty English counties: W. Farrer, *Honors and Knights' Fees*, 3 vols, Manchester 1923–25, ii (Chester Fee); *The Charters of the Anglo-Norman Earls of Chester, c.1071–1237*, ed. G. Barraclough, Rec. Soc. of Lancs. and Cheshire 1988, xii; GEC, iii, 164–7; H. A. Cronne, *The Reign of Stephen 1135–54: Anarchy in England*, London 1970, map on p. 137.
[4] W. Stubbs, *The Constitutional History of England*, Oxford 1880, i, 372.

mould as Geoffrey de Mandeville, 'the most perfect and typical presentment of the feudal and anarchic spirit that stamps the reign of Stephen'.[5] Round argued that, with the exception of a brief period from 1142 until 1146, when he considered Ranulf to have adopted a position of 'armed neutrality', the earl changed sides from the royalist to the Angevin party and vice versa no less than seven times in Stephen's reign.[6] His views were challenged by the late Professor R. H. C. Davis who argued that Ranulf's changes of sides were far less frequent. Davis was convinced that the earl supported Stephen until 1140 when he rebelled and seized Lincoln castle, and thereafter, with the exception of only a brief period in 1146 when he was temporarily reconciled with the king, remained in revolt as a hesitant supporter of the Angevin cause until his death in 1153.[7]

In undermining Round's chronology Davis appears to have rejected his concept of armed neutrality. He portrayed the major baronial figures of Stephen's reign, the earl of Chester included, as *either* supporters of King Stephen *or* supporters of the empress. If the magnates were not on one side in the civil war, then they are usually assumed to be on the other.[8] I intend to suggest, however, that while this 'black and white' assessment may accurately reflect the policies of some magnates in the anarchy, it misinterprets the nature and the chronology of the allegiance offered by Ranulf earl of Chester (and possibly many other barons) to the rival political factions, and oversimplifies a sophisticated aristocratic response to the disputed succession which can usefully be summarised by the term armed neutrality. It is a suggestion based partly upon an examination of the complicated and historically controversial nature of ties of allegiance in this period; an examination which, within the confines of this paper, cannot hope to be comprehensive, but which I hope will make a contribution to the debate.

The definition of armed neutrality employed in this paper is not the one used of certain nation states in the late eighteenth century to describe non-combatants prepared to resort to action to force those engaged in war to respect their rights.[9] By these standards there is no doubt that the earl of Chester was not neutral. He became involved directly in the conflict, and could hardly have avoided doing so. But if we consider the nature of this involvement, in particular the crucial question of what Ranulf *saw himself* as fighting for, and if we confine ourselves to a consideration of his position with regard to the specific issue of the final resolution of the succession dispute, another possible and perfectly applicable definition of armed neutrality emerges. It will be the argument of this paper that when Ranulf fought in the civil war he saw himself as fighting primarily for his own interests rather than for those of the rival factions in the succession dispute; that the allegiance he offered to the rival factions was not an absolute allegiance offered alternately to one side and then the other for the purpose of resolving the succession dispute according to their wishes, but a crucially limited allegiance

---

[5] J. H. Round, 'King Stephen and the Earl of Chester' *EHR* x, 1895, 87; and his *Geoffrey de Mandeville*, v.
[6] Round, 'King Stephen', 87–91, quotation from p. 89.
[7] R. H. C. Davis, 'King Stephen and the Earl of Chester Revised' *EHR* lxxv, 1960, 654–60; Davis, *King Stephen*, 76, 93, and see also Appendix II. His interpretation appears to have been supported by Professor Barraclough: *Chester Charters*, 98, 101.
[8] Davis, *King Stephen*, 76, 93, and Appendix II.
[9] *A Dictionary of British History*, ed. consultant, J. P. Kenyon, London 1981, 19. I am grateful to Dr David Martin for this reference.

offered (perhaps simultaneously on occasions) to both sides with the object simply of minimising the problems and taking advantage of the opportunities posed by the succession dispute; and that so far as *the resolution of that dispute* was concerned *in his own mind* Ranulf supported the *ultimate* goals of neither faction and was effectively neutral.

The primary objective of the earl of Chester and his half-brother and ally, William of Roumare, in Stephen's reign was the preservation and expansion of their power within the localities, rather than the resolution of the succession dispute. This can only be understood by considering their familial and tenurial background.[10] Outside Cheshire their lands were mainly concentrated in Lincolnshire, which was one of the main theatres of their political activities during the anarchy. Their interests here derived primarily from their mother, Countess Lucy of Bolingbroke, and their great uncle, Hugh d'Avranches the second earl of Chester, who held considerable estates in the county in 1086. In addition, either then or later, Lucy enjoyed possession of some part of the Lincoln castle complex, possibly one of the towers or a separate motte distinct from the royal fortifications. Domesday records Lucy's Lincolnshire estates in the possession of her first husband, Ivo Taillebois, sheriff of Lincolnshire, and they passed with her to her second and third husbands, Roger Fitz Gerold and Ranulf Meschin, the respective fathers of her two sons, William of Roumare and Ranulf II earl of Chester. In c.1120, however, Ranulf Meschin surrendered the bulk of Lucy's lands and his own lordship of Carlisle to the king in order to secure his succession to the vacant earldom of Chester, and retained control of only those of Lucy's estates which she had inherited from her kinsman (possibly father) Thorold, the pre-conquest sheriff of Lincolnshire. In spite of this, Ranulf II and William of Roumare were determined to preserve their claims to the lands and offices held by their ancestors. In 1122 Roumare went into rebellion against Henry I in Normandy after the king refused to grant him the recently surrendered lands of his mother. Although restored to the *magnam partem juris quod proposcerat* in c.1127 Roumare failed to recover all of Lucy's estates, and it appears that twenty of her sixty Lincolnshire knights' fees passed to his half-brother Ranulf II. Debts recorded in the Pipe Roll of 1129 x 1130 suggest, however, that both Ranulf and his mother Lucy only managed to retain their estates belonging to the lordships of Bolingbroke and Chester at a heavy price.

In the reign of Stephen, Ranulf II and his half-brother worked closely together to continue their policy of preserving the integrity of their family lordships, and to advance and realise their claims to the powerful administrative offices formerly attached to them (including the shrievalty of Lincolnshire and, probably, the constableship of Lincoln castle). Their ultimate aim was both aggressive and acquisitive: to use this landed and administrative power base as a springboard from which to expand their tenurial and governmental control over large areas of territory throughout the midlands and north through the exercise of regalian rights, the acquisition of jurisdictional seats, and the domination of the lesser aristocracy; often at the expense of the authority of the crown. To them the

---

[10] For the details in this and the following paragraph, see P. Dalton, 'Aiming at the Impossible: Ranulf II Earl of Chester and Lincolnshire in the Reign of King Stephen' in *The Earldom of Chester and its Charters: A Tribute to Geoffrey Barraclough*, ed. A. T. Thacker (Journal of the Chester Arch. Soc., 71) 1991, 109–34 and the sources cited there.

succession dispute was of secondary importance, and their involvement in that dispute was conditioned to a large extent by their private local objectives rather than the ultimate goals of the rival political factions.

There can be little doubt that the earl of Chester and William of Roumare submitted and paid homage to King Stephen in 1136. Ranulf was in attendance on the king by 22 March that year when he was among a group of magnates who withdrew from court in opposition to the prominent place occupied there by Henry of Scotland, to whom Stephen had recently granted Ranulf Meschin's former lordship of Carlisle in the first treaty of Durham.[11] The rift between king and earl, however, was short-lived and Ranulf returned to court a few weeks later for the important Easter festival (22 March).[12] His half-brother Roumare also appears to have accepted Stephen's authority and, although apparently absent from court in 1136, attested two royal charters during the king's visit to Normandy in 1137, appears to have been made earl of Cambridge by Stephen after the forfeiture of the earldom of Huntingdon by the Scots in January 1138, and acted as a royal justice in Normandy later that year.[13]

The submission of the earl of Chester and his half-brother to the king was logical. Stephen was in the right place at the right time, and initially there were no rival contenders for the crown on the scene. But when the empress arrived in England in September 1139 to stake her claim to the royal dignity Earl Ranulf and his fellow magnates were confronted with a new and difficult political situation. Ranulf's response to this situation can first be judged in the complicated events of 1140–41 which appear at first sight to show him deserting the king for the cause of the Angevin party, but which on closer analysis reveal that he placed his own local interests before those of the rival factions and *in his own mind* considered himself to be neutral so far as the resolution of the succession dispute was concerned.

At some time before Christmas in 1140 Earl Ranulf is described as fraudulently seizing the royal castle of Lincoln after Stephen had prevented him from capturing Henry of Scotland with whom Ranulf was in dispute over possession of the lordship of Carlisle. The king responded by going to Lincolnshire, renewing a pact with the earl and leaving for London in peace. But later, at the request of the bishop and citizens of Lincoln, he returned to the city during the Christmas festival and besieged Ranulf and William of Roumare in the castle. Leaving Roumare to hold the fort, Ranulf escaped to his estates in Cheshire, appealed for help to his father-in-law, Robert earl of Gloucester, promised him a lasting fealty to the empress, and together with Robert defeated and captured Stephen at the

---

[11] *Symeonis Monachi Opera Omnia*, ed. T. Arnold, 2 vols, RS 1882–85, ii, 287 (hereafter cited as Symeon); *Chronicles of the Reigns of Stephen, Henry II and Richard I*, ed. R. Howlett, 4 vols, RS 1884–89, iii, 146 (hereafter cited as *Chronicles of the Reigns*). Earl Ranulf's individual sensitivity over matters of prestige is suggested by his prominence in the witness clauses of the royal charters he attested before 1140, and it is noteworthy that his name took precedence over that of Henry of Scotland in the one charter of Stephen they attested together at Easter 1136: *Regesta*, iii, no. 944.
[12] *Regesta*, iii, no. 271. He witnessed a further six royal charters before 1140, five of them granted at Westminster or Gillingham in 1136, and the last at an unspecified place between December 1138 and June 1139: *Regesta*, iii, nos. 818, 945–8, 819. His recognition of Stephen's position as king is also clear from one of his own charters granted to Basingwerk Abbey before 1140: *Chester Charters*, no. 37.
[13] *Regesta*, iii, p. xxi, nos. 67, 598; Orderic, vi, 495; Davis, *King Stephen*, 135.

battle of Lincoln in February 1141.[14] Professor Davis depicted Ranulf's seizure of Lincoln castle as an act of rebellion provoked by the second treaty of Durham of April 1139 in which Stephen regranted the Scots the lordships of Huntingdon and Carlisle, thereby depriving William of Roumare of the earldom of Cambridge and Ranulf of Chester of a Cumbrian honour considered by Davis to have been part of the earl's patrimony and the mainspring of his political policy; a rebellion which resulted in the earl deserting the king and, after Stephen's Christmas siege, becoming an adherent of the Angevin cause.[15] If the historical sources are re-examined, however, they will bear a rather different interpretation of the events of 1140–41. It is an interpretation which suggests that the crux of the troubles between Ranulf and Stephen was Lincoln rather than Carlisle, that Ranulf was fighting principally for his local objectives rather than the objectives of the Angevin party, and that he continued to accept Stephen as king.

To begin with the assumption that Carlisle was the mainspring of the earl of Chester's political policy. Although Ranulf's claims to Carlisle almost certainly explain his attempt to capture Henry of Scotland in 1140 and sparked off his conflict with the king, it is clear that his claims to Lincoln quickly came to predominate and were a far more important influence on his policy. As Professor Holt has pointed out, Carlisle was never, in fact, the patrimony of either Ranulf or his father; and Ranulf's claims to it were relatively weak.[16] Before 1140 there is little or nothing to indicate either that the earl's claims to Carlisle were of primary importance to him, or that they seriously undermined his relationship with the king. In 1136 the rift between Ranulf and Stephen over Henry of Scotland's presence at court lasted only a matter of weeks; and in 1139 the earl made no immediate response to the second treaty of Durham, in spite of Henry being at Stephen's side throughout the summer. Ranulf's attempt to capture Henry took place at least ten months later on a different visit to England.[17] It was in Lincolnshire, the Welsh frontier, and the midlands rather than Cumberland where Ranulf had his strongest claims to land, and where his political activities were concentrated.[18] The lordship of Carlisle receives no mention in the great royal and ducal charters bestowed upon the earl; and in 1149 Ranulf was quite prepared to abandon his claim to Carlisle in return for the lordship of Lancaster.[19] Taken together, the evidence points to the conclusion that Ranulf's claim to Carlisle was not his principal priority, that he was far more concerned with his position in Lincolnshire and the midlands, and that he seized Lincoln castle in 1140 primarily because he wanted control of the fortress for its own sake, rather than because he was aggrieved by the second treaty of Durham.

When Ranulf fought the king at the battle of Lincoln it is clear that he was fighting for himself rather than for the cause of the empress. It is clear from a

---

[14] *Gesta Stephani*, ed. K. R. Potter and R. H. C. Davis, Oxford 1976, 110–114; *Historia Novella*, 46–50; Symeon, 306–309; Orderic, vi, 538–46.
[15] Davis, 'The Earl of Chester Revised', 659; Davis, *King Stephen*, 46–8, 134–5; *Regesta*, iii, no. 178 and note.
[16] J. C. Holt, 'Politics and Property in Early Medieval England' *Past & Present* lvii, 1972, 51–2.
[17] Symeon, 300.
[18] Dalton, 'Aiming at the Impossible', 109–34; Holt, 'Politics and Property', 51; *Gesta Stephani*, 110, 116, 128, 166, 184, 192–6, 198–202, 216, 220, 236, 238; *Historia Novella*, 46–7; Huntingdon, 268, 272–4, 277, 279; Symeon, 306–8, 310, 323–4, 331.
[19] *Regesta*, iii, nos. 178, 180; Symeon, 323.

comparison of the testimony of two independent chroniclers. William of Malmesbury informs us that when besieged at Lincoln Ranulf,

> sent to [Robert of Gloucester] promising by the messengers a lasting fidelity to the empress if . . . he would rescue from wrong those who were in danger and on the very brink of captivity . . . The earl of Gloucester was not hard to persuade since he could not bear the shame of the thing; and at the same time, loathing delay because his noble country, for the sake of two persons, was being tormented by the plunder and slaughter of civil war, he preferred . . . to hazard a final decision . . . So, to avenge God and his sister and to free his relatives, he took the risk . . . though he cunningly concealed his purpose all the way from Gloucester to Lincoln . . . The time of decision came on the very day of the Purification of the most blessed Mary, by the river . . . Trent . . . Only then did the earl disclose his intention to [Earl Ranulf] . . .[20]

The earl of Chester was simply appealing to a powerful relative to help him out of a dangerous situation. But the earl of Gloucester wanted to make the imminent confrontation with the king the occasion for a final settlement of the succession dispute. That he kept his objective hidden from Ranulf until the last moment reveals that the earl of Chester had no knowledge of his father-in-law's plans, and suggests that he may not have been sympathetic towards them.

More evidence that the two earls had markedly different objectives in fighting Stephen at Lincoln is to be found in the speeches put into their mouths by Henry of Huntingdon in his description of the haranguing of the troops immediately prior to the battle. Although speeches related by chroniclers must be treated with caution, Henry of Huntingdon's position as an archdeacon of Lincoln suggests not only that he may have been well-acquainted with local events, but also that he may have been just as aware of public opinion as some monastic chroniclers. This awareness, and the accuracy of his testimony in this instance, is indicated by the fact that the elements in the speeches concerning the arguments being advanced by the rival factions in support of the legitimacy of their causes, are entirely in accord with the arguments related in other sources.[21]

Earl Ranulf is made to say that,

> since it is through me you are called to encounter this peril, it is fitting that I should myself bear the brunt of it, and be foremost in the attack on this faithless king, who has broken the peace to which he is pledged. While I, therefore, animated by my own valour, and the remembrance of the king's perfidy, throw myself on the king's troops . . . it will be your part . . . to follow up my success.[22]

Earl Robert, on the other hand, is made to reply that although it was fitting that Ranulf should ask for the honour of striking the first blow on account of his high rank and valour,

---

[20] *Historia Novella*, 47–8.
[21] See below, note 47.
[22] Huntingdon, 268.

I am actuated by considerations of a very different kind. The king has inhumanly usurped the crown, faithless to the oath which he swore to my sister, and by the disorder he has occasioned has caused the slaughter of many thousands; and by the example he has set of an illegal distribution of lands, has destroyed the rights of property.[23]

The earl of Gloucester was speaking the language of the Angevin party manifesto. He was aggrieved by a faithless king who had broken his oath of fealty to Matilda and engaged in an illegal distribution of property; and he was clearly fighting for the cause of the empress.[24] The earl of Chester was speaking about personal grievances, about the king's breaking of a peace pledge; and he was clearly fighting for his own interests.

But what *exactly* were those interests? To find our answer we must look forward to the events of 1146 and compare them with those of 1140. It was in 1146 that the earl of Chester,

came to the king in humility and submission and, repenting at last of the cruelty and treachery he had shown to him when he stretched forth his hands against his king and lord at the capture of Lincoln and when he encroached for his own aggrandizement on a very wide extent of the royal possessions, was restored to favour after the pact of their old friendship had been renewed between them.[25]

Was this the same pact renewed between king and earl in 1140, and if so what did it involve? An indication of the terms of the 1140 pact is provided by William of Malmesbury who, although not specifically referring to a pact, states that in that year the king had gone away in peace from Lincolnshire before Christmas and had made grants (*honoribus auxerat*) to the earl of Chester and his half-brother.[26] There is evidence to suggest that these grants included the right to exercise some form of administrative and military powers over the castle and city of Lincoln, and possibly even the whole county of Lincolnshire. The author of the *Liber Eliensis*, who may be giving a version of Ranulf's story in 1140, wrote: 'Nam postea rex cum castellum Lincollie repeteret a comite Ranulfo Cestrie, quod ad custodiendum ei tradiderat, et ipse non solum illi reddere negavit, sed conducto illic secum plurimo comitum et baronum agmine bellum parabatur in-

---

[23] Huntingdon, 268–9.
[24] For Robert's loyalty to the empress's cause, see the comments of William of Malmesbury: *Historia Novella*, 64.
[25] *Gesta Stephani*, 184. See also *ASC*, 201; William of Newburgh, *The History of English Affairs*, ed. P. G. Walsh & M. J. Kennedy, Warminster 1988, 72 (hereafter cited as Newburgh); Huntingdon, 279.
[26] *Historia Novella*, 46. See also Orderic, vi, 538–40.
[27] *Liber Eliensis*, ed. E. O. Blake, Royal Hist. Soc. Camden 3rd ser. xcii, 1962, 320–1. I owe this reference to Dr Chibnall who has suggested to me that it seems to indicate that there was either a misunderstanding between the king and Ranulf about the exact rights that were conceded to Ranulf in the castle, or that the earl deliberately misrepresented the position to justify his action. Dr Chibnall has also pointed out to me that it is difficult to know whether Stephen was trying to insist on making Lincoln a royal castle, or whether he was prepared to allow Ranulf to hold it provided that the earl recognized the king's right to place his own men in the garrison in times of emergency. This was a right claimed by Henry I in castles held by others, and Stephen seems to have attempted to assert it, as when he seized the castles of the bishops. The situation at Lincoln is complicated by the existence there of two mottes, one of which probably belonged to Ranulf's

ferre'.[27] Ranulf's acquisition of some form of rights in the castle and city in 1140 is also indicated by his issuing of 'harsh orders to the townsmen and the people of the neighbourhood', and by his confident possession of the fortress after the king had left in peace early in the year.[28] When Stephen returned to besiege the fortress at Christmas he found that it was 'almost empty', and that the half-brothers had 'settled without a care [there]' and were expecting 'nothing less than the king's arrival'.[29] Moreover, the creation of William of Roumare as earl of Lincoln, which probably took place in 1140, may also suggest the conveyance of rights in the castle.[30] Although Roumare seems to have received the earldom without the county, he is known to have been closely involved in his half-brother's seizure and occupation of the castle in 1140, and to have acquired (possibly in the same year) judicial rights over the city authorities in Lincoln as well as control of the important Mowbray Lincolnshire manor and administrative centre of Gainsborough, where he constructed a castle.[31]

For the details of the 1146 pact we are more fortunate. We have a charter. It is an abbreviated charter referred to by its fourteenth century copyist in the margin of his parchment as a *Concordia inter regem Stephanum et Rannulfum comitem Cestr(ie)*. In it the king gives and concedes to the earl the castle and city of Lincoln until he is able to make Ranulf have his Norman lands and all his castles. The charter then stipulates that after recovering his continental possessions Ranulf was to hold one of the king's towers of Lincoln castle until the king was free to give him the fortress of Tickhill, whereafter Stephen was to recover the castle and city of Lincoln, and Ranulf was to retain the tower which his mother had founded together with the constableship of Lincoln castle and Lincolnshire in hereditary right. Finally, the charter grants Ranulf a series of northern and midland lordships held by other magnates.[32] In addition the peace arrangements also appear to have involved Stephen's concession to William of Roumare of the castle and bridge of Gainsborough with an additional grant of the important royal soke manor and wapentake seat of Kirton-in-Lindsey.[33] The apparent concordance between the pacts of 1140 and 1146, the king's grants to Ranulf and his half-brother in 1140, the earl's confident possession of Lincoln immediately after

---

mother, Countess Lucy of Bolingbroke. A further problem concerns the exact position in Stephen's reign of Ralph de la Haye whose father Robert held the constableship of Lincoln castle in the reign of Henry I, and who witnessed a number of the earl of Chester's charters in the 1140s. For notes on Lincoln castle, see *History of the King's Works*, ed. H. M. Colvin, 6 vols, London 1963–77, ii, 704; J. W. F. Hill, *Medieval Lincoln*, Cambridge 1965, 87–9; D. J. Cathcart King, *Castellarium Anglicanum: An Index and Bibliography of the Castles of England, Wales and the Islands*, 2 vols, London 1983, i, 261–2 and note 24; J. A. Green, *The Government of England Under Henry I*, Cambridge 1986, 258; GEC, iii, 164–8; vii, 666–71, 743–6.

[28] *Gesta Stephani*, 110.

[29] *Historia Novella*, 46. See also Orderic, vi, 540; H. A. Cronne, 'Ranulf de Gernons, Earl of Chester, 1129–53' *TRHS* 4th ser. xx, 1937, 115–17. K. R. Potter's translation of the *Historia Novella* states that the brothers had 'settled unsuspiciously' in the castle.

[30] *Gesta Stephani*, 110; Davis, *King Stephen*, 134. Although I do not believe that comital titles necessarily carried with them administrative and military powers over counties, county towns and castles, it was common for magnates who enjoyed the right to exercise powers of this nature to possess such titles.

[31] *Regesta*, iii, no. 472. For Roumare's control of Gainsborough by c.1142 at the latest, and his construction of a castle there, see Dalton, 'Aiming at the Impossible', 117–18.

[32] *Regesta*, iii, no. 178.

[33] *Regesta*, iii, no. 494.

these grants, and the *concordia* of 1146 is too close to be mere coincidence. The different strands of evidence suggest the same thing: that the pacts and the *concordia* were one and the same; that the royal charter granted to Earl Ranulf in 1146 was at least partially a reissue of an earlier document granted in 1140; that although the tenor of the later charter is likely to have been substantially different from that of its predecessor owing to the confiscation of Ranulf's Norman estates and a degree of political realignment in England in the period that separated them, an important element in both the 1140 and 1146 pacts remained unchanged; and that this element was the grant to the earl of Chester of effective control of the castle and city of Lincoln which were the key centres of royal administration in Lincolnshire.[34]

The pact of 1140 was itself a renewal of an earlier agreement which may have been made in 1136 when Stephen made many concessions and pacts in order to secure acceptance, homage and support.[35] That Stephen had made important grants to the earl of Chester and his half-brother before 1140 is suggested by the fact that when he heard of the seizure of Lincoln castle the king 'was very angry at the news and astounded that his close friends, on whom he had heaped lands and honours, should have committed such a crime'.[36] If, as seems likely, these gifts incorporated the castle and city of Lincoln it would make more sense of the events of 1140–41 than previous historical interpretations, and would support the case that the earl of Chester's aims at this time had little if anything to do with the succession issue. It would explain Ranulf's seizure of Lincoln not as a rebellion provoked by the loss of his patrimonial lands in Carlisle, but simply as an independent and personal attempt to secure possession of something to which he felt he had a right. It would explain the king's initial willingness to renew his pact with the earl, acquiesce in Ranulf's control of Lincoln, and leave in peace. It would explain the earl's confident possession of the fortress after the king's departure, and his failure to take precautions against the possibility of an attempt by Stephen to recover what he had bestowed. Finally, and most significantly, it would explain why William of Malmesbury regarded Ranulf as being 'in no wise at fault' in 1140, and why on the battlefield of Lincoln the earl was concerned to correct a perfidious king who had broken a peace to which he was pledged, rather than to support the cause of an empress whose claim to the crown he had been prepared to ignore in 1136.[37]

What effect did the events of 1140–41 have upon Ranulf's position vis-à-vis the succession dispute? There is no doubt about King Stephen's view of those who fought against him at Lincoln. According to the *Gesta Stephani*, he declared that these men were 'not innocent of a monstrous crime in breaking their faith,

---

[34] The possessions of William d'Aubigny *Brito* and the honour of Tickhill (Blyth) which were included in the 1146 charter are unlikely to have been granted to Ranulf in 1140. William d'Aubigny appears to have been loyal to Stephen until 1144, and the honour of Tickhill had been granted by Stephen to the counts of Eu who held it until 1141 and who may have been loyal to the king until 1149: *Regesta*, iii, nos. 271, 437, 655, 442(?), 383, 396, 406, 402; I. J. Sanders, *English Baronies: A Study in their Origin and Descent 1086–1327*, Oxford 1960, 147.

[35] In and after 1136 King Stephen made a series of pacts with the magnates, the church and the citizens of London granting a range of concessions, some of which clearly qualified the homage performed to him: *Gesta Stephani*, 12, 14, 24, 186; *Historia Novella*, 15, 18–23, 32; Orderic, vi, 456, 484; *Regesta*, iii, no. 271; Davis, *King Stephen*, 17–18.

[36] Orderic, vi, 540.

[37] Quotation from *Historia Novella*, 47–8.

condemning their oath, caring nothing for the homage they had pledged him, and rebelling so wickedly and abominably against the man they had chosen of their own will as their king and lord'.[38] But how did the earl of Chester see things? In seizing Lincoln castle, offering his fealty to the empress, and fighting Stephen at Lincoln was he rejecting Stephen's right to be king? Was he, in other words, a supporter of the ultimate objectives of the Angevin cause? It is my belief that he was not. There is no direct evidence that Ranulf ever formally terminated his homage and fealty with Stephen in this period by a ceremonial act of defiance, or that he performed homage to the empress. If the earl had defied Stephen he would have been following widely accepted procedure, and there would have been no grounds for the *Gesta Stephani*'s description of his actions at Lincoln as treacherous.[39] The bond of allegiance between them was almost certainly still intact when the king besieged the earl and his half-brother at Christmas 1140. According to William of Malmesbury the siege 'seemed unfair to many because . . . [Stephen] had left them before the festival without any suspicion of ill-will and had not, in the traditional way, renounced his friendship with them, what they call defiance'.[40] It only needed one of the parties to a bond of allegiance to break the covenant for it to cease to exist, and if Ranulf had already defied the king there would have been no reason for Stephen to be required to defy the earl.[41] Even Ranulf's promise of a lasting fealty to the empress and participation at the battle of Lincoln need not necessarily have been regarded *by the earl* as a formal termination of his acceptance of Stephen's royal lordship and a commitment to the ultimate objectives of the Angevin party.[42] The parties in a bond of allegiance might interpret their obligations in different and conflicting ways.[43] Men could fight against their lords without necessarily rejecting their lordship, and could do

---

[38] *Gesta Stephani*, 112–14.

[39] *Gesta Stephani*, 184. It was still widely believed that men who had never done fealty to the king, or who had terminated their fealty by defiance, could not be accused of treachery for opposing him. This is suggested, for example, by the plea made to the king by some of his barons on behalf of the besieged at the siege of Exeter in 1136: *Gesta Stephani*, 42. For late twelfth century continental evidence illustrating the point, see the renunciation of homage by Raoul de Cambrai cited in J. Le Goff, *Time, Work, & Culture in the Middle Ages*, Chicago 1980, 247. See also the statement that Ranulf and William of Roumare 'fought fiercely on Candlemas Day against *their liege lord*' (my italics): *ASC*, 201.

[40] *Historia Novella*, 47.

[41] For the implications of the act of defiance, see F. L. Ganshof, *Feudalism*, trans. P. Grierson, 3rd edn 1964, 98; M. Bloch, *Feudal Society*, 2 vols, 2nd edn London 1962, i, 228; Sir Frederick Pollock and F. W. Maitland, *The History of English Law before the Time of Edward I*, 2 vols, 2nd edn Cambridge 1968, i, 303. For continental examples of the act of defiance, see *The Murder of Charles the Good Count of Flanders, by Galbert of Bruges*, trans. James Bruce Ross, New York 1967, 170–1, 269–70.

[42] In 1152 the adherents of Henry of Anjou in England are described as binding themselves to Stephen by pledges of peace and friendship. They had apparently offered their faith to Stephen, but had not abandoned Henry. Similarly in 1153 some of the magnates on Stephen's side, described as slack and casual in their service, made a compact with Henry: *Gesta Stephani*, 228, 234. The comments of John of Salisbury on the election of Gilbert Foliot to the bishopric of Hereford also imply that Gilbert had sworn fealty to both King Stephen and Henry of Anjou: *The Historia Pontificalis of John of Salisbury*, ed. and trans. M. Chibnall, London 1956, 47–9.

[43] See, for example, the letters that passed between Bishop Henry of Winchester and Brian Fitz Count in the early 1140s: H. W. C. Davis, 'Henry of Blois and Brian Fitz-Count' *EHR* xxv, 1910, 300–303. For eleventh century continental evidence illustrating this point, see the letter of Fulbert of Chartres written on behalf of Count Odo II of Chartres to King Robert of France: *The Letters and Poems of Fulbert of Chartres*, ed. and trans. F. Behrends, Oxford 1976, 152–4.

so without considering themselves to be treacherous or dishonourable, particularly when their private interests were at stake.[44] It was for these interests rather than the ultimate objectives of the Angevin party that Ranulf was fighting in 1140–41. One of the earl's own tenants viewed the battle of Lincoln 'as essentially an engagement between King Stephen and his lord'.[45] To Ranulf, Stephen may have been a perfidious oath-breaker who had to be brought to rights by force, but he was still the king.

During the empress's bid to secure the acceptance of the Church and a coronation in London the earl of Chester appears to have kept his distance. In April 1141 the Church pronounced against Stephen, and in doing so effectively released the magnates from the obligations inherent in the homage and fealty they had performed to him in 1136. But a number of them, both ecclesiastics and laymen, and including devotees of the empress as well as of the king, were clearly reluctant to renounce their allegiance to Stephen and did so only after receiving permission from the king or instructions from the Church.[46] Their hesitation is easy to understand. They regarded the renunciation of their homage and fealty as a mark of perjury. And this mortal sin was all the more ignominious because in the debate over legitimacy that was raging in Stephen's reign, the king had the upper hand. He was the Lord's anointed.[47] Robert of Gloucester had only been

[44] For the 'classic' idealistic view of the obligations inherent in fealty, see *The Letters and Poems of Fulbert of Chartres*, 90–3, 20–3; Ganshof, 31, 35, 83–95, esp. 83–4. It was noted long ago that the sources which extol lordship as the most cherished of all bonds, and which set great store by the virtue and devotion required of men by their lords, are frequently the same ones which provide us with a long recital of the wars conducted by these men against their lords: Bloch, i, chap. XVII. Some sources give the impression that men were reluctant to formally defy even the most deleterious and obstructive lords, and employed this sanction only as a last resort. In reply to the king's demand that the castle of Bedford be handed over in 1138 the castellan, Miles de Beauchamp, declared that 'if the king was in earnest and really determined to do him this wrong he would endure his anger with what patience he could': *Gesta Stephani*, 48. For continental examples of the durability of bonds of allegiance in similar political circumstances, see the hostilities between Henry of Anjou and King Louis of France in the Vexin between 1152 and 1154, between William Clito and the citizens of Ghent after the murder of Charles the Good count of Flanders in 1127, and between Count William V of Aquitaine and his man Hugh IV of Lusignan in the county of Poitou in the early eleventh century: *The Chronicle of Robert of Torigni*, in *Chronicles of the Reigns*, iv, 162, 165–6, 169–71, 174–5, 180; *The Murder of Charles the Good*, 268–9; Jane Martindale, 'Conventum inter Guillelmum Aquitanorum Comes et Hugonem Chiliarchum' *EHR* lxxxiv, 1969, 529, 541–8. I am grateful to Mr Stephen Church for pointing out the relevance of the last two references cited here.
[45] Stenton, *First Century*, 243.
[46] *Historia Novella*, 51. Brian Fitz Count, who was devoted to the empress, had to be commanded by the bishop of Winchester to help her secure what she was claiming. After the Church acknowledged Stephen as king again in 1141, however, the bishop advised Brian to move with the times and warned him that if he did not do so he would be regarded as faithless. Brian's response to this reveals just how sensitive even the most loyal adherents of the empress were to charges of being faithless to an anointed king. Brian defended himself on his honour, and above all on his obedience to 'the precepts of Holy Church'. See Davis, 'Henry of Blois and Brian Fitz-Count', 301, and the comments in King, 'King Stephen and the Anglo-Norman Aristocracy', 190–1; *The Letters and Charters of Gilbert Foliot*, eds. A. Morey and C. N. L. Brooke, Cambridge 1967, no. 26; and their *Gilbert Foliot and his Letters*, Cambridge 1965, 105–10.
[47] For the debate over legitimacy, see Edmund King, 'The Anarchy of King Stephen's Reign' *TRHS* 5th ser. xxxiv, 1984, 134. See also Huntingdon, 272–3 (the speech made by Baldwin Fitz Gilbert at the battle of Lincoln); *ASC*, 198–9; Newburgh, 52, 58, 126; *English Lawsuits from William I to Richard I*, ed. R. C. Van Caenegem, Selden Soc. London 1990, i, no. 292; *Historia Pontificalis*, 84–6.

prepared to defy him after much soul searching and excusing himself on the grounds that his homage had been conditional; and even then appears to have continued to recognise Stephen's royal title in the early 1140s.[48] Others clearly were not prepared to go as far as defiance; and that one of them was the earl of Chester is suggested by his actions at the siege of Winchester in September 1141.

Although the *Gesta Stephani* lists the earl among the magnates who were with the empress at Winchester, William of Malmesbury merely records that Ranulf's arrival was late and ineffective, and John of Hexham states that the earl had initially been among the group of magnates supporting Stephen's queen until 'a murmuring of those in the army who dreaded some treachery' caused him to go 'over to the besieged'.[49] Davis acknowledged Ranulf's willingness to join the queen, but suggested that it was due to the presence at the empress's court of the earl's rival for control of Carlisle, King David of Scotland.[50] David's presence, however, neither compelled Ranulf to offer his assistance to the queen (he could have remained aloof), nor prevented him from eventually joining the empress. As a late comer, arriving as he did after the events in London and the defection from the empress of Bishop Henry of Winchester, it is possible that Ranulf had waited for the tide to turn against Matilda and was acting opportunistically. There were those among the queen's counsellors who suspected his motives and regarded him as treacherous. It is a suspicion which surfaces in all the key episodes in Ranulf's career.[51] In view of the extensive scope of his local ambitions it is a suspicion which is hardly surprising. But it reflects only one side of the political argument. The other side was voiced by Ranulf at the battle of Lincoln when he accused Stephen of perfidy. Whether simply squaring his conscience, or stating firmly held beliefs, the earl of Chester felt his case not only one worth making, but one worth fighting for.[52]

The earl of Chester is described as 'going over' to the besieged at Winchester. But 'going over' in what sense? Davis, and Professor Cronne before him, argued that the earl was an adherent of the Angevin cause, and supported their case with evidence that Ranulf was actively engaged on behalf of the empress in warfare against Stephen in 1143 x 1144.[53] If Ranulf was an adherent of the empress at Winchester, however, he was, as William of Malmesbury informs us, an ineffective adherent. Moreover, there is once again nothing to indicate that the earl either formally defied the king or performed homage to the empress. He never attested a single charter issued by Matilda and was certainly not an adherent of her cause in 1142 when Geoffrey of Anjou and Robert of Gloucester seized his

---

[48] *Historia Novella*, 23, 18. Robert refers to 'the war between the empress and King Stephen' in his *conventio* with Miles earl of Hereford agreed between 25 July 1141 and 22 December 1143: R. H. C. Davis, 'The Treaty between William Earl of Gloucester and Roger Earl of Hereford' in *A Medieval Miscellany for Doris Mary Stenton*, ed. Patricia M. Barnes and C. F. Slade, Pipe Roll Soc. ns 1962, 145–6; *Earldom of Gloucester Charters*, ed. Robert B. Patterson, Oxford 1973, no. 95.

[49] *Gesta Stephani*, 128; Davis, 'Henry of Blois and Brian Fitz-Count', 302; *Historia Novella*, 59; quotation from Symeon, 310.

[50] Davis, 'The Earl of Chester Revised', 659.

[51] *Historia Novella*, 47; *Gesta Stephani*, 184, 192–8; Symeon, 323.

[52] Davis acknowledged that the king was untrustworthy in his dealings with his magnates: R. H. C. Davis, 'What Happened in Stephen's Reign 1135–54' *History* xlix, 1964, 2–4.

[53] Davis, 'The earl of Chester Revised', 657; Cronne, 'Ranulf de Gernons', 122–5.

Norman *caput* of Briquessart and castle of Vire.[54] Moreover, the evidence that
Ranulf was fighting for Matilda in 1143 x 1144 is highly suspect. It is based upon
three short chronicle references. John of Hexham describes how William earl of
York, 'troubled by the hostility of Ranulf earl of Chester and Gilbert of Gant
converted the monastery of Bridlington into a castle'.[55] The *Gesta Stephani* states
that Ranulf was engaged in a persecution of the North during which, 'all the
king's barons who were near him he burdened with constant attacks'.[56] And
Henry of Huntingdon relates how the earl resisted a royal siege of Lincoln
castle.[57] Cronne went so far as to argue that these references reveal that Ranulf
had been drawn into an Angevin plot designed to immobilise the royalist forces in
the northern counties while Geoffrey of Anjou sailed to England from Normandy
and marched on London.[58] His argument is open to serious objections. Firstly, its
premise that Geoffrey of Anjou intended to come to England is contradicted by
William of Malmesbury's account of the difficulties faced by Robert of Gloucester in persuading the count to join his wife in 1142.[59] And secondly, it is more
than clear that Ranulf's war with the earl of York in 1143 was stimulated by local
territorial and jurisdictional rivalries rather than the politics of the succession
dispute.[60] Nor should the royal siege of Lincoln in 1144, or the *Gesta Stephani*'s
description of Ranulf's attack on the king's barons, necessarily be taken as evidence that the earl had deserted Stephen for the cause of the empress.

In December 1141 the Church had acknowledged Stephen as the rightful king
and judged that the reign had begun again at dawn on the day when he was
captured at Lincoln.[61] In Stephen's second charter for Geoffrey de Mandeville he
makes grants by reference to the day *qua impeditus fui apud Linc(olniam) et
captus*. The Church was wiping out the events that had occurred in the ten
months after Stephen's capture: most significantly the acceptance of the empress
as Lady of England and the transference of allegiance to her by some of the lay
and ecclesiastical magnates. What had happened between 2 February and 7
December 1141 was now viewed as illegitimate. The Church was saying that the
magnates were still bound by the homage relationships that existed at dawn on 2
February 1141.[62] The earl of Chester, in short, was still regarded as the king's
man. Although his homage was still viewed as binding, however, his fealty would
have to be renewed. This is what Ranulf appears to have been doing when he
came to the royal court in 1146 and renewed his pact of peace and friendship with

---

[54] *Historia Novella*, 73. See also, *Regesta*, iii, no. 58.
[55] Symeon, 315.
[56] *Gesta Stephani*, 166–8.
[57] Huntingdon, 277; Newburgh, 72.
[58] Cronne, 'Ranulf de Gernons', 123–5.
[59] *Historia Novella*, 73.
[60] P. Dalton, 'William Earl of York and Royal Authority in Yorkshire in the Reign of Stephen' *The
Haskins Society Journal* ii, 1990, 155–65.
[61] *Regesta*, iii, no. 276.
[62] Stephen does not appear to have required the magnates to renew their homages in 1141. When
he entered the Church council convoked in December 1141 he referred to the magnates who had
captured him at Lincoln as 'homines sui'. To have required the renewal of homage would have
been an acknowledgement that there had been a break in his kingship, a notion which Stephen was
anxious to suppress. Although recrowned it is significant that Stephen did not allow the Church to
restore or reconsecrate him. His brother Bishop Henry was at pains to stress in the December
council that Stephen was the anointed king. See Davis, *King Stephen*, 63; *Historia Novella*, 62–3.

Stephen.[63] It was a pact which did not last long. When Ranulf came to court a second time in 1146 in August at Northampton to ask for assistance against the Welsh who he said were ravaging his lands, he was arrested while under a safe conduct and placed in prison. When released later that year he flew to arms against the king, a campaign which Davis equated with a return to his former adherence to the Angevin party. Once again, however, all is not quite as it might at first appear.

The reason for Ranulf's arrest, according to the *Gesta Stephani*, was that he refused to 'restore the king's property that he had unjustly taken for his own use and afford greater security by giving a guarantee and offering hostages'.[64] Once again Ranulf had fallen foul of the suspicion of the king's counsellors who viewed his accumulation of power at Stephen's expense and his failure to provide security as a sign of treachery. But whatever the suspicions there is a case to be made on the other side. Ranulf had clearly gone out of his way in 1146 to assist the king with a large force at the capture of Bedford and siege of Wallingford.[65] When confronted by the demands of Stephen's counsellors 'the earl at once answered that he had not come to court for this purpose, had not even been given any notice of the matter or deliberated over it with his advisers'.[66] The demand for hostages from a magnate was in any case hardly conventional, and the ferocity of the military campaign Ranulf launched against Stephen after his release suggests that he was a man who felt that he had been wronged.[67] For Ranulf the obligations inherent in his bond of allegiance with the king were binding enough, and his refusal to provide hostages and guarantors illustrates his reluctance to commit himself completely to the royal cause. There was no disloyalty in this. The treachery in 1146, if there was a treachery, was the king's rather than the earl's.[68]

Ranulf's military campaign against the king after his release is assumed to mark his return to the Angevin party. While it is certainly possible that Ranulf defied Stephen at this time, there is no direct evidence to show this. Moreover, it appears that when Ranulf fought against Stephen he was fighting as he had fought on previous occasions, for the recovery of castles to which he felt he had a right, rather than for the ultimate objectives of the empress. His military operations were focused on Coventry and Lincoln, and were conducted 'sometimes against his opponents, sometimes even against those who favoured his cause'.[69] Ranulf witnessed none of the extant charters issued by the empress in the period 1146–48, and although his half-brother, William of Roumare, was resident in

[63] *Gesta Stephani*, 184. This peace pact appears to have a parallel in the pact agreed in 1144 or 1145 between the king and Nigel bishop of Ely, who had also fortified a castle against Stephen, which refers to the bishop as now to hold freely, *quoniam pacem de me habet et concordiam mecum fecit*: *Regesta*, iii, no. 267.

[64] *Gesta Stephani*, 196, and see 184.

[65] *Gesta Stephani*, 184.

[66] *Gesta Stephani*, 196.

[67] Although it was common for the peace pacts of the anarchy to include the provision of hostages, in previous reigns the magnates would not normally have been required by the king to surrender them. For the pacts, see Symeon, 287, 300; *Regesta*, iii, nos. 272, 275; *Gesta Stephani*, 16, 34–6, 186; *Historia Novella*, 61–2, 67–9; Davis, 'Treaty', 139–46; *Chester Charters*, no. 110; Stenton, 286–8.

[68] After the author of the *Gesta Stephani* turned against Stephen he admitted that the king's arrest of the earl in 1146 had been wrong because the earl had come to court under a safe conduct: *Gesta Stephani*, 236 note 2; Davis, *King Stephen*, 93. See also, Newburgh, 72.

[69] *Gesta Stephani*, 198–200, 208; Huntingdon, 279.

Normandy by October 1147, his presence there is almost certainly more a reflection of the weakness of his family's standing with the Angevin party rather than its strength.[70] William was probably there to try to recover, or at least to protect, the family estates which had been seized by Geoffrey of Anjou.

What, then, should we make of the overtures which Ranulf appears to have been making to the Angevin party in 1148 and 1149? For Professor Barraclough the appearance of some of the leading supporters of the empress in the witness clauses of a number of the earl's charters issued in Chester at this time was evidence that Ranulf had assumed the leadership of the Angevin party after the death of Robert of Gloucester in October 1147.[71] The evidence would appear at first sight to be strengthened by the hostilities between Ranulf and Stephen's son Eustace in 1147, and by the earl's participation in the knighting of Henry of Anjou at the court of the king of Scotland at Carlisle in 1149. Here Ranulf 'laid aside the animosity with which he had been wont to claim Carlisle as of hereditary right, and did homage to King David. It was agreed between them, that instead of Carlisle he should have the lordship of Lancaster, and Earl Ranulf's son should marry one of the daughters of Henry, son of the king of Scotland'.[72] Ranulf also appears to have accepted the lordship of Henry of Anjou. A charter issued by the earl at about the same time refers to Henry as 'my lord', and also reveals that Ranulf had accepted the allegiance of Robert Fitz Harding a leading adherent of the empress (albeit for an isolated manor which the earl had little hope of controlling), and had visited the Angevin stronghold of Bristol.[73]

After 1149 there can be no question that the earl of Chester was an adherent of Henry of Anjou and a focal point for Angevin resistance. But an adherent in precisely what sense? Had the Angevin cause 'at last secured the whole-hearted loyalty of Earl Ranulf'?[74] If we are talking about furthering Henry's succession rather than that of Eustace after Stephen's death I believe the answer to be yes. If we are talking about securing Henry's succession by force in Stephen's lifetime the answer must be no.[75] Ranulf had performed homage to King David and, by implication from the earl's reference to the future duke as *dominus*, to Henry of Anjou. But homage *for what*? In the case of David it was probably homage for Lancaster, which illustrates again the importance attached by Ranulf to his local ambitions. In the case of Henry it was homage to the lawful heir; in other words homage for the future, for a time when Henry would be duke of Normandy and king of England.[76] The knighthood Henry received at Carlisle marked his coming of age, the transformation of his legal status, and was an important step towards securing the two realms.[77] But many more steps were needed, and these lay in the

---

[70] *Regesta*, iii, nos. 599, 779, 325.
[71] *Chester Charters*, nos. 64, 84–6, and notes.
[72] Symeon, 323.
[73] *Chester Charters*, no. 87.
[74] Davis, *King Stephen*, 104.
[75] It is possible, of course, that the Angevin party may have contemplated achieving Stephen's departure by peaceful resignation.
[76] Although the young man's succession to the Norman duchy was probably regarded as imminent in 1149, strictly speaking he held no fiefs either in Normandy or in England at that time. Henry formally succeeded his father as duke of Normandy by March 1150, and had been honoured by the people of the duchy as their lord on his return from England in January that year: *Regesta*, iii, p. xxxii; *Gesta Stephani*, 224.
[77] On the implications of knighthood, see G. Duby, *The Three Orders*, Chicago 1980, 296–301; Bloch, ii, 313.

future. In the present Stephen was still the anointed king of England, had the support of the Church, and enjoyed the military upper hand. The prospect of removing him must have seemed very unlikely. Although Ranulf entered into an alliance with Henry of Anjou and the king of Scotland with the purpose of attacking Stephen and capturing York, when called upon to act he 'fulfilled none of the things which he had promised' and abandoned the project.[78] For the earl of Chester adherence to the Angevin cause in the future was one thing, adherence in the present was quite another.

It is significant that when Ranulf next appears in the chronicle sources it is in Lincolnshire fighting a series of campaigns against Stephen and his new earl of Lincoln, Gilbert of Gant, who was set up in 1149 in opposition to the existing earl, William of Roumare, Ranulf's half-brother and ally.[79] The campaigns involved an attempt by the earl of Chester to capture Lincoln castle, and have been seen as part of a plan to create a diversion designed to interrupt Stephen's siege of Henry of Anjou in Devizes after the disintegration of the 1149 alliance.[80] It is clear, however, that this was a private war fought for personal control of regalian rights and the centres of governmental, military and economic power within Lincolnshire. It was a war which probably had little, if anything, to do with an attempt to save Henry of Anjou or with the succession dispute generally.[81] Despite his performance of homage to Henry in 1149, the earl of Chester, it seems, was still more concerned with protecting his local interests in Lincolnshire than with promoting the cause of the leader of the Angevin faction in England.

The idea that the earl of Chester had offered his allegiance to Henry of Anjou in 1149, but was reluctant to back his plans for the final resolution of the succession dispute, is supported by the evidence of the famous *conventio* agreed between Ranulf and his midlands rival Robert earl of Leicester at some point between 1149 and 1153.[82] Here the two earls were concerned to define their spheres of influence in the midlands, to establish a demilitarised zone, and to limit their obligations to their liege lords. Ranulf promised to keep faith with Robert saving the faith due to his liege lord, to bring only twenty knights if forced to go against Robert with his liege lord, and to prevent his liege lord from using his castles and land to attack Robert. And Robert gave an undertaking in the same words. The terms of the *conventio* leave little doubt that the earls of Chester and Leicester were trying to lessen the effect of having to fight for different lords over the issue of the succession, that they were prepared to offer their liege lords only the minimum amount of military support permitted by custom and sanctioned by the Church, and that they were concerned to be seen to be behaving honourably.[83]

[78] Symeon, 323. Ranulf may have attended the initial rendezvous with his allies at Lancaster: *Chester Charters*, no. 88.
[79] *Gesta Stephani*, 220; M. R. Abbot, 'The Gant Family in England, 1066–1191' Univ. of Cambridge Ph.D. thesis, 1973, 45, and no. 59.
[80] Davis, *King Stephen*, 106.
[81] Dalton, 'Aiming at the Impossible', 124–6.
[82] Stenton, 250–3, 286–8; *Chester Charters*, no. 110; Davis, *King Stephen*, 108–9. Dr Golob has dated the *conventio* to the early months of 1153, but it is more likely, as Dr Crouch believes, that it was roughly contemporary with other treaties made by Earl Robert in the late 1140s: P. E. Golob, 'The Ferrers Earls of Derby: a Study in the Honour of Tutbury (1066–1279)' Univ. of Cambridge Ph.D. thesis, 1984, 127–34; D. B. Crouch, *The Beaumont Twins*, Cambridge 1986, 83–5.
[83] Edmund King, 'Mountsorrel and its Region in King Stephen's Reign' *Huntington Library Quarterly* xliv, 1980, 8. Ranulf and Robert were using the concept of liege lordship to allow them

In their *conventio* the earls of Chester and Leicester were not ignoring their obligations to their lords, but merely limiting these obligations in accordance with accepted and legitimate practices concerning conditional allegiance.[84] They were doing so in order to avoid committing themselves to the ultimate objectives of either side in the succession dispute and (in their own minds) were on neither side and effectively neutral so far as the issue of the resolution of that dispute was concerned.[85] They were all the more able to do so because, as the terms of numerous *conventiones* imply, 'royal and with it all lordship was weakened'.[86] This weakness is reflected also in the great charter granted by Henry of Anjou to Earl Ranulf in the early months of 1153.[87] This was yet another conditional pact.[88] Like the Chester-Leicester *conventio* it mirrors the limitations of Ranulf's attach-

---

an honourable method of working their way around the implications of the homages they had performed to different and potentially hostile lords. The same ideas of conditional/limited allegiance can be found in the pacts agreed with the king by Robert of Gloucester and the Church in 1136, in the pact of 1141 between Henry bishop of Winchester and the empress, and in the treaty of Winchester of 1153 which Bishop Henry played a key part in drafting (linked here with liege lordship): *Historia Novella*, 18, 50–1, 63; *Gesta Stephani*, 118; *Regesta*, iii, no. 272. Bishop Henry's 1141 pact is particularly significant. Here he made his fealty to the empress as Lady of England conditional on her accepting his counsel on matters of Church and state and allowing him to continue to aid the king with a maximum of twenty knights, the number reserved for the service of the liege lords in the Chester-Leicester *conventio*. The same ideas go back even further to the reign of Henry I, and appear in the treaty of Dover between the king and Robert II count of Flanders in 1101. Here the count considered it possible to save his fealty to his liege lord King Philip of France despite providing King Henry with 1000 knights to fight Philip, by assisting the latter with *tam parvam fortitudinem hominum secum adducet quam minorem poterit, ita tamen ne inde feodum suum erga regem Francie forisfaciat* if the fighting occurred in England, and with *xx militibus tantum* if it occurred in Normandy: *Diplomatic Documents Preserved in the Public Record Office, I: 1101–1272*, ed. P. Chaplais, London 1964, 1, 3. The incorporation of very similar ideas concerning liege lordship within the late twelfth century legal treatise ascribed to Glanvill reinforces the impression that conditional/limited allegiance was not only customary in the twelfth century, but that it was also legitimate: *Tractatus de Legibus et Consuetudinibus Regni Anglie qui Glanvilla vocatur*, ed. and tr. G. D. G. Hall, Edinburgh 1965, ix, 1, p. 104. It has been suggested that this section of the treatise was prompted by the law suits generated by Stephen's reign: M. Chibnall, *Anglo-Norman England 1066–1166*, Oxford 1986, 98. I am grateful to Dr Chibnall for her suggestion that the attitude of the magnates to liege lordship in Stephen's reign was somewhat anachronistic, and that Henry II was not prepared to tolerate such attitudes when he was securely on the throne.

[84] The twenty knights offered by the earls amounted to only a small fraction of the number they normally owed to the king. In the case of Leicester this may have been as high as 125 knights; and in the case of Chester as high as 198 knights: Sanders, *English Baronies*, 61 note 2, 32 note 2. It should be noted that although limited allegiance may have been legitimate in theory, in practice lords may not have been prepared to accept it. According to Orderic's account of the meeting held by the Anglo-Norman magnates to discuss the division of England and Normandy between William Rufus and Robert Curthose after the death of the Conqueror, the magnates expected to have to choose between their two lords and to suffer the confiscation of their estates on one or the other side of the Channel as a result: Orderic, iv, 122.

[85] For an alternative interpretation of the Chester-Leicester *conventio*, see Crouch, *Beaumont Twins*, 83–6.

[86] Edmund King, 'The Foundation of Pipewell Abbey, Northamptonshire' *The Haskins Society Journal* ii, 1990, 174.

[87] *Regesta*, iii, no. 180.

[88] This is implicit in the form of the witness list of the charter which is divided into two parties of ten magnates who attested on behalf of Henry and Ranulf respectively. For other examples of this practice in treaties, see *Chester Charters*, no. 110; Stenton, 286; *English Diplomatic Documents*, 1.

ment to the Angevin party. Henry was having to buy support, and at some cost – albeit largely with things he did not yet control. The gifts conferred upon Ranulf, which included an impressive array of castles, lordships and rights belonging to the king/duke and a series of magnates throughout western Normandy and the northern and midland shires of England, provide another indication of the importance attached by the earl to his local interests and suggest that his loyalty to Henry was conditional and limited.[89] The conditions we see in the treaty are Ranulf's. What he was offering in return is uncertain. What does seem clear, however, is that he was not offering a whole-hearted commitment to the deposition of King Stephen.

There is no doubt that the earl of Chester was a close adherent of Duke Henry in 1153 and assisted him during the course of his summer campaign.[90] But an adherent in what sense? A close examination of his attacks on the king's party in 1153 suggests that the earl may have been fighting primarily for his own interests rather than those of the Angevin party. Ranulf's hand 'was against every man, and every man's hand against him', and his hostility was directed principally against William Peverel, lord of Nottingham, whose fortress and honour he coveted.[91] The earl's potential for placing self-interest before Henry's cause is also reflected by a charter issued by the duke at the siege of Stamford in late August. The cautious terms of the charter give notification of the reparation promised by Ranulf for the damage he had done to the church of Lincoln, and 'seem to indicate that even now [the earl] was not entirely trusted'.[92] They also provide another illustration of the weakness of Henry of Anjou's lordship. The charter is not a regular lordly confirmation, but a *conventio*. It is yet another of those conditional pacts which peppered the earl of Chester's career. Duke Henry stood as surety (*fideiussor*) for Ranulf and pledged that if the earl defaulted on his promise of reparation he would provide it himself from his own demesne. We are a long way here from the potent *nisi feceris* clauses of the stern writs of Henry I. Implicit in this *conventio* is the possibility that Ranulf could and might still go his own way; that his commitment to Henry was strong but not absolute.[93] Henry I might have turned in his grave at this, but the future Henry II, his succession not yet secure, could press his authority no further.[94]

Both duke and king were having trouble imposing their authority on many other magnates in 1153; and for reasons very similar to those behind Henry's difficulties with the earl of Chester. Their two attempts to settle the issue by battle

---

[89] For an analysis of the gifts conferred, see G. White, 'King Stephen, Duke Henry and Ranulf de Gernons, Earl of Chester' *EHR* xci, 1976, 555–65.

[90] *Regesta*, iii, nos. 840, 44. We are informed that 'the earl, as long as he lived, exerted all his efforts to attack the king's party': *Gesta Stephani*, 236.

[91] *Gesta Stephani*, 236. Nottingham was besieged and burnt in autumn 1153: Huntingdon, 288. Ranulf was granted the castle and borough of Nottingham and all the fee of William Peverel by Duke Henry, unless Peverel came and cleared himself of treachery in the duke's court: *Regesta*, iii, no. 180.

[92] *Chester Charters*, no. 106 and note; *Regesta*, iii, no. 492.

[93] Suretyship was one of the forms of personal engagement by which men sought to keep each other honest: W. Davies, 'Suretyship in the Cartulaire de Redon' in *Lawyers and Laymen: Studies in the History of Law Presented to Professor Dafydd Jenkins on his Seventy-Fifth Birthday Gwyl Ddewi 1986*, ed. T. Charles-Edwards *et al.*, Cardiff 1986, 72–91.

[94] On the weakness of Henry's position in 1153, see Graeme J. White, 'The End of Stephen's Reign' *History* lxxv, 1990, 3–22, esp. 6.

near Malmesbury and at Wallingford failed because the magnates refused to fight.[95] At Malmesbury in March or April some of Stephen's barons were 'slack and very casual in their service and had already sent envoys by stealth and made a compact with the duke'.[96] Later at Wallingford in August, where Ranulf himself was probably with Duke Henry,

> the traitorous nobles interfered, and proposed among themselves the terms of peace . . . they had no inclination for war, and felt no desire to exalt either one or the other of the pretenders to the crown, so that by humbling his rival they themselves might become entirely subject to the other. They preferred that, the two being in mutual fear, the royal authority should, with respect to themselves, be kept in abeyance. The king and the duke, there-fore, being sensible of the treachery of their adherents, were reluctantly compelled to make a truce between themselves . . .[97]

In Davis's own words, 'it looks as if quite a number of the magnates had adopted an attitude of neutrality, or suspended animation, on the lines suggested by the Church. They remained loyal to Stephen in that they obeyed his summons to the army, but they refused to fight against Duke Henry because he was the lawful heir to the kingdom'.[98] But what the magnates on both sides were doing in 1153 was what the earl of Chester had been doing since 1139. They were refusing to fight whole-heartedly for their accepted lords over the issue of the succession.[99] Most of them had probably also been unwilling to do so at Wilton in 1143, at Tetbury in 1144, at *Lidelea* in 1147, and at York in 1149.[100] For their trouble they, like Ranulf, were branded by King Stephen, Duke Henry and some of the chroni-clers as faithless traitors.[101] But not everybody thought the label fair, and this serves to remind us that there might be perfectly legitimate competing views of allegiance in this period.[102] The magnates were not deserting their lords and swopping sides in 1153. They were simply making use of customs concerning the permissibility of limited allegiance in order to avoid fighting to the death over the issue of the succession. There is no doubt, as the chronicler implies, that this brought them positive advantages. There is no doubt also that it secured them against harm. But, as Davis himself realised, there was more to it than that. The attitude of the Church was crucial. It was an attitude expressed most clearly in the treaty of Winchester which settled the anarchy in 1153, and which was 'a pre-carious compromise made against the wishes of both principals'.[103] Here the Church's policy was that which, with the exception of only a few months in the highly unusual year of 1141, it had almost certainly maintained since 1140: the

---

[95] *Gesta Stephani*, 234–8.
[96] *Gesta Stephani*, 234.
[97] Ranulf attested as first witness a charter for Henry issued at Wallingford between June and November 1153: *Regesta*, iii, no. 44; Huntingdon, 287–8.
[98] Davis, *King Stephen*, 115.
[99] The magnates with Henry also appear to have taken matters out of his hands: *Torigni*, 173–4.
[100] *Gesta Stephani*, 146, 172–4, 208–10, 216.
[101] See *Torigni*, 173–4.
[102] *Gesta Stephani*, 238; *Torigni*, 173–4. Both chroniclers were writing here with the benefit of hindsight.
[103] P. R. Hyams, 'Warranty and Good Lordship in Twelfth Century England' *Law and History Review* v, 1987, 501.

policy of standing squarely behind King Stephen's royal authority and his right to the fealty of his subjects, and the right of Henry of Anjou to succeed him.[104] As with the earl of Chester in 1149, so with the Church in the period 1140–53, allegiance in the future was one thing, allegiance in the present was quite another. For the present there was no hope of deposing the anointed king, and no point in fighting to the death over the issue of the succession. Ranulf had probably realised this all along. By 1153, if not before, most of his fellow magnates realised it too. That is why they were refusing to fight. That is why they were neutral.

The earl of Chester had always refused to fight over the issue of the succession. In 1153 he continued to steer his personal straight course. While the peace negotiations that settled the anarchy were underway in the south of England, Ranulf remained in the midlands conducting his own private peace negotiations with his local rival William Peverel at Nottingham. It was within a short time of these negotiations, only a few miles from where they were held, and possibly as a result of poisoning at Peverel's hands, that Ranulf died at Castle Gresley in Derbyshire in December 1153 on the fee of a tenant of Robert II of Ferrers one of his allies in the Chester-Leicester *conventio*, and close to the region with which that treaty had been primarily concerned.[105] The earl of Chester died as he had lived, a political neutral whose primary concern was the pursuit of his personal objectives within the localities.

In conclusion. This paper has attempted to illustrate that the policy adopted by the earl of Chester (and possibly many other magnates) in Stephen's reign with regard to the specific issue of the resolution of the succession dispute was a far more complicated and (perhaps) honourable policy than has hitherto been re-alised. The view that Ranulf was prepared to switch his allegiance from side to side in that dispute misinterprets a highly sophisticated response to a difficult political situation. It is a misinterpretation resulting from the way in which most historians of Stephen's reign have tended to think about allegiance in absolute terms. In doing so they have made no allowance for the fact that political allegiance is frequently more a matter of degree than of absolutes, and that inter-pretations of this allegiance might vary according to the perspective of the interpreter. The problem with the history of baronial behaviour in Stephen's reign is that the perspective adopted by most historians is that of the leaders of the rival factions in the civil war, for whom the question of allegiance over the succession issue was paramount. But the earl of Chester did not see things that way; and by 1153, if not before, many of his fellow magnates shared his views. Ranulf wanted to avoid committing himself fully to the ultimate objectives of either of the rival factions in the succession dispute. Although he fought in the civil war, *in his own mind* he was fighting primarily for his private local ambitions. He supported neither Stephen's desire to defeat the Angevins and establish his family as a royal dynasty, nor the Angevin wish to remove the king, and he was thus on neither side and neutral so far as the resolution of the succession issue was concerned. At

---

[104] The crucial terms of the treaty had probably been on the table since 1140: King, 'Anarchy', 134; *Historia Novella*, 44–5, 57–8. For the Church's support of Stephen's royal authority, see John of Salisbury's description of the election of Gilbert Foliot as bishop of Hereford in 1148, and the policy of the papacy towards the English succession: *Historia Pontificalis*, 47–9, 83–6. See also the refusal of English ecclesiastical leaders to crown Eustace in 1152: Huntingdon, 283–4; Davis, *King Stephen*, 114.
[105] *Chester Charters*, nos. 34, 117, 118; Golob, 'Ferrers Earls', 138–40.

the same time he was not prepared to ignore the obligations inherent in the homage and fealty he performed to King Stephen and Duke Henry and wanted to maintain a limited form of allegiance with them, perhaps even simultaneously. The king's counsellors and some chroniclers either could not or would not understand Ranulf's position and denounced him as a turncoat, and most historians have accepted their opinion. But this is a view which confuses limited loyalty with disloyalty; and at least one chronicler may have been aware of this. In describing the events of 1140 William of Malmesbury states that Ranulf had long since offended the empress's principal supporter, Robert earl of Gloucester, 'chiefly because he *seemed* faithful to neither side' (*maxime quia in neutro latere fidus videretur esse*).[106] We shall never know whether Malmesbury's uncertainty about the earl's reputation for faithlessness sprang from a belief that there was no treachery in Ranulf's limited allegiance to two hostile lords. But what is almost certain is that this kind of allegiance was sanctioned in Stephen's reign not only by the force of custom, but also by the precepts of Holy Church.

All this should not be seen as an attempt to whitewash Earl Ranulf's career, to argue that he *always* behaved with honour and was a paragon of virtue. There is no doubt, and the point should be stressed, that he was a slippery, highly aggressive and acquisitive self-seeker who was aiming at little short of independent administrative and military control of large areas of the midlands and north.[107] There is no doubt also that he had a reputation for treachery among the chief combatants in the civil war and some of the chroniclers under their influence. But there is a case to be made on the other side, and this paper has attempted to make it. There are grounds for believing that, so far as the specific issue of the ultimate resolution of the succession conflict was concerned, the earl saw his policy as one of legitimate neutrality. He did not share the view that allegiance to either of the chief combatants had to be absolute. For him there was no contradiction between this neutrality, limited allegiance and 'dishonourable' self-help. In combining these policies Ranulf was simply exercising the complicated range of skills which politicians in all ages have endeavoured to exercise. His career can only corroborate a general characterization of the Anglo-Norman magnate made over eighty years ago: that he 'was not to himself or to the majority of those who came in contact with him the mere incarnation of a centrifugal and disruptive individualism'.[108]

---

[106] *Historia Novella*, 47. The italics are mine. I am indebted to Dr Chibnall for her suggestion that although this passage could be taken to mean that Malmesbury thought neither side trusted Ranulf, it might also indicate that the chronicler thought that Ranulf trusted neither side.
[107] For the scope of his ambitions in Lincolnshire, see Dalton, 'Aiming at the Impossible'.
[108] Davis, 'Henry of Blois and Brian Fitz-Count', 297.

HYPOTHESES SUR LA FORTIFICATION DE ROUEN AU ONZIEME SIECLE. LE DONJON, LA TOUR DE RICHARD II ET L'ENCEINTE DE GUILLAUME.*

Bernard Gauthiez

Au travers de cette communication, je voudrais éclaircir certains points de l'histoire de Rouen à l'époque ducale, en particulier ce qui concerne sa fortification.

En l'absence de données archéologiques nouvelles, c'est à partir d'un examen attentif de la topographie de la ville, et d'un relecture des textes disponibles, qu'il est possible de faire un certain nombre d'hypothèses. L'exposé qui va suivre traitera de trois sites particuliers (figure 1).

J'évoquerai tout d'abord le site du Donjon, actuellement non reconnaissable, localisé à l'angle sud-ouest de l'enceinte du Bas-Empire (figure 2).

Plusieurs arguments, outre son nom même, qui apparaît dans une charte de 1231,[1] et celui de l'église voisine de St Pierre du Châtel, montrent qu'il s'agit probablement de la résidence occupée par les premiers ducs normands.

L'endroit est au douzième siècle un fief du chambellan de Tancarville.[2] Il est exclu de l'étendue d'application de l'ordonnance sur les moulins de 1199,[3] pour une surface d'une acre, soit environ 8200 m2. Cette surface correspond à celle que les Cordeliers occupent au treizième siècle, après leur installation sur le site.

D'autre part le duc Richard II donne en 1006 une 'maison dans la Cité de Rouen, avec une chapelle' à l'abbaye de Fécamp.[4] En 1024, il la reprend lors d'un échange, et on apprend à cette occasion que la chapelle et la maison sont localisées 'sur la porte St Clément'.[5] Cette porte, étant donné qu'aucun autre lieu de culte de ce nom n'est connu à Rouen, est à localiser sur le mur de la Cité à proximité de la future paroissiale St Clément, au bas de l'ancienne rue des Iroquois près de la rue des Charrettes, à proximité du Donjon.

L'abbé de Fécamp à cette époque, de 1001 à 1031, est Guillaume de Volpiano.[6]

---

* L'essentiel de cette communication est tiré d'une recherche de doctorat récemment soutenue à l'Ecole des Hautes Etudes en Sciences Sociales, à Paris: Bernard Gauthiez, *La logique de l'espace urbain, formation et évolution; le cas de Rouen*, fév. 1991.

[1] Charles Robillard de Beaurepaire, *Nouveaux mélanges historiques et archéologiques*, Rouen 1904, 431–458.
[2] Robillard de Beaurepaire, 1904, 443, cf. Archives Départementales de la Seine-Maritime (ADSM), Rouen, Fond des Cordeliers: 'tenementum . . . quod videlicet vocatur Donjon', 1231.
[3] Léopold Delisle, *Cartulaire Normand*, Caen 1882, no. 50.
[4] Marie Fauroux, 'Recueil des actes des ducs de Normandie', *Mémoire de la Société des Antiquaires de Normandie (MSAN)*, XXXVI, Caen 1961, 79.
[5] Fauroux, 124.
[6] *Histoire de la Normandie*, sous la direction de Michel de Boüard, Toulouse 1970/1987, 121.

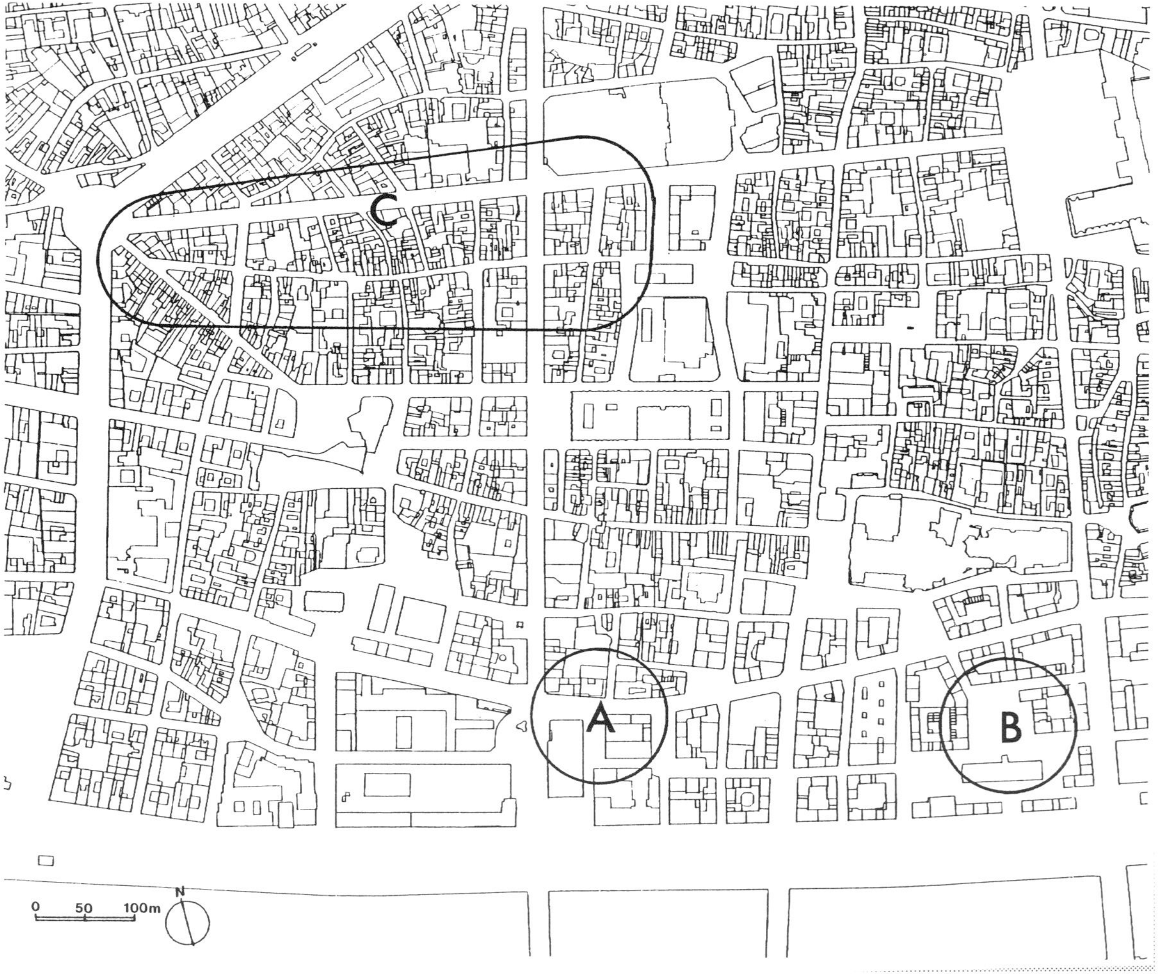

Figure 1
Les sites dont il
est ici question,
reportés sur le
plan de Rouen
en 1980.
A: Le Donjon;
B: La Tour;
C: Une enceinte
hypothétique

L'association topographique du Donjon et de l'abbé de Fécamp incline à penser que Richard II pourrait avoir, comme à Fécamp, associé Guillaume de Volpiano à l'exercice de son pouvoir en lui confiant sa chapellenie rouennaise.

Le vocable de St Clément pourrait être de plus l'indice d'une fondation scandinave. Elle trouve par exemple un parallèle à Londres où existait une église St Clément-aux-Danois, sur la rive de la Tamise.[7] Au sujet de la porte St Clément, il n'est certainement pas indifférent d'ajouter qu'elle donnait directement sur le Vieux-Pont de Rouen, attesté au début du onzième siècle, qui a permis la traversée de la Seine jusqu'à la construction du pont de pierre par Mathilde au douzième siècle[8] (figure 3).

C'est peut-être au Donjon que pense Dudon lorsqu'il cite vers 940–956 la 'domus Willelmi ducis', ou encore la 'domus principum civitatis' et le 'Rotomagensis urbis palatia'.[9] D'ailleurs, à la même époque, la résidence ducale de Fécamp est elle-aussi appelée 'palais'. Il pourrait s'agir de l'ancienne résidence comtale carolingienne.

Voyons maintenant ce qu'il en est de la Tour de Rouen.

De manière un peu surprenante, peu de publications y ont trait, et pourtant son site est assez bien défini par les textes médiévaux, qui permettent d'en cerner à la fois les limites et l'étendue. Le site de la Tour est tout d'abord indiqué de manière évidente par les toponymes de 'place de la Haute Vieille Tour', 'place de la Basse Vieille Tour' et 'Halles de la Vieille Tour', sur le plan de la ville avant les destructions de 1940 et 1944, et plus encore au début du dix-huitième siècle (figure 4). Il est cependant possible de le définir plus en détails.

Au nord le mur d'enceinte du château ducal était probablement situé à l'alignement de la halle au nord de la place de la Haute-Vieille-Tour, le long de la rue Neuve-des-Halles. En effet l'octroi en 1259 d'une rente par le roi au chapitre cathédral, 'pour des dommages supportés tant en maisons, places, jardins et en toutes autres choses, en raison des Halles nouvellement construites à (la Vieille Tour)',[10] se comprend aisément si l'on considère que la rue Neuve-des-Halles a été établie sur le fossé du château, concédé au chapitre en 1171/90.[11]

A l'ouest existait aussi un fossé. Il est attesté au début du douzième siècle à proximité de l'église St Candé-le-Vieux,[12] à l'est de la rue du Bac. Il était à l'emplacement de la rue du Hallage, encore en 1398 un espace vide, un 'clos', où

[7]   Tim Tatton-Brown, 'The topography of Anglo-Saxon London', *Antiquity*, LX, 27, d'après E. Cinthio, 'The churches of St Clement in Scandinavia', *Archeologia Ludensia*, 3, 103–116.
[8]   Sur la question du Vieux Pont, voir Robillard de Beaurepaire, 1904, 441; Georges Dubosc, 'La Maison des Templiers à Rouen', *Bulletin des Amis des Monuments Rouennais (BAMR)*, 1911, 75, et Gauthiez, 133–35.
[9]   Dudon de St Quentin, 'De moribus et actis primorum Normanniae ducum', publié par Jules Lair, *MSAN*, XXIII, Paris 1865, pp. 194, 225, 227 et 264.
[10] Delisle, *Cartulaire Normand*, no. 631: 'in domibus, plateis, jardinis quam possessionibus et rebus aliis quibuscumque, ratione Halarum nostrarum Rothomagensium de novo constructarum ibidem'.
[11] Le fossé est signalé lors de la cession d'un terrain situé au sud de la rue St Denis. Bibliothèque Municipale de Rouen (BMR) ms. Y.44, nos 228 et 229: 'masuram cum gardino et tota terra de retro supra fossatum a dextris et a sinistris sicut terra se extendit a turrenula muri castelli usque ad antiquum murum Civitatis versus Rodobeccam'.
[12] A côté de la résidence de l'évêque de Bayeux à Rouen, située 'juxta Sanctum Candidum et fossatum castelli, contigua muroque Civitas clauditur a parte Franciae', *MSAN*, VIII, 427.

s'entrainaient les arbalètriers.[13] Le fossé y a été rencontré par Léon De Vesly en 1898 lors d'une fouille, sous la forme d'une structure maçonnée, vers la Seine.[14]

Les côtés est et sud du château reprennent apparemment l'enceinte édifiée au quatrième siècle.

La concession du site de la Tour après sa désaffection comme résidence royale donne d'autres précisions.

En juillet 1216 Philippe-Auguste concède 'toute la place où est le Vieux Château de Rouen, jusqu'au cours de la Seine, telle que l'ont tenue Henri et Richard autrefois rois d'Angleterre'.[15] Un peu plus tard, en 1224, Louis VIII concède à la commune de Rouen 'la tierce partie (du) Vieux Château de Rouen près de la Seine, à savoir la partie qui est vers le Pont de Rouen'.[16] Nous savons par ces textes que le terrain du château ducal avait alors été divisé en trois tiers, se succédant d'ouest, vers le Pont de Rouen, en est. Après la concession d'un tiers à la Commune en 1224, le roi ne disposera plus que des deux tiers restants du site pour y construire des halles au XIIIème siècle. De fait en plan la distance entre la rue du Bac et l'extrémité ouest de l'ancienne Halle aux Toiles, 48 mètres, est la moitié de la distance entre cette même extrémité et le mur d'enceinte du quatrième siècle, 96 mètres. Ceci signifie que le château ducal s'étendait à l'ouest jusqu'à la rue du Bac.

L'étendue du château ducal ainsi déterminée, d'ailleurs bien reconnaissable sur le plan de la ville au début du dix-huitième siècle, est de l'ordre de 15 000 m2.

Au douzième siècle, il comprenait la Tour elle-même, une Grande Salle (aula) devant la Tour,[17] des appartements princiers,[18] des prisons,[19] et une chapelle dédiée à St Romain,[20] près de la Grande Salle.[19] L'église St Candé, collégiale créée par le duc Robert avant 1035, faisait fonction de chapelle princière, la 'dominica capellaria'.[21] Elle était patronnée par l'évêque de Lisieux. On accédait au château par une porte[22] que desservait un pont-levis.[23] A l'ouest, l'espace compris entre le fossé à l'emplacement de la rue du Hallage et la rue du Bac avait peut-être une fonction de basse-cour.

Les fouilles archéologiques effectuées dans le courant de ce siècle, trop sommaires, n'ont pas permis de préciser la situation des éléments composant le

[13] BMR, Inventaire des délibérations de la ville, reg. A4, 30 mars 1397.

[14] *BAMR*, 1902, 105–106, figure IV.

[15] Pour 30 £ tournois de rente annuelle: 'totam plateam nostram in qua vetus castrum rothomagi sedet cum toto porprisio usque ad canellum Secane sicut Henricus et Ricardus quondam reges Anglie illam tenuerunt tenendam', *MSAN*, XV, 157.

[16] Il s'agit de la partie autrefois concédée à Jean Luce avec l'accord de son fils Pierre, pour 10 £ de rente annuelle, soit le tiers de la rente de 1216: 'tertiam partem quam habebat idem Petrus in veteri castro rothomagensi juxta Secanam, eam videlicet partem que est versus Pontem de Rothomago, prout metata est', BMR, Tiroir 63, vidimus de 1279.

[17] *MSAN*, VIII, 436.

[18] Robert de Torigni, *Chronique*, publiée par Léopold Delisle, Rouen 1872, 164: 'Henricus rex circa Turrem Rothomagi, quam aedificat Primus Ricardus dux Normannorum, in palatium sibi murum altum et latum cum propugnaculis aedificat, et aedificia ad mensionem regiam congrua infra eundem murum parat. Ipsi vero Turri propugnacula quae deerant, addit.'

[19] *MSAN*, XV, 22.

[20] Lucien Musset dans *Histoire de Rouen*, sous la direction de M. Mollat, Toulouse 1979, 47.

[21] Masselin, *MSAN*, XXV, 327.

[22] Delisle, *Cartulaire normand*, no. 583.

[23] *MSAN*, XVI, 99.

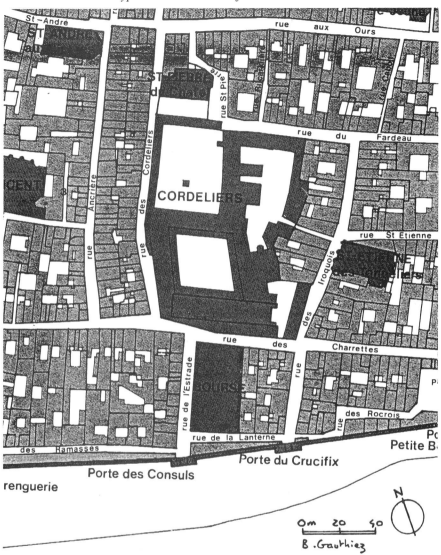

Figure 2 Le site du Donjon vers 1730. Le Donjon est acquis par les Cordeliers au treizième siècle. Sa topographie est encore sensible au dix-huitième siècle, à l'angle de l'enceinte antique qui longeait la rue des Cordeliers à l'est et la rue des Charrettes au nord. La chapelle des Cordeliers, dédiée à St Clément, le long de la rue des Charrettes, rappelle l'ancienne chapelle du même nom placée sur une porte de la ville donnant sur le Vieux Pont, dans l'axe de la partie sud de la rue des Iroquois, qui portait ce nom au treizième siècle, à l'emplacement de la rive remblayée de la Seine

Figure 3   Restitution des abords de la Seine aux onzième-douzième siècles. Les plus anciennes mentions topographiques rencontrées sont indiquées. Le fossé de la Cité à l'ouest du Donjon était vraisemblablement le site où venaient s'ancrer les navires ducaux. Le nom de la 'rue as Ancres', plus tard rue Ancrière, en serait le souvenir

Figure 4 (opposite)   Le site de la Tour de Rouen vers 1730. De Même que pour le Donjon, et de manière plus nette encore, l'emplacement du château est bien lisible dans la topographie du quartier, marquée par le quadrilatère des Halles qui reprennent son pourtour

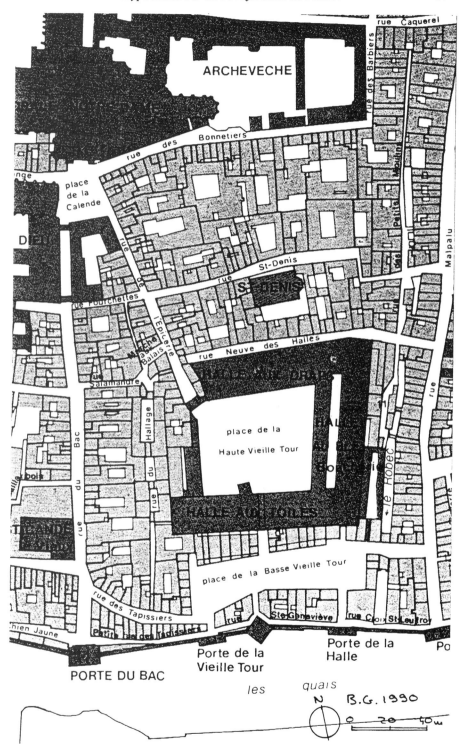

ARCHEVECHE

rue des Bonnetiers

place de la Calende

St-DENIS

rue St-Denis

rue Neuve des Halles

place de la Haute Vieille Tour

HALLE AUX TOILES

place de la Basse Vieille Tour

Ste Geneviève

PORTE DU BAC

Porte de la Vieille Tour

Porte de la Halle

les quais

N

B.G. 1990

0   20   40 m

château ducal, et particulièrement celle de la Tour elle-même, qui devait se trouver proche du mur vers la Seine.[24]

Voici donc les principaux traits de la topographie du site (figure 5). Quant à la datation de la construction de la Tour, Robert de Torigni nous enseigne que Richard Ier la fît édifier pendant son règne, soit avant 996.[25] Il semble cependant qu'elle n'ait été édifiée que plus tard, au début du onzième siècle, et par Richard II.

Que peut en effet signifier la reprise de la chapelle St Clément à l'abbaye de Fécamp en 1024, si ce n'est que le duc n'a plus l'utilité de disposer de l'abbé et des moines au Donjon, donc que la Tour est construite?

C'est probablement pour des raisons de droits antérieurs sur le site de la Tour que le duc n'a pas confié à l'abbaye de Fécamp la chapelle du nouveau château ducal, en effet Guillaume de Volpiano ne meurt qu'en 1031. L'évêque de Lisieux en est le nouveau bénéficiaire, d'où la création d'une collégiale peu après dans l'église St Candé-le-Vieux, dont les chapelains sont attestés dès cette époque, en 1028–33.[26] C'est peut-être en compensation de la perte de la chapellenie ducale que l'abbaye de Fécamp fut très richement dotée à Rouen à partir de 1024.

Il est ainsi probable qu'en 1006, la résidence ducale est encore le Donjon, et que le nouveau château de la Tour n'est mis en service qu'en 1024 ou peu avant. C'est donc plutôt à Richard II qu'il faut en attribuer pour l'essentiel la construction, son père Richard Ier l'ayant, si l'on suit la chronique, peut-être commencé.

La Tour servira de résidence ducale puis royale probablement jusqu'à sa cession en 1216 par Philippe-Auguste, après l'achèvement d'un nouveau château construit après la prise de la Normandie en 1204. Le rôle de la Vicomté de Rouen en 1210, en comportant un certain nombre de dépenses relatives à la Tour de Rouen, notamment au 'chapelain de la Tour', au 'gardien de la Tour', au 'géolier de la Tour' et au 'chapelain de la grande salle de la Tour', implique que la Tour est en effet encore en fonction à cette époque. Il devait en subsister des éléménts significatifs encore en 1240, peu avant la construction des halles vers 1257.[27]

---

[24] Que ce soient celles de Guy Dubois en 1956, *Actes du 81ème congrès des Sociétés Savantes*, Rouen-Caen 1956, 39; les observations de Daniel Lavallée en 1955–56, *Bulletin de la Commision Départementale des Antiquités de la Seine-Maritime (CDA)*, XX, 95 et 110; ou le relevé effectué par l'architecte des Monuments Historiques M. Jullien lors de la reconstruction de la Halle aux Toiles en 1956, voir Archives de la Circonscription des Antiquités Historiques de Haute-Normandie, à Rouen, 4/1966. A cette occasion, il fut demandé à l'entreprise chargée de reconstruire la Halle aux Toiles de faire le plan des murs rencontrés lors de l'établissement des fondations. L'entreprise devait être payée en fonction de la quantité de murs . . .
[25] Robert de Torigni, 28.
[26] Fauroux, 201.
[27] Les rôles de l'Echiquier de 1180 et 1195, *MSAN*, XV, 22 et 47; de 1198, Delisle, *MSAN*, XVI, 7; et celui de la Vicomté de Rouen en 1210, Delisle, *Cartulaire Normand*, no. 210, ont exactement les mêmes postes de dépenses relatives au château de la Tour. Après sa cession en trois parts en 1216, il semble que la Tour a été reprise par le roi, ce que l'on constate à l'occasion de la concession par Louis VIII d'un des trois tiers en 1224 à la Commune, mais aussi lorsque Louis IX donne en 1240 ce qui doit correspondre aux deux tiers restants aux Frères Prêcheurs pour leur installation à Rouen. La lettre de remerciement que ceux-ci lui envoient indique que le site du château royal (de la Tour) pouvait encore être utile au roi, voir Jean-Louis Eloy, *Le couvent de St Jacques de Rouen 1224–1790*, Bayeux 1965, 28. Ce don n'aura cependant de suite, du fait de la ferme opposition du chapitre cathédral en 1245, cf. ADSM G 3658. Les Frères Prêcheurs trouveront à s'installer à l'angle sud-ouest de l'enceinte du onzième siècle, voir Gauthiez, 242.

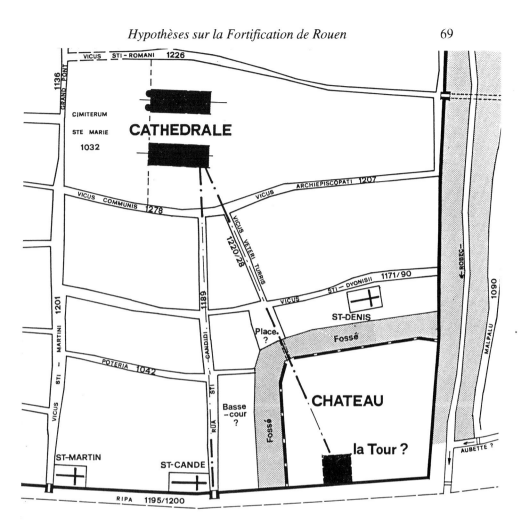

*Figure 5   Restitution du site de la Tour peu après son achèvement,
probablement vers 1024. Les plus anciennes mentions topographiques
rencontrées sont indiquées. La rue de la Vieille Tour, ainsi appelée au
treizième siècle, pourrait avoir été percée à l'occasion de la construction de la
Tour, de manière à créer un lien non seulement symbolique, mais aussi visuel,
avec la Cathédrale et l'Archevêché, alors étroitement associé au pouvoir*

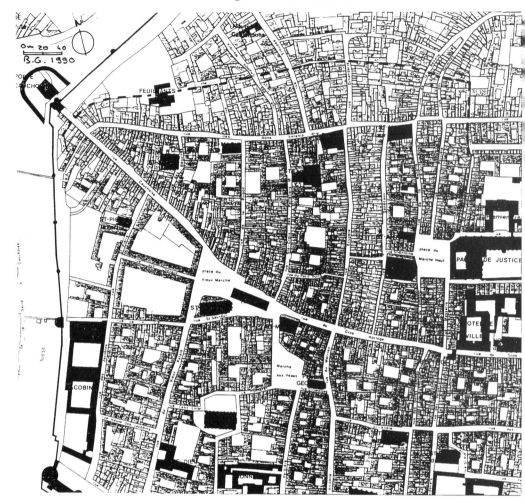

*Figure 6   La partie ouest de Rouen vers 1730. Le pointillé indique un tracé
qui pourrait correspondre à celui d'un rempart, les bandes de parcelles
l'accompagnant suggérant un fossé*

Si la question des châteaux ducaux ne laisse pas trop d'incertitude quant à leurs
sites et à leur chronologie relative, il n'en est pas de même pour l'enceinte de la
ville, sur laquelle les textes sont particulièrement muets.

   Il est cependant possible de faire l'hypothèse de la construction d'une enceinte
au onzième siècle.

   Le plan actuel de Rouen ne nous renseigne que de manière très approximative
sur la ville médiévale, du fait d'importantes modifications intervenues depuis le
dix-neuvième siècle, avec notamment la Reconstruction du dernier après-guerre.

   Mais la forme de Rouen au dix-huitième siècle, telle que l'on peut la restituer
au travers des plans d'archives, est plus parlante. Parmi les structures géomé-

triques que l'on peut y lire, et plus particulièrement parmi celles qui suggèrent des murs d'enceinte, l'ensemble de tracés situés entre la place Cauchoise et l'allée Eugène Delacroix, et suivant l'emplacement de l'actuelle rue Thiers, n'a pas jusque-là attiré l'attention des historiens[28] (figure 6).

Cet ensemble de tracés est composé d'une ligne de limites parcellaires longé par une bande de propriétés, large d'environ trente mètres, formant une discontinuîté entre deux parties de la ville, et qui pourraient correspondre à l'emplacement d'un mur et d'un fossé.

L'archéologie est muette sur un tel mur, et les textes guère plus explicites. Un ensemble d'éléments permet cependant d'étayer cette hypothèse.

Des travaux effectués rue Thiers en 1862 ont remué, entre la rue Etoupée et la rue des Champs-Maillets, un terrain 'argileux et sans vestiges', puis, entre la rue des Champs-Maillets et la rue Porte-aux-Rats, un 'sol qui a du être remué dans bien des circonstances'. Il contenait du mobilier gallo-romain et médiéval.[29] Une telle description est celle d'un remplissage de fossé avec des terres vierges provenant de l'extérieur de la ville, et celle de terres de déblai repoussées sur les terrains voisins lors du creusement.

Les textes n'ont livré qu'une mention d'un mur d'enceinte différent de celui existant plus au nord, datable de Henri II.[30] La *Chronique Normande* de Pierre Cochon mentionne en 1430 la première et la deuxième porte Cauchoise, et plus loin sur le même parcours la porte Massacre, au Gros-Horloge actuel, à l'occasion de l'arrivée à Rouen d'un personnage important.[31] Venant de l'extérieur de la ville, la première porte Cauchoise correspond au mur de Henri II, la deuxième pourrait être un vestige de l'enceinte supposée ici.

Son existence au nord de la rue des Bons-Enfants est étayée par les noms médiévaux des rues Ecuyère et Dinanderie. La rue Ecuyère s'appelait au début du XIIIème siècle Vieille rue Ecuyère.[32] Le 'vieille' de la rue Ecuyère s'oppose au 'neuve' de la Neuve Rue que l'on rencontre paroisse St-Pierre-l'Honoré en 1206–17, et qui n'est autre que la rue Dinanderie.[33] Or les deux rues sont pratiquement l'une dans le prolongement de l'autre. La rue Dinanderie va de la rue des Bons-Enfants à la rue des Maillots, qui suivant l'hypothèse de tracé longe le fossé contigu au mur supposé.

Autre élément, le nom de la rue Etoupée (= fermée) évoque à l'évidence l'existence d'un obstacle. Et pourtant il s'agit au début du treizième siècle de l'un

[28] Cette hypothèse d'enceinte a déjà fait l'objet d'une note, aux conclusions maintenant dépassées, rédigée bien avant que je n'entreprenne ma thèse, voir B. Gauthiez, 'Les enceintes médiévales de Rouen', *Bulletin des Amis des Monuments Rouennais*, oct. 1984–sept. 1985, 35–39. La question des enceintes à Rouen, jusqu'à ce jour plutôt controversée, a pu être approfondie, et notablement éclaircie, à l'occasion de ma thèse.
[29] Paul Baudry, *Le Nouvelliste de Rouen*, 10 octobre 1862, et Archives Municipales de Rouen, carton rue Thiers, pour le positionnement des travaux de l'égoût dont il est ici question, mis en place dans l'axe de la rue. L'absence du mur sur le tracé des travaux est cohérente avec l'hypothèse, qui le fait passer à quelques mètres plus au sud.
[30] Gauthiez, 183–189.
[31] Pierre Cochon, *Chronique Normande*, éditée par Charles Robillard de Beaurepaire, Rouen 1870, 312–313.
[32] Le nom est valable aussi bien pour la partie paroisse St Jean, ADSM G 4304, que pour celle située paroisse St Pierre-l'Honoré, ADSM G 4344.
[33] ADSM G 4370, et BMR ms Y 44, no. 248. L'indentité de la Rue Neuve et de la rue Dinanderie est donnée par un texte de 1477, Nicétas Périaux, *Dictionnaire indicateur des rues et places de Rouen*, Rouen 1870, 174.

des accès à la ville. Une porte s'y trouvait en 1231, datant probablement de la construction en ce point de l'enceinte de Henri II.[34] La rue Etoupée n'est donc pas fermée à cette époque, et se prolonge en ville par le 'vicus Stopatus'.[35] Tout s'accorde si l'enceinte ici supposée a effectivement fermé cette rue, et que, à l'occasion de la construction de l'enceinte de Henri II, il a été jugé utile de rétablir cet accès à la ville.

D'autre part il semble bien que le fossé ouest du 'castrum' a été comblé, ou abandonné, antérieurement à ceux situés au nord et à l'est, dont la suppression est autorisée en 1224[36] par Louis VIII. Le fossé ouest de la Cité, après sa désaffection, a servi de décharge aux bouchers qui exerçaient aux environs de la porte Massacre au Gros-Horloge.[37] De grandes masses d'ossements ont été rencontrées entre la rue Percière et la rue du Tambour.[38] Les rues sur l'emplacement de ce fossé apparaîssent bien avant 1224. La rue Percière est citée en 1201, plus au sud on trouve en 1201–03 l'actuelle rue Massacre, et en 1193–1201 la 'rue du Temple', l'ancienne rue des Cordeliers.[39] Le fossé ouest de la Cité était donc supprimé et loti bien avant que les fossés vers le nord et l'est suivent le même sort.

C'est ce que suggère aussi la double localisation du toponyme Ganterie, d'une part la partie de la rue du Gros-Horloge hors la porte Massacre, appelée en 1189–94 Wanteria,[40] d'autre part l'actuelle rue Ganterie, nommée le Fossé-aux-Gantiers en 1293.[41] Les gantiers, perdant l'usage d'une partie du fossé à l'ouest de la Cité lors de sa désaffection, auraient été amenés à se déplacer pour occuper un site proche d'un fossé actif, et donc libre.

Ainsi, il est vraisemblable qu'une enceinte a existé autour de la partie ouest de la ville antérieurement à la construction de l'enceinte de Henri II (figure 7).

On a vu quel pouvait être son tracé au nord, où les éléments disponibles semblent confirmer l'hypothèse. Au sud, le parcellaire ne livre pas de tracé suggérant un mur. Il ne semble pas y avoir eu de clôture du côté du fleuve, le long de la rive située jusqu'au treizième siècle au niveau de la rue des Charrettes.[42] Il faut cependant mentionner la palissade citée en 1202 sur la rive de la Seine, à proximité de la Cité, qui pourrait toutefois être d'origine plus ancienne.[43]

Le tracé ouest est déjà probablement celui où le mur de la ville subsistera jusqu'au dix-huitième siècle. En effet aucun élément, que ce soit en plan ou dans les textes, ne permet de supposer un autre tracé. De ce côté, le mur d'enceinte

---

[34] Un faubourg est dit en 1231 tout au long de la 'rue Etoupée hors la Porte', BMR reg. U2, fo. 56 recto.
[35] ADSM G 4608; on trouve aussi 'vicus Obtrusus', ADSM G 4352; et encore 'vicus Obstructus', dans la paroisse St Pierre-l'Honoré, ADSM G 2094, 135.
[36] BMR, Tiroir 63, Vidimus de 1279.
[37] Appelée 'porte de la Boucherie' en 1219, BMR Tiroir 52, 'Porta Macellaria'.
[38] A l'occasion de la construction de la partie ouest du Palais de Justice, Lecoeur, *CDA*, VI, 5.
[39] ADSM G 4324, et BMR ms Y 44, no. 243, 1201–03, 'vicus Percamenariorum', pour la rue Percière; la 'rue de la Boucherie', ADSM 20 H 6, 'vicus Macelli', pour la rue Massacre; et Robillard de Beaurepaire, 1904, 431, note 1, pour la rue du Temple. L'adéquation rue du Temple = rue des Cordeliers est confirmée par un texte de 1244, Archives Nationales, S.5199, no. 42, qui nous dit que la rue du Temple est parallèle à la Renelle, elle-même parallèle au mur de la Cité.
[40] ADSM G 4306 et G 4301.
[41] ADSM G 4305.
[42] La rue des Charrettes est dite 'super ripam' en 1206–17, ADSM G 4289.
[43] T. D. Hardy, *Rotuli Normanniae in Turri Londinensi*, I, 49.

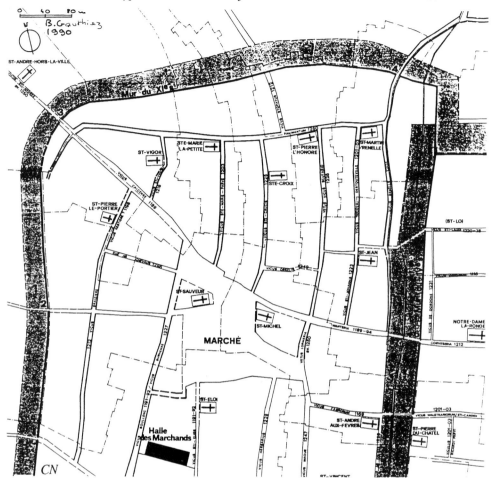

Figure 7 Hypothèse de restitution de la partie ouest de Rouen peu après la construction de l'enceinte qui l'enclôt, réalisée peut-être par Guillaume entre 1067 et 1087. Les plus anciennes mentions topographiques rencontrées sont indiquées. Les numéros indiquent les portes vraisemblables, dont en 3, la porte Cauchoise. En CN, au sud-ouest, était situé le 'clos des Galées', chantier naval royal

descendait au delà de la rue des Charrettes et de la rive vers la Seine, comme l'indique l'acte de cession du 'lieu où l'on construisait les galées' en 1283 par le roi à la ville,[44] à l'emplacement du Vieux-Palais, forteresse construite par Henri V après 1420.[45] Il protégeait ce chantier naval, dont l'origine pourrait ainsi être ducale.

[44] L'emplacement est en effet délimité 'entre le mur de la clôture de la ville d'une part et le tènement de Nicaise d'Orbec d'autre part, du chemin par devant jusqu'à la Seine par derrière', BMR Tiroir 324.
[45] Gauthiez, 294.

L'ensemble de ces éléments et de ces indices est à mon sens probant. La datation de ce mur est plus problématique. Il n'est en effet explicitement évoqué dans aucun document, on l'a vu.

Cependant le récit par Orderic Vital de la sédition organisée à Rouen par Conan au profit du roi Guillaume le Roux en 1090, sédition visant à lui livrer la ville alors tenue par le duc Robert, est suffisamment précis dans ses données topographiques pour que l'on puisse raisonnablement penser que cette enceinte existait à ce moment.[46]

La ville apparaît dans ce récit comme un ensemble clos, avec des dépendances à l'est, le faubourg Malpalu, et au sud, sur l'autre rive de la Seine. Les partis en présence s'affrontent à l'intérieur de cet ensemble, les bourgeois eux-mêmes étant divisés entre partisans et adversaires du duc Robert. Le seul élément de la ville topographiquement indépendant dans ce texte est le château, d'où assiste impuissant le duc à la bataille, avant de tenter une sortie qui se termine par sa fuite par la porte de la rue St Romain, vers l'est.

Dans cet ensemble clos, lieu d'une furieuse guerre urbaine, essaient alors de pénétrer des troupes au secours du duc par la 'porta méridionalis', la porte St Martin ou St Clément, menées entre autres par Henri Cliton, et des troupes en faveur de Guillaume à la porte Cauchoise.

Ce texte montre bien l'unité que forme la ville, à laquelle il donne une limite, la porte Cauchoise, à l'extrémité nord-ouest de la rue du même nom. Il ne peut s'agir de la porte située au Gros-Horloge, toujours appelée porte Massacre ou de la Boucherie dans les actes. Il exclut de fait la présence d'un faubourg non protégé du côté ouest de la ville.

On voit mal le duc Robert construire cette enceinte dans les trois années de son fragile pouvoir après la mort de Guillaume. Il faut donc certainement en faire remonter l'édification avant 1087. Une charte nous enseigne que c'est de fait à son règne qu'il faut l'attribuer, puisqu'elle indique que les églises St Sauveur et Ste Croix (des-pelletiers) sont 'hors les murs' alors que Guillaume est roi.[47] L'archevêque Maurille est témoin de cette charte de donation, ce qui pourrait la dater de 1067, année de sa mort. Le quartier aurait ainsi été enclos après cette date.

Il reste que l'on aimerait bien disposer de preuves archéologiques sur un élément aussi déterminant de Rouen à cette époque. La situation de l'archéologie dans la capitale normande est si difficile, à la remarquable exception des fouilles menées par Jacques LeMaho sur l'ensemble cathédral, qu'il faudra vraisemblablement être patient.

Ainsi, Guillaume pourrait avoir construit une nouvelle enceinte à Rouen, peut-être à la même époque qu'à Caen, vers les années 1060–70.[48] La superficie enclose, avec ce nouveau mur, passe d'environ 24 ha à 49 ha (figure 8). Si Guillaume a favorisé Caen, il ne semble donc pas pour autant qu'il ait délaissé Rouen.

[46] Orderic, iv. 220–6; Orderic Vital, *Histoire de Normandie*, éditée par Guizot, III, Caen 1826, 308–313.
[47] ADSM 14 H 18, no. 273.
[48] Michel de Boüard, *Archéologie Médiévale*, numéro spécial 'Le château de Caen', Caen 1979, 10–11.

Figure 8   Hypothèse de restitution de Rouen vers la fin du onzième siècle. Les éléments remontant au onzième siècle sont reportés sur le plan de la ville actuelle

La fonction de cette nouvelle enceinte est assez claire. En effet le quartier concerné, tout en englobant l'ancien 'portus' situé en bordure du fleuve, est constitué pour l'essentiel d'un important développement de la ville, au nord et à l'ouest de la place du Vieux-Marché, réalisé au début du onzième siècle probablement par le duc Richard II. Ce quartier n'est autre, les textes permettent d'en être sûr, que le Bourg cité dans la charte des Libertés octroyées aux citoyens de Rouen par Henri II, dont une partie des articles remonte précisément certainement à Richard II.[49]

L'action de Guillaume à Rouen pourraît ne pas s'être limitée à construire une enceinte défendant le Bourg à l'ouest de la ville. On peut en effet se demander s'il n'a pas associé à sa construction le chantier naval dont il a déjà été question. Les navires ducaux étaient auparavant vraisemblablement stationnés au débouché du fossé ouest de la Cité, à côté du Donjon, sur un site que longe la rue Ancrière, dont le nom lui-même est évocateur. La possible création par le duc Guillaume d'un nouveau chantier naval, protégé par une avancée du nouveau mur d'enceinte dans la Seine, nous ramène aux évènements qui ont donné son nom au lieu où nous nous trouvons. Ne peut-on penser, en effet, qu'une partie de la flotte du Conquérant a pu être construite et armée dans ce nouveau chantier naval rouennais?

---

[49] Gauthiez, 82–85 pour le 'portus', 140–151 pour le Bourg.

ANGLO-SCANDINAVIAN EQUESTRIAN EQUIPMENT IN ELEVENTH-CENTURY ENGLAND

James Graham-Campbell

At the 1987 Battle Conference, Professor Ralph Davis concluded that:

> Evidently, horses were far more important in England than in Normandy during the period 946–1020, but after that the balance began to change and by 1045 had been reversed completely; Duke William's Normandy was far more horse-minded than Edward the Confessor's England. What could have been the reason for the sudden decline in English horses? . . . the most likely cause would have been the disruption of the English studs during the disastrous wars of the reign of King Æthelred II (978–1016). It is true that King Cnut (1016–35) restored peace to the land, but since his organization of the army was by ships and 'shipfulls' there would not have been much incentive for him or his subjects to invest large sums of money in the production of larger and heavier horses.[1]

At the same time, however, Davis admitted that 'strictly speaking it is impossible to answer the question' as to how the horses of the Normans would have compared with those of the Anglo-Saxons, 'but we can compare our knowledge of the two' from the record evidence.[2] It is the intention of this paper to broaden the basis of this enquiry by bringing to bear artefactual evidence for the importance of the warhorse in eleventh-century England, from the Danish conquest to the Battle of Hastings.[3]

The warhorse was far more costly than any other horse and was always a stallion, as can be clearly appreciated from their depictions in tenth- and eleventh-century English manuscript illumination, sculpture and tapestry. In addition to his warhorse, an equestrian warrior required one or more lesser horses; the medieval knight had need of at least three – one to ride before battle and one for his squire (who had the care of the warhorse), and one for the baggage (including his armour) – as well as others for a mounted escort.[4] In the Bayeux Tapestry, Duke William's squire is shown bringing his warhorse to him at the onset of battle.[5]

The Bayeux Tapestry, in Davis's words, 'makes a great feature of horses . . . there are at least 179 in the main tapestry and perhaps as many as 186 . . . The

---

[1] R. H. C. Davis, 'The Warhorses of the Normans', *ante*, x, 1987, 67–82, at 81.

[2] Davis, 'Norman Warhorses', 80.

[3] Regrettably, there appears to be no modern survey of such material from Normandy to allow comparisons to be made.

[4] R. H. C. Davis, *The Medieval Warhorse: Origin, Development and Redevelopment*, London 1989, 24–6.

[5] D. M. Wilson, *The Bayeux Tapestry*, London 1985, pls 51–2.

artist has made it his business to show William's army as an army of cavalry'.[6] It is difficult to be sure of the size of the horses depicted in the Tapestry, but they were clearly small by later standards; archaeological evidence reveals Anglo-Saxon horses barely larger than ponies.[7] Given that the Tapestry does not distinguish in size between the horses of England and of Normandy, there seems to be no clear basis for the observation that 'the Bayeux Tapestry leaves one in no doubt that in 1066 the Norman's horses were thought marvellous in both quantity *and quality*' [my italics].[8] Quantity is not of course in doubt, given the estimate that the Norman army had mustered between two and three thousand horses (however many actually crossed the Channel), but the Tapestry can scarcely be used as evidence for the *extra* quality of the Norman horses. On the other hand, Norman interest in the quality of horses is amply demonstrated in their record sources, the evidence being their widely differing values[9] – a concern for prices not matched in the extant English sources, although it does not necessarily follow, as Davis suggested, that the Anglo-Saxons treated all horses 'equal' for distinctions are made in their wills between horses, wild horses, stallions, geldings, mares and colts (with studs mentioned specifically on two occasions in the eleventh century).[10]

However, in both Normandy and England, it was not just the quality of the mount that mattered – or that reflected its owner's status – but also that of the horse's equipment. Horse-trappings, as much as a man's weapons, had become status symbols,[11] reflected in both material quality and decorative appearance. It is thus essential to pursue the artefactual reality behind the references in Old English sources to *gereade* (and its related forms) – to be translated prosaically as 'tack' (bridle and saddle), if more poetically as 'horse-trappings'.[12]

An eighth-century date has been proposed by the Biddles for a remarkable stone fragment, excavated by them at Repton in Derbyshire, carved on one of its faces with a depiction of an equestrian warrior.[13] It is probable that this sculpture formed the upper part of a cross-shaft, but only the ornament of the 'rider face' is of concern here.

The horse is a clearly denoted stallion, but of small size in relation to its rider who controls it by means of a bridle having a complex bit, with a ring-shaped cheek-piece through which is passed the rein to be held loosely at shoulder height. The warrior is seated astride a saddle, held in position by a breast strap and a crupper, whilst the girth is not shown, being hidden behind his clothing and leg. There is an ornamental band, above which rises the front of the saddle; its back is said by the Biddles to end 'flat (or less high – it is concealed by the

---

[6] Davis, 'Norman Warhorses', 68.
[7] J. Langdon, *Horses, Oxen and Technological Innovation*, Cambridge 1986, 18.
[8] Davis, 'Norman Warhorses', 69.
[9] Davis, 'Norman Warhorses', 81.
[10] Davis, 'Norman Warhorses', 82, Appendix.
[11] See, for example, N. P. Brooks, 'Arms, Status and Warfare in Late-Saxon England', in *Ethelred the Unready*, ed. D. Hill (British Archaeological Reports 59), Oxford 1978, 81–103, and G. R. Owen-Crocker, 'Hawks and Horse-Trappings: the Insignia of Rank', in *The Battle of Maldon AD 991*, ed. D. Scragg, Oxford 1991, 220–37.
[12] Owen-Crocker, 229–30.
[13] M. Biddle and B. Kjølbye-Biddle, 'The Repton Stone', *Anglo-Saxon England*, 14, 1985, 233–92.

weapon at the waist)'. There are no stirrups and stirrup leathers and the rider is not equipped with spurs.

The Repton rider is a fine representation of an equestrian warrior on parade in Late Anglo-Saxon England (even if based on a Late Antique or Byzantine model). On the other hand, it provides no evidence that the Anglo-Saxons used horses in battle, as distinct from riding to battle or for pursuing a defeated army. In the illustrated Canterbury Hexateuch (British Library, MS. Cotton Claudius B.iv, fol. 25r), from the second quarter of the eleventh century, the Hebrew warriors pursue Lot's captors on horseback, using stirrups and spurs, but the actual engagement takes place on foot.[14]

Such representations of riders support the observation of Seaby and Woodfield that there is no archaeological evidence for the use of metal stirrups in Britain before the Viking age – or indeed for their widespread adoption by the English before the eleventh century, although it is impossible to rule out the use of rope or leather slings for this purpose.[15]

The use of spurs certainly began earlier in England than that of metal stirrups, as there is archaeological evidence for their occasional use before the tenth century. One example is on record from an Anglo-Saxon pagan grave, but there is some evidence for their manufacture in ninth-century England. Although the supposed bronze spur from Pakenham in Suffolk has not been universally accepted, it remains hard to see what else it could have been, however idiosyncratic its form, as well as a very similar (but more acceptable) example also found in Suffolk, at Icklingham.[16] A bronze spur from the Thames at Kingston, ascribed to the Carolingian period, has the long U-shaped arms characteristic of the continental spurs that doubtless formed the stimulus behind the adoption in England of this article of equestrian equipment – and potential status-symbol.

In this connection, it is worth noting the recent suggestion that a set of two silver strap-slides and two tongue-shaped strap-ends in the Trewhiddle hoard from Cornwall (deposited c.868) are from spurs.[17] In form, this strap-set appears to follow a Carolingian prototype, like the spur-fittings in the late ninth/early tenth-century Norse boat-burial at Balladoole on the Isle of Man.[18] The latter were found together with simple iron spurs and stirrups, forming the earliest such set of horse-equipment from Britain, although the burial is contemporary with two graves of Viking equestrian warriors found in north-west England – at Aspatria, from which a horse-bit and a spur were recorded (now lost), and at Hesket-in-the-Forest, where the grave-goods included a horse-bit and spurs (the latter now lost). However, neither of these two Cumbrian burials contained stirrups, although both were well-furnished in other ways.[19]

---

[14] J. Kiff, 'Images of War: Illustrations of Warfare in Eleventh-Century England', *ante*, vii, 1984, 177–94, at pl. 6; R. Abels, 'English Tactics, Strategy and Military Organization in the Late Tenth Century', in ed. Scragg, 143–55, at pl. 7.1.
[15] W. A. Seaby and P. Woodfield, 'Viking Stirrups from England and their Background', *Med. Arch.*, xxiv, 1980, 87–122.
[16] D. A. Hinton, *Catalogue of the Anglo-Saxon Ornamental Metalwork, 700–1100, in the Department of Antiquities, Ashmolean Museum*, Oxford 1974, no. 29.
[17] L. Webster in *The Making of England: Anglo-Saxon Art and Culture, AD 600–900*, ed. L. Webster and J. Backhouse, London 1991, no. 264, i.
[18] G. Bersu and D. M. Wilson, *Three Viking Graves in the Isle of Man*, London 1966, 36–9, pl. vii, b–d.
[19] B. J. N. Edwards, 'The Vikings in North-West England', with refs, in *Viking Treasure from the*

Stirrups are still not in evidence on the Anglo-Scandinavian sculpture of the next generation in northern England, such as a tenth-century hogback fragment from Sockburn in County Durham, although several features are omitted, including bridle and girth.[20] On the other hand, the Sockburn saddles are clearly depicted with raised backs – the high cantle required to prevent a cavalryman from being thrust back off his saddle in combat. Indeed, in this respect, they are no different from the saddles of the Bayeux Tapestry which Davis believed to be the earliest attested examples of this feature.[21]

On the Tapestry saddles are depicted in a uniform manner, with pommel and cantle, and stirrup-irons with their leathers attached well forward of the buckled girth-strap.[22] Stirrups in this forward position were well in front of the rider's centre of gravity and meant that he had to sit with his legs sticking out forward, toes pointing down. In this position, 'with legs braced against the stirrup-irons, buttocks pressed hard back against the cantle, he was locked in position in moments of stress or emergency'.[23]

It is regrettable that no Anglo-Saxon or Norman saddle is preserved for detailed study, but this is scarcely surprising given their organic construction (of wood, leather and cloth). However, the fragment of a late ninth/early tenth-century oak bow from the Coppergate excavations in York (with horn inlay, held in place by silver rivets) gives an impression of how a saddle-bow might have been decorated in England at that period.[24]

The same problem of the poor survival of organic material means that few details are known of the bridle by which the horse is controlled and guided (comprising the head-stall, bit and reins). Cow-hide will have been used for the main elements, both for strength and because it is available in long lengths. Bits were of iron, although their cheek-pieces were sometimes of copper alloy (as discussed below), whilst the straps might be decorated with ornamental metal-work. Two sets of gilt chains, from London, with distributors and pendant discs decorated in a late ninth-century style, have been identified as harness-mounts, although 'their light construction would suit dogs rather than horses'.[25] It is not surprising therefore that horse-harness could be of high value in Late Anglo-Saxon England, as is evident from its inclusion in wills, and from the occasion when a stolen bridle was precious enough to fight to death over (as mentioned in a charter of 995).[26] Its general appearance can be deduced from depictions (such as in the Bayeux Tapestry) and from comparanda found in Viking graves both in Britain and in Scandinavia. For example, the bridle from the Balladoole boat-burial on the Isle of Man, already cited (p. 79), is in the native Insular tradition of

North-West: the Cuerdale Hoard in its Context, ed. J. Graham-Campbell, Liverpool 1992, 43–62, at 43–6 (nos 1 and 2, figs 5.1 and 2).

[20] Sockburn 9: J. T. Lang, 'The Hogback: a Viking Colonial Monument', *Anglo-Saxon Studies in Archaeology and History*, 3 (1984), 85–176, at 166–7; Owen-Crocker, pl. 13.15.

[21] Davis, *Medieval Warhorse*, 15.

[22] A particularly clear example is Wilson, *BT*, pl. 11; but see also Taylor, this vol., illustration inside back cover.

[23] C. Chevenix Trench, *A History of Horsemanship*, London 1970, 76.

[24] Webster, in ed. Webster and Backhouse, no. 253 (illustrated upside down).

[25] Webster, in ed. Webster and Backhouse, no. 252 (illustrated upside down).

[26] P. H. Sawyer, *Anglo-Saxon Charters*, London 1968, no. 883.

Late Celtic metalwork, with decorated copper-alloy mounts and an openwork pendant ornament (fig. 1).[27]

The importance of horses to the Danish forces active in England during the late ninth century is well documented in the Anglo-Saxon Chronicle; their use by leaders of the Norse settlement of northern England in the early tenth century has been indicated above from the archaeological evidence of grave-goods and sculpture. It is thus necessary to review briefly aspects of the Viking-age evidence from Scandinavia in order to consider further the potential contribution of the Danes to the development of cavalry in eleventh-century England.

The unique group of so-called 'picture-stones', on the Baltic island of Gotland, some of which date from the beginning of the Viking Age, in the eighth century, include scenes of warriors on horseback, but combat on foot.[28] Naturalistic depictions of any kind are rare in Scandinavian art of the Viking age, but an equestrian warrior occurs in an unusual set of openwork roundels (from c.900) that was deposited in the Gokstad ship-burial, Vestfold, Norway. It has been suggested by some Scandinavian authorities that these mounts are Norse copies of Anglo-Saxon work, despite the absence of any obvious English prototypes.[29] In any case, the rider appears to be mounted side-saddle, wearing an ankle-length costume, so that the design was most probably copied from some eastern model.[30]

Many pieces of standard horse equipment were deposited as grave-goods in Scandinavia, for example over one thousand bits are known from Norway; some bridles were very showy. Stirrups were introduced to Scandinavia as early as the eighth century, but did not become common before the tenth century when highly ornamented examples were being made, sometimes with matching spurs; they have encrusted and inlaid ornament to complement that used on sword-hilts, spear-sockets and even axes.[31]

The rising importance of the equestrian warrior in tenth-century Scandinavia, most notably Denmark, is clear from the grave-goods of the rich, even at a time when pagan burial practices were in decline in the face of Christianity.[32] Indeed, one of the most interesting equestrian burials, from the English point of view, dates to the early eleventh century and thus well after the official conversion of Denmark – a barrow-grave at Velds, near Viborg in Jutland, containing a splendid set of gilt-bronze harness-mounts and a fine pair of stirrup plates.[33] The ornament of the latter has recently been described as 'an amalgam of Late Saxon acanthus

---

[27] Bersu and Wilson, 19–26, figs 11–16, pls iv, c–vi (the reconstruction reproduced here is fig. 16).

[28] S. Lindqvist, *Gotlands Bildsteine*, 2 vols, Stockholm 1941–42; E. Nylén and J. P. Lamm, *Stones, Ships and Symbols*, Stockholm 1988.

[29] H. Arbman, *The Vikings*, London 1962, 131, fig. 33; D. M. Wilson and O. Klindt-Jensen, *Viking Art*, London 1966 and 1980, 91.

[30] Cf. Chevenix Trench, 66 (illustration after a wall-painting in a catacomb at Kerch).

[31] For an illustrated selection, with refs, see J. Graham-Campbell, *Viking Artefacts: a Select Catalogue*, London 1980.

[32] K. Randsborg, *The Viking Age in Denmark*, London 1980, 127–9; but see also, E. Roesdahl, *Viking Age Denmark*, London 1982, 139.

[33] Owen-Crocker, pl. 13.12 (although they should be dated to the eleventh rather than to the tenth century, along with the associated stirrup plates).

and bird decoration and Scandinavian Ringerike-style tendrils', in such a manner that Leslie Webster concluded:[34]

> It may be that they were made for a Scandinavian follower of Cnut in early
> eleventh-century southern England, or that a Danish craftsman adapted a
> set of Anglo-Saxon ornamental motifs to a native Scandinavian style of
> stirrup for a home-coming Viking.

The term 'Ringerike style' is applied to a late phase of Viking art – that which provides the key to the recognition of the wider group of eleventh-century horse-equipment that highlights the links between England and southern Scandinavia during the reign of Cnut. The Ringerike style combines foliate patterns drawn from west European art with the Scandinavian tradition of stylised animal ornament in compositions based on axiality which stand out against their background; innovations include tight clusters of intertwined tendrils and the use of alternating tendril/lobe schemes.[35] This style is considered to have emerged around the millennium and its 'classic' phase is dated within the first half of the eleventh century. It was thus at its height of fashion during the reign of Cnut and so it is reasonable to suppose that it was his followers who commissioned the famous stone found in St Paul's churchyard, London,[36] from a sculptor who had been trained in the mainstream Ringerike style. This displays a magnificent backward-looking animal (or 'great beast'), with flowing mane and tail in the form of tendril clusters, preceded by a serpent-like lesser animal, its open-jawed head topped with a tendril crest.

The Ringerike style was widely used in the Scandinavian world and was thus naturally employed for the embellishment of horse equipment, although often poorly executed (e.g. the 'great beast' on a stirrup-plate from Stenåsa, on Öland,[37] and in yet more simplified form on the cheek-piece of a horse-bit from Lund, in southern Sweden,[38] excavated in a context dating from 1020–50).

Of particular importance for the study of the material from England is the equestrian equipment in this style found in a grave in central Sweden (at Lundby, Fors, Södermanland),[39] comprising a pair of copper-alloy stirrups (fig. 2), with openwork sub-foliate ornament decorated in a rocked-graver technique, and an iron bit with matching copper-alloy cheek-pieces (fig. 3), composed of paired animal-heads, with open jaws and tendril extensions to their contoured bodies. Characteristically, the knobbed side-links have three ornamental projections; such are known from England, even if their significance has not always been recognised.[40]

A preliminary survey of these decorated stirrups and cheek-pieces was published in 1980 by Signe Horn Fuglesang, who noted that their distribution covered

---

[34] L. Webster in *The Golden Age of Anglo-Saxon Art, 966–1066*, ed. J. Backhouse, D. H. Turner and L. Webster, London 1984, no. 98.
[35] Wilson and Klindt-Jensen, 134–46; but see now, S. H. Fuglesang, *Some Aspects of the Ringerike Style*, Odense 1980.
[36] Wilson and Klindt-Jensen, 135–6, pl. lviii,a; Graham-Campbell, no. 499; Fuglesang, no. 88.
[37] Wilson and Klindt-Jensen, 117 and 140, pl. lxii,a.
[38] K. Bergman and I. Billberg in A. Mårtensson, *PK Banken i Lund*, Lund 1976, 229, pl. 176.
[39] *Fornvännen*, 4, 1909, 245–6, figs 36–7 (SHM 13,703).
[40] A fragment of one from the Winchester excavations has recently been published as a '?mount', by D. A. Hinton in M. Biddle, *Objects and Economy in Medieval Winchester* (Winchester Studies 7:2), Oxford 1990, 770 (no. 2345).

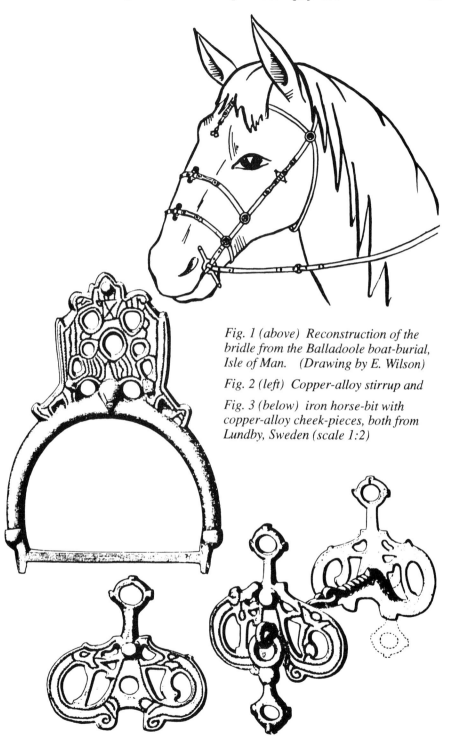

Fig. 1 (above) Reconstruction of the bridle from the Balladoole boat-burial, Isle of Man.   (Drawing by E. Wilson)

Fig. 2 (left) Copper-alloy stirrup and

Fig. 3 (below) iron horse-bit with copper-alloy cheek-pieces, both from Lundby, Sweden (scale 1:2)

Fig. 4 (above)   Copper-alloy cheek-piece fragment from Cambridgeshire (scale 1:1)

Fig. 5 (right)   Copper-alloy cheek-piece fragment from Stoke Holy Cross, Norfolk (scale 1:1). (Drawing by K. Penn)

central and southern Sweden, Denmark, England and Iceland.[41] The garbled nature of their Ringerike-style ornament suggested to her that this new style equestrian equipment was based on Anglo-Saxon prototypes, but such were left unspecified and the material so far known, including that surveyed above, includes no obvious exemplars. Indeed, the reverse trend now seems the more probable, in the light of the detailed arguments since published for the general introduction of the metal stirrup into England from southern Scandinavia during the reign of Æthelred.[42]

In fact, when Dr Fuglesang published her provisional list, it contained only one stirrup, a lost example from Mottisfont, Hants,[43] and one cheek-piece fragment, from Cambridgeshire (fig. 4),[44] which is a well-made example of one of these artefacts, although it displays their inherent weakness – a tendency to break across the central perforation.[45] The last decade has seen a considerable increase in the number of fragments on record, some recovered through excavation and others by metal-detecting, to the point at which this (and related) material would benefit from cataloguing and detailed study; only a selection will be presented here.

One such cheek-piece fragment from Norfolk (fig. 5) has been published as a 'mount';[46] another such crested animal-head terminal is mentioned as having been excavated in Norwich. Their design is closely paralleled by a complete example from central Sweden (fig. 6).[47] A couple of fragments from Suffolk are debased in style, being simplified in form and having punched rather than graved

---

[41] Fuglesang, 132–5, Appendix 5.
[42] Seaby and Woodfield, 101–4.
[43] Seaby and Woodfield, no. 9.
[44] *Viking Antiquities in Great Britain and Ireland*, iv, ed. H. Shetelig, Oslo 1940, 68, fig. 40.
[45] Cf. the Danish example illustrated as Fuglesang, pl. 79,b.
[46] S. Margeson, 'A Ringerike-style Mount from Stoke Holy Cross', *Norfolk Archaeology*, xl, 1987, 126–7, fig. 4.
[47] Ångsby, Lena, Uppland (Uppsala Museum: UMF 4573).

Fig. 6   Copper-alloy cheek-piece from Ängsby, Sweden (not to scale)

Fig. 7 (left) Copper-alloy pendant in Ringerike style, from ?Norwich (scale 1:1)

Fig. 8 (below left) Copper-alloy pendant from near Basingstoke, Hants (scale 1:1)

Fig. 9 (below right) Copper-alloy pendant from Northampton (scale 1:1)

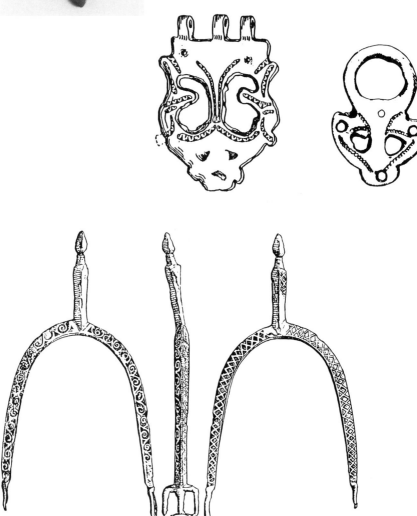

Fig. 10   Spur with brass inlay from Canning Town, London (scale 1:2)

ornament.[48] More in the mainstream, except for its small size, is an animal-head cheek-piece excavated recently at Llanelen in the Gower peninsula, S. Wales.[49] This style and technique of decoration is also found occasionally in England on weaponry, a spearhead socket from York providing a fine example.[50]

Some D-shaped buckles with related Ringerike-style ornament might well have been girth-buckles, including the unfinished example with cast ornament from the Thames at Barnes.[51] Whether or not this is the case, a distinctive group of pendant ornaments in the same basic decorative tradition may now be recognised – pendants which, it is suggested here, may best be identified as horse-trappings.

Chief amongst these decorative dingle-dangles is a previously unpublished example purchased in Norwich (fig. 7);[52] its relatively fine quality allows the ornament to be interpreted on a cruder version (fig. 8), excavated on the medieval site of Brighton Hill South, Basingstoke, Hants.[53] The excavator of a related openwork object from Northampton (fig. 9) was at a loss to explain its function (or even to date it), although noting that its loop showed wear.[54] It is doubtless a yet further simplification of this hitherto unrecognised group of Anglo-Scandinavian horse-trappings, although in form it seems to hark back to the ninth/tenth-century pendant of Insular manufacture that forms part of the Balladoole bridle (fig. 1).[55] These pendants have no obvious Scandinavian parallels so that they would seem to be an English addition to the repertoire of equestrian equipment in Ringerike-related style, bearing in mind the use of decorative pendants on the ninth-century harness from London, mentioned above (p. 80).

A stirrup from Seagry, Wilts.,[56] serves to link such Anglo-Scandinavian Ringerike-style ornaments to the well-known English group of eleventh-century stirrups, that were developed out of those introduced from Scandinavia around the millennium.[57] The finest examples of the decorated English group have a predominance of scrolled ornament, reflecting that known on contemporary swords and spurs, as well as on spears and battle-axes – evidence of an integrated 'look' for the fashionable equestrian warrior of the early to mid-eleventh century. The Canning Town spur from London, embellished in this mannner (fig. 10),[58] has the developed form of those depicted in the Bayeux Tapestry, with distinct

[48] From Nedging and ?Wangford; information from the late Mrs Owles of Moyses Hall Museum, Bury St Edmunds.

[49] Information in advance of publication from the Pendragon Society, Bristol, and Dr Ewan Campbell, Cardiff.

[50] Fuglesang, 139, pl. 79,a, whose dating is to be preferred to that suggested in J. T. Lang, 'A Viking Age Spear-Socket from York', *Med. Archaeol.*, xxv, 1981, 157–60, pl. xv, a.

[51] D. M. Wilson, *Anglo-Saxon Ornamental Metalwork, 700–1100, in the British Museum*, London 1964, no. 34; Graham-Campbell, no. 185; Fuglesang, no. 48.

[52] Information in advance of publication from Dr Susan Margeson, Castle Museum, Norwich.

[53] Information in advance of publication from Dr Richard Newman, Trust for Wessex Archaeology.

[54] J. H. Williams, *St Peter's Street, Northampton: Excavations 1973–1976*, Northampton 1979, 253, fig. 108 (Cu 18).

[55] The Irish cheek-pieces described by Bersu and Wilson (p. 25) as 'closely related' to this openwork pendant are different in form from those under consideration here and are most probably later in date.

[56] Seaby and Woodfield, no. 35; C. Haith in ed. Backhouse *et al.*, no. 99.

[57] Seaby and Woodfield, 'English Type 2C'.

[58] R. E. M. Wheeler, *London and the Vikings* (London Museum Catalogues, No. 1), London 1927, 42, fig. 19.

neck and goad, as also has, for example, a plain one found in the earliest occupation level of Winchester Castle.[59] It is considered, however, that the decorated English stirrup is not the type represented on the Tapestry, where they appear to be more triangular in shape with the loop forming an integral part of the bow, as known from both England and Scandinavia.[60]

The evidence reviewed by Seaby and Woodfield lead them to conclude that it is the finds of stirrups from the first half of the eleventh century that give 'the first indication of the extensive use of stirrup-using horsemen in Saxon England'.[61] This development can now be seen to have been complemented by the appearance of a range of horse-trappings, not previously used in England, showing design influences from Scandinavia in the time of Cnut.

How does this archaeological picture fit with that drawn by Professor Davis from the documentary record (as above, pp. 77–8)? The answer would appear to be not very well, for it seems to illustrate a significant growth in the use of horses by the military elite at this period. Given that the surviving material is both widespread in distribution and generally poor in quality, there must then have existed much prestige horse-equipment for it to have been so commonly imitated. In fact, the artefactual evidence accords better with the conclusions of a second paper by Professor Davis,[62] in which, after quoting the laws of Cnut (about 1023) laying down that an earl's heriot included eight horses (four accoutered and four not), whilst a thegn's heriot included four horses (two accoutered and two not), he went on to comment:

> Another fact that suggests that the English army was becoming increasingly cavalry-minded is the introduction of the office of staller . . . by King Edward the Confessor at the beginning of his reign (1042).

Davis thus chose to identify himself with those who have interpreted the post of staller as that of 'a military officer whose control of the stables suggested the existence of a cavalry force'.[63] Indeed, by 1989, his considered opinion was that:

> If we consider the introduction of stallers together with the evidence of the heriots, it becomes extremely difficult to argue that the use of warhorses in pre-Conquest England was either unknown or totally different from that of Northern France or Normandy.[64]

In conclusion, even if Normandy was more horse-minded than England by the mid-eleventh century, it does not follow that the English horse had experienced a sudden decline as a result of Danish activity. On the contrary, England seems to have owed much to the Danes, during the tenth and eleventh centuries, for innovations and improvements in horse-equipment. It remains therefore to explain why, in Professor Allen Brown's words, there was at Hastings 'a total and fatal absence of cavalry' on the English side,[65] although for Professor Warren

[59] B. Ellis in Biddle, *Winchester*, 1037 and 1039 (no. 3862).
[60] Seaby and Woodfield, 101.
[61] Seaby and Woodfield, 102.
[62] R. H. C. Davis, 'Did the Anglo-Saxons have Warhorses?', in *Weapons and Warfare in Anglo-Saxon England*, ed. S. Chadwick Hawkes, Oxford 1989, 141–4.
[63] Davis, 'Anglo-Saxon Warhorses', 143.
[64] Davis, *Medieval Warhorse*, 77.
[65] R. Allen Brown, *The Normans and the Norman Conquest*, 2nd ed., Woodbridge 1985, 144.

Hollister cavalry only 'constituted a larger percentage of the total Norman force'.[66] It is reasonable to suppose that the English horses, after the ride south from York to London and a forced march to the place of battle, were not fresh enough to consider using in combat. There was nothing peculiar in opting to fight on foot, as the English army had just done so successfully at Stamford Bridge. Indeed, as Hollister has pointed out, even afterwards 'in every important battle of the Anglo-Norman age, the bulk of the feudal cavalry dismounted to fight' – at Northallerton, in 1138, the Anglo-Norman knights 'dismounted to a man and fought behind a shield wall such as had been employed earlier by the Anglo-Saxon armies'.[67]

[66] C. Warren Hollister, *Anglo-Saxon Military Institutions on the Eve of the Norman Conquest*, Oxford 1962, 140.
[67] Hollister, 131–2.

Note (added in press): an important contribution to the above review is provided by the recent re-interpretation as stirrup-mounts of a substantial group of Late Saxon (including Anglo-Scandinavian) and Saxo-Norman copper-alloy fittings, previously identified as book- or chest-mounts; see P. Robinson, 'Some Late Saxon Mounts from Wiltshire', *Wiltshire Archaeological and Natural History Magazine*, 85 (1992), 63–9.

Acknowledgements
I am most grateful to Dr Susan Margeson (fig. 7) and to Dr Richard Newman (fig. 9) who have both generously provided illustrations of material prior to their own publications. Fig. 4 is copyright of the Museum of Archaeology and Anthropology, Cambridge, fig. 7 of the Norwich Castle Museum (photo. D. Wicks, Norfolk Museum Services), and fig. 9 of the Trust for Wessex Archaeology. Fig. 6 is copyright of Signe Horn Fuglesang, Oslo, courtesy of Uppsala Museum, Sweden. The other plates are reproduced, with due acknowlegement, directly from the sources cited in the relevant footnotes.

FINANCING STEPHEN'S WAR [1]

Judith Green

Stephen, having inherited his uncle's treasure at Winchester, was in financial difficulties within three to four years, and matters can hardly have improved in the climacteric year of 1141. Yet when Stephen was released from captivity he carried on fighting and did not noticeably run out of funds. He was even able to pay off Henry of Anjou's mercenaries in 1147, and it was not financial exhaustion that brought him to terms with his rival in 1153, so where did the money come from? [2] As no financial records survive, the historian has to calculate those counties where Stephen had enough support for his revenues to be paid, and those sources likeliest to have been productive. One factor in the calculation was the degree to which he could command the loyalty of the sheriffs. In the search for finance contributions from townsmen were likely to be of particular importance, and those from the Londoners most of all. Stephen established a close relationship with the Londoners which paid dividends not just in political and military terms, but also financial. The city gave Stephen access to the money markets which could provide the cash he needed for his knights; it also may have been the base for the exchequer. In the 1140s there was what might be described as a shift in the centre of gravity in royal finance towards the south-east and towards London, using a group of officials whose responsibilities were organized to meet Stephen's needs. The first part of this paper looks at political geography as an aid to understanding from which areas Stephen could have raised money, then at his relationship with the Londoners, and finally suggests how financial administration evolved to deal with the new situation.

Stephen presumably inherited a full set of sheriffs in December 1135, the fiscal year having begun at Michaelmas. Following the precedent of his Norman predecessors, he is unlikely to have made many changes, and there are indications that several Henrician sheriffs remained in post: Ansfrid in Kent,[3] Warin in Dorset (and possibly his other counties, Somerset and Wiltshire).[4] William de Pont de l'Arche presumably continued to hold Hampshire, for he gave his allegiance and the keys of the treasury at Winchester to the new king.[5] Miles of Gloucester

---

[1] I should like to thank Dr Emilie Amt, Dr David Crouch, Dr Derek Keene, Dr Jane Martindale, Professor Edmund King, Mr John Prestwich, and Miss Susan Reynolds for references and comments.
[2] For a general discussion of Stephen's finances see H. V. A. Cronne, *The Reign of Stephen*, London, 1970, chapter 8; for the situation between 1135 and 1140 see J. O. Prestwich, 'War and Finance in the Anglo-Norman State', *TRHS*, 5th ser., iv, 1954, 19–43 at 37–43; and for the aid given by Stephen in 1147 see *Gesta Stephani*, ed. and trans. K. R. Potter with a new introduction and notes by R. H. C. Davis, Oxford, 1976, 204–8.
[3] *Regesta*, iii, no. 142.
[4] *Regesta*, iii, nos. 434, 818.
[5] *Gesta Stephani*, 8; *Historia Novella*, 15.

(Gloucestershire) and Payn FitzJohn (possibly sheriff in Shropshire and Here-fordshire) delayed coming to Stephen's court, though both appear as witnesses to the Oxford Charter of Liberties in April 1136.[6] Challenges to royal authority soon occurred in various parts of the country. A few sheriffs were directly involved; the position of others as royal officials was affected by revolt; most of all, though, it was Stephen's response to revolt, in appointing a whole series of earls, which was to affect the shrievalty.

In the Norman period there were very few earls. In 1135 there were earls of Chester, Leicester, Warwick, Gloucester, Buckingham, Surrey, Northamp-ton/Huntingdon, and the bishop of Durham in Durham. In Chester and Durham, the bishop and earl had extensive powers which included control of the sheriff; in other counties in 1135 earls had precedence over sheriffs in the address clauses of royal writs, and possibly a share in the proceeds of the shire courts.[7] Sheriffs were usually appointed and controlled by the crown, and the counties were also subject to the visitation of royal justices. The creation of earldoms by Rufus and Henry I had thus not brought a major diminution of royal authority. The title *comes* was one of very high social standing, and one could argue that Anglo-Norman earls would be alert to any possibility of exercising the powers of their continental counterparts, but before 1135 this had not occurred.

R. H. C. Davis calculated that between 1136 and 1140 Stephen created earls in another fourteen English counties, that the Empress created several more, and there were possibly one or two later additions, so that there were only five counties with no known earl at any stage (Kent, Hampshire, Berkshire, Middle-sex, and Shropshire). Davis argued persuasively that the earldoms were intended to have real powers: that the king, worried about the loyalty of his sheriffs, created a

> new set of provincial governors who could oversee the work of the sheriffs and suppress incipient rebellion . . . He was not bestowing empty honours, but trying to ensure that local government was controlled by his friends rather than by the bureaucrats whom Henry I and Roger of Salisbury had installed.[8]

---

[6] *Gesta Stephani*, 24; *Regesta*, iii, no. 271. Payn's position in Shropshire and Herefordshire is not made clear in the sources. He seems to have been Henry I's chief agent in both counties in the last years of the reign, but whether he held a formal office as justiciar or sheriff, is not certain. See Judith A. Green, *English Sheriffs to 1154*, Public Record Office Handbooks no. 24, London, 1990, 72, 45, and cf. W. E. Wightman, *The Lacy Family in England and Normandy 1066–1194*, Oxford, 1966, 178–9.

[7] For the earls created by the Conqueror see C. P. Lewis, 'The Early Earls of Norman England', *Anglo-Norman Studies*, xiii, 1990, 207–223. The evidence for the creations of Rufus and Henry I is briefly reviewed by Judith A. Green, *The Government of England under Henry I*, Cambridge Studies in Medieval Life and Thought, 4th ser. iii, Cambridge, 1986, 118–119. Robert earl of Gloucester may have enjoyed greater powers than the other earls created between 1087 and 1135, for William of Malmesbury refers to the subordination to the earl of Miles of Gloucester, sheriff and castellan, *Historia Novella*, 35. The earl's 'part of the county', presumably the earl's third penny, was an allowance against the county farm of Gloucestershire in 1130, *Pipe Roll 31 Henry I*, ed. J. Hunter for the Record Commission, London, 1833, 77.

[8] R. H. C. Davis, *King Stephen*, 3rd edn, London, 1990, 30–1, 125–141. On the implications of the arrest of the bishops in 1139 see K. Yoshitake, 'The arrest of the bishops in 1139 and its consequences', *Journal of Medieval History*, xiv, 1988, 97–114.

It is in fact very difficult to connect any of the sheriffs at the start of Stephen's reign directly with Roger, but that does not mean Roger did not exercise very considerable influence over the sheriffs, or that the king thought that he did. One might suppose that all Stephen had to do was to make a clean sweep of the sheriffs, but Davis pointed out that the king through 'inclination and policy' was likely to look to the upper nobility, to men who had the background and resources to protect the shires, and the appropriate rank for them was that of earl. In other words, Davis was suggesting that Stephen was thinking of men who were not just superior in rank to sheriffs, but who filled a different role that was military and more broadly governmental. Davis was right to stress that the creation of earls has to be seen in a wider context than the king's suspicions about Roger, for the process had begun some time before the bishops' arrest. What he did not spell out was how Stephen envisaged the earls' powers. If they were to defend the shires, were they, for instance, to supervise military obligations owed to the crown, to take over money paid in commutation of that service, or to assume custody of royal castles?[9] Were they entitled to the third penny of the shire courts, or to a greater share of royal revenue? Above all it is impossible to know whether Stephen intended his earls to take on major powers as has been suggested recently, or whether the more enterprising simply took advantage of the situation.[10] Moreover, once the process had begun, it would have been hard to stop, and it may have been this, rather than a conscious master plan, that explains why there were earls in most counties by 1140.

Davis drew attention to the way some earls came to control the sheriffs. At the start of Henry II's reign he wrote that 'eight counties were controlled directly by their earls'. Accounts for Norfolk and Suffolk (1154–5), Devon (1154–7), Wiltshire (1154–1160), were presented at the exchequer by their earls, whilst Maurice sheriff of Herefordshire and Osbert of Westbury sheriff of Gloucestershire are both known to have been at some stage stewards of the earl of Hereford.[11] No accounts were made for Cornwall, Chester, and, it might be added, Durham.

Davis's total of counties whose earls controlled the sheriffs can, however, be increased. Of the sheriffs of 1154–5, Robert de Perer, (Nottinghamshire and Derbyshire) can be identified as a steward of Robert de Ferrers earl of Derby,[12] Robert Grimbald (Northamptonshire), as a steward of Simon de Senlis,[13] and

---

[9] There is no evidence to indicate that earls did take over performance of military obligations, though it is worth remembering that pre-Conquest earls had led out the fyrd. Sheriffs as earls' deputies may well have had some organisational duties. The military role of sheriffs *qua* sheriffs is not well documented in the first century after the Conquest. Nevertheless there is also an intriguing comment by a minor tenant-in-chief, William de Colecherche, in 1166 that he had done homage to the king and his son for the half a knight's fee he held in Norfolk, and had performed the service to the sheriffs, *Red Book of the Exchequer*, ed. H. Hall, RS, London, 1896, i, 400.

[10] W. L. Warren, *The Governance of Norman and Angevin England*, London, 1987, 89–95; cf. Paul Latimer, 'Grants of "Totus Comitatus" in Twelfth-Century England: their Origins and Meaning', *Bulletin of the Institute of Historical Research*, lix, 1986, 137–45 for the suggestion that three grants of 'totus comitatus' in Stephen's reign were of all the ruler's rights in the counties concerned.

[11] Davis, *King Stephen*, 128; *Charters of the Earldom of Hereford*, ed. D. Walker, Camden Miscellany, xxii, Camden Society, 4th ser., i, 1964, nos. 43, 27, 36.

[12] *Sir Christopher Hatton's Book of Seals*, ed. L. C. Loyd and D. M. Stenton, Northamptonshire Record Society, xv, 1950, 104.

[13] BL Royal MS 11 B IX, f. 12; see also W. Farrer, *Honors and Knights' Fees*, 3 vols., London and Manchester, 1923–5, ii, 302.

Geoffrey l'Abbé (Leicestershire) as a steward of Robert earl of Leicester and son of his butler.[14] The limits of dating of private charters make it impossible to say if these men were stewards at the time that they were sheriffs. It is more likely that the offices of steward and sheriff were kept distinct, but the recruitment as sheriffs of men closely identifiable with the interests of the earls must have strengthened the earls' influence over the counties concerned. The Scots controlled Northumberland until 1157. In the last years of Stephen's reign the sheriff of Warwickshire was probably Hugh FitzRichard, a leading tenant of the earl.[15] Thus sheriffs of almost half the English counties were under the authority of earls in 1154. In some counties it is clearer than in others how long this had been the case: Chester and Durham and possibly Gloucestershire throughout the reign, Northumberland from 1139, Cornwall from c.1140, Herefordshire probably from 1141, and Norfolk and Suffolk since 1153. The geographical plotting of these counties, moreover, supports the case which Professor King made in his paper to the Royal Historical Society, that by the 1140s, Stephen was strongest in the east and south-east of England.[16]

In the north, the Scots made inroads as soon as the news of the old king's death reached the Scottish court. Of the shired regions, they controlled Northumberland between 1139 and 1157, put Durham under pressure for a time in the early 1140s, and were not without ambitions in Yorkshire.[17] In Yorkshire Stephen was fortunate to be able to rely on William of Aumale lord of Holderness, whom he had made earl after the battle of the Standard and who remained loyal to his cause, not least because he was able to increase his own power in the process, being described as 'more truly the king beyond the Humber'.[18] However influential William was, Yorkshire was far too large to be controlled by one man, and local conflicts are known to have occurred.[19] Royal control over the coinage in the region broke down.[20] It is not clear who controlled the king's castles at York. A charter of Roger de Mowbray dated between 1143 and 1153 referred to his hoping to recover 'the castle at York' – which of the two royal castles is not

---

[14] D. Crouch, *The Beaumont Twins. The Roots and Branches of Power in the Twelfth Century*, Cambridge Studies in Medieval Life and Thought, 4th ser., i, Cambridge, 1986, 142, citing F. M. Stenton, *Documents Illustrative of the Social and Economic History of the Danelaw*, British Academy Records of Social and Economic History, London, 1920, 248–9.

[15] *PRs 2–4 Henry II*, 87; *Red Book of the Exchequer*, i, 325.

[16] 'The Anarchy of King Stephen's Reign', *TRHS*, 5th ser., xxiv, 1984, 133–53.

[17] For a recent review of the evidence see Judith A. Green, 'Anglo-Scottish Relations 1066–1174', *England and Her Neighbours 1066–1453. Essays in honour of Pierre Chaplais*, ed. M. Jones and M. Vale, London, 1989, 53–72.

[18] William of Newburgh, 'Historia Rerum Anglicarum' in *Chronicles and Memorials of the Reigns of Stephen, Henry II, and Richard I*, ed. R. Howlett, 4 vols., RS, London, 1884–90, i, 103; cf. *Chronicon Monasterii de Melsa*, ed. E. A. Bond, 3 vols., RS, London, 1866–8, i, 76; on William of Aumale see B. English, *The Lords of Holderness 1086–1260*, Oxford, 1979, 16–28.

[19] For conflict between William of Aumale, Gilbert de Gant, and Ranulf earl of Chester in Lincolnshire and Yorkshire, see William of Newburgh, i, 47; John of Hexham in Symeon of Durham, *Opera Omnia*, ed. T. Arnold, 2 vols., RS, London, 1882–5, ii, 315. Roger de Mowbray joined Henry of Anjou and David of Scotland in 1149 and may have been in arms subsequently, *Charters of the Honour of Mowbray 1107–91*, ed. D. E. Greenway, British Academy Records of Social and Economic History, new ser., i, London, 1972, xxvi–xxvii. For conflict between Henry de Lacy and Gilbert de Gant see Wightman, *Lacy Family*, 76–80.

[20] G. C. Brooke, *A Catalogue of Coins in the British Museum. The Norman Kings*, 2 vols., London, 1916, i, cvi–cxvi.

specified.[21] In 1148 William of Aumale and the citizens prevented Archbishop Henry Murdac from entering York; later in the same year Stephen visited York, and handed over a small fortification to the citizens for destruction.[22] Only one sheriff has been positively identified, Robert of Octon. He was a tenant of William of Aumale and may well have been William's sheriff of Holderness.[23] Two other sheriffs, William and Ralph, may also have been baronial rather than royal officials.[24] The Henrician sheriff, Bertram de Bulmer, lived to take up office again in January 1155 and it is even possible he had never formally been replaced. Bertram was a man of relatively modest standing who held some estates in chief and the bulk as a tenant, but not of William of Aumale. His principal estates were at Bulmer and Sheriff Hutton, where he is thought to have been responsible for building the stone castle.[25] We thus do not know if there was a sheriff accountable to Stephen: certainly, none was addressed by him by name in any surviving document.

In the south-west and west it was the Empress' supporters who prevailed. Baldwin de Redvers held large estates in Devon, Hampshire, and the Isle of Wight; these had been given to Richard de Redvers by Henry I.[26] Geoffrey de Mandeville (of Marshwood), probably sheriff of Devon in the early years of Henry's reign, had been Richard's tenant, but subsequently the office was held by Richard FitzBaldwin, son of the Domesday sheriff, before reverting to another Redvers tenant, Geoffrey de Furneaux, who held Devon and Cornwall in 1130. Geoffrey was still living in 1136 and was possibly still sheriff; if so, he was soon replaced by Richard FitzBaldwin.[27] Baldwin de Redvers fortified Exeter castle against the king in 1136 and was driven out of England, returning three years later. He was created earl of Devon by the Empress in 1141 and seems to have recovered a measure of his authority over his estates.[28] The Angevins were strong in Devon: of the chief lay magnates only Henry de Tracy lord of Barnstaple from 1139 seems to have been a whole-hearted supporter of Stephen.[29]

From 1141 the dominant figure in Cornwall was the Empress's half-brother Reginald. Cornwall in 1086 had been dominated by Robert count of Mortain. The

[21] *Charters of the Honour of Mowbray*, no. 255.
[22] John of Hexham in Symeon of Durham, *Opera Omnia*, ii, 323.
[23] English, *Lords of Holderness*, 138, 158; William's charter enfeoffing Robert with land at Holmpton is edited by B. English in 'The Counts of Aumale and Holderness 1086–1260', St Andrews University Ph.D. thesis, 1977, Appendix A no. 11.
[24] Green, *English Sheriffs*, 90.
[25] For Bertram's lands see Green, *Government of England*, 238–9; for the castle at Sheriff Hutton *VCH North Riding*, ii, 176.
[26] For the estates see R. Bearman, 'Charters of the Redvers Family and the Earldom of Devon in the Twelfth Century', London University Ph.D. thesis 1981, chapter 3.
[27] *Regesta*, ii, nos. 633, 649, 662, 773; 1131, 1493; *PR 31 Henry I*, 152; *Regesta*, iii, no. 500.
[28] *Gesta Stephani*, 30–46; Bearman pointed out that the charters issued by Baldwin suggest that he soon recovered authority over his English estates, 'Charters of the Redvers Family', 38. He may have been in Exeter in 1142 when he gave the chapel of the castle to Plympton priory, F. Liebermann, *Anglo-Normannische Geschichtsquellen*, Strassburg, 1879, 29. This may have been the occasion when he gave the priory of St James at Exeter to St Martin des Champs, Paris, a grant confirmed by the Empress *Regesta*, iii, no. 651.
[29] The chief landholders in Devon were Robert earl of Gloucester, Robert of Bampton and Fulk Paynel (Bampton), Henry de Tracy (Barnstaple), Alfred son of Juhel (Totnes and a claim to Barnstaple), Henry de Pomeroy (Berry Pomeroy), William de Tracy (Bradninch), William son of Odo (Great Torrington), Baldwin de Redvers (Plympton), and Guy de Nonant (Totnes). For Henry de Tracy, *Gesta Stephani*, 82–4, 150, 210–212, 222.

counts had enfeoffed a small handful of men in relatively compact lordships; after the forfeiture of Count William the under-tenants became tenants-in-chief, and the most powerful of them, William FitzRichard, arranged the marriage of his daughter to Reginald.[30] Stephen had thereupon appointed Count Alan of Brittany as earl, and for a short time he ousted Reginald. The latter however managed to establish himself permanently as earl, and held the county until his death in 1175.[31] Richard of Raddon occurs as sheriff of Cornwall in the 1140s.[32] The 'Raddon' from which he took his name seems to have been West Raddon.[33] In 1166 Richard de Raddon held the land and service of Raddon which William FitzJohn of Harptree claimed to hold in chief. Richard also held two fees of the bishop of Exeter and one of William FitzRobert of Torrington.[34] He witnessed several of Earl Reginald's charters and his gift of land at Trewanta in Cornwall to Launceston priory was confirmed by the earl.[35] Two other sheriffs of Cornwall occur in the cartulary of Launceston. Durand is called Durand the clerk in one document whilst Bernard is presumably to be identified with Bernard the chaplain who accounted at the exchequer in 1175 for the farm of the earl's land in Cornwall.[36]

In the west William FitzAlan was described by Orderic Vitalis as sheriff of Shropshire and castellan of Shrewsbury in 1138. William had claims to the shrievalty which his father, but not he himself, had held. He may have been appointed by Stephen after the death of Payn FitzJohn in 1137, or his claim may have been passed over by Stephen, and this would have given him an obvious motive for revolt. In either case, his declaration for the Empress in 1138 proved to be premature. He was expelled from the county, and was formally restored to lands and the shrievalty by Henry II.[37] By contrast in Gloucestershire and Herefordshire the Angevins, led by Earl Robert and Miles of Gloucester, waited until 1139 to rebel, and despite royalist attacks could not be dislodged.

Powerful earls were also to be found in the midland counties. Ranulf II controlled the county and sheriff of Cheshire, and he was also influential though not all powerful in neighbouring Staffordshire. Not only did he have extensive estates here but he also attracted to his entourage Robert of Stafford, the most important lay landholder and the likeliest candidate for the shrievalty.[38] Nottinghamshire

---

[30] Ian N. Soulsby, 'Richard FitzTurold, Lord of Penhallam, Cornwall', *Medieval Archaeology*, xx, 1976, 146–8.

[31] *Gesta Stephani*, 100–4, 116.

[32] *The Cartulary of Launceston Priory*, ed. P. L. Hull, Devon and Cornwall Record Society, new ser., xxx, 1987, no. 244 (as Richard the sheriff).

[33] Of the three Raddons in Devon in 1086, William the Usher held two estates in East Raddon, one of Tavistock abbey and one in chief, *Domesday Book*, i, 103b, 117b. Raddon in Marystowe was held of the honour of Totnes, *Domesday Book*, i, 108b. There were two estates in West Raddon, one held of the count of Mortain and the other of Walter de Clavile, *Domesday Book*, i, 104b, 112. It seems to have been the Mortain estate in West Raddon from which the sheriff came. By the thirteenth century this had passed to Baldwin II de Raddon, whose predecessor Baldwin I seems to have been the successor of Richard, *Book of Fees*, London, 1920–31, ii, 761; *Cartulary of Launceston*, nos. 277–8, 332–4.

[34] *Red Book of the Exchequer*, i, 219, 248, 256.

[35] *Cartulary of Launceston*, nos. 11–13, 415, 538, 114, 115.

[36] *Cartulary of Launceston*, nos. 556, 194, 11, 538; *PR 21 Henry II*, p. 65.

[37] Orderic, vi, 520; *Regesta*, iii, nos. 378, 461; for William's career see R. W. Eyton, *Antiquities of Shropshire*, 12 vols., London and Shifnal, 1854–60, vii, 232–7.

[38] Robert the sheriff witnessed Geva Ridel's foundation charter for Canwell priory, *Monasticon*,

and Derbyshire shared a county court and probably a sheriff in this period. The only known sheriff, Robert de Perer, was the steward of Robert II de Ferrers, who inherited the title of earl from his father and for a time, possibly when William Peverel was imprisoned after the battle of Lincoln, styled himself earl of Nottingham.[39] In the later years of the reign local politics are difficult to disentangle. Earl Robert remained loyal to Stephen until 1153 but was also the ally of Ranulf II and potentially the heir of William Peverel, as the husband of William's daughter. William however was so antagonistic to Ranulf II that he tried to poison him.[40]

The sheriff of Worcestershire in the later eleven-thirties was William de Beauchamp, son and possibly successor as sheriff of Walter de Beauchamp. Stephen created Waleran of Meulan earl of Worcester and Waleran subordinated to his lordship the lands and office of William.[41] In 1141 first William and later Waleran transferred their allegiances to the Empress; thereafter Waleran stayed out of England whilst William seems to have held the castle at Worcester until imprisoned for a time in 1151.[42] In the account for Worcestershire of 1156 Payn the sheriff is referred to in the past tense, perhaps as a former sheriff or under-sheriff, whilst in 1154–5 the sheriff was William Comin, either the unsuccessful contender for the see of Durham or, more probably, his nephew and namesake.[43] By Michaelmas 1155 William de Beauchamp once again held the county.

As already mentioned King David of Scotland held by right of marriage the midland earldom of Northampton/Huntingdon, but his support for the Empress inevitably threw his tenure into jeopardy. Stephen soon created a rival earl, Simon II de Senlis. Simon styled himself Earl Simon or earl of Northampton. Stephen allowed Prince Henry of Scotland to hold his father's midland estates between 1138 and 1138, and again from 1139 until they were lost to the Scots in 1141. Robert Grimbald, Simon de Senlis' steward, was sheriff of Northamptonshire in 1154–5 and was mentioned as a past sheriff of Huntingdonshire.[44] There is one other known sheriff of Huntingdonshire, Payn of Hemingford. It is not clear when Payn took up office. He was sheriff of Cambridgeshire in 1139 or 1140 and again from 1154 and was also probably sheriff of Surrey.[45] He held an estate at Heming-

---

[39] iv, 105; Robert of Stafford was sheriff in 1154–5, *Red Book of the Exchequer*, ii, 652; for attestations of Ranulf's charters, *The Charters of the Anglo-Norman Earls of Chester c.1071–1237*, ed. G. Barraclough, Record Society of Lancashire and Cheshire, cxxvi, 1988, nos. 62, 65.

[39] M. Jones, 'The Charters of Robert II de Ferrers, earl of Nottingham, Derby and Ferrers', *Nottingham Medieval Studies*, xxiv, 1980, 7–26.

[40] Robert is mentioned as Ranulf's ally in the latter's treaty with the earl of Leicester, F. M. Stenton, *The First Century of English Feudalism*, 2nd edn, Oxford, 1961, 286–8. It is not clear precisely when the poisoning attempt was made, but it presumably accounts for the reference to *scelus et traditio* in *Regesta*, iii, no. 180 issued in the early months of 1153.

[41] Crouch, *Beaumont Twins*, 39–51.

[42] *Gesta Stephani*, 228.

[43] *PRs 2–4 Henry II*, 64; *Red Book of the Exchequer*, ii, 656; *Hatton's Book of Seals*, nos. 507, 509; William Comin the younger attests a deed of Countess Gundrada of Warwick, BL Cotton MS Julius C vii, f. 217r. I owe the references to William Comin junior to Dr David Crouch.

[44] Farrer, *Honors and Knights' Fees*, ii, 296–8; *Regesta Regum Scottorum*, i, *Malcolm IV 1153–65*, ed. G. W. S. Barrow, Edinburgh, 1960, 102; *Red Book of the Exchequer*, ii, 655; *Regesta*, iii, no. 611; *PRs 2–4 Henry II*, 41, 42.

[45] A. Saltman, *Theobald, Archbishop of Canterbury*, London, 1956, nos. 301, 302; *English Episcopal Acta*, i, *Lincoln 1067–1185*, ed. D. M. Smith, London, 1980, no. 267; *Regesta*, iii, no. 410; *Red Book of the Exchequer*, ii, 655; Payn's career possibly began before 1135, for there was a Payn collector (of geld) in Hunts. in 1130, *PR 31 Henry I*, 49. Payn had evidently succeeded to the

ford Grey as part of his tenancy of three knights' fees held of Aubrey de Vere, and gave the tithes of Hemingford and Yelling to the priory of St Melaine Rennes at Hatfield Broad Oak.[46] Aubrey III de Vere was made an earl by the Empress in 1141 in a charter designating Cambridgeshire unless the king of Scots were to have the county (about which the Empress was at that time unclear), or one of four other counties. The Empress may have been thinking that Aubrey would have been well placed to take over Cambridgeshire as the sheriff was his tenant.[47] Payn may have built the mid-twelfth century stone hall that still survives at Hemingford Grey, and if he did, we must assume that he enjoyed a degree of material prosperity in troubled times.[48]

In a number of counties the situation was less clear-cut, and the scanty evidence about sheriffs has to be fitted into the context of a shifting balance of power. Dorset, Somerset, Wiltshire, Lincolnshire, Bedfordshire, Berkshire, and Oxfordshire, all come into this category.[49] To take just one example: Oxfordshire was one of the counties most keenly contested. Two leading local magnates, Robert II d'Oilly, sheriff in 1130, and John de St John, went over to the Empress in 1141.[50] Stephen in response established William de Chesney at Oxford in 1142, gave him the d'Oilly lands plus Deddington in the north of the county where Odo of Bayeux had built a large motte, and gave another of his supporters, Richard de Camville, some of the St John lands.[51] Azor, sheriff in the late 1140s, witnessed a charter of William de Chesney.[52] His successor may have been 'John the sheriff' mentioned in a document from St Frideswide's, possibly John de St John, and by Michaelmas 1154 the shrievalty had passed to Henry of Oxford, already sheriff of

---

land held in 1086 by Ralph son of Osmund, and before 1066, significantly, by Aluric the sheriff, *Domesday Book*, i, 208.

[46] *Red Book of the Exchequer*, i, 352; BL Additional Charter 28,337.

[47] *Regesta*, iii, no. 634.

[48] *VCH Huntingdonshire*, ii, 309.

[49] There is no evidence for Dorset and Somerset after Warin until 1154–5. In that year Richard de Raddon, sheriff of Cornwall, also held Dorset, and Richard de Montacute, probably the lord of Montacute, held Somerset, *Red Book of the Exchequer*, ii, 657, 654. Wiltshire seems to have returned to the descendants of Edward of Salisbury, the Domesday sheriff, first Walter *Regesta*, iii, no. 684; then, possibly, William, castellan of Salisbury in 1143, *Gesta Stephani*, 148; and, finally, Earl Patrick, who was sheriff by 1153, *PRs 2–4 Henry II*, 56–7. Two sheriffs of Lincolnshire have been positively identified: Hugh FitzEudo lord of Tattershall, *Registrum Antiquissimum*, ed. C. W. Foster and K. Major, Lincoln Record Society, vii, 1953, no. 2050; and Jordan de Blosseville, *Red Book of the Exchequer*, ii, 656. Jordan is perhaps to be identified with the man of this name who witnessed charters for William II and William III de Warenne, *Early Yorkshire Charters*, viii, ed. C. T. Clay, Yorkshire Archaeological Society, Record Series, Extra Series, vi, 1949, 80, 91, 93–4, 99; cf. *Regesta*, iii, no. 212. The only known sheriff of Bedfordshire was William Bacon, *Regesta*, iii, no. 683. A man of this name attested four charters of Ranulf II of Chester and was perhaps related to Richard Bacon, Ranulf's kinsman, *Charters of the Earls of Chester*, nos. 40, 66, 67, 68. Apart from Henry of Oxford, for whom see below note 54, the only other possible sheriff of Berkshire was Jordan de Podiis, *Regesta*, iii, no. 2; cf. no. 89. He was possibly one of Stephen's captains.

[50] *Regesta*, iii, nos. 571, 644.

[51] *Gesta Stephani*, 180; *Regesta*, iii, no. 633.

[52] *Cartulary of Oseney Abbey*, ed. H. E. Salter, 6 vols., Oxford Historical Society, lxxxix–xci, xcvii–xcviii, ci, 1929–36, iv, 87; 'Acsur', presumably the sheriff, occurs in a list of witnesses with William de Chesney c.1150, and he gave land to Eynsham, *Eynsham Cartulary*, ed. H. E. Salter, 2 vols., Oxford Historical Society, xlix, li, 1907–8, ii, 103, 44.

Berkshire.[53] He was a man of native extraction whose rise had evidently been assisted by Brian FitzCount.[54]

Stephen's support was strongest in the east and south-east of England. In East Anglia, first of all, he had large estates even before 1135 as lord of the honours of Eye and Boulogne; the sheriff of Norfolk and Suffolk between about 1115 and 1128 was Robert FitzWalter (de Chesney), an under-tenant of the honour of Eye.[55] In 1148 Stephen's second son William succeeded through marriage to the Warenne estates, clustered thickly in Norfolk. Norfolk and Suffolk were thus counties in which Stephen might feel, with some confidence, that he could beat off any challenge to his authority. The challenge came as early as 1136 from Hugh Bigod, who had sworn that on his deathbed Henry had changed his mind about the succession and had designated Stephen as his heir.[56] Hugh was doubtless hoping for advancement from Stephen, perhaps custody of Norwich castle and the title of earl. If so, he was to be disappointed, for it was the Empress not the king who created him earl of Norfolk in 1141.[57] The shrievalties of Norfolk and Suffolk were kept in the hands of men loyal to the king at least until the early 1150s. Two sons of Robert FitzWalter, John and William, were successively sheriffs,[58] and then in the early 1150s Roger Gulafre and William de Fresney were sheriffs of Norfolk and Suffolk.[59] The two may have been joint-sheriffs, but if each was sheriff of a county it is not clear who held which. Roger came from a family established on the honour of Eye in 1086 and attests a charter of William Martel at a time when the latter may have been in charge of the honour of Eye,[60] whilst William de Fresney, about whom less is known, held some land of Hugh Bigod.[61] It is particularly unfortunate that the precise dates and counties of these men cannot be identified, because they bear on the question of Earl Hugh's authority in Norfolk. In the treaty of 1153 between Stephen and Henry the county of Norfolk, seven hundred pounds of land, and custody of Norwich castle were ceded to Stephen's son William, whilst Hugh's right to the third penny of Norfolk was recognised, the first clear evidence that Stephen was prepared to acknowledge Hugh's earldom.[62] In 1154–5 Hugh accounted for Norfolk and Suffolk at the exchequer. William de Neville, who accounted for the old farm of Norfolk at

---

[53] *Cartulary of St Frideswide*, ii, 297–8; *Red Book of the Exchequer*, ii, 657.
[54] *Book of Fees*, i, 114; *Cartae Antiquae 1–10*, Pipe Roll Society, new ser., xvii, 1939, no. 141; see most recently K. S. B. Keats-Rohan, 'The Making of Henry of Oxford: Englishmen in a Norman World', *Oxoniensia*, liv, 1989, 287–309.
[55] J. H. Round, 'The Early Sheriffs of Norfolk', *EHR*, xxxv, 1920, 481–496; *Regesta*, ii, nos. 1218, 1219, 1321 (all Suffolk), 1461, 1597, 1598 (with Norfolk), *PR 31 Henry I*, 90.
[56] *The Historia Pontificalis of John of Salisbury*, ed. M. Chibnall, Edinburgh, 1956, 83–5.
[57] Davis, *King Stephen*, 138–9.
[58] John seems to have succeeded his father as sheriff of Suffolk in 1137 or 1138, *Regesta*, iii, no. 288. He was sheriff of Norfolk between 1140 and 1146, when he was succeeded by his brother William, *Regesta*, iii, no. 399; A. Jessopp and M. R. James, *The Life and Miracles of St William of Norwich*, Cambridge, 1896, xxxiv, 29, 111–112, 128, 172.
[59] H. Cam, 'An East Anglian Shire-Moot of Stephen's reign 1148–1153', *EHR*, xxxix, 1924, 571.
[60] *Domesday Book*, ii, 305, 305b, 306, 310, 316b, 321, 326, 327b; *PR 31 Henry I*, p. 97; *Red Book of the Exchequer*, i, 411; Cartulary of Eye priory, Essex Record Office D/DBy Q 19, f. 23v.
[61] *Red Book of the Exchequer*, i, 395.
[62] *Regesta*, iii, no. 272. By this treaty the *castra et villas* of Norwich with £700 of lands, and the whole county of Norfolk except the lands of churches, prelates, abbots and earls and Earl Hugh's third penny were granted to William.

Michaelmas 1156 and had presumably been sheriff or under-sheriff before Michaelmas 1155, was also Hugh's tenant.[63]

In Essex Stephen was rich in land, both as king and as count of Boulogne. In the early years of his reign he had the support of Geoffrey de Mandeville, the most powerful magnate in the west of the county. Stephen created him earl, probably between December 1139 and December 1140, possibly at Whitsun 1140.[64] Subsequently Geoffrey was able to negotiate better terms from the Empress: in the first of her two charters, probably issued in Midsummer 1141, she added to the earldom of Essex, the shrievalty and justiciarship of that county, custody of the Tower of London and various other grants of land.[65] She later raised her bid; Stephen issued a second charter, probably after his release from captivity, granting the shrievalties and justiciarships of Essex, (London and) Middlesex, and Hertfordshire, custody of the Tower, and further grants of land.[66] It would appear that Geoffrey held the three shrievalties from the time of his reappearance fighting for the queen at the siege of Winchester in 1141 until his downfall in 1143.

Perhaps as a consequence of Geoffrey's fall, a new sheriff appeared in Essex, Maurice of Tilty. He may have started his career as Geoffrey's deputy, for his father had been the earl's steward.[67] Maurice was not simply a tenant of the Mandevilles. He held land of several lords and Tilty itself was held of the Ferrers family.[68] Maurice survived Geoffrey's downfall and continued as sheriff subordinate to Richard de Lucy, who became a key figure in Stephen's regime in the last decade of the reign. Richard received estates in Essex centred on Ongar, and acted as local justiciar.[69] What happened in Hertfordshire after Geoffrey's fall is not clear. In 1154–5 two sheriffs accounted, each for half of the year. Guy son of Tyece (? Thierry or Teutonicus) witnessed for Stephen on several occasions, and a 'plea of Guy son of Tyece' is mentioned in 1156 in the account of London; otherwise this sheriff is unknown.[70] The other sheriff was Henry of Essex, a man

---

[63] As joint heir with his brother Henry, William quitclaimed to the abbey of St Benet of Holme land at Heigham and Hardley. In 1166 both William and Henry held land of Earl Hugh, *St Benet of Holme 1020–1210*, ed. J. R. West, Norfolk Record Society, ii, iii, 1932, ii, 232; *Red Book of the Exchequer*, i, 396, cf. 348 where William held three fees of Walter FitzRobert in Essex.

[64] *Regesta*, iii, no. 273. For discussion of the dates of the two surviving charters issued by Stephen and two by the Empress to Geoffrey de Mandeville see J. H. Round, *Geoffrey de Mandeville*, London, 1892, 37–200; Round's dates for the Empress's second charter (M2) which produced an order of S1 M1 S2 M2 were revised by R. H. C. Davis, 'Geoffrey de Mandeville Reconsidered', *EHR*, lxix, 1964, 299–307 and the revised order (S1, M1, M2, S2) was followed by Davis and Cronne in *Regesta*, iii; J. O. Prestwich, 'The Treason of Geoffrey de Mandeville', *EHR*, ciii, 1988, 283–312 argued for a return to Round's order, but Davis disagreed in *EHR*, ciii, 1988, 313–17; further contributions were made by Prestwich in 'Geoffrey de Mandeville: a further comment', *EHR*, ciii, 1988, 960–6; by Davis in *King Stephen*, 156–60; and by both in 'Last Words on Geoffrey de Mandeville', *EHR*, cv, 1990, 670–2.

[65] *Regesta*, iii, no. 274.

[66] *Regesta*, iii, nos. 275, 276.

[67] *Regesta*, iii, nos. 544, 546–8, 552; *Monasticon*, iii, 434 and cf. Essex Record Office D/DBa T/2/1: a notification of Geoffrey II de Mandeville attested by Geoffrey the steward.

[68] *Domesday Book*, ii, 56b.

[69] Emilie M. Amt, 'Richard de Lucy, Henry II's Justiciar', *Medieval Prosopography*, ix, 1988, 61–85.

[70] *Red Book of the Exchequer*, ii, 651; *Regesta*, iii, nos. 456, 590, 874, 938–941; *PRs 2–4 Henry II*, 5.

who had been loyal to Stephen. He was lord of Rayleigh in Essex and, from 1152, constable.[71]

In Kent and Surrey again, Stephen was relatively strong. Kent has been studied by Dr Eales, who pointed out that the two most powerful lords were the archbishop of Canterbury and William of Ypres.[72] The two known sheriffs of the reign, Ansfrid in 1136 and Ralph Picot, were both connected with the archbishop. Ansfrid, who is mentioned in 1136 and had been sheriff under Henry I, was probably the archbishop's steward.[73] Ralph Picot appears in the later years of the reign. He was both the archbishop's tenant and his constable.[74] The archbishops in the early twelfth century may even have received the earl's third penny, as had happened for a time before the Conquest.[75] In Surrey Earl William de Warenne was loyal to Stephen, and his estates passed by marriage to Stephen's second son. The other important local lord was Gilbert FitzRichard of Tonbridge, who was loyal to Stephen except for a short time in 1147.[76] Payn of Hemingford, as mentioned above, was sheriff at some point under Stephen and again in 1154–5, and the other possible sheriff, of whom we shall hear more later, was William Martel, Stephen's steward.[77]

Gilbert FitzRichard was also lord of the castle and rape of Pevensey, one of the six lordships into which Sussex divided. These were units where the lords controlled all the land not held by the church; they had considerable rights of jurisdiction, and each had a sheriff.[78] It would appear nevertheless that there was a royal sheriff before 1135 to administer the king's rights. Hugh de Warelvilla who accounts for the 'farm of Sussex' in 1130 was presumably the king's sheriff.[79] Ailwin the sheriff, a man who is otherwise unknown, occurs under Stephen.[80] Between January and Michaelmas 1155 the bishop of Chichester was sheriff.[81] Although the Rapes were not palatine lordships, Stephen's authority would obviously depend to a very considerable extent on the allegiance of the lords: Stephen could clearly count for the most part on Gilbert FitzRichard, William de Warenne (Lewes), and William d'Aubigny (Chichester). Henry and John, counts of Eu and lords of Hastings, witnessed occasionally for Stephen; Philip de Briouze does not occur, and his son William de Briouze only as witness to three confirmations for Lewes priory evidently issued by Stephen on the same occasion.[82] Stephen presumably could also depend on his brother the bishop of

---

[71] *Regesta*, iii, xx; cf. xxiii for the suggestion that Henry may have been a royal justice before 1141; for Rayleigh, I. J. Sanders, *English Baronies*, London, 1960, 139.
[72] R. Eales, 'Local Loyalties in Norman England: Kent in Stephen's Reign', *Anglo-Norman Studies*, viii, 1986, 88–108.
[73] Green, *Government of England*, 205; *Regesta*, iii, no. 142.
[74] Eales, 'Local Loyalties', 102.
[75] A memorandum from a plea of 1078–9 stated that Archbishop Aethelnoth had received the third penny of the shire of Kent, but that King Edward had given it to Godwin in Archbishop Eadsige's time, BL Cotton MS Aug. II. 36 cited by N. Brooks, *The Early History of the Church of Canterbury*, Leicester, 1984, 301.
[76] *Regesta*, iii, nos. 169, 170, 460, 853, 276, 494; *Gesta Stephani*, 200–2.
[77] BL Cotton MS Domitian A X, f. 143v; *Regesta*, iii, no. 934; *Red Book of the Exchequer*, ii, 654.
[78] Green, *English Sheriffs*, 80–2.
[79] *PR 31 Henry I*, 68.
[80] BL Cotton MS Faustina A III, f. 258b, printed *Monasticon*, i, 310. There was a moneyer called Ailwin at Pevensey in Stephen's reign, Brooke, *Catalogue of Coins . . . Norman Kings*, i, ccxxxii–ccxxxiii.
[81] *Red Book of the Exchequer*, ii, 654.
[82] *Regesta*, iii, nos. 402, 406, 188, 383, 396; 448–50.

Winchester to ensure a degree of stability in Hampshire after 1141. William de
Pont de l'Arche had gone over to the Empress by that year and tried to combat
Bishop Henry's control of the city, but his efforts backfired and he ended in
prison in the royal castle. He may have been succeeded as sheriff by his clerk
Thurstan.[83]

What does it mean to say that earls dominated sheriffs, and, more specifically,
how much revenue had reached Stephen from such counties? Some earls, such as
Reginald of Cornwall, evidently were able to take over royal revenue, for no
revenues from Cornwall were accounted for at the exchequer until after his death.
When Ranulf earl of Chester was reconciled with Stephen, probably in 1146, he
was still regarded with suspicion because 'he neglected to return the revenues of
the royal lands and castles he had seized'.[84] If it is borne in mind that earls may
have been expected to take over the defence of their counties, and that they could
bring strong pressure to bear on the sheriffs, it is possible that they siphoned off
royal revenue in recompense for their expenditure on the king's behalf. Clearly,
though, the evidence is much too scanty to be certain how much or for how long
powerful earls could divert royal revenues to their own coffers.

For other possible insights into Stephen's finances, there is, first of all, the
numismatic evidence, which, broadly speaking, reinforces the above sketch of
local politics. Stephen inherited a system whereby the crown had a monopoly of
coining silver pennies produced in local mints to a weight standard of about 21.5
grains established by the Conqueror. From time to time new types were issued,
and when this happened old coins were reminted to the new design. In the early
twelfth century there was a shortage of silver and Henry I, in common with other
rulers, had had problems with debased and lightweight coins.[85] Stephen too
experienced difficulties. William of Malmesbury reported that in 1140 there were
problems with counterfeit money (*pro falsitate*), and that the king himself had
ordered the weight of pennies to be lightened.[86] William of Newburgh, writing
later, commented on the private coinage issued by lords of castles.[87] In the *British
Museum Catalogue* surviving examples of Stephen's coins were classified in
seven types, of which four (I, II, VI, VII) are now regarded as substantive.[88] Type
I was issued coins from mints widely distributed round the country. It is not clear
when the first type was replaced: the traditional view that the second type followed Stephen's release from captivity has been disputed though not over-
turned.[89] It is evident, however, that with the escalation of conflict the royal

---

[83] *Gesta Stephani*, 150–2; Thurstan was confirmed in his lands by the Empress in 1141 and held
much property in Winchester in 1148, *Regesta*, iii, no. 897; F. Barlow, M. Biddle, D. J. Keene,
Winchester in the Early Middle Ages. Winchester Studies, i, Oxford, 1976, 175 (index listing
Thurstan's holdings); J. H. Round, 'The Rise of the Pophams', *Ancestor*, vii, 1903, 59–66.
[84] *Gesta Stephani*, 184.
[85] The most recent survey is that by M. Blackburn, 'Coinage and Currency under Henry I: a
Review', *Anglo-Norman Studies*, xiii, 1990, 49–81.
[86] *Historia Novella*, 42.
[87] William of Newburgh, i, 70.
[88] Brooke, *Catalogue of Coins . . . Norman Kings*; cf. R. P. Mack, 'Stephen and the Anarchy
1135–54', *British Numismatic Journal*, xxxv, 1966, 38–112; for a recent survey taking account of
the important 1980 find at Wenallt, George C. Boon, *Coins of the Anarchy*, Cardiff, 1988.
[89] M. Dolley, 'The Anglo-Norman Coins in the Uppsala University Cabinet', *British Numismatic
Journal*, xxxvii, 1967, 34; R. J. Seaman, 'A Re-examination of some hoards containing coins of
Stephen', *British Numismatic Journal*, xlviii, 1978, 58–72; P. Seaby, 'King Stephen and the
Interdict of 1148', *British Numismatic Journal*, l, 1980, 50–60 and *The Story of British Coinage*,

monopoly of coinage broke down. The Empress issued coins at Bristol, Cardiff, Oxford, and Wareham, and Henry of Anjou at Hereford, Gloucester, Malmesbury, Sherborne and Bristol. Various irregular and baronial issues survive, plus coins issued in the north by David of Scotland and his son Henry. Very few examples survive of types III, IV, and V survive, and they are thought to have been localized productions from the east midlands rather than substantive issues. Type VI is regarded as a substantive issue, but its timing is uncertain, whilst type VII probably followed the peace treaty of 1153 and again came from widely distributed mints. The average weight, as against the weight standard established by the Conqueror, is types I and II 21.5, III 18.5, IV 18.0, V 16.0, VI 20.5 whilst VII is between 21 and 23.[90] In other words, at the start of the reign the coinage held up well, but then Stephen's political difficulties were reflected in private issues and lightweight coins, with a recovery at the end of the reign.

A second source is the early pipe rolls of Henry II's reign. Some of the information they record is clearly retrospective and raises possibilities about the situation at the end of Stephen's reign but no more, bearing in mind that there may have been a measure of financial recovery in the months following the peace treaty between Stephen and Henry. Moreover, it is evident that it took time for the pipe roll scribes to re-establish the form and arrangement of entries.

The most important annual revenues at the start of Henry's reign were the county farms. Professor King has pointed out that several sheriffs accounted for their farms tale rather than blanch at the first exchequer sessions of Henry's reign, and he believes that this 'retrograde' practice may give an indication that these farms had at least been paid, albeit not in assayed coin. The counties concerned were Norfolk and Suffolk, where Stephen was strong, Essex (under Richard de Lucy), Somerset, Devon, (where the Angevins were strong) and Sussex and Shropshire which always had accounted tale.[91] Mr Yoshitake has taken the argument further by suggesting that payment blanch in 1154–5 or 1155–6 may also indicate that these farms also had been paid.[92] It seems more likely, though, that it took the exchequer a few years to enforce blanch payment generally. The long lists of *terre date* (lands granted out of the farm) in the early rolls have been studied in detail by Dr Amt.[93] These can usually only be assigned on grounds of probability to Stephen or Henry. Clearly the large grants to William of Ypres, the commander of Stephen's Flemish troops, must have been made by Stephen.[94] A major programme of restocking of royal manors was necessary at the start of the

---

London, 1985, 49. For a different view, see M. Archibald, 'Coins', *English Romanesque Art 1066–1200*, Catalogue of 1984 exhibition at Hayward Gallery, London, 1984, 321. The dating of Stephen's types is currently a matter of debate. In June 1991 the British Numismatic Society held a meeting at Oxford titled 'Stephen and the Anarchy', and it is to be hoped that the papers presented there will appear in print in due course. I owe information on this point to Professor Edmund King, who kindly sent me a copy of his own paper 'What sort of anarchy?'

[90] Mack, 'Stephen and the Anarchy 1135–54', 40, 48, 51, 52, 55. It is significant that type VI is of a reasonable weight and all the more regrettable that it cannot be dated precisely.

[91] King, 'Anarchy of Stephen's Reign', 152.

[92] K. Yoshitake, 'The Exchequer in the Reign of Stephen', *EHR*, ciii, 1988, 950–9.

[93] Emilie M. Amt, 'From Tempus Werre to Pax Publica: the Reconstruction of Royal Government in England c.1149–c.1159', Oxford University D.Phil. thesis 1988, chapter 5.

[94] *Red Book of the Exchequer*, ii, 648–9; *PRs 2–4 Henry II*, 65, 101, 102. Biographical details are to be found in the *Dictionary of National Biography*.

new reign, suggesting either war damage or simply running down because of economic dislocation.

So far as danegeld is concerned, Stephen is alleged to have promised to abolish the tax, but not to have kept his promise.[95] He may well have received danegeld from those counties in his control, simply because it would have been the easiest tax to collect. Two lawsuits, one relating to Kent and the other to Hampshire, suggest danegeld may have been levied in those counties. In Kent the sheriff Ralph Picot was accused by the monks of Christ Church Canterbury of having demanded scot, danegeld, the murder fine and other dues from Elverton, which they claimed as exempt demesne, the case being heard before the shire court in 1153.[96] In Hampshire a dispute seems to have arisen at the end of Stephen's reign between Southwick priory and Herbert of Boarhunt and his son Alexander about pastures, and refers to the king (not named, and not clear from the context whether this was Stephen or Henry) having taken danegeld.[97] It is not impossible that some earls had the tax collected and kept the receipts. A. L. Poole drew attention to a charter of Waleran of Meulan as earl of Worcester exempting the prior and monks of Worcester from *gildum regis quod ad me pertinet* and from all customs, services, and forest rights *quae prius regis erant et postea mea* at Tibberton.[98] The accounts for the first levy of Henry's reign, that of 1155–6, are conspicuous for the large sums written off in waste, and these indicate disputes over liability, the effects of war, either direct or indirect, and possibly out-of-date assessments. It is also possible that in some counties sheriffs had levied the tax but had been more liberal with exemptions than Henry II's exchequer was prepared to allow.[99] What we simply do not know is how much sheriffs outside Stephen's sphere of influence forwarded to the king either by way of farms or other revenues. Earls could have expended large sums locally to defend their shires, and have reclaimed them from royal revenues. The early pipe rolls of Henry II's reign thus do not provide much help about the sources of Stephen's revenues after 1141, and we have to base our assumptions on what we know of political allegiances in the shires.

[95] Huntingdon, 258.
[96] R. C. Van Caenegem, *English Lawsuits from William I to Richard I*, Selden Society, cvi, 1990, no. 340. I owe this and the following reference to Miss Susan Reynolds.
[97] Van Caenegem, *English Lawsuits*, no. 343.
[98] A. L. Poole, *From Domesday Book to Magna Carta* 2nd edn, Oxford, 1955, 158; citing H. W. C. Davis, 'Some Documents of the Anarchy', *Essays in History presented to R. L. Poole*, Oxford, 1927, 168–189 at 170–1.
[99] See most recently G. White, 'Were the Midlands "Wasted" during Stephen's Reign?' *Midland History*, x, 1985, 26–46 and Emilie M. Amt, 'The meaning of waste in the early pipe rolls of Henry II', *Economic History Review*, xliv, 1991, 240–8. The subject was touched on by the present author in 'The Last Century of Danegeld', *EHR*, xcvi, 1981, 252, where the question whether the waste totals are to be explained by disputes or war damage was left open. It now seems to me, however, that disputes over liability were more likely to be hidden in the payments into the treasury in 1156, lower in many counties than in 1130, than in waste. If so, waste has to be explained otherwise. If the term was used in the same sense as in 1086, then it referred to the non-productiveness of arable, perhaps directly because of war damage, or indirectly because of depressed market conditions. Amt raises two further considerations (p. 247), out-of-date assessment lists, and sheriffs claiming for larger amounts than were justified by local conditions. She points out that the sheriff of Warwickshire and Leicestershire, Robert FitzHugh, was removed from office in disgrace not long after 1156. She does not, however, raise the possibility that particularly generous pardons had been allowed in some counties, as, for instance, the pardon granted by Waleran of Meulan cited in the text above.

The king could also call for assistance from wealthy groups in the community, voluntary (or involuntary) donations, or loans. The church was one obvious source. Some churchmen, especially wealthy clerics such as his brother, may have been persuaded to proffer 'aids'.[100] Monasteries were soft targets. According to the *Historia Novella*, his counsellors urged Stephen that he should never lack money whilst the monasteries were full of treasure.[101] There are references to a raid on Abingdon made by William Martel on Stephen's orders, and to the abbot of St Albans being compelled to melt down treasure and hand it over to royalist commanders.[102]

Possible lenders in this period were the Templars, the Jews, and the Flemings. Dr Amt has drawn attention to the possibility that the Templars may already have been lending to the crown in Stephen's reign.[103] Stephen as a member of the house of Blois and his wife as countess of Boulogne were both drawn to the order, and it does not seem to have been noticed that Osto of Boulogne, who may have been an early master of the Templars in England, witnessed a charter issued by Stephen and his wife before 1135.[104] Osto also witnessed Queen Matilda's grant of Cressing to the Templars, their first major estate in England.[105] Patronage by the supporters of Stephen and Matilda was indeed striking, and far outweighed that of the Empress and her party.[106] It is possible at least that the Templars' role as bankers to the crown began in this period. The relationship between Jewish communities and the crown is obscure in this period. Jews were contributing to the crown by 1159 and it is at least a possibility that they were already contributing to Stephen's finances.[107]

The activities of the Flemish banker, William Cade, may well have started before 1154, as Professor Cronne pointed out.[108] Moreover, Cade is hardly likely

[100] Dr Jane Martindale kindly drew this possibility to my attention.

[101] *Historia Novella*, 20.

[102] *Gesta Abbatum Monasterii Sancti Albani*, ed. T. Riley, 3 vols., RS London, 1867–9, i, 94; *Chronicon Monasterii de Abingdon*, ed. J. Stevenson, 2 vols., RS, London, 1858, ii, 292.

[103] Amt, 'From Tempus Werre to Pax Publica', 192–3; for Louis VII and the Templars, L. Delisle, *Mémoire sur les Opérations Financières des Templiers*, Mémoire de L'Institut National de France, Paris, 1889, 15, 20.

[104] BL MS Harley 4757, f. 8d; for Osto of Boulogne see *Records of the Templars in England in the Twelfth Century*, ed. B. A. Lees, British Academy Records of Social and Economic History, London, 1935, xxxix, xlviii; 'Otun miles Templi' witnessed the treaty of 1153, *Regesta*, iii, no. 272.

[105] *Regesta*, iii, no. 843.

[106] In *Regesta* iii there is only one charter from Matilda or Henry for the Templars, and that is a confirmation, no. 867. It is thus hard to concur with the view implicitly advanced by Lees that both sides in the civil war were equally generous patrons, *Records of the Templars*, xl.

[107] H. G. Richardson, *The English Jewry under the Angevin Kings*, London, 1960, 50, 60, played down the potential role of the Jews as creditors of the crown in the 1140s and 1150s. We know nothing of the wealth of Jewish communities in England at this date, or whether the crown would borrow from or tax them. Yet the huge payment of £2000 accounted for by the London Jews in 1130 which was clearly punitive suggests that royal officials were already exploiting their wealth for the benefit of royal finance. Jews in turn were accounting for the king's help to recover debts from two of the great magnates, *PR 31 Henry I*, pp. 149, 148. 'The Life of St William of Norwich' is also worth noting in this context, for the author, Thomas of Monmouth, includes an imaginary reconstruction of a meeting between the Jews and King Stephen at Norwich when the Jews told the king 'Nos iudei tui sumus, tui quotennes tributarii, tuisque crebro necessarii necessitatibus, tibi siquidem semper fideles regnoque tuo non inutiles,' *Life*, 100.

[108] Cronne, *Reign of Stephen*, 235–6; on William Cade see E. King, *Dictionary of National Biography. Supplementary volume: from the beginnings to 1985*, forthcoming.

to have been the only Flemish merchant with an eye to profiting from a war in a country that supplied cloth to the Flemish wool towns, and in which Flemish mercenaries played a conspicuous role. The two trades may even have been linked. In this context we may note the comment by Jordan Fantosme about the Flemings who accompanied Robert earl of Leicester to England in the revolt of 1173–4 were that they were weavers who wanted English wool.[109]

Likely contributors to the king's coffers were concentrated in towns and cities. The role of urban wealth in the war finance of the Norman kings is a topic about which little is known because it barely surfaces in the records, yet in a time of civil war it may have been of critical importance. Bristol was the headquarters of the earl of Gloucester and its growing trade must have helped sustain the Angevin cause.[110] The king, on the other hand, could look to Winchester, York, Lincoln (for a time), and, most of all, to London.

Stephen's excellent relationship with the Londoners, it has been suggested, was because as count of Boulogne he controlled their most important trading outlet, and because of his large estates in Kent and in Essex which 'took his power up to the city walls'.[111] Stephen certainly had more influence as count and king than his rivals, but did he 'dominate' the city? The overseas trade of early twelfth-century London was not only with Flanders, and her political society was far from subservient. If Stephen could not dominate, then he needed to conciliate, and the basis of his good relationship with the Londoners needs further explanation.

In 1135 Stephen had gone straight to London from Winchester and made a deal with the Londoners, who chose him as their king. In return he promised them good laws, and the right to form a commune.[112] He presumably confirmed their privileges, and may even have granted new ones. Henry I had conceded the valuable privilege of freedom of election of sheriffs, mentioned in the 1130 pipe roll. The text of Henry I's charter to the Londoners also conceded to the Londoners the right of holding the farm at £300, the figure at which the Empress granted it to Geoffrey I de Mandeville in 1141. The timing and even the authenticity of this text have been much discussed. It is after all hard to see why Henry should have conceded election of sheriffs in 1130 and on a later occasion reduced the farm from the level at which it stood in 1130 by forty per cent.

The possibilities of fabrication or forgery, and when these might have occurred, were discussed by Brooke, Keir, and Reynolds.[113] One was that what survives may represent Stephen's charter with the initial of the king altered from S to H. Any such change, or even a forgery, is likely to have occurred not long after 1135. Those who have studied the witness list point out that it is credible for a date around 1130. Warren Hollister however pointed out that one of the witnesses, Alfred son of Joel, was in revolt against Stephen in 1136 and would hardly

---

[109] *Jordan Fantosme's Chronicle*, ed. R. C. Johnston, Oxford, 1981, lines 991–5; for the (unprovable) assumption that the Anarchy ruined Anglo-Flemish trade, Gaston G. Dept, 'Les Marchands Flamands et le Roi d'Angleterre (1154–1216)', *Revue du Nord*, xii, 1926, 303–4.

[110] For the career of Robert FitzHarding, who helped to finance Henry of Anjou see especially Robert B. Patterson, 'Robert FitzHarding of Bristol: Profile of an Early Angevin Burgess-Baron Patrician and his Family's Urban Involvement', *Haskins Society Journal*, i, 1989, 109–22.

[111] E. King, 'King Stephen and the Anglo-Norman Aristocracy', *History*, lix, 1974, 180–194 at 183.

[112] *Gesta Stephani*, 4–6; *Historia Novella*, 54–5.

[113] C. N. L. Brooke, G. Keir, and S. Reynolds, 'Henry I's Charter for the City of London', *Journal of the Society of Archivists*, iv, 1972, 558–578.

have attested for him after that date, and on that score ruled out the possibility that the charter was issued by Stephen in 1135, opting instead for a date of 1133.[114] Yet Alfred was a man with a claim to two honours, Barnstaple and Totnes, and it is not inconceivable that he might have presented himself at court at the very start of Stephen's reign in the hope of having his right to Totnes, which he never seems to have possessed, recognised. His sworn ally, Baldwin de Redvers, is said by one chronicler to have rebelled because Stephen refused him *quendam honorem*.[115] Both men could have been hoping for recognition of territorial claims, and have rebelled when they were disappointed. It thus remains one possibility that it was Stephen who reduced the farm to £300, and this would give the Londoners a strong incentive to remain loyal. If the text was an outright forgery, it is tempting to associate it with the events of 1141, as Brooke, Keir, and Reynolds point out, when the citizens might well have wished to have a charter backdating the concession of the farm at £300 in their negotiations with both sides.

The Londoners however did not confine their contributions to the farm. In 1141 they claimed they had seriously impoverished themselves in helping the king.[116] Evidence of one notable Londoner's contributions have survived. Gervase of Cornhill received from the queen ten marks' worth of land she mortgaged at Gamlingay, and was granted land by Stephen for service to be paid in coin at London.[117]

London remained strikingly loyal to the king as Archbishop Hugh of Rouen commented in a letter addressed to the 'senators, honoured citizens, and whole commune of London'.[118] They only reluctantly admitted the empress in 1141, and when the queen appeared at Southwark, rose up and threw the empress out. In the weeks following there were Londoners in the queen's army; they were present at Faringdon in 1145, and again at Wallingford in 1152.[119] Later tradition held that the armed forces of London were under the command of the lord of Baynard's, namely, Robert FitzRichard, who seems to have died in 1137, and his son Walter.[120] Robert was prominent at Stephen's court, whereas Walter only attested once for the king.[121]

Stephen took care to build up good relations with the major religious houses. His illegitimate son Gervase was appointed abbot of Westminster in 1138, and Stephen wrote to the pope to support the attempt to canonize Edward the Confessor.[122] Henry of Blois was dean of the collegiate church of St Martin le Grand, a house of which the counts of Boulogne were patrons.[123] Both Stephen and his

---

[114] C. Warren Hollister, 'London's first Charter of Liberties: is it genuine?', *Journal of Medieval History*, vi, 1980, 289–306, at 290–2.
[115] Richard of Hexham, 'De Gestis Regis Stephani et de Bello Standardi', *Chronicles of the Reigns of Stephen, Henry II and Richard I*, iii, 143.
[116] *Gesta Stephani*, 122.
[117] *Regesta*, iii, nos. 243–4.
[118] Cited by Round, *Geoffrey de Mandeville*, 116.
[119] *Gesta Stephani*, 128, 226; Huntingdon, 278.
[120] M. Bateson, 'A London Municipal Collection of the Reign of John', *EHR*, xvii, 1902, 480–511, 707–30, at 486.
[121] *The Pinchbeck Register*, ed. F. Hervey, 2 vols., Brighton, 1925, ii, 299; *Regesta*, iii, no. 814; Amt, 'Richard de Lucy', 68.
[122] H. G. Richardson and G. O. Sayles, *The Governance of Mediaeval England*, Edinburgh, 1963, 413–21.
[123] *Regesta*, iii, no. 527.

queen were benefactors of Holy Trinity Aldgate; two of their children were buried there, and Prior Ralph was the queen's confessor.[124] The exception to this harmony, and the Empress' notable success, was in securing the see of London in 1141 for Robert de Sigillo, keeper of the seal in her father's day.[125] The last bishop had died in 1134 and the chapter had been divided over a successor, one faction electing Abbot Anselm of Bury, and its opponents appealing to Rome. Anselm had returned to his abbey, and the see was temporarily in the charge of Henry of Blois when Matilda decided that Robert was the man for the job. It was hard for the chapter to object to Robert on the grounds of character, for he had retired from the court to be a monk at Reading. He was also the son of a canon of St Paul's, and perhaps the Empress hoped that he would be able to win friends there.[126] In the event he found himself caught up in the events of 1141 when Geoffrey de Mandeville descended on the bishop's manor at Fulham and bore off the bishop, apparently as a hostage.[127] At Easter 1142 Bishop Robert issued a confirmation for St Paul's at London, a document which survives in the original. The scribe is *scriptor* xiii, who has been nominated as the author of the possibly forged charter of Henry I for London.[128] The bishop's relations with Stephen were difficult: the king was said by St Bernard to have prevented the bishop from entering his see and on a later occasion Eugenius III wrote individually to Stephen and his queen about the oath of fealty the king required.[129]

If we turn from the ecclesiastical to the secular sphere, it must be borne in mind that there was a greater variety of officials and agents Stephen could use here than elsewhere. The justiciar and sheriff were mentioned in Henry I's charter; there were in addition the constables of the royal castles and the king's chamberlain of London, who was responsible for purchasing wine for the royal household, and seems to have had some authority over the Lotharingian merchants.[130] There were also the moneyers who, it has been suggested, were royal agents.[131] At least five justiciars, election of whom was conceded in Henry I's charter, are mentioned in Stephen's reign: Andrew Buccuinte, Geoffrey de Mandeville, Gervase

[124] *Cartulary of Holy Trinity Aldgate*, ed. G. A. J. Hodgett, London Record Society, vii, 1971, 3.

[125] Florence of Worcester, *Chronicon ex Chronicis*, ed. B. Thorpe, 2 vols., London, 1848, 1849, ii, 131; M. Chibnall, 'The Empress Matilda and Church Reform', *TRHS*, 5th ser., xxxviii, 1988, 107–130, at 114–115.

[126] J. Le Neve, *Fasti Ecclesiae Anglicanae 1066–1300, I St Paul's Cathedral*, compiled by D. E. Greenway, London, 1968, 2; for the disputed election at London, Ralph of Diceto, *Opera Historica*, ed. W. Stubbs, 2 vols., RS, London, 1876, i, 248–254.

[127] Nicholas Trivet as cited by Round, *Geoffrey de Mandeville*, 117.

[128] London, Guildhall, St Paul's Cathedral Dean and Chapter Muniments, A40/1443, printed *Early Charters of St Paul's*, ed. M. Gibbs, Camden Society 3rd ser., lvii, 1939, no. 219. For *scriptor* xiii, T. A. M. Bishop, *Scriptores Regis*, Oxford, 1961, notes to plate xvii (a); *Regesta*, iii, xiii–xiv. For his possible authorship of any doctoring of Henry I's charter for London see, Brooke, Keir, and Reynolds, 564.

[129] Bernard, *Opera*, ed. J. Leclercq, C. H. Talbot and H. M. Rochais, 8 vols. in 9, Rome, 1957–77, viii, 70; *Patrologiae cursus completus series latina*, ed. J.-P. Migne, 221 vols., Paris, 1844–64, clxxx, cols. 1248–9.

[130] For the chamberlain of London, W. Kellaway, 'The Coroner in Medieval London', *Studies in London History presented to Philip Edmund Jones*, ed. A. E. J. Hollaender and W. Kellaway, London, 1972, 75–91, at 76–7; D. Keene, 'New Discoveries at the Hanseatic Steelyard in London', *Hansische Geschichtsblätter*, Köln, Wien, 1989, 15–25 at 19.

[131] P. Nightingale, 'Some London Moneyers and Reflections on the Organization of English Mints in the Eleventh and Twelfth Centuries', *Numismatic Chronicle*, cxlii, 1982, 34–50.

of Cornhill, and Richard de Lucy with Theodoric son of Deorman.[132] Osbert Huitdeniers may have been at different times both justiciar and sheriff.[133] His links were with the Angevins. He held land of the earl of Gloucester, and a grant of land to him by the Empress is mentioned in her second charter to Geoffrey de Mandeville.[134] Gervase of Cornhill also held both offices, for he was a justiciar under Stephen and sheriff in the following reign.[135] Andrew Buccuinte, justiciar at the start of Stephen's reign, was a Londoner, as was Theodoric; the latter was also a moneyer.[136] Richard de Lucy was a key agent of Stephen but perhaps should not as yet be seen as a magnate, and, that being the case, Geoffrey de Mandeville stands alone as the only great magnate to be justiciar.

The same is true of the known sheriffs: Osbert Huitdeniers, 'N', Gilbert Becket, Ranulf, Gilbert Proudfoot, Geoffrey de Mandeville, and John, possibly John FitzRalf who held office under Henry II. Gilbert Becket, the father of Thomas, was sheriff, possibly in the 1130s. He also was well to do. His son's biographer William FitzStephen claimed that Gilbert was not engaged in money-lending or full-time business, but lived on his rents.[137] Gilbert Proudfoot was evidently a Londoner, whilst John, Ranulf and 'N' remain totally obscure.[138]

Geoffrey de Mandeville thus stands out as the only sheriff who was a definitely a leading magnate. He gained possession of the Tower, probably when news of the king's capture at Lincoln reached him.[139] At midsummer 1141 the Empress appointed him justiciar and sheriff of London as well as constable, and he was confirmed in these positions by Stephen about December 1141, holding them until his downfall in 1143. Geoffrey was hated by the Londoners: the Empress's second charter refers to the Londoners as his mortal enemies and promises that she and count Geoffrey would not make a separate peace with them. Geoffrey's father-in-law, Aubrey de Vere, was killed in a rising of the citizens in 1141.[140] One could argue, therefore, that Stephen would have been unlikely to relish the

---

[132] *Regesta*, iii, xxv. Andrew's role is not specified in the charters cited here, but he was described as the king's justiciar in a lawsuit said to have taken place in the second year of Stephen's reign, Round, *Commune of London*, 99–100.

[133] FitzStephen says that Becket was a clerk in the household of his kinsman Osbert, whilst Edward Grim states that Becket was clerk to an (unnamed) sheriff, *Materials for the History of Thomas Becket*, i–vi ed. J. C. Robertson, vii ed. J. C. Robertson and J. B. Sheppard, RS, London 1875–85, iii, 14; ii, 363. The suggestion that he was justiciar is based on a group of writs issued for St Martin le Grand, *Regesta*, iii, nos. 527–9, 531.

[134] *Red Book of the Exchequer*, i, 189; Osbert witnessed once for Earl Robert, and was a guarantor of the earl's treaty with Earl Miles of Hereford, *Earldom of Gloucester Charters*, ed. R. B. Patterson, Oxford, 1973, nos. 6, 95. Brian FitzCount mentioned Osbert in a list of those who could vouch for his veracity, H. W. C. Davis, 'Henry of Blois and Brian FitzCount', *EHR*, xxv, 1910, 302.

[135] Round, *Geoffrey de Mandeville*, 304–12.

[136] Round, *Commune of London*, 108–112; Nightingale, 'Some London Moneyers', 35; Theodoric married a relation of Gilbert FitzRichard, *Calendar of Charter Rolls*, ii, 71–2.

[137] *Materials for the History of Thomas Becket*, iii, 14.

[138] *Historical Manuscripts Commission 9th Report*, Appendix, pp. 60a, 62a, 63b; *Cartularium Monasterii de Ramesia*, ed. W. H. Hart and P. A. Lyons, 3 vols., RS, London, 1884–93, i, 161; Dugdale, iii, 310; *Westminster Abbey Charters c.1066–1214*, ed. E. Mason assisted by J. Bray, London Record Society, xxv, 1988, no. 274; BL Additional Charter 65,175: a charter of Earl Robert de Ferrers attested by Ranulf sheriff of London; *Regesta*, iii, no. 530.

[139] William of Newburgh, i, 45, and see Prestwich and Davis, *EHR*, cv, 1990, 670–2.

[140] *The Chronicle of Melrose*, facsimile with an introduction by A. O. Anderson and M. O. Anderson, London, 1936, 34.

disturbance to his good relations with the Londoners by making Geoffrey sheriff and justiciar. Yet Geoffrey evidently was able to attract Londoners to his entourage at some stage, because he issued from the Tower a charter addressed to Bishop Robert and his archdeacon restoring to the canons of St Martin le Grand their Essex manors. The charter was witnessed amongst others by Gilbert the sheriff (? Gilbert Proudfoot sheriff of London), Ailwin son of Leofstan, Robert de Ponte, and Hugh son of Ulger, all notable Londoners. The charter was issued by Geoffrey as earl of Essex so its date must therefore lie between 1141 and 1143, and possibly close to his death.[141]

It is possible to suggest that in the 1140s the centre of gravity of Stephen's financial administration shifted towards London and the south-east. The semi-autonomous midland earldoms, the strength of the Angevin cause in the west, the sack of Winchester, and the loss of Normandy all played a part. Winchester had been a place where royal treasure was stored before 1066; that role continued under the Norman kings, with treasure being stored either in the royal palace or, more probably, in the castle built in the south-west of the city.[142] When the court of the exchequer is first mentioned it met at Winchester, though whether it always met there we cannot be sure.[143] Westminster in the early twelfth century was an important royal residence, but it is not clear if it was already a seat of royal administration. Winchester on the other hand was convenient for transporting treasure to Normandy via Porchester, where a strong keep was built in Henry I's reign and entrusted to the custody of a chamberlain.[144] After Stephen's campaign of 1136–7 he did not cross to Normandy again, and the progressive loss of the duchy to Duke Geoffrey obviated the need to transport large supplies of coin from Southampton Water. Meanwhile the royal palace at Winchester was taken over by Henry of Blois and was fortified by 1141.[145] The arrest of Roger of Salisbury and his nephews in 1139 and the king's resulting quarrel with his brother, may have dislocated the machinery of the exchequer, though the Empress seems to have believed that it was still functioning in 1141 when she issued a writ of *computate* in favour of the canons of Oseney.[146] Winchester was sacked in 1141; William de Pont de l'Arche the sheriff remained loyal to the Empress and was at odds with Bishop Henry. In these circumstances Winchester, no longer particularly convenient as a financial headquarters, was not even particularly secure, either.

At a date before 1154 exchequer operations had moved to London, for there is a reference to expenditure on repairing the 'houses of the exchequer' in the pipe

[141] Extracts from the charter are printed by Round, *Commune of London*, 118; for Ailwin and Hugh see Round, *Commune of London*, 105–6, 101, 102, 120–1; *HMC 9th Report*, Appendix, 62a; cf. 68a for Robert de Ponte, and 66a for Hugh son of Ulger. For Hugh son of Ulger see also H. W. C. Davis, 'London Lands and Liberties of St Paul's, 1066–1135', *Essays in Medieval History presented to Thomas Frederick Tout*, Manchester, 1925, 45–59.

[142] *Winchester Studies*, i, 304–5.

[143] *Regesta*, ii, no. 1000: a court meeting at Winchester in the treasury in the presence of the queen, Bishop Roger, and others; cf. nos. 963, a writ issued at Westminster addressed to the barons of the exchequer, and no. 1514, issued at Winchester and addressed to Bishop Roger and the barons of the exchequer. T. F. T. Tout argued that there would be no need for the latter writ if the exchequer met at Winchester, but this does not necessarily follow, *Chapters in the Administrative History of Mediaeval England*, 6 vols., Manchester, 1920–37, i, 96.

[144] *History of the King's Works. II. The Middle Ages*, ed. R. A. Brown, H. M. Colvin and A. J. Taylor, London, 1963, 783–4.

[145] *Winchester Studies*, i, 297–301.

[146] *Regesta*, iii, no. 628.

roll account for London in 1156.[147] The entry is tantalisingly brief. It could mean that the houses had fallen into disrepair, from which we might infer that they had not been used in the recent past and could push the date for meetings of the exchequer at Westminster to Henry I's reign, or it might indicate the need for refurbishment, which would not rule out their use in Stephen's reign. The houses presumably formed part of the palace of Westminster, and could have been on the site of the later treasury of receipt, or lower exchequer.[148] After 1154 the court of audit usually, but not always, met at Westminster. Winchester for a few years had renewed importance as a principal royal treasury, but by the end of Henry II's reign had been eclipsed by London. In the later twelfth century, as Allen Brown pointed out, treasure was stored in London at the Tower and at the New Temple as well as Westminster.[149]

Between 1142 and 1154 we can also see signs of change in that financial administration which had developed to satisfy the priorities of the Norman kings. In 1130 William de Pont de l'Arche had been based at Winchester and Porchester whilst his brother Osbert had an office in the chamber. Geoffrey de Clinton, who like William was described as chamberlain and treasurer, seems to have been the link with the itinerant household, whilst William Mauduit seems to have been the chief financial officer based in the chamber. Bishop Roger himself presided at meetings of the exchequer, whilst his nephew Nigel acted as the co-ordinator, the first in a line of clerical treasurers.[150]

This situation had begun to change even before Henry I's death. Geoffrey de Clinton was accused of treason in 1130. He may have died not long afterwards and though his son called himself chamberlain and treasurer he was not active in royal administration.[151] Nigel was appointed to the see of Ely in 1133 and was not apparently replaced until Bishop Roger secured the position for his kinsman Athelelm from Stephen.[152] Bishop Roger's influence seems to have been unchallenged until 1139, and he is said to have been arrested whilst in the *camera curie*.[153] Afterwards Nigel returned to his see, Athelelm was dean of Lincoln, and Roger of Fécamp is said (though not on any strong evidence) to have been put in charge of the finances.[154] By 1141 William Mauduit as well as William de Pont de

---

[147] *PRs 2–4 Henry II*, 4.

[148] H. Hall, *The Antiquities and Curiosities of the Exchequer*, London, 1891, 68; *History of the King's Works*, I, 538–9.

[149] R. A. Brown, 'The "Treasury" of the Later Twelfth Century', *Studies presented to Sir Hilary Jenkinson*, ed. J. Conway Davies, Oxford, 1957, 35–49.

[150] Green, *Government of England*, 31–4, 38–50; C. Warren Hollister, 'The Origins of the English Treasury', *EHR*, xciii, 1978, 262–75.

[151] Geoffrey did, however, attend Duke Henry and his army at Torigny in 1154, *Regesta*, iii, no. 66. The Empress referred to 'Geoffrey the chamberlain of Clinton' in her confirmation for Oseney, whilst Stephen's confirmation for Kenilworth simply refers to 'Gaufridus de Glint(ona) junior', *Regesta*, iii, nos. 629, 418. Geoffrey styled himself 'chamberlain of Clinton' in his own charters, *Cartulary of Oseney*, iv, 60; H. E. Salter, *Facsimiles of Early Charters preserved in Oxford Muniment Rooms*, Oxford, 1929, nos. 71, 102; *Hatton's Book of Seals*, nos. 194, 508.

[152] Hollister, 'Origins of the English Treasury', 272; *Regesta*, iii, xix; *Historia Novella*, 38–9; E. Kealey, *Roger of Salisbury*, Berkeley and London, 1972, 274.

[153] *Historia Novella*, 29.

[154] *Liber Eliensis*, ed. E. O. Blake, Camden Society, 3rd ser., xcii, 1962, 316–94 *passim*. Yoshitake suggested that Roger of Fécamp may have taken charge of Stephen's finances, 'Arrest of the bishops in 1139', 106. Roger was a royal clerk whom C. H. Haskins identified as treasurer of Normandy, *Norman Institutions*, Cambridge, Mass., 1918, 110 but for criticism see Judith A. Green, 'Unity and Disunity in the Anglo-Norman State', *Historical Research*, lxii, 1989, 120 n. 24.

l'Arche and Geoffrey II de Clinton had gone over to the Empress, and none of them returned to Stephen's allegiance.[155] William Mauduit survived long enough to obtain a charter of confirmation for the chamberlainship he himself had held, plus that of William de Pont de l'Arche held earlier by the Mauduits.[156]

What is interesting is that Stephen did not take steps to replace the three Henrician chamberlains. From 1141 the most conspicuous chamberlain was Hubert, who was evidently chamberlain of the honour of Boulogne and must have been the vital link between the Boulogne estates and the king.[157] This situation does however fit into the general picture of Stephen's tendency to rely on a small inner group and not to replace defectors from the main household offices. Again and again his documents were witnessed by William Martel the steward, Robert de Vere the constable (later succeeded by Henry of Essex), and men such as Richard de Lucy and Richard de Camville.

Of these the likeliest to have run the household side of Stephen's finances was surely William Martel as Professor Cronne suggested.[158] William's family came from upper Normandy.[159] In 1086 Geoffrey Martel, William's father, had held land in Hertfordshire as a tenant of Robert d'Oilly, and in Essex as an under-tenant of Geoffrey de Mandeville.[160] His uncle Walter son of Grip was a tenant of the honour of Eye.[161] William had been a butler of Henry I; he joined Stephen's household as steward on or before the latter's accession to the throne and he may have been sheriff of Surrey for a time.[162] Stephen greatly prized William's services: it was to secure William's release that Stephen handed over Sherborne castle.[163] There is a reference to land which Stephen had granted to William at North Baddesley in Hampshire, and he may have granted William additional estates of the honour of Eye.[164] William had extensive property in Winchester in 1148, and he may have been responsible for acquiring the Martel lands in London.[165] Major

[155] *Regesta*, iii, no. 581.
[156] *Regesta*, iii, no. 582.
[157] *Regesta*, iii, nos. 162, 207, 244, 510, 516, 517, 541, 553, 554, 830, 843, 509; Hubert was the father of Richard of Anstey, P. Brand, 'New Light on the Anstey Case', *Essex Archaeology and History*, xv, 1983, 68–72.
[158] Cronne, *Reign of Stephen*, 198–200.
[159] J. Le Maho, 'L'Apparition des seigneuries châtelaines dans le Grand-Caux à l'époque ducale', *Archéologie Médiévale*, vi, 1976, 12, 23.
[160] *Domesday Book*, i, 137b; ii, 57b, 60, 61, 61b, 62.
[161] *Domesday Book*, ii, 329, 329b, 330.
[162] *Regesta*, ii, nos. 1562, 1689–90, 1696, 1749, 1776*, 1822–3, 1835. For William's office, *Historia Novella*, 55–6. His son Geoffrey accounted for land attached to the butlership, *Red Book of the Exchequer*, i, 217–18. William Martel was the sole witness of Stephen's first Charter of Liberties; he attested the second as steward whilst his brother Eudo attested the latter as butler, *Regesta*, iii, 270, 271; for William's possible shrievalty of Surrey, *Regesta*, iii, no. 934; *Red Book of the Exchequer*, ii, 654.
[163] *Gesta Stephani*, 148.
[164] *Regesta*, iii, no. 828; for Eye see Cartulary of Eye priory, Essex Record Office D/DBy Q 19, f. 23v: William confirmed the gift of Osbert de Conteville, and quitclaimed the men and land concerned from all customs and exactions which had been exacted either at Eye or at Thorndon, and referred to exactions of William's *ministri* at Eye or Thorndon. Mrs Vivien Brown kindly drew my attention to the possible implication that William had been put in charge of the whole honour of Eye for a time.
[165] *Winchester Studies*, i, 177: entries nos. 41, 51, 54, 35, 490, 467, 488, 489, 492, 490; in London William Martel, 'steward of the king of England' gave land to Holy Trinity Aldgate, London PRO E40/7364, transcribed by Colin Taylor, Museum of London, text made available by Dr Derek

enduring territorial gains eluded him, however. Reliance on a single rather than several stewards was a development which J. E. A. Jolliffe placed in the Angevin period, but its origins evidently go back to the time of William Martel.[166]

William's responsibilities would have prevented him from overseeing financial operations at Westminster. Richard de Lucy, on the other hand, could have fulfilled this role. In Essex Richard had been the chief beneficiary of Geoffrey de Mandeville's fall, and he was the father-in-law not only of Walter FitzRobert lord of Baynard's Castle in the south-west of London, but also of Gilbert de Montfitchet, lord of Montfitchet's castle, close to or part of, Baynard's.[167] Richard was justiciar of London and may have had custody of the Tower, for the castle was committed to him by the terms of the treaty of Westminster. If he did, then he was obviously well placed to supervise operations.[168] Unlike William Martel, Richard was able to come to terms with Henry II. His guardianship of the Tower and Windsor in 1153 suggests that he was considered trustworthy. Henry II chose him as co-justiciar with Robert earl of Leicester, and as Richardson and Sayles pointed out, this choice is more easily comprehended if Richard had had a comparable job under Stephen.[169]

This is as far as the evidence takes us. In the absence of pipe roll records there must always be an element of speculation about Stephen's finances, and the publication of further private charters may, by adding a new name or revising a date, cast new light on local politics, even if the general picture is tolerably clear. The conclusions of this paper prompt the thought that we have tended to see Stephen's finances from the standpoint of Richard FitzNigel who, when he came to write the *Dialogue of the Exchequer* in 1177, looked back on Stephen's reign as a time when knowledge of the exchequer had almost perished. His father, Nigel bishop of Ely, had to be brought out of retirement to set the wheels in motion again.[170] The low receipts and the disorder of the early pipe rolls of Henry II's reign bear out his verdict. Moreover, the new king was committed to a return to 1135, with an exchequer to enforce accountability. Winchester recovered some of its former importance as a base from which coins could be moved down to the south coast for transshipment. Because Henry II's reign witnessed a restoration of his grandfather's financial system, we may have judged Stephen's reign by the extent to which that system survived, and thus have missed signs of an alternative arrangement, based on a secure control of rather fewer counties, perhaps more

Keene, Centre for Metropolitan History, University of London, Institute of Historical Research. It is not clear from the context whether the grantor was William I or his grandson William II. On the loss of Normandy in 1204 William Martel adhered to Philip Augustus, and the soke of his London property was acquired by Joce FitzPeter, G. Williams, *From Commune to Capital*, London, 1963, 53. For a possible reference to a donation by William I to the Templars, *Regesta*, iii, no. 849.

[166] J. E. A. Jolliffe, *Angevin Kingship*, 2nd edn, London, 1963, chapter 10.

[167] Amt, 'Richard de Lucy', 66; for varying assessments of Montfitchet's see Henry Johns, 'Introduction to the Maps', *British Atlas of Historic Towns*, III, *The City of London*, ed. Mary D. Lobel, Oxford, 1989, 59–62; A. Vince, *Saxon London: An Archaeological Investigation*, London, 1990, 39.

[168] *Regesta*, iii, no. 272.

[169] Richardson and Sayles, *Governance of Mediaeval England*, 166. Note, however, that the evidence does not really support Richardson and Sayles' suggestion that Richard was Stephen's chief justiciar.

[170] *Dialogus de Scaccario*, ed. and trans. C. Johnson, with corrections by F. E. L. Carter and D. E. Greenway, Oxford, 1983, 50.

heavily reliant on credit, and using different channels between the localities and the itinerant household. That arrangement provided Stephen with the resources to continue fighting to the bitter end, and acted as a stimulus to the rise of London or more properly Westminster as the capital of royal administration.

DISPUTE SETTLEMENT IN ANGLO-NORMAN ENGLAND

Edmund King

In the year 1154 Geoffrey de Waterville gave to Kirkstead Abbey in Lincolnshire his lands of Thimbleby and Buckland, to hold in alms and in fee-farm for the service of eight marks a year. It is a grant in standard form, addressed to his men and his friends, a little unusual in having a precise date, but otherwise with little to attract our interest.[1] Except that is for a word not usually found in grants of this kind: it is described as an agreement – a *conventio* – and the phrase is insisted on. Why? Some clues may be offered if I say a little more about Geoffrey de Waterville. He was the younger son of one of the knightly tenants of Peterborough Abbey. But he had come up in the world and had wider horizons than this.[2] The legend on his seal reads: SIGILLUM GAUFRIDI DE WATERVILLA DAPIFERO CONSULIS. He was the steward of Robert earl of Gloucester. In the charters of earl Robert, and of the protagonists in the civil war of Stephen's reign, Geoffrey is often found at his lord's side. He is first found there in a *conventio* which Robert of Gloucester made with the abbey of Fécamp in 1128. He is one of the chief witnesses in the *confederatio amoris* which the earls of Gloucester and Hereford made before Robert sailed to Normandy in 1142; he attended the *conventio* which Robert made in the presence of the Empress with the Bishop of Bayeux in 1146.[3] The language of compromise runs through his career.

I start with the proposition that the *conventio*, an agreed settlement of a dispute, a conditional agreement predicated on future events, was a routine way of doing business in the local communities of Anglo-Norman England, as elsewhere in western Europe at the same time.[4] It is to these communities that we must look for the ideas which underpin the *conventiones* of King Stephen's reign, which are my

[1]   BL Harley Charter 57 F 14, reproduced in *Facsimiles of Royal and Other Charters in the British Museum*, ed. G. F. Warner and H. J. Ellis, London 1903, no. 36.
[2]   *Henry of Pytchley's Book of Fees*, ed. W. T. Mellows, Northamptonshire Record Society, ii, 1929, 41–5 E. King, *Peterborough Abbey 1086–1310. A study in the land market*, Cambridge 1973, 32–3, and more fully in 'The knights of Peterborough Abbey', *Peterborough's Past* 2, Peterborough Museum Society 1986, 36–50.
[3]   *Earldom of Gloucester Charters*, ed. R. B. Patterson, Oxford 1973, nos. 70, 95, 6 (= *Regesta*, iii, no. 58).
[4]   F. L. Cheyette, 'Suum Cuique Tribuere', *French Historical Studies* vi, 1970, 287–99; 'The "sale" of Carcassonne to the counts of Barcelona (1067–1070) and the rise of the Trencavels', *Speculum* 63, 1988, 826–64; S. D. White, ' "Pactum Legem Vincit et Amor Judicium". The settlement of disputes by compromise in Eleventh-Century Western France', *American Journal of Legal History* xxii, 1978, 281–308; 'Inheritances and legal arguments in Western France, 1050–1150', *Traditio* xliii, 1987, 64–70; Jane Martindale, 'Conventum inter Guillelmum Aquitanorum comes et Hugonem Chiliarchum', *EHR* lxxxiv, 1969, 528–48; Emily Z. Tabuteau, *Transfers of property in eleventh-century Norman law*, Chapel Hill 1988, 31–3, 163–9.

main topic. The texts are to be found in charters, and in the charter-narratives that
are a characteristic feature of the archives of several of the major monasteries.
Many of the texts are unprinted, including those from Peterborough and Thorney,
while of the printed editions many are old. Marjorie Chibnall's chapter, 'Towards
a Common Law', in her survey of Anglo-Norman England, provides an admirable introduction to them. And now Van Caenegem's major edition of the texts of
English lawsuits for the Selden Society, replacing Bigelow's *Placita Anglo-
Normannica* of 1879, provides a reader focussing on the procedures involved.[5] It
must be noted, however, that this invaluable new work 'is a collection of narrative
and non-narrative texts from the period 1066–1199 which contain information on
English law as it was practised in the courts'.[6] The texts of *conventiones* or
agreements will only appear here if they proceed from or are cited in connection
with adjudication; and this is only one form of dispute settlement. Indeed it was a
commonplace of contemporary thought about procedure that agreement and
judgement were antithetical: *pactum enim legem vincit et amor judicium*, said the
author of the *Leges Henrici Primi*, 'an agreement supersedes the law and amic-
able settlement a court judgement'.[7]

The land might seem to have as many lords as it had neighbours.[8] Disputes
between neighbours needed to be settled by their coming together, by discussion
and by agreement, all of which concepts are included in the *conventio*. One area
where neighbours jostled, and where monasteries clustered almost 'horn under
horn', was in the fenland. It is not surprising to find that in Domesday Book, from
where my first examples are taken, one of the *conventiones* recorded concerns
Whittlesey Mere, and the four boats which the three monasteries of Ramsey,
Thorney and Peterborough sailed upon it. Those rights were customary. The
agreement concerned the terms on which Peterborough as it were leased from
Thorney one of its two boats: *hec conventio T.R.E. facta est inter eos.*[9] The jurors
here and elsewhere are going back to pre-Conquest times: x had been given rights
in Worthy, Hampshire, *eo pacto et conventione* that the church should return to
the bishop of Winchester after the third heir; y had an estate in Seckford in
Suffolk, *eo conventione . . . testante hundredo* that after the tenant's death the
estate should return to Ely Abbey.[10] Finally, and most interestingly here there are
the references in the Suffolk Domesday of the terms by which the reeve then held
from the king the valuable hundredal manor of East Bergholt, held in 1066 by
Harold and thereafter by Robert Malet and Roger Bigod. The last-named, in
dispute with the reeve, offered to bring as witnesses the men present at their
discussions (*uult probare per illos homines qui ad suas conventiones fuerunt*).
And as to the terms on which the reeve then held, there was a further agreement

5 *English Lawsuits from William I to Richard I*, ed. R. C. Van Caenegem, 2 vols, Selden Society
cvi, 1990, cvii, 1991.
6 *English Lawsuits* i, xi.
7 *Leges Henrici Primi*, ed. L. J. Downer, Oxford 1972, cap. 49, 5a; and see the valuable comments in M. T. Clanchy, 'Law and love in the middle ages', in *Disputes and Settlements. Law and
human relations in the West*, ed. J. Bossy, Cambridge 1983, 47–67; White, '*Pactum legem vincit*'.
8 J. Laporte (ed.), 'Epistolae Fiscannenses: lettres d'amitié, de gouvernement et d'affaires',
Revue Mabillon xi, 1953, 30.
9 *Domesday Book*, i, fol. 205a (= Phillimore edn 19, *Huntingdonshire* 7/8).
10 *Domesday Book*, i, fol. 46d (= Phillimore edn 4, *Hampshire* 29/3); ii, fol. 373a (= Phillimore
edn 34, *Suffolk*, ii, 16/3).

that he should render to the king £60 in profit. In one entry both Saxon reeve and Norman lord refer to their *conventiones*.[11]

The Domesday enquiry brought numerous disputes into focus, and must have been the stimulus to the making of many *conventiones*. Van Caenegem collects most usefully texts of documents relating to a dispute between the abbot of Evesham and the bishop of Worcester regarding particular estates within the hundred of Oswaldslaw.[12] When the matter first came to judgement the abbot withdrew his claim, and an agreement was made. The laity played a major role in bringing the two churchmen to judgement, and the particular roles they played were laid down by the normal procedures of dispute settlement.[13] On one side came the friends who characteristically persuaded one of the parties, here the abbot, to withdraw. On the other came a array of witnesses, *legitimi testes* prepared to prove *per sacramentum et bellum* the agreement that had been made. There were also men in holy orders 'prepared to confirm this by the judgement of God'. The abbot did not go away empty-handed, however, for the specific lands in question were conceded to him to be held by proper recognition and service. (The public acknowledgement was just as important as the money payment). These agreements were acknowledged when the two parties appeared before the Domesday commissioners, who are named along with their entourage.[14] This, before a unique tribunal, was the recognition promised. The record was a *confirmatio conventionis*. The *conventiones* were the discussions themselves.

The records of *conventiones* surviving from the reigns of the first two Norman kings of England are disappointingly meagre. There is nothing, however, to suggest that they were not routine. They would not normally be put in writing. A agreement made late in the 1080s between two lords as important as bishop Gundulf of Rochester and Gilbert de Tonbridge was noted as being put in writing at the express command of archbishop Lanfranc.[15] Those that were written down, for reasons that will be examined in the last section of this paper, stood a poor chance of being preserved. An agreement between Ivo Taillebois and abbot Turold of Peterborough, providing for the return to the abbey of two manors in Lincolnshire, is identified by being referred to as a cirograph in a charter of William Rufus.[16] A rare survival from the reign of the Conqueror, relating to the grant of land in fee, is Robert bishop of Hereford's grant of Holme (Lacy) to Roger son of Walter (de Lacy).[17] The grant had been sought *per amicos et per pecuniam*; it was made *ea conventione* that Roger perform the service of two knights. It was drawn up in the form of a cirograph, and it was noted by the Hereford archivist that 'the other part' was deposited in Gloucester abbey.

---

[11] *Domesday Book*, ii, fol. 287b (= Phillimore edn 34, *Suffolk*, i, 1/103).

[12] *English Lawsuits*, i, no. 15.

[13] See the works cited note 4; and for comparative purposes S. Roberts, *Order and Dispute. An introduction to legal anthropology*, Harmondsworth 1979, 69–79; 'The study of dispute: anthropological perspectives', in *Disputes and settlements*, 1–24.

[14] *English Lawsuits*, i, no. 15 document E. The entourage was largely English-speaking, as I suggested (without knowledge of this text) it must have been in 'The making of the Rutland Domesday', *Rutland Record* 7, 1987, 231–5.

[15] *English Lawsuits*, i, no. 136.

[16] *Regesta*, i, no. 409. A date of c.1086 x c.1094 may be suggested for the chirograph, since the manors were not in dispute in Domesday and Ivo Taillebois is reckoned to have died c.1094: GEC, vii, 743.

[17] V. H. Galbraith, 'An episcopal land-grant of 1085', *EHR* xliv, 1929, 353–72 (with facsimile).

In the reign of Henry I the texts become more plentiful, and allow us to focus in a little more detail on some of the dynamics of dispute settlement. They show the workings of the new social groupings that the Conquest had brought about, the groups of feudal tenants clustered round their lords, in particular in the rather unusual circumstances caused by the feudalisation of the Anglo-Saxon monasteries. The honorial courts can be seen operating in relation one to another, and to the established local courts of shire and hundred.

One group which they had in common was their suitors. And among the suitors a distinctive place appears for the senior members of the honorial baronage who held office as stewards. These were men at what we might now term the interface of feudal, local and clerical custom and procedures. Geoffrey de Waterville, steward of Robert of Gloucester, came from one such family. His father and his elder brother were successively stewards of Peterborough Abbey.[18] Another such was the family of le Moine, stewards of Ramsey Abbey, prominent in the records of this and of neighbouring monasteries. In the 1120s the abbot of Thorney was successful in recovering land that had been granted to Robert of Yaxley, the nephew of his predecessor. In the county court of Huntingdon on 21 September 1127 Robert of Yaxley swore fealty to the abbot 'as Hervey le Moine best knew how to set it out (*sicut Herveius Monachus melius scivit distingere*), namely that he will be faithful to him and all of his as to his lawful lord, and that he will never make any claim or suit against the abbot, and that he will keep the aforesaid agreements (*conventiones*) for ever'. The stewardship of Ramsey at this time was far from being a sinecure. It involved a lot of travel. The same man served as the go-between, for example, in agreements reached with Holy Trinity Priory, London, regarding the lands of the English *cnightengild*; and in negotiating the terms on which Hugh son of Ailfwold obtained property in the market-place of St Ives. The Ramsey cartulary also makes room for a lengthy document recording deliberations preceding the foundation of Sawtry Abbey. Again we are looking at pasture in Whittlesey Mere. Here we find Hervey le Moine, surrounded by his men, telling the abbot of Thorney, 'it's no use you thinking you can make yourself rich by making other people poor'. *Sicque discessit*; he said his piece and left.[19]

If some of these *conventiones* are made between two church corporations, a more typical agreement involved one clerical and one lay party. In one of the earliest originals that survive, from the 1120s, Robert de Ferrers made a *conventio* with the abbot of Burton upon Trent regarding some woodland: it was made in the castle of Tutbury and confirmed in the chapter-house. There is a reference in some of the Ramsey texts to agreements being confirmed in the court of Simon de Beauchamp.[20] With so many competing jurisdictions the texts have to be careful to spell out just what was done where.

Agreements of this kind continue through the reign of Stephen, preserved most characteristically in charters of confirmation by a variety of lords. In one case that lord was the king. Stephen confirmed an agreement made between Gervase of

---

[18] Above note 2.

[19] On le Moigne see J. A. Raftis, *The Estates of Ramsey Abbey*, Toronto 1957, 28, 43 (which, however, confuses the family with that of Mohun). The examples of Hervey le Moigne's activities given here are from: *English Lawsuits*, i, no. 272; *Cartularium monasterii de Rameseia*, i, ed. W. H. Hart, RS 1884, 133–4, 144–5, 165.

[20] *English Lawsuits*, i, no. 252; and in facsimile in Warner and Ellis, *Facsimiles*, no. 9; *Ramsey Cartulary*, i, 136, 147.

Cornhill and Hubert the queen's chamberlain as to the terms of his tenure, where Gervase was to hold *sicut conventio est inter eos.* To have this one example in an archive of over a thousand royal charters is useful in establishing that such a confirmation was exceptional. In the archives of lay and ecclesiastical magnates the matter was quite different. Between 1135 and 1140 archbishop Thurstan of York confirmed a *conventio* made between the church of Beverley and the canons of Bridlington, 'as in the charter issued by each of them and sealed with the seal of St John' of Beverley. The Mowbray charters are particularly fruitful here. To take just two examples. Between 1138 and 1148 Roger de Mowbray confirmed an agreement made between one of his men and St Leonard's hospital, York. About the middle of that time he confirmed agreements made between the abbot of Byland and the canons of Hood, saying that he stood as witness to and surety for agreements that had been made.[21] While the northern archives are particularly rich, and have been notably well-edited, the reader can look for *conventiones* with some confidence in any cartulary which preserves texts from this time.

King Stephen's reign concluded with what Ralph Davis, in a memorable phrase, termed 'the magnates peace'. It rested on what he termed 'an elaborate patchwork of alliances' between the great magnates who controlled the midlands of England, which he set out in diagrammatic form.[22] He had himself edited the two agreements between successive earls of Gloucester and Hereford;[23] while the best known *convencio* of all was the agreement between the earls of Chester and Leicester, which provided a key text for Sir Frank Stenton is his examination of 'the end of Norman feudalism'.[24] Churchmen played an important role in developing the ideas of the peace, and citing agreements which involve ecclesiastical lords only strengthens the general argument.[25] Here, it might appear, the *convencio* becomes the key to what our modern colleagues like to term 'high politics'.

In fact there is little difference, in this respect, between the end of the reign and the beginning. Stephen's reign is jam-full of *convenciones.* I start with two examples, both of them well known. The first is the first peace treaty between Stephen king of England and David king of Scots, after David had invaded the north of England. 'A conference was held in that province, and a treaty was concluded between the two kings.' Richard of Hexham goes on to give the detail of a carefully worked-out *conventio.*[26] The concessions made by each party were

---

[21] *Regesta,* iii, no. 244; *Early Yorkshire Charters,* ed. W. Farrer, i, Edinburgh 1914, no. 103; *Charters of the honour of Mowbray 1107–1191,* ed. D. E. Greenway, London 1972, nos. 298, 194.
[22] R. H. C. Davis, *King Stephen,* 3rd edn, London 1990, 108–24.
[23] There are two texts, hereafter cited as Gloucester-Hereford 1 and Gloucester-Hereford 2. *Gloucester-Hereford 1*: date 1141 x 1143 and probably 1142 from *Historia Novella,* 72, *Gloucester Charters,* no. 95, facsimile copy in *Sir Christopher Hatton's Book of Seals,* ed. L. C. Loyd and D. M. Stenton, Oxford 1950, no. 212. *Gloucester-Hereford 2*: 1147 x 1150, *Gloucester Charters,* no. 96 (facsimile plate XIV), R. H. C. Davis, 'The treaty between William Earl of Gloucester and Roger Earl of Hereford', in *A medieval miscellany for Doris Mary Stenton,* ed. P. M. Barnes and C. F. Slade, Pipe Roll Society, ns 36, 1962, 139–46 (with facsimile plate XI).
[24] *The Charters of the Anglo-Norman Earls of Chester c.1071–1237,* ed. G. Barraclough, Record Society of Lancashire and Cheshire, cxxvi, 1988, no. 110, also in F. M. Stenton, *The First Century of English Feudalism,* 2nd edn, Oxford 1961, 250–3, 286–8, with facsimile in *New Palaeographical Society,* ii, plate 40.
[25] E. J. King, 'The anarchy of King Stephen's reign', *TRHS* 5th ser. 34, 1984, 133–53.
[26] *Chronicles of the reigns of Stephen, Henry II, and Richard I,* ed. R. Howlett, iii, RS 1886, 145–6.

carefully balanced. And the first concession was made by the Scots. 'Henry, son of David king of Scotland, did homage to King Stephen at York.' Richard of Hexham has the detail from someone who was there: 'according to the account of some, who state that they were present at that *conventio*,' Stephen promised not to grant out the earldom of Northumberland without having his court consider the claims of Henry to it. William of Malmesbury, writing in 1140, in considering this episode gives no detail but writes of the Scots king (who lived until 1153) as one of yesterday's men.[27] Now as he came south King David had taken the fealty of, and had taken hostages from, the northern magnates that they maintain faith with the Empress. As he headed north after this *conventio*, and his son travelled south to Stephen's Easter court, he had abandoned the high moral ground. It was there, in the early months of Stephen's reign, that the battle was fought.

It was fought also in patient dealing with individual members of the nobility, which only quite exceptionally became a matter of record. Such exceptions are to be found in the *conventiones* noted in charters issued by Stephen to Miles of Gloucester at Reading, all but certainly on the occasion of Henry I's burial early in January 1136.[28] They take the form of grants by Stephen. And very generous grants: 'the whole of his honour of Gloucester and Brecon, with all his lands, shrievalties, etc.,' some of them spelt out in a second document: *et ego ei in convencionem habeo sicut rex et dominus baroni meo*. John Horace Round was not impressed. 'Possibly the most instructive feature to be found in each charter is the striking illustration it affords of the method by which Stephen procured the adhesion of the turbulent and ambitious magnates. It is not so much a grant from a king to a subject as a *convencio* between equal powers.'[29]

It should rather be seen as both. We need to look for the arrangements which lie behind these parallel charters. The first question must be, has Miles of Gloucester done homage to Stephen? I would answer yes. But a further question arises, homage for what?[30] One of the charters for Miles of Gloucester concludes with this sentence: 'and know that I as lord and king make this agreement with him (*convencionavi ei*) as my baron and justice that I will not implead him concerning any tenancy which he held on the day on which king Henry was alive and dead, nor will I implead his heir'.[31] It should be noted that the *convencio* does not relate to his honour or to his lands. He had done homage in respect of these, and concerning them no more need be said. It relates rather to the *tenaturae*, here generally described as consisting of sheriffdoms and other things, with more detail being given in the other charter (and where you have more detail so that charter is much more clearly a *convencio*). In his treatment of the Treaty of Durham Richard of Hexham had similarly used the word *convencio* in the context of discussions in respect of an office, there not a sheriffdom or castellanship but an earldom, that of Northumberland.

Such an approach may offer a clue as to why these particulars charters survive. In the course of his debate with J. O. Prestwich over the detail of the charters issued to Geoffrey de Mandeville the late and much lamented Ralph Davis

---

[27] *Historia Novella*, 16.
[28] *Regesta*, iii, nos. 386–7. On multiple documents relating to the same transaction, see Cheyette, 'Sale of Carcassonne', 838.
[29] Round, 14.
[30] J. C. Holt, '1086', in *Domesday Studies*, ed. Holt, Woodbridge 1987, 43.
[31] *Regesta*, iii, no. 386.

referred to certain charters which in his view must have been part of the Mandeville archive, though they had since been lost. 'There must also have been at
least one lost charter of the king, for as a tenant-in-chief Geoffrey must have got
his lands confirmed when he gave Stephen his allegiance at the beginning of his
reign.'[32] He went on to say some interesting things; his dating of the key charter
of the Empress was in my view correct; but the assumption behind this statement
I think is wrong. If all of the laymen who did homage to Stephen in the first few
months of his reign were issued with charters in recognition of that fact, we have
to ask why none of the others have survived. And we need not presume that they
did homage. We have the *ipsissima verba* of Henry of Blois. 'King Henry my
uncle having gone the way of all flesh, and my brother Stephen having succeeded
in the kingdom, the aforesaid Robert [fitz Walter the Fleming] did homage and
swore an oath of fealty as was the custom, together with the other magnates of the
land.'[33] The relationships formed by these acts of homage might last the whole
reign.

The remaining *conventiones* to be considered here, which include the magnate
treaties already mentioned, date from the period after the Empress landed. It was
a period of civil war, and the first point that must be made about this group of
agreements is that they were entered into in time of war. In Gloucester-Hereford 1
this was specified as 'the war now going on between the Empress and King
Stephen'. The two earls looked to the end of the war, to the time when both of
them 'would have their lands and their rights again (*terras suas et sua recta
rehabuerint*)'. Until that blessed time came their freedom of action, and the scope
of their realistic ambition, were severely curtailed. A number of things they felt
they could do, and they used the existing routines of dispute settlement, familiar
to themselves and their followers, to provide for them. Records of agreement
were drawn up in duplicate: in Chester-Leicester CIROGRAPHUM and in Gloucester-Hereford 2 HEC EST COMPOSICIO AMORIS were cut through. The two Gloucester-Hereford agreements were sealed.[34]

The *conventio* during the civil war might be used for a variety of purposes.

1. It could record promises made regarding future alliances. Thus the Empress
in the summer of 1141. *Et convenciono*: 'I make this agreement with the same
Geoffrey earl of Essex that neither my lord the count of Anjou nor myself nor our
sons will make any peace or concord with the burgesses of London, without the
consent of earl Geoffrey, for they are his mortal enemies (*quia inimici eius sunt
mortales*).' Robert of Gloucester in the following year undertook not to make
peace or conclude a truce with anyone who sought to do down (*malum facere vel
de aliquo decrescere*) Miles of Gloucester earl of Hereford. In the agreement
between their sons in the late 1140s William of Gloucester promised Roger of

---

[32] R. H. C. Davis, comment on J. O. Prestwich, 'The treason of Geoffrey de Mandeville', *EHR*
ciii, 1988, 315.
[33] *English Lawsuits*, i, no. 292, from *Adami de Domerham Historia de rebus gestis Glastonien-
sibus*, ed. T. Hearne, Oxford 1727, ii, 310.
[34] Gloucester-Hereford 2 retains the imprint of the seal; only the stub of Gloucester-Hereford 1
survived in 1640 when the facsimile was made: *Book of Seals*, no. 212. Round, 380, noted
similarities between the latter agreement and Henry I's treaty with Robert count of Flanders in
1110, an early example of a sealed chirograph: *Diplomatic Documents preserved in the Public
Record Office*, i (1101–1272), ed. P. Chaplais, London 1964, no. 2.

Hereford assistance 'specifically to disinherit Gilbert de Lacy (*nominatim ad exherandum Gillebertum de Lasci*)'; while Roger of Hereford in his turn promised not to make peace nor any truce with Gilbert de Lacy unless with the assent of William de Braose.[35]

2.   It could provide its own form of castle-guard. The chronicles are full of the tyrannies of the castlemen. It is not surprising that so many of the *conventiones* of the reign come to focus on the control of castles. This is most obvious in the case of the agreement between the earls of Chester and Leicester: 'the earl of Leicester has promised earl Ranulf that he will destroy the castle of Ravenstone unless earl Ranulf shall allow that it shall remain'. This was another of the Empress's promises to Geoffrey de Mandeville in the summer of 1141: 'if I cannot gain the bishop of London's castle at Stortford, then I promise him that I will cause it to be razed to the ground (*tune eo convenciono quod faciam illud prosternere et ex toto cadere*)'. Roger de Mowbray granted Selby Abbey a small manor next York, 'on this understanding that when I have recovered custody of the castle of York (*ea tamen conventione ut quando recuperabo custodiam castelli Eboraci*) I will give the monks an exchange'. Both in 1149 and in 1153 Henry of Anjou was brought into agreement with bishop Jocelin of Salisbury regarding the custody of Devizes castle. And, as we shall see, a number of castles were specified in the final peace settlement of 1153.[36]

3.   It could be used to spell out the precise terms of a warranty.[37] 'The bond of trust arising from lordship and homage should be mutual,' says *Glanvill,* 'so that the lord owes as much to the man on account of lordship as the man owes to the lord on account of homage, save only reverence. Therefore if anyone gives to another a tenement in return for service and homage, and a third party afterwards proves his right to it against the tenant, the lord will be bound to warrant him that tenement or give him equivalent lands in exchange.' Some of the texts from the end of the civil war, anticipating the general settlement, spell out the warranty in some detail. An example was the grant by the earl of Chester to Lincoln Cathedral of two manors in Northamptonshire in recompense for damage done in time of war. One of the possible claimants, Walter de Wahull, remitted his rights; but claims were also anticipated from the heir of Norman de Verdun or the heirs of William Meschin. A *convencio* related to these, and was confirmed by Duke Henry: *ego autem hanc conuencionem firmam esse uolens interposui me fidejussorem hac conditione,* that if necessary he would give the diocese demesne lands to the equivalent value.[38]

4.   It could provide security for the future performance of promises made. David

---

[35] *Regesta,* iii, no. 275; Gloucester-Hereford 1; Gloucester-Hereford 2; Z. N. Brooke and C. N. L. Brooke, 'Hereford cathedral dignitaries in the Twelfth Century – Supplement', *Cambridge Historical Journal* 8, 1944–6, 185.

[36] Chester-Leicester; *Regesta,* iii, no. 275; *Mowbray Charters,* no. 255; *Regesta,* iii, nos. 795–6; *Regesta,* iii, no. 272.

[37] The starting-point of any discussion on warranty is now P. R. Hyams, 'Warranty and good lordship in Twelfth Century England', *Law and History Review* 5, 1987, 437–503. Note also D. Postles, 'Gifts in frankalmoign, warranty of land, and feudal society', *Cambridge Law Journal* 50, 1991, 330–46.

[38] *Tractatus de legibus et consuetudinibus regni Anglie qui Glanvilla vocatur,* ed. G. D. G. Hall, Nelson's Medieval Texts, London 1965, IX, 4; *Regesta,* iii, nos. 491–2.

of Scotland had taken hostages from the northern magnates in the early months of the reign. The concern for security is an insistent concern of the *conventiones* made during the civil war. 'They are all confirmed by oaths and are guaranteed by leading vassals as *obsides*: that is, guarantors or hostages.'[39] Matilda, responding to Geoffrey de Mandeville's demands in the summer of 1141, made sweeping concessions in this regard. The count of Anjou her lord would give Geoffrey security *manu sua propria*, as would Henry her son. If it were possible the king of France would be a hostage; if not he would offer his hand. There were *obsides per fidem et testes*, present at the making of the agreement, and others, *obsides per fidem*, who were not. Henry did indeed guarantee the parallel charter which Matilda issued at the same time for Aubrey de Vere.[40]

At the end of the same charter Matilda promised the security of the community of the English church, *Christianitas Anglie*. Here we are on difficult ground, difficult for all parties. What part should the church properly play in the making of these *conventiones*? In the autumn of 1141 Archbishop Theobald and Henry of Blois, 'the archbishop and the legate,' offered themselves as hostages for the performance of the most complicated *conventio* which secured the exchange of Stephen and Robert of Gloucester.[41] (More work here for Geoffrey de Waterville.) 'It is the height of folly to achieve nothing but hatred by one's efforts,' Henry of Winchester had mused, after his mediation in 1140 had failed;[42] but this is indeed what he and Theobald achieved during the following year. A very clear indication of just how angry the Empress's followers were made by their treatment by the higher clergy in 1141 is provided by Brian fitz Count's letter to Henry of Blois. 'I am sorry for the poor and their plight, when the church provides scarcely any refuge for them, for they will die if peace be longer delayed.'[43]

It is not surprising that in the treaty which survives from elsewhere in the Empress's camp around the same time, i.e. Gloucester-Hereford 1, the clergy are nowhere mentioned. But by the end of the reign the clergy are more in evidence. In Chester-Leicester the bishop of Lincoln, who presided, was prepared to be named as a security for the agreement, on his Christianity (*posuerunt eundem episcopum obsidem huius convencionis super Christianitatem suam*). Theobald now legate received the affidation of Duke Henry and named followers, and of the bishop of Salisbury, in their 1153 agreement regarding Devizes Castle. Affidation *in manu* was routine in agreements at all levels. And in some charters from late in the reign there is at least the suggestion that groups of individuals and communities were working out how far their responsibilities could extend. In 1154 a grant by Roger de Mowbray to Rievaulx Abbey was secured in this way: 'we have sworn in the hand of Robert the dean in the presence of the lord Roger the archbishop and the whole chapter of York and the same church of York'.[44]

---

[39] M. M. Chibnall, 'Anglo-French relations in the work of Orderic Vitalis', in *Documenting the past. Essays in honour of G. P. Cuttino*, ed. J. S. Hamilton and P. J. Bradley, Woodbridge 1989, 17.
[40] *Regesta*, iii, no. 275; *Regesta*, iii, nos. 634–5; and the comments of M. M. Chibnall, *The Empress Matilda*, Oxford 1991, 108–12.
[41] *Historia Novella*, 69–70.
[42] *Historia Novella*, 45.
[43] H. W. C. Davis, 'Henry of Blois and Brian Fitz-Count', *EHR* xxv, 1910, 301–3.
[44] On affidation *in manu* see Round, 384–7; F. M. Stenton (ed.), *Transcripts of Charters relating to Gilbertine Houses*, Lincoln Record Society, 18, 1922, xxix–xxx; Chibnall, 'Anglo-French relations', 17–18. The examples cited in this paragraph are from: Chester-Leicester; *Regesta*, iii,

Who was responsible for negotiating these agreements? The clergy, as has been seen, were not altogether trusted at times, and for their part had misgivings as to what was properly their role. They might at times mediate, but this was not seen as their primary function. It did, however, lie at the heart of the role of those identified in the texts as the men (*homines*) or friends (*amici*) of the disputing parties. It is they who were the *nuntii*, the go-betweens, who can be seen criss-crossing England at certain key periods of Stephen's reign. The *conventiones* are their hard-bargaining, their long drawn-out discussions. Their aims were the same whether their principals were in dispute as to the succession or, as in a case involving Southwick Priory, Hampshire, 'because of some exchanges of land . . . and because of some common pastures'. In the latter case, which spanned a number of years, 'the justice of the lord of Porchester and neighbours and friends of the church met several times without managing to end the business so as to take the interests of both parties into account'.[45] The lord of Porchester here was Richard du Hommet, the constable of Duke Henry. In Gloucester-Hereford 1 it is seen as the job of the sound men of each earl to arrange (*de probis hominibus utriusque comitis considerabuntur*) for a permanent peace between their lords.[46] The magnates' peace was the work of their officials.

In these discussions the stakes were high, for in discharging their duty to counsel their lord, his men and his friends were protecting his and their own integrity. The idea of integrity leads naturally to considering problems of divided loyalty. There is much discussion in the documents, particularly from those late in the reign, about the constraints upon individuals' freedom of action presented by homage, and it may be that we see a development of the idea of liege homage. Book IX of *Glanvill* starts with various definitions about homage and what constitutes liege homage: *unum . . . oportet esse precipuum et cum ligeancia factum*. 'It is evident from this that a vassal may not attack his lord without breaking the faith of his homage, except perhaps in self-defence or when he goes by royal command with the king's army against his lord. . . . If anyone has done several homages for different fees to different lords who are attacking each other, and his liege lord commands him to go personally with him against another of his lords, he must obey his command in this matter, but saving to that other lord the service for the fee which he holds of him.'

This passage leads the reader straight back to the final years of the anarchy. It calls to mind most clearly Chester-Leicester, which in terms of feudal obligation is exemplary. It is useful to bear in mind that Robert of Leicester served as justiciar until his death in 1168, and himself played a major part in the negotiation of the 1153 peace settlement.[47] This agreement is predicated on homage and its obligations. The two earls envisaged a situation in which they might have to fight

no. 796; *Early Yorkshire Charters*, ix, ed. C. T. Clay, Yorkshire Archaeological Society Record Ser., Extra Ser., vii, 1952, no. 151 (= *Mowbray Charters*, no. 236).

[45] *English Lawsuits*, i, no. 343, translated in *The Cartularies of Southwick Priory*, ed. K. A. Hanna, i, Hampshire Record Series, ix, 1988, I no. 121. The texts in this cartulary would seem to support the suggestion that William Mauduit did not secure the custody of Porchester: J. H. Round, *The Commune of London and other studies*, London 1899, 82; *The Beauchamp cartulary*, ed. Emma Mason, Pipe Roll Society, ns 43, 1980, liii–liv, no. 167.

[46] Stenton, *First Century*, 286; *Mowbray Charters*, no. 318; *Gloucester Charters*, no. 95.

[47] *Gesta Stephani*, ed. K. R. Potter and R. H. C. Davis, Oxford 1976, 234; D. Crouch, *The Beaumont Twins*, Cambridge 1986, 86.

against each other for different lords: 'if it be necessary for the earl of Leicester to go upon the earl of Chester with his liege lord'. They had not started with *Glanvill*. They had started with their own private quarrels, but almost immediately they had found their freedom of action constrained by having to recognise their obligations to, having to reserve, the fealty owed to their liege lord (*salva fide ligii domini sui*). They had to work their way around the implications of the homages they had performed, and which their men had done to them. Gloucester-Hereford 2 allowed each earl to aid the other against all men, unless against his lord Henry in person. In the case to Gloucester's undertaking to Hereford, this was followed by the promise to disinherit Gilbert de Lacy, but then saving the position of hostage in which Gloucester served in the agreement of Hereford with Leicester.[48] The securing of one agreement could easily come to constrain future alliances.

The final document of the reign to be discussed is the peace settlement of 1153, headlined in the *Regesta* as a 'treaty between King Stephen and Duke Henry'.[49] As a *conventio* it is exemplary. It is exemplary because it is predicated on the understanding that the act of homage was substantive, while the *conventio* qualified it in some way. In return for the transfer of the kingdom, described as a gift and a confirmation, Henry did homage to Stephen 'in the terms of the agreements that have been made between us, as set out in this charter (*per conventiones inter nos prolocutas, que in hac carta continentur*)'. Then Stephen's heir did liege homage to Henry, in return for the grant of lands carefully specified, for it was understood that only specific grants would be honoured. The next set of concessions were made to Stephen: the earls and barons of the duke, who had never been his men, because of the honour done to their lord, did homage to Stephen, *salvis conventionibus inter me et ducem factis*. Those who had previously done him homage swore fealty. Then, to balance this concession in its turn, the earls and barons of the king did liege homage to the duke, saving their fealty to the king.

A number of points may be highlighted here, as they concern those who had been Angevin supporters during the anarchy, here described as 'the earls and barons of the duke'. By the terms of the agreement, they were to do homage to King Stephen. Again the question may be asked, homage for what? The charter makes it clear that the question had been asked; and the answer had been *pro honore*, 'for the honour done to their lord'. We may detect an echo of this in *Glanvill* IX, 2: 'for mere lordship no homage is done except to the king'. The homage that they did was conditional, *salvis conventionibus*, saving the conditional agreements that had been made. There is at least the suggestion here of another echo, here from the passage in William of Malmesbury in which he described Robert of Gloucester as having done homage to Stephen in 1136 *sub conditione quadam*, 'that is to say, for as long as the king maintained his rank unimpaired and kept the agreement'.[50] The Angevin party were particularly sensitive on these matters, but all were affected. The performance of these homages, in the terms of the agreement, recognised the integrity and protected the tenures of those who had taken different parts in the civil war. Two charters survive (prob-

---

[48] *Gloucester Charters*, no. 96.
[49] *Regesta*, iii, no. 272.
[50] *Historia Novella*, 18. There has been extensive commentary on this passage, which I shall consider in my revised edition for Oxford Medieval Texts.

ably) from the Easter court of 1154 in which lands are confirmed up to that date.[51] It may be suggested that it was presumed that by then all the necessary homages would have been performed.

This is a short paper under a broad title, one which can be defended if at all only by the addition of the phrase, 'some reflections'. The main reflection in conclusion must be that any longer study must start from the diplomatic. Galbraith in printing the grant of Holme Lacy in 1085, said that the evidence on which he relied to put it in context provided 'an unsafe foundation for the history of this critical period owing to the neglect of its diplomatic.' Were he writing today, he would surely except the study of episcopal *acta*, but for acts of laymen would hardly need to modify his judgement. The document he printed 'still uses the venerable form of the chirograph, which seems to have been the normal species of private deed at least as far back as the early tenth century'.[52] By the late Saxon period it had become very popular, and particularly, it has been suggested, among the laity, since the document's 'authenticity could be tested by illiterates with a practised eye'.[53] In the Norman period it seems to lie dormant, until the Angevins rediscovered its utility.[54]

Why had this happened. To the monk of Crowland who wrote the pseudo-Ingulf, surveying an archive to which he did little credit, the story seemed clear. Chirographs had disappeared because the Normans did not like the look of them. 'Chirographs made in the English way, which up until the time of King Edward were ratified by the faithful who were present by gold crosses and other sacred signs, were condemned by the Normans who termed chirographs charters.'[55] This may be bad history, but it was good diplomatic; what the Normans did not like, it was suggested, was that the chirograph was written in English, and it was authenticated in the wrong way. The Norman Conquest was indeed marked by a change in the language of dispute-settlement. This marked a very clear disjunction in any archive. I have noted only one post-Conquest chirograph in English, preserved in the cartulary of Bath priory.[56]

Chirographs written in Latin had a better chance of survival in the Anglo-Norman period, but none the less those chances were not good, and those that did survive are not always identified as chirographs. To take one example, which could serve for a number of others. The Ramsey chronicle preserves the text of a

[51] *Regesta*, iii, nos. 696, 866.
[52] Galbraith, 355. A range of examples of chirographs will be found among the 'miscellaneous texts' in P. H. Sawyer, *Anglo-Saxon Charters. An annotated list and bibliography*, London 1968, nos. 1429–81.
[53] P. Wormald, 'Charters, law and the settlement of disputes in Anglo-Saxon England', in *The Settlement of Disputes in Early Medieval Europe*, ed. W. Davies and P. Fouracre, Cambridge 1986, 161–2.
[54] M. T. Clanchy, *From Memory to Written Record*, London 1979, 65–7; and note J. C. Holt, 'Magna Carta 1215–127: the legal and social context', in *Law in medieval life and thought*, ed. E. B. King and S. J. Ridyard, Sewannee 1990, 15–16.
[55] *Rerum Anglicarum Scriptorum Veterum Tom. I*, ed. W. Fulman, Oxford 1684, 70.
[56] Cambridge, Corpus Christi College, MS 111, p. 95 contains a *forewarde* between abbots Wulfwold and Aelfsige and William Hoset regarding land in Charlcombe, identified as a chirograph by the rubric; printed T. Madox, *Formulare Anglicanum*, London 1702, 73 (where it is Madox who has supplied the facing Latin text); *Monasticon*, ii, 264; *Two Chartularies of the Priory of St Peter at Bath*, ed. W. Hunt, Somerset Record Society, vii, 1893, i, no. 48.

notification of Herbert abbot of Ramsey dated 17 June 1088 of the terms on which William Pecche and his wife were to hold Over for the terms of their lives. It was a grant on certain conditions, and bore all the marks of a chirograph, but it is only a later reference in a charter of Henry I that allows it to be identified as such.[57] More often still, it is the rubricator, with the text in front of him, who notes that the original of the document was in chirograph form. Thus in the case of an exchange of land between Faritius abbot of Abingdon and Ansketillus one of his men, dated 7 March 1105. After noting the witnesses, the Abingdon chronicler goes on to note that for the further security of the lay party two sealed writs were issued by Henry earl of Warwick, the lord of Chesterton, one of which remained in the treasury of the abbey and the other with Ansketil.[58]

This leads on to the second point to which the monk of Crowland drew attention. The chirograph was not sealed.[59] The scribe of the Red Book of Thorney, writing in the mid thirteenth century, felt it necessary to preface two of his earliest documents with an apology: 'it is to be noted that the two following charters are without seals and old, and yet they are authentic (*caracterate*), for in the old days the faithful offered their goods and possessions upon the altar with charters of this kind'. There followed *conventiones* of Aubrey de Vere and of his son relating to their holding Twywell in fee-farm.[60] Where the agreement which the chirograph recorded was confirmed perhaps a little later by the sealed writ or charter of a lord, it was easy to lose even the clue offered by the word *conventio*. Thus c.1150 Roger de Mowbray issued a general notification 'that I have granted and by my charter have confirmed' to Durham cathedral priory land in Blyborough Lincs that had been given them by Robert of St Martin. Behind this lay a gift drawn up in the form of a chirograph, attached to which there is preserved the knife by which seisin was delivered to the church.[61] In these two documents, the terse charter with its impressive seal, and the much more long-winded chirograph with its rusty knife, we see the new and the old – or so at least it appeared to the monastic archivists on whom we depend for so much of our knowledge of the Anglo-Norman world.

The famous story of Richard de Lucy pronouncing *ex cathedra*, 'it was not the custom in the past for every petty knight to have a seal', turns on this point: earlier in the proceedings, 'by the king's permission, the chirographs of purchase and gifts were read before everyone, as were charters of confirmation', and Gilbert de Baillol had objected that his ancestor's chirographs were not sealed.[62] The test of authenticity of the chirograph lay not in a seal but in the signatures of those present, as the monk of Crowland noted, and as Gilbert would have known perfectly well. The point is nicely developed in another of the Bath texts, which

---

[57] *Chronicon Abbatiae Ramseseiensis*, ed. W. D. Macray, RS 1886, 228–9 (royal charter = *Regesta*, ii, no. 1629), 233 (1088 chirograph). The case is fully discussed in J. Hudson, 'Life-grants of land and the development of inheritance in Anglo-Norman England', *ante* xii, 67–80.

[58] *Chronicon Monasterii de Abingdon*, ed. J. Stevenson, ii, RS 1858, 136–7; and for other chirographs identified in this way, ii, 18–19 (dated 14 March 1089), 27–8, 176–7.

[59] The sealed chirograph is a hybrid document. It may be in recognition of this that neither of the Gloucester-Hereford agreements is termed a chirograph, though using its form: above, p. 121. The matter needs better attention than it has been given here.

[60] Cambridge University Library, Additional MS 3021, fol. 227v–228r.

[61] *Mowbray Charters*, no. 89; K. Major, 'Blyborough Charters', in *Stenton Miscellany*, 206–7 (with facsimiles); Clanchy, 24.

[62] *Battle Chronicle*, 214–15.

shows abbot John 'sitting at his court with his friends and his barons', engaged in the most earnest discussion of diplomatic. It came to judgement (and so to Van Caenegem's collection): 'the man who purports to be the legal heir shall prove irrefutably what he has just claimed in support of his case by at least two free and lawful witnesses . . . or by a signed and credible chirograph (*chirographo credibiliter signato*)'. It was part of the obligations of those who are named in chirographs and *conventiones* to appear in court to make what was termed 'a legal record'; the phrase is found, for example, in Gloucester-Hereford 1 where it is seen as the particular responsibility of the go-betweens. A slight contrast is offered by a document of more local interest, a grant to Sawtry Abbey by Henry of Costentin. 'This agreement was fully recognised thereafter and recorded (*tota recognita fuit postmodum et recordata*) before Henry archdeacon of Huntingdon, and Adam his son, and Alexander his nephew.' Of all the chroniclers of Stephen's reign, Henry of Huntingdon was the one most familiar with local dispute settlement.[63]

By the agreement that settled the civil war it was made clear that the future Henry II would not recognise claims to title based on grants made in Stephen's reign. It was necessary for the grants to Faversham Abbey to be confirmed in it for him to rest in peace. In terms of record-keeping, this provided a further disjunction. And within a few years of Stephen's death the unsealed chirograph had lost much of any residual authority it might have claimed. This was because of changes in the common law which withdrew the protection of the royal court from what Glanvill referred to as *privatae conventiones*. 'He could', suggests Paul Hyams, 'be enunciating a rule that would offer remedies for wrongs connected with agreements only if they had in some way ceased to be "private", by acquiring some royal or public interest.' He discusses proceedings in the royal court in 1201 relating to the manor of Cockfield, in which we have Jocelin of Brakelond to put flesh on the bones of the official record. The abbey's case against its tenant turned on the validity of a number of its chirographs. 'The knights having been sworn said they knew nothing about our charter or our private arrangements (*privatae conventiones*), but that they believed Adam his father and grandfather had for a hundred years back held the manors in fee-farm, one after the other on the days when they were alive and dead.' Lords hereafter would need professional advice in drafting documents 'from someone skilled in the practice of the *curia regis*'.[64] This is the last of the disjunctions which have contributed to the paucity of the surviving archives. Once the Angevin royal court refused to recognise what it termed *privatae conventiones*, it sentenced to oblivion many of the routine records of dispute settlement in Anglo-Saxon and Anglo-Norman times.

This change must have happened quite suddenly. It is not suprising to find, and it is perhaps worth noting, that a majority of the records used in this discussion either survive as originals or are taken from cartularies made in the mid-twelfth

[63] *English Lawsuits*, i, no. 226; Gloucester-Hereford 1; BL, Harley Charter 83 B 6, facsimile in *Palaeographical Society*, 2nd ser., ii, plate 39; and compare Henry of Huntingdon's description of Stephen at Oxford in 1136, 'ubi recordatus est et confirmavit pacta que . . . concesserat in die coronationis sue', Huntingdon, 258.

[64] P. R. Hyams, 'The charter as a source for the early common law', *Journal of Legal History* 12, 1991, 173–89; *The Chronicle of Jocelin of Brakelond*, ed. H. E. Butler, Nelson's Medieval Texts, London 1949, 123–4.

century. Here the Abingdon chronicle is a key text, established by Stenton's study to be 'the work of an author who ceased writing early in the reign of Henry II'.[65] Of like date, and no less important though much less well-known, is the cartulary of Bath Priory.[66] They are full of *privatae conventiones*, many of them relating to the establishment of feudal tenures; and these are documents of a distinctly consensual kind. In the Abingdon chronicle grants of land in fee, for services that can be seen coming to be more closely specified, are several times described as *pactiones*.[67] In the Bath cartulary there are a number of texts that might be taken to typify the *privata conventio*, and they were indeed taken by Madox as the earliest representatives in a group of texts which he categorised as 'covenants of divers kinds'.[68] *Hec est conventio et concordia* by which William Hoset on 20 February 1123 was reconciled with the monks on all matters of dispute between them. 'He was received into fraternity, swearing on the text of the gospels and by the same gospels, that he would be a true friend and faithful man to the monks in all places as to his lords.'[69] Friendship, brotherhood, lordship, all together in a single package, mixed together in men's minds. In the earliest texts particularly grants of fraternity play a key role in dispute settlement.[70] It would be difficult, without a good deal of qualification, to argue from such texts that we are here in 'a truly feudal world'.[71] In these texts relationships that we would regard as feudal are part only of a much broader package.

The evidence that has been discussed in this paper might be held to support the approach of such scholars as Paul Hyams and Stephen White, in questioning when if at all the 'truly feudal world' ever existed. 'It is more an Angevin lawyers' ideal of how lordships ought to have been run in the old days,' it has been suggested, 'than any memory of how they actually were run.'[72] The documents printed by F. M. Stenton in his classic study of the *First Century*, suggested Stephen White, 'reveal honorial courts arranging or ratifying concords, rather than making judgments'.[73] Stenton was concerned primarily with lay lordships, but while procedures might differ in church lordships, in essence their work was the same.

The story of Stephen's reign is the story of a disputed succession. It is hardly surprising that the records which tell this story have much to offer those who are interested in dispute settlement. Stephen became king because of a coup, but his position was only confirmed because of an agreement with the church as an estate and of individual agreements with the lay magnates, of which those with Miles of

---

[65] F. M. Stenton, *The Early History of the Abbey of Abingdon*, Reading 1913, v, 4–6.
[66] Corpus Christi College, Cambridge MS 111, where the final text in the main hand, pp. 128–9 is dated by James to 1165: M. R. James, *A descriptive catalogue of the manuscripts in the library of Corpus Christi College, Cambridge*, Cambridge 1912, 242.
[67] *Chron. Abingdon*, ii, 131–2, 134–5.
[68] Madox, *Formulare Anglicanum*, 73–4.
[69] *Monasticon*, ii, 269.
[70] E.g. *Chester Charters*, no. 2 (date 1090, from *Chron. Abingdon*, ii, 19); *Ramsey Cartulary*, i, 127–8 (date 1081), 129 (date 1091 x 1102). For grants of fraternity attached to gospel books see C. Clark, 'British Library Additional MS. 40,000 ff. 1v–12r', *ante* vii, 1985, 50–68.
[71] The phrase is that of S. F. C. Milsom, 'Introduction' to F. Pollock and F. W. Maitland, *The History of English Law*, 2nd edn revised, 2 vols, Cambridge 1968, i, xxxvi, reflecting ideas more fully developed in his *The Legal Framework of English Feudalism*, Cambridge 1976.
[72] P. Hyams, reviewing Milsom, *Legal Framework*, in *EHR* xciii, 1978, 858.
[73] 'Inheritances and Legal Arguments', 102.

Gloucester and Robert of Gloucester are the best known.[74] When faced with Scottish invasions, he concluded compromise agreements with King David and Henry his son.[75] In just such a way had William Rufus and Henry I dealt with their brother Robert.[76] The northern barons made agreements with the Scots in their turn;[77] just as did those with lands on the Welsh marches with the princes and chiefs of the Welsh.[78] This was how things were done, by an exchange of messengers, and by face to face discussions, 'so as to take the interests of all parties into account'. It was the tragedy of England that for so long the interests of the protagonists as to the succession could not be reconciled, though in 1140, 1141 and 1146 the terms of a possible agreement were tabled for discussion. They can have differed little in their essence from the terms which were accepted in 1153. It might be possible to argue, though it would have to be on another occasion, that in the context of medieval disputes, 'nineteen long winters' was not a particularly long time.

---

[74] *Regesta*, iii, no. 271, and the comments of *Historia Novella*, 15, and Huntingdon, 258; above, p. 120.

[75] In 1136: see Richard of Hexham, 144–6, discussed above, pp. 119–20. In 1139: Richard of Hexham, 176–8; John of Hexham, in *Symeonis Monachi Opera Omnia*, ed. T. Arnold, ii, RS 1885, 300 (*pax convenit inter duos reges*), discussed by Judith Green, 'Anglo-Scottish relations, 1066–1174', in *England and her neighbours, 1066–1453. Essays in honour of Pierre Chaplais*, ed. M. Jones and M. Vale, London 1989, 66.

[76] In 1091: *The Peterborough Chronicle 1070–1154*, ed. Cecily Clark, 2nd edn, Oxford 1970, pp. 18–19; *De Gestis Regum*, ii, 363. In 1101: *Peterborough Chronicle*, p. 29; *De Gestis Regum*, ii, 472. For a useful discussion focussing on the role of pledges see Tabuteau, 163–9.

[77] E.g. the terms on which Ranulf of Chester did homage to David of Scotland, *convenit enim sermo inter eos ut pro Karlel haberet honorem de Lanecastre*: John of Hexham, 323.

[78] Rice Merrick in *Morganiae Archaiographia. A book of the antiquities of Glamorganshire*, ed. B. Ll. James, South Wales Record Society, i, 1983, 39, 54 provides only notes of documents, but sufficient clues as to the diplomatic; and see D. Crouch, 'The earliest original charter of a Welsh king', *Bulletin of the Board of Celtic Studies* xxxvi, 1989, 125–31. While this paper has been in press, Dr Crouch has been kind enough to send me a further important paper on the themes I have discussed: 'A Norman *conventio* and the bonds of lordship in the reign of Stephen', forthcoming in *Studies presented to Sir James Holt*, ed. J. Hudson and G. Garnett, Cambridge 1993.

ADELA OF BLOIS AND IVO OF CHARTRES:
PIETY, POLITICS, AND THE PEACE IN
THE DIOCESE OF CHARTRES

Kimberly A. LoPrete

In January 1101 as regent for her crusading husband, Adela, countess of Blois, Chartres, Châteaudun, and Meaux, convoked before the assembled members of her *curia* at Coulommiers the bishops of Meaux and Troyes, the abbots of Lagny and Rebais, and representatives of the abbot of Ste Foi, Conques. These high-ranking ecclesiastics, assisted by other clerics from their own entourages as well as by clerics from Adela's household staff, were enjoined by Adela to settle the dispute between the abbeys of Rebais and Conques over possession of Ste Foi, Coulommiers purportedly given to each house by Adela's father-in-law, Thibaud III, sometime between 1065 and his death in 1089. Meeting under lay auspices at Adela's court, this special ecclesiastical tribunal heard the pleadings of both parties to the dispute and rendered judgment. According to the document recording these proceedings, drawn up by one of Adela's chaplains and sometime chancellor, the tribunal's judgment was respected and thus, after a series of solely ecclesiastical councils had earlier failed to impose a settlement, this long-standing inter-monastic dispute was finally peaceably resolved.[1]

This case illustrates how, at the opening of the twelfth century, the perceived duties of lay lords as protectors of the church could intersect and, indeed, overlap those of churchmen themselves, even with the acknowledgment of distinct spheres of lay and ecclesiastical jurisdiction. In a society whose members believed that all power came ultimately from God (whatever the various means for mediating that power to individuals of diverse stations), both high-ranking ecclesiastics and lay princes comprised a ruling earthly elite that was deemed responsible for maintaining social order and dispensing justice so that *Christianitas* could flourish and all people some day attain their eternal rewards.[2] Despite the tensions and even open conflicts that erupted over the precise demarcation of jurisdictional boundaries between lay lords and members of the ecclesiastical hierarchy concerned to reform the institutional church of their day, it remained true that churchmen often chose to support powerful lay lords who respected certain ecclesiastical prerogatives as a means both to ensure a modicum of stability in their circumscriptions and to foster the actual implementation of their reforming ideals.

---

[1] Gustave Desjardins, ed., *Cartulaire de l'abbaye de Conques en Rouergue*, Paris 1879, 340–42 no. 470.

[2] For a discussion of *Christianitas* as 'a common religious observance (*cultus*) overseen and enforced by the king together with his lords and bishops', see John Van Engen, 'The Christian Middle Ages as an Historiographical Problem', *American Historical Review* 91, 1986, 539–41.

At the same time, lay lords who acted as sponsors of church reform were often spared the potentially debilitating effects attendant upon the imposition of ecclesiastical sanctions and could benefit from the enhanced authority which accrued, in the eyes of their contemporaries, to protectors of the church and promoters of the fully religious life. These lords were also believed to benefit from divine support of their position as earthly rulers through the intercession of churchmen's prayers. Though it is difficult for the historian to gauge the level of any divine support, as it is likewise difficult to measure degrees of enhanced authority, both could be reflected in practice in the continued loyalty of powerful followers and military victories. While at first sight the implementation of reform measures could undercut traditional sources of a lay lord's power, more intangible factors such as enhanced authority and the support of influential ecclesiastics could increase a given lord's power in relation to competing lords in a wider political arena; in addition, certain reform measures could be implemented in ways that resulted in the confirmation of specific lay juridical or economic prerogatives.[3] It should also be noted that some churchmen could actively impede ecclesiastical reform as effectively as some lay lords.

This paper examines the interpenetration of piety and politics as it was played out in the diocese of Chartres during the episcopacy of Ivo, a leading reformer and canonist, at which time (November 1090 through December 1115) the most powerful lay lord in his bishopric was the count (or countess) of Blois, Châteaudun, Chartres, and Meaux, the preponderance of whose core patrimonial domains (including the castles at Blois, Châteaudun, and Chartres) lay within the diocese of Chartres.[4] At the time of Ivo's consecration, Stephen-Henry, the eldest son of Thibaud III, had been acting as count for just over one year. Stephen ruled with the active assistance of his royal-born wife, Adela, the daughter of William the Conqueror, until his departure on the first crusade in October 1096, at which time Adela ruled as regent for their minor sons. Stephen returned to France sometime in 1099 but, late in 1100, would depart again for the Holy Land where he would die a martyr's death in May 1102. Adela assumed authority as regent during her husband's second absence and, as I have demonstrated elsewhere, would continue to act as acknowledged head of both branches of the Thibaudian family after Stephen's death until her own retirement to a monastery, about four-and-a-half years after the death of the bishop Ivo.[5]

In addition to detailing comital-episcopal relations in the diocese of Chartres, this paper will argue that Adela, especially, fostered good relations with the influential Ivo as a means to undergird her exercise of comital authority across the

---

[3] The role of lay lords in ecclesiastical affairs is the subject of a growing body of literature; for an exemplary recent study of one region of France, see Constance B. Bouchard, *Sword, Miter and Cloister: Nobility and the Church in Burgundy, 980–1198*, Ithaca, N.Y., 1987. Gregory VII's contrasting attitudes to Adela's father, William the Conqueror, and king Philip I of France as well as the reform measures of Adela's father-in-law, Thibaud III, are discussed in my unpublished Ph.D. dissertation, 'A Female Ruler in Feudal Society: Adela of Blois (ca. 1067–ca. 1137)', University of Chicago, 1991, ch. 5.4.

[4] For overviews of the life and career of Ivo, see Rolf Sprandel, *Ivo von Chartres und seine Stellung in der Kirchengeschichte*, Stuttgart 1962; and Lynn K. Barker, 'History, Reform, and Law in the Work of Ivo of Chartres', unpublished Ph.D. dissertation, University of North Carolina at Chapel Hill, 1988.

[5] LoPrete, 'Adela' (as in n. 3); see also Kimberly A. LoPrete, 'The Anglo-Norman Card of Adela of Blois', *Albion* 22, 1990, 5692–89.

widespread domains she ruled. Comital-episcopal cooperation appears most clearly in the promulgation and enforcement of peace statutes in the diocese of Chartres and in the promotion of ecclesiastical reform and renewal. Likewise, despite a few incidents of open conflict, it will be seen that Ivo could and did use both his ecclesiastical authority and legal acumen to support Adela's political agenda. Circumstances suggest that Adela, as a female ruler who, 'according to the custom of the day' (as Baudry of Bourgueil felicitously phrased it) was not personally trained in mounted armed combat, had a particular interest in working to gain the support of influential ecclesiastics such as the bishop Ivo in order to enhance her effective authority as a ruler.[6]

Underlying the presentation of this material is a more general concern to counter the prevailing view in the modern historical literature of the presumed weakness of the Thibaudian counts vis-à-vis their princely peers in northern France from the family's loss of Tours to the Angevins in 1044 until the emergence of a county of Champagne in the second half of the twelfth century.[7] Evidence adduced to support such a view of Thibaudian weakness includes the family's inability consistently to control or influence episcopal elections in dioceses where they exercised diverse prerogatives of lordship. However, consideration of both the extent and location of Thibaudian lands and rights indicates that the family's on-the-ground situation was not strictly comparable to that of their contemporaries and peers.

During Adela's tenure as countess the lands and rights of the senior line of the Thibaudian family lay in twelve different dioceses; counting those of the cadet branch of the family, Thibaudian lands and rights fell in a total of thirteen episcopal sees.[8] Granted, significant concentrations of Stephen and Adela's domains lay in the dioceses of Chartres, Orleans, Bourges, Sens, and Meaux, but only in the bishoprics of Chartres and Meaux can it be said that their holdings corresponded to a major extent of the diocese. And these two dioceses bordered

[6] Baudry, carmen 134 v. 35, ed. Karlheinz Hilbert, *Baldricus Burgulianus Carmina*, Heidelberg 1979, 150.
[7] The chimera of Thibaudian family weakness is in part attributable to varying critera of assessment; it is compounded by the lack of any thorough study of all the lands, rights, and effective power in the hands of any one count in the context of the shifting political and territorial alignments of the eleventh and early twelfth centuries. Until such a study is undertaken, Henri d'Arbois de Jubainville, *Histoire des ducs et des comtes de Champagne* vols 1–3, Paris 1859–61; Karl F. Werner, 'Königtum und Fürstentum des französischen 12. Jahrhunderts', *Vorträge und Forschungen* 12, 1968, 177–225, English trans. by Timothy Reuter, 'Kingdom and Principality in Twelfth-Century France,' in *The Medieval Nobility*, ed. Reuter, Amsterdam 1978, 250–60 and 280–87; André Chédeville, *Chartres et ses campagnes (XIe–XIIIe s.)*, Paris 1973; Guy Devailly, *Le Berry du Xe siècle au milieu du XIIIe*, Paris 1973; Michel Bur, *La formation du comté de Champagne, v.950–v.1150*, Nancy 1979; Yves Sassier, *Recherches sur le pouvoir comtal en Auxerrois du XI au début du XIIIe siècle*, Auxerre 1980 – all works written for different ends – provide the best introduction to the sources concerning the Thibaudians; a preliminary re-assessment of the situation of the Thibaudians in the second half of the eleventh century is available in LoPrete, 'Adela', ch. 1.2–3.
[8] By province: Tours – Tours, Le Mans; Sens – Chartres, Orleans, Auxerre, Sens, Troyes, Meaux; Rheims – Soissons, Rheims, Châlons-sur-Marne; Bourges – Bourges. The cadet branch's holdings also fell in the diocese of Langres (province of Lyons) though they controlled more significant lands than the senior family line in the dioceses of Troyes, Rheims, and Châlons-sur-Marne; see the works cited in n. 7, and Jacques Dubois, 'La Carte des diocèses de France avant la révolution', *Annales* 20, 1965, 865.

directly on the royal domain of the Capetian kings, while the Capetians also both controlled important lands in these two bishoprics and were the predominant lay lords in the dioceses of Orleans and Sens.[9] Whatever the relative power and influence of any individual Capetian king or Thibaudian count in the eleventh and twelfth centuries, the Capetian kings were the Thibaudians' socio-political superiors; no other princely family in northern France had the kings of France as immediate neighbors on as many fronts. Examination of Thibaudian relations with the many bishops who acted as their diocesans across their widespread domains indicates that Thibaudian power and influence was stronger than is generally portrayed; such examination, of course, surpasses the scope of this paper.[10] Nonetheless, in the dioceses of both Chartres and Meaux it was the Thibaudian counts who exercised the important *jus spolii* – rights over episcopal goods during vacancies – from at least the mid-eleventh century and examination of comital-episcopal cooperation in the diocese of Chartres during the tenure of Ivo reveals the ways and means by which the Thibaudians enhanced their power and authority as a ruling family even when they could not reasonably be expected to control episcopal elections.[11]

The accession of Ivo, prior of the canons at St Quentin, Beauvais, at the time of his election to the see of Chartres, was not uncontested. In 1089 the pope, Urban II, had seen to the deposition of Ivo's predecessor, Geoffrey I, and apparently proposed Ivo to the cathedral chapter as a worthy successor. Duly elected, Ivo, acknowledging royal prerogatives in the see of Chartres, received pre-consecration investiture at the hands of king Philip but was refused consecration by Richer, the archbishop of Sens, who claimed that his authority had been impugned by the papal deposition of Geoffrey and Urban's role in the new election. Ivo thus sought out the pope at Capua and was consecrated by Urban himself in November 1090.[12] Back in Chartres by April 1091, Ivo was summoned to appear before Richer and his suffragans at Etampes, where only Ivo's threat to appeal to Rome kept Geoffrey from being restored. Envisioning such a summons, Ivo agreed to go to Etampes on condition that count Stephen-Henry, delegated by Richer and the king, personally guarantee his safety.[13] Ivo's request shows not only his respect for the *de jure* hierarchy of authority in his diocese, but also indicates that he knew Stephen supported his position as rightful bishop. At some stage during the opening years of his episcopacy Ivo acknowledged the *de facto*

[9] See especially William M. Newman, *Le Domaine royal sous les premiers Capétiens*, Paris 1937; and Elizabeth M. Hallam, *Capetian France, 987–1328*, London 1980.

[10] See LoPrete, 'Adela', esp. chs 3 and 4.1.

[11] Comital exercise of *jus spolii* is known only from eventual renunciations, that for Chartres discussed below, pp. 141–2, that for Meaux renounced by Adela's son Thibaud IV during the decade after Adela's retirement (Arbois de Jubainville, iii 424, no. 91). Most convenient introduction to literature and summary of complex relations between king, count, and bishop in the dioceses of Chartres and Meaux is Reinhold Kaiser, *Bischofsherrschaft zwischen Königtum und Fürstenmacht*, Bonn 1981, 395–98; 410–17.

[12] Ivo, epp. 1, 2, 8, ed. Jean Leclercq, *Yves de Chartres: Correspondance*, Paris 1949, 2/4, 4/8, 34; on Richer's dispute with the pope over the primacy of Gaul, see Alfons Becker, *Studien zum Investiturproblem in Frankreich*, Saarbrücken 1955, 70–71.

[13] Ivo, ep. 12, ed. Leclercq, 54 (see Sprandel, 178 for date); and ep. 8, ed. Leclercq, 36: '. . . paratus ero tempore opportuno et loco tuto . . . si conductum tutum, comitem videlicet Stephanum ex parte domini nostri regis et vestra [Richer] propter circumstantes inimicos habuero, paratus, inquam, ero vobis occurrere . . .'

position of the counts of Chartres in his swearing of the (by then) traditional oath of *securitas*.[14]

Once established as bishop, Ivo's relationship with his sovereign deteriorated rapidly when Philip started (in 1092) an adulterous liaison with Bertrada of Montfort, then married to Fulk Rechin of Anjou, which the king wanted to legitimize by setting aside his first wife and solemnly marrying Bertrada. Ivo refused absolutely to countenance this clear breach of his strict interpretation of marriage vows and he castigated his episcopal colleagues who willingly sanctioned Philip's actions. The result for Ivo was imprisonment at Le Puiset (in the diocese of Orleans) at the hands of the joint royal and Thibaudian vassal Hugh I, almost certainly acting at the behest of his royal overlord.[15] However, prior to Hugh's move against him, Ivo met with the countess Adela and Adela voluntarily swore that both she and her husband would protect Ivo in his role as defender of God's law.[16] According to a letter Ivo wrote during his captivity, it appears that Stephen and Adela moved to act on their oath by planning to spring Ivo by force, but Ivo counseled against the use of violence and his counsel was heeded. By October 1093 Ivo had been released, thanks to a negotiated ransom supplied by the people of Chartres.[17]

This double series of events, known primarily from Ivo's own correspondence, reveals both Thibaudian support of Ivo from the start of his tenure and the potential political ramifications of such support in terms of Thibaudian relations with their own neighbor and king. Ivo's description of Adela's oath also indicates the active and acknowledged public role she played in comital governance alongside her husband after the death of her father-in-law. It was also in these troubled early years of Ivo's episcopacy that Adela requested Ivo to intervene in the case of a Norman kinswoman (most likely the granddaughter of her paternal aunt Adelaide) involved in an adulterous liaison with one William, traditionally identified as William of Breteuil.[18] Ivo politely rebuked Adela for condoning the

---

[14] Referred to in Ivo, ep. 49, ed. Leclercq, 200; I follow the interpretation of Kaiser, 415–16.

[15] Augustin Fliche, *Le Règne de Philippe Ier, roi de France (1060–1108)*, Paris 1912, 40–51 provides most detailed account of this incident; see also Sprandel, 103–6. On the Le Puiset family, vassals of the Thibaudians for the viscounty of Chartres, see Adolphe de Dion, 'Le Puiset aux XIe et XIIe siècles', *Mémoires de la société archéologique d'Eure-et-Loir* 9, 1889, 1–34 and 71–85; and John L. LaMonte, 'The Lords of Le Puiset on the Crusades', *Speculum* 17, 1942, 100–118.

[16] As recounted by Ivo in a letter to his former *confrères* at St Quentin, ep. 17, ed. Leclercq, 74: 'Ligat me etiam charitas cleri, devotio populi, benevolentia principis, quæ ita se mihi gratuito contulit, ut etiam comitissa, me non petente, imo renuente, in manu mea quam sancte spoponderit pro se et pro comite se mihi omnem fidem servaturos et in nulla persecutione quam pro lege Dei patiar aliquatenus defurturos'; see Sprandel, 186, for date prior to 1095.

[17] Ivo, epp. 20, 21, ed. Leclercq, 86/90; see also Leclercq, 82 n. 1 and Sprandel, 178.

[18] Ivo, ep. 5, ed. Leclercq, 14/16, datable to before the death of William of Breteuil in January 1102, though the place of the letter in the collection as a whole speaks for a date soon after Ivo's accession. For the correct filiation of Ivo's 'Adalaide' (known to Orderic Vitalis, 11.10, ed. vi, 54, as Adeliza) as the daughter of Judith, daughter of Lambert of Lens and William the Conqueror's sister, Adelaide, see Marjorie Chibnall at Orderic, vi, 54 n. 6; Orderic refers to Adeliza's mother as king Henry I's *consobrina*, as Ivo likewise calls 'Adalaide' Adela's *consobrina*, a fitting term for who would be first and second cousins of both Henry and Adela. The tradition that the 'Adalaide' in question was the daughter of Ebrard I of Le Puiset, popularized by Lucien Merlet (ed. and trans., *Lettres de Saint Ives*, Chartres 1885, 7 n. 2), is based on reading back two generations the later family relationship between the Thibaudians and the Le Puisets established by the marriage of Hugh III and a daughter of Stephen-Henry in the early decades of the twelfth century (on which see LoPrete, 'Anglo-Norman Card', 584); besides, even if such a family tie between the Thibau-

couple's adultery but agreed to accede to Adela's unspecified request on the couple's behalf. In light of events after the death of William of Breteuil, it is plausible to suggest that Adela's request was to see to the legitimation of the couple's son, who became a supporter of Adela's brother Henry in Normandy.[19] While Ivo's intransigence towards king Philip and Bertrada remained unabated, he could clearly temper his rigor in regards to uncanonical behavior in certain circumstances so as not to provoke an open conflict with those whose support he needed and would receive.

Three years after Ivo's release from captivity, Stephen-Henry was preparing to leave for the Holy Land on what became known as the first crusade. Prior to Stephen's departure (and perhaps prior even to the council of Clermont) Ivo penned an open letter to all the faithful in his diocese in which he sketched a theology of Christian peace applicable to Christian knights. Acknowledging the impossibility of maintaining a perpetual peace in this sinful world, Ivo called for a cessation of armed combat from Thursday through Sunday (the traditional term of the truce of God) which he grounded in typological parallels drawn from the life of Christ. With explicit reference to the decrees of his *majores*, Ivo concluded with a call for all to swear on sacred relics to observe the peace statutes he was sending them.[20] Then, on 26 October 1096, Ivo presided at a synod convoked 'according to the custom of our church' to treat 'ecclesiastical affairs and peace in the entire country [*patria*]'.[21] No peace statutes from the diocese of Chartres have survived and what can be known about them will be discussed below. For the present it is important to note that, whatever the precise terms of the peace, Ivo arranged for it to be reconfirmed in the most solemn of manners on a diocesan-wide basis within the very month of Stephen's departure. While such a reaffirmation of the peace was also doubtless partly in response to the decrees of the council of Clermont, Ivo explicitly stated that peace synods were already custom-ary in his diocese.[22] Thus, at this critical juncture, as Adela was assuming comital authority as regent, Ivo saw to it that the weight of the church would be brought to bear on any who might conceive of the count's absence as an opportunity to disrupt good order in the diocese.

By the later eleventh century in northern France it was increasingly customary for episcopally-sponsored peace legislation to be confirmed by publicly-sworn oaths and enforced through a combination of ecclesiastical sanctions and penal-

---

dians and the LePuisets existed by the end of the eleventh century (and there is no evidence for such a link), the relationship between 'Adalaide' and Adela would be one by marriage only and more distant than that between Adela and the granddaughter of Adelaide.

[19] Orderic, 11.4, ed. vi, 40, relates that William of Breteuil had no offspring by his legitimate wife, Adeline of Montfort, and was eventually succeeded by his *de concubina filius*, Eustace, who won the support of king Henry and other Norman neighbors in the disputed succession because of his fully Norman parentage; see LoPrete, 'Adela', chs 4.2 and 5.1.

[20] Ivo, ep. 44, ed. Leclercq, 174/84: 'Quorum [majorum nostrorum] vestigia pro posse nostro sequentes, exhortando præcipimus et præcipiendo exhortamur ut pacem, cujus constitutionem vobis scriptam dirigimus, sine disceptatione servetis et servandam tactis sacrosanctis reliquiis manu propria firmetis' [184]; on date, see Hartmut Hoffmann, *Gottesfriede und Treuga Dei*, Schriften der Monumenta Germaniae historica 20, Stuttgart 1964, 196.

[21] Ivo, ep. 62, ed. Leclercq, 258; for date see Hoffmann, 197 n. 7.

[22] On the Clermont decrees see Hoffmann, 222–24; and Robert Somerville, *The Councils of Urban II. Volume I: 'Decreta Claromontensia'*, Annuarium Historiae Conciliorum, Suppl. 1, Amsterdam 1972, 73–74; 81; 106; 116; 124; 143.

ties imposed by secular authorities. Whether their cases were heard before ecclesiastical, lay, or special peace tribunals, alleged peace offenders were subject to increasingly well-defined juridical procedures. Both the exact terms of any known peace and the precise relations between bishop and secular authorities in enforcing it, however, varied from place to place.[23] That the peace statutes in the diocese of Chartres entailed episcopal-comital cooperation in enforcement is evident from diverse references throughout Ivo's extant letters.[24]

Indeed, one of the clearest statements to this effect is in a letter Ivo directed to Stephen after his return from the crusade in order to reprimand the count for refusing to bring to justice some of his men charged with breaking their peace oaths, as Stephen had earlier promised to do. Ivo related that he would interpret Stephen's continued inaction as meaning that Stephen, in all his power and lordship, could apparently manage without the peace so that Ivo would dissolve it rather than continue to bear the expenses and burdens attendant on overseeing it; Ivo nonetheless promised to continue to obey Stephen, as the '*magnus et potentus vir*' he was, in other matters.[25] Whatever this letter reveals about the potential for a breakdown in relations between Ivo and Stephen-Henry, Adela's situation as a female ruler was different from that of her husband and the peace would be promulgated regularly throughout Ivo's remaining years as bishop. Adela, as acting countess, would publicly swear to observe the peace in 1104 (after the resolution of a dispute in which she herself had acted as a peace breaker) and again in 1107, on the occasion of a papal visit to Chartres.[26]

Ecclesiastical-secular oversight of the peace in the diocese of Chartres is also revealed in a case concerning despoilers of the possessions at a priory of the major Benedictine abbey in Chartres, St Père, known from a series of acts re-

---

[23] For a review of the vast literature on the peace of God, see Frederick S. Paxton, 'The Peace of God in Modern Historiography: Perspectives and Trends', *Historical Reflections/Réflexions historiques* 14, 1985, 385–404; in addition to Hoffmann, as in n. 20, I have found most useful (though I disagree on some points) the discussions by Aryeh Graboïs, 'De la trêve de Dieu à la paix du roi: Etude sur les transformations du mouvement de la paix au XIIe siècle', in *Mélanges offerts à René Crozet*, edd. Pierre Gallais and Yves-Jean Riou, Poitiers 1966, i, 586–91; H. E. J. Cowdrey, 'The Peace and Truce of God in the Eleventh Century', *Past and Present* 46, 1970, 58–67, rpt in his *Popes, Monks and Crusaders*, London 1984, no. VII; and Thomas N. Bisson, 'The Organized Peace in Southern France and Catalonia, ca. 1140–ca. 1233', *American Historical Review* 82, 1977, 293–95.

[24] Hoffmann, 195–206, provides the most complete summary but he has not discussed all instances; that specific statutes were the result of consultation with lay people (and hence could be modified) and were not necessarily committed to writing is clear from Ivo, ep. 90, in J. P. Migne, *Patrologiae cursus completus . . . series latina*, 221 vols, Paris 1844–64 (henceforth cited as *PL*), 162:111, to the archbishop of Sens: '. . . trevia Dei . . . pro communi tamen utilitate hominum ex placito et pacto civitatis ac patriæ, episcoporum et ecclesiarum, ut nostis, est auctoritate firmata. Unde judicia violatæ pacis modificari oportet, secundum pacta et diffinitiones quas unaquæque ecclesia consensu parochianorum instituit, et per scipturam vel bonorum hominum testimonium memoriæ commendavit'. Ivo's discussion of the truce in his *Panormia*, 8, 147, ed. *PL* 161:1343, is understandably devoted solely to ecclesiastical sanctions and inter-diocesan treatment of condemned peace breakers – an arena in which Ivo himself had disputes with other bishops in specific instances, as discussed in LoPrete, 'Adela', ch. 5.3.

[25] Ivo, ep. 86, ed. *PL* 162:107: 'Quod si refutaveritis, scimus quia potentia vestra et principatus vester pace ecclesiastica non eget. Nos vero erimus contenti terminis nostris; et pacem istam, quæ ecclesiæ valde est onerosa et sumptuosa, quam contra vos tenere non possumus, dimittemus; in aliis autem sicut magno et potenti viro serviemus.'

[26] Ivo, ep. 179, ed. *PL* 162:181a.

corded in the house's cartulary that were not edited in full in Guérard's standard edition.[27] Though the secular authorities involved in the settlement of this case were castellans in the *mouvance* of the Thibaudians, it should be noted that at the time of the various court proceedings (29 October 1104 through 15 May 1105), Adela herself was either elsewhere in her extensive domains or lying seriously ill at Blois.[28] The case in question became a peace case when, at Epiphany, lay claimants to some of the priory's possessions refused to abide by an earlier settlement worked out at the court of the local castellan and proceeded, with a gang of followers, to destroy monastic properties. The monks excommunicated the alleged peace breakers and appealed to the local castellan to oblige the despoilers to make satisfaction. The court of the local castellan condemned the accused parties after they failed to appear to defend themselves. Four months later the monks arraigned the peace breakers at Chartres before a tribunal consisting of the bishop Ivo, several chapter officials, and several important vassals of Adela, including the viscount of Châteaudun (the comital castle closest to the disputed properties), though how the accused were compelled to attend this second hearing was not specified. At Chartres, damages and terms for a final settlement were fixed, to be implemented by the peace breakers at the court of the local castellan. Two days later, then, the original despoilers renounced all claims to the disputed properties and swore to make restitution for damages. At the same time, the peace was reconfirmed on oath by all present (ninety people were named in the document) and forty-pound pledges were apportioned out amongst the various peace breakers until such time (fifteen days was specified) as the restitutions were made good.

Other evidence reveals that members of the castellan family involved in the settlement of this dispute (most of the hearings were presided over by the castellan's wife and second son) frequented the comital entourage and were consistently loyal to the Thibaudian counts despite their own extensive holdings.[29] Such was likewise true of the comital vassals, most notably the viscount of Château-

---

[27] M. Guérard, ed., *Cartulaire de l'abbaye de Saint-Père de Chartres*, 2 vols, Paris 1840, ii, 481 for brief summary; acts were published by the Abbé Peschot (from a transcription provided by Charles Métais), 'Notice historique sur la paroisse de Chapelle-Royale', *Bulletins de la Société Dunoise* 9, 1898, 285–88 no. 8; see LoPrete, 'Adela', ch. 5.1, for full details.

[28] 13 November 1104 Adela was at Sancerre (M. Gemähling, *Monographie de l'abbaye de Saint-Satur près Sancerre (Cher)*, Paris 1867, 137–38 no. 2 [= Louis Raynal, *Histoire du Berry*, 3 vols, Bourges 184[4]–47, i, 480–81 no. 14]); she was back in Blois by January 1105 (Jean-Martin Demézil, 'Les forêts du comté de Blois jusqu'à la fin XVe siècle', *Mémoires de la Société des Sciences et Lettres de Loir-et-Cher* 34, 1963, 197–203) where she fell seriously ill, not to recuperate until May (Eadmer, 163–64).

[29] On this family, surnamed Gouet, see Chédeville (as in n. 7), 257–58; 264; 284; and LoPrete, 'Adela', ch. 5.1; of especial interest in the present context is William Gouet's presence at St Père in 1104 when Adela restored some vineyards to a priory and renewed her oath as the house's protector (Guérard, ii, 408–9 no. 10); William had crusaded with Stephen-Henry (Ernest Laurain, ed., *Cartulaire Manceau de Marmoutier*, 2 vols, Laval 1911–15, i, 117 no. 1) and his second son was present in 1101 when Adela reconfirmed the comital family's renunciation of its *jus spolii* at Chartres (Eugène de Lépinois and Lucien Merlet, edd., *Cartulaire de Notre-Dame de Chartres*, 3 vols, Chartres 1862–65, i, 108 [name corrected according to Gaignières copy in Paris, BN MS latin 17033, p. 66]; William's heir, William Gouet, Junior, fought for the Thibaudians in the wars of the second decade of the twelfth century (see Emile Mabille, ed., *Cartulaire de Marmoutier pour le Dunois*, Châteaudun 1874, 84–86 no. 94; and Lucien Merlet, ed., *Cartulaire de l'Abbaye de la Sainte-Trinité de Tiron*, 2 vols, Chartres 1883, i, 104–6 no. 85) and would be rewarded for his

dun, who participated in the hearing at Chartres.[30] As the resolution of this affair indicates, it was due in part to episcopal-secular cooperation in enforcing peace statutes in the diocese of Chartres and in part to Adela's ability to command the loyalty of castellans and vassals powerful in their own right, that Adela was able to act as a competent detainer of Thibaudian comital authority even when she was occupied elsewhere in her widespread domains or temporarily indisposed.

This overview of the evidence for ecclesiastical-secular cooperation in the promulgation and enforcement of the peace in the diocese of Chartres makes it plausible to suggest that the peace statutes referred to by Ivo were similar to those known from extant legislation emanating from the Norman council of Lillebonne in 1080 and from a Rheims provincial synod held in Soissons sometime 1083– 1095 (perhaps in 1092), both of which were likely known to Ivo and/or Stephen and Adela.[31] The Lillebonne statutes were issued at a ducal assembly of lay and ecclesiastical lords convoked soon after the cessation of hostilities between William the Conqueror and king Philip that provided the immediate backdrop to the negotiations for Adela's marriage; close Thibaudian relations to the Normans date from the mid-1050s.[32] Ivo, prior of St Quentin in 1080, had been with William and Philip at Gerberoi in January of the previous year.[33] Probably a former student at Bec, Ivo was in touch with other Bec alumni as they advanced in the Norman or English ecclesiastical hierarchy. Moreover, the cathedral of Chartres had landed possessions in three Norman dioceses and the proximity of Chartres to the dioceses of Sées and Evreux brought Ivo into contact with affairs in those bishoprics.[34]

Significant aspects of the Lillebonne statutes included ducal initiative in the promulgation of the peace (unlike Chartres), episcopal oversight of enforcement backed both by ecclesiastical sanctions and by the active intervention of local lay lords should alleged peace breakers prove recalcitrant, and a special charge to the king's viscount in cases of recalcitrant local lords.[35] This latter clause is not

loyalty to the Thibaudian – Anglo-Norman cause with a wife who was an illegitimate daughter of Adela's brother, king Henry I (Robert of Torigni's interpolations in Jumièges, 8.29, ed. 308).
[30] The viscount, Hugh IV, was the paternal uncle of Rotrou III of Nogent (on whom, see below, pp. 148–9).
[31] See below, nn. 32, 35, 36.
[32] Orderic 5.5, ed. iii, 24/36, esp. 26 and 32 for specific statutes; discussed by Hoffmann, 172–73. On Norman-Thibaudian relations, see LoPrete, 'Adela', ch. 1.2, and summary in LoPrete, 'Anglo-Norman Card', 572–75.
[33] Maurice Prou, *Recueil des actes de Philippe Ier*, Paris 1908, 242–45 no. 94.
[34] Lynn K. Barker, 'Ivo of Chartres and Anselm of Canterbury', *Anselm Studies: An Occasional Journal* 2, 1988, 15–19; and Barker, 'Ivo of Chartres and the Anglo-Norman Cultural Tradition', *Anglo-Norman Studies* 13, 1991, 17–19. The cathedral had been given lands in the dioceses of Rouen, Evreux, and Lisieux by duke Richard II (de Lépinois and Merlet, i, 12; discussed by Sprandel, 90; 105). For Ivo and Audoin, bishop of Evreux, see Ivo, epp. 223 and 242, ed. *PL* 162:227–78; 249–50; Ivo and William Bona Anima, archbishop of Rouen, ep. 185 and add. ep. 4, ed. *PL* 162:185–86; 289–90; Ivo's intervention in the 1103–7 disputes in the see of Lisieux, epp. 149, 153, 154, 157, ed. *PL* 162:154–55; 157; 157–78; 162–63, and Chibnall at Orderic, v, 322–23 nn. 3–4.
[35] Orderic 5.3, ed. iii, 26: 'Qui uero [the peace] seruare contempserint, uel aliquatenus fregerint episcopi secundum quod prius statutum est eos iudicando iusticiam faciant. Si quis uero episcopo suo inde inoboediens fuerit, domino in cuius terra habitat episcopus hoc demonstret, et ille subdat eum episcopali iusticiæ. Quod si et dominus facere contempserit.' regis uicecomes per episcopum inde requisitus omni remota excusatione faciat.'

without interest in terms of the appearance of the viscount of Châteaudun in the St Père case discussed above. Though his precise role cannot be determined with certainty, it is possible that he was one of the men responsible for obliging the already once contumacious parties to attend the hearing at Chartres.

The statutes issued at Soissons indicate that the observance of the peace, promulgated by ecclesiastical authorities throughout the province of Rheims, had to be general enough to account for the wide-array of local customs and laws that characterized the diverse secular jurisdictions prevailing in that province where not only members of both branches of the Thibaudian family acted as counts, but likewise both the kings of France and the counts of Flanders were among the most powerful lay lords. Peace oaths were to be sworn in the hands of the appropriate bishop or his representative by all 'lords of cities, castles, and forti-fied sites'; the diverse fines and restitutions imposed in the course of enforcing the peace were to be made according to local law or custom. In some instances the fines were collected by the local lord while episcopal consultation with local 'good men' was mandated before peace militias were mustered, thus indicating secular cooperation in the enforcement of the peace.[36]

It should be pointed out that five of the major castles controlled directly by Stephen and Adela in what was known as the county of Meaux were in the province of Rheims and four of these were in the diocese of Soissons.[37] In the opening years of the 1080s, Thibaud III had been able to assure the election of one, and perhaps two, candidates to the see of Soissons though neither (if there were two) was able to maintain his position for long.[38] From 1095–1100 the bishop of Châlons-sur-Marne was none other than Stephen-Henry's half-brother, who had been elected in 1093.[39]

The bishops of Soissons at the time these peace statutes were issued were known personally to both Stephen and Adela. Adela would continue to have

[36] Max Sdralek, *Wolfenbüttler Fragmente: Analekten zur Kirchengeschichte des Mittelalters aus Wolfenbüttler Handschriften*, Münster 1891, 140–42, esp. no. 5: 'Hoc iterum statuimus, ut omnes domini civitatum et castellorum et munitionum hanc constitutam pacem per sacramentum vel per dextere dacionem in manu episcopi sui confirment'; no. 4: 'Quod si hoc fecisse [despoiling pilgrims or merchants] convicti fuerint, emendationem faciant domino patrie secundum consue-tudinem patrie illius'; no. 10: 'Si quis vero pacem infregerit et eam emendare voluerit post episcopi sui vel legati eius ammonitionem, episcopo pro infracta pace IX libras persolvat et ei, cui iniuriam intulerit, sua restituat et secundum legem patrie iusticiam faciat'; no. 6: 'Statuimus iterum, ut si episcopus ex consilio bonorum virorum super excommunicatum illum, qui pacem non confirmaverit vel confirmatam infregerit, exercitum ducere decreverit . . .'; see also Hoffmann, 186–88. Roger Bonnaud-Delamare discusses earlier legislation in this province, stressing its relationship to earlier Norman statutes, in his 'Les Institutions de paix dans la province ecclésias-tique de Reims au XIe siècle', *Bulletin philologique et historique jusqu'à 1715 du Comité des Travaux Historiques et Scientifiques* année 1955–56, 1957, 143–200.
[37] See Bur (as in n. 7), 234: Vertus (diocese of Châlons-sur-Marne); Oulchy, Château-Thierry, Châtillon-sur-Marne, and Montfélix (diocese of Soissons); note that the comital couple also controlled other lands and rights in these dioceses, as well as in the diocese of Rheims itself (see Bur, *passim*).
[38] Arnoul of Tiegem in 1081 and perhaps the chancellor of the Chartres cathedral, Ingelrannus, in 1084; see esp. 'Vita S. Arnulfi, suessionensis episcopi', ed. *MGH* 15:884–85; Nicolas Huyghe-baert, 'Saint Arnould de Soissons et la consécration de l'église du prieuré de Coincy (1082)', *Analecta Bollandiana* 85, 1967, 317–18; and discussion in LoPrete, 'Adela', ch. 5.4.
[39] Bur, 230; *Gallia Christiana in provincias ecclesiasticas distributa*, 16 vols, Paris 1715–1865 (henceforth cited as *GC*), ix, 875–76; for his death on 3 April, see necrology of Molesme, Paris, BN MS nouv. acq. lat. 2057, p. 376.

relations with bishop Hilgod (1085–1087/88) after he resigned and became a monk, then abbot (in 1100), of Marmoutier. Hilgod's successor, Henry, would also resign after serving four or five years; he was purportedly related to Adela's brother, king Henry (and thus to Adela herself) and had an eventful future career in the Anglo-Norman church. The bishop from 1092 to 1102, Hugh of Pierrefonds, had the closest working relationship of these three bishops to the count and countess of Meaux; he accompanied Stephen-Henry to the Holy Land in 1101 but died on the course of the expedition.[40] As a canon at St Quentin Ivo had known the bishop Hilgod; Ivo was likewise a correspondent of both the bishops Hugh and Henry after his resignation.[41]

Given this nexus of relations, it seems reasonable to infer that both the bishop of Chartres and the Thibaudian counts of Chartres were familiar with the peace statutes, stipulating episcopal-secular cooperation in the promulgation and enforcement of the peace, issued at Soissons in the closing decades of the eleventh century. Likewise, given Adela's Norman origins, Thibaudian relations with the Normans from the mid-eleventh century, and Ivo's diverse relations with various Norman prelates, it appears likely that both bishop and count or countess knew about the application of peace legislation in Normandy. Whether or not the peace statutes in these two regions actually were used by Ivo in the formulation of his peace provisions, the fragmentary evidence emanating from the diocese of Chartres itself indicates that the peace statutes observed there similarly entailed episcopal-comital cooperation in its promulgation and enforcement, thus pointing to an arena in which lay and ecclesiastical lords worked together in attempts to maintain stability and order in their respective, but overlapping, circumscriptions. Stephen-Henry, and especially, Adela, had shown themselves to be strong supporters of Ivo in the troubled early years of his episcopacy; Ivo himself saw that the peace was reconfirmed at the time Adela began to rule as regent. Though Stephen, as an able warrior in his own right, might well have been capable of maintaining order in his domains without reliance on episcopal oversight of peace legislation, Adela had no such immediate access to policing power and it appears that cooperation with Ivo in the enforcement of peace statutes did, indeed, serve to undergird her authority as ruling countess.[42]

Another arena in which the bishop Ivo and, especially, the countess Adela cooperated was in the promotion of ecclesiastical reform and renewal of the religious life. Shortly after Stephen's return to France from the siege of Antioch, when his authority as count could have been undermined by ecclesiastical sanctions against his failure to complete his pilgrim's vow, Stephen and Adela, at Ivo's behest, issued a privilege renouncing their traditional claim to control episcopal properties on the bishop's decease. In exchange, the couple received annual anniversary prayers and the assurance that the episcopal residence, newly rebuilt in stone by Ivo, would not be fortified by the bishop. Issued first before the chapter and an assembled host of sixty-five episcopal *casati*, comital officials, burghers from Chartres, and important castellan-vassals from across their

---

[40] See LoPrete, 'Adela', ch. 3, for these comital-episcopal relations.
[41] Ivo, epp. 88, 42, 233, ed. *PL* 162:108–9; 53–55; 235–36.
[42] The commonplace that Stephen was, if not a total coward, a generally ineffectual leader and fighting man is based on an uncritical reading of select sources; a reassessment of Stephen's abilities is found in LoPrete, 'Adela', appendix 2.

domains (several of whom would accompany Stephen on his return to the Holy Land), the exemption was first applied to the episcopal residence and immovable goods outside the city; it was subsequently extended in a second document issued under comital seal.[43]

The importance of this privilege was underscored by its being subscribed by all of Stephen and Adela's sons, including the sickly Odo. Its public issuance was staged to make its provisions known to all assembled as well as to enhance the prestige of the comital couple as they acted as sponsors of reform at the diocesan level.[44] Ivo subsequently had the privilege confirmed by the archbishop of Sens, the pope, and, after the lifting of his excommunication, the king of France.[45] In the year after Stephen's second departure Adela reissued the privilege in the presence of two papal legates and two visiting abbots, as well as key vassals; she also arranged for it to be confirmed by her two sons who would act with comital authority in Chartres.[46]

Stephen had earlier come into conflict with Ivo over the immunity of the cathedral close and Stephen's authority could be called into question until he fulfilled his vow to reach Jerusalem (a situation which doubtless prompted his decision to return to the Holy Land).[47] The council of Clermont had prohibited the despoiling of the goods of deceased bishops, and even those of all clerics generally.[48] Thus, Ivo, in requesting that the count and countess issue a written privilege renouncing their customary *jus spolii*, was merely acting in conformity with church law. That he took such action when he did (four years after the council of Clermont) and obtained the desired result without protest could reflect as much his good relations with Adela as Stephen's anomalous situation. Besides, in view of Stephen's imminent re-departure, this was the ideal time for confirming comital-episcopal concord and bolstering comital authority through the granting of an important reforming privilege. Though traditionally interpreted as a major concession on the part of the Thibaudians, the privilege also explicitly reserved a significant component of comital authority in the clause prohibiting

---

[43] These two acts are now known from seventeenth-century copies and an early twelfth-century copy in the Archives d'Eure-et-Loir (Chartres), liasse G 709; another seventeenth-century copy (from the original) of the long form is available in Paris, BN MS lat. 17033, pp. 64–66, which describes the now-lost seals. The edition in de Lépinois and Merlet, i, 104–8 no. 24 is not, as the editors claim, after the original but from the twelfth-century copy where the long form of the act, preceded by copies of the papal confirmation of 14 February 1100 (ed. *PL* 163:35–36 no. 8) and the royal confirmation of 1105 (ed. Prou, 383–85 no. 152), have all been copied in the same hand.

[44] Note subscription clause of first version: 'Ut autem hoc firmum et inconcussum per succedentia tempora permaneat, non defuit communia assensus optimatum tam laicorum quam clericorum, quorum nomina diligentissime curavimus subscibere . . .'; see also Werner (as in n. 7), 254 and 281 n. 34.

[45] See n. 43 and Jean-Baptiste Souchet, *Histoire du diocèse et de la ville de Chartres*, ed. A. Lecocq, 4 vols, Chartres 1866–73, ii, 333.

[46] De Lépinois and Merlet, i, 106–8 and BN MS lat. 17033, p. 66.

[47] Ivo, ep. 49, ed. Leclercq, 196/98; on sanctions, see general discussion in James A. Brundage, *Medieval Canon Law and the Crusader*, Madison 1969, 37–39, 127–29; despite the well-known 'speech' of Adela urging her husband to return to the Holy Land in order to salvage his shaken reputation penned by Orderic Vitalis (10.20, ed. v, 324), Orderic had earlier written that the threat of ecclesiastical sanctions was enough to send Stephen back at the head of a large host (10.23, ed. v, 268).

[48] Somerville (as in n. 22), 111 no. 9 and 147 no. 34; Paschal's confirmation (see n. 43) cites the Clermont decrees in its preamble.

fortification of the episcopal residence.[49] Moreover, according to Ivo's letter to Paschal requesting papal confirmation of the privilege, Ivo had apparently also provided some kind of counter-gift to the comital family, though he was studiously ambiguous about its precise nature.[50]

Extant evidence also provides information about seven instances in which the bishop Ivo and the countess Adela cooperated in the promotion of reform and religious renewal on several fronts – the establishment of new parish churches, the reform of nunneries and houses of canons, and the sponsorship of newer forms of religious community, both *leprosaria* and hermitages.[51] Two of these reform projects were undertaken on Adela's initiative during her husband's absence on the first crusade. In one instance Adela sought to ensure episcopal approval for the creation of a parish church at the new town of 'Francheville', established under the direction of monks from Marmoutier on recently cleared forest land from Adela's dower.[52] In the other, Adela enlisted Ivo's support in her attempt to oblige the nuns at Faremoutiers to reform themselves. Interesting in this case is that Faremoutiers lay in the diocese of Meaux and the first prompting for reform seems to have come from the Marmoutier monks installed with Thibaudian consent in 1081–82 at the nearby monastery of La-Celle-sur-Morin. Instead of appealing to the royal nominee and supporter of the then excommunicate king, the bishop Walter of Meaux, Adela addressed her concerns to Ivo with whom she apparently had a closer working relationship. Responding to Adela's express desires, Ivo then followed proper ecclesiastical channels and helped set in motion the events that led to reform of the nuns' way of life.[53]

Two other cases in which Adela initiated reform concern houses of secular canons that had long been treated as virtual private possessions of the Thibaudian counts; significant in both cases is that, however laudatory Adela's undertakings appeared to her diocesan, Adela's reform measures were only partial by strict canonical standards and full reform would not be implemented at either house until after Adela's retirement. In 1105 Adela restored to the canons of Bourgmoyen, Blois, their *libertas*, or immunity, but apparently continued to exercise certain prerogatives such as naming priors and disposing of prebends at the related establishment of canons installed at the chapel of the comital castle. She petitioned Ivo to confirm her undertaking by sanctioning the excommunication of

---

[49] That the early twelfth-century chapter copy omits this clause, contained in all other known versions (see n. 43), can be attributed to scribal error as much as to any deliberate attempt on the part of the chapter scribe to suppress an important comital privilege; for a contemporary dispute between William Rufus and Hildebert, bishop of Le Mans, over episcopal fortifications, arguably well-known to Stephen and Adela, see Frank Barlow, *William Rufus*, Berkeley 1983, 402–6.

[50] Ivo, ep. 94, ed. *PL* 162:114: 'Quoniam divino adjutorio Carnotensis comes pravas consuedtudines quas habuerant antecessores sui et ipse in domibus et rebus Carnotensis episcopi defuncti vel depositi, multo meo labore et sumptu ecclesiæ dimisit . . .', which is not to say that Ivo actually supplied the money for Stephen's second trip to the Holy Land, as asserted by Souchet, ii, 323–33, and Merlet, 193 n. 1.

[51] Full details about these cases are given in LoPrete, 'Adela', ch. 5.2.

[52] Mabille, 148–49 no. 158; see also Chédeville, 181 and n. 185, and Mabille, 78–82 no. 92, and 62 no. 68.

[53] Ivo, ep. 70, ed. *PL* 162:89–90: 'Quod ideo suggero dilectioni vestræ [bishop Walter], quia tam ex verbis Turonensium monachorum, quam ex litteris dominæ Adelæ venerabilis comitissæ audivi turpissimam famam de monasterio Sanctæ Faræ . . .'; see also Prou, 272–73 no. 107; and Toussaints du Plessis, *Histoire de l'Eglise de Meaux*, 2 vols, Paris 1731, ii, 11–14 nos. 17–18.

infringers of the canons' immunity, which Ivo did in June in a privilege issued in the presence of the visiting archbishop of Canterbury, Anselm. Ivo described Adela as 'burning with the flame of divine love and inflamed with the desire to augment religion' and her restoration of the canons' *libertas* as 'most diligent' reform – doubtless appropriate if high-blown language to characterize the countess as she prepared to accompany Anselm to Normandy for his important negotiations with her brother, Henry I.[54] Nonetheless, it was only in 1120–23 that Adela's son, with the support of Ivo's successor, regularized the life of the Bourgmoyen canons by instituting the Augustinian rule and a canonically elected prior; at the same time Thibaud IV renounced his ancestors' claims to install canons at the castral chapel and made them fully dependent on Bourgmoyen.[55]

At about the same time as her initiatives for Bourgmoyen, Adela, as lay prior, was moved to restore the canons at St Martin au Val, Chartres, to their original monastic state by granting the house to Marmoutier; Ivo authorized Adela's undertaking on her request and papal confirmation of the intended reform was obtained, perhaps on Paschal's visit to Chartres in 1107.[56] Subsequently, however, Ivo had to write to Adela in an attempt to persuade her to bring her plans to fruition. Though Ivo claimed he feared no earthly cupidity on Adela's part, Adela clearly found it easier to continue profiting from St Martin's revenues and the patronage potential of its prebends. Still, Ivo did not insist that the reform be implemented; doubtless, as war erupted in the Chartrain in the closing years of his tenure, Ivo saw no need to undercut either the Thibaudians' power base or their authority.[57] Only in 1128 did Thibaud IV, goaded by his mother's letters from Marcigny, remit the St Martin prebends into the hands of Ivo's successor so that they could be canonically granted to the abbot of Marmoutier. As Thibaud rather lamely explained at that time, 'certain unfortunate circumstances' had arisen which prevented Adela from implementing her projected reform; he was fulfilling his mother's wishes and saw that their vassal and supporter in the wars of the second decade of the twelfth century, Hugh III of Le Puiset, did likewise.[58]

[54] Ivo, *diplomata* 1, ed. *PL* 162:289–290: 'Ego Ivo . . . notum esse volo . . . quia Adela comitissa, Stephani comitis uxor, divini amoris igne successa, augmentandæ religionis desiderio inflammata, humilitatem nostram humiliter adiit petens ut libertatem ecclesiæ Sanctæ Mariæ de Burgomedio, ejus canonicorum et aliorum clericorum eidem ecclesiæ famulantium, nec non eorum servientum, ab Odone comite et Berta uxore ejus olim factam per antiquitatem aliquantulum imminutam, sed per eam diligentissime reformatam, auctoritate nostræ excommunicationis confirmaremus'; for Adela, Anselm, and Henry see Eadmer, 164–65; Anselm, ep. 288, ed. F. S. Schmitt, *S. Anselmi . . . Opera Omnia*, 6 vols, Rome 1938–61, v, 331–32.
[55] Paris BN MS collection Anjou vol. 12[1], fols 59v–60r no. 1091 (partial ed. in Ch. Hardel, 'La Chapelle de Saint-Calais ou Sainte-Chapelle du château de Blois,' *Le Loir-et-Cher historique . . .* 9, 1896, 370); see also Hardel, 371; *GC* viii, *instr.* 420–21 no. 8; and *PL* 163:1271–72.
[56] Paris, BN MS lat. 12776, p. 421; Samuel Loewenfeld, ed. *Epistolae Pontificum Romanorum ineditae*, Leipzig 1885, 74 no. 149.
[57] Ivo, add. ep. 2, ed. *PL* 162:288–289: 'Semota omni mundana cupiditate, piam vestram intentionem laudato quod ecclesiam S. Martini de Valle, quæ olim monasterium fuit, in antiquum statum reformare desideratis.' For Adela acting as lay prior, see Guérard, ii, 309–10 no. 57, and 454–55 no. 60; for context, see Adela, 'Anglo-Norman Card', 584.
[58] De Lépinois and Merlet, i, 131–34 no. 43: 'Verumtamem, quibusdam causis impedientibus, non statim fuerunt monachi corporali investitura investiti; in quo intervallo, contigit ipsum papam [Paschal, d.1118] et ipsum episcopum [Ivo, d.1115] de hoc mundo migrasse, et matrem meam vitam monachilem accepisse [April–May 1120], et dominium Carnotensis comitatus in manum meam devenisse. Dolens igitur valde mater mea quod prefata elemosina non satis plene consum-

Adela also acted as lay defender of, and approved donations to, the canons of St Jean en Vallée, Chartres, where Ivo had instituted the Augustinian rule and clarified the canons' relationship to the nearby cathedral chapter in 1099–1101 so that those cathedral canons desiring to live a regular life could do so.[59] In gratitude for Adela's intervention on behalf of a *conversus* of the canons from Adela's Meaux domains, Ivo instituted prayers on Adela's behalf and renewed his pledge of faithful service to the countess.[60] Though the St Jean canons had been granted immunity in the bourg of Muret in the first quarter of the eleventh century, Adela and her successors continued to exact *taille* payments there until 1140.[61] Again, though Ivo was the initiator of reform at this house of canons – in part because he was unable fully to reform his own chapter – Adela continued to reap both spiritual and material benefits from her position as the canons' protector.[62]

Both Adela and Ivo also promoted the expanding *leprosarium* outside of Chartres that had been founded by Thibaud III in 1054.[63] Adela placed the house under comital protection and granted certain exemptions to those who cared for the sick while Ivo prepared a set of statutes to govern the life of the inmates and acted as both spiritual and administrative overseer of the hospice. Adela's brother, king Henry I, also became a patron both of the Beaulieu *leprosarium* and of Ivo's statutes which were imported into Normandy and England.[64] This case, especially after examination of the links between other supporters of the hospice, indicates the growing network of patronage and piety that underlay the renewal of religious life in the diocese of Chartres as a result of both Adela's Norman connections and her prestige as protector of the church and churchmen. Related to this case in terms of the extended network of actors and solidarities confirmed through com-

---

mata remanisset . . . sepe et sepius, preces jungens precibus, me rogavit . . .'; BN MS lat. 12776 p. 241 [Adela's letter], and pp. 242–44 [Hugh of Le Puiset].

[59] Jean Becquet, 'La réforme des chapitres cathédraux en France aux XIe et XIIe siècles', *Bulletin philologique et historique (jusqu'à 1610) du Comité des Travaux Historiques et Scientifiques*, Paris 1975, 37–38 and 41; rpt in his *Vie canoniale en France aux Xe–XIIIe siècles*, London 1985, no. 11.

[60] Ivo ep. 91, ed. *PL* 162:112; note that *regulas* in line 16 is a misprint for *reculas*: 'Pro hoc enim a fratribus prædictæ ecclesiæ habebitis munus orationum, et a nobis fidele servitium.' For other benefactions by Adela, see René Merlet, ed., *Cartulaire de Saint-Jean-en-Vallée de Chartres*, Chartres 1906, 4 and 9, nos. 4 and 14.

[61] R. Merlet, xii–xvi and nos. 1 and 51; see Sprandel, 99.

[62] Note also Ivo, ep. 91, ed. *PL* 162.112: 'Rogo autem pro remedio animæ vestræ [Adela] ut ecclesiam beati Joannis Baptistæ, in qua regularem vitam Deo donante ordinavimus, diligatis, et res ad ipsam ecclesiam pertinentes contra insidiantes et incursantes pro posse vestro defendatis . . .'

[63] Thibaud's foundation charter is no longer extant, but see Paul-M. Renard, *Le Séminaire du Grand-Beaulieu-lès-Chartres*, 3 vols, Chartres 1890–92, i, 5; and de Lépinois and Merlet, i, 17 n. 3; the first extant reference to lepers there is in 1109 (Paris, BN MS nouv. acq. lat. 608, p. 37).

[64] Adela's grants are known only from later confirmations by her son (Paris, BN MS nouv. acq. lat. 1408, fols 26v–29r) and grandson (René Merlet and Maurice Jusselin, edd., *Cartulaire de la léproserie du Grand-Beaulieu et du Notre-Dame de la Bourdinière*, Chartres 1909, 16–17 no. 36); see also her consent to donations in BN MS n. a.l. 608, p. 34, and the cathedral chapter's request for her intervention in Lucien Merlet, 'Lettres d'Ives de Chartres et d'autres personnages de son temps, 1087–1130', *Bibliothèque de l'Ecole des Chartes* 16, 1855, 469 no. 34. For Ivo, see Sprandel, 146; BN MS n. a.l. 608, pp. 90–91; and Edward J. Kealey, *Medieval Medicus: A Social History of Anglo-Norman Medicine*, Baltimore 1981, 112–16, 200–1 (though his chronology for the Thibaudians is confused). For Henry, see Kealey, as indicated; Merlet and Jusselin, 1–2 nos. 1 and 2; and Robert of Torigni in Jumièges, 8.32, ed. 313.

mon support of an ecclesiastical establishment is the joint comital and episcopal fostering of the new hermitage at Tiron founded on land first granted by the Chartrain vassal of Adela and son-in-law of Henry I, Rotrou III of Nogent.[65] However, examination of these extended networks and the political ramifications of early donations to this establishment would require discussion of the wars that erupted in northern France in the second decade of the twelfth century and surpass the space allotted to me.[66]

What is perhaps most significant about these diverse reform undertakings is the frequency of Adela's initiative, which could be attributed to her personal piety alone. However, the limited extent of some of her projects, together with the retention of some key lay prerogatives (as was also underscored in the comital couple's privilege for the cathedral), indicates Adela's ability both to act as a sponsor of reform and supporter of her bishop's reform agenda without seriously undercutting traditional sources of comital income and patronage potential. Indeed, as expectations of lay behavior in regard to ecclesiastical establishments changed as the reform movement gained momentum, Adela's authority was doubtless enhanced in the eyes of both the influential clerics and powerful laymen whose active service she commanded as countess.

Moreover, it should be noted that Adela continued to benefit materially as well as spiritually from her position as protector of the major Benedictine monasteries of St Père (Chartres), St Lomer (Blois), and St Florentin (Bonneval), in the diocese of Chartres. Writing in the midst of a dispute between Adela and the monks of Bonneval triggered by the monks' men killing a noble vassal of Adela, Ivo both praised Adela as a noted patron of religious establishments and acknowledged that several monasteries in his diocese were under her control. Still, given Adela's angry reaction to the monks' actions, Ivo advised Adela to moderate her behavior so that her earthly reputation should not be diminished in the eyes of her contemporaries.[67] Ivo clearly recognized the important, if often intangible, ties linking lay lords' prestige and authority to their active protection of the church and the historian would be mistaken to ignore the pragmatic political consequences of Ivo's promulgation of the peace, support for those reform measures Adela was willing to implement, and both his actions during moments of conflict

---

[65] On foundation, see Geoffrey Grossus, 'Vita Bernardi Tironiensis', ch. 8, ed. *PL* 172:1409; Ivo ep. 283, ed. *PL* 162:283 [= L. Merlet, ed., *Tiron* (as in n. 29), i, 13–14 no. 2]; and L. Merlet, *Tiron*, i, 1–2 no. 1. For Adela's benefactions, see 'Vita', ch. 9, ed. *PL* 172:1413; L. Merlet, *Tiron*, i, 14–15; 28–29; 40–41; 104–6; nos. 3–4, 14, 24, 85; Orderic 8.27, ed. iv, 330.

[66] See LoPrete, 'Adela', ch. 6.2.

[67] Ivo, ep. 187, ed. *PL* 162:190: 'Præterea debetis consulere saluti vestræ et famæ vestræ, ne vanum videatur quod monasteria quæ non sunt juris vestri, muneribus vestris sustentatis, et quibus modis potestis ampliatis, ea autem quæ vestri juris sunt, minuitis et quasi servili oppressione subjugatis. Unde, ne ista ad aures multotum perveniant, et famæ vestræ, sicut saluti, plurimum detrahant, sicut monui iterum moneo, ut mitius agatis, ne insolita et intolerabilis severitas posteris vestris sit in exemplum, et vobis in peccatum æternum'; on this dispute, see LoPrete, 'Adela', ch. 5.3. After the dispute was settled, king Louis VI formally installed Thibaud IV and his vassal, Hugh, the viscount of Châteaudun, as Bonneval's lay defenders, a position previously held by Stephen-Henry (V. Bigot, ed. *Histoire abrégée de l'abbaye de Saint-Florentin de Bonneval des RR. PP. Dom Jean Thiroux et Dom Lambert continuée par l'abbé Beaupère et M. Lejeune*, Châteaudun 1875, 58–60; see also Achille Luchaire, *Louis VI le Gros: Annales de sa vie et de son règne*, Paris 1890, 55–56 no. 102).

and interventions on behalf of Adela's vassals – these latter to be discussed presently.

According to extant evidence (primarily Ivo's own correspondence), during the thirteen years between the deaths of Stephen-Henry and Ivo, the countess Adela came into conflict with her bishop on only three occasions.[68] One of the disputes was over jurisdiction in the case of goods seized from a *'pseudomonacha'* who had been hiding out in Blois – doubtless a rare event and a technical issue that could not be expected seriously to undermine generally good relations between bishop and countess.[69] A more violent dispute occurred shortly after Easter 1107 and, though details are lacking, was apparently provoked by the cathedral canons. Ivo intervened because he claimed Adela had not followed proper procedure in her reaction to the canons' behavior (not because she did not have a legitimate grievance); though he threatened Adela with ecclesiastical sanctions, the dispute was apparently resolved before sanctions were imposed.[70]

The one major dispute between bishop and countess broke out in the fall following Stephen-Henry's death and was embedded in a deeper dispute between both Ivo and Adela and the cathedral chapter. This underlying dispute had been triggered by Ivo's attempts to admit low-born men from the *familiæ* of both Adela and the king of France to the cathedral priesthood. Though the chapter imputed simoniacal intent to their bishop, Ivo insisted to the papal legate who investigated this affair that his support of these men had nothing to do with comital or royal *quid pro quos*; when this dispute was definitively settled two years later the chapter was obliged to promote whatever men from the comital *familia* Ivo selected.[71] In the mind of Anselm of Canterbury, who intervened with the pope on Adela's behalf after the dispute widened, the scandalous behavior of the chapter was the ultimate cause for the entire complex conflict.[72]

The dispute became one between bishop and countess only when Ivo placed his concern to impose the moral-legal principle of the inviolability of sworn oaths over his concern to preserve peaceful relations with Adela. Adela apparently interpreted Ivo's insistence on the need for a papal dispensation of the chapter's oath (to prohibit the admission of low-born men), sworn early in the dispute, as Ivo's abandonment of the struggle to advance men from her *familia*.[73] As a result of what Ivo maintained was Adela's misunderstanding of his stance towards the chapter, Adela ordered the seizure of cathedral commodity stores and assented to a general roughing up of the canons and their men. The chapter moved to place the diocese under interdict but Ivo continued to seek a negotiated settlement with Adela, despite her violent depredations.[74] The honorable reception accorded to

---

[68] Full accounts of these disputes in LoPrete, 'Adela', ch. 5.3.
[69] Ivo, ep. 101, ed. *PL* 162:120.
[70] Ivo, ep. 179, ed. *PL* 162:180–181.
[71] Ivo, ep. 147, ed. *PL* 162:152c; for simony allegations, see Paschal, ep. 81 (to Ivo), ed. *PL* 163:100; and Ivo, ep. 133, ed. *PL* 162:141–43; for settlement, see Ivo, ep. 147, ed. *PL* 162:152–53; and Paschal, ep. 403, ed. *PL* 163:365 [= de Lépinois and Merlet, i, 112 no. 403].
[72] Anselm, ep. 340, ed. Schmitt, v, 278: 'De causa quae est inter Carnotensem ecclesiam et comitssam Carnotensem unde vestrae celsitudini Romae locutus sum, vestra prudentia non eget nostro concilio; sed rei necessitas nostram et omnium pacem et utilitatem eiusdem ecclesiae amantium precem ad vestram pietatem expostulat, quantum intelligo, quatenus quod a clericis in grave scandalum factum esse cognoscitur, apostolicae sapientiae discretione a pacem revocetur.'
[73] Ivo, ep. 126, ed. *PL* 162:138.
[74] Ivo, epp. 116, 121, 126, ed. *PL* 162:131; 134; 138.

Anselm by both bishop and countess at Pentecost 1103 indicates that the threatened sanctions were not imposed and Anselm was able to negotiate a truce between Ivo and Adela.[75] Several months later the papal legate negotiated a truce between Adela and the cathedral chapter until such time as a definitive resolution of the diverse issues raised as the dispute progressed could be worked out under papal auspices (since Ivo's one non-negotiable claim was that only the pope could dispense the canons from the terms of their oath, however ill-advised Ivo thought it had been).[76]

Despite the rash intervention of Adela's eldest son at this stage in the negotiations, Ivo refrained from sanctioning him and continued to treat with Adela as acting countess.[77] While it took another year for the papal dispensation to reach Chartres, the dispute between Ivo and Adela was effectively resolved in about seven months, that between Adela and the cathedral chapter in less than a year. Over the course of the conflict (only summarized here), Ivo addressed Adela with respect, appealed to their decade-old spirit of cooperation, created opportunities for Adela to come to terms with the cathedral chapter, and studiously respected the terms of his truce with Adela negotiated by Anselm of Canterbury; threatened ecclesiastical sanctions were apparently never pronounced. Thus, it would be a mistake to see in this complex affair any deep-seated antagonism between Ivo and Adela or, indeed, any dispute over fundamental principles of the role of lay lords in ecclesiastical affairs. Rather, as the underlying dispute was one over the promotion of low-born men from the comital *familia* in the cathedral chapter, it appears that, despite Ivo's denial of the charge of simony, he was on certain occasions able to accommodate his reform principles to promoting Adela's interests.

Ivo's correspondence also provides evidence for the bishop of Chartres' willingness both to tap his knowledge of law and risk censure from his ecclesiastical superiors in order to support the interests of the men on whom Adela relied to preserve order in her domains. While it is not possible now to discuss each of these cases in terms of their broader political implications, two in particular merit a brief airing.[78] The first of these concerned Adela's Chartrain vassal, Rotrou III of Nogent, and Adela's backing of Rotrou's new fortifications on land west of Chartres over against the protestations of Hugh II of Le Puiset and his vassal, Ivo of Courville.[79] The Le Puisets, also viscounts of Chartres, were vassals of both the

[75] Anselm, epp. 286–87, ed. Schmitt, iv, 205–7; Ivo, ep. 134, passage omitted in *PL* 162:144b supplied from Paris, BN MS lat. 2887a, fols 66v–67r: '. . . cum etiam respectus esset inter me et comitissam *mediante canturiensi archiepiscopo, respectus etiam inter clericos et comitissam* mediante apostolico . . .'

[76] See above, nn. 71 and 75.

[77] Ivo, epp. 134, 136, ed. *PL* 162:144b; 145b.

[78] These and three more cases are discussed fully in LoPrete, 'Adela', ch. 5.3; I have found no cases in which Ivo's interventions in the affairs of Thibaudian vassals could be construed as detrimental to Adela's political agenda.

[79] On the family of the castellans of Nogent and viscounts of Châteaudun, see Charles Cuissard, 'Chronologie des vicomtes de Châteaudun (960–1395)', *Bulletins de la Société Dunoise*, 1894, 23–48 (to be used with caution); Jacques Boussard, 'Les évêques en Neustrie avant la réforme Grégorienne', *Journal des savants*, 1970, 174–76; Philippe Siguret, 'Recherches sur la formation du comté du Perche', *Bulletin de la Société Historique et Archéologique de l'Orne* 79, 1961, 17–39, and 80, 1962, 3–42; Lynn H. Nelson, 'Rotrou of Perche and the Aragonese Reconquest', *Traditio* 26, 1970, 113–33; LoPrete, 'Anglo-Norman Card', pp. 581–82.

Thibaudian counts and the Capetian kings; leading members of this family frequently rallied to the Capetians until Adela was able to win Hugh III over to the Thibaudian cause late in 1111. Hugh II, son of the man who had imprisoned Ivo in the early 1090s, had been excommunicated by Ivo as a peace breaker and despoiler of episcopal property in 1097–1099 and 1102–1104.[80]

This dispute opened as Hugh was preparing to leave for the Holy Land in 1106–1107. Rotrou defended his right to fortify the land on the grounds that the parcel he was fortifying was mostly allodial land he had purchased and not the adjacent land Ivo of Courville held from Hugh of Le Puiset. Though Hugh and Ivo of Courville took their counter-claims to bishop Ivo's episcopal court, claiming protection owed to crusaders and charging Rotrou with breaking the peace, the bishop referred the case to Adela's court because he considered it to be a case of disputed land lordship rights over land ultimately held of the countess. At Adela's court, Hugh of Le Puiset renounced his claims but Ivo of Courville responded to Adela's judgment in Rotrou's favor by attacking Rotrou; in the ensuing skirmishes, Ivo was captured by Rotrou's men.[81]

Hugh of Le Puiset, meanwhile, on his way to the Holy Land, took his complaint to the pope who ordered the case to be judged before an ecclesiastical tribunal consisting of the archbishop of Sens and his suffragans from Paris, Orleans, and Chartres; Rotrou was to be excommunicated until the hearing. Hugh's brother, a former cleric and viscount of Etampes (in the royal domain), as guardian of his brother's lands, demanded application of the papal mandate while Ivo prevaricated, not wanting to excommunicate Rotrou without a formal hearing. Ivo, responding to allegations of disobedience, defended his inaction to his archbishop and the bishop of Paris on the grounds of Adela's prior judgment and Rotrou's assent to a hearing in an ecclesiastical court.[82] The first hearing before the papally-mandated tribunal came to naught when the spokesmen for the Le Puiset/Courville side refused to treat without prior satisfaction on Rotrou's part; they even rejected a truce in which Rotrou would halt his fortifying and ransom Ivo. As these men demanded immediate judgment, Rotrou expressed to his bishop Ivo his fears about attaining a just verdict from the tribunal as constituted (stacked in favor of royal bishops) and Ivo agreed to support Rotrou in an appeal direct to Rome by writing him letters of introduction to the pope while also requesting clarification of the applicability of crusader privileges to the case.[83]

Whatever personal reservations Ivo may have had about new crusader privileges and their relationship to peace legislation, they were manifested in the broader context of his concern to uphold the authority of Adela's prior judg-

---

[80] See above, n. 15; LoPrete, 'Anglo-Norman Card', 584; Ivo, ep. 60, ed. Leclercq, 252/54; epp. 76–77, 111–12, 114, 124, ed. *PL* 162:97–98; 129–31; 136.

[81] For date, see Sprandel, 192; for place, see Chédeville, 278 and 290 n. 246; Ivo, ep. 68, ed. *PL* 162:170d–171c, note esp.: '. . . judicatumque est quia hæc causa sine monomachia terminari non poterat, et judicium sanguinis nobis agitare non licebat, ut utraque pars irent in curiam comitissæ, ad quam talia judicia pertinebant, et de cujus feudo ista tenebant. Sicut judicatum erat, venerunt utrique in curiam comitissæ, et actionibus utrinque ventilatis nescio quibus de causis vicecomes a causa cecidit.'

[82] Ivo, epp. 168–169, ed. *PL* 162:170d–173a; and later to Daimbert, ep. 170, ed. *PL* 162:173c–174a: 'Si relatum fuerit ad vos nos Rotrocum nondum excommunicasse, sciatis nos non inobedienter fecisse, sed rationabili et legitima causa distulisse . . .'

[83] Ivo, ep. 173, ed. *PL* 162:176–77, esp.: 'Quo judicio cum se prægravari timeret comes Rotrocus, audientiam apostolicam appellavit, cujus eum auctoritate premebamus.'

ment.[84] He flatly refused to excommunicate Rotrou, despite a papal mandate and the risk of ecclesiastical censure. Never denying the competency of ecclesiastical courts in the case, Ivo displayed the consummate technical skill of an able lawyer by arguing for a change of venue for the judgment so as to minimize the risk of Rotrou's condemnation at the hands of an ecclesiastical tribunal stacked in favor of his enemies. No record of the papal judgment survives, but the name La Motte-Rotrou speaks for Rotrou's ultimate success in his fortifying endeavor undertaken with the support of both Ivo and Adela.

A second case concerns Raoul of Beaugency and shows how comital and episcopal interests coincided in the disposition of Raoul's holdings near Adela's *Silva Lognia* dower disputed between the important Angevin foundation of La Trinité, Vendôme, and the Thibaudian abbey of St Lomer, Blois. Vassal of the counts of Anjou, the kings of France, and the Thibaudians for his scattered holdings in northern Anjou, southern Maine, the Loire valley, the Vendômois, and around Châteaudun, Raoul's father had gravitated to the powerful counts of Anjou – the direct competitors of the Thibaudians – in the second half of the eleventh century. Imitating his Angevin overlord, Raoul's father was an important patron of La Trinité, Vendôme, a focal point of expanding Angevin power in the diocese of Chartres.[85] In 1085, following in his father's footsteps, Raoul donated to La Trinité his castral chapel at 'Montfollet' and nearby land for the construction of a bourg and parish church; whether or not he truly favored Raoul's action, Stephen-Henry, as overlord of the lands granted, assented to Raoul's donation.[86] Raoul, however, gravitated more and more to the Thibaudian court, especially after crusading with Stephen, and would prove to be a particularly effective and loyal military vassal of Adela.

In 1106–7 Adela made a major donation to the important Thibaudian abbey in Blois, St Lomer. A key component of this donation was a tract of the *Silva Lognia*, from Oucques to 'Montfollet', as a means to gain the assistance of the St Lomer monks in organizing the clearing and economic valorization of this vast forest from which both countess and the monks would profit.[87] At the same time, the monks decided to contest La Trinité's right to the 'Montfollet' properties granted originally by Raoul's father, which they claimed belonged to their church at Oucques. They took their claims to the bishop Ivo, no supporter of La Trinité's abbot, Geoffrey, who had resorted to forgery in his attempts to win for his house full exemption from episcopal jurisdiction. During his investigation into these disputed claims, Ivo discovered that Raoul's father had originally usurped St Lomer's rights over the properties handed over to La Trinité by Raoul.[88] After

---

[84] See James A. Brundage, 'Anslem, Ivo, and the Ideology of the First Crusade', in *Les Mutations socio-culturelles au tournant des XIe–XIIe siècles: Actes du colloque international du CNRS, Le Bec-Hellouin 1982*, ed. Raymonde Foreville, Paris 1984, 178–79; and Hoffmann, 200–2.

[85] On Raoul and his family, see LoPrete, 'Anglo-Norman Card', p. 583.

[86] Charles Métais, ed. *Cartulaire de l'abbaye cardinale de la Trinité de Vendôme*, 4 vols, Paris 1893–1903, ii, 34–35 no. 324, and Noël Mars, *Histoire du royal monastère de Sainct-Lomer de Blois de l'ordre de Sainct-Benoist*, ed. Alexandre Dupré, Blois 1869, 368, give variant versions of this act; further research is needed to determine whether the records of one house have been willfully changed (perhaps because of the subsequent dispute), though the variations do not impinge on the fact of the donation.

[87] Mars, 142–45 (cf. Jean Bernier, *Histoire de Blois . . .*, Paris 1682, *preuves* v–vi); Martin-Demézil (as in n. 28), 232.

[88] Ivo, ep. 172, ed. *PL* 162.175–76; see also Sprandel, 151–54.

Ivo's judgment, Raoul, accepting the usurpation interpretation, formally donated the properties to St Lomer, along with further land to support the creation of yet another parish church in this area of burgeoning new settlements.[89] With these properties, the St Lomer monks could effectively consolidate the land they had just acquired from Adela.

Whatever the precise motivation of the various actors in this poorly documented affair, it was the intervention of Ivo on the side of the Thibaudian abbey of St Lomer that allowed Raoul of Beaugency to revoke an earlier donation to the Angevin house of La Trinité, Vendôme. Legally empowered to re-donate these properties to St Lomer, Raoul, now following in the footsteps of Adela, proceeded to do so, thereby both affirming his solidarity with the Thibaudians and assuring that the rapidly increasing wealth from *Silva Lognia* assarts would accrue to the benefit of the largest Thibaudian abbey in Blois. Despite abbot Geoffrey's appeal to Rome, Ivo's judgment in favor of St Lomer stood unshaken and Ivo's support of St Lomer in this case shows how both countess and bishop could work together to promote shared comital-episcopal interests in limiting Angevin influence in the Chartrain.

To conclude, this paper represents an attempt to describe the interpenetration of piety and politics that characterized the structuring of both religious institutions and power relations among lay lords in northern France in the late-eleventh and early-twelfth centuries as it was played out in the diocese of Chartres during the episcopacy of the justly famous bishop Ivo. The predominant lay power in this diocese was exercised by the Thibaudian counts of Blois, Chartres, Châteaudun, and Meaux, the preponderance of whose core patrimonial domains lay in Ivo's bishopric. For seventeen of the twenty-five years Ivo served as bishop, comital authority was exercised primarily by the countess Adela, royal-born daughter of William the Conqueror, who had also played an active role in comital affairs during her husband's lifetime. Both Stephen-Henry and Adela were key supporters of the bishop Ivo in the troubled early years of his episcopacy despite their negligible role in Ivo's election and the close working relationship that Adela, especially, fostered with her influential diocesan both resulted in episcopal support of Adela's political agenda and allowed Adela to be spared the undermining of her comital authority through the imposition of ecclesiastical sanctions despite moments of conflict with her bishop.

Indeed, it has been argued that Adela, as an able protector of the church and sponsor of ecclesiastical reform, actually benefited (in both material and spiritual terms) from the enhanced prestige and authority accorded to her by both influential clerical and powerful lay contemporaries. By strict standards several of Adela's reform undertakings were incomplete, but Ivo displayed a keen pragmatic sense in accepting the measures Adela was willing to take while continuing to acknowledge comital prerogatives at religious establishments as they existed. Even the comital couple's important reform privilege for the Chartres cathedral was issued at a time and place signficiant for undergirding Adela's authority while it also confirmed episcopal acceptance of ultimate comital prerogatives in matters of defense. Clearly, Adela was able effectively to balance the perceived need for reform as championed by her diocesan against the maintenance of certain comital

---

[89] Métais, ii, 134–36 and J.-B. Souchet edition of variant version of this act from a St Lomer source in *PL* 162:478 (see comment above, n. 86).

prerogatives over ecclesiastical establishments so as to strengthen her position as countess without undercutting key components of Thibaudian status, power, or income.

It was the institutionalization of peace legislation in the diocese of Chartres that allowed for the greatest degree of comital-episcopal cooperation while also serving to undergird the interests of both bishop and countess. Although there are no extant peace statutes from the diocese of Chartres in this period, other evidence indicates that they would have been similar to contemporary statutes in Normandy and the province of Rheims, two regions to which both Ivo and Adela had strong ties. While a churchman's interest in peace and general stability is self-evident, what needs to be stressed is how episcopal oversight of peace statutes applied in ways that relied on lay enforcement of specific provisions could undergird the position of a female ruler who had no direct recourse to arms. Ivo's promulgation of a diocesan-wide peace at the time of Stephen's departure on the first crusade brought the full weight of ecclesiastical authority to bear on potential peace-breakers as Adela assumed sole rule for the first time; the peace would be solemnly reconfirmed at regular intervals during Adela's tenure as countess – once on the occasion of a papal visit to Chartres. Of course, Adela's authority over her officials and powerful vassals was critical to the maintenance of order in her domains, but Adela could also clearly rely on the support of the bishop Ivo in the enforcement of the peace.

Though it has not been possible to detail the full extent of the political ramifications either of Adela's patronage of certain religious establishments or of Ivo's interventions on behalf of key vassals of Adela, the cases of Rotrou of Nogent and Raoul of Beaugency that were briefly summarized indicate that Ivo was both willing and able to tap his legal acumen while using his position in the church hierarchy to promote Adela's political agenda at critical junctures. Full examination of these and related cases reveals not only what must have been Ivo's real respect for Adela both as a person and as countess of Blois, Chartres, Châteaudun, and Meaux, but also the positive political consequences attendant upon his proffered support. Nonetheless, even the various events reviewed in this paper suggest that the portrayal of the Thibaudian counts as ineffectual and poorly-respected lords after their loss of Tours in 1044 and prior to the formation of a county of Champagne needs to be recast, not the least because of the countess Adela's astute manipulation of the prerogatives of lordship as they were exercised within the religious and ideological structures of her day.

THE ANGLO-NORMAN FAMILY: SIZE AND STRUCTURE [1]

John S. Moore

The size and structure of the West European family and household has long been a matter of interest and debate amongst historians and sociologists for a variety of reasons. Even economic historians with only a passing interest in the family or household *per se* nevertheless needed estimates of average family or household size to use as 'multipliers' in converting contemporary enumerations of heads of household produced by ecclesiastical or fiscal authorities into estimates of total populations.[2] Social historians and sociologists concentrated their attention more on the structure and role of the family, and thus became entangled in the attempt to establish whether the typical family of the pre-industrial period in Western Europe was the 'nuclear family' predominant since the Industrial Revolution (parents and unmarried children, perhaps with one widowed grandparent) or was some more complex structure containing more than one married couple, either of the same or different generations, with all their children.[3] Increasingly, a consensus seems to be emerging amongst historians dealing with 'Western' societies in the early modern and modern periods that the typical family was indeed the small nuclear family and that, in consequence, the normal household, i.e. the nuclear family plus unrelated co-residents (e.g. lodgers, apprentices, servants), was also small outside the landowning classes, containing an average of about five persons.[4] It has also long been known that landowners' households were

[1] My debt to the late Cecily Clark (whose studies of the as yet unpublished Thorney Abbey *liber vitae* (see references cited in n. 44) are fundamental to all work on this class of document) will be apparent to all readers; I am grateful to her for extended discussions and help with this article. I must also acknowledge the interest of my students in my 'Domesday England' course over several years and the stimulus of my colleagues in the department of Economic and Social History, University of Bristol, who have agreed to the introduction of a new course on the 'History of the Family' and thus unwittingly provoked the production of this article. I am grateful to Robert Smith, Chairman of the Manorial Society of Great Britain, for his invitation to read an early version of this paper to the Society's 1990 Conference; the comments of the audience then and those of my colleagues at a Staff Seminar in Economic and Social History, University of Bristol, have been of great value. The necessary inspection of MSS in Durham, London and Winchester was aided by a generous grant by the Twenty-Seven Foundation, for which I am most grateful. Finally, I am very happy to acknowledge the help and the stimulating comments of participants at the Battle Conference, the kindness of Dr Diana Greenway and Mrs Mary Cheney for answering queries before the Conference, and Dr Marjorie Chibnall's patience and knowledge in assisting the preparation of the final version.
[2] T. H. Hollingsworth, *Historical Demography*, London 1969, esp. 118–22, 125; J. S. Moore, 'Demographic Dimensions of the Mid-Tudor Crisis', *Econ. Hist. Rev.* (forthcoming).
[3] M. Anderson, *Approaches to the History of the Western Family, 1500–1914*, London 1980, esp. 22–38.
[4] P. Laslett, R. Wall, *Household and Family in Past Time*, Cambridge 1974, esp. introduction and

much larger because of the large number of servants needed to staff their houses, and this conclusion has recently also been documented for the medieval period.[5]

But the size of the normal family and household in medieval England has remained a matter of controversy even in the relatively well-documented period from the thirteenth century onwards – one eminent historical demographer committed himself to 3.5 as an estimate of average size,[6] though most medievalists have tended to accept as reasonable the early modern average of 4.75 suggested by Laslett[7] – whilst the period before 1200 has remained *terra incognita*. At the other end of the tunnel there was the evidence of the Carolingian *polyptyques* that the average size of the peasant family in France, the Low Countries, Western Germany and Italy was also of the same order, about five persons.[8] We may note *en passant* that such evidence had begun to come into print before the French sociologist Frédéric Le Play adumbrated his theories about the complex family of pre-industrial Europe.[9] Evidently sociologists then were as unwilling to learn from historians as they are now. In the absence of any *polyptyques* for England, is it possible to arrive independently at any valid conclusions about the average size and normal structure of the family in Anglo-Norman England?

A major problem in trying to write the economic and social history of the

chaps 1–7, is the *locus classicus*; for a recent extension of these results to the later medieval period, see R. A. Houlbrooke, *The English Family, 1450–1700*, London 1984, 10, 18–26.

[5] F. M. Stenton, *The First Century of English Feudalism, 1066–1166*, Oxford, 2nd edn 1961, chap. 2; C. Given-Wilson, *The English Nobility in the Later Middle Ages*, London 1987, chap. 4; K. Mertes, *The English Noble Household, 1250–1600*, Oxford 1988, esp. Appendix C; J. F. A. Mason, 'Barons and their officials in the later eleventh century', *Anglo-Norman Studies* xiii, 1991, 242–60.

[6] J. C. Russell, *British Medieval Population*, Albuquerque (USA) 1948, 23–32, 50, 61–9, 366.

[7] J. T. Krause, 'The Medieval Household: Large or Small?' *Econ. Hist. Rev.* 2nd ser., 9, 1957, 420–32; H. E. Hallam, 'Some thirteenth century censuses', *Econ. Hist. Rev.* 2nd ser., 10, 1958, 340–61; Houlbrooke, 10, 18–26; C. Dyer, *Lords and Peasants in a Changing Society: the Estates of the Bishopric of Worcester, 680–1540*, Cambridge, 1980, 230–2; T. Lomas, 'South-East Durham: the late fourteenth and fifteenth centuries' in P. D. A. Harvey, ed., *The Peasant Land Market in Medieval England*, Oxford 1984, 257–8; E. D. Jones, 'Going round in Circles: some new evidence for population in the later Middle Ages', *Journal of Medieval History* xv, 1989, 338. Although Jones' averages may be slightly high, as argued in M. Bailey, 'Blowing up Bubbles: some new demographic evidence for the fifteenth century', *Journal of Medieval History* xv, 1989, 347–58, there is no reasonable doubt about their order of magnitude, and the typical family is clearly nuclear (Jones, 334; Bailey, 353).

[8] For three recent studies based on such evidence, see R. R. Ring, 'Early Medieval Peasant Households in Central Italy', *Journal of Family History* 4, 1979, 2–25; D. Herlihy, *Medieval Households*, London 1985, chap. 3, esp. 62–72; G. M. Schwarz, 'Village Populations according to the polyptyque of the abbey of St Bertin', *Journal of Medieval History* xi, 1985, 31–41. The study of tenth-century French private charters also suggests the prevalence of the conjugal family (G. Duby, *La Société au XIe et XIIe siècles dans la région mâconnaise*, Paris (France) 1953, repr. 1971, 65–6, 122, 221; R. Fossier, *La terre et les hommes en Picardie jusqu'à la fin du XIIIe siècle*, Paris (France) 1968, I, 262–77).

[9] B. Guérard, *Polyptych de l'abbé Irminon*, Paris (France), 2 vols, 1844, was the first classic edition of a Carolingian *polyptyque*, followed by his *Polyptyque de l'abbaye de Saint Remi de Reims*, Paris (France) 1853; a useful bibliography of the MSS of *polyptyques* and printed editions is in R. H. C. Davis, 'Domesday Book: Continental Parallels' in J. C. Holt, ed., *Domesday Studies*, Woodbridge 1987, 30–9. See also J. Percival, 'The Precursors of Domesday Book' in P. H. Sawyer, ed., *Domesday Book: a reassessment*, London 1987, 5–27. F. le Play's views on the family were elaborated in *La Réforme sociale en France déduite de l'observation comparée des peuples européens*, Paris (France), 2 vols, 1864 and *L'Organisation de la Famille*, Paris (France) 1871.

pre-industrial period is that the interests of the present-day economic and social historian were not usually shared by the contemporaries who produced the surviving evidence. As a result, the economic and social historian to a far greater extent than a political or military historian is generally forced to press into service materials which were not intended for his (or her) purposes. Such a procedure necessarily has its recognized dangers: a corollary less obvious but equally valid is that economic and social historians must not allow their specialized interests (and their understandable concentration on the source-materials most obviously relevant to their purpose) to narrow their vision to the extent that they fail to perceive the utility of types of evidence which they would not normally consider to be useful because these sources were not intended by their originators to provide economic and social information. Here, modern historians are peculiarly likely to suffer from the inbuilt presuppositions of their own, largely Godless, age when trying to understand the Middle Ages. Whether or not 'all our ancestors were literal Christian believers, all of the time,'[10] – a view that I beg leave to doubt – the Catholic Church, its institutions, beliefs and value-systems certainly permeated and largely determined medieval life. Yet economic and social historians, whilst duly grateful for estate-surveys, account-rolls and court-rolls often produced by clerics for mainly episcopal or monastic masters, rarely pause to consider other records produced by the same clerics for the same masters which both masters and clerics would indubitably have considered to have much greater significance. But monastic records, for example, only existed as a means to facilitate the end, the due performance of the *opus dei*. As I hope to show, the economic historian, and even more the social historian, who ignores apparently uninteresting records is thereby the loser.

Nevertheless, medieval elites were not entirely uninterested in demographic matters, since a shortage of people would have military and fiscal repercussions for rulers and political and economic repercussions for lords. And it is clear from the 'terms of reference' entered at the beginning of the *Inquisitio Eliensis* that obtaining information on the number of individuals within various socio-economic classifications in 1086 was one of the original motives behind the Domesday survey: '*quot homines* . . .?' The perceived need for this information is highlighted by the account in the *Anglo-Saxon Chronicle* of the crisis created by the threatened Danish invasion of 1085 which is immediately followed in the *Chronicle* by its coverage of the 'deep and long discussion' at Gloucester in January 1086 leading to the inception of the 'survey of all England'. Using Domesday Book for demographic purposes is not therefore as anachronistic as some modern commentators have asserted. In addition, given the gradual spread after 1066 of more formalized 'feudal' land-tenure, all lords from the King downwards would need to know the ages of their tenants' male heirs (if any), the number and ages of coheiresses (if not) and the existence of widows in order to enforce the 'feudal incidents' of 'wardship' and 'marriage'. There are in fact six kinds of historical document whose evidence can be used to determine the size and structure of the medieval family; of these two can also be used to to establish the size of the medieval household.

Of these records, I shall not be touching on manorial court-rolls. Such records,

---

[10] P. Laslett, *The World We have Lost further explored*, London, 3rd edn 1984, 71.

especially in the east midlands, have long been exploited by members of the 'Toronto School' of historians led by Professor J. Ambrose Raftis;[11] more recently, Dr Zvi Razi of the University of Jerusalem in a classic study of Halesowen (Worcs.) has brilliantly exploited the method of 'family reconstruction' pioneered by early modern demographers to demonstrate the size and structure of local families and households in the west midlands.[12] There are, however, three drawbacks to using court-rolls, assuming that the methodology is valid: the first is that the results are, by definition, local and at best only of regional validity: a series of studies all over England where suitable records exist would be necessary before a national pattern would begin to emerge. Secondly, to be successful, the method requires long and continuous sets of court-rolls which are rarely to be found. Thirdly, using family-reconstruction, whether on medieval court-rolls or on the early modern parish registers for which it was originally devised, is extremely time-consuming, even using a computer. Most crucially for my present purpose, manorial court-rolls only start in the middle decades of the thirteenth century.

Similarly, I shall also ignore the inquisitions post mortem, which have been analysed extensively by J. C. Russell and T. H. Hollingsworth, because these are only extant from the 1230s onwards.[13] Putting the court-rolls and I.P.Ms to one side, we are thus left with four main sources for the demographic history of the Anglo-Norman family and household: in chronological order of origin, these are *libri vitae* and other records of religious confraternity; cartularies and original deeds; the unique *Rotuli de Dominabus* of 1185; and royal judicial records at both national and county level.

Since there is plenty of surviving evidence, it is first worth asking why the history of the medieval family has not received more attention. In part, this is because most medieval historians are not trained in the specialist techniques and approaches of economic and social history, and, even more, because most economic and social historians are neither interested in the medieval period nor qualified to study it. But a more valid reason is that our knowledge of the size and composition of families and households from the sixteenth century onwards has derived mainly from full 'listings' at parish level since the 1520s and detailed national censuses since the 1840s.[14] Apart from the 'serf-lists' for Spalding Priory in the later thirteenth century and those for some manors in Durham, the east

---

[11] J. A. Raftis, *Tenure and Mobility*, Toronto (Canada) 1964; E. B. De Windt, *Land and People in Holywell-cum-Needingworth*, Toronto (Canada) 1972; J. A. Raftis, *Warboys*, Toronto (Canada) 1974; E. Britton, *The Community of the Vill*, Toronto (Canada) 1977; J. A. Raftis, *Pathways to Medieval Peasants*, Toronto (Canada) 1981; see also G. C. Homans, *English Villagers of the Thirteenth Century*, Cambridge (USA) 1941.

[12] Z. Razi, *Life, Marriage and Death in a Medieval Parish: Economy, Society and Demography in Halesowen, 1270–1400*, Cambridge 1980. The use of manorial court-rolls for demographic purposes has been reviewed in J. M. Bennett, 'Spouses, Siblings and Surnames: Reconstructing Families from Medieval Court Rolls', *Journal of British Studies* 23, 1983, 26–46; L. R. Poos, R. M. Smith, ' "Legal Windows onto Historical Populations"? Recent Research on Demography and the Manor Court in Medieval England', *Law and History Review* 2, 1984, 128–52; Z. Razi, 'The Use of Manorial Court Rolls in Demographic Analysis: a Reconsideration', *Law and History Review* 3, 1985, 191–200; L. R. Poos, R. M. Smith, ' "Shades still on the Window": a reply to Zvi Razi', *Law and History Review* 3, 1985, 409–29; Z. Razi, 'The Demographic transparency of Manorial Court Rolls', *Law and History Review* 5, 1987, 523–35.

[13] Russell, 92–117; Hollingsworth, 220–2, 362, 375–87. See refs cited in n. 19.

[14] Laslett and Wall, chaps 1, 4, 6–7.

midlands and Worcestershire in and after the 1470s,[15] such 'listings' only start with the Coventry City enumeration of 1523 and the Lichfield Abbey confraternity register of c.1532–3.[16] In the absence of any 'listings' for the period before the mid-thirteenth century, the historian wishing to investigate the composition of the earlier medieval family is, in the main, forced back on a reconstruction of individual families, from whatever sources are available, in the hope that there will be a sufficient number of families to afford a usable sample for analysis. 'In the main' but not quite entirely.

Although they are not a 'listing' as demographers studying the early modern and modern periods would understand the term, the unique *Rotuli de Dominabus* of 1185 do nevertheless permit the reconstruction of 128 families of royal tenants by knight-service or serjeanty whose husbands died in the four decades preceding 1185. These *Rotuli*, whose full title is cynically but accurately translated by Cecily Clark as 'Register of Rich Widows and of Orphaned Heirs and Heiresses',[17] comprise an apparently unique survey by royal officials, now surviving only for parts of twelve counties, of the lands of these royal tenants which were in the king's hands in 1185 because the tenants had died leaving either minors as heirs or widows (or both). The survey was required so that the king could give or more commonly sell the 'wardship' of the minor (or minors if girls) and the 'marriage' of the minor(s) and any widows. In order that the available opportunities could be accurately evaluated, the survey also generally included the names and ages of the widows and children of the deceased tenants. J. H. Round, who edited the *Rotuli* as long ago as 1913, gave reasons for thinking that there had been an earlier survey in 1177;[18] if so, it no longer exists, and there was no later survey: the Crown's need for such information was largely supplied from the 1230s onwards by the inquisitions post mortem taken after the death of individual tenants-in-chief by knight-service.[19] Despite his largely justified reputation as a reactionary and narrow-minded 'feudal' historian, Round was at pains to point-out the value of the *Rotuli* for demographic as well as genealogical purposes;[20] nevertheless, demographic and social historians have almost entirely ignored them. J. C. Russell, often accused of scraping the bottom of the evidential barrel for medieval demography, did not use them, and they are not mentioned in Hollingsworth's near-exhaustive survey of the sources for demographic history:

---

[15] Hallam; Dyer, 230–2; Lomas, 257–8; Jones, 329–45.
[16] C. Phythian-Adams, *Desolation of a City: Coventry and the Urban Crisis of the Late Middle Ages*, Cambridge 1979, esp. Appendix 1; A. Kettle, 'A list of families in the archdeaconry of Stafford, 1532–3', *Staffordshire Record Society* 4th ser., 8, 1976.
[17] C. Fell, C. Clark, *Women in Anglo-Saxon England*, Oxford 1986, 149.
[18] J. H. Round, 'Rotuli de Dominabus et Pueris et Puellis de XII Comitatibus', *Pipe Roll Society* 35, 1913, xviii, 2, 15, 23, 29, 36, 45, 52, 57, 59, 63–5, 78.
[19] The *Calendar of Inquisitions Post Mortem*, i–xviii, London 1904–88, summarises inquisitions from 1234 to 1405, dealing principally with tenants-in-chief by knight-service. Tenants holding land only by serjeanty were normally excluded, and serjeanty holdings were increasingly fragmented and converted to socage tenure (or less frequently to knight-service) after the late twelfth century (H. C. Maxwell-Lyte, ed., *Book of Fees*, London 1920, I, 4–8, 10–11; C. D. Ross, ed., *The Cartulary of Cirencester Abbey* i, Oxford 1964, 43n.; J. H. Round, *The King's Serjeants and Officers of State*, London 1911, 17–19, 28–9, 38–43, 93–4, 111, 123–4, 134–5, 167, 173–6, 226, 233, 256, 280, 283, 286, 305; E. G. Kimball, *Serjeanty Tenure in Medieval England*, New Haven (USA) 1936, vii, 5, 31, 33–4, 44, 86, 124, 148–9, 194, 199–241).
[20] Round, 'Rotuli', xxv, xxxviii–ix.

TABLE 1 Family size and composition in the *Rotuli de Dominabus*

ENTRY NO.	*ROTULI DE DOMINABUS* PAGE NOS.	NAME OF LATE HUSBAND	HUSBAND	WIDOW
Baronial families				
1	4–7, 62, 84	Conan, Earl of Richmond	1	1
2	66, 76	Gilbert, Earl of Pembroke	1	1
3	15–16	Hugh, Earl of Chester	1	1
4	1, 63	William D'Aubigny	1	1
5	2, 16	Thomas de Arci	1	1
6	43, 45	John de Bidun [senior]	1	1
7	43, 49, 55, 87	John de Bidun, junior	1	1
8	47, 63	William Blund	1	1
9	62, 84	Humphrey de Bohun	1	1
10	34, 40, 86	Walter de Bolbec	1	1
11	11, 45	William de Bussei	1	1
12	17	Simon de Canci	1	1
13	13–14	Robert de Cauz	1	1
14	60–1	Philip de Columbariis	1	1
15	20	Reginald de Crevequer	1	1
16	7, 18	Simon de Crevequer	1	1
17	73	William de Curci	1	1
18	14–15, 27	William de Diva	1	1
19	18–9	John D'Eincurt	1	1
20	23–4, 27	Richard Engaine	1	1
21	5, 9, 11	Robert Fitz Hugh	1	1
22	26–7, 30, 38–9	Hamo Fitz Meinfelin	1	1
23	29–30, 76–7	Roger Fitz Richard	1	1
24	4, 14, 48, 62	Albert Gresle	1	1
25	12	Richard de la Haie	1	1
26	59	William de Helion	1	1
27	51	Gerard de Limesi	1	1
28	38, 50, 54, 58	Warin de Mountchesney	1	1
29	85	William de Mountfitchet	1	1
30	24–5, 28	Geoffrey Ridel	1	1
31	1	Everard de Ros	1	1
32	47, 66, 70, 80	Hubert de St Clair	1	1

(By Social Group)

BOYS	GIRLS	MEN	WOMEN	SEX RATIO	TOTAL SIZE OF FAMILY
0	1	1	2	50	3
1	1	2	2	100	4
1	4	2	5	40	7
1	0	2	1	200	3
3	4	4	5	80	9
0	5	1	6	17	7
0	0	1	1	100	2
1	0	2	1	200	3
1	2	2	3	67	5
0	1	1	2	50	3
2	2	3	3	100	6
1	0	2	1	200	3
0	1	1	2	50	3
1	0	2	1	200	3
2	0	3	1	300	4
2	2	3	3	100	6
1	1	2	2	100	4
2	2	3	3	100	6
1	0	2	1	200	3
1	0	2	1	200	3
10	0	11	1	1100	12
1	4	2	5	40	7
2	1	3	2	150	5
1	3	2	4	50	6
0	3	1	4	25	5
1	0	2	1	200	3
2	2	3	3	100	6
3	2	4	3	133	7
2	2	3	3	100	6
2	1	3	2	150	5
2	0	3	1	300	4
0	1	1	2	50	3

ENTRY NO.	*ROTULI DE DOMINABUS* PAGE NOS.	NAME OF LATE HUSBAND	HUSBAND	WIDOW
33	46, 49–50	William de Say	1	1
34	69–70	Robert de Stuteville	1	1
35	77	Ralph de Tony	1	1
36	31	Geoffrey de Trailly	1	1
37	1, 27–8	William Trussebut	1	1
38	67, 77, 87	Roger de Valognes	1	1
39	9–10	William de Vesci	1	1
40	35, 40, 88	William de Windsor	1	1
Sub-totals:	**(40 families)**	**(31.3%)**	**40**	**40**

Knightly families

ENTRY NO.	*ROTULI DE DOMINABUS* PAGE NOS.	NAME OF LATE HUSBAND	HUSBAND	WIDOW
41	44	Richard Albus	1	1
42	25, 61, 68–9	Stephen de Beauchamp	1	1
43	25, 45, 57–8	Thomas de Belfou (*Bellofago*)	1	1
44	3–4	Peter de Bilingeia	1	1
45	43	Gilbert de Bolebec	1	1
46	16	Robert de Bonesboz	1	1
47	56	Hugh de Burdeleis	1	1
48	81	Ralph de Busseville	1	1
49	55–7	William Buteriz	1	1
50	39–40	William de Cauz	1	1
51	72	Godfrey *Camerarius*	1	1
52	32	Robert *Camerarius* (I)	1	1
53	82	Robert Camerarius (II)	1	1
54	61–2, 68–9	Gilbert de Coleville	1	1
55	61–2	William de Coleville	1	1
56	20	Peter de Cotes	1	1
57	23	Ingelram de Dumard	1	1
58	71–2	William de Elinton	1	1
59	80, 82	William Fitz Alured	1	1
60	36–7	Angot Fitz Anketil	1	1
61	49, 55, 77, 87	Thomas Fitz Bernard	1	1
62	79	William Fitz Gerard	1	1
63	31	Henry Fitz Gerold	1	1
64	8, 10	Herbert Fitz Gilbert	1	1

BOYS	GIRLS	MEN	WOMEN	SEX RATIO	TOTAL SIZE OF FAMILY
0	2	1	3	33	4
1	2	2	3	67	5
1	0	2	1	200	3
2	2	3	3	100	6
2	3	3	4	75	7
2	0	3	1	300	4
1	0	2	1	200	3
1	7	2	8	25	10
58	**60**	**98**	**100**	**98**	**4.95**
2	9	3	10	30	13
1	5	2	6	33	8
1	0	2	1	200	3
1	0	2	1	200	3
1	0	2	1	200	3
1	3	2	4	50	6
6	2	7	3	233	10
2	2	3	3	100	6
1	0	2	1	200	3
1	0	2	1	200	3
1	0	2	1	200	3
2	3	3	4	75	7
3	4	4	5	80	9
2	6	3	7	43	10
1	0	2	1	200	3
1	0	2	1	200	3
0	0	1	1	100	2
0	1	1	2	50	3
3	4	4	5	80	9
4	4	5	5	100	10
3	1	4	2	200	6
0	1	1	2	50	3
2	0	3	1	300	4
7	0	8	1	800	9

ENTRY NO.	*ROTULI DE DOMINABUS* PAGE NOS.	NAME OF LATE HUSBAND	HUSBAND	WIDOW
65	49	Robert Fitz Ralph	1	1
66	13	William Fitz Ranulf	1	1
67	21–3	Hugh Fitz Robert	1	1
68	40–1, 44, 56	Geoffrey Fitz William	1	1
69	51–2	William de Gernemuwe	1	1
70	81	William Granvel	1	1
71	32–3	Richard Gubiun	1	1
72	28	[ ] Gulafre	1	1
73	12	Walter de Hacunbi	1	1
74	5–6	Gilbert Hansard	1	1
75	60	Ralph de Haudeboville	1	1
76	47, 55	Theobald Hautein	1	1
77	79	William de Howe	1	1
78	85	[William] de Huntingfelde	1	1
79	48–9, 54, 56	Richard La Veile	1	1
80	48	Eustace de Leiham	1	1
81	24	Fulk de Lisores	1	1
82	33–4	Roger le Lohereng	1	1
83	75–6	Geoffrey de Luci	1	1
84	67	William de Luvetot	1	1
85	30–1	William Malbanc	1	1
86	26, 38	Robert Mantel	1	1
87	29	Gilbert de Monte	1	1
88	42	Peter Morel	1	1
89	38	William de Noers	1	1
90	83	[ ] de Pappewurthe	1	1
91	6	Peter Paynel (*Pounel*)	1	1
92	20–1	William Paynel	1	1
93	52–3	Peter de Peleville	1	1
94	83–4, 86	Aubrey Picot	1	1
95	73	Guy de Rocheford [senior]	1	1
96	84	William de Ros	1	1
97	81	[Robert] de Ruilia	1	1
98	70	Jordan de Sacqueville	1	1
99	53	[Richard] de Saiton	1	1
100	42	William de Schirinton	1	1

BOYS	GIRLS	MEN	WOMEN	SEX RATIO	TOTAL SIZE OF FAMILY
3	0	4	1	400	5
1	0	2	1	200	3
5	2	6	3	200	9
0	2	1	3	33	4
3	0	4	1	400	5
3	0	4	1	400	5
7	6	8	7	114	15
3	2	4	3	133	7
2	2	3	3	100	6
1	0	2	1	200	3
1	0	2	1	200	3
3	0	4	1	400	5
2	2	3	3	100	6
5	5	6	6	100	12
2	5	3	6	50	9
2	2	3	3	100	6
4	9	5	10	50	15
1	0	2	1	200	3
1	1	2	2	100	4
0	1	1	2	50	3
0	4	1	5	20	6
3	1	4	2	200	6
1	4	2	5	40	7
1	0	2	1	200	3
1	0	2	1	200	3
4	2	5	3	167	8
1	0	2	1	200	3
1	0	2	1	200	3
2	2	3	3	100	6
2	3	3	4	75	7
3	1	4	2	200	6
3	4	4	5	80	9
1	0	2	1	200	3
1	0	2	1	200	3
6	1	7	2	350	9
3	3	4	4	100	8

ENTRY NO.	*ROTULI DE DOMINABUS* PAGE NOS.	NAME OF LATE HUSBAND	HUSBAND	WIDOW
101	48	Hugh de Scotia	1	1
102	13	Osbert Selvein	1	1
103	80	Robert de Setvans	1	1
104	83	Gumer de Stanton	1	1
105	72	Nicholas de Stelbing	1	1
106	30–1	Robert de Surive	1	1
107	71–3, 87	Picot de Tany	1	1
108	51	[ ] de Tony	1	1
109	57, 78	Geoffrey de Tresgoz	1	1
110	43–4	[William] Visdelu	1	1
111	36	Ginant [de Wicumbe]	1	1
112	60	[ ] de Winemersse	1	1
Sub-totals:	**(72 families)**	**(56.3%)**	**72**	**72**

Freemen's families:

113	36, 43	Walter de Burton	1	1
114	82	Walter English (Anglicus)	1	1
115	9	William Fitz Chetel	1	1
116	60	William Fitz Mabel	1	1
117	82	Robert Fitz Odo	1	1
118	62	Herbert Fitz Rolland	1	1
119	35	Stephen Forester	1	1
120	17–18	Walter Furmage	1	1
121	66–7	Robert de Habingwurthe	1	1
122	60	Warengar de Hocxene	1	1
123	16–17	[Ivo] de Humestain	1	1
124	59	Walter Pikard	1	1
125	37	David Pinel	1	1
126	37	Roger Pinel	1	1
127	44	Robert de Riblemunt	1	1
128	78	Turstin de Waltham	1	1
Sub-totals:	**(16 families)**	**(12.5%)**	**16**	**16**
TOTALS:	**(128 families)**		**128**	**128**

Source: J. H. Round (ed.), 'Rotuli de Dominabus et Pueris et

BOYS	GIRLS	MEN	WOMEN	SEX RATIO	TOTAL SIZE OF FAMILY
3	0	4	1	400	5
1	0	2	1	200	3
1	0	2	1	200	3
0	2	1	3	33	4
2	0	3	1	300	4
1	0	2	1	200	3
5	2	6	3	200	9
1	5	2	6	33	8
1	4	2	5	40	7
1	0	2	1	200	3
1	2	2	3	67	5
4	3	5	4	125	9
149	**127**	**221**	**199**	**111**	**5.83**
0	1	1	2	50	3
1	0	2	1	200	3
2	0	3	1	300	4
0	0	1	1	100	2
1	0	2	1	200	3
1	5	2	6	33	8
0	3	1	4	25	5
0	1	1	2	50	3
1	0	2	1	200	3
1	3	2	4	50	6
2	1	3	2	150	5
1	0	2	1	200	3
1	1	2	2	100	4
0	0	1	1	100	2
0	1	1	2	50	3
2	2	3	3	100	6
13	**18**	**29**	**34**	**85**	**3.94**
220	**205**	**348**	**333**	**105**	**5.32**

Puellis de XII Comitatibus', *Pipe Roll Society* 35, 1913

Herlihy, who does mention them, states erroneously that they refer to 'the Anglo-Norman nobility . . . the high English aristocracy', and his analysis of them is also faulty, as we shall see.[21]

As Table 1 shows, the *Rotuli* were very far from being confined to 'the high English aristocracy': the greater tenants-in-chief holding *per baroniam* constitute less than one-third (31.3 per cent) of the 128 families which can be reconstituted; even if we add from the ranks of the 'knights' some important royal officials such as Thomas Fitz Bernard and Robert Mantel, and some major 'honorial barons' such as William de Luvetot, lord of Hallamshire (Yorks.), and William Malbanc of Cheshire, the number of dead husbands who were major landholders is still little more than a third of the total. An outright majority (56.3 per cent) of the royal tenants in the *Rotuli* were of knightly rank, and one-eighth were serjeants, most of whom were little if at all superior to free peasants. Robert de Habingwurthe (no. 121), apparently the most prosperous of the 'freemen', held two and a quarter hides (perhaps 300 acres) in Wallington and Clayhall (Herts.): he may perhaps have ranked as a knight. Robert Fitz Odo (no. 117) may also just have ranked as a knight, since he held one-tenth of a knight's fee in Essex, but it is recorded of his son that 'He and his mother can scarcely have their food from it.'[22] Robert Chamberlain I (no. 52) has been classified as a knight because his holding was later represented by the manor of Dunton Chamberlain (Beds.), but its demesne comprised only two carucates (240 acres); the land of Robert de Surive (no. 106), again classified as a knight, had a demesne of the same size (two hides, about 250 acres) in Wimmington (Beds.). Walter Furmage (no. 120) who had two holdings, each of a half-carucate, in total 120 acres, in Crosholm and Snitterby (Lincs.), Turstin de Waltham (no. 128) holding a hide (about 100–150 acres) in Waltham (Essex) and Ivo de Humestain (no. 123), apparently only holding six bovates (about ninety acres) in Humberston (Lincs.), to judge from his widow's dower of two bovates, were all no more than prosperous peasants. Two other freemen, Walter de Burton (no. 113) and Warengar de Hoxne (no. 122) each held half a hide or carucate (about sixty acres), whilst two brothers, David and Robert Pinel (nos. 125–6), in succession held a half-hide in Wycombe (Bucks.), but it is stated that 'the widows can scarcely live off the produce of this land'.[23] The eighty-year-old widow of Robert de Riblemunt (no. 127) had to survive on no more than forty acres in the two common fields of Buckingham, and the three daughters of Stephen Forester (no. 119) had only a half-virgate (about fifteen acres) in Iver (Bucks.) as 'their inheritance': it is to be hoped that they had beauty to attract suitors, for their land would not. The Pinel brothers, Robert de Riblemunt and Stephen Forester, holding between fifteen and sixty acres apiece, were typical of the ordinary peasant of the twelfth century: only in their legal tenure and social status were they different from their neighbours.

---

[21] Herlihy, 102, 105. I regret very much having to report my divergence from David Herlihy, with whom I had corresponded for many years. I was about to write to him to discuss this discrepancy between our results when I heard of his sadly premature death at the height of his powers.

[22] Round, 'Rotuli', 82.

[23] Round, 'Rotuli', 37. I have converted tenemental units into acres for illustrative purposes, taking hides and carucates to average 120 acres, virgates 30 acres and bovates 15 acres. I have myself shown that hides especially could vary between extremes of 40 and 1,500 acres (J. S. Moore, *Laughton: a study in the evolution of the Wealden landscape*, Leicester 1965, 30, 53–5).

The stringent economic conditions under which the peasantry generally lived probably explains the great difference in average family-size between the 'freemen' (3.94) and their betters (4.95 – 5.83) shown in Tables 1–2. Since families headed by widows are clearly atypical – early modern 'listings' suggest that households headed by widows were about thirteen per cent of all households[24] – I have 'restored' the dead husbands for the purpose of calculating both the completed family-size and the normal sex-ratio. With regret I report that I have been quite unable to replicate Herlihy's finding that 'Among the offspring females outnumber males by 155 to 138.'[25] Theoretically, this 'restoration' of husbands will lead to a slight over-estimate of both the completed family-size and the sex-ratio. If we adjust the 'Summary' figures in Table 2 to allow for the 'normal' absence of about one-eighth of the 'restored' husbands, we obtain the following results:

Baronial families	Sex-ratio:	93	Average family-size:	4.83
Knightly families	Sex-ratio:	107	Average family-size:	5.71
Freemen's families	Sex-ratio:	79	Average family-size:	3.59
All families	Sex-ratio:	100	Average family-size:	5.20

What is abundantly clear from Tables 1–2 and from their source is that, at all social levels, the nuclear family of husband, wife and unmarried children was the norm in Henry II's England; the only other kin occasionally noticed in the *Rotuli* are widows surviving from a still earlier generation. Thus both Maud, widow of Earl Ranulf II of Chester, d.1153, and her daughter-in-law Bertreia, widow of Earl Hugh of Chester, d.1181, occur in the *Rotuli*.[26] There is no evidence whatsover of more than one married couple sharing a holding, much less living in one household: David Pinel only succeeded his brother Roger because the latter died childless. And it must be emphasized that this negative conclusion is not the result of absence of evidence, because the existence of any other dependent kin would have had clear implications for the Crown's calculations of the value of 'wards'. Since, however, the *Rotuli* in their present form only cover the east midlands and East Anglia from Lincolnshire to Middlesex, much of which was within the 'Danelaw' with its legal and social peculiarities,[27] it could perhaps be argued that the results obtained from the foregoing analysis may not be representative of the rest of England. It could also be argued that, since the *Rotuli* mainly reflect families of baronial and knightly status, the few freemen's families may not be typical of the majority of families in the entire population. For both these reasons we must therefore turn to other sources.

Among the records produced by the medieval Western Church were what were known as *libri vitae* – 'books of life'. The name originated in Biblical texts such as *Exodus*, XXXII, 32; *Psalms*, LXIX, 29; *The Epistle to the Philippians*, IV, 3;

---

[24] Laslett and Wall, 147 (Table 4.9).
[25] Herlihy, 102.
[26] Round, 'Rotuli', 15–16.
[27] F. M. Stenton, *Documents illustrative of the social and economic history of the Danelaw*, London 1920; F. M. Stenton, *The Free Peasantry of the Northern Danelaw*, Lund (Sweden) 1926; F. M. Stenton, *The Danes in England*, London 1927; D. C. Douglas, *The Social Structure of Medieval East Anglia*, Oxford 1927; G. C. Homans, 'The Frisians in East Anglia', *Econ. Hist. Rev.* 2nd ser., 10, 1958, 189–206.

TABLE 2 Distribution of family sizes and population in the *Rotuli de Dominabus*

Family size:	2	3	4	5	6	7	8	9	10	11	12	13	14	15
Baronial families														
Number of families:	1	13	6	5	7	5	0	1	1	0	1	0	0	0
% of families:	2.5	32.5	15.0	12.5	17.5	12.5	0	2.5	2.5	0	2.5	0	0	0
Pop'n in families:	2	39	24	25	42	35	0	9	10	0	12	0	0	0
% of pop'n:	1.0	19.7	12.1	12.6	21.2	17.7	0	4.6	5.1	0	6.1	0	0	0
Knightly families														
Number of families:	1	23	5	6	10	5	4	9	3	0	1	1	0	2
% of families:	1.4	34.7	6.9	8.3	13.9	6.9	5.6	12.5	4.2	0	1.4	1.4	0	2.8
Pop'n in families:	2	75	20	30	54	35	32	81	30	0	12	13	0	30
% of pop'n:	0.5	17.9	4.8	7.2	14.3	8.3	7.6	19.3	7.1	0	2.9	3.1	0	7.1
Freemen's families														
Number of families:	2	7	2	2	2	0	1	0	0	0	0	0	0	0
% of families:	12.5	43.8	12.5	12.5	12.5	0	6.3	0	0	0	0	0	0	0
Pop'n in families:	4	21	8	10	12	0	8	0	0	0	0	0	0	0
% of pop'n:	6.4	33.3	12.7	15.9	19.0	0	12.7	0	0	0	0	0	0	0

Family size:	2	3	4	5	6	7	8	9	10	11	12	13	14	15
ALL FAMILIES														
Number of families:	4	45	13	13	19	10	5	10	4	0	2	1	0	2
% of families:	3.1	35.2	10.2	10.2	14.8	7.8	3.9	7.8	3.1	0	1.6	0.8	0	1.6
Pop'n in families:	8	135	52	65	114	70	40	90	40	0	24	13	0	30
% of pop'n:	1.2	19.8	7.6	9.5	16.7	10.3	5.9	13.2	5.9	0	3.5	1.9	0	4.4

Summary

	Number of families		Total population in families		Average Family Size	Sex Ratio
	N	%	N	%		
Baronial:	40	31.3	198	29.1	4.95	98
Knightly:	72	56.3	420	61.7	5.83	111
Freemen's:	17	13.3	63	9.3	3.94	85
ALL:	128	100.1	681	100.1	5.32	105

Source: Table 1

Social Classification

'Baronial': Included in I.J. Sanders, *English Baronies: their origin and descent, 1086–1327* (Oxford 1960)
'Knightly': Non-baronial holders of knights' fees and manors
'Freemen': Holders of sub-manorial property

Book of Revelations, III, 5, XVII, 8, XX, 12 and XXII, 19. The original purpose of such books was to record the names of members of the monastic community, but it was soon extended to include benefactors and other laity who were joined to the community by confraternity. At Thorney the *liber vitae* appears not to have any new entries after the 1190s; the Hyde liber went out of use rather earlier, but a few entries were added in the five decades before the Dissolution;[28] at Durham additions were still being made to the *liber vitae* down to the end of the fifteenth century,[29] whilst its use as a memorial at the high altar was still remembered in an account written in 1593.[30] Later, as Hamilton-Thompson noted,[31] the *liber vitae* often developed into a more specialised *liber confraternitatum*,[32] supplemented by obituary and mortuary rolls[33] and letters of confraternity,[34] whilst the notes of gifts sometimes found in a *liber vitae* were subsequently elaborated in cartularies. These cartularies may contain agreements for confraternity as at Thorney (occasionally) and Rochester (frequently).[35] The *libri vitae* are of considerable historical value from several viewpoints, including onomastics, etymology and prosopography, but for historical demographers their interest lies in their occasional inclusion of the wives and children of lay donors (and in the eleventh and twelfth centuries of a few married clergy as well). There was no legal or customary rule which required the inclusion of kin other than children – unlike the contemporary French *laudatio parentum* and the later French *offre aux parents*, *retrait lignager* and *réserve coutumière*[36] – and most frequently male donors are listed either alone or only with their wives, but the context suggests that when children were mentioned, usually all were included who were alive at the time.[37] Even more valuable from a demographic viewpoint, such information, sparse

[28] W. de G. Birch, 'Liber Vitae: Register and Martyrology of New Minster and Hyde Abbey, Winchester', *Hampshire Record Society* 5, 1892, 177–8, 180, 188–9.
[29] A. Hamilton-Thompson, 'Liber Vitae Ecclesiae Dunelmensis: a collotype facsimile of the original manuscript', *Surtees Society* 136, 1923, ix.
[30] Hamilton-Thompson, xxviii, citing J. T. Fowler, 'The Rites of Durham', *Surtees Society* 107, 1903, 16–17.
[31] Hamilton-Thompson, xiv–v, xxvi.
[32] E.g. Kettle, 'A list of families'.
[33] E.g. Birch, 135–52; J. Raine, 'The Obituary Roll of William Ebchester and John Burnby, priors of Durham', *Surtees Society* 31, 1856; W. H. St John Hope, *The Obituary Roll of John Islip*, London 1906; M. V. Taylor, 'Liber Luciani de laude Cestrie', *Lancashire and Cheshire Record Society* 64, 1912.
[34] E.g. J. Stevenson, 'Liber Vitae Ecclesiae Dunelmensis', *Surtees Society* 13, 1841, xv–vi, 32–3, 71–3; Birch, 293; Raine, 106–20; J. B. Sheppard, 'Literae Cantuarienses', RS 85, 1887–9, I, 10–13; II, 456–7; III, 137–8, 140–3, 152, 288, 315, 368–9; J. H. Bloom, 'Liber Ecclesiae Wigornensis', *Worcestershire Historical Society* 28, 1912, 52.
[35] Thorney: 'Red Book' (Cambridge University Library, MSS 3020–1); Rochester: '*Textus Roffensis*' (Rochester Cathedral Library, MS. A.3.5, fos 119–235, ed. T. Hearne, *Textus Roffensis*, Oxford 1720, 62–242, from a sixteenth-century transcript (B.L. Cotton MS Julius C ii); printed in facsimile in P. Sawyer, ed., '*Textus Roffensis*, part II', *Early English Manuscripts in Facsimile* xi, Copenhagen (Denmark) 1962).
[36] S. D. White, *Custom, Kinship and Gifts to Saints: the Laudatio Parentum in Western France, 1050–1150*, Chapel Hill (USA) 1988, 3, 53, 199, points out that English practice required only the consent of heirs, not of other near-kin, hence the early rise of warranty against heirs in England, and that, apart from *retrait lignager* in a few boroughs, the later French practices were unknown in England. I am most grateful to Dr Marjorie Chibnall for bringing Dr White's work to my notice.
[37] Again, there is a contrast with France, where, although challenges to monastic donations were normally confined to the wives/widows, sons, daughters and sons-in-law of donors, the presence of other kin means that there can be no 'routine equation' of kin with the co-residential family,

though it admittedly is, comes mainly from the eleventh and twelfth centuries when little other information on the size of families is available.

Three *libri vitae* survive from Anglo-Norman England: one developed at Durham out of a record begun at Lindisfarne;[38] another began at New Minster, Winchester, and was continued at Hyde Abbey;[39] the third was maintained at Thorney Abbey.[40] Even as liturgical documents they have not received overmuch attention: the original edition of the Durham *liber* did little more than provide a usable text, and its palaeographical element was rudimentary; a re-edition did not proceed beyond a useful facsimile, the promised second volume of text with a proper study of the various handwritings and a prosopographical index never materialising.[41] The edition of the Hyde Abbey *liber*, whilst again giving a usable text, was hardly notable for palaeographical expertise, as well as citing the wrong reference (B.L. Stowe MS 960) for the original manuscript,[42] and neither the Durham nor the Hyde *libri* were collated with the available cartularies,[43] a task which Cecily Clark has demonstrated in her preliminary studies of the Thorney Abbey *liber vitae* is essential to the successful identification and dating of the individuals involved.[44] We look forward eagerly to the appearance of her edition of the text. The necessity for collation with the evidence of cartularies, original charters and any other external dating-material arises from the fact that though originally entries would have been made in chronological sequence on each manuscript folio, any spaces left blank were likely to be filled-in at a later stage, sometimes decades or even centuries later. In addition, in some cases entries from another source were inserted into a *liber vitae* at a much later date; in other cases, such entries did not reach the *liber vitae*.[45] Nevertheless, what is available constitutes a small but useful sample of families in three widely separated regions of Anglo-Norman England, the north (Durham Priory), the east midlands (Thorney Abbey) and the south (Hyde Abbey).[46] Although I shall try to analyse the evi-

---

though there was an 'overwhelming preponderance of conjugal pairs and full or truncated conjugal kin' (White, 62, 96, 119, 124–6).

[38] B.L. Cotton MS Domitian A VII, printed in Stevenson, 1–134.

[39] B.L. Stowe MS 944, printed in Birch.

[40] B.L. Add. MS 40,000, fos 1v–12r; an edition by C. Clark is in preparation.

[41] Hamilton-Thompson, vii.

[42] Birch, i.

[43] The cartularies are listed in G. R. C. Davis, *Medieval Cartularies of Great Britain*, London 1958, 39–41 (Durham Priory), 121 (Hyde Abbey). The numerous Durham cartularies, mostly still in the Dean and Chapter muniments, are all unprinted, as are the four post-Conquest cartularies in the British Library for Winchester Cathedral, Hyde Abbey and Holy Cross Hospital; the latter, however, contain very few copy-deeds and virtually none before the thirteenth century. The Hyde Abbey chronicles (E. Edwards, 'Liber Monasterii de Hyda', RS 45, 1866) do not contain any information on the abbey's dealings with land in the Anglo-Norman period. The other major source of relevant documentary evidence is edited in M. Biddle, *Winchester in the Early Middle Ages*, Oxford 1976.

[44] C. Clark, 'British Library Additional MS 40,000, ff. 1v–12r', *Anglo-Norman Studies* vii, 1985, 50–68; C. Clark, 'The *Liber Vitae* of Thorney and its "catchment area" ', *Nomina* 9, 1985, 53–72; C. Clark, 'A witness to post-Conquest English cultural patterns: the *liber vitae* of Thorney Abbey', *Studies in honour of Rene Derolez*, ed. A. M. Simon-Vandenbergen, Ghent (Belgium) 1987, 73–85.

[45] Birch, 148, prints a twelfth-century confraternity-agreement for Ansketil Fitz Gilbert from the rear paste-down of a Durham obit-book.

[46] Professor Hirokazu Tsurushima's paper on 'The Fraternity of Rochester Diocese, c.1100' (below, pp. 313–37) has revealed the existence of numerous confraternity agreements between the

dence on families recorded in all three *libri vitae* for Durham Priory, Hyde and Thorney Abbeys, I shall not now discuss the problems of dating the entries in these *libri*, which I hope to accomplish elsewhere.[47]

It has to be confessed that the dating of undated medieval documents or parts of them such as individual entries in *libri vitae* by means of identifying the individuals concerned or, in default, by establishing a chronological context, is one of the more tedious tasks of the medieval specialist: it is a necessary chore. At least with the Hyde Abbey *liber*, there is a reasonable hope of identifying many of the heads of families and other individuals commemorated, because the large amount of documentation available for the Winchester monasteries is augmented by the eleventh- and twelfth-century surveys in the 'Winton Domesday' so superbly edited by Frank Barlow.[48] By comparison, the documents available in print to identify individuals in the Durham *liber* are much more sparse before the thirteenth century, although the Durham Cathedral manuscripts are arguably the largest surviving English monastic archive.[49] Nevertheless, it seems highly probable that most of the entries of families from the Durham *liber* analysed in Table 3 antedate 1220, since a change of practice in entering names can be seen from about the second quarter of the thirteenth century. From page 85 onwards in Stevenson's edition (fol. 54 in the original manuscript), the entries are all in scripts of the thirteenth to fifteenth centuries, and contain extremely few family entries and relatively few entries of husbands and wives. For Thorney I have been able to draw on Cecily Clark's expert knowledge and on the late Olof Von Feilitzen's notes which she has kindly made available to me. In fact, the vast majority of the heads of families can be adequately identified and dated sufficiently closely to be included in my analysis in Tables 3–4.

It will, I hope, be clear from what I have said that the most relevant entries in the *libri vitae* can be dated within reasonably close limits: it now remains to demonstrate their so far unrecognised importance as a source for the history of the medieval family. There was no legal or moral compulsion on the laity to enter into confraternity with a monastery and thus ensure their inclusion in a *liber vitae*, nor was there any further sanction to ensure the mention of family members, much less other kin, alongside the individual *confrère* – unlike the contemporary French *laudatio parentum* – and in fact the vast majority of secular entries in all three *libri vitae* refer to individuals. The impulse came from the potential donor, leading one eminent Scottish historian to describe the Durham *liber vitae* as 'That incomparable tourist Visitors' Book'.[50]

1080s and the 1140s in the Textus Roffensis, many of which include details of families. I hope to analyse the families in these agreements in the future in conjunction with Prof. Tsurushima.

[47] The chronology and identification of family-entries are studied in a 'Corpus of Families extracted from English *Libri vitae*' circulated at the Battle Conference; this is too large to be printed as an annex to this paper, but I hope to publish it in instalments in *Nomina*. Entry numbers in the remainder of this paper refer to this 'Corpus'.

[48] Davis, 120–2; Biddle, 32–141.

[49] J.A. Conway-Davies, 'The Muniments of the Dean and Chapter of Durham', *Durham University Journal* 13, 1952, 77–87, esp. 78–9. Some Durham charters of the eleventh to thirteenth centuries have been printed in the notes to J. Greenwell, 'Feodarium Prioratus Dunelmensis', *Surtees Society* 58, 1872, and in H. S. Offler, 'Durham Episcopal Charters, 1071–1152', *Surtees Society* 179, 1968.

[50] G. W. S. Barrow, *The Anglo-Norman Era in Scottish History*, Oxford 1980, 158–9.

The corollary is that it is difficult to regard the people entered in a *liber vitae* as in any sense a random sample. Geographically, as might be expected, the visitors to Durham come overwhemingly from north-east England and southern Scotland, those to Hyde from southern England and those to Thorney from the east midlands.[51] Until the task of personal identification is complete, a full social classification is impossible, but in all three places the visitors are mostly from the baronial and knightly groups, albeit with a sprinkling of local freeholders and townsmen. It is, however, fair to say that the families of the barons and knights do not seem to be markedly different in either size or composition from the families of the freeholders and townsmen, though admittedly the number of the latter is too small to be a satisfactory sample. It is also clear from the sex-ratio (i.e. the number of men per 100 women) that men are considerably over-represented in the reconstructed families at all three centres. These sex-ratios are 151 (Durham), 163 (Hyde), 182 (Thorney). Now it is not necessary to indulge, as French historians did when confronted with the same apparent sexual imbalance in the Carolingian estate-surveys or *polyptyques*, in fantasies about massive female infanticide: where they were observed, the feast-days commemorating the death of the Eleven Thousand Virgins (22 August and 21 October) were not occasions for culling surplus young girls. The truth is more prosaic: it is not that women were missing, rather that men were more likely to be represented, for the very obvious reason that men did matter more in the feudal age.[52] Visits to all three religious houses may well often have followed, and been in thanksgiving for, the birth of a son and heir, which was vital to the family's survival. The over-representation of men is therefore entirely explicable in terms of the value-system and ethos of the lordly classes in 'the first century of English [and Scottish] feudalism'; it does not weaken the value of the *libri vitae* for historical demography.

We can now turn to consider the results of analysing the 'family' entries in the Durham, Hyde and Thorney *libri vitae* for the 'Anglo-Norman' period, which I have defined as the period from c.1050 to c.1250. Table 3 presents the data for both 'Anglo-Norman' and later medieval families, under two headings: for those entries where the statement of family-size is unambiguous and those where there is some imprecision. So far as the structure of the Anglo-Norman family is concerned, the very great majority of entries for families refer to nuclear families consisting of a married couple and their children and thus containing only two generations.[53] Since the sole difference between the families whose size I have classified as 'certain' or 'uncertain' relates to the exact number of children, we can consider both categories when examining the structure of the family. No more than seventeen families out of 162 (10.5 per cent) were headed by a widowed parent. That at least seems a reasonable deduction from the non-mention of the missing parent. Where other kin are concerned, there is always the possibility that an entry was partly commemorating past generations: this is probably true of

---

[51] For Thorney, see Clark, 'The *Liber Vitae* of Thorney and its "catchment area" '.

[52] Cf. E. R. Coleman, 'Medieval Marriage Characteristics: a neglected factor in the history of medieval serfdom' in T. K. Rabb, R. I. Rotberg, eds, *The Family in History*, New York (USA) 1976, 4–13 and Herlihy, 62–8, on the illusory surplus of men on the estates of St Germain des Prés in the ninth-century *polyptyque*.

[53] The reason for this prevalence of nuclear families in the record-evidence partly results from the absence of the *laudatio parentum* in England (White, 3, 53, 199).

Waltheof Fitz Gospatric (entry no. 100) and Thomas de Amundeville (entry no. 107), and is certainly true of the extended kin-group intertwined with Gilbert Fitz Richard's family (entry no. 152). It is therefore uncertain whether kin other than parents and children were co-resident or were only associated for the spiritual benefits of confraternity. Nevertheless, even if all the other kin mentioned in the *libri vitae* (apart from the Clares) were co-resident, this only affected a small minority of families. At most, therefore, only three families (nos. 51, 100, 107) contained one set of grandparents (1.9 per cent), and another three families (nos. 24, 50, 53) contained a single, presumably widowed, grandparent; five families (nos. 4, 50, 51, 53, 60) apparently included unmarried brothers of the husband (3.1 per cent); two more families (nos. 45, 109) may have included the eldest son's wife (1.2 per cent); one family (no. 92) possibly had a nephew living with them; another family had the wife's mother living with them (no. 45) and a third (no. 122) clearly had three generations, including the daughter's children. Because of overlaps in these sub-categories, only twelve out of 162 families (7.4 per cent) were structurally abnormal: the norm, in the Anglo-Norman period, as now, was a two-generation family consisting of either one or two parents and their children.

Although there are 162 entries of families for our period, in only 128 can the family-size be unambiguously deduced, and I have initially concentrated on analysing these 128 entries in Tables 3 and 4. Table 3 presents the data for each family in a standardized manner, whilst Table 4 analyses the distribution of family-sizes in greater detail. Two regional differences seem to be apparent: the first is that the average family-size in the Hyde *liber* is lower than that in the Durham and Thorney *libri*, both in the Anglo-Norman and in the later medieval periods. But the difference is not significant and may be a statistical vagary resulting from the small number of family-entries in the Hyde record. Secondly, the average family-size in the Durham area (4.26) is definitely smaller than in the Thorney area (4.74), which may partly reflect the known lower population-density in the 'highland zone' compared to the densely populated area of East Anglia and the fenland region, a difference apparent throughout the medieval period. (The survival of partible inheritance in East Anglia well into the Middle Ages is another possible explanation for the larger average family-size seen in the Thorney *liber vitae*.)[54] Nevertheless, the overall average size of 4.34 for the Anglo-Norman family based on the 128 families whose size is not in doubt seems entirely reasonable.

Is it possible to improve on this estimate by including the remaining thirty-four families of 'uncertain size' where the scribes have used the unspecific *filii et filiae* formula? In strict theory this ought to indicate a minimum family-size of six (parents, at least two boys and at least two girls). On this assumption I have calculated averages of 'unmodified estimates' and incorporated these in overall averages including the 'certain size' families, resulting in a final figure of 4.53. But since scribes sometimes used plurals where singular cases should have been employed – e.g. 'et eorum filii Rodbertus' (entry no. 4, Hyde) – I have also produced 'modified estimates' on the basis that the *filii et filiae* formula must imply at least one child of each sex, and have recalculated on the basis that such

---

[54] I owe this suggestion to Dr Marjorie Chibnall.

TABLE 3 Family-size and composition in the *Libri Vitae*

1. FAMILY SIZE CERTAIN

ENTRY NUMBER	DATE	HUSBAND	WIFE/ WIDOW	CHILDREN BOYS	GIRLS	TOTAL SIZE OF FAMILY
A. HYDE ABBEY				,		
Anglo-Norman						
28	c.1060	1	1	0	1	3
17	c.1060	1	1	2	0	4
1	c.1070	1	1	2	0	4
27	c.1070	1	1	1	0	3
2	c.1080	1	1	0	1	3
29	c.1080	1	1	3	1	6
16	c.1090	1	1	2	1	5
24	c.1090	1	0	1	0	2
24	c.1090	1	1	0	0	2
18	c.1110	1	1	2	0	4
15	c.1120	1	1	2	0	4
21	c.1120	1	1	2	2	6
14	c.1130	1	1	1	1	4
Average:						3.85
Later medieval						
8	C13	1	1	0	2	4
30	c.1485	1	1	1	2	5
31	c.1510	1	1	1	1	4
32	c.1530	1	1	1	0	3
33	c.1530	1	1	1	0	3
Average:						3.80
B. DURHAM PRIORY						
Anglo-Norman						
69	c.1090	1	0	2.5	1.5	5
72	c.1090	1	1	2	0	4
57	c.1100	1	1	1	0	3
63	c.1100	1	1	3	0	5
73	c.1100	1	1	2	0	4
141	c.1100	1	1	3	2	7
43	c.1110	1	1	1	0	3
74	c.1110	1	1	1	1	4
97	c.1110	1	1	2	0	4
35	c.1130	1	1	2	2	6
56	c.1130	1	1	1	0	3

ENTRY NUMBER	DATE	HUSBAND	WIFE/ WIDOW	CHILDREN BOYS	CHILDREN GIRLS	TOTAL SIZE OF FAMILY
B. DURHAM PRIORY (cont.)						
58	c.1130	1	1	1	0	3
67	c.1130	1	1	4	2	8
109	c.1130	1	1	4	2	8
44	c.1140	1	1	2	0	4
45	c.1140	1	1	3	1	6
46	c.1140	1	1	0	0	2
47	c.1140	1	1	1	0	3
48	c.1140	1	0	1	0	2
49	c.1140	1	1	1	0	3
50	c.1140	1	1	2	0	4
66	c.1140	1	1	5	2	9
92	c.1140	1	0	2	3	6
36	c.1150	1	1	4	0	6
37	c.1150	1	0	0	4	5
100	c.1150	1	1	1	0	3
102	c.1150	1	1	1	0	3
55	c.1160	1	0	0	1	2
61	c.1160	1	1	2	0	4
80	c.1160	1	1	1	1	4
93	c.1160	1	1	3	0	5
98	c.1160	1	1	2	0	4
99	c.1160	1	1	1	0	3
107	c.1160	1	1	1	0	3
113	c.1160	1	0	1	0	2
114	c.1160	1	1	1	0	3
119	c.1160	1	0	3	0	4
121	c.1160	1	1	0	2	4
122	c.1160	1	1	0	1	3
54	c.1165	1	1	1	0	3
81	c.1165	1	1	2	1	5
38	c.1170	1	1	0	4	6
83	c.1170	1	1	1	0	3
94	c.1170	1	1	1	0	3
42	c.1175	1	1	1	1	4
51	c.1175	1	1	5	1	8
52	c.1175	1	1	2	0	4
39	c.1180	1	1	2	2	6
53	c.1180	1	1	0	1	3
60	c.1180	1	1	1	1	4
62	c.1180	1	1	3	0	5
65	c.1180	1	1	1	1	4

ENTRY NUMBER	DATE	HUSBAND	WIFE/ WIDOW	CHILDREN		TOTAL SIZE OF FAMILY
				BOYS	GIRLS	
B. DURHAM PRIORY (cont.)						
70	c.1180	1	1	3	0	5
71	c.1180	1	1	2	0	4
82	c.1180	1	1	1	0	3
101	c.1180	1	1	1	0	3
103	c.1180	1	1	0	1	3
112	c.1180	1	1	3	4	9
104	c.1180	1	1	1	0	3
64	c.1185	1	1	2	2	6
91	c.1185	1	1	3	0	5
75	c.1190	1	1	1	1	4
77	c.1190	1	1	0	5	7
110	c.1190	1	1	1	1	4
123	c.1190	0	1	4	2	7
85	c.1195	1	1	2	3	7
117	c.1195	1	1	1	0	3
118	c.1195	1	1	1	0	3
40	c.1200	1	1	0	0	2
95	c.1200	1	1	3	2	7
105	c.1200	1	1	1	1	4
76	c.1210	0	1	1	0	2
84	c.1210	1	1	0	0	2
90	c.1215	1	1	1	0	3
79	c.1225	1	1	2	2	6
86	c.1225	1	1	1	0	3
115	c.1240	1	1	4	0	6
78	c.1245	1	1	1	0	3
87	c.1250	1	1	1	0	3
88	c.1250	1	1	0	1	3
89	c.1250	1	0	0	2	3
Average:						4.26
Later medieval						
120	C14	1	1	11	4	17
126	C14	1	0	3	0	4
127	C14	1	1	2	0	4
128	C14	1	1	5	4	11
124	C15	1	1	1	0	3
125, 133	C15	1	1	3	5	10
129	C15	1	1	6	4	12
130	C15	1	1	6	6	14
131	C15	1	1	0	2	4

ENTRY NUMBER	DATE	HUSBAND	WIFE/ WIDOW	CHILDREN		TOTAL SIZE OF FAMILY
				BOYS	GIRLS	
B. DURHAM PRIORY (cont.)						
132	C15	1	1	1	1	4
134	C15	1	1	3	2	7
135	C15	1	1	2	5	9
136	C15	1	1	5	2	9
137	C15	1	1	3	0	5
138	C15	1	1	6	6	14
139	C15	1	1	4	2	8
140	C15	1	1	3	0	5
Average:						8.24
C. THORNEY ABBEY						
Anglo-Norman						
168	c.1100	1	1	1	0	3
169	c.1100	1	1	0	1	3
170	c.1100	1	1	1	0	3
171	c.1100	1	1	1	0	3
174	c.1100	1	1	4	0	6
179	c.1100	1	1	1	0	3
182	c.1100	1	1	6	4	12
183	c.1100	1	1	10	0	12
185	c.1100	1	1	1	0	3
186	c.1100	1	1	1	1	4
188	c.1100	1	1	0	1	3
166	c.1110	1	1	1	0	3
167	c.1110	1	1	0	1	3
158	c.1125	1	1	1	0	3
159	c.1125	1	1	5	0	7
160	c.1125	1	0	2	1	4
162	c.1125	1	0	3	1	5
163	c.1125	1	1	0	1	3
143, 146	c.1135	1	1	3	2	7
144	c.1135	1	1	3	0	5
145	c.1135	1	1	2	0	4
147	c.1135	1	1	1	2	5
148	c.1135	1	1	2	0	4
149	c.1135	1	1	1	0	3
150	c.1135	1	1	3	0	5
151	c.1135	1	1	1	0	3
152	c.1135	1	1	6	4	12
164	c.1135	1	1	1	0	3
165	c.1135	1	1	2	2	6

ENTRY NUMBER	DATE	HUSBAND	WIFE/ WIDOW	CHILDREN BOYS	CHILDREN GIRLS	TOTAL SIZE OF FAMILY
154	c.1150	1	1	2	0	4
155	c.1150	1	1	0	1	3
156	c.1150	1	1	4	2	8
157	c.1150	1	1	1	0	3
142	c.1180	1	1	0	1	3
Average:						4.74

AVERAGE, ALL ANGLO-NORMAN FAMILIES, CERTAIN SIZE: 4.34

2. FAMILY SIZE UNCERTAIN

ENTRY NUMBER	DATE	HUSBAND	WIFE/ WIDOW	CHILDREN BOYS	CHILDREN GIRLS	TOTAL SIZE OF FAMILY
A. HYDE ABBEY						
Anglo-Norman						
25	c.1060	1	1	2	2	6
26	c.1060	1	1	2	2	6
3	c.1090	1	1	2	2	6
4	c.1090	1	1	2	2	6
10	c.1090	1	1	3	2	7
19	c.1100	1	1	2	2	6
5	c.1110	1	1	2	2	6
6	c.1110	1	1	2	2	6
11	c.1110	1	0	2	2	5
12	c.1110	0	1	2	2	5
22	c.1110	1	1	2	2	6
23	c.1110	1	1	2	2	6
20	c.1120	1	1	3	2	7
9	c.1130	1	0	2	0	3
13	c.1130	1	1	2	2	6
7	c.1140	1	1	2	2	6
Average:						5.81
Average (modified):						4.88
B. DURHAM PRIORY						
Anglo-Norman						
68	c.1090	1	0	2	2	5
34	c.1130	1	1	2	2	6
106, 116	c.1140	1	1	2	2	6
59	c.1160	1	1	2	2	6

ENTRY NUMBER	DATE	HUSBAND	WIFE/ WIDOW	CHILDREN BOYS	CHILDREN GIRLS	TOTAL SIZE OF FAMILY
41	c.1170	1	1	2	0	4
108	c.1170	1	1	2	2	6
111	c.1175	1	1	2	0	4
Average:						5.29
Average (modified):						4.57

Later medieval

96	C15	1	0	2	2	5

C. THORNEY ABBEY

Anglo-Norman

ENTRY NUMBER	DATE	HUSBAND	WIFE/ WIDOW	CHILDREN BOYS	CHILDREN GIRLS	TOTAL SIZE OF FAMILY
172	c.1100	1	1	2	0	4
173	c.1100	1	1	2	0	4
175	c.1100	1	1	2	0	4
176	c.1100	1	1	2	0	4
177	c.1100	1	1	2	0	4
178	c.1100	1	1	2	0	4
180	c.1100	1	1	2	0	4
181	c.1100	1	1	2	0	4
187	c.1100	1	1	1	0	3
161, 184	c.1125	1	1	2	2	6
153	c.1135	1	1	2	2	6
Average:						4.36
Average (modified):						4.18

AVERAGE, ALL ANGLO-NORMAN FAMILIES, CERTAIN SIZE, AND UNCERTAIN SIZE (UNMODIFIED ESTIMATES):   4.53

AVERAGE, ALL ANGLO-NORMAN FAMILIES, CERTAIN SIZE, AND UNCERTAIN SIZE (MODIFIED ESTIMATES):   4.40

families probably contained five rather than six people. This leads to an overall average family-size of 4.40. Such calculations are speculative, but they do establish that the first overall average of 4.34 derived from the 128 families of 'certain size' would not be significantly raised if we had accurate data for the other thirty-four families. Table 4 explores the composition of families in greater detail. Generally about two-thirds of all families contained no more than four people, though about half the population were in families of six or more. In this as in other ways, there was much more continuity between the medieval and later periods than used to be supposed, for these results are strikingly similar to those established by Peter Laslett for the better-documented centuries after 1538.

The problem of dating confronts us again when we turn to the third source, namely cartularies (and modern printed editions and calendars of deeds). A cartulary was in essence simply a register into which, for reasons of both safety and convenience of reference, clerks copied the deeds by which donors (and often sellers) notified and confirmed their transfer of land to the monastery, cathedral chapter, bishop or secular lord. Before the mid-thirteenth century private deeds were rarely dated, and even royal charters were often undated in the twelfth century; they can nevertheless usually be dated within reasonably close limits either when the donor is a well-known individual or when the cartulary includes the names of witnesses to the transaction: in the latter case the charter can obviously only have been made when all the witnesses were alive, and in consequence can usually be dated to within a known period of about thirty years at most.

Again, we must bear in mind the purpose for which the deeds were made in order to understand both their value and possible drawbacks to their use. The donor normally was conveying land (or rights over land) to an ecclesiastical body in return for future benefits, to wit prayers for the souls of the donor, his wife, children, parents, ancestors, etc., many of whom would thus be named in the body of the deed(s) concerned. The recipient was equally concerned to ensure that it had what we would call 'clear title' to the land it was being given, and would often require – shades of modern 'requisitions on title' – further deeds to be made by anyone whom 'counsel learned in the law' considered could have a valid claim to the land in question: wives above all, younger sons, daughters, brothers, sisters, cousins, feudal superiors, etc., and both Crown and Papacy would often be requested to confirm new grants or series of grants. At the very least, wives and sons were normally required to witness such charters as evidence that they knew of and willingly consented to the gift. Consequently such deeds, and series of earlier deeds, contain, when assembled, an enormous amount of information on the membership of medieval families, especially in the eleventh, twelfth and thirteenth centuries when giving land to the Church was most in vogue. By the end of the thirteenth century Crown and Parliament were becoming concerned about the amount of land being transferred to the Church and were restricting this possiblity by acts against 'mortmain'; partly as a result, patterns of piety were also changing and increasingly donors were tending to give money rather than land, though gifts of land never entirely ceased in the later medieval period.

A single example of a family reconstructed from deeds copied into cartularies must suffice. Gospatric son of Orm son of Ketel was lord of Workington (Cumb.) from c.1145 to c.1180; both he and his eldest son Thomas, d.1201–2, were benefactors to St Bees Abbey, whose cartulary has been utilised. Three charters

TABLE 4 Size-distribution of Anglo-Norman families in *Libri Vitae*

NUMBER OF PERSONS IN FAMILY

	2	3	4	5	6	7	8	9	10	11	12	Total
HYDE ABBEY												
Certain:	2	3	5	1	2	0	0	0	0	0	0	13
%:	15.4	23.1	38.5	7.7	15.4	0	0	0	0	0	0	
All:	2	4	5	3	13	2	0	0	0	0	0	29
%:	6.9	13.8	17.2	10.3	44.8	6.9	0	0	0	0	0	
Population in all families:	4	12	20	15	78	14	0	0	0	0	0	143
% of total population:	2.8	8.4	14.0	10.5	54.5	9.8	0	0	0	0	0	
DURHAM PRIORY												
Certain:	7	28	19	8	9	5	3	2	0	0	0	81
%:	8.6	34.6	23.5	9.9	11.1	6.2	3.7	2.5	0	0	0	
All:	7	28	21	9	13	5	3	2	0	0	0	88
%:	8.0	31.8	23.9	10.2	14.8	5.7	3.4	2.3	0	0	0	
Population in all families:	14	84	84	45	78	35	24	18	0	0	0	382
% of total population:	3.7	22.0	22.0	11.8	20.4	9.2	6.3	4.7	0	0	0	

THORNEY ABBEY

Certain:	0	17	5	4	2	2	1	0	0	3	34
%:	0	50.0	14.7	11.8	5.9	5.9	2.9	0	0	8.8	
All:	0	17	14	4	4	2	1	0	0	3	45
%:	0	37.8	31.1	8.9	8.9	4.4	2.2	0	0	6.7	
Population in all families:	0	51	56	20	24	14	8	0	0	36	209
% of total population:	0	24.4	26.8	9.6	11.5	6.7	3.8	0	0	17.2	

ALL SERIES

Certain:	9	48	29	13	13	7	4	2	0	3	128
%:	7.0	37.5	22.7	10.2	10.2	5.5	3.1	1.6	0	2.3	
All:	9	49	40	16	30	9	4	2	0	3	162
%:	5.6	30.2	24.7	9.9	18.5	5.6	2.5	1.2	0	1.9	
Population in all families:	18	147	160	80	180	63	32	18	0	36	734
% of total population:	2.5	20.0	21.8	10.9	24.5	8.6	4.4	2.5	0	4.9	

by Gospatric giving the township and wood of Salter (in Workington) and the church of Workington were all witnessed by his wife Egliva and his son and heir Thomas; one was also witnessed by 'Adam and Robert, his [Thomas'] brothers', the other two by 'Alan my son'.[55] Another charter by Gospatric adding the church of Harrington and common pasture at Arlecdon was also witnessed by his wife,[56] whilst two charters by Thomas son of Gospatric adding an annual render of twenty salmon were both witnessed by 'Alan son of Gospatric and Adam his brother'.[57] The confirmation of Thomas' gift of a saltworks at Culwen in Galloway by his Scottish overlord Roland son of Uctred son of Fergus was witnessed by 'Gilbert son of Gospatric' and an antiquary's note of the now lost grant by Roland to Thomas recorded that this grant was witnessed by Thomas' brothers 'Alexander and Gilbert, sons of Gospatric'.[58] Finally, another confirmation-charter by William le Gros, Count of Aumale, d.1179, was witnessed by 'Gospatric son of Orm and Adam his son',[59] whilst a charter relating to land in Gilcrux was witnessed by 'Gospatric son of Orm, Thomas his son, and Adam the clerk son of Gospatric'.[60] This series of deed-copies thus makes possible a full reconstruction of Gospatric's family, in all comprising eight people:

> Gospatric son of Orm son of Ketel, his wife Egeliva, his sons Thomas, Alan, Adam, Robert, Alexander and Gilbert.   [8]

Clearly, this method, if pursued energetically, will facilitate a large increase in our knowledge of families especially in the Anglo-Norman period (c.1050–c.1250): there are at least 760 cartularies for England and Wales known to survive, of which about 125 are now in print: many contain deeds dating back at least to the twelfth century.[61] I do not claim as yet to have done more than scratch the surface of this material, sufficient to satisfy myself of its potential utility.

Two points may be made about family-reconstruction using such evidence: the first is that the evidence, like that of the *Rotuli de Dominabus* and the *Libri vitae* is obviously socially biased towards those of baronial or knightly rank, since in general only people of this level could afford to give land to the Church, though certainly in the midlands and north quite a large number of freeholders and townsmen also appear as donors, and members of this group of substantial peasants and burgesses can be found as donors elsewhere in medieval England. The second is related to the nature of the process which brought the deeds into being: as we have seen, both donor and recipient of land had an interest in seeing that the completed family at the time of the gift was listed accurately; the donors wished to secure their family's spiritual wellbeing by ensuring that all were

---

[55] J. Wilson, 'The Register of the priory of St Bees', *Surtees Society* 126, 1915, 61–3, charter nos. 32–3; 383–4, charter no. 384.

[56] Wilson, 63–4, charter no. 34.

[57] Wilson, 64–7, charter nos. 35–6.

[58] Wilson, 92–3, charter nos. 61–2.

[59] Wilson, 249–50, charter no. 224.

[60] Wilson, 551, App., no. 33.

[61] There are 1356 entries in Davis, *Medieval Cartularies of Great Britain*; of these, 375 do not relate to cartularies proper, 137 to lost or untraced cartularies and 77 to Scottish or Irish cartularies; one cartulary (no. 620) is 'almost entirely illegible'. My calculations of printed editions allow for editions since 1958.

remembered by name in the prayers offered by monks and priests, whilst the grantee wished to ensure that everyone who might claim against it was effectively barred by consenting to the gift. Consequently, the average family size as derived from cartularies and deeds may in the end prove to be larger than averages calculated from the *libri vitae* or the *Rotuli de Dominabus*: the cartularies will reflect completed families at the end of child-bearing, whilst the families will often appear in the latter sources at earlier stages in the life-cycle.[62]

I now return to my initial distinction between 'family' (the group of co-resident kin) and 'household' (all those, whether related or not, living in one house under the control of its head). For most people below knightly level the difference will be slight: at most a few domestic servants in a farmhouse or more prosperous parsonage, a couple of apprentices or an unmarried time-served journeyman in a burgess' house or craftsman's cottage. Only at knightly and even more baronial level was the biological core likely to be swamped by the surrounding shell of domestic servants, chaplains, estate-officials, scribes, and, particularly in castles , men-at-arms, squires undergoing military training and knights not yet given land by their lord. To judge from the relatively plentiful available contemporary and later medieval evidence, knights' households normally contained over ten people, perhaps usually ten to twenty, whilst baronial households ranged from fifty up to some hundreds in the case of national magnates.[63] For the lower orders the evidence is normally thought to be non-existent, but this conclusion is unduly pessimistic. Many years ago, Helen Cam pointed to the genealogical evidence on peasant families to be found in the rolls of the *Curia Regis*, although she was mainly concerned to demonstrate the incidence of marriage between 'free' and 'unfree' in village society.[64] More recently, J. C. Russell made some desultory use of similar records to support his theory of a 'small' medieval household averaging 3.5 persons,[65] whilst two other American scholars have used both eyre rolls and coroners' records to study homicide in England during the thirteenth and four-teenth centuries, incidentally throwing much light on the size of medieval families.[66] I have already shown that the evidence of the Gloucestershire eyre roll

---

[62] In discussion after the delivery of this paper, it was suggested that the existence of bastards, who would not appear in most records because they could have no claim to land as heirs, would affect calculations of total family size. This is of course true, but calculations from early modern parish registers suggest that bastards formed an insignificant proportion (well under five per cent) of the total population before the later eighteenth century (P. Laslett, *Family Life and Illicit Love in earlier generations*, Cambridge 1977, chap. 3; P. Laslett, K. Oosterveen, R. M. Smith, *Bastardy and its comparative history*, London 1980, chaps 2–6). Peter Laslett specifically remarks of the low early modern levels of bastardy, 'Indeed we know of no reason why such a pattern should not have existed indefinitely' (Laslett, Oosterveen and Smith, 31). It was also suggested that sons may be more likely to be recorded in deeds than daughters – as in France (White, 96–7, 108, 119) –, which may throw still more doubt on calculations of family-size using such evidence. This may well be true for England but only further work on these sources will show whether this objection is decisive.

[63] See references cited on p. 154, n. 5.

[64] H. M. Cam, 'Pedigrees of Villeins and Freemen in the Thirteenth Century', *Liberties and Communities in Medieval England*, Cambridge 1944, 131–5.

[65] J. C. Russell, 'Late Ancient and Medieval Population', *Transactions of the American Philosophical Society* 48, pt 3, 1958, 17.

[66] J. B. Given, *Society and Homicide in Thirteenth-Century England*, Stanford (USA) 1977, chap. 3, 'Homicide and the Medieval Household', studied relatives as both accomplices and victims, but did not try to estimate the size of family and household; Barbara Hanawalt's *Crime and Conflict in*

for 1221 suggests that the medieval household comprised about five people, rarely contained more than one married couple and their children or more than three generations, and, in short, was in no way perceptibly different from its better-documented early modern counterpart.[67] But the evidence is so voluminous that a more detailed analysis is both possible and desirable.[68]

It is convenient to start with the division between 'Crown Pleas' and 'Civil Pleas', since the latter will generally yield only information on the size and composition of families, whilst the former may include information on the size and composition of both families and households. The 'Civil Pleas' section of the eyre rolls, the Assize rolls that developed separately from the mid-thirteenth century, and the civil pleas entered on the *Curia Regis* rolls, consisted mainly of the possessory assizes introduced by Henry II: these can be made to yield valuable data on family size within certain limits. An assize of *mort d'ancestor* merely telling us that X held certain lands which his son Y claimed is normally useless for our purpose, given primogeniture, since it will not tell us if Y had younger brothers (unless a younger brother tried to take over the inheritance) or if Y had any sisters. If, however, X left only daughters, or if Y then or later had no direct male heirs leaving only descendants from his younger brothers or sisters, we can hope to reconstruct X's family. But cases of *mort d'ancestor* involving only sons are of use if the land in question is held in gavelkind: thus William and Elias, sons of Edwin de Wolferton, were both found to be Edwin's heirs for his lands in 'Wolferton' (Kent) in 1194; equally, if only one son was named as a Kentish heir, as in the case of John son of Gilbert in Langport in 1200, this was because he was the only son.[69] Assizes of *novel disseisin* can also be helpful if family-groups are involved. So far I have only found two examples of the assize *utrum* that contain information on families,[70] but cases of *darrein presentment* can often yield worthwhile data, if the last presentation was made by a father who either left only daughters to succeed him or whose son or sons died childless leaving only their sisters.[71] Various other civil actions apart from the possessory assizes can also be of use; of these, actions for dower and for what later became an action for pourparty are the most obvious. Less frequently, actions for warranty can provide the same kind of information about coheiresses as actions for dower.[72] Occasionally, other civil actions such as entry by writ of right and nuisance can also be of value. All these civil actions provide the basis for the reconstruction of families since it is reasonable to assume that the information they contain is accurate: it

---

English Communities, 1300–1348, Cambridge (USA) 1979, 27–8, included a preliminary analysis of household-size, which receives extended treatment in her *The Ties that bound*, Oxford 1986, chap. 6.

[67] J. S. Moore, 'The Sudeley and Toddington area in Domesday Book' in Lord Sudeley, *The Sudeleys: Lords of Toddington*, London 1987, 60.

[68] D. Crook, *Records of the General Eyre*, London 1982, provides an admirable list of surviving eyre records and of printed editions; regrettably, there is no list of assize records of similar quality, assize and eyre records being intermingled in *PRO List and Index* iv, London 1910. The records utilised for my own analysis are listed in the Appendix.

[69] Maitland, 'Three Rolls of the King's Court', 39; *Curia Regis Rolls*, i, 96.

[70] Fowler, 'Some Lost Pleas of 1195', 405; Wrottesley, 'Curia Regis Rolls of . . . Richard I and King John', 51.

[71] E.g. Stenton, 'Rolls . . . for Lincolnshire, 1218–19', 205–7 (case no. 445).

[72] E.g. Stenton, 'Rolls . . . for Lincolnshire, 1218–19', 259–61 (case no. 552).

was an obvious basis for rebuttal if a defendant could point to a brother or sister not mentioned in a plaintiff's suit.

The 'Crown Pleas' section of the eyre rolls are principally concerned with criminal matters, and although some criminals and some victims are isolated individuals, it is frequently clear from the context that the rolls are concerned with families and households. Even where the numbers involved are not stated, the victims are often said to be a man 'and all his family' or 'his whole family'[73] or 'all his children',[74] a husband and wife 'and their whole family',[75] a widow 'and all her family',[76] a 'husband, wife and all whom they found in the house';[77] sometimes, even when members of the family or household have been listed, a note is added, 'to wit, everyone in that house' or 'all those in these houses'.[78] With care, it therefore seems possible to extract a considerable amount of information on family and household size and composition from the 'Crown Pleas' section of the county eyre rolls of the itinerant justices who perambulated England at intervals from 1194 onwards, particularly in cases involving arson of, theft from, and assault or murder in victims' houses.

The following analysis is not based on a complete survey of all the available data: it is confined to printed editions of the local eyre and assize rolls and to the printed rolls of the *Curia Regis* up to the end of 1200.[79] Even so, the data covers over twelve hundred families, a figure that will probably rise by between one-third and a half when the families recorded in the remaining printed *Curia Regis Rolls* have been added. Because of the non-survival of judicial records, especially those of the itinerant justices, in the period 1194–1272,[80] as well as the differing activities of local record societies, the geographical coverage of the material surveyed is uneven: whilst all the Bedfordshire records from 1194 to 1247 have been printed, no judicial records have been printed for Cumberland, Dorset, Hampshire, Kent, Nottinghamshire, Sussex and Westmorland, so that the north-west, south and south-east are unrepresented except in the rolls of the *Curia Regis*. This is particularly unfortunate in the case of Kent, where the prevalence of gavelkind would have yielded valuable information on the number of sons in Kentish families. Chronologically, all surviving eyre and assize records before 1222 are in print, but thereafter the printed coverage is increasingly patchy; and although no records before 1194 now survive, the families recorded often date far back into the twelfth century: indeed, in at least one case, oral memory preserved details of the family of a Domesday tenant, Geoffrey Malesoures. And all social levels are represented – barons, knights, freemen and villeins – though the villeins are obviously under-represented for well-known reasons. Nevertheless, no very obvious 'class differences' in the size and composition of families can be

[73] Stenton, 'The Earliest Northamptonshire Assize Rolls, A.D. 1202 and 1203', 17 (case no. 77); Maitland, *Pleas of the Crown*, 19 (case no. 79); Wrottesley, 'Plea Rolls of the reign of Henry III', 69; Harding, 232 (case no. 629); Palmer, 35–6.
[74] Maitland, *Pleas of the Crown*, 83 (case no. 346); Summerson, 10 (case no. 9); Clanchy, 386–7 (case no. 1011).
[75] Stenton, 'Rolls . . . Worcestershire, 1221', 538, 555, 563 (case nos. 1083, 1132, 1145).
[76] Chew and Weinbaum, 49 (case no. 121); Harding, 216 (case no. 568).
[77] Stenton, 'Rolls . . . for Yorkshire, 1218–19', 303 (case no. 830).
[78] Maitland, *Pleas of the Crown*, 82–3, 104 (case nos. 345, 437).
[79] The editions of judicial records searched for data on families and households will be found in the Appendix.
[80] Crook, 12–14.

TABLE 5   Social analysis of families in judicial records, 1194–1279

	Number of	*Size of families*				
Classification	*families*	MIN.	MAX.	MODE	MEDIAN	AVERAGE
Barons	13	3	6	4	4	4.15
Knights	113	2	11	4	4	4.55
Freemen	1084	1	10	4	4	4.23
Villeins	14	3	6	4	4	4.36

Sources: As listed in the Appendix

discerned from Table 5, except that the knights and freemen appear to have a wider spread of family-sizes than the barons or villeins. This, however, is probably a statistical oddity resulting from the small sample-size of the two latter groups. Certainly there is no great divergence between any of the 'class' averages and the overall average family-size.

In all, 1,236 households and 1,234 families have so far been analysed by computer, with the following results.[81] The average size of family (husband, wife and children) is 4.25, the average size of household (family with any servants, lodgers or visitors) is 4.38. A fuller analysis is given in Table 6.

Again, nearly two-thirds of families consist of four or less people, whilst over forty per cent of the population live in families of five or more. These figures are so near to those calculated both by Peter Laslett for the early modern period and by myself from the *Rotuli de Dominabus* (Table 2) and from the *libri vitae* (Table 4) that the temptation to accept the conclusion that the normal family in both periods was identical is strong. But the temptation ought to be resisted for a while. Firstly, as with the *Rotuli de Dominabus*, in order to ensure comparability fathers (and mothers) have been 'restored', so that the above averages are bound to be over-estimates. A minority of families (about one in eight) in reality would have had a widow or widower as head: this would reduce the average family-size to about 4.15 and the average household-size to about 4.26. Secondly, the families thus reconstructed are much closer to the completed families recorded in deeds and cartularies than to the chronologically random sample (i.e. at varying stages in the life-cycle of each family) of families in the *Rotuli de Dominabus* or in early modern 'listings', modern censuses and social surveys. Again, there is likely to be a degree of over-estimation. Thirdly, the sex-ratio of the members of the 1,234 families is 85, suggesting that men are under-represented. This in fact is not too serious an objection: it can be explained by reference to the nature of the cases from which the data on families have been extracted. It is much easier to be certain that the membership of families where daughters were co-heiresses was completely recorded than with other kinds of case, where sons were more likely to be mentioned than daughters. For this reason, Table 7 analyses those families in which only female children were recorded. Since demographic theory states that in a 'normal' population males and females ought to be equal in number, the distribution and size of families with daughters only should be a mirror image of

---

[81] The numerical difference between families and household totals is attributable to the exclusion of two London brothels.

TABLE 6 Family-size calculated from judicial records, 1194–1279:

NUMBER IN FAMILY

	1	2	3	4	5	6	7	8	9	10	11
All Families											
Number of families	12	41	208	559	272	88	32	13	6	1	2
% of all families	1.0	3.3	16.9	45.3	22.0	7.1	2.6	1.1	0.5	—	—
People in families	12	82	624	2236	1360	528	224	104	54	10	22
% of all people	0.3	1.6	11.9	42.5	25.9	10.0	4.3	2.0	1.0	0.2	0.4

Average family: 4.25 Min.: 1 Max.: 11 Mode: 4 Median: 4
Average household: 4.38 Min.: 1 Max.: 12 Mode: 3 Median: 4

Sources: As listed in the Appendix

those for families with boys only, and ought to be a good guide to the family-characteristics of the whole population.

Table 7 therefore summarizes the distribution of family-sizes for those families who only had daughters recorded in the judicial records. By definition, childless couples have been excluded, and consequently Table 7 is not directly comparable with Tables 6 and 8, since there can be no families totalling one or two. Although in practice there would be families consisting of a widowed parent and one daughter, it is extremely difficult to detect such families in the available sources. To permit a degree of comparability, the data on the percentage-distribution of family-sizes in Tables 6 and 8 has therefore been reworked by excluding families of one or two people. Although the distributions are not identical, they are similar to each other and to the average of the data from all three tables. Given that the data employed in Table 7 ought to be more reliable than that in Tables 6 and 8 because the quality of the sources for female coheiresses is better than that for male heirs, this inspires more confidence in the calculations of family-size based on the main sample of families from the judicial records.

The analysis of household-size is more difficult, partly because far fewer definable households were recorded than families. The average household-size of 4.38 calculated above is based on the unlikely assumption that those families without recorded non-family co-residents were also households, hence the real average household-size is effectively understated. In many cases – all barons and knights, and at least some freemen – it would be ludicrous to assume that the household contained no servants and other members apart from the biological family. The reason for the under-recording of households lies in the nature of the sources I have studied, which are biassed towards families rather than households. To rectify this situation, we need to look at those instances where the records suggest that we are dealing with complete households, whether or not these contained individuals apart from the nuclear family. For this purpose, Table 8 analyses those households recorded in the 'Crown Pleas' sections of local eyre rolls. Alas, not all the recorded households can be used in this analysis. Two London brothels with three and six prostitutes have been omitted as clearly atypical, and because nine other households may be atypical – the London lodging-house of Robert the Cook containing twelve residents, a London crafts-man's establishment containing eight people, four inns outside London, and three households each containing two families – two sets of calculations have been made, excluding (A) and including (B) these nine households. As will be seen from Table 8, apart from increasing the maximum household-size, including these nine households makes very little difference to the average household-size, which rises only from 3.98 to 4.18 persons. Indeed, this average is well below that suggested by the entire set of families, but this is because the average family-size in the 'household' set is itself lower than that of the entire set of families, namely 3.22 (basis A) or 3.14 (basis B). A probable explanation is that since the great majority of these households were the victims of criminals, they may not have been typical families, and their below-average size may have been a factor encouraging their predators to prey on them; the larger the family, one imagines, the more difficult it would be to kill everyone or to ransack the house undetected. In short, therefore, Table 8 is not as useful as one could wish in providing a safe basis for a direct calculation of average household-size, and it is perhaps more useful in enabling us to calculate the difference between the family and household

TABLE 7 Family-size calculated from judicial records, 1194–1279

FAMILIES WITH DAUGHTERS ONLY

	NUMBER IN FAMILY										
	1	2	3	4	5	6	7	8	9	10	11
Number of families	—	—	171	257	96	28	10	7	2	1	1
% of all families	—	—	29.8	44.9	16.8	4.9	1.7	1.2	0.2	0.2	0.2
People in families	—	—	513	1028	480	168	70	56	18	18	11
% of all people	—	—	21.7	43.5	20.3	7.1	3.0	2.4	0.8	0.8	0.5

Average family: 4.11 Mode: 4 Median: 4
Average household: 4.14 Mode: 3 Median: 4

PERCENTAGE-DISTRIBUTION OF FAMILIES (SIZES 3 – 11)

	NUMBER IN FAMILY									
	3	4	5	6	7	8	9	10	11	12
Table 6	17.6	47.3	23.0	7.5	2.7	1.1	0.5	0.1	0.2	0
Table 7	29.8	44.9	16.8	4.9	1.7	1.2	0.3	0.2	0.2	0
Table 8 (B)	34.7	25.8	14.5	13.7	7.3	2.4	0.8	0	0	0.8
Average	27.4	39.3	18.1	8.7	3.9	1.6	0.6	0.1	0.1	0.3

Sources: As listed in the Appendix

TABLE 8 Size of selected households (Crown pleas), 1194–1279

NUMBER IN HOUSEHOLD

	1	2	3	4	5	6	7	8	9	10	11	12	12+
Number of households													
A:	1	16	43	32	16	15	7	2	0	0	0	0	0
B:	1	16	43	32	18	17	9	3	1	0	0	1	0
% of all households													
A:	0.8	12.1	32.6	24.2	12.1	11.4	5.3	1.5	0	0	0	0	0
B:	0.7	11.3	30.5	22.7	12.8	12.1	6.4	2.1	0.7	0	0	0.7	0
People in households													
A:	1	32	129	128	80	90	49	16	0	0	0	0	0
B:	1	32	129	128	90	102	63	24	9	0	0	12	0
% of all people													
A:	0.2	6.1	24.6	24.4	15.2	17.1	9.3	3.0	0	0	0	0	0
B:	0.2	5.4	21.9	21.7	15.3	17.3	10.6	4.1	1.5	0	0	2.0	0

Household Data Summary

A: Average: 3.98   Mode: 3   Median: 4   Min.: 1   Max.: 8
B: Average: 4.18   Mode: 3   Median: 4   Min.: 1   Max.: 12
Difference (household minus family):   A: 0.76   B: 1.04

Sources: As listed in the Appendix

averages, namely 0.76 (basis A) and 1.04 (basis B). Of these, the former seems the safest to use.

Is it now possible to reach some provisional conclusions on the size of families and households from all the available records for the Anglo-Norman period? First, all the sources exploited show the same type of family to be the norm: basically a two-generation unit of one set of parents and their children. Second, average family-sizes calculated from differing sources are of the same order of magnitude: 5.32 (*Rotuli de Dominabus*: Table 2), 4.34 – 4.40 (*libri vitae*: Table 3), 4.25 (judicial records: Table 6). The aberrant high figure obtained from the *Rotuli de Dominabus* is a result of the very high proportion of baronial and knightly families included (nearly ninety per cent of all families). Reworking the data in Table 2 on the assumption that the baronial and knightly classes together might have accounted for ten per cent of the population would produce an overall average family of the order of 4.15 persons. For the household, the total body of 1,236 entries produces a minimum estimate of 4.38 which I have suggested above is unrealistically low. Applying the calculated difference between household and family from Table 8 (0.76 on basis A) to the range of possible family averages (4.15, 4.25, 4.34) results in a household multiplier perhaps as high as 5.1. At all events, the average size of the Anglo-Norman household, ranging between 4.38 and 5.10, is of the same order as Laslett's famous early modern estimate of 4.75; indeed, the mid-point of that range is 4.74.

This paper has tried to show some of the results of analysing the size and composition of the Anglo-Norman family and household drawn from widely differing sources within the Anglo-Norman period – the *libri vitae* covering the period from the eve of the Norman Conquest to the early thirteenth century, the monastic cartularies again going back at least to the early twelfth century, the *Rotuli de Dominabus* of 1185, the *Curia Regis* rolls from 1194 to 1200, the 'Crown Pleas' and 'Civil Pleas' sections of the itinerant justices' court-rolls from c.1200 onwards. Some of this is work 'still in progress': this is particularly true of the monastic cartularies. Even with the *libri vitae* some problems of personal identification and therefore dating still await final solution in Durham and Winchester. And whilst I initially began my analysis using a 'spreadsheet' computer-program, under the mistaken idea that there was very little data to be processed, I now realise that a data-base program is essential to avoid the increasing risk of duplicating entries derived from different sources. It will also be apparent that I have said nothing about non-demographic aspects of the family, not because there is nothing to be said but rather that there is plenty. Let me therefore simply state that I do not believe some fashionable hypotheses current among some social historians about love, whether between spouses or between parents and children, being an invention of the twelfth, or of the sixteenth, or of the eighteenth century. And I remain convinced that the results from all the types of record that I have tried to explore are mutually consistent and converge on a single conclusion: the nuclear family was as typical of the England of William I as it was of the England of George I. In this respect as in others, the division between 'medieval' and 'early modern' history is more than a little artificial. Above all, the complex family beloved equally by French sociologists and American television script-writers is quite simply a myth.[82] 'However, we would not end

---

[82] Thus the original Ewing household at 'Southfork' in the T.V. series *Dallas* consisted of three

this essay upon a discord. Therefore a last and peaceful word.' The great Maitland, of course. The history of the Anglo-Norman family, to use Maitland's words
about Domesday Book, 'appears to me not indeed as the known but as the
knowable'.[83]

APPENDIX

List of Judicial records consulted

The following editions of judicial records have been searched for data on families
and households.

Curia Regis, 1194–1200: F. Palgrave, *Rotuli Curiae Regis*, London 1835, I,
1–148; II, 1–281; F. W. Maitland, 'Three Rolls of the King's Court', *Pipe Roll
Society* XIV, 1891, 1–59, 214–44; *Curia Regis Rolls* I, HMSO 1922, 1–373; VII,
HMSO 1935, 327–51.

Itinerant Justices: Bedfordshire, 1202: G. H. Fowler, 'Roll of the justices in
eyre at Bedford, 1202', *Bedfordshire Historical Record Society*, I, 1913, 144–247;
D. M. Stenton, 'The Earliest Lincolnshire Assize Rolls', *Lincoln Record Society*
XXII, 1926, 213–15; D. M. Stenton, 'The Earliest Northamptonshire Assize
Rolls', *Northamptonshire Record Society* V, 1930, 87–97; **1227–8:** G. H. Fowler,
'Roll of the justices in eyre at Bedford, 1227', *Bedfordshire Historical Record
Society* III, 1916, 10–202; **1240:** G. H. Fowler, 'Roll of the justices in eyre, 1240',
Bedfordshire Historical Record Society IX, 1925, 75–143; **1247:** G. H. Fowler,
'Calendar of the roll of the justices on eyre, 1247', *Bedfordshire Historical
Record Society* XXI, 1939. **Berkshire, 1248:** M. T. Clanchy, 'The Roll and Writ
file of the Berkshire Eyre of 1248', *Selden Society* XC, 1973. **Buckinghamshire,
1194–5:** Maitland, 'Three Rolls of the King's Court', 119–48; G. H. Fowler,
'Some lost pleas of 1195', *EHR* XXXVII, 1922, 403–5; **1227:** J. G. Jenkins,
'Calendar of the Roll of the Justices in Eyre, 1227', *Buckinghamshire Record
Society* VI, 1945 [for 1942]). **Cambridgeshire, 1261:** W. M. Palmer, *The Assizes
held at Cambridge, 1260 (sic)*, Linton 1930, 1–43. **Cornwall, 1201:** D. M. Stenton, 'Pleas before the king or his justices, 1198–1212, I–IV', *Selden Society* 67–8,
83–4, 1952, 1967, II, 30–178. **Derbyshire, 1269:** M. K. Dale, C. E. Lugard,
Cases for Derbyshire from Eyre and Assize Rolls, 1256–1272, Barnston 1938,
52–192. **Devon, 1219:** L. G. Cruwys, 'Abstracts from the Devon Assize Rolls for
1218–19', *Devon and Cornwall Notes and Queries* XX, 1939, 338–52, 395–416;
1238: H. Summerson, 'Crown pleas of the Devon Eyre of 1238', *Devon and
Cornwall Record Society* NS 28, 1985. **Durham, 1235–6:** K. E. Bayley, 'Two

---

married couples: 'Jock' and 'Mizz Ellie', their eldest son 'J.R.' and his wife Sue-Ellen, their
younger son Bobbie and his wife Pam, as well as their unmarried granddaughter Lucy. Whether
such a family is typical of Texas oil-barons in real life I know not.
[83] F. W. Maitland, *Domesday Book and Beyond*, Cambridge 1897, v, 520.

thirteenth century assize rolls for the county of Durham', *Surtees Society* 127, 1916, 75–105; **1242:** Bayley, 1–74. **Essex, 1198:** Palgrave, I, 173–4, 178–211. **Gloucestershire, 1221:** F. W. Maitland, *Pleas of the Crown for the County of Gloucester . . . 1221*, London 1884; D. M. Stenton, 'Rolls of the Justices in Eyre for Gloucestershire, Warwickshire and Staffordshire' [*sic*; *recte* Shropshire], *Selden Society* 59, 1940, 1–143. **Hertfordshire, 1198:** Palgrave, I, 149–78. **Lancashire, 1246:** J. Parker, 'Calendar of Lancashire Assize Rolls, I', *Lancashire and Cheshire Record Society* XLVIII, 1903, 6–120. **Lincolnshire, 1202:** Stenton, 'The Earliest Lincolnshire Assize Rolls', 1–84, 93–194; **1206:** Stenton, 'The Earliest Lincolnshire Assize Rolls', 235–77; **1208:** Stenton, 'Pleas before the king or his justices, 1198–1212', IV, 118–30; **1218–19:** D. M. Stenton, 'Rolls of the Justices in Eyre for Lincolnshire, 1218–19, and Worcestershire, 1221', *Selden Society* 53, 1934, 1–440. **London, 1244–6:** H. M. Chew, M. Weinbaum, 'The London Eyre of 1244', *London Record Society* VII, 1970; **1276:** M. Weinbaum, 'The London Eyre of 1276', *London Record Society* XII, 1976. **Middlesex, 1198:** Palgrave, I, 211–19. **Norfolk, 1198:** Stenton, 'Pleas before the king or his justices, 1198–1212', II, 1–15; **1202:** Stenton, 'Pleas before the king or his justices, 1198–1212', II, 226–89; **1209:** Stenton, 'Pleas before the king or his justices, 1198–1212', IV, 168–282. **Northamptonshire, 1202:** Stenton, 'The Earliest Northamptonshire Assize Rolls', 1–86 and Stenton, 'The Earliest Lincolnshire Assize Rolls', 195–212. **Northumberland, 1256:** W. Page, 'Three Assize Rolls for the County of Northumberland', *Surtees Society* LXXXVIII, 1891, 1–133; **1269:** Page, 134–222; **1279–80:** Page, 223–399. **Rutland, 1202:** Stenton, 'The Earliest Northamptonshire Assize Rolls', 1–86, and Stenton, 'The Earliest Lincolnshire Assize Rolls', 195–212. **Shropshire, 1203:** Stenton, 'Pleas before the king or his justices, 1198–1212', III, 63–122; **1221:** Stenton, 'Rolls of the Justices in Eyre for Gloucestershire, Warwickshire and Staffordshire' [*sic*; *recte* Shropshire], 430–585; **1256:** A. Harding, 'The Roll of the Shropshire Eyre of 1256', *Selden Society* 96, 1980. **Somerset, 1201:** Stenton, 'Pleas before the king or his justices, 1198–1212', II, 179–225, superseding C. E. H. Chadwyck-Healey, 'Somerset Pleas, I', *Somerset Record Society* XI, 1897, 4–24; **1225:** Chadwyck-Healey, 28–107, case nos. 102–389; **1243:** Chadwyck-Healey, 137–324, nos. 421–1264; **1280:** L. Landon, 'Somerset Pleas, IV, pt. 1', *Somerset Record Society* XLIV, 1929. **Staffordshire, 1199:** G. Wrottesley, 'Curia Regis Rolls of the reigns of Richard I and King John', *Staffordshire Historical Collections* III, pt. 1, 1882, 33–65, and Stenton, 'Pleas before the king or his justices, 1198–1212', III, 1–3; **1203:** Wrottesley, 'Curia Regis Rolls', 85–128; **1227:** G. Wrottesley, 'Plea Rolls of the reign of Henry III', *Staffordshire Historical Collections* IV, pt. 1, 1883, 47–74; **1272:** Wrottesley, 'Plea Rolls of the reign of Henry III', 191–215. **Suffolk, 1198:** Stenton, 'Pleas before the king or his justices, 1198–1212', II, 16–29; **1202:** Stenton, 'Pleas before the king or his justices, 1198–1212', II, 226–89; **1203:** Stenton, 'The Earliest Northamptonshire Assize Rolls', 131–53. **Surrey, 1235:** C. A. F. Meekings, D. Crook, 'The 1235 Surrey Eyre', *Surrey Record Society* 31–2, 1979, 1983. **Warwickshire, 1221–2:** Stenton, 'Rolls of the Justices in Eyre for Gloucestershire, Warwickshire and Staffordshire' [*sic*; *recte* Shropshire], 144–429, 586–650. **Wiltshire, 1194:** Maitland, 'Three Rolls of the King's Court', 65–118; **1249:** C. A. F. Meekings, 'Crown Pleas of the Wiltshire eyre, 1249', *Wiltshire Record Society* 16, 1961; M. T. Clanchy, 'Civil Pleas of the Wiltshire eyre, 1249', *Wiltshire Record Society* 26, 1971. **Worcestershire, 1221:** Stenton,

'Rolls of the Justices in Eyre for Lincolnshire, 1218–19, and Worcestershire, 1221', 441–655. **Yorkshire, 1204:** Stenton, 'Pleas before the king or his justices, 1198–1212', IV, 125–75, superseding C. T. Clay, 'Three Yorkshire Assize Rolls', *Yorkshire Record Series* XLIV, 1910, 2–25; **1208:** Stenton, 'Pleas before the king or his justices, 1198–1212', IV, 94–117, superseding Clay, 25–42; **1218–19:** D. M. Stenton, 'Rolls of the Justices in Eyre for Yorkshire, 1218–19', *Selden Society* 56, 1937; **1251–2:** Clay, 43–87; **1260:** Clay, 88–139.

The following editions contain no relevant cases.

Derbyshire, 1219: Stenton, 'Rolls of the justices in eyre . . . Lincolnshire, 1218–19, and Worcestershire, 1221', 202–14, 321–51. **Herefordshire, 1203:** Wrottesley, 'Curia Regis Rolls', 124–5. **Huntingdonshire, 1208–9:** Stenton, 'Pleas before the king or his justices, 1198–1212', IV, 130–5, 156–7, 158–62. **Leicestershire, 1202:** Stenton, 'The Earliest Lincolnshire Assize Rolls', 84–8 (Lincolnshire pleas only). **Northamptonshire, 1203:** Stenton, 'The Earliest Northamptonshire Assize Rolls', 99–131, 153–63. **Nottinghamshire, 1219:** Stenton, 'Rolls of the justices in eyre . . . Lincolnshire, 1218–19, and Worcestershire, 1221', 202–14, 321–51. **Oxfordshire, 1203:** Stenton, 'Rolls of the justices in eyre . . . Lincolnshire, 1218–19, and Worcestershire, 1221', 90, and Wrottesley, 'Curia Regis Rolls', 127. **Suffolk, 1209:** Stenton, 'Pleas before the king or his justices, 1198–1212', IV, 153–5, 162–7. **Warwickshire, 1202:** Stenton, 'The Earliest Lincolnshire Assize Rolls', 88–92 (Lincolnshire civil pleas only). **Worcestershire, 1203:** Stenton, 'Pleas before the king or his justices, 1198–1212', III, 116–19 (Shropshire entries only); Wrottesley, 'Curia Regis Rolls', 125–7.

THE AUTHOR OF THE 'MARGAM ANNALS': EARLY THIRTEENTH-CENTURY MARGAM ABBEY'S COMPLEAT SCRIBE

Robert B. Patterson

The 'Margam Annals', have long been known through H. R. Luard's Rolls Series edition of Trinity College Cambridge, MS 0.2.4 entitled 'Cronica Abbreviata a tempore Sancti Edwardi Regis ultimi de progenie Anglorum'.[1] The work is only one of four or possibly five books which have been traced to the Cistercian abbey's medieval library and enjoys a varied reputation as a source for the Anglo-Norman and early Angevin periods.[2] Its yearly entries range from local events pertaining to the abbey and its Glamorgan environs to *gesta* of more realm-wide significance, such as the fealty sworn to William aetheling in 1116 and a few morsels of even broader interest like the succession of popes and several notable Crusader victories.[3]

As is well known, from the dramatic moment when the Margam account commences in 1066 with its recording the appearance of Halley's Comet and the death of Edward the Confessor to approximately the third quarter of the twelfth century, the work is heavily derivative; but from this point until their final, incomplete entry for 1232, the 'Annals' become an important original source for the history of Glamorgan.[4]

[1] This is a much revised version of a paper originally read in 1990 at The Ninth International Conference of the Charles Homer Haskins Society. I am extremely grateful for their comments on the present text to members of the Fourteenth Annual Conference on Anglo-Norman Studies such as Susan Reynolds and John Gillingham and especially Martin Brett, whose comments on manuscripts of annals associated with Glamorgan and South Wales helped me to hone my own ideas. Research for this paper was made possible by grants from the University of South Carolina Venture Fund, the USC Research and Productive Scholarship Committee, and the Southern Regional Education Board.

Annales Monastici, ed. Henry Richards Luard, 5 vols, London, 1864–69, 1: 3–40.
[2] Walter de Gray Birch, *Margam Abbey*, London, 1897, 277–79; *Medieval Libraries of Great Britain*, ed. N. R. Ker, 2nd edn, London, 1964, 129; Ceri W. Lewis, 'The Literary Tradition of Morgannwg down to the Middle of the Sixteenth Century', in *Glamorgan County History* 3, ed. T. B. Pugh, Cardiff, 1971, 537; W[illiam] Greenway, 'The Annals of Margam', *Transactions of the Port Talbot Historical Society* i, 1963, 29; F. G. Cowley, *The Monastic Order in South Wales 1066–1349*, Cardiff, 1971, 144–45 and nn.; *A Bibliography of Celtic-Latin Literature 400–1200*, eds Michael Lapidge and Richard Sharpe with Foreword by Proinsias Mac Cana, Dublin, 1985, no. 141; *Medieval Libraries of Great Britain; Supplement to the Second Edition*, ed. Andrew G. Watson, London, 1987, 49; *Trinity College Dublin: Descriptive Catalogue of the Medieval and Renaissance Latin Manuscripts*, ed. Marvin L. Colker with Introduction by William O'Sullivan, 2 vols, Aldershot and Brookfield, VT, 1991, no. 939.
[3] 'Annales de Margan', 4, 6–7, 9–13.
[4] See in general, Antonia Gransden, *Historical Writing in England c.550 to c.1307*, London, 1974, 332 and n.; Lewis, 'Literary tradition', 537; the interruption in the entry for 1232 and

The 'Annals'' most notable claim to fame – popularized by the works of scholars such as Sir Maurice Powicke, Sidney Painter, and W. L. Warren – is their account of King John's murder of his nephew Arthur of Brittany.[5] Indeed it has been widely held that the Trinity College Cambridge manuscript is the only source for this version of the politically important episode aside from the French epic poem, Guillaume le Breton's the 'Philippid'.[6] This view almost certainly has depended heavily upon widespread acceptance of Luard's belief in MS O.2.4 as the sole text of 'Margam Annals' entries.[7] As will be seen, this belief is quite incorrect, but nonetheless the Cambridge manuscript still can be regarded as the 'Annals' text.[8] Furthermore, until now the manuscript's Margam scribe has remained unknown.[9] However, new evidence has revealed the individual's identity.[10]

As to the textual status of MS O.2.4, Powicke long ago claimed (without generating any noticeable revision of Luard's belief in the uniqueness of his manuscript source) that Trinity College Cambridge, MS O.2.4 was not alone as a Margam chronicle: a manuscript in the library of Trinity College Dublin contained a similar text.[11] It is now catalogued as MS 507, a text written in a single hand about the same time as MS O.2.4. Several reference works have classified it as another text of the 'Margam Annals', the most recent being a catalogue of the Dublin library's manuscript collection by Prof Marvin L. Colker.[12] Folio 7v carries the identical reference to King John's murder of his nephew, which fact disposes of the claimed prominence of the Trinity College Cambridge manuscript in this regard; but most importantly the likeness of the Dublin text to MS O.2.4 might appear to undermine the latter's status as the sole text of the 'Margam Annals'.[13]

Collation of MS 507 with MS O.2.4 reveals that in many ways the two texts are almost identical. Excluding from consideration 507's entries from 1232 to 1235,

---

absence of subsequent entries have resulted from two folios having been cut away from the original 18 in bound MS O.2.4; see also supra, n. 3.

[5] Sir Maurice Powicke, *The Loss of Normandy 1189–1204*, 2nd edn rev., Manchester, 1961, 316–22, 324: followed by Sidney Painter, *William Marshal*, Baltimore, 1933, 161–62, and *The Reign of King John*, Baltimore, 1940, 7, 27, 236 and n.; W. L. Warren, *King John*, New York, 1961, 82, 107; 'cum rex Ioh(anne)s cepisset Arthuru(m), eumque aliquamdiu in carcere vivum tenuisset, in turre tandem Rothomag(e)nsi, feria quinta ante Pascha, post prandium, ebrius et demonio plenus, propria manu interfecit, et grandi labide ad corpus eius alligato, proiecit in Secana(m)': Cambridge, Trinity College Library, MS O.2.4, a. 1204, fol. 22; 'Annales de Margan', 27; Arthur's murder occurred in 1203.

[6] Powicke, *Loss of Normandy*, 321; Greenway, 'Annals of Margam', 29; Lewis, 'Literary Tradition', 537; Cowley, *Monastic Order*, 149; Gransden, *Historical Writing*, 332 and n.; for the relationship of *Histoire de Guillaume le Maréchal* to the account of Arthur's murder, see M. Dominica Legge, 'William Marshal and Arthur of Brittany', *BIHR* lv, 1982, 18–24: I am indebted to Dr Marjorie Chibnall for this reference.

[7] 'Annales de Margan', xiii; Greenway, 'Annals of Margam', 21; Gransden, 332 and n.

[8] See infra, 198–99.

[9] Luard referred to him as a single 'clear hand', 'Margam annalist', and 'chronicler': 'Annales de Margan', xiii–xv.

[10] See infra, 202–3.

[11] Powicke, *Loss of Normandy*, 316 and n.

[12] *The Western Manuscripts in the Library of Trinity College Cambridge* 3, ed. M. R. James, Cambridge, 1902, 84; Watson, *Medieval Libraries; Supplement*, 49; Colker, *Descriptive Catalogue*, 939.

[13] See supra, and n. 12.

which 0.2.4 may be missing, and variations in orthography and word order, most entries in MS 507 either are identical to MS 0.2.4's or are obvious abbreviated or rewritten versions.[14] Parhelia appear in approximately the same locations as in MS 0.2.4.[15] Dates attributed to annual entries generally are those used in the Cambridge manuscript.[16] The two texts even repeat the same mistake of recording the death of Pope Honorius II and the accession of Innocent II in 1130 as the entry for 1110;[17] and MS 507's account for 1232 provides the remainder of MS 0.2.4's missing text.[18] Can then the scribe of Luard's Cambridge manuscript any longer be considered the author of the 'Margam Annals'?

Certain differences between the two manuscripts provide the answer. The most obvious of these is that the Cambridge manuscript contains language and script which show that it was written by a Margam scribe for his community. Thus, the scribe recorded that Earl Robert of Gloucester founded *our* abbey; that the Welsh burned *our* barn and attacked *our famuli*; and that Earl Gilbert de Clare confirmed lands and liberties to *us*. The Dublin text reveals no such evidence of affiliation. Only four of its entries mention events affecting Margam, and no possessive adjectives or personal pronouns expressing the scribe's membership in Margam accompany the details.[19] In referring to Earl Gilbert's confirmations, the scribe of MS 507 merely designates 'abbatie de Margan' not *nobis* as the beneficiary.[20] Furthermore, paleographical evidence, as will be seen, demonstrates that MS 0.2.4 was the work of a member of Margam Abbey's scriptorium, while the same cannot be said for MS 507.[21] Consequently, it is not a mere exercise in semantics to call the scribe of MS 0.2.4 the author in some sense of the 'Margam Annals'.

Judging by other material in MS 0.2.4, but missing from MS 507, the scribe of the former also was more explicitly sympathetic to the ecclesiastical reform tradition in England represented by Archbishops Anselm (1093–1109) and Thomas Becket (1162–1170) than the Dublin annalist. The Margam annalist not only recorded more details about Anselm than MS 507's scribe, he, and not the latter, denounced as 'tyrannical abuses' the royal customs relating to the Church; and he attributed the conflicts between Anselm and both William Rufus and

---

[14] For the rest of the 1232 entry, see MS 507, fols 10–10v; this text continues with entries to 1235 on fols 10v–13v; Prof Colker estimates that this latter material 'may not derive from a Margam chronicle': *Descriptive Catalogue*, 939; for difference in spelling, see a. 1100, *interficeret* (MS 507, fol. 3) and *inficeret* (MS 0.2.4, fol. 4); for an example combining differing word order and spelling, see a. 1190 'expulit a Conveitreya' (MS 507, fol. 6v) vs. 'a Conventreia expulit' (MS 0.2.4, fol. 17); the two manuscripts' accounts for 1172 are typical of identical entries (MS 507, fol. 54v; MS 0.2.4, fol. 13); MS 507's entry for 1191 is a dramatic case of its abbreviation of a corresponding entry in the Cambridge manuscript (fol. 6v; compare with MS 0.2.4, fol. 17); for one of MS 507's rewritten versions of the Cambridge manuscript's entries, see the two texts' accounts for 1206 (MS 507, fols 7v–8; MS 0.2.4, fols 22–23).
[15] MS 507, a. 1104, 1233, fols 3v, 10v; MS 0.2.4, a. 1104, 1232, fols 6, 32–33.
[16] See infra, 200 and n. 26.
[17] MS 0.2.4, fol. 7; 'Annales de Margan', 9; MS 507, fol. 3v.
[18] MS 507, fols 10–10v; see also supra, n. 14.
[19] MS 0.2.4, a. 1147, 1161, 1224, fols 11–12, 26–27; see also a. 1187, 1223, 1227, fols 16, 27, 29 and a. 1213, 1214, fol. 26; 'Annales de Margan', 14–15, 20, 32, 34–36; compare with MS 507, a. 1151, 1213, 1216, 1223, fols 5, 8v–9; Abbot Gilbert's death at Kirkstead Abbey is recorded under 1214: ibid. fol. 8v.
[20] MS 507, a. 1216, fol. 8v.
[21] Infra, 202–3.

Henry I and between Becket and Henry II to these efforts 'to subvert ecclesiastical liberty.'[22] The Margam scribe also sided with the territorial claims of the bishop of St David's against Bishop Urban of Llandaff, whereas the scribe of MS 507 ignored the issue.[23]

While the similarities between MSS 0.2.4 and 507 show that they are related, differences between the two along with those already cited suggest that the manuscripts' texts are different adaptations, variants, of a common proximate textual progenitor. As already seen, the Cambridge and Dublin manuscripts appear to have different origins – the one, Margam; the other, an unknown location.[24] Based on a comparison of the two texts, the scribe of MS 0.2.4 seems to have added the special Margam references to 'customise' a common source for his monastery's use. On the other hand, the Dublin manuscript's scribe apparently edited this common source in several ways. In some places he simply cut; in others, he rewrote to achieve greater brevity; and in at least one passage, the entry for the year 1232, he interpolated the account of an attack by Welshmen on the abbot of Grace Dieu and a monk engaged in a peace mission to them.[25] Furthermore, the text of MS 507 contains other material which could hardly have been borrowed from the Cambridge manuscript. It attributes the date of Margam's foundation and the death of its founder Earl Robert of Gloucester to 1151 instead of 1147, the date used in MS 0.2.4; and several other of MS 507's entries are dated differently from the corresponding accounts in the Cambridge text.[26]

Behind this Glamorgan/South Wales/West Country chronicle (see infra, table, *G*), the proximate textual source for MSS 0.2.4 and 507, lay a collection of sources (infra, table, *Q*). Its existence is supported by certain entries in MSS 0.2.4 and 507 which also are found verbatim or virtually so in other roughly contemporary but unrelated South Wales/West Country annals. It seems unlikely that the immediate textual source of MSS 0.2.4 or 507 provided these texts; otherwise these other annals would resemble the Cambridge and Dublin works more closely.[27]

One of these is contained in a late thirteenth-century manuscript in the Public

---

[22] In the Cambridge and Dublin manuscripts, see particularly the entries a. 1093, 1097, 1102–4, 1109, 1170–71: MS 0.2.4, fols 3–7, 13; 'Annales de Margan', 5–9, 16–17; compare with MS 507, fols 2v–3v, 5v; according to both texts, Becket died 'pro defensione ecclesiasticae libertatis'. Luard commented on the singularity of MS 0.2.4's denunciation of the royal customs: 'Annales de Margan', xv.

[23] See a. 1131, MS 0.2.4, fol. 10; MS 507, fol. 4v.

[24] See supra, 199.

[25] See supra, 199; the entry for 1125 reveals both cutting and rewriting: MS 507, fol. 4v; compare with MS 0.2.4, fol. 9; 'Annales de Margan', 11–12; for the interpolation, see MS 507, fol. 10.

[26] For the different foundation and obit dates, see MS 507, a. 1151, fol. 5; MS 0.2.4, a. 1147, fol. 11; 'Annales de Margan', 14; MS 0.2.4 has no entry for 1086; MS 507 does, and it is an only slightly changed version of the Cambridge manuscript's account for 1087: MS 507, a. 1086, fols 2–2v; MS 0.2.4, fol. 2; for other examples of differences in dating, see for the years 1138, 1144–47, 1151, 1153–55 in MS 0.2.4, accounts for 1139, 1143–45, 1151, 1154–56 in MS 507: MS 0.2.4, fols 11–12; MS 507, fol. 5.

[27] For other annals covering 1066–1268 which may have emanated from a cell of Tewkesbury Abbey (Gloucs.) at Cardiff, or possibly from Margam and do not appear to be derived from *Q*, see B.L., MS Royal 6.B.XI, fols 105–108v; the work is said to have descended from the 'Tewkesbury Annals': *Descriptive Catalogue of Materials Relating to the History of Great Britain and Ireland*, ed. Thomas Duffus Hardy, 3 vols in 4, London, 1862–71, 3: no. 297; Ker, *Medieval Libraries*, 48; Lewis, 'Literary Tradition', 538 & n.; Cowley, *Monastic Order*, 145.

Table

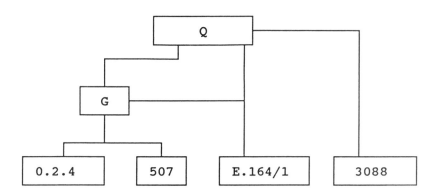

Record Office known as the 'Exchequer Domesday'.[28] From their contents, the annals have a clear affinity with the Cambridge and Dublin manuscripts. For example, seven of the annual entries between 1066 and 1100 are completely or partially identical to corresponding accounts in MSS 0.2.4 and 507 or can be considered paraphrases of them.[29] In the 'Exchequer Domesday's' 1088 account of the translation of St Nicholas's body to Bari, only one word of the passage is changed.[30] Yet the PRO annals borrow from a source different from the proximate source of the Cambridge and Dublin texts. The PRO annals begin with a brief mention of St Augustine of Canterbury's sixth-century mission to England, not with the death of Edward the Confessor as do the other two texts.[31] On the other hand, the PRO annals ignore the succession-oath sworn to William aetheling in 1116, an event recorded in the other manuscripts.[32] While the 'Exchequer' text mentions Earl Robert of Gloucester's foundation of Margam in 1147, it adds details of his construction of Bristol Castle and of the Priory of St James not found in the other texts. And lastly, the PRO annals lack the Margam-centered events of the Cambridge text except for mention of the abbey's foundation.[33]

Annals in British Library, Egerton MS 3088, which belonged to Abbey Dore, support to a lesser degree the existence of *Q* as the ultimate source from which the texts under consideration descended.[34] A number of entries record portions of

[28] PRO, E.164/1, fols 14v–17v; printed in 'Chronicle of the Thirteenth Century', in *Archaeologia Cambrensis*, 3rd ser. 8, 1862, 273–83; it is considered to be a transcript made in a Glamorgan or Gwent monastery from some other manuscript ('Chronicle', 272).

[29] E.164/1, a. 1066, 1081, 1087, 1088, 1095, 1098, fol. 14v.

[30] E.164/1, a. 1088, fol. 14v.

[31] E.164/1, fol. 14v, where the date is incorrectly stated to be A.D. 600; the annals' next entry is for the year 1066 and they continue to 1298.

[32] MS 0.2.4, fol. 7; 'Annales de Margan', 10; MS 507, fol. 4.

[33] E.164/1, a. 1147, fol. 14v.

[34] Fols 118–134v; partially printed in 'Annales Dorenses', ed. R. Pauli in *MGH Scriptorum* 27, 514–31; Ker, *Medieval Libraries*, 58; *The British Museum: Catalogue of Additions to the Manuscripts 1931–1935*, Trustees of the British Museum, London, 1967, 306–7, esp. 309; I am indebted to Dr Martin Brett for calling my attention to this text.

comparable ones in MSS 0.2.4 and 507 using identical or very similar wording. The range of similarity extends from the identical wording to record lightning damage to the roof of Salisbury Cathedral tower in 1092 and the death of Bishop Herewald of Llandaff in 1104 to the manuscript's very similar descriptions of the famine of 1094 and the discord beween Kings Henry I of England and Louis VI of France.[35] Egerton MS 3088 even repeats the story of Arthur of Brittany's murder, although in a different version and not under the same year.[36]

Nevertheless, the proximate chronicle source of the Cambridge and Dublin manuscripts clearly is not also the immediate source of Egerton MS 3088. The Abbey Dore annals cover a different time span. The account written in a single thirteenth-century hand begins with the reign of Emperor Augustus and the Nativity and runs to 1243, after which it is continued by several other hands to 1362.[37] Its different version of Arthur of Brittany's murder already has been noted. And within the chronological period covered by MSS 0.2.4 and 507, the Egerton text contains many other entries both completely and partially different from those of the two annals.[38]

So some ultimate source material, Q, seems to have existed which provided data for all of the annals so far mentioned (infra, table). How distant it was from MS 3088 and indeed what changes the scribe of the pre-1244 entries introduced I cannot say. The affinity between Q and MSS 0.2.4 and 507 and the likelihood of a common proximate source for the two seem established beyond doubt. Differences between the 'Exchequer Domesday' and the two annals are best explained by the text's independent descent from Q. Since both MS 507 and the 'Exchequer Domesday' are non-Margam in focus, Q would seem to have been as well.

As for Q, the process of its formation and a thorough survey of its composition await further study. However, component sources such as 'Florence of Worcester,' William of Malmesbury's *Gesta regum* and *Historia novella*, and an annals of Winchester have long been known through the works of various commentators on the 'Margam Annals' from T. D. Hardy and Walter de Gray Birch to Felix Liebermann, William Greenway, F. G. Cowley, and Antonia Gransden.[39]

With the textual status of the 'Margam Annals' clarified, it is appropriate to consider the paleographical evidence already alluded to which establishes its scribe's membership in the Margam community: the Cambridge manuscript is written in the hand of a Margam Scribe. The manuscript came to the fore in

[35] MS 3088, a. 1092, 1094, 1104, 1115, fol. 131v; 'Annales Dorenses', 521–22.

[36] MS 3088, fol. 133; 'Annales Dorenses', 527: Arthur is said to have been run through with a sword at Mirebeau; a superscript gloss corrected the site to Rouen; see supra, n. 5.

[37] Fols 118–33; *B.M., Catalogue*, 309.

[38] For completely different entries than corresponding ones in MSS 0.2.4 and 507: e.g., a. 1158: MS 3088, fol. 132; 'Annales Dorenses', 524; MS 0.2.4, fol. 12; 'Annales de Margan', 15; MS 507, fol. 5; for entries partially different: e.g., a. 1081, MS 3088, fol. 131v; 'Annales Dorenses', 521; MS 0.2.4, fol. 2; 'Annales de Margan', 4; MS. 507, fol. 2; for entries in years for which MSS 0.2.4 and 507 lack accounts, e.g., a. 1072–74, MS 3088, fol. 131; 'Annales Dorenses', 521.

[39] Hardy, *Catalogue*, 77; Luard, 'Margam Annals', xiii–xiv; Liebermann, 'Ex Annalibus de Margan', 428–30 and nn.; Greenway, 'Annals of Margam', 21, 26–27; Lewis, 'Literary Tradition', 537; Cowley, *Monastic Order*, 150; Gransden, *Historical Writing*, 332.

connection with a study of secretarial bureaucracies in the lordship of Glamorgan nearing completion.[40] It was logical to investigate whether any of the scribes of the lordship's honorial abbey, Margam, whose hands I had identified, could have written the 'Annals'. A printed facsimile of folio 11 in Walter de Gray Birch's *Margam Abbey* seemed to be written in the hand of a Margam scribe who had been assigned the work number **24**.[41]

Comparison of the entire Cambridge manuscript with the *acta* written by **Scribe 24** of my Glamorgan study has confirmed that the script of the literary and diplomatic sources is the same. So far 25 of **Scribe 24**'s original *acta* have been located.[42] The script of these is a consistent thirteenth-century semi-cursive business hand dating from approximately 1225 to mid-century.[43] It reveals **Scribe 24** to have been an experienced clerk who wrote *acta* with a flair, drawing ascenders boldly and thickening his strokes on ascenders, diagonal and horizontal tops of *f* and *s*, the loops of currently written *d*'s, suspension signs and trailing-headed *a*'s. *A*, *H*, and *M* can be 'filled in', *M* being the prime example. Obvious descenders are rare. Characteristic forms are *M*, *R*, *g* and terminal *s*. Lower-case *g* is found with the tail finished in two principal forms: frequently tightly drawn with two or three-strokes; calligraphically looped; and horizontal stroke with and without a slight *ductus*. [44]

Although the script of the 'Annals' is less calligraphic than the style **Scribe 24** employed in his *acta*, it is clearly **24**'s work. In the 'Annals', the script has been adapted for book writing. This has resulted in few dramatic strokes on letters like those found in **24**'s *acta*. However, the scribe continued to 'fill in' capitals such as *M*. On folio 2 can be found virtually all of the forms which characterize **Scribe 24**'s writing, including the two principal types of *g*.[45]

The effect of this scribal identification has been to identify for the first time the author of what has been called one of 'two . . . surviving Welsh monastic chronicles of importance'.[46] Regrettably a named member of the Margam community does not emerge from this process. Few scribes in this period did identify

---

[40] Robert B. Patterson, *Margam Abbey and the Scribes of Early Angevin Glamorgan: Secretarial Clerks and Bureaucracies in a Marcher Barony c.1150–1218*, forthcoming.

[41] Birch, *Margam Abbey*, plate facing p. 277.

[42] Aberystwyth, National Library of Wales, Penrice and Margam Charters, nos. 69–70, 73–74, 76, 121, 136–37, 146, 1961, 1967, 1973, 1977, 1992, 1994–96, 2036; London, British Library, Harley Charters, 75.A.35, 75.B.39–40, 75.C.22, 75.C.29, 75.C.41, 75.C.52; *Cartae et alia munimenta quae ad Dominium de Glamorgancia pertinent*, eds George T. Clark and Godfrey L. Clark, 2nd edn, 6 vols, Cardiff, 1910, 2: nos. 239, 372, 376 (without witnesses), 377 (without witnesses), 383 (without witnesses), 384 (without witnesses), 472, 484, 490, 505, 512, 551, 604; 3: nos. 716 (without witnesses), 813, 820–21; 6: nos. 1576, 1578, 1581, 1589.

[43] For *f*, *fideliter*, l.8, P. and M., no. 1995 (infra, plate 1), *filius*, l.1, P. and M., no. 1996 (infra, plate 2); *s*, *scriptum*, l.1, no. 1995, l.1., no. 1996; *d*, *domino*, l.1, no. 1995, l.1, no. 1996; *a*, *Margan*, l.3, no. 1995, l.3, no. 1996; *A*, *Audituris*, l.1, no. 1995, P. and M., no. 137, *Audituris*, l.1, P. and M., no. 137; *H*, *Hiis*, l.9, no. 1995, l.12, no. 1996; *M*, *Marie*, l.3, no. 1995, l.3, no. 1996; for suspension signs, *presens scriptum*, l.1, no. 1995, l.1, no. 1996; for variations in *g*: tail looped in *Margan*, l.3, closed and tight, *ego*, l.2, no. 1996, open, *ego*, l.10, no. 1996 and *ego*, l.5, no. 1995, a variation.

[44] Powicke, *Loss of Normandy*, 316, dates MS 0.2.4 to c.1240.

[45] Compare in MS 0.2.4: *f*, *Weldeofus*, fol. 2. l.2 (infra, plate 3); *s*, *sedem*, l.15, *comitis*, l.2; *d*, *tradere*, l.1; *a*, *decollatur*, l.2; *A*, *Andree*, l.30; *H*, *Hoc*, l.30; *M*, *Matildis*, l.14; suspension signs, *Will(el)m(um)*, l.1; *t(er)remotus*, l.26; *g*, *pugna*, l.3, *fulgurum*, l.35.

[46] Cowley, *Monastic Order*, 149.

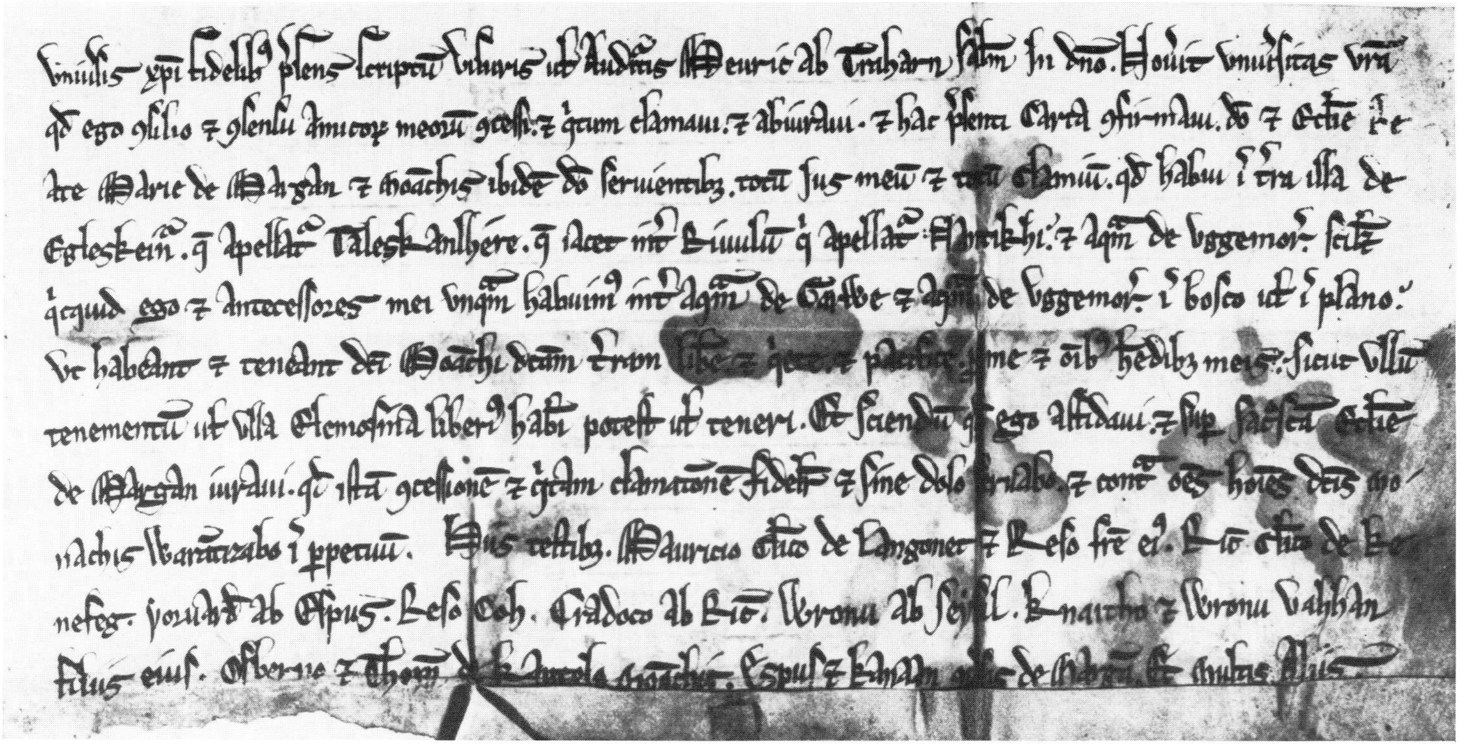

Plate 1 (above) National Library of Wales, Penrice and Margam Charter, no. 1995 (with permission of The National Library of Wales and by courtesy of Mr C. P. M. Methuen-Campbell)

Plate 2 (below) National Library of Wales, Penrice and Margam Charter, no. 1996 (with permission of The National Library of Wales and by the Courtesy of Mr C. P. M. Methuen-Campbell)

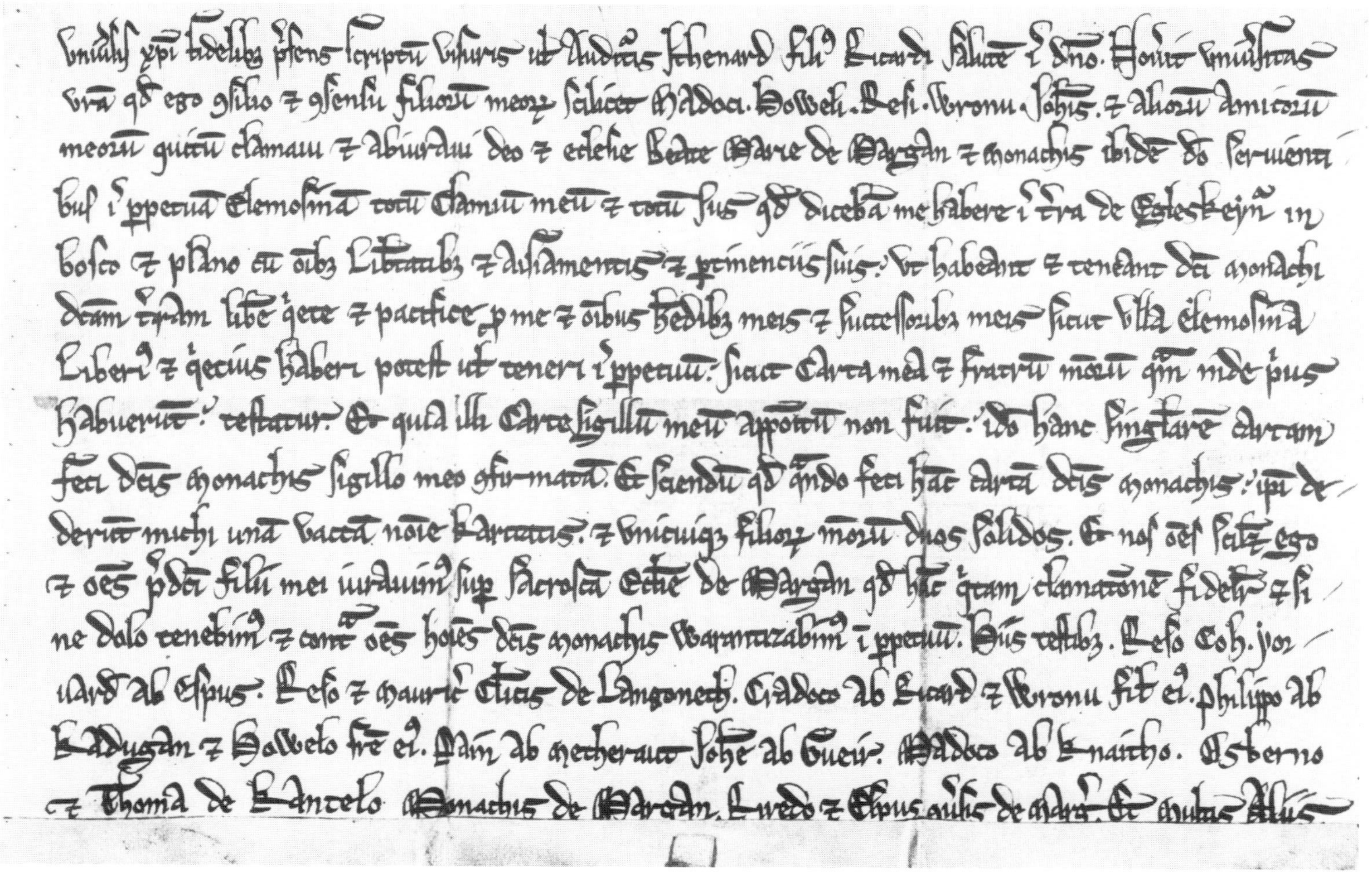

noluerint tradere Regem Willm̄

Waldeofus Dux syluardi comitis fili' decollat';
iste ī pugna eboracensi plures normannorū solus
obtruncauerat: unos ⁊ unos p portam egredientes
decapitans.

Primus fuit uent' ī nocte Natal' dn̄i.
IN festiuitate sce helene magnū incendiū fuit
Wintonie. Et edificata ÷ villa Cardiuie sub Rex
selmio Rege.

Obiit Matildis Regina.
Withbert' papa sedem accepit.
erdalac Rex hibernie obiit.

Obiit Wills Rex Anglie senior .viii. id' septēbr̄
anno Regni sui .xxi. Comitat' Lxu. uixit .l. ix.
corp' ei sepultū ÷ apud cadomensē cenobiū ī Nor-
mannia qd' ipe edificauerat. Eode anno Wills rex
Willi filius cepit regnare.
Corpus sci Anastasii Nicholai de Myreā ciuitate
ī locum qui Barim dr̄ ix. die mensis maii trāslā-
tum est.

Factus est tremotus .iii. id' augusti. unde totam In-
glia tremor iualit. Cernebant nāq; edificia emin'
resilire ⁊ mox pristino modo residere. Secuta ē inopia
fructuum. edita in seuis frugū rel ut ad festū sca
Andree uix messes reconderent in horreis. Hoc anno obiit ⁊ Lanfrancus Cantuar' archiepc. ⁊ Alanus
Comes Rufus.

Tumult' fulguru.⁊ mor' Dn̄iu etiāin' Deniq; id'

Plate 4a (above)
National Library of Wales, Penrice and Margam Charter,
no. 127 verso (with permission of The National Library of Wales
and by the courtesy of Mr C. P. M. Methuen-Campbell)

Plate 4b (below)
National Library of Wales, Penrice and Margam Roll, no. 293/15 (with
permission of The National Library of Wales and by the courtesy of Mr C. P. M.
Methuen-Campbell)

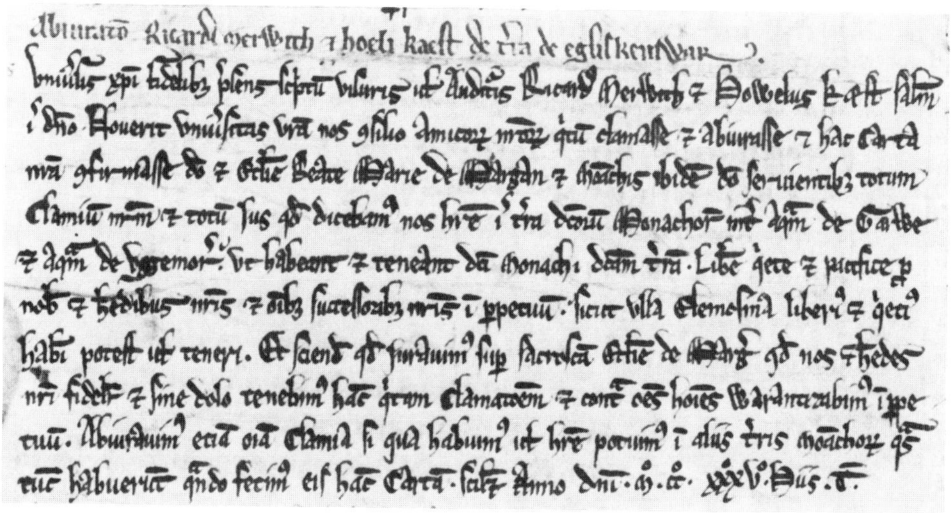

themselves as the executors of the charters they wrote.[47] It was equally unusual for Cistercian literary monastic-copyists to do so, as Prof C. R. Cheney has written.[48]

With only a few exceptions, the Cambridge manuscript is in **Scribe 24**'s hand, and the condition of the text provides a few opportunities for the annalist to be observed at work. He seems to have written the entire text, then corrected by erasing or adding a word superscript or a new detail to his account of King Richard I's return from his crusade.[49] A marginal gloss on folio 1 may be an afterthought of his on the appearance of Halley's Comet in 1066.[50] When he felt the need to squeeze more words to a folio, he could reduce his script in size.[51] And as he so often did with his charters, **Scribe 24** set out his text between ruled margins and lines.[52] Either **24** or possibly another scribe added filled out initial uncials.[53] Other scribes annotated parhelia and some time after the text was completed, two different scribes added respectively material on the captives of Mirebeau in the account of 1202 and details of the Fourth Lateran Council.[54]

This physical evidence shows that **Scribe 24** was no mere copyist, although one must agree in general with Powicke that the Margam scribe's text is not the original work.[55] Yet in assessing the nature of **Scribe 24**'s authorial role, his Margam-focused additions and expressions of religious political sympathies should be remembered.[56] He also demonstrates some originality in material not found in MS 507 which he included in his text, such as his description of the Cathari.[57] There is evidence that the scribe used charter evidence, to which he had access as a member of Margam's scriptorium, as the basis for his 1217 entry about Gilbert de Clare's patronage of Margam.[58]

The preceeding puts more than a little 'flesh' on an otherwise paleographical

---

[47] Among Gloucester comital *acta* issued between c.1147 and 1217, only one scribe, Master Herveus, identified himself: Robert B. Patterson, *Earldom of Gloucester Charters: The Charters and Scribes of the Earls and Countesses of Gloucester to A.D. 1217*, Oxford, 1973, 17; for Mr T. A. M. Bishop's identification of named twelfth-century Chancery scribes, see his *Scriptores Regis*, Oxford, 1960, 23, plates XVII (a) and n., XXI (a) and n., XXXI (b); M. T. Clanchy, *From Memory to Written Record*, Cambridge, Mass., 1979, 242–43.

[48] Christopher Cheney, 'Les Bibliothèques Cisterciennes en Angleterre au XIIe Siècle', in *Mélanges Saint Bernard*, Association bourguegnonne des sociétés des savants, Dijon, 1953, 376.

[49] MS 0.2.4, fol. 22, l.33; fol. 18, l.17.

[50] MS 0.2.4, fol. 1.

[51] MS 0.2.4, fol. 17, ll.10–11.

[52] E.g., P. and M. Chs, nos. 1995–96 (infra, plates 1 & 2); not all of **Scribe 24**'s *acta* have ruled lines and margins.

[53] The difficulty in deciding this question is that there are no examples of such uncials in **24**'s other work for purposes of comparison.

[54] MS 0.2.4, fols 6, 32–33; fol. 21, ll.16–19; fol. 26, ll.28–34.

[55] Powicke, *Loss of Normandy*, 316.

[56] Supra, 199–200.

[57] MS 0.2.4, a. 1163, fol. 12; 'Annales de Margan', 15.

[58] MS 0.2.4, a. 1217, fols 26–27; 'Annales de Margan', 33; an excellent charter source candidate would be P. and M. Ch., no. 2045; Clark, *Cartae*, 4: no. 969, pp. 1221–23 printed the text from an *inspeximus*; the charter was issued after 18 November 1217 and before 12 November 1218: *Handbook of British Chronology*, eds F. Maurice Powicke and E. B. Fryde, 2nd edn, London, 1961, 429 (Gilbert de Clare styled earl of Gloucester and Hertford); *Llandaff Episcopal Acta 1140–1287*, ed. David Crouch, South Wales Record Society 5 (1988), xv (death of witness, Bishop Henry of Llandaff); see also Michael Altschul, *A Baronial Family in Medieval England: The Clares 1217–1314*, Baltimore, 1965, 26–27 and nn.

phantom. But the fortunate survival of other samples of his hand enlarges the image of the Margam annalist still further, thereby providing an unusually detailed career cameo of a secretarial scribe and evidence of several significant bureaucratic procedures followed by his scriptorium.

Scribe 24 was one of at least fifteen secretarial scribes who served in Margam Abbey's scriptorium during the early thirteenth century. It is possible that he succeeded as principal scribe **Scribes 15** and **16** who wrote respectively 22 and 15 *acta* for the abbey during their careers.[59]

Most of the charters written by **Scribe 24** recorded lay landlords' pious donations and quitclaims to Margam Abbey, which often were reinforced by oaths sworn on relics. At least one of these transactions took place in the chapter before the entire community; others, possibly there or in the abbey church.[60] A quitclaim involving land Rhys Goch *iunior* held at Egloskeinwir occurred at the abbey on November 1, 1234 in the presence of Elias, bishop of Llandaff.[61] In 1239 **Scribe 24** wrote a charter in the name of Bishop Elias recording an agreement reached in the bishop's presence between Robert, abbot of Tewkesbury, and Margam providing for Tewkesbury's renunciation of tithes and other parochial rights in the parish of Kenfig in return for an annual rent.[62] Still another charter he wrote for Bishop Elias was an *inspeximus* of an earlier one of Elias's predecessor Bishop Henry of Abergavenny in favor of Margam.[63] One quitclaim took place sometime between 1219 and 1240 at Llandaff before the cathedral chapter.[64] Many of the pious grants **Scribe 24** recorded probably were disguised business transactions. One of his charters was explicitly this kind of record, i.e., a 1230 chirograph detailing Raymond de Sully's sale of rental rights over Bonvileston to Margam for five years.[65]

Scribe 24 also played minor roles in two other major activities of the Margam scriptorium. Ever since the second half of the twelfth century, the scriptorium had implemented a system to facilitate identification of original *acta* the community had received, folded, and stored in some sort of chest or press for future reference. To make it unnecessary to unfold the *acta* to determine their contents, clerks wrote endorsements on the dorse sides of the folded documents, indicating the donor or relevance of the charter by some cryptic wording. This archival personnel I have labeled the scriptorium's filing clerks. From the end of the twelfth century until about the first quarter of the thirteenth, most of this work was done by a secretarial scribe **15**, assisted by a few other secretarial scribes and filing clerks. With few exceptions, like **Clerk 1**, these latter types were casual recruits: none endorsed more than six *acta*.[66] **Scribe 24** was one of the first type, a secretarial scribe who temporarily helped out in filing. At least one of his endorse-

---

[59] Patterson, *Margam Abbey*, appendices I and II.
[60] The proceedings of Harl. Ch. 75.B.39 (Clark, *Cartae*, 2: no. 372) took place 'in Capitulo coram toto Conventu super sacrosancta ecclesie de Margan'; many others were recorded as having been sworn 'super sacrosancta', without indication of place.
[61] Harl. Ch. 75.B.40; Clark, *Cartae*, 2: no. 490.
[62] P. and M. Ch., no. 136; Clark, *Cartae*, 2: no. 505; Crouch, *Llandaff Acta*, no. 78.
[63] P. and M. Ch., no. 137; Crouch, *Llandaff Acta*, no. 80.
[64] P. and M. Ch., no. 1977 (Clark, *Cartae*, 6: no. 1581) mentions the 'sacrosancta Ecclesie de Landaf'; the witness-list is dominated by members of the chapter and the episcopal *familia*; for the dating, see Crouch, *Llandaff Acta*, xix–xxi, xxiv.
[65] Harl. Ch. 75.A.35; Clark, *Cartae*, 2: no. 474.
[66] Patterson, *Margam Abbey*, Appendix V.

ments has been found on a charter another unidentified scribe wrote for Hywel ap Grono Goch.[67]

In the early thirteenth century Margam refined its archival procedures still further by taking the precaution against possible loss of original *acta* by enrolling copies. The scriptorium ultimately produced seventeen rolls dating from the thirteenth through the fifteenth centuries.[68] Some secretarial scribes were engaged in copying activities. **Scribe 34** wrote over sixty copies on several rolls.[69] Some archival copyist-scribes whose hands cannot be found in other types of *acta* must have served in the scriptorium entirely in this capacity. Still others only dabbled as copyists. **Scribe 24** was one of these latter types. At least ten of his copies have been found. Several groups of consecutive entries argue for service on two single occasions or relatively closely connected ones.[70]

Scribe 24 was engaged in four major activities – secretarial scribe, filing clerk, archivist-copyist, and in a qualified sense, author – more than can be documented for any other Margam scribe. His activities reveal the bureaucratic versatility Margam Abbey's scriptorium had developed by the mid-thirteenth century. In his literary role, by transforming his chronicle source **Scribe 24** was more than a mere copyist. In **24**'s hand the identity of the author of the 'Margam Annals' has finally been discovered. It is not surprising that he turns out to be the great abbey's most versatile scribe.

Note:
Two pertinent studies have come to my attention since the completion of this paper: Kathleen Hughes, 'The Welsh Latin chronicles: *Annales Cambriae* and related texts' in her *Celtic Britain in the Early Middle Ages*, ed. David Dumville, Woodbridge, 1980, 67–85 – called to my attention by Mr Daniel Huws, Keeper of Manuscripts and Records, The National Library of Wales; and Marvin L. Colker, 'The "Margam Chronicle" in a Dublin Manuscript', forthcoming in *The Haskins Society Journal: Studies in Medieval History* iv, 1992. In her discussion of Glamorgan annals Hughes overlooked Trinity College Dublin, MS 507 (81 and n.–84); she argued for a Neath Abbey provenance for PRO, E.164/1 (82 and n.–83 and n.). Prof Colker's paper contains the first published text of the Dublin manuscript from the point where Trinity College Cambridge, MS 0.2.4 breaks off through 1235 and a collation of the two manuscripts for the years 1066–1232. Colker believes that MS 507 derives from Grace Dieu Abbey. Finally, I am grateful to Dr Rodney M. Thomson for his advice on an aspect of this paper.

[67] P. and M. Ch., no. 127v [infra, plate 4 (a)]; Clark, *Cartae*, 2: no. 375.
[68] P. and M. Rolls, nos. 288–96, 543–46, 2089–92; the list in Birch, *Margam Abbey*, 281 and n. is incomplete. My count is based on the current catalogue numbers; several groups of these items formed the actual rolls.
[69] Patterson, *Margam Abbey*, Appendix II; P. and M. Rolls 288/1–9; 289/1–27; 292/1–10; 293/1–6; 543/1–11.
[70] P. and M. Rolls 289/37–41; 293/14–15 [supra, plate 4 (b)]; see also Rolls 290–91/52, 57; 293/23; 2089/(8).

BOOKLAND, FOLKLAND AND FIEFS

Susan Reynolds

For someone who studies Old English history only tangentially to reopen the question of bookland and folkland may seem to be the height of rashness.[1] But it is a mere foothill compared with the high foolhardiness of the project of which it forms part. I am writing a book that I plan to call *Fiefs and Vassals*, and that is to examine the evidence of the medieval phenomena which lie somewhere behind the meanings which medieval historians seem to attribute to these two words. At present I am thinking about the phenomena that lie behind the word fief, which are, I take it property relations among the upper or landed classes of the middle ages, whatever the words used to describe them, and however people at the time thought about them. I am deliberately separating property relations from the personal and political relationships that lie behind the word vassalage in order to be able to clarify my ideas about each before looking at the way they were related. People at the time did not do this and may not have articulated their ideas about either at all clearly but that is at this stage irrelevant: we cannot penetrate vague ideas by being vague ourselves. As Maitland said of the 'happy haze' in which, he said, some people in his day wished to leave another set of medieval ideas: 'Now I am very ready to believe that haze is its native atmosphere, and that, when we have plucked it out and inspected it in the modern daylight, we must once more tenderly put it back into the medieval muddle . . . Only let us know that haze is haze.'[2]

The scholars of the seventeenth and eighteenth centuries who first worked out the ideas about feudal law and feudal society from which all subsequent ideas of feudalism have derived did not base them on the records of law as practised in the so-called feudal monarchies of the middle ages. They based them on the twelfth-century Lombard treatise known as the *Libri Feudorum* and the comments on it of academic lawyers, who studied it along with Roman law in medieval universities.[3] Some of their glosses and commentaries reflected current issues but some were more concerned with distinctions and hypothetical hard cases. The resulting 'feudal law', like most of the 'feudal theory' which has been deduced from it, was alien to the customary law of the earlier middle ages, when fiefs are supposed to have emerged, and impinged on the professional law of the later middle ages

[1] I am grateful to members of the conference for references and ideas but especially to Chris Lewis for discussing commendation and, above all, to Pauline Stafford for references and repeated and clarifying discussions.
[2] F. W. Maitland, *Township and Borough*, Cambridge 1898, 31–2.
[3] *Das Langobardische Lehnrecht*, ed. Carl Lehmann, Göttingen 1896. Cf. D. R. Kelley, 'De origine feudorum', *Speculum*, xxxix, 1964, 207–28 and 'Clio and the lawyers', *Medievalia et Humanistica*, N.S. v, 1974, 25–49; Alan Watson, *Making of the Civil Law*, Cambridge, Mass.,/London 1981, 12, 25, 29, 44, 60.

chiefly when it provided useful tags or arguments for professionals who had studied Roman law. Modern ideas of feudalism are still marked by the context in which ideas of feudal law and feudal property were worked out in the seventeenth and eighteenth centuries. Feudal property was then seen as incomplete in contrast to the absolute property which Locke, for instance, derived from Natural Rights and used as an argument against taxation and tyranny. As more knowledge about the middle ages has been accumulated, ideas of feudal property – feudal 'tenure' as medieval historians like to call it – have been elaborated and endlessly debated but not seriously rethought.

Marc Bloch was still a prisoner of a very old tradition when he explained that in the middle ages 'the word "ownership" [*propriété*], as applied to landed property [*un immeuble*], would have been almost meaningless.'[4] A more recent writer who, though not a professional medievalist, seems to me to sum up the general view of those who see the fief as embodying the characteristically medieval – or feudal – idea of property, puts it like this: 'Land, in fact, was not "owned" by anyone; it was "held" by superiors in a ladder of "tenures" leading to the king or other supreme lord. ("Tenure", derived from the Latin word *tenere*, "to hold", itself means "a holding").'[5] But the distinction between 'ownership' or 'property' on the one hand and 'tenure' on the other, or between 'owner' and 'tenant', is a distinction between words – our words. In so far as it bears any relation to legal realities (and that is not tremendously far) they are the realities of our legal system. Absolute property exists nowhere but in the minds and polemics of those who claim it in order to defend their rights against governments which threaten to tax them or confiscate their possessions. In trying to make sense of the rules and practice of property-holding by nobles and free men in medieval Europe, one cannot rely on residues of seventeenth- and eighteenth-century ideas – even if we label them 'feudal theory'. Serious modern students of comparative law and property look at property in rather different terms.[6] As L. C. Becker puts it: 'property rights are typically aggregates of different sorts of rights and rights-correlatives.'[7] They need to be analysed. If we are to treat fiefs as something one could call a category of property, which is what many medievalists seem to think it was, then we need to establish what were the rights and obligations of the properties that we call fiefs or that were called fiefs at the time, and how these rights and obligations differed from those of other property. I have used Andrew Reeve's discussion of A. M. Honoré's eleven possible 'incidents of ownership' to construct a check-list of rights and obligations, whether I am dealing with fiefs,

[4] *Feudal Society*, London 1962, 115 (*La Société Féodale*, i, Paris 1939, 183).
[5] H. J. Berman, *Law and Revolution*, Cambridge, Mass., 1983, 312. The use of 'tenure' for a holding rather than a method of holding, not recorded in *Oxford English Dictionary*, 2nd edn, 1989, xvii, 791, after 1766, seems to have come into writing about medieval history quite recently.
[6] E.g. W. N. Hohfeld, *Fundamental Legal Conceptions*, New York/London 1919, 28, 69–91; A. M. Honoré, 'Ownership' in *Oxford Essays in Jurisprudence*, ed. A. G. Guest, Oxford 1961, 107–47; J. H. Merryman, 'Ownership and Estate', *Tulane Law Review*, xlviii, 1974, 916–45; L. C. Becker, *Property rights: Philosophical foundations*, London 1977; Andrew Reeve, *Property*, London 1986; Sally Falk Moore, *Social Facts and Formations*, Cambridge 1986, 38–40, 64–80; Jack Goody, *Death, Property and the Ancestors*, Stanford 1962, 284–303; Max Gluckman, *The Ideas in Barotse Jurisprudence*, Manchester 1972, 75–112. I have largely ignored what any of them says about European feudalism which is generally derived from the tradition which their own material and arguments undermine.
[7] Becker, 21.

alods, bookland, or whatever. Generally, of course, the sources tell me about few of the items on my list, but I have found it helpful to think about them nevertheless.

The rights or claims of property on my check-list are the rights to use and manage the thing concerned and to receive its produce or income; the right to pass it on to one's heirs and the right to dispose of it to others – these two being liable to conflict with each other when exercise of the second disappoints potential heirs. There are also the questions of the term, or absence of term, during which all the other rights and obligations exist, and of who gets the ultimate reversion. Last but far from least, there is the right to have one's title protected. In all societies these rights will be limited or regulated in some way, for instance by the degree to which one's use of property is exclusive or by the possibility, however restricted, of its confiscation. Property also always carries obligations, even if people within a society do not perceive the connection very clearly and some theorists of modern property rights prefer to play them down. In most societies there is an obligation not to use one's property in ways officially considered harmful. Property normally carries some kind of obligation to taxation or service, even if, in a lot of relatively simple societies, the obligation is thought of as voluntary or contractual and as owed by the property-holder rather than imposed on the property. Such conceptualizations are revealing and important but we need to distinguish them – especially if the evidence of them is slight – from the conceptualizations that we impose.

Rights and obligations do not always come in solid packages. There is no reason to say that there are no true property rights in a society just because the packages are different from ours. Neither in our society nor, I think, in any other, do all the rights in landed property normally belong to only one person. They are often both divided and shared, sometimes in several layers. My landlord and I each enjoy some of the rights of property against each other and against others, including both local and central government. Each of us has obligations to each other and to outsiders, including both local and central government. Rights can be combined into various packages, even in a single society, and it seems to me extremely likely that the packages should have varied in England between the seventh and eleventh centuries, even if the same words were sometimes used for different packages or bits of them. In smaller and simpler societies it is often impossible to distinguish between rulers and landlords, taxes and rents, not because simple people confuse them but because the distinction does not exist.[8] If seventh-century England was perhaps in that category then worrying whether early grants to churches conveyed immunity – which presumably meant something like rights of government – or conveyed 'simply land' may be missing the point. In any case, grants could not convey 'simply land' because rights in land are seldom simple. Land granted to churches presumably had peasants on it who owed something – rent or taxes? – but who themselves had some of the rights of property: that is, they used their land and took its produce subject to renders which were effectively limited by custom. By the eleventh century conditions had changed radically: England formed a single kingdom with taxes apart from rents, even if for some people, on some estates, the two were in practice indistinguish-

---

[8] Lucy Mair, *Introduction to Social Anthropology*, Oxford 1965, 137–42 is suggestive. On confusion: F. W. Maitland, *Domesday Book and Beyond*, Cambridge 1907, 224.

able. Of course, people in the eleventh century got on with paying or collecting rent and taxes without agonizing about the difference, let alone explaining it to us. But some of the confusions are more ours than theirs. It is modern historians who are so obsessed with the origins of what is called a hierarchy of tenure that they envisage relationships of government or patronage in (to use the same weasel word) tenurial or proto-tenurial terms. It is modern historians who say that under feudalism all land 'really' belonged to the king: I'd be interested to have any reference to the expression of such an idea in the middle ages.

I am not suggesting that there was no difference between property rights in the middle ages and now. On the contrary. Property rights vary in different societies and need to be analysed in context, not lumped into crude categories constructed by noticing only one or two kinds of right or obligation, sticking a label on them so that we do not need to look behind it. At different times and in different places in the middle ages people thought of some property as carrying what they thought of as full or complete rights. In general people of high status had more rights in their property and owed lighter obligations than people of low status. People of high status, however, sometimes also held property granted to them by churches or kings with fewer rights and, sometimes, more obligations. Political favour, power politics, the growth of a land-market, and the drift of custom constantly introduced anomalies. All human life outside textbooks is full of anomalies, particularly human life under customary law. Customary law, although perceived as old and fixed, is bound to vary from time to time as well as from place to place: the precedents followed are the precedents that are remembered and seem right at the time. Early medieval custom, moreover, like all law and all morality, embodied conflicting norms, while giving fewer opportunities for formal and authoritative discussion and resolution of conflicts of principle than professional law would later provide. Apparent statements of principle were often not rules of law but maxims that were stated just because there were doubts and disagreements – doubts and disagreements that may have been resolved differently the year before and would be resolved in yet another way the year after or in the next county.[9] Property rights could be affected by some of the most fundamental conflicts in medieval values: between hierarchy, obedience, and loyalty on the one hand and custom, immanent justice, mutuality of obligations, and collective judgement on the other.[10] A man's claim to pass on his property to his children or other close kin was liable to frustrate the claim of a ruler to keep some control over land in his territory. All those whose land was protected by their rulers owed some obligations in return even if they thought of their rights in it as complete and whether or not anyone thought that the ruler or one of his predecessors had given it in the first place. The terms on which any particular estate was held must often have been uncertain. Even if it had originally been granted by a ruler or other lord, gratitude and a sense of obligation are perishable: the bond between grantor and grantee would be bound to erode as time and generations passed. Rulers hoped to maximize dues and controls, subjects hoped to secure maximum rights and minimum obligations. The normative working of custom would tend to turn any vindicated claim into right by the mere passage of time. In these conditions I suspect that – to use the terminology of modern historiography – individual fiefs

---

[9] Cf. Moore, *Social facts*, 38–40 and *Law as process*, London/Boston 1978, 169–70.
[10] Discussed in S. Reynolds, *Kingdoms and communities*, Oxford 1984, chapters 1–2 et passim.

would tend with the passage of time to become assimilated to the condition of alods even while powerful rulers would be trying to assimilate alods to the condition of fiefs.

The idea that the words bookland, folkland, or laenland represent consistent categories of property rights depends on assuming that such categories existed and then interpolating the words into centuries and contexts where they are not found.[11] Folkland occurs only in five texts, all but one between about 858 and the early tenth century. In the fifth (The Wife's Lament) it means something like 'a country'.[12] To approach the subject of property rights from a supposedly technical vocabulary is, in any case, to ignore how language works. Words do not have fixed and agreed meanings and the more important the element of social life they refer to the more likely they are to have multiple meanings.[13] Words are used precisely or technically only within particular disciplines in which precision is necessary. In the context of property and political relationships precise and consistent usage could come from lawyers, but only if they are professional lawyers working in a legal system that has acknowledged authorities, written documents in which their pronouncements are recorded, and some system of publishing and enforcing those pronouncements. Even then the more general and important words will be vulnerable to ambiguity and change from social and political influence.

To begin – at length – at the beginning, I think that Patrick Wormald was right in suggesting that analogies from outside England make it highly probable that before the conversion customary law allowed nobles to pass on their lands to their children.[14] The instability of the early English kingdoms may have entailed frequent confiscations and redistributions, while their smallness would have made it harder for nobles to keep their heads down in distant areas than it was for Frankish, Saxon, or Lombard nobles in the same period. All this, however, need not imply that nobles were not considered to have a right in principle, provided they were loyal subjects of their kings, to pass on their holdings or that they never did so. There are several suggestions of an assumption of inheritance, and when Bede complained that, under the pretext of founding monasteries, people were getting lands ascribed to them by royal edicts in hereditary right, he need not have meant that hereditary right was in itself new.[15] Any periods of local stability would accumulate precedents to strengthen the claims of heirs. Whether we call

[11] E.g. Eric John, *Orbis Britanniae*, Leicester 1966, 74–5, 117–22.
[12] R. L. Venezky and A. di P. Healey, *Microfiche Concordance to Old English*, Toronto 1980: Folcland, folclande, folclondes. For another possible reference (as *terrulas sui propriae publicae juris*) see H. Vollrath-Reichelt, *Königsgedanke und Königtum bei den Angelsachsen*, Cologne/Vienna 1971, 216. Unlike 'bookland', folkland is not apparently used in any glosses to explain a Latin word. Vollrath-Reichelt's suggestion (*ibid.* 192–225) that folkland was royal domain which the king could not alienate without consent could be right for the contexts of the charters she discusses but on other aspects of her argument see Nicholas Brooks, 'Anglo-Saxon Charters', *Anglo-Saxon England*, iii, 1974, 210–31, at 221–2. The *Concordance* suggests that folkright (folcriht, folcryht, folcryhte) also had a fairly wide range of meanings: cf. folclaga, folclage.
[13] M. Gluckman, *Politics, Law and Ritual in Tribal Society*, Oxford 1977, 199.
[14] P. Wormald, *Bede and the Conversion of England*, Jarrow 1984, 19–22.
[15] Bede, *Historia Ecclesiastica*, ed. C. Plummer, Oxford 1896, i. 413–14 (Epist. ad Ecgbertum, c. 12); cf. 375–6 (Hist. Abbatum, c. 11); Eddius Stephanus, *Life of Bishop Wilfrid*, ed. B. Colgrave, Cambridge 1927, 140 (c. 65).

noble landowners governors or landlords at this stage is our choice: presumably they received some or all of the tribute from the land and functioned in some sense as local governors. Whether they could alienate their property is unknowable: if there were few occasions to do so there would also be few occasions for rules to develop.

From very soon after the conversion of England began in the seventh century royal gifts of land to the church began to be recorded in charters known in the vernacular as *landbocan* or simply *bocan*, so that, although the word bookland occurs less often in the charters than modern commentaries suggest, land conveyed in this way came to be called bookland or booklands.[16] The church's tenure of land was in some respects inevitably different from that of lay nobles, so that the word bookland must have implied some difference of rights. Church property was granted not merely with the traditional hope or expectation of inheritance but for ever, while bishops and monks did not perform the military services demanded of lay nobles. That need not have exempted the peasants on church lands from their obligations to the king until the churches got formal immunities. Practice may have varied between kingdoms and estates.[17] The freedom of alienation noted in some early charters to individual bishops, abbots, and abbesses, was presumably intended to allow them to be succeeded in their offices and the attached property by non-kinsmen within their communities rather than by the kinsmen who would otherwise have hoped to inherit their property. It was also essential when kings gave lands to laymen who wanted to endow monasteries.[18] It seems to me possible, incidentally, that some of these grants to subjects for churches may have been royal confirmations rather than royal gifts: in other societies it is not unknown for nobles to attribute their pious benefactions to their rulers. It flatters the ruler and secures his authority and protection.[19] It need not mean that it was absolutely impossible for anyone but a king to give land to a church. However that may be, lay nobles soon began to get royal charters for themselves, even when no transfer to the church was apparently envisaged. In 779 Offa granted his faithful follower Dudda three *cassati* for ever *in ius ecclesiasticae liberalitatis*, with permission to leave this land to any of his kin that he chose,

[16] Venezky and Healey, *Concordance*. The word is not used e.g. in the charter referred to in *EHD*, i, no. 88 as 'a most important document for understanding the meaning of "bookland" ': Peter Sawyer, *Anglo-Saxon Charters*, London 1968, no. 298. But cf. Sawyer no. 1622 (which seems to be the earliest reference; cf. comments by Nicholas Brooks, *Early History of the Church of Canterbury*, Leicester 1984), 139. A. R. Rumble's interesting suggestions ('Old English *Boc-Land* as an Anglo-Saxon estate-Name', *Leeds Studies in English*, xviii, 1987, 219–30) about the significance of the placename Buckland are not affected by my doubts about the certainty of bookland 'as a legal term'.

[17] For the debate: Eric John, *Land tenure in Early England*, Leicester 1960, 64–79, and *Orbis Britanniae*, Leicester 1966, 64–8; Nicholas Brooks, 'The development of military obligations in eighth and ninth century England', *England before the Conquest*, ed. P. Clemoes and K. Hughes, Cambridge 1971, 69–84 (which I follow); P. Wormald, 'The Age of Bede and Aethelbald', in *The Anglo-Saxons*, ed. James Campbell, Oxford 1982, 95–8; Richard P. Abels, *Lordship and military Obligation in Anglo-Saxon England*, Berkeley/London 1988, 43–57.

[18] Michael Sheehan, *The Will in Medieval England*, Toronto 1963, 86–97. Wormald, *Bede*, 27–8 lists works on the early charters.

[19] K. N. Panikkar, 'A Historical Overview', *Anatomy of a Confrontation*, ed. Sarvepalli Gopal, New Delhi 1991, 22–37 at 27.

and a promise that if any of them committed a crime it would not be forfeit.[20] The word bookland thus came to be applied to lay property.

Bookland cannot always have carried the same rights and obligations. Initially its chief advantage was that, even while it granted its holder *ece erfe*, or land *in sempiternum hereditatem*, or *in hereditatem propriam*, it rather contradictorily allowed him to alienate it. There was always liable to be tension between the rights of a current owner and the expectations of his heirs, for most people (though not all) held their land individually rather than in family groups. With a charter the current owner could secure unilateral power, backed by royal authority, to ignore the expectations of his nearest and dearest: most recorded claims to inherit came from quite close kin. But the terms of charters varied. Dudda's allowed him to choose among his heirs, not to ignore them all. Alfred the Great ordered that restrictions imposed by past owners of bookland on its alienation should be enforced. Whether they generally were is another matter. Alfred himself wanted his bookland kept in the male line but his own will exemplifies the difficulty of controlling events after one's death even if one is a king.[21] A prudent testator leaving either bookland or other acquired land away from his family, or from the most obvious heir within it, might still think it wise ask for royal approval.[22] In the later ninth century ealdorman Alfred did this and at the same time sought permission to bequeath his *erfe* and his folkland – perhaps both in this context meaning much the same: the rest of his inheritance.[23] Whatever the terms of charters, many alienations must have been subject to family negotiation, social values, and political pressures, just as they were in France, though there royal grants that included freedom of disposition did not create a separate category of property with a separate name. There acquisitions were regarded as more freely disposable than old family land. Perhaps a similar freedom was sometimes claimed in England, though the evidence is late and dubious: the development of bookland may have made it less useful.[24]

Doubts about freedom of disposition as a defining characteristic of bookland are intensified by consideration of church property. The church provided the first model of bookland but some donors said that churches were not to alienate their gifts and, even if they did not, church councils forbade it.[25] Churches might need to grant lands to nobles for all kinds of reasons, but they were not supposed to alienate them permanently. Churches in England therefore, like churches elsewhere, normally made grants for one or more lives.[26] We have relatively little evidence of such grants, except from Worcester, but what English documents sometimes call a *laen* (and British historians sometimes call a lease) was very

---

[20] Sawyer, no. 114; cf. F. M. Stenton, *Latin Charters of the Anglo-Saxon Period*, Oxford 1955, 59–61.
[21] *Die Gesetze der Angelsachsen*, ed. F. Liebermann, Halle 1916, i, 74 (Alfred c. 41); Sawyer, nos. 509, 1507.
[22] Cf. Sawyer, no. 155: Offa said that his *minister* should not give away land given by his lord (though this had been king Egbert) without his permission.
[23] Sawyer, no. 1508. But in 946 Sawyer, no. 1504, uses *yrfe* to cover laenland.
[24] See e.g. Moore, *Social Facts*, 38–40.
[25] G. Le Bras and others, *Histoire du droit et des institutions de l'église en occident*, Paris 1958–, iii. 310–11; Brooks, *Early History*, 159.
[26] E.g. Sawyer, nos. 1260–1, 1297–1374; Reginald Lennard, *Rural England*, Oxford 1959, 159–70.

similar to the benefices or *precaria* granted by churches elsewhere.[27] As elsewhere, kings begged church land for themselves and their followers, some donors were probably allowed to keep a life interest in donations, and solemn agreements to protect the church's reversionary interest were sometimes forgotten or ignored.[28] I shall argue in my book that the resulting disputes were caused as much by conflicting norms as by sin and greed: temporary inheritance did not seem right to laymen.

Meanwhile, royal authority was developing. What seems to be the earliest reference to folkland occurs in a note on the Wassingwell/Mersham charter of 858. It seems there to mean land owing obligations from which bookland was normally exempt – though bookland is not explicitly mentioned in the charter.[29] Any such exemptions were, however, offset by the reservation on all land of the three burdens of military service, bridge-building, and fortress-building.[30] Increased royal authority meant increasing royal demands. It also meant increased royal responsibility. When kings granted exemptions and privileges they were supposed to do so with formality and consultation.[31] The charters that allowed kings to turn royal estates into bookland, so as to leave them to those they chose, look like a consequence of distinctions, provoked by increasing royal reponsibilities, between the king's private capacity and property and what belonged to him *ex officio*.[32] One advantage of bookland, apart from any privileges it might carry, remained the book itself, especially if it had names of authority on it. Not that royal charters (if all the references to landbooks are to royal charters[33]) always constituted incontrovertible evidence. Their content might be mulled over and one might still have to muster an oath.[34] And charters were not inviolable. Land held by charter, like other land, could be forfeit. After king Alfred had

---

[27] F. W. Maitland, *Domesday Book and Beyond*, Cambridge 1907, 293–318. *Beneficium* and *praestare* occur occasionally, e.g. Sawyer, nos. 1274, 1368.

[28] Sawyer, nos. 215; 356 and 1797; 693, 1077–8, 1274, 1297–1374; 1420, 1444, 1456, 1458; R. Fleming, 'Monastic Lands and England's Defence in the Viking Age', *EHR*, c, 1985, 247–65; J. L. Nelson, 'A King across the Sea', *TRHS*, ser. 5, xxxvi, 1986, 45–68; *Hemingi Chartularium*, ed. T. Hearne, Oxford 1723, 253–4, 257–60, 264–5. For life interests of donors: Lennard, 161–2.

[29] Sawyer, no. 328. I find H. Vollrath-Reichelt, 65–8, 192–225 unpersuasive: cf. N. Brooks, 'Anglo-Saxon Charters', 222.

[30] Brooks, 'Development of Military Obligations'.

[31] Sawyer, nos. 168, 298, 328, 335, 715, 1438.

[32] Sawyer, nos. 298, 715, 717; possibly also 1258. The conversion to folkland in no. 328 presumably recognizes the same responsibility. Cf. P. Sawyer, 'The Royal Tun in Pre-Conquest England', *Ideal and Reality in Frankish and Anglo-Saxon Society*, ed. P. Wormald *et al.*, Oxford 1983, 273–99 at 288. Cf. Liebermann, i, 458–9 on the king's wergeld.

[33] Sawyer, nos. 1445 (even if the key *boc* here was royal, rather than a private charter strengthened by some kind of royal subscription, it was evidence of a transaction between subjects, not of a royal grant), 1460 (*boc* giving free disposition, made at royal command but about a transaction between subjects); *Liber Eliensis*, ed. E. O. Blake, RHS Camden ser. 3, xcii, 1962, 99, 101 (*cyrographa*). *Chronicon Monasterii de Abingdon*, ed. J. Stephenson, RS 1858, i. 475 is late and seems to overstate the force of charters. Wills could be called *yrfebec*: J. Bosworth and T. N. Toller, *Ango-Saxon Dictionary*, Oxford 1898, 598, and one (Sawyer, no. 1536) was called a *freolsboc*. Sawyer, no. 1444 uses *bociunnæ* for a life-grant.

[34] Patrick Wormald, 'Charters, law and the settlement of disputes in Anglo-Saxon England' in *The Settlement of Disputes in Early Medieval Europe*, ed. W. Davies and P. Fouracre, Cambridge 1986, 149–68.

confiscated a traitor's inheritance his son ordered that any old charters (*antiqui libri*) concerning it that anyone might have should be cancelled.[35]

By about 900 there seem to have been three main categories of property, excluding that of the less free peasants. First there was the ordinary hereditary property of nobles and free men, with obligations that varied according to local custom and, probably, the status of the owner; second, property, often called bookland, that was held by charters granting special privileges, often including some freedom of disposition, at least for the first grantee, and freedom from obligations beyond the three general burdens; third, property that nobles or free men held on restricted rights, generally from a church or king. In the larger kingdom of the tenth and eleventh centuries royal and noble estates were more widely scattered, so that the scope for temporary grants of lay property must have been greater than before.[36] Kings and lay nobles, however, had different priorities from churches in granting land and the rights and obligations in what they granted were consequently liable to be different. Much of the idea of feudalism, and much of its nonsense, has come from deducing general rules of property and of relations between warrior lords and their followers from records of church property. However that may be, after the mid tenth century the distinction between the first two categories I have mentioned – ordinary free property and bookland – seems to have become blurred. King Eadric's seems to be the last will to say whether land bequeathed was bookland and Edgar was, I think, the last king recorded as turning land into bookland.[37] Thereafter, the word may, I suggest, have indicated rather the status of the landowner than any specific grant or privilege. Without entering into the argument about the literacy and efficiency of late Old English government, it seems to me improbable that all thegns, even all king's thegns (however that is understood), acquired charters, let alone that all of them preserved their charters.[38] Maybe, as the kingdom grew, kings used charters both to make grants to their carpet-bagging followers and to confirm the title of their new subjects, but, if they did, charters to the latter would presumably not always have conferred new privileges. If Bishop Aethelwold got royal charters to confirm his purchases his *Libellus* did not bother to mention them any more than it bothered to use the word bookland.[39] Bookland was, I suggest, by and large, what belonged to thegns – though a thegn's property could alternatively be defined in terms of a minimum hidage.[40] Those who held bookland were likely to have sake and soke, at least over peasants on their land and perhaps over others, though whether all the land of those under soke would count as part of the lord's bookland is difficult to say.[41] Domesday, combined with the various eleventh-

---

[35] Sawyer, no. 362.

[36] *King Alfred's Version of St Augustine's Soliloquies*, ed. T. A. Carnicelli, Cambridge, Mass., 1969, 48; cf. the *læn* in Sawyer, no. 1445; Lennard, 142–75.

[37] Sawyer, nos. 715, 727, 1515.

[38] For the latest contribution: Simon Keynes, 'Royal Government and the Written Word in late Anglo-Saxon England' in *The Uses of Literacy in Early Mediaeval Europe*, ed. R. McKitterick, Cambridge 1990, 226–57.

[39] Cf. A. G. Kennedy, 'Disputes about Bocland: the Forum for their Adjudication', *Anglo-Saxon England* xiv, 1985, 175–95, at 186.

[40] Liebermann, i, 196, 294, 444, 456 (II Edgar 2, I Cnut 11, *Rectitudines, Gethynctho*); cf. the various categories in *Anglo-Saxon Charters*, ed. A. J. Robertson, Cambridge 1956, no. 84 and the lack of any in e.g. S 1460, 1462.

[41] E.g. Abels, 123–4; D. Roffe, 'From Thegnage to Barony', *ante* xii, 1989, 157–76 and 'Domes-

century classifications, suggests that it was as difficult to put people and their property into tidy categories then as it is in all but the smallest and simplest societies.[42] Homilies use the word bookland to mean apparently nothing more specific than one's own land.[43] When Aethelred ordered at one stage that *wita* and *bote* from people with bookland were to go to the king, and at another that only the king could have soke over a king's thegn, he was presumably claiming penalties over everyone who mattered.[44] Similarly when Cnut ordered that all bookland forfeited by an outlaw should go to the king he presumably meant to get all estates that mattered.[45] If I am right in postulating that bookland and other free or noble property had become indistinguishable by 1000, one reason may have been that both kinds of property were subject to the same social norms and political pressures. That, however, is very tentative: I do not want to fall into the historical trap of suggesting an explanation for something that may not have happened and seeming to suggest that the explanation is evidence that it did.

Altogether, the rights and obligations of property in 1066 (TRE) look very different from those of 700. The free disposition that had originally been conferred by royal charters was now enjoyed not only by nobles but by fairly ordinary looking commoners. Perhaps ordinary freemen were in some cases more free to dispose of their land than were the great: they might be bullied by the great but the great were bullied by the king.[46] Bishop Aethelwold's purchases of many small parcels of land for his monasteries, like other purchases which are referred to in tenth- and eleventh-century wills and charters, occasionally ran into trouble from the kinsmen of vendors, but freedom of disposition seems to have been taken for granted, *prima facie*, by people who surely did not all have royal landbooks.[47] Though Domesday's concern was with freedom from constraint by lords, not families, its frequent notes about whether people of fairly humble status were free to alienate or not would have been pointless if families had regularly exercised an acknowledged right to stop them anyway.[48] Military service or payment instead seems to have been owed in principle by all landowners, probably more or less in proportion to their holdings, subject to privilege, bargaining,

day Book and Northern Society', *EHR* cv, 1990, 310–36, esp. 335; Ann Williams, 'How Land was Held Before and After the Norman Conquest', *Domesday Book Studies*, ed. A. Williams, London 1987, 37–8.

[42] G. W. S. Barrow, *Kingdom of the Scots*, London 1973, 9–28, esp. 17, 19, 27. Some thegns with bocriht owed more than the three burdens: Liebermann, i, 444 (*Rectitudines*). Some of the classification for heriots in II Cnut 71 (Liebermann, i, 356–7) looks ad hoc. III Aethelred talks of senior (*yldestan*) thegns in 3.1, good thegns in 4, and king's thegns in 11, all of which suggests vague and varied gradations (Liebermann, i, 228, 230). If 'king's thegn' always meant a great man rather than a thegn of the king then the Domesday scribe misunderstood it. Cf. Geoffrey Barrow, *Kingdom of the Scots*, London 1973, 13, 16; P. Stafford, *The East Midlands in the Early Middle Ages*, Leicester 1985, 156–7.

[43] Venezky and Healey, *bocland, boclanda, boclande, boclond*.

[44] Liebermann, i, 218, 230 (I Aeth. 1. 14, III Aeth. 11).

[45] Liebermann, i, 316, 364 (II Cnut 13, 77), though cf. *Domesday Book*, i, fol. 280v.

[46] E.g. Sawyer, nos. 1484, 1497, 1504, 1535; P. Stafford, *Unification and Conquest*, London 1989, 159–61. Cf. Liebermann, i. 366 (II Cnut 79)

[47] *Liber Eliensis*, 75–117; claims from kin (both after sales and wills): *ibid.* 87, 94, 97, 101, 104.

[48] *Pace* Carl Stephenson, 'Commendation and Related Problems in Domesday', *EHR* lix, 1944, 289–310, at 309–10, and S. F. C. Milsom, introduction to F. Pollock and F. W. Maitland, *History of English Law*, Cambridge 1968, pp. xxxii, xlv.

and local custom.[49] Though lords – probably soke lords – had some responsibility for their men, the service, at least in Berkshire and Worcestershire, was nonetheless owed to the king and organized by shires, while penalties for non-performance went to him too.[50] Taxation seems also to have been levied on all land. In the eleventh century non-payment is known to have incurred confiscation – once again to the king, though third parties prepared to make good the unpaid geld could take over the property.[51] Foreshadowings of the so-called 'feudal incidents' of relief, wardship, and marriage which would later loom so large in the relations of English kings with their subjects can be seen both in heriots and in early eleventh-century laws about the rights and remarriage of widows.[52] Nicholas Brooks has shown how the right of a lord, enshrined in tradition, to a gift from his dead follower's arms and goods was translated by kings in the tenth century (if not before) into a regular tariff of death duties – a tariff that went up in the eleventh century.[53] Though the laws make the tariff one of status, heriots were in practice sometimes related to the size of estates.[54] In late tenth-century Huntingdonshire responsible opinion was that there was no land there so free that it could not be forfeit.[55]

If a hierarchy of tenure is taken to mean a division of property rights and obligations between two or more layers of people – which is what I take it to mean – then I suggest that it may be misleading to think of all or even most pre-Conquest property above the peasant level as normally forming one. English society was very unequal but not all unequal relationships affected property rights, let alone property rights arranged in a hierarchy. I know of no evidence that *medemra thegna* were in the middle of a hierarchy of property (or even of commendation) rather than being middling in status.[56] Land held by nobles from churches formed a two-tier hierarchy – or three-tier, if one includes peasant holdings. So, presumably, did that held *ex officio* or for life from the king and, no doubt, some that was managed on similar restricted terms for earls and other great landowners, but I have not found evidence that heritable grants from kings or other laymen normally created permanent layers of rights. The hierarchy of government was by now at least partially distinct from any hierarchy of property. Earls – or some of them – got a share of heriots as of other royal income from their shires and they had much opportunity for influence and patronage, but none of that gave them a formal share in the property rights of people within their earldoms. Sokes had survived the last reorganization of local government as an anomalous relic from the time when government and property were indistin-

[49] For evidence of bargaining by townspeople: S. Reynolds, 'Towns in Domesday Book', *Domesday Studies*, ed. J. C. Holt, Woodbridge 1987, 295–309, at 306–7; cf. J. Gillingham, 'The Introduction of knight service into England', *ante* iv, 1982, 53–64, at 61–4.
[50] *Domesday Book*, i, fols. 56v, 172; cf. 354, 375v.
[51] M. K. Lawson, 'The Collection of Danegeld and Heregeld in the Reigns of Aethelred and Cnut', *EHR*, xcix, 1984, 721–38.
[52] Liebermann, i, 242, 254, 356–8 (V Aethelred 21; VI Aethelred 26; II Cnut 70–4).
[53] N. Brooks, 'Arms, status and warfare in late Saxon England' in *Ethelred the Unready*, ed. David Hill, Oxford 1978, 81–103.
[54] *Domesday Book*, i, fols. 280v, 298 (other heriots or reliefs: i, fols. 1, 252, 262v, 336v, ii, fol. 119). For heriots as designed to secure inheritance: e.g. Sawyer, nos. 939 (cf. 1501), 1484, 1486, 1536; cf. *Liber Eliensis*, 100–1, 117.
[55] *Liber Eliensis*, 98–9.
[56] Liebermann, i, 358–9 (II Cnut 71. 2); cf. *Domesday Book Studies*, ed. Williams, 158 (glossary).

guishable but it is not clear how significant a share soke lords had in the property rights of their free subjects. What they had was jurisdiction and quasi-governmental rights. While jurisdiction over the property of many free men seems now to have lain in the county, subject to royal intervention, soke lords may still have retained jurisdiction over property within their sokes, as well as taking some of the penalties incurred by their subjects in county or other courts.[57] Military service may have been organized through sokes, though that involves generalizing from the customs of Worcestershire, where most sokes belonged to churches and were therefore dominated by a distinctive proprietary relationship.[58] Some soke lords took heriots and no doubt a variety of other dues.[59] Nevertheless, despite these obligations, some, though not all, of the property of sokemen or free men under soke, and *a fortiori* of any thegns who may have been under soke, carried pretty full rights.[60] Even if property under soke was never called bookland (and we cannot be sure it was not), some of it was freely alienable and some of its owners could choose patrons outside the soke. The variety created by local custom and varying status must have been increased by individual bargains and judgements. As the *Rectitudines* put it, *landlaga syn mistlice*: the laws and customs of lands are multiple and various.[61] To call people under soke tenants and to see sokes as part of a 'tenurial hierarchy' is to darken counsel.

So it is to see commendation as tenurial. *Commendare, commendatio* etc. were words of many meanings.[62] The sense that is at issue in Domesday Book seems to be that which denotes a relationship of patronage or protection. This could affect land. A patron might bargain for rights over property he protected but Domesday does not suggest that commendation automatically gave him any.[63] Many clients probably gravitated to their lord's banner in war, especially if they were not committed to a soke contingent, but that does not make it helpful to call them tenants, let alone subtenants, of their patrons. Some people were recorded as having held land under (*sub*) or from (*de*) their patrons but that need not mean that their property rights were reduced.[64] The right to choose a protector for one's property seems often to have gone together with the right to alienate it, though it must be wrong to describe them roundly as 'identical in meaning'.[65] Round's confusion arose, I suggest, because in 1086 both rights illustrated a roughly similar and significant status, so that they came to much the same thing for the purposes of the enquiry. Sometimes the Domesday information about commendation seems to be part of a general desire to explain what rights a church or other lord of a soke or manor had enjoyed over relatively free property TRE, and what

[57] *Domesday Book*, i, fols. 1, 172, 172v, 280v; cf. Kennedy.

[58] Above n. 42; Abels, 121–31.

[59] *Domesday Book*, i, fol. 1; cf. Sawyer, no. 1519, in which the archbishop was perhaps Ketel's soke lord.

[60] Thegns apparently under soke: Barrow, 17 and n. 43 (esp. *Inquisitio Eliensis*, ed. N. E. S. A. Hamilton, London 1876, 67, 74, 93).

[61] Liebermann, i, 452 (*Rectitudines* 21).

[62] *Dictionary of Medieval Latin from British Sources*, Oxford 1975–, 391–2.

[63] Relationships of this kind are suggested in *Liber Eliensis*, 106; Sawyer, nos. 1447, 1462, and (much earlier) 1187; Maitland, 71–4.

[64] Maitland, 72–3, 154–5.

[65] J. H. Round, *Feudal England*, London 1895, 22. Round cited cases where one became the other at different stages of the text, but circuit and county practice varied. Both were given e.g. in *Domesday Book*, i, fol. 199v.

the TRW holder could therefore now claim.[66] In a good many cases, however, it looks as though commendation needed to be mentioned only because new lords who had come to make their fortunes in England had taken a broad view of the rights of the predecessors from whom they were supposed to have derived their titles. County and hundred juries made some attempt to record the resulting usurpations.[67] Patronage links before 1066 sometimes formed hierarchies but it was one that could, then as later, cut across other hierarchies. The relative scarcity of evidence about personal clientage after 1066 does not mean that all clientage was from now on attached to landholding. It just did not need to be recorded in the same way. We cannot penetrate the obscurities of pre-Conquest property if we lump evidence of commendation and sokes in with that about the variously restricted and subordinate terms on which church and royal lands were certainly held, and some lands of great lords were probably held, and see them all as part of a proto-feudal hierarchy.

Before we come to the effects of 1066 it may be useful to say something about French property in the eleventh century. Arguments and references must await my book, but in the meantime I am pretty sure that the various Latin words we translate as fief did not yet represent anything like a distinct category of property. They were often applied to property, including church property, held with subordinate rights, by peasants as well as others. Often, however, the word fief was non-committal, denoting a unit of property with no indication of its status, rights, or obligations. It could also be used to denote the area under the authority of a superior, whether king, count, or other lord: property being conveyed was said to belong to his fief or be in his fief. In this usage there is no implication that the fief itself, within which the property conveyed lay, was subject to anyone else. Nor was the property that was said to be in a lord's fief when it was conveyed, itself normally called a fief or, apparently, held with less than full rights. Before the thirteenth century noble property in France (except that held from churches) was normally described as a fief only in this kind of context, to indicate its owner's authority over other property.[68] In the eleventh century the properties of nobles were described as their inheritances, *propria*, *proprietates*, or alods, though by the end of the eleventh century I have the impression that in northern France the word alod was coming to be restricted to the holdings of relatively humble people. Both nobles and others were often said to hold their property, but *tenere* seems to have no juridical significance. Though some property held from (*de*) someone else had restricted rights or more obligations the expression could indicate nothing more than political subordination. In Normandy alods were said to be held both from Richard II and William the Conqueror.[69]

---

[66] E.g. *Domesday Book*, i, fols. 50v, 62v, 72, 163, 164v–165, 172–172v, 174–175v, 179–180v, 190v–192, 199v.

[67] E.g. *Domesday Book*, i, fols. 44v, 137v (cf. J. H. Round in *VCH Herts.* i. 267–9), 199v, 211v, 225v; ii, fols. 5v–6, 40v, 71v, 148, 187v, 287, 310v–311, 313–313v, and cases cited by P. Sawyer, '1066–1086. A Tenurial Revolution', *Domesday Book: a Reassessment*, ed. P. Sawyer, London 1985, 71–85, at 78–80. Rights of alienation could also be involved, e.g. *Domesday Book*, i, fols. 133 (Round, *VCH Herts.* i. 275), 137v.

[68] There are exceptions, e.g. Orderic, iv. 180. I would put this one under my second head of units of property of indeterminate rights.

[69] E.g. Fauroux, nos. 36, 45–6, 93, 113, 137, 142, 156.

The rights and obligations of noble property in eleventh-century Normandy were naturally different from those of Carolingian alods, just as they were different from those of English bookland or from twelfth- or thirteenth-century English fiefs. Custom developed variously as economies, politics, and legal procedures changed. There may perhaps have been less freedom of alienation than in England. Because French churches had long found it prudent to get the consent of counts, lords, and kinsmen for their acquisitions of property, consent, at least for grants to churches, came to seem necessary, though the frequency with which lords gave general permissions must have undermined the rule. By 1066 Duke William had become rather good at getting obedience and military service from his subjects, but there is no evidence that this had much to do with the formal status of their property or the terms of any remembered grant. Churches used grants of land to get military service but lay lords recruited their forces more widely. The idea of specifying precise obligations in terms of knights' fees seems, outside church lands, to have originated in England and been introduced to Normandy from here.[70] It never spread significantly to the rest of France. The only people outside Normandy whose military obligations were normally specified precisely before the reign of Philip IV were those who owed garrison duties – and, of course, peasants. The so-called 'feudal aids', which may have originated in Anjou, were owed only by the relatively humble, while reliefs, which I suspect had first been demanded on church land, had not as yet spread far off it.[71]

I suggest that the Norman Conquest did not change ideas about the rights and obligations of property in England very much. All the references to the legal changes William introduced imply a background of similar assumptions about custom and right. In so far as rights changed in practice it was because of the turmoil of the times. Englishmen were expropriated in hundreds and thousands, but that was ostensibly because they rebelled. Title in 1086 officially depended on the title of one's predecessor TRE, though it needed more explicit acceptance by the current government than is necessary in quieter times.[72] Henry I's charter suggests that Normans had much the same expectation of inheritance as their predecessors and that Henry accepted it – in principle.[73] The king's right to a relief was not supposed to amount to confiscation and resale. Arguments that the principle of inheritance was not yet accepted rely heavily on reasoning developed later by common lawyers, while much of the evidence cited to support them concerns church land. At best this is irrelevant to the heritability of lay property. At worst it illustrates the troubles that lay norms of inheritance caused to

---

[70] See D. R. Bates, *Normandy before 1066*, London 1982, 168–9, 258–9; M. Chibnall, 'Military Service in Normandy before 1066', *ante* v, 1982, 65–77; E. Tabuteau, 'Definitions of Feudal Military Obligations in Eleventh-Century Normandy' in *On the Laws and Customs of England*, ed. M. S. Arnold and others, Chapel Hill 1981, 18–59.

[71] Pending my further discussion of this, see Carl Stephenson, *Medieval Institutions*, Ithaca 1954, 1–40: essay on 'Aids of French Towns' translated and revised from *Le Moyen Age*, ser. 2, 24 (1922), 274–328; and, for Normandy, Emily Tabuteau, *Transfers of Property in Eleventh-century Norman Law*, Chapel Hill/London 1988, 56–7, 59–61. The earliest references to the three aids I have seen are *Cartulaire de Saint-Vincent de Mâcon*, ed. M. C. Ragut, Mâcon 1864, 751, 807.

[72] G. Garnett, 'Coronation and Propaganda', *TRHS* ser. 5, xxxvi, 1986, 91–116; J. C. Holt, '1086', *Domesday Studies*, Woodbridge 1987, 41–64 at 62.

[73] J. C. Holt, 'Feudal Society and the Family in Early Medieval England: II', *TRHS*, ser. 5, xxxiii, 1983, 193–220 at 218.

churches.[74] How far freedom of alienation was affected by the Conquest is unclear. Most restraints should probably, like the ending of freedom of bequest, be seen in the context of longer-term developments of government and law. Some testators had always asked for royal approval of their bequests of land and for a while some went on doing so.[75] It seems to me difficult to draw any hard and fast line between English wills and Norman post-obit gifts.[76] Taxes and dues became very heavy, except on lands that were sometimes or regularly exempt from geld. If tenants in chief were normally exempt – and the evidence is far from clear – it may have been more because the geld was such an appalling shock to Normans than because tenants in chief were identified from the first as a distinct legal category. It would be some time before taxes on tenants in knight service were distinguished from others. The tax Henry I took in 1110 on his daughter's marriage does not seem to have been restricted to them.[77] What does seem to have changed significantly and permanently was the obligation of landowners to military service, but even here the evidence of immediate, deliberate, and systematic change looks weaker than Round maintained.[78] William I no doubt made some new and explicit arrangements about the services that his followers would owe in respect of their new lands, but there is absolutely no evidence that a 'precise definition of service' formed an automatic part of each grant.[79] The imposition of new quotas of what became a distinctly new sort of service look to me less like the result of a new political and tenurial ideology than a response to the urgent needs of conquest which then became fixed in custom.

The biggest change in ideas about property that can be directly attributed to the Norman Conquest came from Domesday Book. It was the record itself and the way it was arranged that gave such a strong impression of a hierarchy of property and of a hierarchy created by grants. The orders to produce information which went out at the beginning of 1086[80] must have been addressed to important people rather than tenants in chief. Geld lists would have said who owned (or had owned) estates but, given the variety of ways in which property had been acquired, it may have been hard, before the survey was made, to draw up reliable

[74] Mary Cheney, 'The Litigation between John Marshal and Archbishop Thomas Becket in 1164', *Law and Social Change in British History*, London 1984, 9–26; John Hudson, 'Life-grants of Land and the Development of Inheritance in Anglo-Norman England', *ante* xii, 1989, 67–80. Cf. e.g. apart from many entries about church land in Domesday Book: J. A. Robinson, *Gilbert Crispin*, London 1911, 38; V. H. Galbraith, 'An Episcopal Land-grant of 1085', *EHR* xliv, 1929, 353–72 at 372; *Cartularium Monasterii de Ramseia*, ed. W. H. Hart and P. A. Lyons, RS 1884–93, no. 166; *Placita Anglo-Normannorum*, ed. M. M. Bigelow, London 1879, 114–17; *Reading Abbey Cartularies*, ed. B. R. Kemp, RHS Camden ser. 4, xcii, 1962, nos. 1, 27.
[75] Stafford, *Unification and Conquest*, 159–61; Sheehan, 19–21, 106–19, 267–74.
[76] Sheehan, 267–74; Pollock and Maitland, ii. 326–31; cf. Holt, 'Feudal Society and the Family in Medieval England: I', *TRHS*, ser. 5, xxxii, 1982, 193–212 at 197–8; Tabuteau, *Transfers*, 24–7.
[77] S. Harvey, 'Taxation and the Economy', *Domesday Studies*, 249–64; *Two Saxon Chronicles*, ed. C. Plummer and J. Earle, Oxford 1892, i. 243 (1110); Judith A. Green, 'The Last Century of Danegeld', *EHR* xcvi, 1981, 241–58 at 245–6 and *The Government of England under Henry I*, Cambridge 1986, 83–4.
[78] Among the vast literature: Gillingham, 'Introduction of Knight Service' and J. C. Holt, 'The Introduction of Knights Service into England', *ante* vi, 1983, 89–106.
[79] F. M. Stenton, *First Century of English Feudalism*, Oxford 1961, 130.
[80] V. H. Galbraith, *The Making of Domesday Book*, Oxford 1961, 121–2; H. B. Clarke, 'The Domesday Satellites', *Domesday Book: a Reassessment*, ed. P. H. Sawyer, London 1985, 50–70 at 61.

lists of those who held their land directly from the king. Take the church. Few of its lands had been granted to it by William and some had not been granted by previous kings either. Great churches now generally appeared at the head of each list of tenants in chief because if church lands were to be listed, as they needed to be, the prestige of the church demanded that position.[81] At the other end of the lists came all those miscellaneous little people who had to be listed with the tenants in chief because they were royal servants or did not fit in anywhere else. All this fostered ways of looking at property rights which may have strengthened the king's hand when he made demands on those who became known as his tenants in chief:[82] in practice, however, he probably profited less from such conceptualizations than from the precedent of English royal rights, bolstered by hard military facts and hard political bargaining. That the hierarchy of 1086 appears so clearly as a hierarchy of property or tenure rather than of status or authority is to be explained partly by the sensitivity of titles to property in 1086.[83] Partly it was because property and jurisdiction had been, and would be, relatively separate in England, even if the Norman conquerors did not yet realize it. Partly, however, it is the effect of a long tradition of anachronistic deductions drawn from the vocabulary of the survey.

The most important of these is the belief that, because to us the word tenant implies restricted rights, holding in Domesday meant less than having or owning. But most of the lists of those *tenentes terras* in each county in Domesday Book are headed by King William, who *tenet* his individual manors just as King Edward *tenuit* his. 'Holding from' may, in any case, not have implied, any more than in France, an actual reduction of rights or increase of obligations. As for the word fief, it is rare in Domesday, except in the sense, derived from French usage, of superior estates or units of authority.[84] The king's fief is not mentioned in England until a little later but, on the French analogy, other lords' fiefs do not imply restricted or subordinate rights.[85] Otherwise most properties that Domesday says were held *in feudo* or *ad feudum* seem to have been smallish and some paid rent. Maybe the word was useful, as in France, because it was noncommittal.[86] In circuit 1, however, *in feudo* sometimes seems to mean much the same as *in alodio* or *in alodium*. *Alodiarii* here look rather like sokemen elsewhere. Some are explicitly said to have had the right to sell their land. Others lacked it, but they all look like people who may have had enough rights to create a presumption of free disposition.[87] Exceptions had to be noted. Maybe property that Domesday describes as held *in alodio* or *in feudo* would have been called bookland by Englishmen talking English. In the twelfth century *on his boclande* was translated variously as *in feudo suo*, *in hereditate sua terram*, or *in alodio suo*; *bocland* as *terra testamentalis*, *alodium*, or *libera terra*; and *bocrihtes wyrthe* as *dignus*

[81] Though not e.g. York Abbey: *Domesday Book*, i, fols. 298v, 305, 314.
[82] *Oxford Dict. of Medieval Latin*, i. 278: *caput*, 20: note the citation from Ralph of Diss.
[83] J. C. Holt, '1086'.
[84] Maitland, 152–4; in addition to his examples: *Domesday Book*, i, fols. 44, 32v, 155v; ii, fols. 175v, 176–176v, 187v.
[85] For the king's fief in England: *Oxford Dictionary of Medieval Latin*, 1. 920 (*feodum* 4b).
[86] Pamela Taylor in this volume discusses its use in Domesday for certain bishops' estates.
[87] H. C. Darby and E. M. J. Campbell, *Domesday Geography of South-East England*, Cambridge 1962, 254, 258, 382, 518; Maitland, 153–4.

rectitudine testamenti sui.[88] By then bookland was a memory but, after all, there had never been an authoritative definition of it that had got lost.

Domesday Book, like the Lombard *Consuetudines Feudorum*, contributed a great deal to later ideas of feudalism, but it did so because scholars approached it with the idea of feudalism already in their heads. What it implies about the law of property can be deduced better by looking at it in the context of eleventh-century law, practice, and terminology. It was produced for a very powerful king – in itself a paradox in terms of ideas of feudalism everywhere but England – but for a king who had interfered much more with the practice of property-holding than with its principles and rules. The further development of royal control over property would take place against the background of Domesday Book's classifications but in a new age of record-keeping and professional law which the great survey only foreshadowed. We cannot understand the customary law of the early middle ages in terms of later medieval professional law or of theories of feudal law that were worked out in the seventeenth century.

[88] Liebermann, i, 196–7, 294–5, 316–17, 444, 612.

PATRONS AND POLYGLOTS:
FRENCH LITERATURE IN TWELFTH-CENTURY ENGLAND

Ian Short

The aim of this paper is as straightforward as it is modest: to provide non-specialists with an idea of the scope, diversity, originality and importance of the French literature produced in England during the twelfth century. The dangers of attempting to produce any sort of unstructured overview will be self-evident, and I shall, unless I am careful, run the risk of incurring the same reproach that Abelard levelled at a professor under whom he studied, namely that any fire he managed to kindle filled the house with more smoke than light. I have, as it happens, no blinding insights to offer, but I do, I hope, have a small glimmer of new light to shed, through the prism of the polyglots and patrons of my title, on the much neglected origins of French literature in the twelfth century. Such origins have, as we shall see, little to do with the Continent and a great deal to do with Insular culture;[1] and if I describe them as much neglected, it is only because standard histories of Medieval French literature persist in ignoring the fact that French literature begins, to all intents and purposes, in twelfth-century Anglo-Norman England.

The first adventure narrative (or proto-romance) in French literature; the earliest example of historiographic writing in French; the first eye-witness history of contemporary events in French; the earliest scientific texts in French; the first administrative texts in French; the first Biblical translations into French; the earliest French vernacular versions of monastic Rules; the first scholastic text to be translated into French; the earliest significant examples of French prose; the first occurrence of the French octosyllabic rhyming couplet (the standard verse-form of Medieval French narrative); the first explicit mention of secular *courtoisie* (courtly culture) in vernacular French; the first named women writers in French; the earliest named and identifiable patrons of literature in French – an impressive list of firsts by any standards, and all to be credited not to Continental French culture, but to Insular Anglo-Norman society of the twelfth century.[2]

Most French medievalists will shrug their shoulders in disbelief, and, if

---

[1]   In this paper, the terms Insular and Continental are used, for convenience, in a linguistic rather than geographic sense; the former embraces the duchy of Normandy as well as Britain, the latter all other *langue d'oïl* areas. It is difficult to make any clear or consistent distinction between British and Norman French in the twelfth century, though traditionally writers such as Wace and Etienne de Fougères are regarded as Norman. For the MS survivals, see Brian Woledge & Ian Short, 'Liste provisoire de mss. du XIIe siècle contenant des textes en langue française', *Romania* cii, 1981, 1–17 [= Liste provisoire]. For cross-Channel relations in general, see C. Warren Hollister, 'Normandy, France and the Anglo-Norman *regnum*', *Speculum* li, 1976, 202–42; David Bates, 'Normandy and England after 1066', *EHR* civ, 1989, 851–80.

[2]   To this list might be added the *Jeu d'Adam* as the earliest surviving example of twelfth-century

pressed, fall back on a complacent ignorance of what they perceive to be an Insular backwater culture out of the Continental mainstream, some sort of peripheral activity (its unarticulated centre being, of course, Paris) in a bastardised, inferior form of French. Those who are better informed, who might even have read Dominica Legge or Reto Bezzola,[3] will remain sceptical and ask difficult questions, for example, on the role that accidental manuscript preservation could have played in accounting for this manifestation of exceptional literary precocity vis-à-vis what was happening (or not happening, apparently) on the other side of the Channel. Those who have made a special study of twelfth-century Britain, on the other hand, will need little convincing that the richness of its society was such as to confer on it a cultural specificity well capable of initiating, fostering and sustaining a wide range of literary innovation.

One of this society's most productive characteristics, as I see it, is to be found in its multi-culturalism and its concommitant multi-lingualism, and I am convinced that England's unique trilingual culture holds at least one of the keys for unlocking the mystery of its literary precocity. Where you have cultures in contact, you have unrivalled opportunities for literary symbiosis through the intermediary of polyglots, both clerical and secular. Where you have a social climate conducive to the arts of peace and an intellectually curious aristocracy, you have enlightened literary patrons. And patronage, of course, is a necessary condition for the production of medieval literature, and a leisured and cultured nobility a sufficient condition for its reception.

But there is a broader context still into which I would place the early blossoming of French literature in England, that of the *translatio studii*, the contemporary notion that there was continuity of culture between Antiquity and the intellectual centres of northern France and Anglo-Norman Britain, the humanistic concept of a progressive transmission of learning from Greece to Rome and ultimately to the French-speaking world of the twelfth century.[4] Far from being exclusive to

drama (see W. Noomen's ed., CFMA, Paris 1971, 6–7). My premise is that such firsts are more likely to be a function of precocious literary production than of chance textual survival. A comparative account of twelfth-century Continental literature naturally lies outside the scope of this paper.
[3] M. D. Legge, *Anglo-Norman Literature and its Background*, Oxford 1963 [= ANL], also 'La Précocité de la littérature anglo-normande', *Cahiers de civilisation médiévale* viii, 1965, 327–49; R. R. Bezzola, *Les Origines et la formation de la littérature courtoise en Occident (500–1200)*, Paris 1958–63, ii/2 391–548, iii/1 3–311 (*La Cour d'Angleterre comme centre littéraire sous les rois angevins*). Cf. also A. Press, 'The precocious Courtesy of Geoffrey Gaimar', *Court and Poet: Selected Proceedings of the Third Congress of the International Courtly Literature Society . . .*, ed. G. S. Burgess, Liverpool 1981, 267–76; A. Bell, 'Gaimar as Pioneer', *Romania* xcvii, 1976, 462–80; C. Warren Hollister, 'Courtly Culture and Courtly Style in the Anglo-Norman world', *Albion* xx, 1988, 2–17. The theory of peripheral Insular conservatism (particularly favoured by Belgian and Swiss scholars) is more or less exclusively based on the preservation of epic MSS, including the Oxford *Roland*, and is all the more difficult to sustain when viewed within a wider literary perspective. For the continuing debate, see M. D. Legge, 'Archaism and the Conquest', *Modern Language Review* li, 1956, 227–29; Ian Short, 'An early French epic MS. . . .', *The Medieval Alexander Legend and Romance Epic: Essays in honour of David J.A. Ross*, ed. P. Noble, L. Polak, C. Isoz, London 1982, 173–91 (174); M. Tyssens, 'Typologie de la tradition des textes épiques . . .', *Actes du XIe Congrès international de la Société Rencesvals*, Memorias de la Real Academia de Buenas Letras de Barcelona 22, Barcelona 1990, ii 433–46.
[4] E. Gilson, *Les Idées et les lettres*, Paris 1932, 182–85; H. Grundmann, 'Sacerdotium – Regnum – Studium . . .', *Archiv für Kulturgeschichte* xxxiv, 1951, 5–21; W. Goez, *Translatio Imperii*,

scholastic circles, the process of appropriating the learning of the past to the present comes to affect and to embrace the secular world also. *Translatio* engenders translations and adaptations, breaking the monopolistic hold of Latin over access to the culture firstly of the past and subsequently also of the present, as the French vernacular begins to assume status as an alternative or parallel medium of culture. What I like to refer to globally as the vernacularisation of culture is, for me, one of the most important, and one of the least widely recognised, aspects of the new intellectual vitality of the twelfth century which we fondly refer to as a Renaissance. A re-birth it certainly was, and a return to the learning of the past, but viewed from within the perspective of secular culture, it seems to me to mark first and foremost a decisive new beginning, a coming of age in the status of the French vernacular, and equally importantly a new era in access to literacy. This in turn invites us to look more critically at the validity of the polarised opposition that we all tend to work within between Latin and the vernaculars, and to scrutinise more carefully the many areas of overlap and interdependence between what for our own convenience we categorise as the learned and lay cultures. That the earliest surviving written traces of cross-cultural literary symbiosis should emerge in Anglo-Norman rather than in Continental French raises a whole series of questions, some of which I should like to explore with you.

I shall be looking at Anglo-Norman literature more as a social than as an artistic phenomenon, and attempting to analyse it systematically along axes of production and reception. By concentrating, as I intend to, on those Anglo-Norman works which we know to have been commissioned by particular individuals or communities, I hope to be able to show to what extent vernacular literary production in twelfth-century England can be seen as a function of cultural and linguistic conditions specific to its pluralistic society – a society whose leading members had both the motivation and the wherewithal to widen access to learning and literacy by innovation.[5] Women, as we shall see, played an important role in this process.

Patronage is, of course, a complex phenomenon which, if it is to be a productive analytical tool, needs rigorous definition, failing which it becomes a critical pretext for the sort of speculation that – to take a particularly notorious example – persists in linking the name of Eleanor of Aquitaine with Thomas's *Romance of Tristan*.[6] In the strictest sense of the term, literary patronage involves a specifi-

Tübingen 1958, 117–24; A. G. Jongkees, 'Translatio Studii: les avatars d'un thème médiéval', *Miscellanea mediaevalia in memoriam J. F. Niermeyer*, Groningen 1967, 41–51; D. Kelly, 'Translatio Studii; translation, adaptation and allegory in Medieval French literature', *Philological Quarterly* lvii, 1978, 287–310.

[5] M. B. Parkes, 'The Literacy of the Laity', *Literature and Western Civilization: The Medieval Period*, ed. D. Daiches & A. K. Thorlby, London 1973, 555–77; R. V. Turner, 'The *miles literatus* in twelfth- and thirteenth-century England: how rare a phenomenon?', *AHR* lxxxiii, 1978, 928–45; M. Clanchy, *From Memory to Written Record: England 1066–1307*, London 1979, 177–263; F. H. Bäuml, 'Varieties and Consequences of Medieval Literacy and Illiteracy', *Speculum* lv, 1980, 237–65; M. J. Scholz, *Hören und Lesen: Studien zur primären Rezeption der Literatur im 12. und 13. Jahrhundert*, Wiesbaden 1980; Brian Stock, *The Implications of Literacy: Written Language and Models of Interpretation in the eleventh and twelfth centuries*, Princeton U.P. 1983, 12–87; P. Zumthor, *La Poésie et la voix dans la civilisation médiévale*, Paris 1984, 37–66.

[6] From R. S. Loomis, 'Tristram and the house of Anjou', *Modern Language Review* xvii, 1922, 24–30, through R. Lejeune, 'Rôle littéraire d'Aliénor d'Aquitaine et de sa famille', *Cultura Neolatina* xiv, 1954, 5–57, also 'Rôle littéraire de la famille d'Aliénor d'Aquitaine', *Cahiers de*

cally articulated contract between a named commissioner and an author for the production of an original text, usually in return for remuneration or preferment. Such active patronage needs, as far as possible, to be distinguished from what I would call prospective patronage, that is the speculative dedication of a work to an influential individual in the hope of attracting *post hoc* reward, future commissions or favours. We need also to bear in mind the relationship between individual patronage and public audience, since secular patrons must also have been instrumental in disseminating to a broader public the texts that they had commissioned. Of more far-reaching importance than the personal prestige that patronage and book ownership must have conferred was the socio-literary influence which secular individuals, both women and men, could exert at the wider level of their communities.[7]

A special additional category of patronage needs, however, to be created if we are to be able to take account of a particularly significant and fruitful area of vernacular text production, namely the monasteries. Anglo-Norman was widely used in the cloister throughout the twelfth century, and the French vernacular was recognised, within both monastery and convent, as a perfectly appropriate medium not only for preaching and other didactic purposes, but also for the transmission of religious writing. The best known exemplification of this is perhaps the Eadwine Psalter, a unique and beautifully illustrated book emanating from Christ Church Canterbury between 1155 and 1160.[8] This lavish triple psalter has three additional interlinear texts: between the lines of the Gallicanum and in the margin there is Peter Lombard's Latin commentary, between the lines of the Romanum there is an Old English rendering of the psalter text, and an Anglo-Norman psalter translation between those of the Hebraicum. The French text, which shows clear signs of graphemic interference from English,[9] is a conflation of two separate translations which prove to antedate the Eadwine Psalter and were not therefore made specifically for it. Everything here points to the long Anglo-Saxon tradition of the vernacular glossing of Biblical texts being carried over into post-Conquest monastic culture when the predominant vernacular had become French. The psalter's linguistic plurality is as much a feature of it as a book as it is of the society that conceived and executed it. This society, keenly aware of its Anglo-Saxon inheritance and of the continuum of Insular learning, was no less open to the culture of its Continental neighbours, of whose linguistic hegemony it had been an integral part for several generations.

The interlined Anglo-Norman text seems to have been conceived of originally as a linguistic gloss to the Latin, as an aid to comprehension that is to be seen

---

civilisation médiévale i, 1958, 319–37 (334), up to M. D. Legge, 'La Littérature anglo-normande au temps d'Aliénor d'Aquitaine', *Cahiers de civilisation médiévale* xxix, 1986, 113–18, also ANL 49.

[7] K. J. Holzknecht, *Literary Patronage in the Middle Ages*, New York 1923; J. Bumke, *Mäzene im Mittelalter . . .*, München 1979; D. Tyson, 'Patronage of French vernacular history writers in the twelfth and thirteenth centuries', *Romania* c, 1979, 180–222; Karen Broadhurst, 'Patronage and production of French literature in the twelfth century', unpubl. Ph.D. thesis, U. of London 1991.

[8] *The Eadwine Psalter: Text, Image, and Monastic Culture in twelfth-century Canterbury*, ed. M. Gibson, T. A. Heslop, R. W. Pfaff, MHRA, London [forthcoming].

[9] E.g. eighteen attestations of the Anglo-Saxon digraph *æ* and one of *th*; see W. Schumann, *Vokalismus und Konsonantismus des Cambridger Psalters*, Heilbronn 1883, 27, 47.

more within a long and respectable monastic tradition of textual glossing than as part of an innovative movement of vulgarisation by translation. The vernacular in the Eadwine Psalter, in other words, gives the impression of being a functional adjunct to, and not a substitute for, Latin. There is no reason in principle why the use of this vernacular text should have been limited to the monastic readership whose immediate needs it was originally meant to serve. Whether, however, in practical terms members of the laity could actually have had access to and read the Anglo-Norman in the Eadwine Psalter seems highly doubtful. Secular patronage for the book is, in any case, out of the question. In the final analysis, it could be said that the presence here of the French vernacular in fact transcends the functional and assumes a symbolic value: an acknowledgement that Anglo-Norman occupied a privileged position not only as a cohesive language of the ruling classes, but also as a shared vehicle of expression common to the religious and secular worlds; a recognition of the social status of this imported language of colonialisation as a living medium of culture and devotion, and a legitimisation of it as a mode of expression complementary to Latin and a written adjunct to it. The Psalter was designed as a prestige object, to be not so much used as seen, admired and copied.

Though the Eadwine treasure-book is in every sense a *unicum*, there is ample evidence that there existed an Insular tradition of French psalter translations. It opens in fact, chronologically, not, as one might expect, with an interlinear bilingual version, but with the monolingual Oxford (or Montebourg) Psalter, the earliest recorded in the French language.[10] This is a soberly but handsomely written French vernacular psalter, without illustration, which is almost certainly of monastic origin, and palaeographically unlikely to post-date the middle of the twelfth century. Rather than representing an original exemplar, however, the Oxford Psalter is probably to be seen as a monolingual transcription made from an existing bilingual Gallicanum psalter and as being designed to fulfil some specific *ad hoc* function about which we can only speculate. Its French text, of which more than seven early copies are extant,[11] in fact survives interlined with a Latin psalter in an Old Norse palimpsest originating from mid twelfth-century Britain.[12] The same text reappears in the Winchester (or Henry of Blois) Psalter where it is in parallel columns to the Gallicanum. This psalter also has, accompanying many of its fine illustrations, Anglo-Norman *tituli* (often stating the blindingly obvious) which appear to have been added to the book shortly after it was written towards 1160.[13] The interlined bilingual Arundel Psalter of the second half of the twelfth century again has the same Anglo-Norman translation as the Oxford Psalter, though with modifications that are probably due to independent scribal emendation.[14]

There are other survivals from the twelfth century that enable us to broaden and fill out the picture of vernacular writing in the devotional sphere. Though we know nothing about the circumstances of its composition, the translation (com-

[10] MS Oxford Bodley Douce 320, ff. 37r–75v; D. Sneddon, 'The Anglo-Norman Psalters . . .', *Romania* xcix, 1978, 395–400.
[11] B. Woledge & H. P. Clive, *Répertoire des plus anciens textes en prose française . . .*, PRF 79, Genève 1964 [= Répertoire], no. 42.
[12] P. Skårup in *Romania* xcviii, 1977, 90–94.
[13] K. E. Haney, *The Winchester Psalter: an iconographic study*, Leicester U.P. 1986, 13–14.
[14] Répertoire no. 39, and Sneddon 397–400.

bined with commentary) of the Books of Samuel and Kings, *Li Quatre Livre des Reis*, may well, to judge from its earliest surviving manuscript, have had an Anglo-Norman monastic origin.[15] The oldest extant manuscript of Canon Herman de Valenciennes' *Li Romanz de Dieu et de sa mere* is Anglo-Norman, but this rhymed Biblical paraphrase of 1189–95 is more likely to have been of secular, and perhaps Continental, provenance.[16] The Medieval French *Vie de saint Alexis* is in all probability of Norman origin ultimately.[17] Whatever the explanation for its presence in the St Albans' Psalter (1120–30), of which it is an integral part both palaeographically and codicologically, its vernacular verses were obviously seen as entirely appropriate and acceptable to figure alongside scriptural Latin in such a richly illustrated monastic manuscript.[18] The Anglo-Norman verse translation of, and commentary on, the Book of Proverbs was certainly made, as we shall see later, under secular patronage.

An anonymous Anglo-Norman prose translation of the Book of Judges was specifically undertaken for the edification of the Templars at the request of 'Master Richard and Brother Otho'. These are to be identified as Richard of Hastings, English Provincial Master from 1155 until 1185, and Otho de Saint-Omer, perhaps the same person as Odo de Saint-Amand, Grand Master of the Templars between 1170 and 1179.[19] Henri d'Arci, an influential Templar active in the 1160s and 1170s, was the dedicatee of four Anglo-Norman verse translations, one of the *Vitae Patrum*, another of the *Visio Sancti Pauli*, a Life of Thaïs and a poem on Antichrist. In the prologue to the *Thaïs*, the translator presents his works both to Henri d'Arci and to the members of the Templar community at Temple Bruer, near Lincoln.[20]

The Hospitallers also had recourse to the vernacular, this time for their Rule which, by an unparalleled feat of poetic ingenuity, was turned into Anglo-Norman rhyming octosyllables between 1181 and 1185, thus pre-dating the oldest surviving version of the Latin Rule by over half a century.[21] The choice of French verse for such a document can be interpreted by the uncharitable as an eloquent testimony of the general state of literacy within the English Hospitaller community. A more indulgent critic will recall that Abbot Walthenus of Melrose used French to expound the Rule of St Benedict to his monks, and that French translations of the

[15] Répertoire no. 38.
[16] A. de Mandach, 'A quand remonte la *Bible* de Herman de Valenciennes?', *Valenciennes et les anciens pays bas: Mélanges offerts à Paul Lefrancq*, Publ. du Cercle archéologique et historique de Valenciennes 9, Valenciennes 1976, 53–69, also 'Le "Jeu des Trois Rois" de Herman de Valenciennes . . .', *Vox Romanica* xlviii, 1989, 85–107. The text is edited by I. Spiele, *'Li Romanz de Dieu et de sa mere' d'Herman de Valenciennes . . .*, Leyde 1975; for the oldest MS, unknown to Spiele, see Liste provisoire 5.
[17] U. Mölk, 'La *Chanson de saint Alexis* et le culte du saint en France . . .', *Cahiers de civilisation médiévale* xxi, 1978, 339–55.
[18] O. Pächt, C. R. Dodwell, F. Wormald, *The Saint Albans Psalter*, London 1960; C. M. Kauffmann, *Romanesque Manuscripts: 1066–1190*, London 1975, no. 29; *La Vie de saint Alexis*, ed. C. Storey, TLF, Genève & Paris 1968.
[19] G. A. Bertin & A. Foulet, 'The Book of Judges in Old French prose . . .', *Romania* xc, 1969, 121–31; cf. *Records of the Templars in England in the twelfth century*, ed. B. A. Lees, London 1935, xxxix–xliv [this text not in ANL]. See also Répertoire no. 3.
[20] R. C. D. Perman, 'Henri d'Arci: the shorter works', *Studies in Medieval French presented to A. Ewert . . .*, Oxford 1961, 279–321.
[21] *The Hospitallers' 'Riwle'*, ed. K. V. Sinclair, ANTS 42, London 1984 [text not in ANL].

Benedictine, Cistercian and Templars' Rules also survive from the twelfth century.[22] It remains, however, significant that none of these communities saw fit to abandon prose and embrace, as the Hospitallers did, a popular verse-form with its cogent links to the secular world and also, one conjectures, practical mnemonic advantages for recitation and memorisation. Such texts are proof of the evident need that was felt to have an alternative language to Latin in monastic communities. The patronage of the Masters of the Templars suggests that such use of French probably enjoyed official recognition.

More orthodox religious houses are known also to have permitted, indeed encouraged, the writing of religious poems in Anglo-Norman. Monks composed verse in the vernacular, and Anglo-Norman literature preserves three examples from the twelfth century. Guischart de Beauliu and Beneit both state unequivocally that they were Benedictines, the former at Beaulieu Priory in Bedfordshire, a cell of St Albans, the latter at St Albans itself.[23] The third, Denis Pyramus, writing in the closing years of the century, undertook his translation of the life of St Edmund, he tells us, at the express behest of the monks at Bury ('de l'eglise li segnur').[24] One assumes also, from Beneit of St Albans' constant use of the rhetorical apostrophe 'seignurs' (a well-attested form of address within monastic communities), that he was writing for his brethren. His life of Thomas Becket, a rhymed adaptation of Robert of Cricklade's now lost *Vita*, seems to date from around 1184. Of particular interest is the fact that this text seems to have had both an internal monastic, and an external secular, audience. A recently discovered fragment of it preserves a unique colophon in which the author dedicates a copy of his poem to Simon FitzSimon of Cuckney (Notts) and his wife Isabel, both of whom had died before 1200. Simon had impressive family connections in terms of ecclesiastical patronage: his father had founded Bullington Priory, near Lincoln, his brother Philip Kyme Priory, his sister Hagneby Priory, both in Lincolnshire, and his father-in-law Welbeck Abbey. Hagneby was in fact dedicated to Becket, and one is tempted to conjecture that this must have had some part to play in Simon's acquiring a copy of an enclosed monk's poem, originally designed perhaps for refectory or *collatio* reading at St Albans.[25] Guischart's rhymed *Romaunz de temtacioun del secle* mentions a Lady Dionysa, whom Miss Legge identified as the wife of William Hacon, who had estates in Hertfordshire and Bedfordshire, but it is unlikely that she could have been any sort of patroness.[26] Denis Pyramus was to be followed at Bury in the early thirteenth century by Thomas of Walsingham who wrote a rhymed Anglo-Norman version of the life of St Faith, and later by Everard de Gately who wrote an Anglo-Norman version of the Miracles of the Virgin.[27] At St Albans it was Matthew Paris who was to

---

[22] *Vita S. Watheni Abbatis . . .*, *Acta Sanctorum* Augusti I 261a, cit. by M. Richter, *Sprache und Gesellschaft im Mittelalter: Untersuchungen zur mündlichen Kommunikation in England . . .*, Stuttgart 1979, 92. For the Medieval French monastic Rules, see Liste provisoire 4, 6, and G. Hilty in *Vox Romanica* xxvii, 1986, 176.

[23] ANL 134–38, 250.

[24] ANL 81–85.

[25] Ian Short, 'The Patronage of Beneit's *Vie de Thomas Becket*', *Medium Ævum* lvi, 1987, 239–56. Cf. B. Golding, 'Simon of Kyme: the making of a rebel', *Nottingham Medieval Studies* xxvii, 1983, 23–36; I owe this reference to Emma Mason.

[26] M. D. Legge, *Anglo-Norman in the Cloisters*, Edinburgh U.P. 1950, 33.

[27] ANL 257–58, 267.

continue the tradition of vernacular saints' lives with his Anglo-Norman Alban, Edward, Edmund and Becket, which he copied and illustrated himself and circulated amongst his aristocratic lady acquaintances.[28]

French, of course, was a very important cultural medium for educated women, as much as, or perhaps even more so than, it was for men, and the considerable role played by women patrons in fostering Anglo-Norman literature is well recognised. Women within monastic communities are also found composing vernacular verse. Clemence of Barking's rhymed life of St Catherine is a re-writing of an earlier vernacular life, a fragment of which survives in a later copy and probably represents the oldest surviving Anglo-Norman text.[29] Clemence may well have been the same person as the anonymous nun of Barking who composed her Anglo-Norman life of Edward the Confessor, based on Ailred of Rievaulx's *Vita*, probably between 1163 and 1170, and who modestly – and quite unneccessarily – apologises for her Insular French which she describes as 'false' or inauthentic.[30] Clemence is the earliest recorded woman poet in French literature.

Before leaving Barking, mention should be made of Adgar who dedicated one version of his *Gracial*, a rhymed collection of Miracles of the Virgin in Anglo-Norman, to a certain Lady Maud, whom critics have identified as the natural daughter of Henry II and abbess of Barking.[31] There is not, alas, the slightest justification for this conjecture. Much better substantiated and more interesting is the case of Guernes de Pont-Sainte-Maxence. In an epilogue to the second edition of his verse *Vie de saint Thomas Becket*, completed in 1174, he acknowledges the material help and support that he had received from Archbishop Thomas' sister Marie, who had become abbess of Barking in April 1173, and from the nuns ('les dames') there. Odo, prior of Holy Trinity Canterbury, who the following year was to come to Battle as abbot, is also thanked for his material support, together with his monks.[32] Though such assistance is not patronage in the strict sense of the term, it is certainly a form of financial sponsorship by monasteries of vernacular poets.

The factors governing the production of French texts in the English monastic world of the twelfth century were, one suspects, above all practical. As an alternative to Latin, Anglo-Norman was all the more convenient for being closely related to it linguistically. It was also, of course, the current vernacular of the society's

[28] R. Vaughan, *Matthew Paris*, Cambridge 1958, 169–81; Florence McCulloch in *Speculum* lvi, 1981, 761–85; *La Estoire de seint Ædward . . .*, ed. Kathryn Wallace, ANTS 41, London 1983; N. J. Morgan, *Early Gothic Manuscripts I: 1190–1250*, London 1982, 30–31, 107–8, 130–45, also 'Matthew Paris, St Albans, London, and the leaves of the "Life of St Thomas Becket" ', *Burlington Magazine* cxxx, 1988, 85–96; cf. Suzanne Lewis, *The Art of Matthew Paris in the 'Chronica Majora'*, Aldershot 1986.

[29] *The Life of St Catherine by Clemence of Barking*, ed. W. Macbain, ANTS 18, Oxford 1964; for the earlier version, MS Manchester John Rylands Lib. French 6, ff. 9r–10r (since discovered to have originally been part of MS BL Egerton 2710), see xiii. It has been conjectured that this text may have been the *Ludus de Sancta Katerina* which Geoffrey, later abbot of St Albans, wrote and had performed at Dunstable. Geoffrey was abbot (1119–46) at the time when the St Albans Psalter was made (E. C. Fawtier-Jones, *Romania* lvi, 1930, 86–87; ANL 311).

[30] ANL 60–66.

[31] ANL 187–91; *Adgar: 'Le Gracial'*, ed. P. Kunstmann, Ottawa U.P. 1982, 12. The name of another dedicatee, a certain Gregory, is also found in this text.

[32] *Guernes de Pont-Sainte-Maxence: La Vie de saint Thomas Becket*, ed. E. Walberg, CFMA, Paris 1936, 191–92. Guernes tells us (v. 6158) that he frequently recited his poem at the saint's tomb. On the first edition of Guernes' text, see my article in *Medium Ævum* xlvi, 1977, 20–34.

dominant class as well as an international language. To regard Insular French as a poor relation of Latin, hermetically sealed off from it as a subordinate or inferior linguistic register, would be anachronistically to underestimate its importance and cultural status in a trilingual society where it coexisted naturally and comfortably with Latin as a complementary vehicle of expression. Anglo-Norman was thus able to form a ready and natural bridge between the traditionally juxtaposed religious and secular cultures.

When we leave the cloister, what we may term the collective, institutional patronage of French literature within religious communities gives way, in the secular sphere, to an individual-based or (if you will excuse the term) a private-enterprise patronage. It is no doubt fitting – perhaps even significant – that, chronologically speaking, royalty should open the account. Towards 1106 a monk called Benedeit, surnamed 'li Apostoiles' ('papal envoy', perhaps), was commissioned by Henry I's first queen Edith/Maud to make a French translation of the Hiberno-Latin *Navigatio Sancti Brendani*, and his Anglo-Norman *Voyage of St Brendan* inaugurated what was to prove to be a long tradition of Medieval French quest narratives of Celtic inspiration written in octosyllabic rhyming couplets. Maud's name appears in only one of the four manuscripts and fragments that preserve the prologue to Benedeit's text. That of Adeliza, Henry's second wife, is substituted in what one may assume to have been a rededicated edition dating from after 1121.[33] Both Maud and Adeliza were, of course, educated women and both are known to have been patronesses of literature.

Adeliza's name is linked with two further Anglo-Norman texts. One is a now lost vernacular verse chronicle (a 'chançon') of Henry I's reign written by one David, of which, according to Gaimar, Adeliza had a lavish copy made with its opening verse set to music. Constance FitzGilbert, Gaimar's patron, herself paid a silver mark to have a copy made of David's text and she often read from it in her chamber.[34] The other work is this time clearly dedicated to Adeliza; it is Philippe de Thaon's Anglo-Norman verse translation of the Latin *Physiologus* or Bestiary.[35] As the Queen retained her title after Henry's death up until her remarriage to William d'Albini, Philippe's *Bestiaire* has probably to be dated between 1121 and 1139. Soon after 1154 Philippe rededicated the work to Eleanor. In the interval, probably between 1139 and 1141, he had written another poem, the *Livre de Sibile*, which he speculatively dedicated to the Empress in an effort to have a lost inheritance restored.[36] Philippe also, as we shall see later, wrote for less elevated members of Anglo-Norman society.

Eleanor's name is linked explicitly only to Philippe de Thaon's *Bestiaire*. Her assumed patronage of Wace's adaptation of Geoffrey of Monmouth's *Historia Regum Britanniae*, the *Roman de Brut*, has the authority only of Wace's Middle

---

[33] *Benedeit: The Anglo-Norman Voyage of St Brendan*, ed. Ian Short & Brian Merrilees, Manchester U.P. 1979. Cf. William of Malmesbury's encomium of Maud in *De Gestis regum Anglorum*, ed. W. Stubbs, RS, ii 493–95.
[34] *'L'Estoire des Engleis' by Geffrei Gaimar*, ed. A. Bell, ANTS 14–16, Oxford 1960, vv. 6481–6520. Bell's suggestion that David's 'chançon' was in Latin seems untenable. On Henry I's court, see Gaimar vv. 6495–512; M. D. Legge, 'L'Influence littéraire de la cour d'Henri Beauclerc', *Mélanges offerts à Rita Lejeune*, Gembloux 1969, i 679–87.
[35] ANL 22–25.
[36] *'Le Livre de Sibile' by Philippe de Thaon*, ed. Hugh Shields, ANTS 37, London 1979.

English translator Laȝamon, writing over half a century later.[37] Henry's patronage
of the *Brut*, which was completed in 1155, can at best be inferred; it is certainly
not made explicit within the text.[38] On the other hand, praise of Eleanor and
Henry, and a dedication of sorts, are to be found in Wace's other major chronicle,
the *Roman de Rou*, begun in 1160, interrupted, resumed sometime after 1170, and
completed, one assumes, before Eleanor's fall from grace in 1173.[39] Wace was
also to fall from grace, and he left his *Rou* unfinished when he was replaced at
court as vernacular chronicler by Beneit, the Continental author of the *Chronique
des ducs de Normandie*, and the same person no doubt as the Benoît de Sainte-
Maure who wrote the *Roman de Troie*.[40] It seems clear, however, that Wace had
had a full patronage relationship with Henry II, who had rewarded him for his
pains with a prebend in Bayeux.[41] And Wace it is who expresses with disarming
frankness the twelfth-century vernacular poet's mission when he explains that the
sort of people he addresses are the rich, those with income and cash, who can
afford to buy books and pay for his services.[42] Master Wace (a forename, incidentally)[43] also wrote three other religious pieces, one of which, the *Vie de saint
Nicolas*, was patronised, presumably in Caen, by one Robert FitzTiout.[44] Though
his *Brut*, of which some twenty-six manuscripts survive, was popular enough to
have eclipsed the now lost first part of Gaimar's history, at least one other
twelfth-century Anglo-Norman version of Geoffrey of Monmouth has survived,
albeit in a severely fragmentary form.[45] Wace's French may not qualify as Insular

---

[37] *Laȝamon: Brut*, ed. G. L. Brook & R. F. Leslie, EETS os, London 1963–73, i vv. 21–23.
[38] The text itself contains no information on the circumstances of its production other than that it
was completed 'mil e cent cinquante e cinc anz' (*Le Roman de Brut de Wace*, ed. I Arnold, SATF,
Paris 1938–40, ii v. 14865). Tyson's declaration ([note 7 above] 194) 'That the *Brut* was written
for royal patronage is certain' therefore requires qualification. The most sober and reliable account of literary patronage under Henry II remains W. F. Schirmer & U. Broich, *Studien zum
literarischen Patronat im England des 12. Jahrhunderts*, Köln 1962, 22–203; see also C. H.
Haskins, 'Henry II as a patron of literature', *Essays in medieval history presented to Thomas
Frederick Tout*, ed. A. G. Little & F. M. Powicke, Manchester 1925, 71–77; Peter Dronke, 'Peter of
Blois and poetry at the court of Henry II', *Medieval Studies* xxxviii, 1976, 185–235; D. Tillman-
Bartylla, 'Höfische Welt und Geschichtsbedürfnis: die anglo-normannischen Verschroniken des
XII. Jahrhunderts', *Grundriss der romanischen Literaturen des Mittelalters*, ed. H. R. Jauss & E.
Köhler, xi/1 *La Littérature historiographique . . .*, Heidelberg 1986, 313–50. On the other hand, R.
Lejeune [note 6 above], J.-G. Gouttebroze, 'Henri II Plantagenêt, patron des historiographes
anglo-normands de langue d'oïl', *La Littérature angevine médiévale: Actes du colloque du samedi
22 mars 1980 . . .*, Univ. d'Angers 1981, 91–109, and Bezzola [note 3 above] all, in varying
degrees, take liberties with the evidence. The (too) often repeated view that Henry was deliberately using Wace's vernacular poetry to further his own political ends is challenged by Lesley
Johnson in her unpubl. Ph.D. thesis, U. of London 1990, 'Commemorating the Past: a critical
study of the shaping of British and Arthurian history . . .', 131ff.
[39] *Le Roman de Rou de Wace*, ed. A. J. Holden, SATF, Paris 1970–73, C.A. vv. 1–4, 17–42, ii vv.
4420–25, iii vv. 172–79, 185–90, 11431–38.
[40] *Rou* iii 11419–30. Cf. G. A. Beckmann, *Trojaroman und Normannenchronik: die Identität der
beiden Benoît . . .*, München 1965.
[41] *Rou* iii 171–76, 5313–18.
[42] *Rou* iii 143–66 (163–66).
[43] 'Gace' in Continental spelling. He was mistakenly baptised 'Robert' by the Abbé de la Rue in
1794, an error still perpetuated today by the uninformed.
[44] *La Vie de saint Nicolas par Wace*, ed. E. Ronsjö, Lund 1942, 193–94 and vv. 1546–50.
[45] MS BL Harley 4733, f. 128, published by R. Imelmann, *Laȝamon: Versuch über seine Quellen*,
Berlin 1906, 112–17, though the editor failed to recognise the twelfth-century date of the bifolium
in question.

stricto sensu[46] (he tells us that he was born in Jersey and lived for long periods in Normandy),[47] but his *Brut*, one of the most influential of twelfth-century vernacular texts, and his *Rou* are Anglo-Norman in all but name.

Henry has also been linked – though highly speculatively – with French literature's earliest example of contemporary historical writing in the vernacular, the verse account of the rebellion of the Young King in 1173–74 by the Winchester cleric Jordan Fantosme. Fantosme's largely eye-witness narrative, in which an orthodox providential view of history is dressed up in strongly epic garb, was probably destined for the consumption of the baronial participants in the events.[48] Marie's *Lais*, as we shall see, might have been dedicated to Henry, if not to the Young King or even to John, though there is no means of telling whether or not a genuine patronage relationship ever existed between them. Nor is the evidence for the presence of troubadour poets at Henry's court sufficient to prove active royal patronage.[49] Attempts, finally, to link the Medieval French romances of Antiquity and even Chrétien de Troyes with Henry's court are doomed to remain conjectural.[50]

As for Richard, the attribution to him of two Medieval French lyrics has surprisingly remained unchallenged by literary critics, though I note that Miss Legge grants it only passing and duly dismissive reference.[51] As far as John's tastes in vernacular literature are concerned, all we know is that he once borrowed a verse history of England written in French ('Romancium Historia Angliae') from Reginald de Cornhill. The Close Rolls do not reveal whether he ever returned it.[52]

Royal patronage of Anglo-Norman literature must certainly have stimulated emulation, but when we come to evaluate patronage by members of the higher nobility, we have unfortunately to be content with rather fragmentary evidence. A eulogy of Cecily, countess of Hereford and daughter of Sibyl de Lacy, might allow us to speculate on her possible patronage of Etienne de Fougère's *Livre des Manières*, a somewhat austere moralising treatise on the three estates in verse.

---

[46] Miss Legge, in ANL, excludes the *Brut* and the *Rou* from the Anglo-Norman canon, as she does also Marie's *Lais*.
[47] *Rou* iii 5305–12.
[48] *Jordan Fantosme's 'Chronicle'*, ed. R. C. Johnston, Oxford 1980, also 'The Historicity of Jordan Fantosme's *Chronicle*', *JMH* ii, 1976, 159–68; A. Lodge, 'Literature and History in the *Chronicle* of Jordan Fantosme', *French Studies* xlv, 1990, 257–70.
[49] J. Audiau, *Les Troubadours et l'Angleterre*, Tulle 1927. I owe this reference to Ruth Harvey.
[50] For example: B. Schmolke-Hasselmann, 'Henri II Plantagenêt, roi d'Angleterre, et la genèse d'*Erec et Enide*', *Cahiers de civilisation médiévale* xxiv, 1981, 241–46, also 'The Round Table: ideal, fiction and reality', *Arthurian Literature* ii, 1982, 41–75; C. Bullock-Davies, 'Chrétien de Troyes and England', *Arthurian Literature* i, 1981, 1–61.
[51] ANL 108, 332. Cf. J. K. Archibald, 'La Chanson de captivité du roi Richard', *Cahiers d'études médiévales* i, 1974, 149–58; P. Bec, *La Lyrique française au moyen âge*, Paris 1978, ii 124–25. According to Roger of Howden, Richard's chancellor, William Longchamp, patronised French poetry for personal self-advertisement: 'Hic ad augmentum et famam sui nominis emendicata carmina et rhythmos adulatorios comparabat, et de regno Francorum cantores et joculatores muneribus allexerat ut de illo canerent in plateis, et jam dicebatur ubique quod non erat talis in orbe' (*Chronica*, ed. W. Stubbs, RS, iii 143).
[52] *Rotuli Litterarum Clausarum*, Rec. Com., i 29 (*anno* 1205). For a telling example of Anglo-Norman court life imitating vernacular French literature, see Emma Mason, 'The Hero's Invincible Weapon: an aspect of Angevin propaganda', *The Ideals and Practice of Medieval Knighthood III (Strawberry Hill Conference 1988)*, Woodbridge 1990, 121–37.

Etienne had been a member of the chancery of Henry II from 1157 and the King's chaplain before his eventual elevation to the see of Rennes in 1168. His French is not distinctively Anglo-Norman.[53]

Mention may be here of another putative patronage, that of the chronicle of the Conquest of Ireland which covers the period 1152 to 1175 and is known under the title of *The Song of Dermot and the Earl.* This epic-flavoured octosyllabic text seems to have been composed sometime after 1187 by an outstandingly mediocre poet who claims as his eye-witness source Maurice Regan, latimer to King Dermot of Leinster. Not only has Maurice himself been proposed as a patron, but also Isabel of Clare, granddaughter of Dermot, daughter of Strongbow and, of course, wife of William Marshal.[54] Though we will encounter the Clares again shortly, we must regretfully relegate this particular patronage to the realm of the purely conjectural.

An unidentified Earl William, 'the most valiant in any kingdom . . . the flower of chivalry, learning and courtliness', is the dedicatee of a collection of rhymed *Fables* from the pen of one Marie, universally but erroneously referred to as Marie de France.[55] William, son of Robert of Gloucester, has been suggested as a likely candidate, but there were at the time at least a dozen different Earl Williams (including the Marshal), each of whom is as well – or as badly – qualified for consideration as the other. Marie's more famous *Lais* are equally vaguely dedicated to 'the noble King', presumably Henry or his son.[56] The third work attributed to her, a verse translation of the Latin *St Patrick's Purgatory*, has no evidence of patronage. The identification of Marie herself remains a mystery, despite gallons of scholarly ink. The latest contender to be touted, the daughter of Waleran II, count of Meulan, is, alas, unlikely to be the last in a seemingly endless flow of conjecture.[57] More important for our purposes is the fact that none of Marie's works passes the conventional dialectal test that would admit her into the Anglo-Norman canon. She was a Continental writer from the Ile-de-France who, like Wace and Benoît before her, worked at the Anglo-Norman court, probably in the 1170s. She was a learned woman, knew Latin and probably English, and no doubt also had a smattering of Breton/Welsh. The multi-culturism of twelfth-century Britain inspires and pervades her work. After the Anglo-Norman Clemence of Barking, Marie can be heralded as the second named woman writer of Medieval French literature.

[53] *Etienne de Fougères: 'Le Livre des Manières'*, ed. A. Lodge, TLF, Genève 1979.
[54] *The Song of Dermot and the Earl*, ed. G. H. Orpen, Oxford 1892, vv. 1–11 (a new ed. and translation are in preparation for ANTS by E. Mullally); cf. W. Sayers, 'The Patronage of *La Conquête d'Irlande*', *Romance Philology* xxi, 1967, 34–41; J. Long, 'Dermot and the Earl: Who wrote the *Song*?', *Proceedings of the Royal Irish Academy* lxxv/c, 1975, 263–72.
[55] *Marie de France: 'Fables'*, ed. A. Ewert & R. C. Johnston, Oxford 1942, Prol. vv. 30–32, Epil. vv. 9–10; cf. *Marie de France: 'Fables'*, ed. & trans. H. Spiegel, Toronto U. P. 1987; M. Soudée, 'Le Dédicataire des *Ysopets* de Marie de France', *Les Lettres romanes* xxxv, 1981, 183–98. Marie claims an Anglo-Saxon translation by King Alfred as her source (Epil. vv. 12–19), but no such text is known. The author of *Le Roman de Waldef* (ed. A. J. Holden, Cologny-Genève 1984, vv. 85–86) also refers to a fictitious Anglo-Saxon source. Gaimar, on the other hand, did translate the *Anglo-Saxon Chronicle*.
[56] *Marie de France: 'Lais'*, ed. A. Ewert, Oxford 1944, Prol. vv. 43–53; cf. *Les Lais de Marie de France*, ed. Jean Rychner, CFMA, Paris 1981, viii–ix; G. S. Burgess, *Marie de France: an analytical bibliography*, London 1977, also *Supplement*, London 1986.
[57] P. R. Grillo in *Medium Ævum*, lvii, 1988, 269–74.

In contrast to almost all of the Anglo-Norman romance texts produced in the twelfth century, for which no direct patronage evidence survives (Thomas's *Tristan*, *Horn* by yet another Thomas, Thomas of Kent's *Alexander*, Robert Biket's *Lai du Cor*, *Fergus*, *Amadas et Ydoine*, *Waldef*), Hue de Rotelande's *Protheselaus*, dating from between 1180 and 1190, was, the author tells us, written for Gilbert FitzBaderon.[58] Gilbert was lord of Monmouth and related, on his mother's side, to the Clares. According to Hue, he actually possessed a personal library in his castle, well stocked with volumes in both Latin and Romance (that is, French). This is in fact one of the earliest records of a secular library.[59] In Hue de Rotelande's earlier romance *Ipomedon*, written shortly after 1174, he tells us that he lived at Credenhill, outside Hereford, and it is probable that his patronym refers to Rhuddlan in North Wales, not far from Geoffrey of Monmouth's bishopric of St Asaph.[60] Hue, who has a fine sense of literary irony, wrote very good verse in Anglo-Norman, little different from its Continental counterpart. We may note in passing that another Anglo-Norman poet, Simund de Freine, was a canon at Hereford at around the same time, but neither his *Roman de Philosophie*, a verse vulgarisation of Boethius, nor his *Passion de saint George*, preserve any mention of specific patronage.[61]

The possibility of ecclesiastical patronage of Anglo-Norman literature is raised by the case of Simund's superior at Hereford, Bishop William. This William can perhaps be identified with the William de Vere who, together with a certain Gilbert the Butler, was reportedly instrumental in acquiring, while at Constantinople, the original Latin *Letter of Prester John* which Raoul (or Roanz) of Arundel translated into Anglo-Norman verse, probably at Waltham in the 1180s.[62] William apparently, when he was at Chich, wrote a Latin life of St Osyth, and this was also translated into Anglo-Norman.[63]

The utility of Anglo-Norman literature for seculars can be illustrated by returning to the second decade of the century and to Philippe de Thaon. To Philippe goes the dubious distinction of having written what must surely be the most excruciating hexasyllabic rhyming couplets in Medieval French literature. Admittedly, a Latin computational treatise for calculating movable feasts is hardly inspiring subject matter, and more remarkable than the quality of Philippe's poetry is the fact that he chose to turn such an unpromising text into verse in the first place. Might, one wonders, its recipient have found a rhyming text more easy

---

[58] *'Protheselaus' by Hue de Rotelande*, ed. A. J. Holden, ANTS 47–48, London 1991, ii vv. 12696–710.

[59] Under Henry I, Queen Adeliza and Constance wife of Ralph FitzGilbert are both recorded as owning vernacular books. The notorious Hugh de Morville, when on crusade with Richard in 1194, lent his personal copy of an Arthurian romance to Ulrich von Zatzikoven, who used it as the source for his Middle High German *Lanzelet* (K. Ruh, *Höfische Epik des deutschen Mittelalters*, Berlin 1977–80, ii 35). On the Continent, Marie countess of Champagne is known to have had a personal library; see P. Stirnemann, 'Quelques bibliothèques princières et la production hors-scriptorium au XIIe siècle', *Bulletin archéologique* . . . n.s. xvii–xviii/a, 1984, 7–38, also 'Les Bibliothèques princières et privées au XIIe et XIIIe siècles', *Histoire des bibliothèques françaises, I: Les Bibliothèques médiévales* . . ., Paris 1989, 173–91.

[60] *'Ipomedon': poème de Hue de Rotelande*, ed. A. J. Holden, Paris 1979, 7–11 and v. 10571.

[61] ANL 183–87.

[62] *La Lettre du prêtre Jean*, ed. M. Gosman, Groningen 1982, vv. 1105–96; J. Barrow, 'A twelfth-century bishop and literary patron: William de Vere', *Viator* xviii, 1987, 175–89.

[63] Barrow 175–77; ANL 259–61.

to memorise? The prologue to what is in effect the first scientific popularisation in the French language tells us that the *Comput* is designed 'to enable priests to maintain the laws of the Church'.[64] It is dedicated to Philippe's uncle, Hunfrei de Thaon, chaplain to the King's steward Eudo Dapifer, and can be dated on internal evidence to 1113 (or 1119). By turning Nelson's eye to Phillippe's verse, Miss Legge is able to describe his *Comput* as 'an early monument of "civil service" French'.[65] While the use of the vernacular in the great offices of state is hardly unexpected, what is perhaps surprising is the poor standard of Latin which Philippe's translation seems to presuppose.

The fact that the real, everyday language of royal, seigniorial, civic and commercial administration in twelfth-century Britain was in fact Anglo-Norman sometimes surfaces in the Latin of administrative documents, where the vernacular persists as a tangible substratum.[66] This is most visible at the lexical level when royal scribes, for instance, can be found supplementing their Latin by appropriating vernacular terms: for example, 'reddunt compotum de . . . .x. chasçurs et .v. girfalcs'. It can be seen also in the widespread practice of linguistic back-formation where nouns and verbs of Romance origin are dressed up in borrowed Latin garb: 'scutagium', 'palefridus', 'averia', 'chiminum', 'gaiola', 'saisire', 'adreciare'.[67] In the domain of syntax also, the vernacular frequently makes its presence felt in sentence structure.[68] One suspects that the use of Latin and the vernacular was far from being as hierarchically delineated as our modern perceptions may lead us to suppose, and that the passage from one to the other was, in bureaucratic circles, natural and effortless.[69] Indeed, with the two languages being so closely related, it is not impossible that they could, in certain circumstances, have been thought of as forming a single linguistic spectrum of varying registers and levels of appropriateness.[70]

Evidence would suggest that Anglo-Norman was used in the courts of law from an early date, and that pleading in the vernacular was the normal practice.[71] The

[64] *Philippe de Thaon: 'Comput'*, ed. Ian Short, ANTS, London 1984, vv. 3–4.
[65] ANL 21.
[66] Cf. Cecily Clark, 'People and Languages in post-Conquest Canterbury', *JMH* ii, 1975, 1–33, also 'Women's names in post-Conquest England . . .', *Speculum* liii, 1978, 223–51.
[67] My examples are taken from *Pipe Roll 1 John* 209, and from the glossary to Stubbs' *Select Charters* . . .
[68] A particularly well documented example – from the Continent – is the 'Conventum inter Guillelmum comitem et Hugonem Chiliarchum', ed. J. P. Martindale, *EHR*, lxxxiv, 1969, 541–48, and studied by Mary Hackett, 'Aspects de la langue vulgaire du Poitou . . .', *Mélanges offerts à Rita Lejeune*, Gembloux 1969, i 13–22. I owe these references to Susan Reynolds. See also, for Insular examples, the letters quoted in H. G. Richardson & G. O. Sayles, *The Governance of Medieval England* . . ., Edinburgh U.P. 1963, 275–77.
[69] Clanchy 159–63, 173–74, 261. The absence of correlation between the language of oral transaction and the language of written record is another aspect of this wider phenomenon of linguistic fluidity.
[70] Cf. Suzanne Fleischman, 'Philology, linguistics and the discourse of the medieval text', *Speculum* lxv, 1990, 19–37: 'We might view the relationship between Latin and Old French . . . as one of "complementary distribution". For Latin, the text controlled the voice; speech was modeled on a written idiom with an established tradition of grammar and rhetoric. For French, the voice controlled the text, improvising as best it could a functional *écriture*' (24 n. 16).
[71] Richardson & Sayles 93–95, 278; Clanchy 160–64, 168–74, 220–26; M. D. Legge, 'Anglo-Norman as a spoken language', *ante* ii, 1979, 108–17 (108); P. Hyams, 'The Common Law and the French Connection', *ante* iv, 1981, 77–92 (91–92).

so-called Laws of William the Conqueror (*Leis Willelme*) have come down to us, exceptionally, in Anglo-Norman French in a mid twelfth-century manuscript.[72] A charter of Ralph FitzWalter of Sherington (Bucks) for the Hospitallers, dating from c.1140, is the earliest example of the use of the French vernacular in administrative documents (after the celebrated Strasbourg Oaths of 842.)[73] The next oldest survival, a return to Henry's Inquest of Sheriffs (1170) crudely written in Anglo-Norman,[74] provides another rare glimpse into the realities of bureaucratic life among the lesser nobility.[75]

Two instances of the nobility commissioning Anglo-Norman literary texts are particularly well documented, and I should like to give pride of place in my survey to two patrons from the first half of the century, both women, both from Lincolnshire, and their families related by marriage. Each was innovative in a very special sense. What other than a genuine thirst for knowledge, for access to a Latin learning from which she had apparently been excluded, can explain why Alice, wife of Robert de Condet should have commissioned the unusual text she did? This was a vernacular translation, by one Sanson de Nantuil, of the first nineteen chapters of the Book of Proverbs and its scholastic commentary into over 11,000 rhyming octosyllables (complete with Latin text).[76] Although Alice's genealogy is obscure, it has been suggested that she might have been the daughter of Ranulf le Meschin, earl of Chester, and of countess Lucy. Her first husband, Richard FitzGilbert of Clare, died in battle in 1136, and she subsequently, it would appear, married Robert de Condet, who in turn died somewhere between 1140 and 1145.[77] Alice was still alive in 1154, and it would follow that Sanson's *Proverbes de Salemon*, the earliest scholastic text in the French vernacular, was probably composed in the second quarter of the twelfth century.

Alice had family connections with Gaimar's patron, Constance, wife of Ralph FitzGilbert, who both played an active role in obtaining some of Gaimar's source books for his *Estoire des Engleis*. Clearly a most scholarly author, Master Geffrei Gaimar lists the four principal sources that he used for his ambitious rhymed history of both the British and the English kings, of which only the second part

---

[72] MS BL Addit. 49366, ff. 141r–144v, ed. F. Liebermann, *Die Gesetze der Angelsachsen*, Halle 1903–16, i 492–520, ii 283–92; cf. also J. Wüest, *Die 'Leis Willelme': Untersuchungen zur ältesten Gesetzbuch in französischer Sprache*, Romanica Helvetica 79, Bern 1969 (both critics misdate the MS; see Liste provisoire 6), and Howden's *Chronica*, RS, ii 242.

[73] *The Cartulary of the Knights of St John of Jerusalem in England: Secunda Camera: Essex*, ed. M. Gervers, Oxford U.P. 1982, 169–70, no. 272 (this supersedes an earlier article in *Journal of the Society of Archivists* vi, 1979, 131–35). The charter in question survives only in a later copy.

[74] H. Richardson, 'A twelfth-century Anglo-Norman Charter', *BJRL* xxiv, 1940, 168–72, also [H. Suggett] 'An Anglo-Norman return to the Inquest of Sheriffs', *ibidem* xxvii, 1942–43, 179–81. For the earliest twelfth-century Continental French documents, see Répertoire nos. 6, 7, 54, 55.

[75] Cf. also M. Bateson, 'A London Municipal Collection of the reign of King John', in *EHR* xvii, 1902, 480–511, 707–30 (= Répertoire no. 49). Twelfth-century Insular MSS also provide the earliest examples of Latin/French glosses and of medical receipts in the vernacular; see, for the former, Liste provisoire, and T. Hunt in *Revue de linguistique romane* xliii, 1979, 236–37, and, for the latter, T. Hunt, *Popular Medicine in thirteenth-century England*, Woodbridge 1990, 64–66.

[76] *'Les Proverbes de Salemon' by Sanson de Nantuil*, ed. C. Isoz, ANTS 44, 45, London 1988, i vv. 191–212.

[77] ANL 36–42; C. W. Foster, *The 'Registrum Antiquissimum' of the Cathedral Church of Lincoln*, Hereford 1931, i 277–95; J. W. Alexander, *Ranulf of Chester: a relic of the Conquest*, U. of Georgia P. 1983, 2; cf. T. J. Durnford, 'The incomplete nature of *Les Proverbes de Salemon*', *Romance Notes* xxii, 1981–82, 362–66.

has survived. These were: 'the Winchester History', 'a certain English book from Washingborough' (just outside Lincoln), 'the good book of Oxford' belonging to Walter the Archdeacon, and a book borrowed from Walter Espec at Helmsley which Robert of Gloucester had had translated 'from the books belonging to the Welsh which they had of the British kings'. Let anyone doubting my scholarship – adds Gaimar – ask Nicolas de Trailly, who turns out to be Walter Espec's nephew and a canon of York.[78] Gaimar's source books look, at first sight, suspiciously like two different copies (perhaps versions) of Geoffrey of Monmouth's *Historia Regum Britanniae*, and two different copies (perhaps versions) of the *Anglo-Saxon Chronicle*. Of the latter Gaimar indeed gives a close translation covering the years 495–975 and taking up half the surviving text. The part of his chronicle for which he would have used Geoffrey is lost.

Gaimar, who wrote the whole of his chronicle in fourteen months, probably between March 1136 and April 1137, was clearly at ease in three cultures, Latin, French and English, and his knowledge of the archaic literary *koinè* in which the *Anglo-Saxon Chronicle* was written quite remarkable. But equally remarkable, it seems to me, is his patron, Constance herself, a cultivated woman (Gaimar tells us that she could read French), born in England but French-speaking, clearly motivated by an intellectual curiosity to understand the Insular world in which she lived, and, like many of her contemporaries, no doubt anxious to find some sort of self-legitimisation with regard to the culture of a country that for her parents had been an adoptive one, but which for her was her native one. She knew, one supposes, that she belonged to two cultures simultaneously, but that she had no possibility of gaining access to one of them without an interpreter to help her cross the wide linguistic gulf that separated her from it.[79] Surely only twelfth-century England could have presented not only the cultural problem, but the literary solution to it as well. The patron found her polyglot, and French literature found the very first vernacular chronicle in its history.

The widespread and innovative use of Insular French in the twelfth century was as much a function, I would contend, of England's specifically multi-cultural environment as it was of any particular lack or low level of Latin literacy among the clergy. Twelfth-century England, and even more so Britain, was a cultural and linguistic melting pot. The multi-lingualism that was its overriding characteristic not only facilitated but actively encouraged the symbiosis of cultures in contact. The vernacularisation of learning through *translatio* goes hand in hand with a conscious decompartmentalisation in the use of Latin and the socially dominant Latin-based vernacular of French. Enlightened monastic, ecclesiastical and aristocratic patronage coincides happily with a rich supply of polyglot authors. Conditions of reception and possibilities of production fall into equilibrium. Here women played a significant role and were enabled, through the vernacular, to participate in literature not only as writers and patrons but also, and equally importantly, as audiences. The innovations of these Anglo-Norman authors made

[78] *L'Estoire des Engleis* [above n. 34] vv. 6428–76; cf. A. Bell, 'Maistre Geffrei Gaimar', *Medium Ævum* vii, 1938, 184–98, also 'The epilogue to Gaimar's *Estoire des Engleis*', *Modern Language Review* xxv, 1930, 52–59.

[79] Cf. Ian Short, 'Gaimar et les débuts de l'historiographie en langue française', *Chroniques nationales et chroniques universelles*, ed. D. Buschinger, Göppinger Arbeiten zur Germanistik 508, Göppingen 1990, 155–63.

a highly significant contribution to the history of French literature. This is no-where better illustrated than in the realm of historiography. In an already impressive list of Latin chroniclers which is one of the most enduring achievements of Anglo-Norman culture, vernacular historians such as Gaimar and Wace find a natural place. And let us not forget here the seminal contribution of Europe's most popular twelfth-century historian, Geoffrey of Monmouth, who better than anyone exemplifies the productive and creative potential of Anglo-Norman Britain. A deep sense of – or search for – cultural continuity with the past, in addition to more immediate propagandistic intent, best explains, I think, the peculiarly Anglo-Norman preoccupation with historiography. But other forms of literature grew and flourished, and by the end of the century an infrastructure of lay scriptoria was beginning to emerge to supply the demands of an increasingly literate and cultivated society.[80]

If, for reasons of rhetorical presentation as well as of time, I have neglected to talk about Continental French literary production in the twelfth century, it is not because I see Anglo-Norman literature as functioning in any way in isolation from its Continental counterpart. Indeed, it is my firm conviction that, despite the thematic specificity sometimes claimed for it,[81] Anglo-Norman literature is to be seen as an integral part of Continental French literature and can be properly understood only within this wider cultural context. I am well aware, also, of the risk that I have been running in privileging, as I have done, one particular language of twelfth-century Britain to the exclusion of the others, for, while I may have made some reference to Latin in passing, it will not have escaped your notice that that I have more or less totally ignored contemporary English, not to mention Welsh, Gallic and Irish. The risk I run is that of giving a distorting slant to what is, in reality, a much more complex overall socio-linguistic picture, even of inadvertantly, by omission, giving credence to the idea that some sort of monolithic linguistic compartmentalisation could have underpinned this rich and varied culture that I have been attempting to describe.

In order partially to correct any such false impressions, I should like to end by looking forward, from the vantage point of the twelfth century, to the subsequent development of Anglo-Norman and its literary interaction with English over the ensuing two hundred years down to the time of Chaucer.[82] Here I am deliberately trespassing on the preserve of my Middle English colleagues. I do so because many of them, it seems to me, have long been in danger not so much of underesti-

---

[80] Ian Short, 'L'Avènement du texte vernaculaire: la mise en recueil', *Théories et pratiques de l'écriture au moyen âge . . .*, ed. E. Baumgartner & C. Marchello-Nizia, Littérales 4, Paris 1988, 11–24.
[81] For example, S. Crane, *Insular Romance: Politics, faith and culture in Anglo-Norman and Middle English literature*, U. of California P. 1986, whose thesis is that 'the romances of English heroes generate an ideal of achievement that responds broadly to the feudal situation of the Insular barony' (12). Miss Legge also argued that Anglo-Norman literature, though a branch of Old French literature, 'has nevertheless a nature of its own' ('The rise and fall of Anglo-Norman literature', *Mosaic* viii/4, 1974, 1–6). No such claims are made in Brian Merrilees' 'Anglo-Norman Literature', *Dictionary of the Middle Ages*, ed. J. R. Strayer, New York 1982–, i 259–72. On Miss Legge's theory of an Anglo-Norman Ancestral Romance (ANL 139–75), see *Waldef*, ed. A. J. Holden [above n. 55], 33–34; Crane 16–18, also *Romance Philology* xxxv, 1981–82, 601–8.
[82] What follows is a revised version of a paper which I read to the Leeds-York Seminar on the Use of French in Medieval England in January 1991.

mating the role of Anglo-Norman in the development of English literature as of failing to recognise the importance of pluri-lingualism as a cultural and literary phenomenon, and of being unable to break free from an unproductive, indeed misleading, bipolarity which they have inherited from the past. This bipolarity is all the more tenacious for being almost too fundamental to question: it is that between, on the one hand, French speakers, and, on the other, English speakers. I wish to plead in favour of viewing the twelfth and early thirteenth centuries from the synchronic perspective of what makes the era cohere culturally, rather than from a diachronic point of view which divides it up hermetically. My contention is that unarticulated post-Victorian ideologies are still at work encouraging us to adopt an anachronistic frame of reference when it comes to analysing what is essentially a multi-lingual society. Unlike the Swiss, the Belgians, the Québecois and, closer to home, the Welsh, the English seem not to be comfortable, conceptually, with bilingualism, still less with the trilingualism that was the unique cultural characteristic of twelfth-century England.

It may be more perceptible in Birmingham than in Battle, but the fact remains that we today live in a multi-cultural, and therefore multi-lingual society. All around us we see living proof of what we read in socio-linguistic studies of immigrant language acquisition, that is that by the second generation practical bilingualism is invariably the order of the day, and that, by the third, complete linguistic assimilation to the dominant, majority language is achieved as part of an entirely natural process.[83] It is during the third generation that preservation of the mother/grandmother tongue becomes a problem, and needs remedial action if it is not to be irretrievably lost. There is no *a priori* reason why, if this is true of the twentieth century, it should not, *mutatis mutandis*, have been equally true of the twelfth – but with the important difference, of course, that the descendants of the Norman incomers, though still an exceedingly small minority of the total population, themselves formed the high-status culture (in certain, perhaps largely urban, areas), and that for them the acquisition of English was a practical, not a socio-political necessity. Be that as it may, the natural dynamic of diglossia and practical bilingualism would have meant that by the middle of the twelfth century at the very latest the 'Anglo-Normans' (for want of a better term) had not only a passive but also an active command of English. Indeed, it would be no exaggeration to say that before the end of the century their first language must have been English. Evidence survives from the 1160s that Insular French was sensed to be degenerating, and, from the 1180s, that French had lost its status as a true spoken vernacular and become a second, acquired language.[84] Concomitantly, the so-called 'Anglo-Normans' begin to refer to themselves explicitly as English.[85] That

[83] J. F. Hamers & M. Blanc, *Bilinguality and Bilingualism*, Cambridge U.P. 1989, 176.
[84] Ian Short, 'On Bilingualism in Anglo-Norman England', *Romance Philology* xxxiii, 1979–80, 467–79.
[85] Writing in the immediate wake of the civil turmoil of 1173–74, Jordan Fantosme speaks of William the Lion inflicting grievous losses on those loyal to Henry II, whom he describes, in the authorial voice, as 'Engleis d'Engleterre' (*Chronicle* [above n. 48] v. 631). Fantosme also puts into the mouth of the wife of Robert earl of Leicester traditional anti-English insults against Henry II's supporters: 'Li Engleis sunt bon vantur, ne sevent ostëer; mielz sevent as gros hanaps beivre e gueisseiller' (978–79). In c.1184, Beneit, monk of St Albans, shows Henry II swearing, during the Becket controversy, that he will not allow the administration of royal justice to be put in jeopardy 'on account of the English' (*La Vie de Thomas Becket par Beneit*, ed. B. Schlyter, Etudes romanes

Anglo-Norman French should, in such circumstances, have been successfully preserved for more than two centuries to come, as a language of culture and social, ancestral separateness, is truly remarkable – but that, for the moment, must remain another story.

That French, for its part, never penetrated at all significantly into the indigenous population is another well attested fact. But how, in that case, are we to account for what we are told is the disappearance of English from the linguistic map of the twelfth century? There is no direct evidence that English was in any way suppressed – this particular myth was fully articulated only in the fifteenth century, and our perception of it owes much to the nationalistic colouring provided by Walter Scott and Charles Kingsley. The eclipse of English is further overdramatised if one adopts a one-dimensional and diachronic view of language development, and if one fails to distinguish a language's written from its oral functions. A much favoured metaphor is that of English going underground following the Conquest and somehow mysteriously resurfacing at the start of the thirteenth century. Now, a language goes underground only when it no longer has enough speakers with their feet firmly planted in real life, and in that case it simply dies. In the case of English in the twelfth century, there were at least two million speakers of it to ensure its continued wellbeing at ground (grassroots) level. Notwithstanding, the range of its written survival is surprisingly narrow. The monasteries, we know, played an important role in the preservation of the so-called West Saxon *koinè*: Peterborough, Christ Church Canterbury, Worcester; closer to everyday reality, a small number of monumental inscriptions have come down to us; there are some administrative survivals also in charters; some Anglo-Saxon letter forms were assimilated into Anglo-Norman spelling conventions, and others continued throughout the century to appear on coinage.[86]

The lack of new and original literary texts in English is less surprising if one subscribes, as I do, to the view that patronage was a necessary condition for literary production in the twelfth century. But the question that then arises is where the first patrons of the first monuments of Middle English literature in the first two decades of the thirteenth century suddenly emerged from (or in the last quarter of the twelfth century, if you subscribe to the re-dating of the *Orrmu-*

de Lund 4, Lund 1941, v. 491: 'pur Engleis'). In the late 1180s, Gerald of Barri in his *Expugnatio Hibernica* consistently refers to the conquerors of Ireland as 'Angli'. In his *Topographia Hibernica* he identifies with 'noster Anglorum populus' (ed. J. S. Brewer, *Giraldi . . . Opera*, RS, v 183), and elsewhere talks of himself as having been brought up 'inter Anglos' (*Opera*, viii lviii). In the *Expugnatio*, he has Maurice FitzGerald declare: 'Sicut Hibernicis Angli, sic et Anglis Hibernici s[u]mus' (ed. A. B. Scott & F. X. Martin, Dublin 1978, 80). The Yorkshire chronicler William of Newburgh, writing between 1196 and 1198, explicitly entitles a chapter of his *Historia Rerum Anglicarum* 'De expugnatione Hiberniensium ab Anglis' (ed. R. Howlett, *Chronicles of the reign of Stephen . . .*, RS, i 165). I owe the Latin references to John Gillingham. For the use of the term 'Norman(an)gli', see Bates [above n.1] 877–80.

[86] D. A. E. Pelteret, *Catalogue of English post-Conquest vernacular documents*, Woodbridge 1990. Inscriptions include the Norman font at Bridekirk Church, Cumbria, and the relief in St Nicholas' Church, Ipswich (on the latter see *English Romanesque Art*, ed. G. Zarnecki, J. Holt, T. Holland, London 1984, 164–65 no. 123). On letter forms, see, for 'ash', note 9 above, and, for the *th* digraph and 'eth', M. K. Pope, *From Latin to Modern French . . .*, 2nd ed., Manchester U.P. 1952, para. 1215; the letter 'wynn' continues to appear on English coins until the 1160s (*English Romanesque Art* 324–38, nos. 381–457). See also, most recently, C. Franzen, *The Tremulous Hand of Worcester: a study of Old English in the thirteenth century*, Oxford 1991.

lum).[87] Now, new patrons of literature do not self-generate *ex nihilo*, and here surely the synchronism with the linguistic assimilation of the so-called 'Anglo-Normans' into native English-speakers by the turn of the century cannot be simply coincidental. My contention is that it is not the culture that changes, but simply that another medium of linguistic expression becomes available. Instead of looking for English patrons of early Middle English literature, why should we not look for patrons *tout court*? Instead of posing the patronage question in terms of nationality, one could just as easily pose it in terms of languages, more specifically in terms of mother-tongues and bilingualism. People whose grandparents had listened to Wace's *Brut* in French in the 1150s could, by 1210, have been natural listeners to Laȝamon's Middle English version of it; children of parents brought up in the 1180s on a French diet of the *Horn* and *Alexander* romances could be perfectly natural consumers of the same narratives in English once English had become their natural mother-tongue. And not only listeners and consumers, but of course patrons as well – commissioning works in either (or both?) of two languages, depending no doubt on different contexts of reception.[88] Exactly how these contexts were constituted socially remains unknown, but let us not forget that the Anglo-Norman nobility was never a narrow aristocratic élite in the sense that its French counterpart was. The Insular Normans never disdained intermarriage with the natives, and, if Richard FitzNeal's explicit testimony is anything to go by, the free-born English and Normans were already fully assimilated by as early as the 1170s.[89] Since it was not apparently possible to tell which was which (FitzNeal's *ipsissima verba*), we can conclude that they were, to his mind at least, already socially and, therefore (it follows), linguistically integrated.

This neat image of cultural coexistence masks, of course, one absolutely crucial difference, namely that the Norman descendants had – and were long to continue to have – in addition to their by now native English mother-tongue, a command of another, and extremely powerful, acquired language, Anglo-Norman French. The social, political, administrative and other privileges which this second language gave them are as self-evident to us today as they were to certain contemporaries, whose resentment is well documented, especially from the 14th century onwards. But the fact that such resentment surfaces in literary texts is no reason for us to polarise literary production in medieval England into two hermetically separate and socially divided worlds. And to talk of Middle English literature, and romance in particular, as a vehicle by which (and I here paraphrase an anonymous colleague) 'a lower-class audience of social aspirants, an emergent

[87] M. B. Parkes, 'On the presumed date . . . of the MS of *Orrmulum*' in *Five Hundred Years of Words and Sounds: a Festschrift for Eric Dobson*, ed. E. G. Stanley & D. Gray, Cambridge 1983, 115–27.

[88] See, for example, Carol Fewster's analysis of the ancestral appropriation by the earls of Warwick of the Anglo-Norman romance *Gui de Warewic*, *Traditionality and Genre in Middle English Romance*, Woodbridge 1987, 104–28. Cf. also Emma Mason, 'Legends of the Beauchamps' ancestors: the use of baronial propaganda in medieval England', *JMH* x, 1984, 25–40, also 'Fact and fiction in the English crusading tradition: the earls of Warwick', *ibidem* xiv, 1988, 81–95.

[89] 'Sic permixtae sunt nationes ut vix decerni possit hodie – de liberis loquor – quis Anglicus quis Normannus sit genere': *Dialogus de Scaccario*, ed. C. Johnson, rev. F. E. L. Carter & D. E. Greenway, Oxford 1983, 53. The context of this statement is the Presentment of Englishry (cf. G. Garnett, '*Franci et Angli*: the legal distinction between peoples after the Conquest', *ante* viii, 1985, 109–37).

bourgeoisie, attempted to emulate their social betters' is, in my view, quite unten-able. Literature in French inevitably carried with it a cachet of superiority, if only by virtue of its identification with the language of the royal court and the mon-arch himself (up to the accession of Henry IV), not to mention its cultural internationalism. Anglo-Norman literature was, by its nature, class-exclusive; literature in English, by comparison, was class-inclusive in that it was accessible to a wider social stratum comprising both monolingual and bilingual Anglo-phones. The increasingly anachronistic minority who chose to perpetuate their social and ancestral separateness *via* Anglo-Norman French, as a language of record and instruction as well as of literature, did so not from without, as foreign-ers, but from within English culture. They had been part of this culture for generations, just as Medieval Latin authors had always been part of their particu-lar national cultures, despite opting to write in a minority, albeit international, language of learning. Were John of Salisbury and Matthew Paris not English, Geoffrey of Monmouth, Walter Map and Gerald of Barri not Anglo-Welsh, and do their achievements not belong as much to English/British literature as any work written in the English vernacular? And is the same not true of Anglo-Norman writers?

Does this mean, then, that post-Conquest English literature does not begin where our texts books tell us it does, that is at the start of the thirteenth century? Only if one's defining criteria narrowly equate nationality with monolingualism can this time-honoured convention stand. At stake here is something more im-portant than mere taxonomy; it is our collective critical perception of twelfth- and thirteenth-century culture on these islands. Its pluri-lingualism was one of its greatest distinguishing characteristics, and to picture bi- or tri-lingualism cutting the country or society up into two or even three antagonistic camps is to fail to see the cultural wood for the linguistic trees. What we are dealing with (to change metaphors) is a cultural spectrum; not clearly delineated or successive units in confrontation or competition along social lines, but a continuum deriving cohe-sion from its diversity and from the many different possibilities of symbiosis which it afforded. We are talking, in other words, cultural process.

Just as the Eadwine Psalter could be said to embody the initial phase of this process culminating in the 1150s, so it could be argued that the trilingual Gower stands as the exemplification of its literary maturity in the 1390s. Neat though such a picture might be, however, it may be more synthetic than real, for the uncomfortable truth is that Gower's French was more Continental than it was Insular.[90] Though Anglo-Norman must always have acted as a channel of literary communication with the Continent, there had come a time, after the loss of Normandy and with the changing political complexions of Henry III's reign, when what Elizabeth Salter termed the English obsession with the Continent[91] opened the way for a new order of French influences on Insular society. This heralded not so much the close of the Anglo-Norman era as its emergence into a new phase, a more complex stage in the larger-scale evolution of Anglo-French cultural relations.

---

[90] G. C. Macaulay, *The Collected Works of John Gower: The French Works*, Oxford 1899, xvi.
[91] E. Salter, *English and International: Studies in the literature, art and patronage of medieval England*, ed. D. Pearsall & N. Zeeman, Cambridge U.P. 1988, part i.

THE EXPANSION OF THE POWER AND INFLUENCE OF THE COUNTS OF BOULOGNE UNDER EUSTACE II

Heather J. Tanner

Traditionally the counts of Boulogne have been portrayed as loyal followers of the Flemish counts, and therefore relatively unimportant in the political machinations of the northern French territorial princes. The careers of the later tenth- and early eleventh-century Boulonnais counts – Arnulf I (962–c.971), Arnulf II (c.971–c.990) and Baldwin I (c.990–1024) – substantiates the purely local scope of the their activities. However, the relationship between the Flemish and Boulonnais counts was not that of powerful lord and amenable vassal. The counts of Boulogne consistently sought to maintain their independence and to increase their own power. At times the pursuit of these goals led the Boulonnais counts to unite their interests with those of the Flemish counts and at others to pursue opposing goals. Their ability to do so was founded in their deft creation and maintenance of alliances. The careers of Eustace I and especially that of his son Eustace II reveal the vigorous expansion of their power and influence in the tumultuous political climate of the eleventh century.

During the minority of Baldwin IV of Flanders (988–c.995) the Boulonnais counts and other local lords freed themselves from Flemish suzerainty and functioned as independent lords.[1] On attaining his majority in 995, Baldwin IV began to reverse this trend by eliminating independent control of castles and concurrently expanding the borders of Flanders.[2] In the period before 1023, Baldwin pushed both southward into the Ternois and eastward into the Cambresis. This expansion brought the counts of Flanders into conflict with Count Baldwin I of Boulogne and his younger brother, Count Arnulf III of Ternois.[3] Arnulf bore the brunt of Baldwin IV's aggression since his county lay in the Flemish count's path to the Cambresis. Arnulf III died in 1019, probably during Baldwin IV's siege of St Omer. P. Feuchere has suggested that Baldwin I, Arnulf's brother and heir, sought to push back this Flemish incursion with the aid of King Robert the Pious. But this stratagem met with only limited success.[4] In addition to warfare, the

---

I would like to thank Dr C. Warren Hollister, Dr Sharon A. Farmer, the members of Dr Hollister's 1990–91 seminar, and the participants of the 1991 Battle Conference, whose helpful comments and criticisms have made this a better work than it began.
[1] Jan Dhondt, *Les Origines de la Flandre et de l'Artois*, Arras 1944, 50–4; P. Feuchère, 'Les Origines du Comté de Saint-Pol, *Revue du Nord* xxxv, 1953, 128. For example, the incastellation of Lens in 975, Bethune, c.995, and Aubigny, Chacque, and Lillers c.1000.
[2] For a discussion of Baldwin IV's career see F. L. Ganshof, *La Flandre Sous Les Premiers Comtes*, Brussels 1949, 32–6.
[3] For a discussion of Baldwin's activities during this period see Dhondt, 56.
[4] Feuchère, 128. Baldwin kept St Omer and apparently some of northern Ternois, but St Pol remained an autonomous county under the governance of a direct vassal of the count of Boulogne, the first of whom was Count Roger (1023–1067).

GENEALOGY I   BOULOGNE

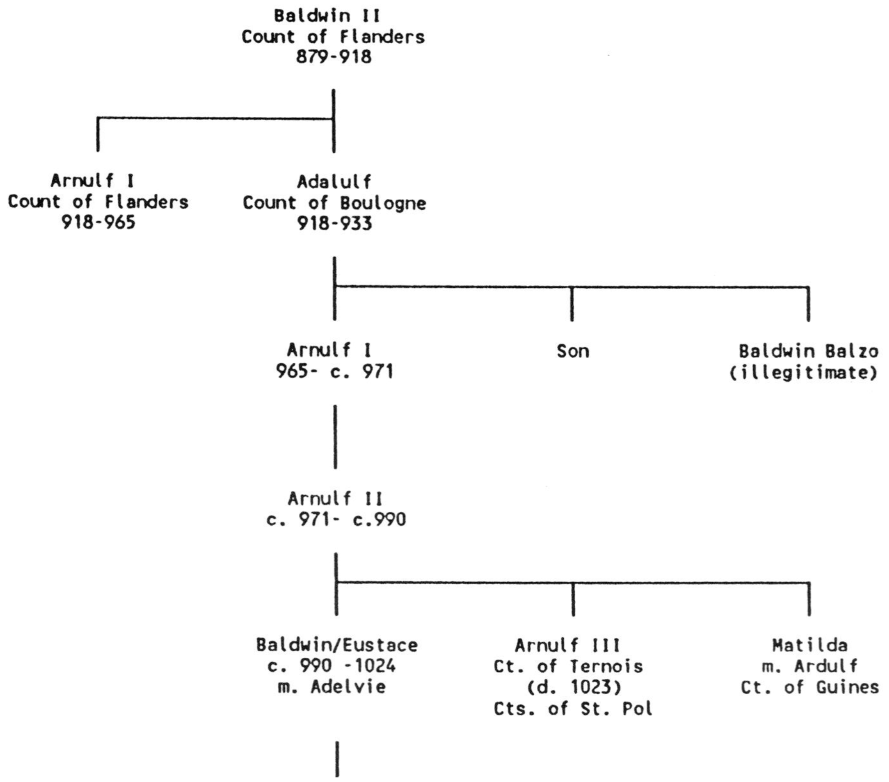

Baldwin II
Count of Flanders
879-918

Arnulf I
Count of Flanders
918-965

Adalulf
Count of Boulogne
918-933

Arnulf I
965- c. 971

Son

Baldwin Balzo
(illegitimate)

Arnulf II
c. 971- c.990

Baldwin/Eustace
c. 990 -1024
m. Adelvie

Arnulf III
Ct. of Ternois
(d. 1023)
Cts. of St. Pol

Matilda
m. Ardulf
Ct. of Guines

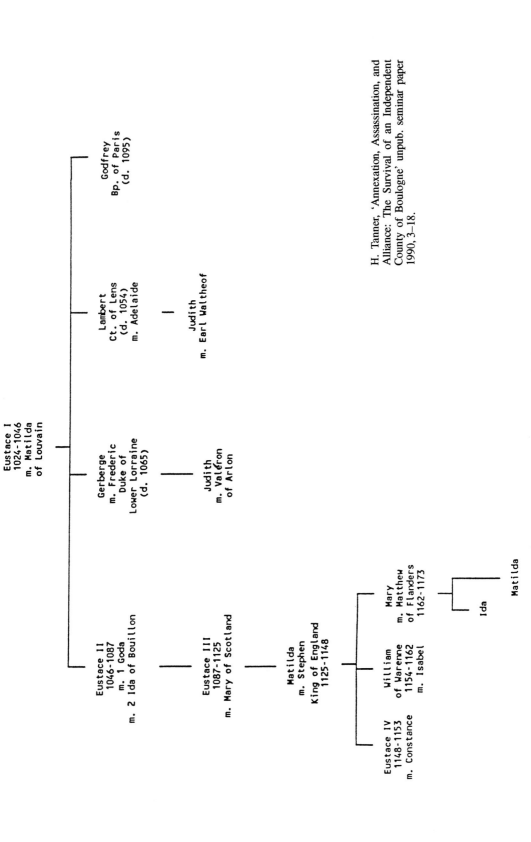

Eustace I
1024-1046
m. Matilda
of Louvain

Godfrey
Bp. of Paris
(d. 1095)

Lambert
Ct. of Lens
(d. 1054)
m. Adelaide

Judith
m. Earl Waltheof

Gerberge
m. Frederic
Duke of
Lower Lorraine
(d. 1065)

Judith
m. Valéron
of Arlon

Eustace II
1046-1087
m. 1 Goda
m. 2 Ida of Bouillon

Eustace III
1087-1125
m. Mary of Scotland

Matilda
m. Stephen
King of England
1125-1148

Mary
m. Matthew
of Flanders
1162-1173

William
of Warenne
1154-1162
m. Isabel

Eustace IV
1148-1153
m. Constance

Ida

Matilda

H. Tanner, 'Annexation, Assassination, and Alliance: The Survival of an Independent County of Boulogne' unpub. seminar paper 1990, 3–18.

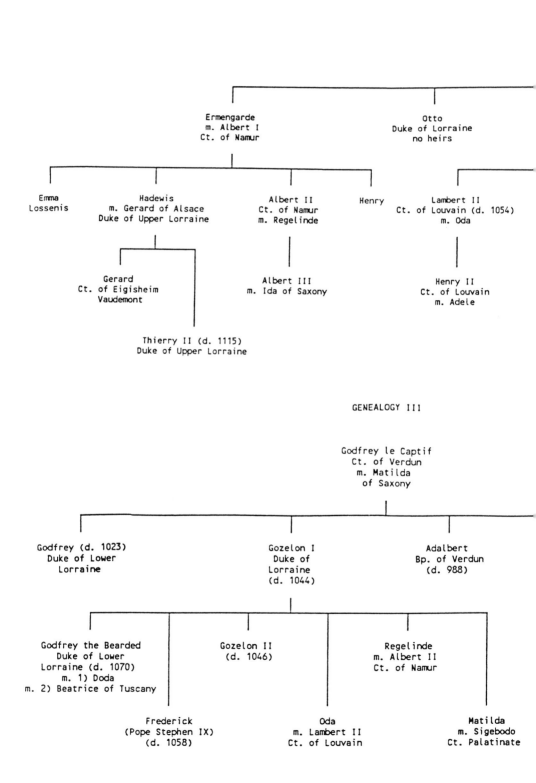

Ermengarde
m. Albert I
Ct. of Namur

Otto
Duke of Lorraine
no heirs

Emma
Lossenis

Hadewis
m. Gerard of Alsace
Duke of Upper Lorraine

Albert II
Ct. of Namur
m. Regelinde

Henry

Lambert II
Ct. of Louvain (d. 1054)
m. Oda

Gerard
Ct. of Eigisheim
Vaudemont

Albert III
m. Ida of Saxony

Henry II
Ct. of Louvain
m. Adele

Thierry II (d. 1115)
Duke of Upper Lorraine

GENEALOGY III

Godfrey le Captif
Ct. of Verdun
m. Matilda
of Saxony

Godfrey (d. 1023)
Duke of Lower
Lorraine

Gozelon I
Duke of
Lorraine
(d. 1044)

Adalbert
Bp. of Verdun
(d. 988)

Godfrey the Bearded
Duke of Lower
Lorraine (d. 1070)
m. 1) Doda
m. 2) Beatrice of Tuscany

Gozelon II
(d. 1046)

Regelinde
m. Albert II
Ct. of Namur

Frederick
(Pope Stephen IX)
(d. 1058)

Oda
m. Lambert II
Ct. of Louvain

Matilda
m. Sigebodo
Ct. Palatinate

LOUVAIN & NAMUR

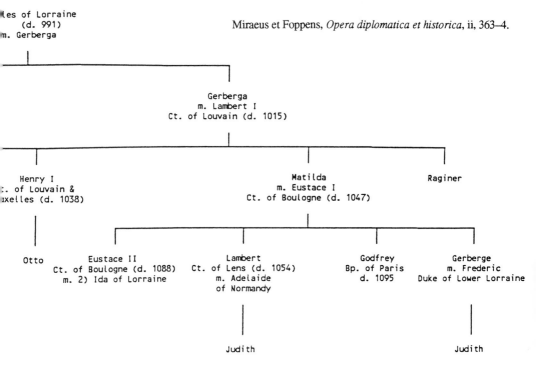

les of Lorraine
(d. 991)
m. Gerberga

Miraeus et Foppens, *Opera diplomatica et historica*, ii, 363–4.

Gerberga
m. Lambert I
Ct. of Louvain (d. 1015)

Henry I
:. of Louvain &
uxelles (d. 1038)

Matilda
m. Eustace I
Ct. of Boulogne (d. 1047)

Raginer

Otto

Eustace II
Ct. of Boulogne (d. 1088)
m. 2) Ida of Lorraine

Lambert
Ct. of Lens (d. 1054)
m. Adelaide
of Normandy

Godfrey
Bp. of Paris
d. 1095

Gerberge
m. Frederic
Duke of Lower Lorraine

Judith

Judith

ARDENNE–VERDUN

Michel Parisse, 'Genealogie de la Maison d'Ardenne' *Publications de la Section
Historique de l'Institut Grand-Ducal de Luxembourg* xcv, 1981, 41.

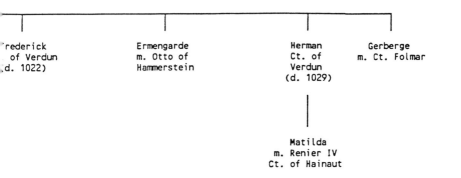

rederick
of Verdun
(d. 1022)

Ermengarde
m. Otto of
Hammerstein

Herman
Ct. of
Verdun
(d. 1029)

Gerberge
m. Ct. Folmar

Matilda
m. Renier IV
Ct. of Hainaut

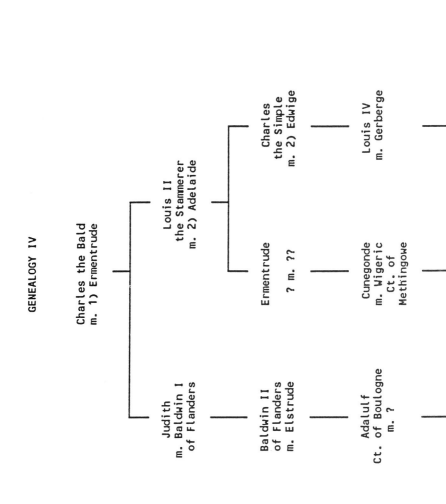

GENEALOGY IV

Charles the Bald
m. 1) Ermentrude

Judith
m. Baldwin I
of Flanders

Louis II
the Stammerer
m. 2) Adelaide

Baldwin II
of Flanders
m. Elstrude

Ermentrude
? m. ??

Charles
the Simple
m. 2) Edwige

Adalulf
Ct. of Boulogne
m. ?

Cunegonde
m. Wigeric
Ct. of
Methingowe

Louis IV
m. Gerberge

Arnulf I
m. ?

Gozelon
m. Uda

Charles
of Lorraine

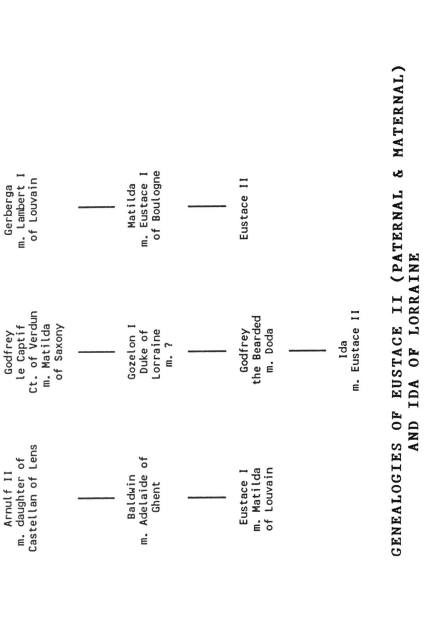

GENEALOGIES OF EUSTACE II (PATERNAL & MATERNAL) AND IDA OF LORRAINE

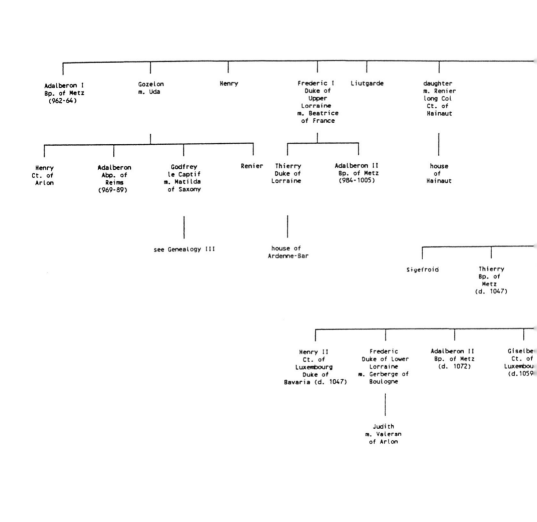

Adalberon I
Bp. of Metz
(962-64)

Gozelon
m. Uda

Henry

Frederic I
Duke of
Upper
Lorraine
m. Beatrice
of France

Liutgarde

daughter
m. Renier
long Col
Ct. of
Hainaut

Henry
Ct. of
Arlon

Adalberon
Abp. of
Reims
(969-89)

Godfrey
le Captif
m. Matilda
of Saxony

Renier

Thierry
Duke of
Lorraine

Adalberon II
Bp. of Metz
(984-1005)

house
of
Hainaut

see Genealogy III

house of
Ardenne-Bar

Sigefroid

Thierry
Bp. of
Metz
(d. 1047)

Henry II
Ct. of
Luxembourg
Duke of
Bavaria (d. 1047)

Frederic
Duke of Lower
Lorraine
m. Gerberge of
Boulogne

Adalberon II
Bp. of Metz
(d. 1072)

Giselbe
Ct. of
Luxembou
(d.1059

Judith
m. Valeran
of Arlon

ARDENNE-LUXEMBOURG

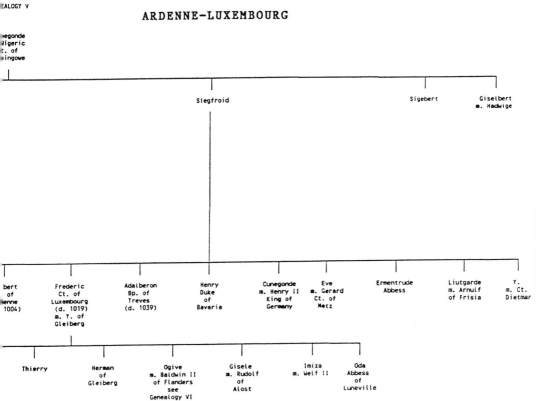

Michel Parisse, 'Genealogie de la Maison d'Ardenne' *Publications de la Section Historique de l'Institut Grand-Ducal de Luxembourg* xcv, 1981, 42.

FLANDERS

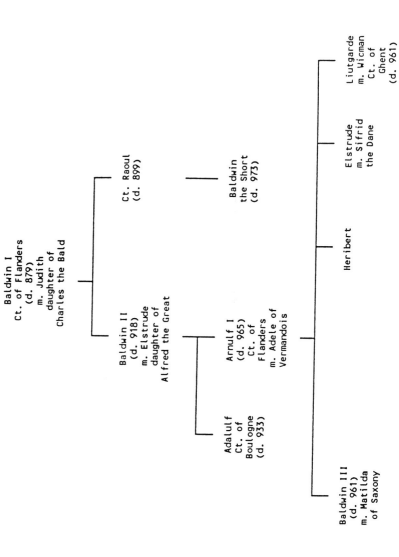

Baldwin I
Ct. of Flanders
(d. 879)
m. Judith
daughter of
Charles the Bald

Ct. Raoul
(d. 899)

Baldwin II
(d. 918)
m. Elstrude
daughter of
Alfred the Great

Adalulf
Ct. of
Boulogne
(d. 933)

Arnulf I
(d. 965)
Ct. of
Flanders
m. Adele of
Vermandois

Baldwin
the Short
(d. 973)

Baldwin III
(d. 961)
m. Matilda
of Saxony

Heribert

Elstrude
m. Sifrid
the Dane

Liutgarde
m. Wicman
Ct. of
Ghent
(d. 961)

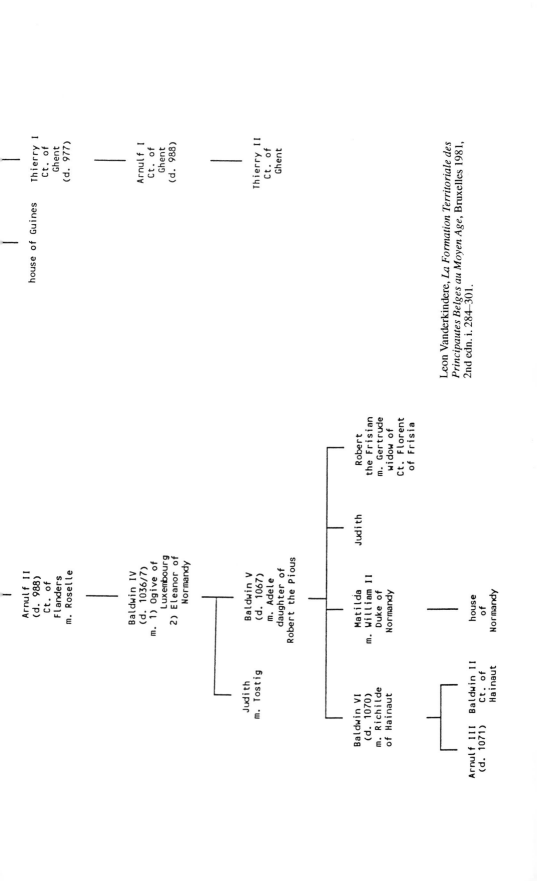

house of Guines

Thierry I
Ct. of
Ghent
(d. 977)

Arnulf I
Ct. of
Ghent
(d. 988)

Thierry II
Ct. of
Ghent

Arnulf II
(d. 988)
Ct. of
Flanders
m. Roselle

Baldwin IV
(d. 1036/7)
m. 1) Ogive of
Luxembourg
2) Eleanor of
Normandy

Judith
m. Tostig

Baldwin V
(d. 1067)
m. Adele
daughter of
Robert the Pious

Baldwin VI
(d. 1070)
m. Richilde
of Hainaut

Arnulf III   Baldwin II
(d. 1071)   Ct. of
              Hainaut

Matilda
m. William II
Duke of
Normandy

house
of
Normandy

Judith

Robert
the Frisian
m. Gertrude
widow of
Ct. Florent
of Frisia

Leon Vanderkindere, *La Formation Territoriale des
Principautes Belges au Moyen Age*, Bruxelles 1981,
2nd edn. i. 284–301.

Boulonnais counts sought to check and counterbalance growing Flemish power through marriages with the children of Flemish border lords and Lotharingian nobles.[5] These alliances provided the foundation for the Boulonnais counts' move from the periphery to the center of political events in northern France, Lorraine, and England during the eleventh century.

As part of their effort to halt Flemish expansion into Lorraine, Eustace I, who succeeded Baldwin I as count of Boulogne in 1024, married Matilda, daughter of Count Lambert I of Louvain, himself a political foe of the Flemish Count Baldwin IV. Lambert I, with several other Lotharingian lords, was involved in a fierce struggle to diminish the effectiveness of imperial overlordship in Lorraine, and through this marriage he hoped to mitigate the effects of an alliance that Baldwin IV had recently concluded with Emperor Henry II.[6] Although Lambert of Louvain's rebellion against the Emperor failed, Eustace I seems to have remained interested in Lotharingian alliances. He allied himself to the house of Ardenne-Luxembourg through the marriage of his daughter Gerberge to Frederic, son of Count Frederic of Luxembourg and later duke of Lower Lorraine (1046–1065). Eustace's brothers-in-law, Henry and Lambert II, succeeded their father, Lambert I, as counts of Louvain, and both were on friendly terms with Duke Gozelon I of Lorraine (1023–1044).[7] Gozelon himself was also at odds with Baldwin IV of Flanders, which may have fostered good relations with Eustace I of Boulogne.[8]

Although Eustace I never reconciled with Baldwin IV, he did establish peaceful relations with Baldwin's son and heir, Baldwin V, who succeeded to the Flemish countship in 1037. Their peaceful relationship was probably rooted in Eustace's aid of Baldwin V's rebellion against his father in 1031. But Eustace did not abandon his independence with this reconciliation; he secured his increased influence in the region through a series of southern alliances. The marriage of his eldest son, Eustace II, to Goda, widow of Dreux of the Vexin, and the marriage of his half-sister to Count William of Arques expanded his political alliances into northern Normandy.[9] Later, Eustace II's marriage to Goda also helped establish an alliance with Goda's brother, Edward the Confessor. Family ties, via Eustace I's mother, Adelvie, and her daughter by her second husband, Count Enguerrand I of Ponthieu, also fostered an alliance with Enguerrand II.

In addition to these southern alliances, Eustace I had maintained control over his own counties of Boulogne and Lens, and influence in the Ternois through the loyal vassalage of Roger of St Pol. Eustace I's alliances placed his son and heir,

---

[5] See Genealogy 1. Since 965, the Boulonnais counts had relied on strategic marriage alliances to strengthen their power within their region and to maintain their independence in the face of Flemish expansion. At first, these alliances were primarily among the local Picard lords. The eleventh-century Boulonnais counts continued this policy of strategic marriages, but on a more ambitious scale from the reign of Baldwin of Boulogne (c.990–1024).

[6] Regnier IV of Hainaut was Lambert's brother and main ally. See Henri Pirenne, *Histoire de Belgique*, Bruxelles 1929, 61–96, 105–19, for a history of Lorraine in the tenth and eleventh centuries.

[7] Gozelon I developed strong ties with the Lotharingian nobility, who had a tradition of rebelling against imperial authority. Gozelon married his daughter, Oda, to Lambert II of Louvain and his daughter, Regelinde, to Count Albert II of Namur.

[8] In 1033, Gozelon and Baldwin IV clashed over the castle at Eaname and Baldwin's expansion into this region. See Pirenne, 108.

[9] William of Arques' wife was the daughter of Eustace's mother, Adelvie, and her second husband, Enguerrand I, of Ponthieu.

Eustace II, in a strong position with allies in Ponthieu, Arques, the Vexin, England, and Louvain. Eustace II built on these alliances, maintained his independence from Flanders and substantially increased the territory under Boulonnais control, thereby expanding his own and his successors' power.

On Eustace I's death in 1047, his counties were divided between his two sons. Eustace II received Boulogne, and his younger brother, Lambert, received Lens. Like his father, Eustace II continued his involvement in Lorraine. He was in attendance, with Baldwin V and Lambert, at the court of Henry III of Germany and witnessed Henry's confirmation of a gift to St Medard in 1047.[10] Shortly afterwards both Eustace II and Baldwin V joined in the rebellion of Godfrey the Bearded, who sought to reunite the duchies of Upper and Lower Lorraine under his control.[11]

The alliance between Eustace and Godfrey was sealed with Eustace's marriage to Godfrey's daughter Ida.[12] Henry's response to this rebellion reveals the strength of the threat to his authority. Not only did Henry gather a large army and invade the Lorraine but he created alliances with the English and Danish kings.[13] Henry also appears to have mobilized ecclesiastical support to undermine the coalition; in 1049 Leo IX excommunicated Eustace for incest and prohibited William the Conqueror's marriage to Baldwin V's daughter, also on the basis of incest.[14]

---

[10] D. Bouquet, *Recueil des Historiens de France*, Paris 1878, xi, 582–3. This charter was issued, most probably, before Godfrey the Bearded, Duke of Lower Lorraine began his second rebellion against Henry III, since Baldwin, abruptly reversing his longstanding allegiance to Henry, joined Godfrey's rebellion; Ganshof, 35–7. Baldwin V had sent his son, Baldwin, to be educated at Henry III's court and had gained the march of Anvers in 1045 or 1046 for his son. Godfrey's successes (or perhaps the opportunity to grab more territory on his eastern borders) seem to have convinced Baldwin V to join his coalition and to abandon his peaceful alliance with Henry III.

[11] Henry, prompted by a desire to protect his own influence in the area, split Lorraine into two duchies on the death of Duke Gozelon I in 1044. Godfrey, Gozelon's eldest son, was given Upper Lorraine and his younger brother, Gozelon II, received Lower Lorraine. Gozelon II's death without heirs in 1047 and Henry's appointment of Frederic of Luxembourg as duke of Lower Lorraine, prompted Godfrey's second rebellion.

[12] Eustace's role in Godfrey's first rebellion of 1044–45 is unknown. Godfrey was supported by the counts of Hainaut, Louvain, Namur, and Holland in 1044–45. Eustace had familial ties to the counts of Louvain and indirectly to Namur, and was a neighbor of the counts of Hainaut. Therefore it is possible that he joined Godfrey in his attempt to win back all of Lorraine. However, Baldwin V's support of the emperor and Eustace's good relationship with Baldwin may have led him to remain neutral or to fight for the emperor. See Edmund Rigaux, 'Recherches sur les premiers comtes de Boulogne' *Bulletins de la Société Académique de l'Arrondissement de Boulogne-sur-Mer* 5, 1894, 166–70, and Frank Barlow, *Edward the Confessor*, Berkeley 1970, 308 for a discussion of the probable date of Eustace's marriage which had taken place by 1049. Central to the argument of both is the excommunication of Eustace in 1049 at the Council of Reims for marrying within the prohibited degrees.

[13] Eustace II and his former brother-in-law, Edward the Confessor, continued their friendly relationship, since each sought to limit Flemish power. See Barlow, 97–9. Barlow argues that Edward's foreign policy was a defensive one against the Danes who received aid from both Flanders and Normandy. Edward therefore cultivated the friendship of the counts of Boulogne, Ponthieu and the Vexin, whose counties lay between Normandy and Flanders. Although Eustace's other kinship ties placed him in Godfrey's coalition, Edward was anti-Flemish not anti-Boulonnais.

[14] In 1049, Leo IX excommunicated both Eustace and Count Enguerrand II of Ponthieu for incest; Bouquet, xi, 523. See Genealogy IV. Eustace and Ida appear to have only barely fallen within the prohibited degrees. The closest blood relative of both Ida and Eustace was Louis II the Stammerer. Briefly, Eustace II's mother, Matilda of Louvain, was the daughter of Lambert I of Louvain and

Although initially successful, the rebellion began to falter in 1049 with Henry III's defeat of Godfrey's ally, the Count of Holland.[15] Shortly after this battle, Godfrey submitted to Henry III, who incarcerated him.[16] Baldwin V, however, remained at war with Henry.[17] Godfrey's defeat led to a parting of the ways for Baldwin and Eustace. For it appears that Eustace joined his father-in-law, Godfrey, in the peace negotiations with Henry III while Eustace's brother, Lambert, remained in Baldwin's camp.[18]

There are several indirect pieces of evidence which suggest that the period of 1049–1056 was one of estrangement between the Flemish and Boulonnais counts. First, the German emperor devastated southern Flanders in 1050 and, until his death in 1056, continued his war with Baldwin V, but Eustace is not mentioned in any of the accounts of these years. Second, Eustace does not attest any of Baldwin's charters between 1049 and 1056. Third, as I will discuss below, the three marriage alliances that Baldwin made in 1051 were at odds with Eustace's interests. And finally, in 1055 at Maestricht, Eustace and Henry III witnessed Godfrey the Bearded's foundation charter of Longliers priory.[19]

In response to Henry III's continued aggression, Baldwin shored up his position through three marriage alliances: the first was the marriage of his daughter, Matilda, to Duke William II of Normandy; the second was the marriage of his eldest son, Baldwin, to Richilde, widow of Count Herman of Hainaut; and the third was between his sister, Judith, and Tostig, son of Earl Godwin of England.[20]

Gerberge, daughter of Charles of Lorraine, whose grandfather was Louis II the Stammerer. Thus, Eustace was related within six degrees to Louis. Eustace's wife, Ida, was the daughter of Doda and Godfrey the Bearded of Lower Lorraine. Godfrey was the son of Gozelon I, whose paternal great-grandmother, Cunegonde, was also a descendant of Louis II the Stammerer. Therefore, Ida was related within nine degrees to Louis. The church only prohibited marriage within seven degrees, see Duby, *The Knight, the Lady, and the Priest: The Making of Modern Marriage in Medieval France*, New York 1983, 35. Eustace and Ida may have been more closely related, but the identities of the wives of Adalulf and Arnulf I of Boulogne, of Gozelon I's wife, and the unknown family of Doda, wife of Godfrey the Bearded, does not allow us to know how closely.

[15] Dhondt, 75.

[16] J. C. Andressohn, *The Ancestry and Life of Godfrey of Bouillon*, Bloomington, Ind., 1947, 12. Godfrey was placed in the charge of the archbishop of Trèves. In early 1051 he was released and given a small fief held of the archbishop of Cologne.

[17] The war between Baldwin and Henry was briefly interrupted with two peace treaties in 1049 and 1050. See Leon Vanderkindere, *La Formation Territoriale des Principautés Belges*, Bruxelles 1981, 2nd edn, i, 108–11. Henry and Baldwin were at war continuously after 1051, when Baldwin married his son, Baldwin, to Richilde, Count Herman of Hainaut's widow. Also in 1051, Godfrey the Bearded, soon after his release from prison, journeyed south and married Beatrice, widow of Boniface of Montferrat, marquis of Tuscany. Henry III immediately gathered an army and invaded southern Italy. Godfrey fled north to Cologne. Godfrey made a separate peace with Henry which was in effect by 1055; see Andressohn, 13.

[18] Lambert died fighting for Baldwin at Lille in 1054; Bouquet, xi, 582.

[19] Miraeus et Foppens, *Opera diplomatica et historica*, Louvain 1743, iv, 183–4.

[20] William II was beginning to make his name as a warrior during this period and therefore would appear to be a useful ally. The county of Hainaut provides access into southern Flanders, therefore Baldwin would be very concerned to secure the goodwill of its count. Baldwin had already established an alliance with Count Herman, and further secured his position with the marriage of his son, to Herman's widow, Richilde. The marriage alliance, which took place in October of 1050, with the house of Godwin was quite astute since Godwin and his family were extraordinarily powerful and Baldwin probably hoped that Earl Godwin and his sons, Tostig and Harold, would advocate an alliance with Flanders to Edward the Confessor. Baldwin and Godwin both enjoyed good relations with the Danes. See Barlow, 108, and *Vita Eadwardi*, 24–5.

Each of these marriages threatened Eustace's influence and power. Although Duke William and Eustace had both been allies of Godfrey, Eustace was aligned with Count William of Arques, the duke's uncle and rival. Thus Duke William's growing power threatened Eustace's allies' and his own influence to the south of Boulogne. The Hainaut alliance also hemmed Eustace in by strengthening the Flemish count's control over the Ternois. The alliance with Godwin undermined the utility and effectiveness of Eustace's alliance with King Edward. Eustace had used the English alliance, in conjunction with his own and Edward's ties to the counts of Ponthieu and the Vexin, as a counterweight in his efforts to remain independent of growing Flemish power. Godwin and his sons were also at odds with Eustace's step-son Ralf, earl of Hereford, and they were generally hostile to Norman and French influence at Edward's court. The tensions between Eustace and the Godwin clan are clearly illustrated in the 1051 incident at Dover.

During a visit to King Edward, Eustace and his men were involved in a skirmish with the men of Dover and several men on both sides were killed.[21] Edward, at Eustace's request, ordered the punishment of the Dover citizens, and when Earl Godwin refused to carry out this command, Edward exiled Godwin and his family. Outlawed, Godwin, his wife, and his son, Tostig, went to Baldwin V's court, while his other sons went to Ireland, and his daughter, Edward's wife, Queen Edith, was placed in a nunnery.

Several scholars have analyzed this incident in an effort to understand the swift fall of Godwin and his sons, who had been the most powerful family in the kingdom until that point, and who were to resume that power in 1052. Both Bertie Wilkinson and Frank Barlow have argued that the Dover incident was only the immediate cause of the falling out between Edward and the Godwin family.[22] Wilkinson argues that the conflict represented Earl Godwin's attempt to restore his authority which had been undermined through the recent failures of his ecclesiastical patronage.[23] Building on Wilkinson's analysis, Barlow also stresses the importance of the mid-Lenten council which was deliberating on a treaty with Normandy to mitigate the possible negative effects of the marriage between William II and Matilda of Flanders. Barlow argues that Godwin may have been advocating a purely Flemish alliance, and that the marriage of his son, Tostig, to Baldwin's sister, Judith, was a reflection of this goal.[24] Both R. Allen Brown and Miles Campbell have also argued that the crisis revolved around the question of

---

[21] The details and chronology of this incident are difficult to state with certainty, primarily because there are three different versions of the event: the *Vita Eadwardi* and the Anglo-Saxon Chronicle versions D and E. *ASC*, i, 116–22; *Vita Eadwardi*, 20–3. Version D is unsympathetic to Godwin and his family, and therefore depicts Eustace as the victim and Godwin as the unfaithful lord. Version E is quite sympathetic to Godwin, portraying him as a victim of evil foreign counsel, while casting Eustace and his men in the role of deliberate aggressors, who put on their armor even before they enter Dover. The *Vita* on the other hand does not mention the Dover incident at all, and reports the ousting of Godwin and his family as the result of a nefarious plot of Archbishop Robert of Jumièges.
[22] Bertie Wilkinson, 'Freemen and the Crisis of 1051' *Bulletin of the John Rylands Library* xxxiv, 1938, 368–87. Barlow, 104–14.
[23] Wilkinson, 373. Godwin's patronage had been checked on two occasions: the first in the appointment of Robert of Jumièges to the archbishopric of Canterbury over his candidate Aelfric, a kinsman, and the second in the contest between Godwin and Robert over Robert's successor to the bishopric of London.
[24] Barlow, 108–9.

an Anglo-Norman alliance and the decision of the witan to name William of Normandy as Edward's heir.[25]

Certainly the tensions between Edward and Godwin were a reflection of their conflicts over foreign alliances, succession concerns, and Norman/French influence at court. What has been largely overlooked in previous analyses is the Boulonnais count's interest in English-continental relations which was founded in the alliance that he and Edward had created.[26] Edward and the counts of Boulogne, Ponthieu, and Vexin had fostered an alliance which provided Edward with a counter-measure against Flemish aid to his Scandinavian enemies and his allies with a counter-weight to maintain their independence from Flanders. Eustace, Enguerrand II of Ponthieu, and Eustace's step-son, Walter of Vexin, were thus vitally concerned with the response of Edward and his nobility to the Norman-Flemish alliance, and in any resulting changes in their relations with England. Thus, the Dover incident was not just the catalyst which precipitated Godwin's defense of his own power but a reflection of Eustace's attempt to preserve his alliance with Edward against Flanders and maintain Boulonnais power in France. Eustace and his allies were also worried about the effects of this new alliance at home; William's marriage strengthened his own position within Normandy and provided him with the means to eliminate the independence of Eustace and his allies in a pincer movement from the north and south of their counties. Eustace's concerns would have been magnified by his own estrangement from the Flemish count.

While his most immediate concern in 1051 was the possible consequences of William of Normandy's marriage, Eustace had other previous connections which fostered his anti-Godwin position – the death of Alfred aethling and his men in 1036 and the newly developed feud between his step-son, Earl Ralf, and Swein,

---

[25] R. Allen Brown, *The Normans and the Norman Conquest*, 2nd edn, Woodbridge 1985, 102–7. Miles Campbell, 'The Anti-Norman Reaction in England in 1052' *Mediaeval Studies*, 38, 1976, 428–41. Brown also interprets Eustace's visit as an embassy from William to accept the witan's offer, p. 106. This I think is highly unlikely since the primary sources give no suggestion of a relationship between Eustace and Duke William. Furthermore, Eustace's ties to William of Arques and his support of Count William's rebellion in 1052 also suggest that Eustace was not a supporter of Duke William and therefore would not have been chosen as the duke's emissary.

[26] The sole exception is a hypothesis of Frank Barlow. He has suggested that Eustace might have had a more direct interest in English politics, based on the possibility that Eustace and Goda had a daughter, who, along with her heirs, would be in a position to inherit the English throne if Edward should die childless. Barlow, 307–8. Since this grandchild was a possible candidate for Edward's throne, Barlow suggests that Eustace's visit was motivated by this concern. The only evidence for this child is the reference to Eustace's 'nepos' in William of Poitiers' and Orderic Vitalis' account of Eustace's 1067 rebellion, who was captured after the attack on Dover failed; William of Poitiers, *Gesta Guillelmi*, 266; Orderic, ii, 206. Although there is a possibility that Eustace and Goda had a grandson of sufficient age in 1067 to be promoted as a candidate for the English throne, the identity of this *nepos* is probably Eustace's known bastard son Geoffrey. See *Regesta*, no. 202 in which William confirms the gift of land in Beddington (Surrey) made by Geoffrey, son of Count Eustace, on behalf of his wife Beatrice, with the consent of his father-in-law Geoffrey de Mandeville, to St Peter's and Abbot Vitalis. See J. H. Round, 'Pharamus of Boulogne' *Genealogist* n.s. xii, 1896, 145–51, for discussion of Geoffrey's parentage. It seems more likely that it was Geoffrey who was captured at Dover, since one of the meanings of *nepos* is descendant, and the euphemism *nepos* is often used to refer to bastards. The argument is further strengthened by the fact that Eustace had no known nephews and his grandson was not born until after 1103. See Genealogies I–III.

son of Godwin. Earl Godwin had been accused in 1036 and again in 1040 of being responsible for Alfred's death, and the death of those in Alfred's largely Boulonnais entourage. Godwin had cleared himself of the charges both times, but the issue was again raised in 1051, according to the author of Edward's *Vita*. The author relates that Robert of Jumièges 'revived' the rumors of Earl Godwin's complicity in Alfred's blinding and death, and Wilkinson suggests that this could help explain Edward's hostility to Godwin and his desire to do battle immediately at Gloucester.[27] The distrust aroused in Edward and Eustace by this rumor was probably compounded by Tostig's marriage to Judith of Flanders, since Flanders was the typical refuge of Edward's political rivals.[28]

In addition to Godwin's culpability in the death of Boulonnais knights, Godwin and his son Swein were at odds with Eustace's step-son, Earl Ralf of Hereford. Ralf had received some, if not most, of Swein's former earldom.[29] Swein, recently reinstated to some of his former lands, seems to have clashed with Ralf and his French enclave in Hereford. Ralf and his men, Osbern Pentecost and Hugh the castellan, were among the first to come to Gloucester after Edward had heard Eustace's complaint; a reflection of both Ralf's own concerns and his support of King Edward and Eustace. Godwin and his sons saw Ralf and his men as enemies.[30] Version D of the Anglo-Saxon chronicle specifically states that Godwin demanded the surrender of Eustace and the Frenchmen in the castle in 1051, while version E states that Godwin and his sons justified the calling up of their armies because of the injuries done to them and the king's men by the foreigners in Herefordshire.[31]

Although Edward was initially successful in eliminating Godwin's influence and a pro-Flemish alliance, Baldwin V un-did Eustace's work through his aid of Godwin's armed return to England in 1052.[32] The royal forces declined to fight Godwin and his sons, and all those who had 'falsely' accused the Godwin clan were outlawed, with the exception of Ralf.[33] The political ramifications of the

---

[27] Wilkinson, 382. *Vita Eadwardi*, 20, 22.

[28] Philip Grierson, 'The Relations between England and Flanders before the Norman Conquest', *TRHS* 4th series 23, 1941, 71–112 at 95–104.

[29] Barlow, 114. For alternative view of what constituted Ralf's earldom see Ann Williams, 'The King's Nephew: The Family and Career of Ralph, Earl of Hereford' in *Studies in Medieval History Presented to R. Allen Brown*, Woodbridge 1989, 329–39.

[30] Williams, 331; Ann Williams has suggested that there was no enmity between Ralf and Godwin's family since Ralf was not exiled with the other men who sided with Eustace in the 1051 conflict. While this interpretation is possible, it seems untenable in the light of Ralf's alliance with the enemies of Godwin and his sons during 1051 and his command of the army which opposed the return of Godwin and his family in 1052. Ralf's relationship with Edward could also explain why he was not exiled in 1052.

[31] *ASC*, 119, [E] 'The foreigners then had built a castle in Herefordshire in Earl Swein's province, and had inflicted every possible injury and insult upon the king's men in those parts . . .' [which is why Godwin and his sons had gathered their armies] 'intending to go to their royal lord and to all the councillors who were assembled with him, so that they should have the advice and support of the king and of all the councillors as to how they should avenge the insult to the king and to all the people.' *ASC*, 117, [D] 'ready to do battle against the king unless Eustace were surrendered and his men handed over to them, as well as the Frenchmen who were in the castle.'

[32] R. Allen Brown, *The Norman Conquest*, London 1984, 64; David Douglas, *William the Conqueror*, Berkeley 1964, 78. When Godwin and his sons returned in 1052, aided by Baldwin V and the Irish king, Ralf was one of the two commanders of the army and fleet raised against them.

[33] *ASC*, 122 ff.

1051 Dover incident were not limited to England. Edward's French allies in Boulogne, Ponthieu, and the Vexin also lost out in the rapid re-arrangement of political alliances in northern France.

After this defeat, Eustace and his southern allies attempted to bolster their position vis-à-vis Normandy and Flanders. Faced with Duke William's growing power, William of Arques, joined by his northern kinsmen and allies, rebelled against his nephew, Duke William II, in 1052.[34] Not surprisingly, Baldwin V and Eustace rallied to the aid of the opposing factions in the battles that followed. The rebellion ended in failure with Duke William's victory at Mortemer in February 1054.

Although there is no specific mention of Eustace's aid to any members of the coalition during the campaigns, there is an enigmatic reference in the chronicle of Alberic of Trois Fontaines to a war in Boulogne, which directly follows his report of the battle of Mortemer.[35] The juxtaposition of the two strongly suggests that Eustace was involved in the fighting and that William retaliated by invading Boulogne. This interpretation is buttressed by William of Arques' retirement to the Boulonnais court after his surrender to Duke William in the autumn of 1053.[36] Although the counts of Boulogne and the dukes of Normandy had never been particularly friendly, William's Flemish marriage transformed their relationship from wary neutrality to hostility.

In 1056, after a nine year hiatus, Eustace appears in two charters of Baldwin V. Although there is no evidence of overt hostility, Eustace and Baldwin had pursued different and conflicting policies in the period between 1049 and 1056. Baldwin's support of the Godwin faction in England – the marriage of Tostig to Judith and his support of Godwin's armed return to England in 1052 – and his provision of refuge to all of Edward's foes were clearly at odds with Eustace's strong ties to Edward and his clashes with Earl Godwin and his sons. The Flemish alliance with William II was in contrast to Eustace's alliances with Enguerrand II and William of Arques, and would have appeared quite threatening, especially after the failure of William of Arques' rebellion. In addition, 1056 marked a turning point in the solidification of Baldwin's increased power, for with the death of Henry III, Empress Agnes negotiated a peace with Baldwin which recognized his control of the eastern lands that he had won during his war with Henry.[37] The substantial increase in Baldwin's territory with the corresponding

---

[34] David Bates, *Normandy Before 1066*, London 1982, 75. This coalition was made up of Enguerrand II, Guy I of Ponthieu, Count Ralph IV of Amiens-Valois-Vexin, King Henry I, and Geoffrey Martel. Enguerrand's death at the battle of St Aubin-sur-Scie, prompted Henry I's invasion.

[35] Bouquet, xi, 356. 'Bellum fuisse apud Mare-mortuum in quibusdam Chronicis annotatur. Item Boloniae bellum, captio Gaufridi, mors Hildoini filii ejus.' Rigaux has identified the Geoffrey as the Count of Sens and suggests that Geoffrey may have come to aid his ally the castellan of Montreuil, whom according to the romance, *Chevalier au Cygne*, Eustace killed; Rigaux, 172. I do not know what role Geoffrey of Sens played at Mortemer; he may have been a member of Henry's army.

[36] Bouquet, xi, 40. 'Willelmus quoque non long post inedia affectus cum suis invitus castellum reddidit, et ipse a nativo solo in exilium discessit. Denique cum uxore sua, sorore scilicet Widonis Comitis Pontivi, Eustachium Boloniae Comitem expetiit; et in ejus familia victum et vestitum percipiens, usque ad morte suam extorris remansit.'

[37] Ganshof, 37–8. These territories were Zeeland, west of the eastern Escaut; Quatre Métiers; Brabant between the Escaut and Dendre; and the county of Hainaut because of Baldwin's son's marriage to Richilde.

expansion of Flemish power added to Eustace's worries.[38] The rapprochement between the two, which appears to have grown slowly between 1056 and 1063, was probably the result of Baldwin's consolidation of power over his newly won eastern territories and the setbacks which Eustace and his allies suffered between 1049 and 1054: Godfrey's failed rebellion of 1047–1049, the triumphant return of the Godwins in 1052, and Duke William's victory over William of Arques in 1054.

The relative shift in power between the two counts is reflected in a charter of 1056. Baldwin V records the settlement of a judicial contest over the seigneurial rights in Harnes between the abbot of St Peter's of Ghent and Eustace which Eustace lost.[39] The adjudication is one of several which Baldwin used to reassert his authority over the monastic advocates within his county. Eustace appears to have been unhappy with the decision, which underlined Baldwin's ability to enforce his feudal rights in Lens, for he did not attest this charter.[40]

Eustace did, however, attest another charter in favor of St Bertin, dated 1056, which also limited the power of an advocate, this time of St Bertin.[41] Eustace's attestation probably reflects his family's longstanding ties to the abbey and its advocate rather than a complete easing of tensions. After 1056, Eustace disappears from the surviving records and does not reappear until 1063, when he once again witnesses a charter in favor of St Bertin.[42]

The early 1060s were a period of consolidation of power for both William II of Normandy and Baldwin V, and a low point in Eustace's political influence. In 1060, both Henry I of France and Geoffrey Martel, Count of Anjou died. Duke William profited by bringing Maine and Brittany under his *mouvance* in the resulting power vacuum. The 1062–4 campaign in Maine pitted William against Eustace's step-son and ally, Walter of Vexin.[43] Walter and his wife were captured in 1063 and died in captivity shortly thereafter. By the mid-1060s, William had

[38] Although Eustace's father-in-law also benefited from Henry's death – Agnes promised formally to invest him with the duchy of Lower Lorraine on the death of Frederick III of Luxembourg – Frederick did not die until 1065 and Godfrey remained active in Italian affairs. Upper Lorraine would remain in the control of the house of Alsace. See Pierre Aube, *Godefroy de Bouillon*, Fayard 1985, 23–4.

[39] Alexandre Teulet, *Layettes du Tresor des Chartes*, Paris 1863, i, 21–2. Edmund Rigaux speculated that this charter suggests that Baldwin V challenged and won from Eustace I the rights to the castellany of Lens after 1036, and that Baldwin had added seigneurial rights to the castellany and sold both to the abbey of St Peter's. Rigaux, 173. However, Lens had not passed into Flemish control after 1036, for Lambert inherited it from his father Eustace I in 1047 and Eustace II had inherited at his brother's death in 1154. Lambert died fighting for Baldwin V at Lille in 1054. Bouquet, xi, 582. This trial is a reflection of Baldwin's efforts to curb the power and independence of the monastic advocates and Baldwin's newly increased ability to enforce his feudal rights over his vassal Count Eustace of Boulogne and Lens.

[40] Teulet, i, 21–2. The witness list is as follows: Marquis Baldwin and his sons Baldwin and Robert, Countess Adèle, Count Roger and his son, Duke Harold [Earl Godwin's son], Count Guy [of Ponthieu], Raingod, Anselm, Werefrid, Baldwin of Warnastun, Drogo son of Rodulf, Count Manasses [of Guines], archdeacon Guy [?later Bishop of Amiens], Isaac, Hugh of Oldenard, Hugh Havet, Baldwin of Wartanbeke, Rodulf son of Rodulf, Herimar and Lantwin, Robert and Wenemar of Lens, Segard son of Ermenfrid, Arnulf son of Herluin (Erlewini) [of Montreuil?], Roric and his son Baldwin, and also Folkard, monk of the latter (bracketed identifications are my own). Harold's presence may have further added to Eustace's chagrin.

[41] B. Guérard, *Cartulaire de l'abbaye de Saint-Bertin*, Paris 1841, 186–7.

[42] Daniel Haigneré, *Les Chartes de Saint-Bertin*, St Omer 1886, i, 30.

[43] Douglas, 174–8. William's claim to Maine was based on his son Robert's betrothal to Heribert's

successfully secured his borders against his neighbors – the counts of Maine, Anjou, Amiens-Valois-Vexin, and Ponthieu.[44]

The death of King Henry also brought increased power to Count Baldwin. Through his marriage to Henry's sister, Adele, Baldwin became the guardian and regent for King Philip I.[45] Eustace's recognition of Baldwin's enhanced status and power can be seen in his 1065 attestation of one of King Philip's charters and the previously mentioned 1063 attestation of Baldwin's gift to St Bertin.[46] Eustace's attestations may also reflect the elevation of his brother, Godfrey, to the bishopric of Paris in 1061, after Baldwin became regent.[47] Although Eustace had assumed a pro-Flemish policy during this period, he had not abandoned his independence. His attendance of Baldwin's court was not frequent and each of the charters which Eustace attested concerned monasteries located near his own lands.[48] Baldwin's and William's successes in the 1060s and the diminished power of his allies in England, Ponthieu, the Vexin, and Lorraine sharply curtailed Eustace's political influence and ability to maneuver independently.

In 1065, the political situation slowly began to shift. In that year Eustace's father-in-law regained the duchy of Lower Lorraine at the death of Frederick of Luxembourg. Godfrey's return provided Eustace with a powerful ally once again. The death of Edward the Confessor in January 1066 and William of Normandy's response to Harold's succession provided Eustace with an opportunity to improve his own fortunes and to attack an old enemy. The primacy of the port of Wissant for access to England meant that William would regard Eustace as a valuable ally. Not only would Eustace's goodwill provide William with some protection from a possible Danish invasion of England, launched from Boulonnais ports, but it would also diminish the danger of any northern attacks on Normandy.

Although both men profited by their new accord, the alliance seems to have been an uneasy one from the beginning. Eustace was required to leave his son as a hostage at the Norman court before setting out on the conquest. And shortly after the Battle of Hastings, Eustace and William had a falling out which led in 1067 to Eustace's rebellion.[49]

Eustace's role in the conquest of England is difficult to determine in its entirety because of the contradictory statements in the surviving accounts of the battle and the preparations for it. The contradictions arise to a great extent through the biases of the contemporary chroniclers; nevertheless, Eustace's role in the Norman success at Hastings appears to have been significant. His importance as a contributor to the Norman conquest and as an ally is corroborated by the extent of

[44] Thus when Harold was shipwrecked in Ponthieu, shortly before the Norman Conquest, and seized by Count Guy, William insisted that Guy release him (Douglas, 176). There is a hint that Eustace may have been involved in this incident for Guy brought Harold to the castle of Belrem, in the county of St Pol, whose count was Eustace's vassal. The incident reflects the continued ties between Boulogne and Ponthieu, later reflected in the *Carmen*, and the continued hostility between Harold Godwinson and Eustace.

(the deceased count) sister who was still an infant. Walter claimed the county through his marriage to Biota, aunt of Count Heribert.

[45] Ganshof, 36, 39.
[46] Miraeus et Foppens, 305–6. The seventeen witnesses after Eustace were all Baldwin's vassals.
[47] See *Gallia Christiana*, vii, 49–52, for a description of Godfrey's career.
[48] Philip's charter confirmed the foundation of the abbey of St Peter's of Hasnon, which is near the county of Lens.
[49] *Gesta Guillelmi*, 264–6.

William's grants to Eustace which made him the tenth largest noble landholder in England and the reestablishment of their political alliance in the mid-1070s.[50]

The contemporary Norman sources for the conquest downplay Eustace's role, and the role of other French nobles, in their victory over Harold's army. Eustace's contribution to William's fleet, which may have been significant since both Wissant and Boulogne were major ports, is also unknown for the Conquest ship list only discusses the Norman contingents.[51] William of Jumièges does not mention Eustace in his account of the conquest and only discusses his rebellion in 1067.[52] William of Poitiers gives us a vivid description of Eustace turning tail at a crucial moment towards the end of the battle and urging retreat upon William.[53] His cowardice was rewarded with 'a resounding blow between the shoulders, the gravity of which was immediately shown by blood spurting from his ears and mouth, and he was borne off by his companions more dead than alive.'[54] Both of these encomiasts would have little reason to praise Eustace and his role in the battle, since both were writing after Eustace's 1067 rebellion.[55]

More positive in their presentation of Eustace's activities during the conquest are the *Carmen de Hastingae Proelio* and the Bayeux tapestry. The latter highlights Eustace's contribution through a depiction of his aid in rallying William's host when the army believed that William had been killed.[56] In the *Carmen*, Eustace plays an important role on three occasions: first, when he offers William his horse, at William's second unhorsing; second, when the poet attributes Harold's death to William, Eustace, Hugh of Ponthieu, and Walter Giffard; and third, when Eustace leads the pursuit of the fleeing English at the end of the battle.[57]

Neither the *Carmen* nor the tapestry is unbiased in its presentation of individual contributions to the victory at Hastings. Frank Barlow, Catherine Morton, and Hope Muntz, among others, have argued that Guy of Amiens, a partisan of Eustace and the count of Ponthieu, wrote the *Carmen*, sometime between 1067 and 1070, to heal the breach between William and Eustace, and to stress the French contributions to the conquest.[58] Shirley Brown has recently argued that

---

[50] See Appendix B.

[51] Elisabeth van Houts, 'The Ship List of William the Conqueror' *ante* x, 1988, 16.

[52] Jumièges, 138; this omission is both a reflection of William's typical brevity when discussing military actions as well as Eustace's recent rebellion which made him a *persona non grata*.

[53] *Gesta Guillelmi*, 202.

[54] Translation from R. A. Brown, 35; for Latin see *Gesta Guillelmi*, 202–4.

[55] William of Jumièges wrote his *Gesta Normannorum Ducum* in late 1070 or early 1071 (Jumièges, xv). William of Poitiers' account was completed by 1077. See R. H. C. Davis, 'William of Poitiers and his History of William the Conqueror' in *Writing of History in the Middle Ages*, eds R. H. C. Davis and J. M. Wallace-Hadrill, 1981, 83.

[56] S. A. Brown, 'The Bayeux Tapestry: Why Eustace, Odo, and William?' *ante* xii, 1990, 8, 9.

[57] *Carmen*, 32–7; see also Appendix D for a discussion of the passage which relates Harold's death.

[58] See Frank Barlow, 'The Carmen de Hastingae Proelio' in *Studies in International History presented to W. Norton Medlicott*, ed. K. Bourne and D. C. Watt, London 1967, 71–100; and *Carmen*, xv–lviii. Barlow has argued that it was written between 1068 and 1070; Morton and Muntz have argued that the poem was completed by Matilda's coronation voyage to England, or by 1068. Barlow, 'The Carmen', 62–3; *Carmen*, xxi–xxii. R. H. C. Davis has argued that the Carmen was a twelfth-century literary exercise and therefore worthless as a historical source; see his 'The Carmen de Hastingae Proelio' *EHR* ccclxvii, 1978, 241–261 and R. H. C. Davis, L. J. Engels, *et al.*, 'The *Carmen de Hastingae Proelio*: A Discussion' *ante* ii, 1979, 1–20.

the Bayeux tapestry, commissioned in late 1081 or early 1082, sought to convey the idea that the victory at Hastings was 'a direct result of an action stemming from the alliance of Odo of Bayeux, Duke William, and Eustace of Boulogne,' in the hopes of stimulating William's mercy towards his brother after the 1082 imprisonment.[59]

While some passages of the *Carmen* are clearly fictitious, Guy of Amiens was in a position to have received a first-hand account of the battle from Eustace himself. Guy was the uncle of Count Guy of Ponthieu and half-uncle to Eustace himself. Guy and Eustace had probably met at the 1056 judicial duel over the village of Harnes, and Eustace's alliance with the counts of Ponthieu and Arques would have provided several other opportunities for these men to meet. It therefore seems likely that Guy's account, although perhaps overemphasizing Eustace's role, would have been believable to the participants. Similarly, the Bayeux tapestry would not have had a chance of encouraging William's mercy if it had not conformed to contemporary recollection of the battle. Thus, I would argue that Eustace did play an important part in William's success at Hastings and that their estrangement was in part the result of the lack of trust between the two men, whatever the proximate cause was.

It is unknown when the falling out between William and Eustace occurred, but none of the contemporary sources indicate Eustace's presence at William's coronation of Christmas 1066. Eustace had definitely returned to the continent by Easter of 1067, for he was present at Bergues when Baldwin V issued a confirmation charter for St Winnoc.[60] The rift was not complete, however, before autumn of 1067, for Eustace was one of the addressees in two of William's acta of 1067, in counties where he is later known to have held land.[61]

However, in the autumn of 1067 Eustace launched an attack on Dover. The rebellion was short-lived and a failure. Odo of Bayeux's men, garrisoned at the castle of Dover, put up a spirited defense, and Eustace's forces fled. Eustace and a few others escaped, but many of his men fell to their deaths from the cliffs, and his *nepos* was captured.[62] At William's Christmas court, Eustace's actions were condemned and his English lands forfeited.[63]

What led Eustace to rebel in 1067? In William of Poitiers' account, Eustace's rebellion was the result of a diplomatic delegation to Eustace from the citizens of Dover. The Dobernians hated the Normans, knew of Eustace's prowess, and preferred to be ruled by a neighbor they knew than by the Normans.[64] More recently, several other theories have been advanced. David Douglas has

---

[59] S. A. Brown, 17.

[60] Miraeus et Foppens, i, 511–13.

[61] For the dating of the rebellion, see Douglas, 212, n. 3. The first was directed to Bishops Herman and Wulstan, Earl Eustace, and other prominent local nobles in Wiltshire and Gloucestershire; *Regesta* i, no. 9. The second was addressed to Archbishop Stigand, Earl Eustace and all the king's thanes in Surrey; *Regesta* i, no. 45.

[62] *Gesta Guillelmi*, 266; '. . . nobilissimus autem tiro nepos ejus comprehensus est . . .;'

[63] *Gesta Guillelmi*, 268.

[64] *Gesta Guillelmi*, 266; 'Nam quia Normannos odere, cum Eustachio pridem sibi inimicissimo concordavere. Eum bellandi peritum atque in praelio felicem experimentis cognoverant. Si erat serviendum non compatriotae, noto servire atque vicino satius putabant.' William of Jumièges' account is very similar to William of Poitiers'; he emphasizes Eustace's wickedness and God's punishment of this in the horrible deaths of his men: '. . . Eustachius Boloniensis comes, quorundam Anglorum intra Cantuariensem comitatum consistentium versutiis depravatus, Dobroberniae

suggested that Eustace's positive response to the Dobernian delegation was influenced by the death of Baldwin V on 1 September 1067, for Baldwin had been 'friendly or at least neutral to William' in 1066.[65] Frank Barlow, on the other hand, has argued that Eustace rebelled in favor of a grandson, his descendant by Goda, and that it was this young man who was captured at Dover.[66]

A simpler solution to this question of motivation may lie in Eustace's long-standing ties to England. Like most of William's companions, Eustace's primary motivation in joining William's expedition was to gain lands and thereby wealth and power. Unlike the other conquistadors, Eustace's previous ties to England may have shaped his expectations of what lands William should grant him in reward for his services. Eustace may have hoped to recover lands held by his former wife Goda, which were probably lost to him at her death.[67] With both of Goda's sons dead – Ralf in 1057 and Walter in 1064 – Eustace may have seen himself as the proper recipient of her lands, or at least of part of them. He may have also hoped to add to these lands some or all of the lands of his step-son Earl Ralf, most of which were held by Harold after 1057.

An analysis of Goda's landholdings reveals that Eustace was not in possession of any of her lands in 1086; the majority were in the hands of the Count of Eu or his vassals, while the remainder were held by the king or Queen, their direct vassals, and or by various monasteries.[68] Eustace may have obtained Goda's Gloucestershire holdings, for William addressed a writ to him and several others with holdings in Wiltshire and Gloucester, but Eustace appears to have forfeited them permanently in 1067. Nor did Eustace receive any of the lands of Earl Ralf in Herefordshire.[69] The writs that were addressed to Eustace prior to the rebellion also corroborate this pattern for they concerned lands in Wiltshire, Gloucestershire, and Surrey, but not in Herefordshire.[70] Thus Eustace's rebellion may reflect his disappointed hopes for the reacquisition of lands that he had previously controlled through his wife.

Alternatively, the two attacks on Dover suggest that Eustace may have hoped to gain control over Dover and the surrounding countryside which would allow

castellum involare est nisus. . . . vindice superni sententia perfidos ac temerarios coterente.' Jumièges, 138.

[65] Douglas, 212.

[66] Barlow, 307–8. See above n. 26, for a discussion of this youth's identity. Catherine Morton and Hope Muntz, building on Barlow's interpretation, have suggested that the quarrel between the count and the duke arose from William's reneging on a promise to share the kingdom with Eustace, whose grandson had a claim on the kingdom. *Carmen*, xxxviii–ix. I think this promise is highly unlikely.

[67] Round has argued that it was 'doubtful' that Edward granted Eustace any lands in England and that on Goda's death her sons, and not Eustace, would be the rightful heirs of her lands; J. H. Round, 'The Counts of Boulogne as English Lords' in *Studies in Peerage and Family History*, London 1901, 147 and 150. However, a gift of land in Surrey, formerly held by Countess Goda, made by Eustace to Rochester may indicate the Eustace continued to control some of Goda's lands after her death. But I have not been able to study the Rochester registers yet in order to establish a date or date range for this gift.

[68] See Appendix A. This appendix is based on the work of Marc Meyer who kindly provided me with this information. For a discussion of the significance of the landholding patterns for women in later Anglo-Saxon England, see his 'The Politics of Possession: Women's Estates in later Anglo-Saxon England' *Haskins Society Journal* iii, forthcoming.

[69] See Appendix B.

[70] *Regesta* i, nos. 9, 45.

him to control the main passageway to and from the continent. Wissant was a principal port to England from the Continent, and Dover was one of the most common landing sites.[71] If Eustace could command access to Dover, he would reap enormous political benefits, as well as substantial economic gains. Whatever Eustace's motivation was – acquisition of Goda's lands or Dover – his rebellion cost him the extensive territories William had granted him immediately after the conquest. But William did not take any further steps against Eustace perhaps because he was too busy securing his new conquest. The failed rebellion did not seem to diminish Eustace's previous power or authority in Boulogne or Lens; it did, however, appear to curtail his interest in foreign exploits for a brief period.

Between 1068 and 1070, Eustace appears to have been active only within his French counties. He witnessed only one charter of Baldwin VI (1067–1070) in 1067, but there is no evidence that the two counts were at odds. Boulogne's economic life was blossoming during this period, and Eustace appears to have profited from this activity. The biographer of Abbot Gervin of St Riquier described Wissant in 1068 as filled with 'a great crowd of soldiers and merchants.'[72] Boulogne and its ports appear to have supported a bustling trade, for Eustace minted his own coins.[73] The count and countess expended some of this wealth on the refoundation of the college of canons at Lens in 1070.[74] Also, during 1070, Eustace witnessed an act of Abbot Fulk of St Peter's of Ghent regarding the rights of the advocates, who were Eustace's vassals, in the village of Harnes.[75]

Eustace reentered regional politics in 1071 when Robert the Frisian rebelled against his young nephew, Count Arnulf III, and Countess Richilde, Arnulf's mother and regent. Eustace chose to support Richilde and her sons, Arnulf III and Baldwin. His decision may reflect his longstanding ties to Louvain, Hainaut, and Lorraine, areas from which Richilde drew her support. Eustace may also have been instrumental in winning King Philip I's aid through his brother Godfrey, bishop of Paris and chancellor to the king. Philip gathered an army to attack Robert which included Eustace, lords from the Ternois, Cambresis, Hainaut, Brabant and a small Norman contingent led by William fitz Osbern.[76] During the battle of Cassel, in February 1071, Eustace captured Robert and put him under the custody of Wulfric Rabel, the castellan of St Omer. Not long after, however, Robert was freed by the citizens of St Omer.[77] Although Robert was captured, Richilde also fell into enemy hands and Arnulf III and William fitz Osbern died in the battle. During the spring, Robert and King Philip came to terms: Robert was recognized as count of Flanders, and Richilde's second son Baldwin became the count of Hainaut.[78] Robert and Philip sealed their

---

71 Grierson, 80–1.
72 Alain Lottin, *Histoire de Boulogne-sur-Mer*, Lille 1983, 47.
73 Lottin, 47. These coins were inscribed with 'URBS B(O)LNIE'. Eustace's interest in coinage is also reflected in the Hertfordshire entry for Tring manor where the value of the manor was '22 pounds of "white pennies" weighed by the Count.' *VCH, Hertfordshire*, i, 320.
74 Miraeus et Foppens, i, 159–61. Bishop Lietbert confirmed their gift; Miraeus et Foppens, 161–2.
75 M. Gysseling and A. C. F. Koch, *Diplomatica Belgica Ante Annum Millesimum Centesimum Scripta*, Bruxelles 1950, 213–14.
76 Charles Verlinden, *Robert Ier le Frison*, Paris 1935, 55–6.
77 *Chronicon S. Andreae*, *MGH*, vii, 538.
78 King Philip's recognition of Robert led Emperor Henry IV to abandon Richilde's cause and accept Robert's homage for his German fiefs. Godfrey the Hunchback, Duke of Lower Lorraine,

alliance, founded in their anti-Norman policy, with Philip's marriage to Robert's step-daughter, Bertha.[79]

Verlinden has suggested that Eustace abandoned Richilde's cause soon after Robert's release and negotiated the settlement between Robert and Philip.[80] However, the *Flandria Generosa* states that Bishop Godfrey, while at Eperlecques, represented Philip in these talks and there seems to be no reason to doubt the accuracy of this information.[81] Eustace may have been a part of this reconciliation, for Philip granted him the forest of Eperlecques, but Eustace's continued hostility to Robert after 1071 renders it improbable.[82] The Eperlecques grant may have been used to placate Eustace for the abandonment of Richilde's cause or as a reward for his services during the battle.

Eustace, his brother-in-law, Duke Godfrey the Hunchback, and the bishops of Utrecht, Cambrai, and Thérouanne, refused to recognize Robert as count, and Eustace himself chose to unite his interests with Duke William.[83] Eustace's alliance to William was probably strengthened when, in 1076, Robert's men killed Godfrey the Hunchback while Godfrey was on his way to aid Bishop William of Utrecht against Robert's step-son and ally, Count Thierry of Holland.[84] There seems to have been a partial thawing in 1080 when Eustace attests a charter Robert issued confirming the possessions of the abbey of Messines.[85] But in the following year, Robert intruded his candidate into the diocese of Therouanne, and the clergy sought Eustace's aid.[86] The ensuing and sometimes violent struggle lasted for approximately three years, generated several papal letters and condemnations, and was finally resolved in 1084.[87]

The last decade of Eustace's life was probably occupied with the management

recognized Baldwin's succession in Hainaut but consistently opposed Robert, as did the Bishops of Utrecht, Cambrai and Thérouanne.

[79] See Elizabeth Hallam, *Capetian France*, 1980, 75–8. Although Eustace maintained a pro-Norman policy after c.1075, he appears to have remained friendly toward Philip I; in 1075 he witnessed charter of Philip in favor of St Peter's of Aire. M. Prou, *Recueil des actes de Philippe Ier, Roi de France (1059–1108)*, Paris 1908, no. lxxii, 182–4.

[80] Verlinden, 68–71.

[81] *Flandria Generosa, MGH* ix, 323.

[82] *Chronicon Sithiense* in E. Martène and U. Durand, *Thesaurum Novus Anecdotorum*, iii, 583.

[83] *Gesta Guillelmi*, 268; in describing the 1067 incident William concludes with, 'But we feel we must in many ways spare this illustrious person, called count, who is now reconciled with the king and is honored by being in his immediate circle.' Since William had finished writing his work by 1077, this passage suggests that he had been recently reconciled. Barlow has suggested a date of c.1074; Barlow, 308.

[84] Lambert of Schafnaburg, *De rebus gestis Germanorum* in Bouquet, xi, 67. See also Andressohn, 18. Because Godfrey died without heirs, he made his nephew Godfrey of Bouillon heir to his property. Young Godfrey only received the March of Anvers from the Emperor in addition to the county of Verdun, and the allodial holdings of Bouillon, Mosay, Stenay, Tellin and Bellou. See Andressohn, 30–41, and H. Dorcy, 'Godefroid de Bouillon, Duc de Basse-Lotharingie' *Revue Belge de Philologie et d'Histoire* xxvi, 1948, 961–99, for discussion of Godfrey's struggles to hold onto his inheritance and earn the duchy of Lorraine from the Emperor.

[85] Miraeus et Foppens, i, 69–71.

[86] See O. Bled, *Régestes des Evêques de Thérouanne 500–1553*, St Omer 1904, i, 74–92; the bishops of Thérouanne usually chose the counts of Boulogne as their ally when they were at odds with the counts of Flanders. See career of Bishop Drogo under Baldwin IV and the intrusion of Lambert by Robert. Bishop Hubert also seems to have been a partisan of Eustace II, see Bled, 84.

[87] Bled, 85–90. In 1082, the canons moved the relics of St Maxima to Boulogne out of fear of Robert.

of his estates in England and France.[88] Eustace's reconciliation with William paid handsome dividends. Domesday book reveals him to be among the ten wealthiest magnates in England. He held lands in eleven counties with the majority of his holdings in Essex, and had an annual income from these lands of approximately £770.[89] An analysis of the distribution of Eustace's lands reveals that he rewarded some of his vassals from Boulogne and the heirs of his allies of 1051, Earl Ralf and Osbern Pentecost.[90] Eustace made several grants to Alvred of Merleberg (Marlborough), nephew of Osbern Pentecost, whose successor was Harold, Earl Ralf's son.[91] Harold was also a knight of Eustace's son, Eustace III.[92]

At his death in 1087, Eustace had increased his power and that of his heirs significantly. His accomplishments were built on the successes of his father. Eustace I and his son manœuvered themselves into the center of political developments in Flanders, Lorraine, and England through their policy of strategic marital and political alliances. The career of Eustace II marks a significant turning point in Boulonnais comital power. His tenth-century predecessors struggled to maintain their freedom in the face of increasing Flemish power. Unlike the counts of Guines, Ghent, and Holland, and the various castellans and monastic advocates in Flanders, the eleventh-century Boulonnais counts increased their own power and autonomy. They achieved this goal through marriage alliances with Flemish political rivals and by carefully maintained alliances with the counts of Ponthieu and the Vexin. The success of these strategies is reflected in King Edward's alliance with Eustace II in the 1040s and 1050s, and Duke William's alliances with Eustace in 1066 and in the mid-1070s, which were sealed by William's generous land grants to Eustace. The pursuance of alliances which were often contrary to the Flemish counts' own interests substantiates the thesis that the Boulonnais counts acted as independent princes and not as obedient Flemish vassals. The long-lived concord between Baldwin V and Eustace I and II,

---

[88] There are two other references to Eustace in the surviving *acta* of the period, each reveals contests over individual estates – one in France with the canons of St Omer which was resolved in 1078 and the other in Suffolk between Eustace's men and the men of Frodo, which can only be dated between 1066 and 1087; Miraeus et Foppens, iv, 5–6; *Regesta* i, no. 242.

[89] C. Warren Hollister, 'Magnates and "Curiales" in Early Norman England' in *Monarchy, Magnates, and Institutions in the Anglo-Norman World*, London 1986, 99. His wife Ida also received six manors from William. See Appendix B.

[90] See Appendix C. Of the 140 land grants recorded in Domesday Book, fifty-two grants were held in demesne, thirty grants were held individually, and fifty-eight grants were divided between thirteen men who held more than three grants from him. Of these frequent grantees, five, can be identified as originating from the Boulonnais territories: Adelulf of Merck and his brother, Ralph of Merck, Arnulf, Lord of Ardres and Eustace's seneschal, Roger of Sombres, and Rumold of Doudeaville. I have not been able to identify the origins of the other grantees. My analysis is based primarily on Round, 156–8. See also André DuChesne, *Histoire Généalogique des Maisons de Guines, d'Ardres, de Gand et de Coucy et quelques autres Familles*, Paris 1631, 80–1 for a discussion of Arnulf of Ardres. David Douglas has also identified several lesser Domesday landowners from the Boulonnais: Gumfrid and Sigar of Choques (Hainaut) held lands in Northamptonshire, the family of Cunchy which later supplied the earls of Winchester, Arnulf of Hesdin who was a tenant in chief in several shires, and Gilbert of Ghent, son of Count Alost; Douglas, 266–7. Eustace may have promoted all of these men, but there is no extant evidence of this.

[91] See Appendix C. Alvred of Merleberg (Marlborough) held four Somerset manors from Eustace. Alvred was the lord of Ewias Harold, a castle on the Welsh border. The successor to his holdings was Harold of Ewias, son of Earl Ralf.

[92] Round, 156.

in the periods between 1038–1049 and 1056–1070, has misled scholars of Flanders and France into assuming that this harmony was typical of Flemish-Boulonnais relations rather than the anomaly that it was. The Boulonnais counts Baldwin I, Eustace I and Eustace II were hostile to Baldwin IV of Flanders, and Eustace II was an enemy of Count Robert I. Eustace II proved himself to be a clever schemer, who rose above his own and his allies' setbacks, and who established the eminence of his family in the rough and tumble political world of eleventh- and twelfth-century northern Europe.

Errata

In Genealogy I (p. 253) the dates given for the Counts of Boulogne should be corrected as follows: Eustace I 1024–1047; Eustace II 1047–1088; Eustace III 1088–1125. The correct dates for Stephen's son, William of Warenne, are 1154–1159.

APPENDIX A

Goda's Landholdings

County	Property		Value		Domesday Holder
Berkshire	Farnam Royal	£ 4			Abingdon Church
Berkshire	Twyford	10			Abingdon Abbey
Dorset	Hinton Martell	19 5s			Hugh Filii Grip, QM
Dorset	Bingham's Melcomb	16			Hugh Filii Grip, QM
Gloucester	Aston Subedge	5			Church of Lambeth
Gloucester	Hasleden	8			Sigar of Chocques, WR
Gloucester	Hawling	7			Sigar of Chocques, WR
Gloucester	Horsley	12			Church of Troarn
Gloucester	Minchinhampton	28			Nun's Ch. of Caen
Gloucester	Yanworth	7			Sigar of Chocques, WR
Middlesex	Harfield	14			Richard, son Ct Gil.
Rutland	Cottesmore	7			Geoffrey, WR
Rutland	Greetham	7			King William (WR)
Surrey	Headley	7			Ralph De Felgères
Surrey	Lambeth	10			Church of Lambeth
Sussex	Alciston			35	Hugh, of Ct of Eu
Sussex	Beddington	4			Ct of Eu
Sussex	Bury	12			Abbot of Fécamp
Sussex	East Dean		13		Ct of Eu
Sussex	Jevington		5		Hugh, of Ct of Eu
Sussex	Lawton	5	3		Ct of Eu, Subtenants
Sussex	Littlehampton			10	William, of E. Roger
Sussex	Mountfield ‹	3			Reinbert, Sheriff
Sussex	Netherfield	5			Herolf, of Ct of Eu
Sussex	Ratton			15	Reinbert, Eu. Clerk
Sussex	Saleshurst	1			Ct of Eu
Sussex	Sedlescomb	?			Walter, of Ct of Eu
Sussex	Warbleton	2			Wibert, of Ct of Eu
Sussex	Willingdon	4			Ct of Eu, Reinbert
Sussex	Winton			5	Reinbert Sheriff

APPENDIX B

Domesday Landholdings of Eustace II and Ida

* — land annexed by Ingelric the priest after Edward's death

^ — of 'white pennies' weighed by the Count's own standard

County	Hundred	Property	Holder	TRE Holder	Value TRE	Value Post TRE	Value DB
BEDFORDSHIRE	WILLEY	PAVENHAM MANOR	ERNULF DE ARDRES	ALEVOLD THEGN	N/A	N/A	N/A
BEDFORDSHIRE	WILLEY	TURVEY	ERNULF DE ARDRES	ALWOLD THEGN	20s	20s	10s
BEDFORDSHIRE	WILLEY	LITTLE ODELL MANOR	ERNULF DE ARDRES	ALWOLD THEGN	L8	100s	60s
BEDFORDSHIRE	WILLEY	STEVINGTON	ERNULF DE ARDRES	ADELOLD THEGN	L30	L20	L14
BEDFORDSHIRE	WILLEY	BROMHAM	ERNULF DE ARDRES	ALWOLD & LEVRIC	N/A	10s	20s
BEDFORDSHIRE	WILLEY	STAGSDEN	GODWI ENGLISHMAN	ALWOLD THEGN	L4	40s	25s
BEDFORDSHIRE	WILLEY	TOFT MANOR	ROBERT FITZ ROZELIN	ALWOLD	L4	40s	40s
CAMBRIDGESHIRE	WETHERLEY	GRANTCHESTER	2 KNIGHTS	ASGAR STALLER	L10	L10	L8
CAMBRIDGESHIRE	THRIPLOW	TRUMPINGTON	ERNULF DE ARDRES	HERULF THEGN	100s	N/A	L4
CAMBRIDGESHIRE	WITTLESFORD	ICKLETON	EUSTACE II	ALSI THEGN	L24	L24	L20
CAMBRIDGESHIRE	WITTLESFORD	DUXFORD, (PART)	HERNULF	HERULF	L7	L7	100s
CAMBRIDGESHIRE	WITTLESFORD	DUXFORD, (PART)	WIDO	ABP. STIGAND	N/A	N/A	28s 8d
DORSET	CULLIFORDTREE	WINTERBOURNE MONKTON	COUNTESS IDA	WULFEVA	L6	N/A	L6
DORSET	ROWBARROW	SWANAGE	COUNTESS IDA	WULFEVA	15s	N/A	0
DORSET	ST. GEORGE	BOCKHAMPTON	COUNTESS IDA	WULFEVA	L3	N/A	L3
ESSEX	FRESHWELL	LITTLE BARDFIELD	ADELOLF DE MERC	NORMAN*	L8	N/A	L10
ESSEX	THURSTAPLE	GOLDHANGER	ADELOLF DE MERC	ELRIC	20s	N/A	30s
ESSEX	HINCKFORD	STEEPLE BUMPSTEAD	ADELOLF DE MERC	FREE MAN	L4	100s	100s
ESSEX	THURSTAPLE	TOLLESBURY	ALMERFRID	GUDMUND, FR'MAN	L4	L4	L3
ESSEX	ONGAR	LITTLE STANFORT	ALVRIC	ALVRIC' FATHER	N/A	N/A	10s
ESSEX	WINKFORD	WESTON	ABBOT OF MERC	FREE MAN	20s	N/A	25

County	Hundred	Place	Tenant-in-Chief	Holder			
ESSEX	DUNMOW	PLESINCHOU	BERNARD	FREE MAN	N/A	N/A	10s
ESSEX	THURSTABLE	TOLLESHUNT (GUINES)	ADELOLF DE MERC	TORBERN	L10	N/A	100s
ESSEX	TENDRING	TENDRING	BERNARD	AETNOD	L4	N/A	L4
ESSEX	UTTLESFORD	SHORTGROVE	ADELOLF DE MERC	FREE MAN	N/A	N/A	40s
ESSEX	HINCKFORD	BELCHAMP (ST. ETHELBERT)	BERNARD	ETNOD, FREE MAN	N/A	N/A	30s
ESSEX	DUNMOW	DUNMOW	ADELOLF DE MERC	EDMAR, FREEMAN	N/A	N/A	L8
ESSEX	TENDRING	LITTLE HOLLAND	ADELOLF DE MERC	LEFSTAN*	L6	N/A	L4
ESSEX	HARLOW	LATTON	ADELOLF DE MERC	ERNULF, FR/MAN	50s	N/A	60s
ESSEX	TENDRING	LAWFORD	ADELOLF DE MERC	ALVRIC*	L10	N/A	L10
ESSEX	HINCKFORD	SHORTGROVE	ADELOLF DE MERC	FREE MAN	30s	30s	33s
ESSEX	HINCKFORD	TOPPESFIELD	BERNARD	FREE MAN	N/A	N/A	20s
ESSEX	ONGAR	LAMBOURNE	DAVID	LEFSI	40s	N/A	60s
ESSEX	WINSTREE	LITTLE WIGBOROUGH (1/2 H.)	EUSTACE	N/A*	N/A	N/A	N/A
ESSEX	WITHAM	RIVENHALL	EUSTACE II	QUEEN EADGYTH	L9	N/A	L12
ESSEX	BARNSTAPLE	FOBBING	EUSTACE II	BRICTMAR THEGN	L32	N/A	L36
ESSEX	WITHAM	WHITE NOTLEY	EUSTACE II	ALVARIC THEGN	L10	N/A	L10
ESSEX	THURSTAPLE	TOLLESHUNT	EUSTACE II, DEMESNE	ALMAR	40s	15s	20s
ESSEX	WINSTREE	LAYER DE LA HAY	EUSTACE II	ALRIC, FREEMAN	L4	N/A	L3
ESSEX	ONGAR	HIGH? LAVER	EUSTACE II, DEMESNE	LEWIN & ALWIN*	L16	L16	L20
ESSEX	WITHAM	RIVENHALL	EUSTACE II	HAROLD	60s	N/A	30s
ESSEX	TENDRING	CHICHE	EUSTACE II, DEMESNE	EDWARD*	L12	40s	L10
ESSEX	ONGAR	LITTLE STANFORD (PART)	EUSTACE II	ALVRIC' FATHER	N/A	N/A	40s
ESSEX	ONGAR	STANFORD (RIVERS)	EUSTACE II, DEMESNE	LEWIN*	L24	L24	L40 BL
ESSEX	LEXDEN	GREAT TEY	EUSTACE II	FREE MAN	L16	L22	L22
ESSEX	TENDRING	TENDRING	EUSTACE II, DEMESNE	FREWIN	40s	N/A	60s
ESSEX	WITHAM	COGGESHALL	EUSTACE II	COLO, FR'MAN	L10	N/A	L14
ESSEX	LEXDEN	BOXTED	EUSTACE II, DEMESNE	ALVRIC	L8	L8	L12
ESSEX	DENGIE	PURLEIGH	EUSTACE II	EDEVA	16s 8d	N/A	23s
ESSEX	WINSTREE	LONGENHOE	EUSTACE II, DEMESNE	INGELRIC	L17	L17 5s	L17 5s
ESSEX	LEXDEN	EAST DONYLAND	EUSTACE II, DESMENE	EDRIC	N/A	N/A	5s

County	Hundred	Property	Holder	TRE Holder	Value TRE	Value Post TRE	Value DB
ESSEX	UTTLESFORD	CRESHALL	EUSTACE II, DEMESNE	INGWAR	L15	N/A	L15
ESSEX	FRESHWELL	NEWENHAM	EUSTACE II, DEMESNE	ALSI*	L11	N/A	L12
ESSEX	FRESHWELL	BENDISH HALL	EUSTACE II, DEMESNE	LEMAR PRIEST*	L11	N/A	L12
ESSEX	DENGIE	ILTNEY	EUSTACE II, DEMESNE	INGELRIC	N/A	N/A	30s
ESSEX		12 HOUSES IN COLCHESTER	EUSTACE/ 1 ENGELRIC	N/A	12s	N/A	0
ESSEX	BARNSTAPLE	GRAVESEND	EUSTACE II	INGELRIC	10s	N/A	20s
ESSEX	HARLOW	HARLOW	GEOFFREY	BRICTNAR, F'MAN	N/A	N/A	11s
ESSEX	ONGAR	CHIPPING ONGAR	EUSTACE II	AILIDA	100s	N/A	L8
ESSEX	HINCKFORD	FINCHINGFIELD	GUY	ULVRIC, FREEMAN	N/A	N/A	16s
ESSEX	THURSTAPLE	BLACHAM	EUSTACE II	4 FREE MEN	10s	10s	7s
ESSEX	HINCKFORD	FINCHINGFIELD	GUY	NORMAN	20s	N/A	40s
ESSEX	ROCHFORD	SHOPLAND	EUSTACE II DEMESNE	FREE MAN*	L6	N/A	L10
ESSEX	UTTLESFORD	LITTLE CHISHALL	GUY [DE ANJOU]	GODRIC, FREEMAN	N/A	N/A	10s
ESSEX	HINCKFORD	CLARET	EUSTACE II, DEMESNE	LEDMAR, FREEMAN	L18	L22	L22
ESSEX	WITHAM	BLUNTS HALL	EUSTACE II	FREE WOMAN	20s	N/A	10s
ESSEX	TENDRING	LAWFORD (PART)	EUSTACE II	8 FREEMEN*	N/A	N/A	N/A
ESSEX	HINCKFORD	RIDGEWELL	EUSTACE II, DEMESNE	GODUIN, FREEMAN	L18	L24	L24
ESSEX	BARNSTAPLE	ORSETT	EUSTACE II	INGELRIC	N/A	N/A	20s
ESSEX	UTTLESFORD	LITTLE CHISHALL	GUY [DE ANJOU]	SIRED, FREE MAN	100S	100s	L16
ESSEX	TENDRING	ALRESFORD	HACON	EDWARD	N/A	N/A	60s
ESSEX	LEXDEN	GREAT BIRCH	HUGH	EDRIC*	L6	L6	100s
ESSEX	LEXDEN	EAST THORPE	HUGH	EDRIC	40s	N/A	30s
ESSEX	HARLOW	GREAT PARNDON	IUNAIN [SIC]	ULF THEGN	N/A	N/A	L4

County	Hundred	Place	Lord	Holder 1066			
ESSEX	CHELMSFORD	BOREHAM	KNIGHT OF EUSTACE'S	RANULF PEVEREL*	12d	N/A	N/A
ESSEX	DENGIE	MALDON	ST. MARTIN OF LONDON	FREE MAN*	N/A	N/A	20s
ESSEX	UTTLESFORD	LEEBURY	ROGER DE SUMERI	BRICTULF, F'MAN	L4	N/A	100s
ESSEX	CHELMSFORD	GOOD EASTER (EU' GIFT TO ST.M)	ST. MARTIN OF LONDON	AELMER,K' THANE	L8	N/A	L10
ESSEX	CHELMSFORD	BOREHAM	LAMBERT	14 FREEMEN	L6	N/A	L8
ESSEX	THURSTAPLE	TOLLESHUNT	ST. MARTIN OF LONDON	ULVRIC, FREEMAN	N/A	N/A	30s
ESSEX	CHELMSFORD	NEWLAND HALL	MAUGER	HAROLD*	100s	N/A	L7
ESSEX	HINCKFORD	BELCHAMP (OTTON)	ULMAR	LEDMAR, FREEMAN	40s	L4	L4
ESSEX	ONGAR	CHIPPING ONGAR	RALF BAIGNARD	FREE MAN	N/A	N/A	N/A
ESSEX	BARNSTAPLE	HORDON ON THE HILL	WARNER	ULVRIC, FREEMAN	60s	N/A	50s
ESSEX	WINSTREE	ABBERTON	RALF DE MARCI	SIWARD, FREEMAN	N/A	N/A	60s
ESSEX	TENDRING	FRINTON	RALF DE MARCI	HAROLD*	60s	N/A	L4 10s
ESSEX	CHELMSFORD	LITTLE WALTHAM	LAMBERT	LEFSTAN*	50s	50s	60s
ESSEX	HINCKFORD	SMEETON HALL	RANER	FREE WOMAN	L7	N/A	L8
ESSEX	ONGAR	LITTLE? LAVER	RICHARD	BRICTMAR	N/A	N/A	10s
ESSEX	WITHAM	WITHAM	RICHARD	HAROLD	N/A	N/A	20s
ESSEX	DENGIE	ULEHAM	ROBERT	FREE MAN*	8s 4d	N/A	14s
ESSEX	CHELMSFORD	RUNWELL	LAMBERT	LEFSTAN*	N/A	N/A	20s
ESSEX	BARNSTAPLE	SHENFIELD	ROGER	BODD	N/A	N/A	60s
ESSEX	UTTLESFORD	CRAWLEYBURY	ROGER DE SUMERI	LEFSI*	N/A	N/A	10s
ESSEX	UTTLESFORD	ELMDON	ROGER DE SUMERI	ALMAR	L16	L16	L20
ESSEX	TENDRING	BIRCHO	ROBERT	INGELRIC	60s	N/A	L4 7s
ESSEX	CHELMSFORD	LITTLE BADDOW	LAMBERT	LEWIN*	100s	100s	L6
ESSEX	ONGAR	HIGH? LAVER (120 ACRES)	RALF	ALWIN/FREEMAN*	N/A	N/A	30s
ESSEX	ONGAR	FYFIELD	RICHARD	BRICTMAR	5s	N/A	10s
ESSEX	LEXDEN	EAST DONYLAND	ROBERT	GODRIC COLCHEST	N/A	N/A	12d
ESSEX	LEXDEN	COLNE ENGAINE	ROBERT	ALVRIC BIGA*	30s	N/A	40s
HERTFORDSHIRE	EDWINSTREE	LAYSTON	2 KNIGHTS OF EUSTACE	GODID	3s	3s	3s

County	Hundred	Property	Holder	TRE Holder	Value TRE	Value Post TRE	Value DB
HERTFORDSHIRE	BRAUGHING	BRAUGHING	EUSTACE II	2 THEGNS, GODID	L20	L16	L16
HERTFORDSHIRE	DACORUM	TRING	EUSTACE II	ENGELRIC	L20	N/A	L22^
HERTFORDSHIRE	EDWINSTREE	BORESON	EUSTACE II	ASGAR STALLER	L4	L3	L3
HERTFORDSHIRE	EDWINSTREE	COCKHAMSTREAD	EUSTACE II	GOUTI THEGN	L7	L7	L7
HERTFORDSHIRE	ODSEY	ANSTEY	EUSTACE II	ALWARD THEGN	L15	L14	L14
HERTFORDSHIRE	EDWINSTREE	WAKELEY (FARM)	ROBERT	ALWARD	5s	5s	5s
HERTFORDSHIRE	EDWINSTREE	BARKSDON (GREEN)	ROBERT	ALWARD	100s	40s	L3
HERTFORDSHIRE	EDWINSTREE	CORNEYBURY IN LAYSTON	ROBERT	ALWARD & GODE	20s	10s	13s 4d
HERTFORDSHIRE	ODSEY	REED	ROBERT FITZ ROZELIN	ALWARD	L4	50s	L4
HERTFORDSHIRE	EDWINSTREE	LAYSTON	RUMOLD	GODID	20s	40s	40s
HERTFORDSHIRE	EDWINSTREE	HORMEAD	2 ENGLISHMEN	WLWARD	100s	L4	L3
HERTFORDSHIRE	EDWINSTREE	BEAUCHAMPS	RUMOLD	GODID	40s	40s	20s
HERTFORDSHIRE	EDWINSTREE	HODDESDON	ST. MARTIN OF LONDON	GODID	40s	5s	15s
HERTFORDSHIRE	EDWINSTREE	HORMEAD (PART)	WILLIAM, OF RALPH B	WULFWARD,ASGAR'	5s	N/A	5s
HERTFORDSHIRE	EDWINSTREE	THROCKING	RUMOLD	ALRIC	2s	2s	2s
HUNTINGDONSHIRE		SIBSON	EUSTACE II	ULF	50s	N/A	50s
HUNTINGDONSHIRE		CHESTERTON	EUSTACE II	ULF	L4	N/A	40s
HUNTINGDONSHIRE		STEBBINGTON	LUNEN	SIBSON	N/A	N/A	N/A
HUNTINGDONSHIRE		GLATTON	EUSTACE II	ULF	L10	N/A	L10
KENT	WYE	BOUGHTON ALUPH	EUSTACE II	EARL GODWIN	L20	L30	L40
KENT	WESTERHAM	WESTERHAM	EUSTACE II	EARL GODWIN	L30	L24	L40
NORFOLK	EYNESFORD	WITCHINGHAM	EUSTACE II	GODWIN, FREEMAN	100s	N/A	L7
NORFOLK	HUMBLEYARD	NEYLAND	EUSTACE II	11 FREEMAN	N/A	N/A	10s

County	Hundred	Place	Tenant 1086	Holder 1066			
NORFOLK	DEPWADE	THORPE (ASHWELL)	EUSTACE II	THEGN, STIGAND'	100s	N/A	L6
NORFOLK	FREEBRIDGE	ANMER	EU., SOKEMEN, OSMUND	ORGAR	40s	N/A	80s
NORFOLK	FREEBRIDGE	LITTLE MASSINGHAM	GUY DE ANJOU	ORGAR, FREEMAN	20s	N/A	50s
NORFOLK	DOCKING	FRENGE	EUSTACE, 2 SOKEMEN	ORGAR, FREEMAN	40s	N/A	60s
OXFORDSHIRE		COWLEY	ROGER	N/A	40s	N/A	40s
SOMERSET		CHELWOOD	ALVRED OF MERLEBERG	THURI	N/A	40s	60s
SOMERSET	STANTON DREW	BELLUTON	ALVRED OF MERLEBERG	TOVI	L3	N/A	L4
SOMERSET	NORTH PETHERTON	NEWTON	ALVRED OF MERLEBERG	LEWIN	L4	N/A	L4
SOMERSET	OTTERHAMPTON	COMBWICH	ALVRED OF MERLEBERG	LEWIN	50s	N/A	40s
SOMERSET		LOXTON	EUSTACE II	ULVEVA	100s	N/A	100s
SOMERSET	ENMORE	LAXWORTHY	EVRARD	ALWARD	30s	N/A	30s
SOMERSET		COMPTON BISHOP	MAUD	ULNOD	N/A	L4	100s
SOMERSET		KINGWESTON	COUNTESS IDA	ULVEVA	L6	N/A	L6
SUFFOLK	SAMFORD	RAYDON	EUSTACE II	WULFWARA, F'WMN	N/A	N/A	N/A
SUFFOLK	SAMFORD	STANFELDA	HATO	AELFRIC, FR'MAN	20s	N/A	40s
SUFFOLK	STOW	LITTLE FINSBOROUGH	EUSTACE II	ENGELRIC	50s	50s	100s
SUFFOLK	LACKFORD	ELVEDEN	EUSTACE II	ALSI,->ENGELRIC	30s	N/A	40s
SUFFOLK	STOW	BUXHALL	EUSTACE II	ENGELRIC	40s	N/A	L4
SUFFOLK	THEDWESTRY	RATTLESDEN	ALDRED	ST. ETHELDREDA	N/A	N/A	10s
SUFFOLK	RISBRIDGE	OUSDEN	EUSTACE II	LEOFRIC	L6	N/A	L7
SUFFOLK	SAMFORD	HIGHAM	RALPH DE MERC	LEDMAR, FR'MAN	10s	10s	20s
SUFFOLK	STOW	LITTLE FINBOROUGH (30 ACRES)	7 FREEMEN	SAME MEN	N/A	N/A	100s
SURREY	REIGATE	NUTFIELD	COUNTESS IDA	ULWI	L13	L10	L15
SURREY	TANDRIGE	WACHELESTEDE, 15 HSE LON/SWARK	EUSTACE II	OSWARD	L20	L16	L20
SURREY	TANDRIGE	OXTED, 1 HOUSE IN SOUTHWARK	EUSTACE II	GIDA, HAR' MOM	L16	L10	L14

APPENDIX C

Most Frequent Holders of Eustace II's Lands

Name	Total number of holdings
Adelulf of Merck	11
Arnulf of Ardres	6
Guy of Anjou	5
Robert fitz Rozelin	5
Alvred of Merleberg	4
Bernard	4
Lambert	4
Robert	4
Ralf of Merck	3
Richard	3
Roger of Sombres	3
St. Martin's London	3 (+ 1 outright gift)
Rumold of Doudeauville	3

THE ENDOWMENT AND MILITARY OBLIGATIONS
OF THE SEE OF LONDON:
A REASSESSMENT OF THREE SOURCES [1]

Pamela Taylor

The history of the see of London displays a recurrent contrast between expectation and reality. This dichotomy was present from the outset, when Pope
Gregory's expectation that London would become the metropolitan see remained
unfulfilled. Augustine stayed on under Aethelbert of Kent's immediate aegis at
Canterbury, and in 604 Mellitus was sent as bishop to the East Saxons, whose
territory included London but whose king was already subject to Aethelbert.[2] The
kings of Kent in turn soon lost their hegemony, and for the ensuing millennium
London – both city and diocese – lay very much on the disputed and shifting
frontiers between first Wessex and Mercia and then Wessex and the Danelaw.

Had London become the archbishopric such a location might not have mattered, and could even have proved advantageous.[3] For an ordinary bishopric,
though, it was a considerable handicap. Although the see retained a high status,
probably reflecting both its Roman metropolitan past and the importance of the
city which was eventually to become the capital, its wealth was never even
remotely comparable.[4] This was primarily because the fortunes of English sees
were tied not to cities but to kings and kingdoms. The bishop of the East Saxons
could not attract the sort of royal endowment available to the bishops of more
powerful kings.[5] Additionally he was particularly disadvantaged when royal
awareness of the importance of London and its hinterland led in the ninth and
tenth centuries to a deliberate restriction of the rights of other lords in the area.

If history itself was not especially kind to the see, historians have largely
neglected it. The underlying structural reasons for the mismatch between status
and endowment have not been appreciated, so that when the gap has been noticed

---

[1] I owe particular thanks to Marjorie Chibnall and Susan Reynolds for their helpful comments on
an earlier draft of this paper, as well as to members of the Battle conference for their discussion of
it.
[2] Bede in *EHD*, 604 *et seq.* There was a further attempt in the late eighth century, both dictated
and defeated by political considerations: D. Whitelock, *Some Anglo-Saxon Bishops of London*,
London 1975, 13–14; N. Brooks, *The Early History of the Church of Canterbury*, Leicester 1984,
123–5.
[3] The archbishops might usefully have been situated between political camps, and their endowment was in any case more widely spread. Brooks, *Canterbury, passim.*
[4] For a correction of the view that the see's status was low see Whitelock, *Bishops*, 12.
[5] P. J. Taylor, 'The estates of the bishopric of London from the seventh century to the early
sixteenth century', London Ph.D. thesis 1976, 22–3. Compare Maitland's comments on Winchester: F. W. Maitland, *Domesday Book and Beyond*, Cambridge 1907, 497–8. See also P. Stafford,
Unification and Conquest, London 1989, 181–3, whose useful summary does not note London's
anomalous position.

individual scapegoats have been suggested.[6] Yet, as with the endowment itself, although the surviving sources cannot compare with those of more fortunate sees they are far from non-existent. In this paper I examine three particularly important ones: the will of bishop Theodred, proved in c.950, the St Paul's list of shipmen of c.1000, and Domesday Book.

As well as seeing what these tell us about the endowment and military obligations of the see on both sides of the Conquest, there are two wider aims. One is to bring into focus an area, roughly coincident with the diocese, which has also so far been curiously neglected. The city itself has not of course been overlooked, but has usually been considered in almost autonomous, though surely unhistorical, isolation. My final object is to suggest that the use of the three sources in wider debates is insecure unless their unusual estate and regional context is appreciated.

The first source, bishop Theodred's will, is an essential baseline for considering the endowment. While it does not itself tell us anything about military obligations, the implications of their distribution as shown in the later sources cannot be appreciated without first understanding the overall endowment pattern. The importance of the will for this purpose is enhanced by the paucity of other evidence. The canons in the twelfth century constructed an all-purpose trio of forgeries which were almost the only early title deeds which they used thereafter. These were supposed to be a seventh-century bull and two charters from Athelstan of Wessex (925–939), one apiece for the privileges and the estates.[7] The bishops too were not outstanding archivists. Nevertheless there survived until the seventeenth century a cartulary with a number of entries concerning what had become bishopric estates. Its disappearance probably predated the Great Fire (whose effect in this area at least can be greatly exaggerated), but eighteen extracts were made by Richard James, who died in 1638. Although clearly incomplete, they are acceptable as reliable copies from a cartulary which in turn accurately recorded authentic originals from the early eighth through to the early eleventh centuries.[8]

This is not the place to describe in detail either the charter evidence or what can be pieced together concerning the early endowment, but two summary points need to be made. First, the extracts made by James (hereafter the James MS) provide enough examples to show a normal pattern of endowment: early, large royal grants, followed by smaller bequests from a range of sources.[9] Secondly, the separation of the episcopal and chapter estates occurred uniquely early. When or why the process started is not at issue here, but it is taken for granted in bishop Theodred's will and in the various authentic donations recorded between then

---

[6]   E.g. F. Barlow, *The English Church 1000–1066*, London 1963, 219–20.
[7]   The charter for the endowments, which gives a long list of estates, was treated by the canons, and later commentators, as a grant. Even if it is taken as a confirmation, which the text warrants and which is inherently more likely, it contains a provable anachronism, and no reassuring traces of anything resembling earlier material incorporated within the obviously fabricated text. On the trio see M. Gibbs, *The Early Charters of St Paul's Cathedral*, Camden Soc. 3rd series lviii, 1939, Introduction x; Taylor, 'Estates', 32–3. The anachronism is the 8 *mansae* at Heybridge, not granted until c.1002: D. Whitelock (ed.), *Anglo-Saxon Wills*, Cambridge 1930, 38–9.
[8]   Gibbs, Introduction, *passim*.
[9]   The 704–5 grant of 50 *manentes* at Fulham by Tyrhtilus, bishop of Hereford (Gibbs, J6) has never been fully explained.

and the Conquest.[10] Domesday Book shows that by 1066 at St Paul's, and at no other English cathedral, the process was almost complete, and in 1086 the canons held almost all their estates directly from the king. The fully-fledged and immutable division between the common fund and the thirty prebends, though, was established by bishop Maurice shortly after 1086, so that here Domesday reflects a more fluid situation.[11]

The weakness of the charter evidence has naturally meant that all my three sources have been particularly valuable for filling gaps in our knowledge of the endowment by providing *termini post* or *ante quem* for gains and losses. In some cases this process is unexceptionable: Dunmow was among bishop Theodred's specific bequests to the canons in c.950 and appears in the ship list in c.1000, but Domesday, and later documents, report no St Paul's interest there, and its loss can therefore be assigned to the period c.1000 to 1066. The three have however been used more comprehensively. Each has been taken to provide a complete tally of the estates, and any alteration has therefore been seen as proof of gain or loss during the intervening period.

There is no major problem in accepting that the ship list and Domesday Book are complete lists, and that comprehensive comparisons between them are therefore valid. The same confidence cannot, however, be placed in Theodred's will. Since to say this is to challenge not just a neat antiquarian framework but also a range of wider conclusions specifically drawn from it, the point is important. A number of other interesting matters, including the evidence that Theodred was bishop not only of London but also of the East Anglian diocese centred on Hoxne in Suffolk, are not at issue here.[12]

The will is carefully ordered, and falls into logical sections. The first concerns grants to the king and (probably) the queen-mother. Next are grants to St Paul's: artefacts and relics for the church and, in each case specifically for the community, estates at Chich (known since the twelfth century as St Osyth), Tillingham and Dunmow in Essex, and Southery in Norfolk. Then follow grants of various estates in Suffolk to individuals, some of them named as kinsmen, and to local churches, including Hoxne. After this comes a section which begins with cash bequests to every see and cash distributions on the episcopal lands at London and Hoxne, and continues (in Whitelock's translation):

> And it is my will that the stock which is at Hoxne, which I have acquired there, be taken and divided into two parts, half for the minster, and (half) to be distributed for my soul. And as much as I found on that estate is to be left on it, but all the men are to be freed for my soul. And it is my wish that at London there be left as much as I found on the estate, and that what I added to it be taken and divided into two, half for the minster and half for my soul, and all the men are to be freed. And the same is to be done at

[10] Taylor, 'Estates', 48–52; compare Canterbury: Brooks, *Canterbury*, 139–41; P. B. Boyden, 'A study in the structure of landholding and administration in Essex in the late Anglo-Saxon period', London Ph.D. thesis 1986, 125–31 disputes the idea of early separation, but does not cite the comparative literature or seem to me to substantiate his case.
[11] Gibbs, xx; C. N. L. Brooke, 'The Composition of the Chapter of St Paul's, 1086–1163', *Cambridge Historical Journal*, x, 1951, 111–32. The cathedral endowments display the same gap between status and economic reality as the bishopric's.
[12] Whitelock, *Wills*, 2–5, 99–103.

Wimbledon and at Sheen. And at Fulham everything is to be left as it now stands, unless one wishes to free any of my men. And at Dengie let there be left as much as I found on the estate and let the rest be divided into two, half for the minster and half for my soul.

The bequests then end with a miscellaneous list of gifts.

The belief that the will refers to all the estates derives from Cyril Hart, whose analysis in *The Early Charters of Essex* led him to the categorical statement:

one cannot avoid the conclusion that in his will Theodred named *all* the estates then held by St Paul's, whether as episcopal property, or as land belonging to the canons.

This conclusion rests on two others: first that in the quoted section of the will Theodred 'disposes of his two episcopal properties. The estate at Hoxne . . . is to go to his successor as bishop of East Anglia, and (the other estates) are left to his successor in the see of London.' Secondly, the grant of the four estates to the canons 'is better regarded as an acknowledgement of their existing rights than as a grant *de novo*.'[13]

In fact the wording supports none of these conclusions. All that Theodred does in the quoted section is to make arrangements for any increase of stock above that which he had inherited with the estate, and for the freeing of slaves. No grant or confirmation of the estate itself is involved.[14] For the four estates given to the canons, conversely, the phrase used is 'And I grant'. It is surely improbable that this formula would have been used indifferently for both grants and confirmations, particularly as it is conspicuously absent from the section quoted above concerning the episcopal demesnes.

If the wording of the will fails to support any theory of an automatic grant or confirmation, so too does what wider knowledge we have of the London endowments. Assuming that the estate referred to as London includes extra-mural Stepney, the five mentioned in the section concerning the episcopal demesnes could in fact be a complete list, not least because of the reference to Fulham where nothing is to be altered.[15] This cannot, though, be said of the four named chapter estates. One of these, Southery, is known to have been granted by king Edmund to Theodred in his personal capacity, and was therefore his to bestow at will.[16] This leaves only three, which would be an impossibly meagre endowment. It is implausible that all the other estates, many of them large, which appear in the c.1000 ship list and subsequently but are only covered by the spurious Athelstan charter, were received in the second half of the tenth century. The James MS, moreover,

---

[13] C. R. Hart, *The Early Charters of Essex*, 2nd edn Leicester 1971, 34.

[14] See Whitelock, *Bishops*, 19, which acknowledges Hart's interpretation but does not fully endorse it, and her comment on l. 14 of the will, *Wills*, 103.

[15] That 'London' includes Stepney is made even more likely by the reference to the cash distributions '. . . at mine biscopriche binnen Lundene and buten Lundene' and at Hoxne, since the context indicates that this refers only to the immediate estates near the cathedrals rather than to the whole endowment, or diocese. Whitelock, *Wills*, 4, 103.

[16] Hart's suggestion, 34, that lands outside the diocese were immediately transferred to the canons is unsubstantiated, and if Wimbledon and Sheen were not then within the diocese (which is uncertain), contradicted by them (see below, pp. 296–97). The canons at Hoxne would in any case have been the more obvious recipients for Southery.

however incomplete, at least shows that the large bishopric estates of Fulham and Southminster were received as one would expect far earlier, in both cases at the start of the eighth century.[17]

It is equally unlikely that the canons' extensive Middlesex lands, perhaps the most conspicuous absentees from the will, were at this stage all subsumed within the bishopric manors of Stepney and Fulham. Even if this was originally so, the Middlesex estates would surely have been among the first rather than the last to be separated: the canons themselves always claimed that the twenty-four hides immediately north of the city were part of their foundation endowment.[18] Finally, a charter partially recorded in the James MS suggests that St Paul's acquired Navestock in the mid-ninth century.[19] It does not lie close enough to any of the named estates to be subsumed within them, and remained a St Paul's possession, but it fails to appear in the will.

Of the three estates other than Southery, the earlier history of Dunmow is unknown, but both Tillingham and Chich had probably long belonged to St Paul's.[20] It must be assumed that the will is simply transferring them from the bishop's to the community's support.

If this interpretation is accepted, various wider generalisations specifically based on Hart's conclusions have to be re-examined. This process turns out to be reassuring, since the generalisations concerned are out of line with our accumulating picture derived from other early foundations. At issue, both directly and indirectly, is the whole subject of the nature of bookland. The subject is obviously relevant to the themes of this paper, but is equally obviously too extensive to be examined comprehensively.[21] I therefore limit myself to a few directly salient points.

An association between wills and bookland is generally recognised, and most would probably accept Eric John's assertion that in the tenth century 'wills and the right of manumission are inseparably connected with bookland'.[22] John however goes farther and, citing Hart's conclusion on Theodred's will, apparently argues that both then and earlier all booked land *had* to be transmitted in each generation by will. The position which is actually reflected is surely both more interesting and more probable, for it shows that the distinction between the person and the office of a bishop was well understood. If bishops had enjoyed a totally free right of bequest, they would have been able, and doubtless all too often willing, to dismember their churches' estates. Lands booked to the bishopric or the cathedral did not belong to the individual bishop and therefore did not have to figure in his will. The understanding of the distinction was not new in the mid-tenth century, and was indeed probably at least as old as the threat of

[17] Gibbs, J6–7, J11.
[18] As in the writ obtained from William I, Gibbs, no. 11.
[19] Gibbs, J4. The grant purports to be from king Edgar (959–975), but from analysis of the witness list Gibbs concludes that Edgar's name has been substituted for Ethelred I of Wessex (866–871) in what is otherwise a genuine deed.
[20] Tillingham was probably a genuine foundation grant, even if the supposed charter of king Aethelbert is unreliable: P. Sawyer (ed.), *Anglo-Saxon Charters: an annotated list and bibliography*, London 1968, nos. 1–5, and 87, footnote 32. For Chich see below, footnote 58.
[21] Susan Reynolds' paper, 'Bookland, Folkland, and Fiefs', above, pp. 211–27, has now provided a valuable reassessment of the general issues.
[22] E. John, *Land Tenure in Early England*, Leicester 1960, 17; see also his statement, 10, on *propria potestas*.

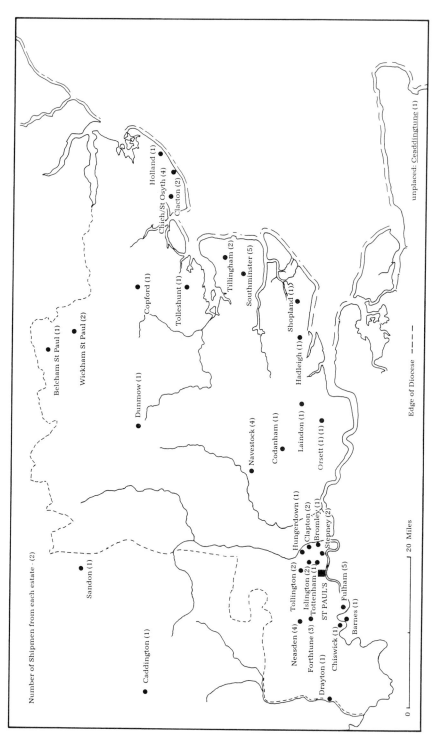

Number of Shipmen from each estate - (2)

Caddington (1)

Sandon (1)

Belcham St Paul (1)

Wickham St Paul (2)

Dunmow (1)

Copford (1)

Holland (1)

Chich/St Osyth (4)
Clacton (2)

Tolleshunt (1)

Tillingham (2)

Southminster (5)

Navestock (4)

Codanham (1)

Shopland (1)

Laindon (1)

Hadleigh (1)

Orsett (1) (1)

Hungerdown (1)

Clapton (2)

Bromley (1)

Stepney (2)

Neasden (4)

Tollington (2)

Islington (2)

Forthune (3)

Tottenham (1)

ST PAUL'S

Fulham (5)

Drayton (1)

Chiswick (1)

Barnes (1)

Edge of Diocese - - - - -

0   20 Miles

unplaced: Ceaddingtune (1)

St Paul's estates from the ship list

dismemberment. Both are clearly visible in the formulae of Canterbury charters of the late eighth and early ninth centuries.[23] The distinction also presumably parallels the one widespread in Germanic societies between inherited property inalienable from the kin and acquired property which could be disposed of more freely.[24]

This reinterpretation of the will's evidence concerning the nature of tenth-century ecclesiastical bookland thus moves it into line with evidence from elsewhere. So too does the associated reinterpretation of the chronology of the endowment. When it was thought that any estate not mentioned in the will must have been a later acquisition, comparison of the relatively few mentioned there with the thirty-three in the ship list led to the inevitable conclusion that St Paul's achieved an enormous expansion of its endowment, including some very large blocks of land, between c.950 and c.1000. Yet if this were so it would have been a remarkable achievement, particularly for an old-established foundation which was not participating in the contemporary Reformation, and would require a radical reassessment of almost all our views on the nature of bookland, royal patronage and the land market both in the second half of the tenth century and earlier.[25]

Once it is no longer necessary to posit this sudden massive increase, we can revert to a more normal and plausible picture of the pattern of the endowment. This is an essential framework for moving on to consider the important changes which genuinely did occur in the late ninth and tenth centuries and which affected the whole nature of legal and military obligations, and their relationship to bookland.

In turning to my next document, the ship list of c.1000, the same themes continue. It is an important source for establishing the St Paul's endowment at the time and, as it was conveniently compiled at almost the mid-point between the deaths of bishop Theodred and Edward the Confessor, it provides some significant evidence concerning intervening gains and losses, including the loss of the bishop's Surrey estates. Setting it in its estate and regional context also allows other interesting and hitherto unexamined implications to emerge.

The list, which survives in a twelfth-century copy now at Cambridge, is as follows. (Modern forms of place names are given in brackets, and the places are mapped in fig.1.)[26]

(S)cipmen. Of Ticc (Chich-St Osyth) IIII. Of Tillingaham (Tillingham) II. Of Dunmaewan (Dunmow) and of Tollesfuntan (Tolleshunt) I. Of Naesing-stoce (Navestock) and of Neosdune (Neasden) IIII. Of Hinawicun (Wickham St Paul's) and of Tollandune (Tollington) II. Of Gnutungadune (Hungerdown) and of Braembelege (Bromley) I. Of Tottanheale (Totten-

---

[23] Brooks, *Canterbury*, 139–42, 158–9.

[24] P. Wormald in J. Campbell (ed.), *The Anglo-Saxons*, Oxford 1982, 95–8. See also Stafford, *Unification*, 170.

[25] Stafford, *Unification*, especially 52–4, 182–4. See also N. Banton, 'Monastic reform in Tenth-Century England', *Studies in Church History*, xviii, 1882, 71–85. Boyden's failure to re-examine Hart and consider this wider context seems to me to undermine his approach and many of his conclusions.

[26] I am very grateful to Laurence Keen for drawing the map. It updates D. Hill's valuable pioneering attempt in *An Atlas of Anglo-Saxon England*, Oxford 1981, map 165.

ham Court) I. Of Clopham (Clapham ?*recte* Clapton) II. Of Baernun
(Barnes) and of Ceswican (Chiswick) I. Of Draegtune (Drayton) I. Of
Caddandune (Caddington) I. Of Sandune (Sandon) I. Of *Ceaddingtune* I.
Of Fullanhamme (Fulham) V. Of Forthune (Fortune Gate) IIII. Of Stybban-
hythe (Stepney) and of Gislandune (Islington) II. Of Orseathun (Orsett) I.
Of Ligeandune (Laindon) I. of Seopinglande (Shopland) and of tham west-
rum Orseathum (Orsett) I. Of Bylcham (Belchamp St Paul's) I. Of Coppan-
forda (Copford) and Holande (Holland) I. Of Suthmynster (Southminster)
V. Of Claccingtune (Clacton) II. Of Haethlege (Hadleigh) and of Codanham (Codham Hall) I.[27]

The heading obviously marks the document as one of rare interest, but its summary nature does not help interpretation. Much has to depend on trying to
establish the rationale behind the grouping of these particular thirty-three places.

St Paul's is not mentioned by name, but the document was originally stored
there. More significantly, as its original editor Liebermann noted, the great majority of the estates listed are known to have belonged to the cathedral and/or
bishop. Liebermann, from whose work all later commentary has been largely
derived, was able to show connections for twenty-five of the thirty-three estates.
Among the remaining eight, he presumed that Clopham was Clapham in Surrey,
and Codanham Coddenham in Suffolk, and suggested that the most likely candidate for Haethlege, since it combined with Codanham to produce one man, was
Hadleigh in Suffolk. For those for which he could find no connection with the
cathedral he hypothesised (in my translation):

> Clapham and Hadleigh lie near London; they might, like Tolleshunt and
> Holland in Essex, which a bishop of London bought in about 1250, have
> called on the protection of St Paul, whom their neighbours served, for their
> ship service duty.[28]

But if this were so it would mean that the bishop was organising his shipfyrd from
estates which were not his, some of them not even within his diocese. If he was in
some way responsible for a whole circle round London, surely the list ought to be
far more comprehensive: why and on what criteria should these few estates have
been selected? Abels, the most recent commentator, skirts the problem by assuming that all the estates belonged to the see, but without re-examining any of
Liebermann's identifications.[29] At the risk of tedium, it is worth attempting to do
this in some detail.

Since Liebermann wrote, connections to St Paul's have been made for some of
the remaining eight estates. The canons' possession of Holland is confirmed by
the *Liber Eliensis*.[30] Two possible links are suggested by Domesday Book: for
Codanham Liebermann could only suggest the similarly named Coddenham in

[27] Corpus Christi College Cambridge MS 383 f. 107; I am grateful to Professor R. I. Page for
providing me with a photocopy when the original was away for repair. First edited by F. Liebermann, 'Matrosenstellung aus Landguetern der Kirche London um 1000', *Archiv fuer das Studium
der Neueren Sprachen und Literaturen*, civ, Brunswick 1900, 17–24. Translated in A. J. Robertson,
Anglo-Saxon Charters, Cambridge 1956, 144–5, with nn. 389–91.
[28] Liebermann, 'Matrosenstellung', 22.
[29] R. P. Abels, *Lordship and Military Obligation in Anglo-Saxon England*, London 1988, 158–9.
[30] Gibbs, xxxix.

Suffolk, but it can perhaps be related to Codham Hall in Warley (Essex) which Domesday Book states had been restored to the bishop by the Conqueror because it had belonged of old to St Paul's.[31] Similarly, Ligenadune is better identified as Laindon rather than Leyton (both in Essex) since the former, despite a different pre-Conquest tenant, was included without explanation in the lands rather than the fee section of the bishopric endowment in Domesday.[32] Post-Conquest restorations may be pointers to the problems posed for ecclesiastical overlords, and historians, by the loss of tenanted lands.

Another relevant problem is that of the use of place-names in administrative contexts. Liebermann refers to the names in the ship list as 'doerfer', most obviously translated as villages, but the obligations were almost certainly imposed on administrative units rather than on settlements. Ealing for example is absent from the list, but although it was the subject of a separate eighth-century grant it was always included within the manor of Fulham.[33] It is now generally understood that since Domesday is organised by manors not settlements it is a very imperfect guide to the latter.[34] The same understanding has to be extended to many other documents. It must be equally true of many charters, and not only early ones conferring overlordship of vast areas, but also later grants of what was often a miscellaneous collection of land lying in neighbouring parishes. Similarly, estates once received could be grouped or regrouped for various purposes, and it is not surprising either that the choice of name for the group could vary or that some settlements are seldom mentioned.

With this in mind, Hadleigh, like Codanham, can almost certainly be safely transferred from Liebermann's Suffolk identification into Essex. The Essex Hadleigh lies close to Shopland and Barling. Shopland is in the ship list, and the James MS includes a charter of 946 in which king Eadred granted twelve mansae there to a nun for religious purposes.[35] As with Hadleigh, no St Paul's interest there is recorded in Domesday Book. Barling was granted to the bishop in 998.[36] It is not in the ship list, but may well either have been received too late for inclusion or subsumed within Shopland. It was soon transferred from the bishop to the canons, who held it in 1086.[37] It is the only place of these three which is recorded in a medieval list of the rotation of the food farm between the canons' estates.[38] Yet Dean Lisieux's mid fifteenth-century catalogue of the cathedral archives has an entry 'de terris in Barlynge Hadley et Sopilande evidencie', and a post-Reformation lease book has details of woods in the Hadleigh area.[39]

A similar explanation could account for the previously unidentified Forthtune.

---

[31] P. Reaney (ed.), *The Place-Names of Essex*, English Place-Name Society xii, Cambridge 1935, 135, 466; Hart, 35.

[32] *Domesday Book*, ii, 9b; see below, pp. 307–08.

[33] Gibbs, J7; *VCH Middlesex* vii, 1982, 144. For the example of Chich see below, n. 58.

[34] P. Sawyer in *Medieval Settlement*, London 1976, 1–7, and in T. Rowley (ed.), *Anglo-Saxon Settlement and Landscape*, British Archaeological Reports 6, 1974, 108–10.

[35] Gibbs, J12.

[36] A. S. Napier and W. H. Stevenson (eds.), *Early Charters and Documents*, Oxford 1895, 9.

[37] Odo of Bayeux held a further half hide there: *Domesday Book*, ii, 13b–14a, 23b.

[38] St Paul's MS WD 4 f. 5, now Guildhall Library MS 25504. The list claims to describe the rotation 'tempore Wulmanni decani'; Wulman occurs as dean 1086 x 1107: D. E. Greenaway (ed.), *Fasti Ecclesiae Anglicanae 1066–1300. I St Paul's, London*, London 1968.

[39] St Paul's MS WD 11 f. 60, now Guildhall Library MS 25111; BL MS Lansdowne 364 f. 364v; see also Hart, 19, 37–8.

The extensive cathedral estates covering the Neasden-Harlesden-Willesden area are entered in Domesday Book under Willesden and Harlesden.[40] The ship list mentions neither of these, but gives us Neasden, and also Forthtune. Fortune Gate Road in Harlesden still preserves a name given as Forton(e)feild in 1300 which in turn probably preserves foran-tune, a settlement in front of the tun of Harlesden.[41] The ship list's Neasden and Forthtune could well equate to Domesday's Willesden and Harlesden. Another name which defeated Liebermann was Gnutungadune, coupled with Bromley. Such couplings are not a consistent guide to proximity, but Bromley is almost certainly Bromley by Bow, which lay within Stepney, and it has now been suggested that Gnutungadune is Hungerdown in Hackney, which was also part of Stepney.[42]

Although some of the identifications are tentative, reasonable links with St Paul's can now be suggested for thirty of the thirty-three places in the list. Of the remaining three, Ceaddingtune remains unidentified;[43] Tolleshunt is in Essex and was probably a small estate whose documentation has vanished.[44] The third, Clopham, or in its modern form Clapham, is however the most crucial of all. Not only was it a substantial estate, producing two shipmen, but the only known Claphams, including the Surrey candidate picked by Liebermann, are outside the diocese.

All the three other estates in the list definitely lying outside the diocese, Sandon in East Herts., Caddington on the Beds./Herts. border, and Barnes in Surrey, were held by the canons in 1066.[45] By that time the bishop had no estates outside his diocese, which had attained its later form, covering Middlesex, Essex and East Herts. Earlier it seems to have been more extensive, and at some points to have included at least part of both West Herts. and Surrey.[46] The details of possible alterations between the seventh and tenth centuries are as complicated as the political history of the area, with which they are of course inseparably connected, and are beyond the scope of this paper.[47] In the tenth century, as earlier, however, the interconnection of dioceses and kingdoms remained a vital reflec-

---

[40] Domesday Book, i, 127d.

[41] G. E. B. Glover *et al.* (eds), *The Place-Names of Middlesex*, English Place-Name Society xviii, Cambridge 1942, 161.

[42] K. McDonnell, *Medieval London Suburbs*, London and Chichester 1978, 19–20.

[43] Ceaddingtune is etymologically unlikely to be the second St Paul's Domesday estate at Caddington: M. Mawer and F. M. Stenton (eds), *The Place-Names of Bedfordshire and Huntingdonshire*, English Place-Name Society iii, Cambridge 1926, 145.

[44] Liebermann was correct, 'Matrosenstellung', 22, in saying that land at Tolleshunt was bought by bishop Fulk Bassett in the mid thirteenth century (*Ancient Deeds*, A 524), but this was a private purchase and assigned to his heirs not his successors. Boyden, 129, corrects my confusion of Tolleshunt and Tollesbury in 'Estates', 41, 127.

[45] *Domesday Book*, i, 136b, 211, 34.

[46] Gibbs, J9 is a grant by the king of the East Saxons to the bishop in c.704–6 of land at Hemel Hempstead, in W. Herts. Hill's *Atlas* assumes that the Thames was the southern boundary throughout. See also Brooks, *Canterbury*, 106–7, 238–50; C. N. L. Brooke, *London 800–1216: the shaping of a city*, London 1975, 17. F. Liebermann, 'Einleitung zum Statut der Londoner Friedensgilde unter Aethelstan', *Mélanges Fitting*, ii, Montpellier 1908, 85–6, points out that the use of the phrase 'south of the boundary' suggests that the area covered extended south of the Thames. It may not have been co-extensive with the diocese, but since the date is c.930 the coincidence is suggestive.

[47] For resumés of what is known of the political position of the various kingdoms see B.Yorke, 'The kingdom of the East Saxons', *Anglo-Saxon England*, xiv, 1985, 1–36; S. Bassett (ed.), *The Origins of Anglo-Saxon Kingdoms*, Leicester 1989; Stafford, *Unification*.

tion of the bishops' multifaceted role, most of which was not shared by the cathedral community. Given the early separation of the estates, it may well have seemed less appropriate for the bishop of London than for his chapter to have lands outside the diocese.

It is however indubitable that in c.950 bishop Theodred, and not the canons, was holding Wimbledon and Sheen in Surrey. Wimbledon is adjacent to Barnes, and Sheen (known since the sixteenth century as Richmond) near by to the west. In c.1000 Barnes alone appears in the ship list. By 1066, as later, Sheen apparently lay within the royal manor of Kingston, and Wimbledon within the archbishop of Canterbury's manor of Mortlake, from which the canons were holding Barnes.[48] Both royal and Canterbury sources are silent, but the absence of Wimbledon and Sheen from the ship list makes it more likely that their transfer occurred between c.950 and c.1000 than between c.1000 and 1066. The most likely occasion is 957 when, following the West Saxon succession crisis, the Thames became the boundary between Eadwig's Wessex and Edgar's Mercia and all the bishops and ealdormen north of the Thames ceased to appear at Eadwig's court and instead attended Edgar's. Although Edgar also gained Wessex in 959, the Thames thereafter remained the boundary between the West Saxon and Mercian parts of his kingdom.[49]

The canons' estate at Barnes may have escaped the transfer which befell Wimbledon and Sheen, but it has to be accounted extremely unlikely that either the bishop or canons was holding a substantial estate in the Surrey Clapham in c.1000, which was in the hands of one Turbern TRE and of Geoffrey de Mandeville in 1086. It has probably only been assumed to be the right place by the usual dangerous argument from silence because its descent between 871 x 889 and 1066 is unknown.[50]

There is a further reason for rejecting this Clapham: the earliest forms of its name, Cloppaham, Clopeham, and Cloppeham, would make the Clopham of the ship list, which is not otherwise anachronistic, a surprising contraction.[51] The earliest forms for Clapham in Bedfordshire, Cloppham, Clopeham and Clopham, are more compatible, but fortunately for historians this estate is known to have been firmly in the hands of Ramsey Abbey throughout.[52] The studies of the clop-element do however support one other possibility: that 'Clopham' is a simple scribal error, either in the original or in the twelfth-century copy, for 'Clopton'. Clapton lies within the manor of Stepney and is an authentic Anglo-Saxon place-name, recorded from 1339 until the mid-sixteenth century as 'Clopton'.[53]

Even on the lowest estimate of fully proven connections, Liebermann's suggestion that other estates might be included in the St Paul's shipfyrd simply because they were near London is, I think, unnecessary. Closer checking of the estate context also strongly suggests that the list is a complete, as well as a discrete, roll of the estates, which leads to the important conclusion that it represents the

---

[48] *Domesday Book*, i, 30, 34.
[49] Stafford, *Unification*, 48; her comments, 183, overlook this evidence for diocesan reorganisation.
[50] *VCH Surrey*, iv, 1967, 39, does not even mention the possibility.
[51] *VCH Surrey*, iv, 1967, 36.
[52] *The Place-Names of Bedfordshire*, 23; *VCH Beds.*, iii, 1912, 128–9.
[53] *The Place-Names of Middlesex*, 105.

bishop's apportionment of his total obligation among all the St Paul's estates.[54] It is from this basis that we can move on to consider what it reveals about both the internal and the external organisation of the obligation.

The question of the internal organisation has puzzled everyone who has used the list. From Liebermann onwards all have assumed that wherever two places occur before a number, as in 'Of Navestock and of Neasden IIII', the places are paired to provide that number. Much time has been spent in trying to make any sense of the pairings, which have no geographical rationale, as well as of the overall basis of the assessment, which shows no correlation with Domesday hidages. Equally surprising has been the total raised: forty-five men rather than the normal sixty.[55]

During discussion at the Battle conference the illuminating suggestion was made that much of the difficulty has been due to a misreading: there are in fact no pairs, and Navestock and Neasden owe four men each.[56] This interpretation is linguistically sound, and makes more obvious sense: why should Navestock and Neasden have combined (and across county boundaries) to produce four men, rather than simply dividing their obligation? The order of the list is basically mnemonic, using a combination of alliteration and geographical proximity.

Even though neither amounts to complete mathematical proof, two further advantages support this interpretation: it produces a much better fit between hidage and obligation, and yields a total of fifty-eight men. The total ought almost certainly to be sixty, but we have to fall back again on probable scribal error, presumably by the twelfth-century copyist, losing what need only be a single minim. The argument over the degree of correlation between hidage and obligation is more subtle. Even if we assume no change in hidation between c.1000 and 1066, it would be impossible to assign Domesday hidages to all the estates in the list. This is not simply because of losses such as Dunmow, where we do not know which Domesday estate is involved: more significant is the problem of choice of place-names for administrative units, discussed above.[57] Even if the suggested identifications of Forthtune, Gnutungadune and Clapton are discounted, it is obvious from even a cursory look that the division of the Middlesex estates in the list and in Domesday is very different. Similarly in Essex, the list's Chich almost certainly includes other estates separately entered in 1086.[58] If place-names do not

[54] For more detail concerning the estates see Taylor, 'Estates', especially chapter 1 and appendix I.
[55] See most recently Abels, 158–9; N. Hooper, 'Some observations on the navy in late Anglo-Saxon England', C. Harper-Bill *et al.* (eds), *Studies in Medieval History presented to R. Allen Brown*, Woodbridge 1989, 203–13. It is worth noting that Abels' choice of examples is in any case unfortunate since it includes both Clapham and Chich: see above, pp. 296–97 and below, n. 58.
[56] Particular thanks are due to Matthew Bennett for the original suggestion, and to Cecily Clark for confirming its linguistic plausibility.
[57] P. 295.
[58] Chich was renamed St Osyth after its transfer to that priory by bishop Richard de Belmeis (1108–27). In Domesday the whole of the clearly defined promontory on which it stands was divided between the bishop's manors of Chich (7 hides) and Clacton (20 hides), the canons' manor of Edulvesnasa (Thorpe and Kirby le Soken and Walton on the Naze, 27 hides), and the 3-hide manor of Bircho removed from the canons by Eustace of Boulogne. (*Domesday Book*, ii, 32b–33a; J. H. Round, 'Birch Hall in Kirby', *Trans. Essex Archaeological Society*, ns xiv, 1918, 363–4; Hart, 30–2; Boyden, 128.) There is no charter evidence, so the first reference to any part comes in Theodred's will, where 'Chich' is transferred and neither Clacton nor Edulvesnasa mentioned, and Clacton's absence from the section detailing demesne stock suggests that it was transferred as

always represent the same area, Domesday hidages cannot reliably be projected backwards. All that can safely be said (and this is a considerable gain), is that with the pairings removed and the new place-name identifications accepted, there seems a reasonable proportionality between the sizes of estates and obligations.

If this is so, and in any case since the list appears to include all the St Paul's endowment, Abels' hypothesis that the obligations were imposed on tenanted lands is improbable.[59] There is the surprising inclusion of both Orsett and west Orsett, as well as the separate mention of subsidiary places within Stepney, which might suggest a division into separately tenanted holdings.[60] But such entries are far fewer than the probable state of the land market would lead us to expect, and they do not bear any significant or remarkable portion of the burden. They are far more likely simply to represent a different division from later either within or between the bishopric and chapter estates.

The list also raises the question of the external organisation behind the imposition. In particular, if the bishop's obligation now appears to have been sixty, or fifty-eight, rather than forty-five, how far are we seeing another example of a three hundred hide-sixty men ship soke? Once again the fundamental starting point is that the list comprises only St Paul's estates. Whatever his other roles, on this occasion the bishop was not acting more widely within his diocese or its constituent shires and hundreds. The exact extent of the London endowment in c.1000 cannot be estimated, but it seems to be between three hundred and 350 hides. The apparent loss of the Surrey estates of Wimbledon and Sheen between c.950 and c.1000 could suggest that here, as at Sherborne, reorganisation took place against some sort of three-hundred-hide benchmark.[61]

Thus far the London evidence seems to confirm the accepted picture. On the other hand, it also suggests the necessity for some refinement. First, in a diocese which, even if it suffered adjustment, was not a new or artificial creation, both the total endowment and the extents of the individual estates were probably not completely amenable to the full one man per five hide formula. Secondly, and more significantly, the distinction between a private three-hundred-hide endowment and a triple hundred needs to be more systematically considered.

Despite the shortage of evidence concerning late Anglo-Saxon naval organisation, there is general acceptance of the importance of units of three hundred hides. It is also accepted that the deliberate royal development of the shires and hundreds during the tenth century included an enhanced role as units of military organisation.[62] One of the standard supporting texts is of course the edict of 1008

part of Chich. In the ship list Clacton occurs as well as Chich but Edulvesnasa does not. We do not know when the Domesday division into two almost equal parts occurred, but it seems certain that in the ship list Edulvesnasa is included within Chich and/or Clacton.

[59] Abels, 158–9, 276. See also D. Roffe, 'From thegnage to barony: sake and soke, title, and tenants-in-chief', *ante*, xii, 1989, 157–76; there are no comparable signs of continuity here, not least because of the radical post-Conquest change in the endowment, see below.

[60] See for instance the Domesday entries for Islington (including the composite make-up of Barnsbury) and Bromley in Stepney: *Domesday Book*, i, 128, 130c; *VCH Middlesex*, i, 1969, 156; viii, 1985, 51; McDonnell, 21. Boyden, 129, suggests that west Orsett is the 1 hide in Orsett held by Engelric of the church TRE and by Eustace of Boulogne in chief in 1086; *Domesday Book*, ii, 26b.

[61] Although it is noteworthy that Stenton, *Anglo-Saxon England*, 439–40, thought this an inadequate endowment. See also Stafford, *Unification*, 188–94.

[62] See especially Abels; Hooper; H. R. Loyn, 'The Hundred in England in the Tenth and early

ordering the provision of a ship from every three hundred, or possibly 310, hides.[63] This may be a little later than the ship list, and could therefore represent a reorganisation, but three-hundred-hide units are definitely earlier. Apart from traces in Domesday we have not only the well known but dubious evidence from Worcester but also the unimpeachable letter from bishop Aethelric of Sherborne. This can only be dated to 1001/2 x 1009/12, but clearly refers to the past since the bishop complains that he is not receiving shipscot from thirty-three hides which his predecessors enjoyed and which are now lacking 'from the three hundred hides which other bishops had for their scyre'.[64]

Insufficient attention has, however, been paid to the significance of the composition of these three hundred hides. 'Scyre' in the tenth century could mean shire, diocese or, in its original and underlying sense, an area of responsibility.[65] Harmer in her influential translation chose diocese, but a glance at the maps in Hill confirms the likelihood of Stenton's assertion, followed the most recent writers, that the three hundred hides refer only to the endowment of the bishopric.[66] If this is so then, like the bishop of London, the bishop of Sherborne was levying his obligations from his own estates. Is it even possible that when the writer of the *Leges Henrici Primi* stated that shires were divided into hundreds and shipsokes he meant not hundreds and triple hundreds but hundreds and estates that provided separate quotas?[67] It is certainly difficult to see how the 1008 edict could have been implemented in counties such as Middlesex where the hundreds were not based on multiples of a hundred hides.[68]

The mention of Middlesex brings us to another important, and hitherto disregarded, context for considering the ship list. The bishop of London suffered distinct disadvantages because of the location of his diocese, or more precisely his cathedral city, and one of these was a failure to hold any private hundreds. This lack was not one of the consequences of the original discrepancy between the status of the cathedral city and the East Saxon kingdom: the endowment could not compare with such as Winchester, but it included large early estates. Instead,

Eleventh Centuries', H. Hearder and H. R. Loyn (eds), *British Government and Administration. Studies presented to S. B. Chrimes*, Cardiff 1974, 1–15.
[63] *EHD*, i, 213.
[64] F. E. Harmer, *Anglo-Saxon Writs*, Manchester 1952, no. 63; Hooper, 209; P. H. Sawyer, 'Charters of the Reform Movement: the Worcester Archive', in D. Parsons (ed.), *Tenth-Century Studies: Essays in Commemoration of the Millenium of the Council of Winchester and 'Regularis Concordia'*, Chichester 1975, 85–7.
[65] D. H. Giffard, 'The Parish in Domesday Book: a study of the mother churches, manorial churches and rural chapels in the late Saxon and early Norman periods', London Ph.D. thesis, 1952, especially 10–13, is illuminating even though he omits the political dimension in the formation of dioceses. See also P. Wormald, 'A handlist of Anglo-Saxon lawsuits', *Anglo-Saxon England*, xvii, 1988, 279.
[66] Not least because one of the estates is outside the diocese. Hill, *Atlas*, nos. 161, 238–241; F. M. Stenton, *Anglo-Saxon England*, 3rd edn Oxford 1971, 439–40; *VCH Dorset*, iii, 1968, 40–1. F. R. Thorn, 'Hundreds and Wapentakes', in A. Williams and G. H. Martin (eds), The Dorset Domesday, London 1991, 38 (my thanks to Laurence Keen for this reference). See also H. Edwards, *The Charters of the Early West Saxon Kingdom*, British Archaeological Reports 198, 1988.
[67] John in Campbell, 172–3 cites this important reference. Although there may have been some difficulties, his view of the probable conflict between royal officials and soke holders seems anachronistic. See also Hooper, 210; J. Gillingham, 'The introduction of knight service into England', *ante*, iv, 1982, 61.
[68] Stafford, *Unification*, 64–5 highlights the local nature of the response at least until 1006.

the restriction has to be seen as a consequence of deliberate royal policy during the establishment of the new shire and hundred structures in the ninth and tenth centuries.

London was a uniquely important town, both economically and strategically. Alfred's grants of land at Queenhithe to the archbishop of Canterbury and bishop of Worcester, with their careful retention of royal tolls on all goods coming into London and on any trade carried on in the public street or on the shore, emphasise how much it was and remained under royal control.[69] It did not, however, have the usual relationship with a single associated shire. Passing over the complex previous history of the East Saxon kingdom, we know from the *Anglo-Saxon Chronicle* that Edward the Elder ordered the building of twin fortifications at Hertford in 913. The associated shire was mainly (if not entirely) drawn from what had previously been a larger Middlesex, which must therefore also have been reorganised, or shired, at this time.[70] Essex followed very shortly, after the reconquest of Colchester in 917.[71] The shire and hundred structure of the three counties was thus a product of the second decade of the tenth century, and very much part of Edward the Elder's general policies for the shiring of Mercia.

Even thereafter there is much that is obscure in the history of the region, and there were almost certainly various modifications. On the one hand we know in general that the full development of hundredal organisation was a little later.[72] More specifically, we have in VI Athelstan, the ordinances of the London Peace Guild, proof of an intermediate stage of organisation in the 930s. This is not one of my three sources, and I shall resist being diverted by it here. For all its interest, it looks like a short-lived product of its transitional period.[73]

It is normally reckoned that the hundreds accommodated many existing estate patterns, so that the holders of large blocks of early endowment, with their associated jurisdictional rights, became the holders of the famous hundreds 'born private.'[74] It has not hitherto been remarked, however, that within the area of the diocese of London private hundreds were systematically aborted. All the six

---

[69] T. Dyson, 'Two Saxon land grants for Queenhithe', J. Bird, H. Chapman, J. Clark (eds), *Collectanea Londinensia*, London and Middlesex Archaeological Soc. Special Paper 2, 1978, 200–15. On the general point see e.g. Brooke, *London, passim*; T. Dyson and J. Schofield, 'Saxon London', in J. Haslam (ed.), *Anglo-Saxon Towns in Southern England*, Chichester 1984, 285–313; P. Nightingale, 'The Origin of the Court of Husting and Danish Influence on London's Development into a Capital City', *EHR*, cii, 1987, 559–78; S. Reynolds, 'Towns in Domesday Book' in J. C. Holt (ed.), *Domesday Studies*, Woodbridge 1987, 295–309.

[70] Middlesex was London's shire, but given the mismatch of scale it is hardly surprising that some obligations were spread more widely. The 1097 entry in the *ASC* bewailing the burdens on the 'many shires whose labour was due at London' for burhbot is far more likely to reflect the delineation of a larger catchment area during the process of shire formation than any vestigial remnant of a much earlier kingdom centred on London.

[71] *ASC*; Bassett, chapters 8–9; Yorke, 27–36; C. R. Hart in K. Neale (ed.), *An Essex Tribute*, London 1987, 57–84.

[72] John in Campbell, 160–4. P. Stafford, 'The reign of Aethelred II, a study in the limitations of royal policy and action', in Hill (ed.), *Ethelred the Unready*, 44, stresses that the shiring was a slow process, but it presumably spread from the south northwards.

[73] F. Liebermann, *Gesetze der Angelsachsen*, iii, Halle 1916, 115–23; Liebermann, 'Einleitung'; Brooke, *London*, 195–7; Loyn, 'The Hundred', 5–6; John in Campbell, 177–80.

[74] H. M. Cam, *The Hundred and the Hundred Rolls*, London 1930, *Liberties and Communities in Medieval England*, Cambridge 1944, and 'The "Private" Hundred before the Norman Conquest', J. C. Davies (ed.), *Studies Presented to Sir Hilary Jenkinson*, London 1957, 50–60, and behind her, Maitland, 84–103.

Middlesex hundreds described in Domesday were in royal hands. They also failed to conform to any pattern of a hundred hides to the hundred, and it seems likely that the original arrangement was of four, each containing around 220.[75] Within Ossulstone hundred (230 hides at Domesday) St Paul's held two continuous blocks of land, each of around seventy-five hides of early endowment, and within Gore (149 hides in Domesday) the archbishop of Canterbury's manor of Harrow, held since the early ninth century, contained a hundred hides.[76] Westminster received substantial endowment both in the later tenth century and from Edward the Confessor, but did not acquire any hundredal jurisdiction in either Middlesex or Essex.[77]

In Essex there were remarkably few private hundreds.[78] In West Herts., which fell to the diocese of Lincoln, St Albans achieved the only one.[79] In East Herts. there were none, and Professor Cam's attribution of the half-hundred of Edwinstree to the bishop of London is a mistake.[80] The charge was brought at the *quo warranto* enquiries, but the bishop's denial was genuine.[81] In addition, the lands in question were late acquisitions, the earliest, Hadham, being obtained in the early eleventh century and the rest shortly after the Conquest.[82]

The post-Conquest bishops had an honorial court at Stortford, view of frankpledge throughout their estates, and a soke (or sokes) within the city, but nothing higher.[83] In thus providing classic evidence for Hurnard's thesis they serve as a reminder that, whatever the normal outcome, bookland and sokeright did not necessarily produce the higher jurisdictions.[84] The tenth-century kings seem to have decided that London and its immediate hinterland were too important to allow the private control, however trustworthy, which the landowning structure might normally have dictated. This means that at the time when the ship list was compiled, and when London was at the centre of resistance to the Danish attacks, its bishop had no private hundredal jurisdiction, and could not play the sort of role apparently allowed to the bishop of Worcester in Oswaldslow or the bishop of Winchester in Taunton.[85]

It is possible that London and its hinterland's combination of particular importance and ready accessibility rendered them the subject of uniquely tight royal control.[86] It is also, however, possible, that our model of the 'normal' evolution of

---

[75] F. Baring, 'The hidation of some southern counties', *EHR*, xiv, 1899, 290–99, remains useful.

[76] *Domesday Book*, i, 127a–128b; Brooks, *Canterbury*, 140–1; see E. John's statement of the normal assumption on the development of such a grant into a private hundred, *Orbis Britanniae*, Leicester 1966, 108–111.

[77] Personal communications from Emma Mason and David Sullivan.

[78] Boyden, especially chapter 7. Since he says, 212, that the Essex hundreds ranged in size from approximately 50 to 300 hides, they were presumably in multiples of 100.

[79] On which see A. E. Levett, *Studies in Manorial History*, London 1938, reprinted 1963.

[80] *The Hundred and the Hundred Rolls*, appendix 4.

[81] Taylor, 'Estates', 144–6.

[82] Gibbs, J1; Whitelock, *Wills*, 140; *Domesday Book*, i, 133c–134a.

[83] Taylor, 'Estates', chapter 3; P. J. Taylor, 'The Bishop of London's City Soke', *BIHR*, liii, 1980, 174–82.

[84] N. D. Hurnard, 'The Anglo-Norman Franchises', *EHR*, lxiv, 1949, 289–323, 433–60; see also P. Wormald, 'Aethelred the Lawmaker', in Hill (ed.), *Ethelred the Unready*, 68. For a recent discussion of sokeright see Roffe.

[85] Hooper, 209–10. See also S. Keynes, 'The declining reputation of King Aethelred the Unready', in Hill (ed.), *Ethelred the Unready*, 232.

[86] The line may have been a little north of Watford, but the north-south divide was an enduring

private hundreds needs to be re-examined. They seem also to be absent from Herefordshire and much of the north, suggesting that the requirements, and solutions, for marcher areas equate to those for London.[87]

One final caveat concerning the ship list is that, as its scrappy form suggests, it may never have been intended to embody a permanent arrangement. This is not simply because the expectation of fixed quotas from this period may in any case be anachronistic.[88] More specifically, the bishop of Sherborne's letter indicates the major drawback to obligations imposed on an individual's estates rather than on a simple territorial basis. The difficulty, though, extended beyond the loss of odd acres or hides to the gain and loss of whole estates. Endowments were never static, and although it might have been possible to exempt gains, losses would always have needed accommodation. For London we know of several early eleventh-century gains, and from Domesday Book of the major loss of Southminster, removed by king Cnut.[89]

Southminster was restored to St Paul's by the Conqueror, and it is to the impact of the Conquest, primarily as reflected in Domesday Book, that I now turn. I shall concentrate mainly on the bishopric endowment, where the changes were substantial, and largely ignore the much less affected cathedral side. The cathedral must, however, have benefited from its bishop's protection.

The bishopric of London did well out of the Conquest, and in this was probably not as unusual as the complaints of the chroniclers suggest. Unlike his immediate predecessors, the Conqueror had no shortage of land at his disposal and this presumably made it easier for him to make ecclesiastical restitutions as well as rewarding his followers.[90] Although Southminster had been removed by the Scandinavian Cnut, both its seizure and return otherwise accord with the recent suggestion that the West Saxon kings financed their military activities in part by expropriating ecclesiastical lands, some of which were restored by the Conqueror.[91] Equally it is likely that some of the sins later attributed to William should really have been assigned to his less hated predecessors.[92] Domesday suggests that many if not all of the estates stretching southwards between Cashio and London which the later St Albans' chroniclers sincerely believed were taken by the Conqueror had in fact gone before 1066. The bishop of London's estates of Finchley and Hornsey, whose origins are totally obscure, could be part of this

reality for kings whose roots were in Wessex or in Normandy. Tom Cain, in a personal communication, confirms how the king operated through agents in the Leicester area. See also Stafford, *Unification*, 29–30; D. M. Metcalf, 'The ranking of the boroughs: numismatic evidence from the reign of Aethelred II', in D. Hill (ed.), *Ethelred the Unready: Papers from the Millenary Conference*, British Archaeological Reports 59, 1978, 220–1.

[87] I owe the information concerning Herefordshire and the north to Chris Lewis and David Roffe respectively.

[88] See Gillingham, 53–64; J. C. Holt, 'The introduction of knight service in England', *ante*, vi, 1984, 89–106.

[89] The gains include Hadham: Whitelock, *Wills*, 34–5. For Southminster, *Domesday Book*, ii, 10a.

[90] For a general summary see W. J. Sheils and D. Wood (eds), *The Church and Wealth*, Studies in Church History xxiv, Oxford 1987, 47–8; for the pressures felt by the late Anglo-Saxon kings, Boyden, 157–74 and the sources there cited.

[91] R. Fleming, 'Monastic lands and England's defence in the Viking age', *EHR*, c, 1985, 247–65.

[92] For similar growths of mythic reputations see Stafford, *Unification*, 106–7; D. Bates, 'The Character and Career of Odo, Bishop of Bayeux (1049/50–1097)', *Speculum*, 50, 1975, 1–20.

belt.[93] The weakness of the Mercian record, destroyed by both West Saxon and Danish hostility, probably assisted the confusion.[94]

If, as Professor Loyn has recently suggested, the Conqueror was heavily reliant on his bishops for all aspects of local government, this must have increased the power of their representations.[95] Here the bishop of London was once again in an unusual position. In 1066 bishop William (1051–75) was the only Norman bishop in England; although close to Edward the Confessor he was also a confidant of the Conqueror, and his advice in the immediate post-Conquest period must have been invaluable. But if the bishop's loyalty was not in doubt, that of the city was. Although the chroniclers' accounts are not totally consistent, it seems clear that London tried initially to resist the Conqueror but was soon forced to abandon its puppet alternative and send emissaries to sue for forgiveness. These according to the *Anglo-Saxon Chronicle* were the archbishop of York, Edgar Atheling, earls Edwin and Morcar and all the best men of London, while Florence of Worcester adds the bishops of Worcester and Hereford.[96] There has been debate about the likelihood of the presence of some of these, but so far as I know no-one has registered the most conspicuous absentee. Had bishop William remained within the city, he would surely have led the delegation, and this would not have been overlooked. Presumably therefore (as before, in 1052) he had fled the city, and may already have been at the Conqueror's side.[97] Whatever his role as mediator none of the chroniclers mentions it, although St Paul's and the city preserved a strong legend that he had interceded, and this was commemorated by an annual procession to his tomb.[98] At the time, of course, gratitude might well have been mixed with resentment.

Against this background, the granting of a castle to the bishop assumes added significance. Because the Conqueror was fully aware of the importance of the city, as well as wary of its loyalty, work rapidly began on the construction of castles at each side, the Tower and Baynards Castle, and probably also of a third, Montfichet.[99] None was entrusted to the bishop, who was instead at some point

---

[93] For archbishop Stigand's activities, including at St Albans, and their subsequent distorted description see Brooks, *Canterbury*, 308–9. St Albans claimed the Conqueror had removed its lands 'between Barnet and Londonstone'. The latter is presumably the one in the City but there is a dearth of identifiable Domesday entries for both Cashio (Herts.) and its immediately southern Middlesex neighbours: P. J. Taylor (ed.), *A Place in Time*, Hendon and District Archaeological Society 1989, 62. Stanmore, which belonged to St Albans in 957, was in lay hands in 1066; *VCH Middlesex*, v, 1976, 96. Significantly, since the county boundary here is manorially defined, it was and remained within Middlesex rather than Herts. despite its restitution to the abbey in 1106. S. Doree, *Domesday Book and the Origins of Edmonton Hundred*, Edmonton Hundred Historical Society Occasional Paper 48, 1986, is interesting, but unreliable on the role of St Paul's, and wrong in interpreting the right of the bishop and his officials to hospitality as anything more than those normally owed to the diocesan (19–20).

[94] N. Brooks, 'England in the ninth century: the crucible of defeat', *TRHS* xxix, 1979, 1–20; P. Wormald in Campbell, chapters 5–6. On the weakness of the St Albans MSS, R. M. Thompson (ed.), *MSS from St Albans Abbey 1066–1235*, Tasmania 1982, 1–2, 8–10.

[95] H. R. Loyn, 'William's bishops: some further thoughts', *ante*, x, 1988, 223–35.

[96] The sources are given and analysed in W. Page, *London, its origin and early development*, London 1923, 67–8. See also Stenton, *Anglo-Saxon England*, 596–9; Brooke, *London*, 27–9.

[97] On the previous flight see Brooks, *Canterbury*, 304.

[98] W. Dugdale, *The History of St Paul's Cathedral . . .*, revised edn London 1818, 37, elaborated in H. H. Milman, *Annals of St Paul's Cathedral*, London 1869, 16–18.

[99] On the increasing importance of London in the tenth century see Nightingale, 559–78; Dyson

between 1066 and 1075 allowed to build one on his newly acquired estate at (Bishops) Stortford in Herts.[100] From the royal point of view this was well placed, guarding Stane Street's fording of the river Stort, but it can hardly have been the bishop's preference.[101] London was his headquarters and even if that was barred he would surely have preferred one of his nearer and longer-established demesne manors.[102] The restriction to a more distant location not only confirms the Conqueror's strategic sense but also indicates how the special position of London once again placed limits on the trust which a king felt able to place in even so reliable a bishop.[103]

On the other hand even though the bishop failed to gain notably in power, he suffered no demotion, and this is well shown by his success in improving his see's endowment.[104] The changes can be briefly summarised: both the bishop and the canons had lost some lands to invaders, but the amounts were small, seldom whole estates, and on balance outweighed by the restitutions. Most strikingly, bishop William had been allowed to purchase a number of new estates, his famous *feudum* or fee. This repays examining in detail not only for what it tells us about the organisation of the endowment but equally for the meaning which the Domesday scribe was attaching to this much debated word.

In the Essex Domesday the bishopric estates are listed in two separate sections, headed respectively 'Land' and 'Fee' of the bishop of London.[105] In Herts there are no separate sections or titles, but the word fee is used in two entries and implied in a third.[106] In Middlesex it does not occur. All the estates in the Essex fee had been acquired since the Conquest. They comprise eighteen holdings in seventeen places, scattered apparently randomly across the county.[107] Only two are in places where lands are also recorded in the first section.[108] None is large, the range being from thirty acres to just over three and a half hides. The entries are in

---

and Schofield, 302–7. The most recent specific discussion of the London castles is R. Mortimer, 'The Baynards of Baynards Castle', in Harper-Bill *et al.*, 241–253. The Baynard fee, which came from various sources, had been assembled by 1072.

[100] Gibbs, no. 5.

[101] For its later efficiency in thwarting Geoffrey de Mandeville's communications see J. H. Round, *Geoffrey de Mandeville*, London 1892, 174.

[102] Stepney was almost in the shadow of the Tower but Fulham, where there was an important early river crossing, would seem ideal. See also Stenton, *First Century*, 63–4.

[103] On the planning behind the location of castles see R. Eales, 'Royal Power and Castles in Norman England', *The Ideals and Practice of Medieval Knighthood*, iii, 1990, 49–78; M. Chibnall, *Anglo-Norman England*, Oxford 1986, 11–13. F. M. Stenton, *Norman London*, Historical Association Pamphlets 93–4, London 1934 (revised and reprinted in G. Barraclough (ed.), *Social Life in Early England*, London 1960 and D. M. Stenton (ed.), *Preparatory to Anglo-Saxon England*, Oxford 1970), 7, says William I's writ to London uses 'both' deliberately to to include the bishop in its injunctions. In fact it is more obviously read as meaning both the French and English burghers in the city, and is so taken by e.g. Brooke, *London*, 29.

[104] Quite apart from the tradition of his mediacy, this alone suggests that John's dismissive judgement, 'Bishop William left little mark on London though he ruled the see for almost a quarter of a century', in Campbell, 230, is ill considered.

[105] *Domesday Book*, ii, 9b–12b.

[106] *Domesday Book*, i, 133c–134a.

[107] Hart's perception of propinquity to long-established estates, *Early Charters*, 39–40, seems to lie in the eye of the beholder, and his comments on their economic importance overlook their subinfeudation.

[108] Laindon and Ramsden Bellhouse, neither of them definitely long-established bishopric manors.

normal form for the county, so that we have all the names of the pre-Conquest holders, but status is given less consistently: we are told seven times that the holder had been a free man and once that he had been a royal thegn. Commendations are not a feature of the Essex Domesday, but one of the free men is noted as having held Little Thurrock under (sub) King Edward.

None of the estates had been shared before the Conquest, and the eighteen had been held by at least eleven differently named individuals. Five names occur twice and one three times, but only once are we told that the same man held two (consecutive) estates. Whether or not any of the other four held more than one, the wide spread shows that at this level there is no possibility of any one predecessor or pre-existing unity. In the absence of evidence the possibility of one predecessor overlord cannot be disproved, but the likelihood seems slim: the estates carry absolutely no pointers to any common source.

This reading is supported by the evidence from Herts. Here the bishop had a total of twenty-five estates in 1086, as opposed to thirty-four in Essex. In conspicuous contrast though, only one of the twenty-five, the seven-and-a-half-hide manor of Hadham, had been held before the Conquest, with a further three being held by his men or women. Within the new acquisitions Stortford, at six hides, was larger than anything in the Essex fee, but otherwise the profile is similar. Apart from Stortford, the other twenty-three new estates (i.e. including the three previously held by his 'men') range from one and a half virgates to three hides one virgate.

The Herts. Domesday, however, gives a wider range of information about the pre-Conquest holders. First, and most importantly, in twenty-one of the twenty-three cases it states that they had right of sale (vendere potuit/potuerunt). Of the other two, Leofwara had only been able to sell a third of her one-and-a-half-hide holding, but it was in any case held of the bishop. Edith the Fair's status was such that her right to sell Stortford was presumably obvious. Additionally, we know that a large number of separate individuals were involved. On each of the fourteen estates previously held by a single person he or she is named, and since commendations are also given we know that there were at least twelve individuals, with a maximum of two, Aldred a thane and Alfward archbishop Stigand's man, occurring twice. The differences in commendations also allow us to be sure that there is no predominant predecessor lurking behind the two thegns, two brothers, and two to five freemen who had held the remaining estates. With the exception of Stortford, the bishop's new Hertfordshire estates were acquired from a number of small men. Not only are there no references to any common overlord, but the range of commendations makes it hard to posit an available candidate.[109]

If the newly acquired estates in the two counties were similar in kind, why were they given a separate section in the Domesday account of Essex but not of Herts.? Two plausible suggestions can be made: first, with only one old-established bishopric estate in Herts., separate sections were not warranted. Secondly, the different scribal conventions of the two circuits may have been significant. The Herts. Domesday, for instance, uses the shorthand of upper case for the

---

[109] I am grateful to David Roffe for helpful discussion of the issue of commendation. See also Reynolds, pp. 222–23.

names of manors held in chief and lower case for the rest, while the scribe of the Essex Domesday does not.[110]

Another obvious possibility is that the word feudum was being used differently in the Essex account, but this is less convincing. The Herts. Domesday contains three relevant references: Stortford is described as 'of the fee which bishop William bought' (de feudo quem emit); one and a half virgates at Wickham is also specifically stated to be 'of bishop William's fee'. Additionally, land at Throcking is said by the bishop's men to be part 'of bishop William's purchase' (de emptione) but this is not confirmed by the men of the shire. These are the three references used by Round to explain the Essex fee and to suggest that its essence lay in its purchase by bishop William.[111]

This interpretation is further strengthened if we go on to ask why these three, but no others, occur, for the answer seems to be that each confirms a special case. The entry for Throcking is unfortunately ambiguous, since it could refer to one mortgaged virgate rather than to the whole estate. The uncertainty of title thus created could have been enough to explain both the explicit reference and the conflicting testimony of the shire and bishop's men. In addition, though, it is worth noting that Throcking was one of only three estates whose pre-Conquest holders had been bishop William's men, and one of the other two was Wickham, where there is also an explicit reference to the fee. In possibly significant contrast, the entry for the third such estate, Leverage, is alone in emphasising both that its TRE tenant had held it from the bishop, and that she could sell only a third of the one-and-a-half-hide estate. The other specific reference occurs at Stortford, which was a unique estate within the fee, much larger than any other, and already bearing the bishop's castle; here it probably underlines the point that, contrary to appearance, this was not a long-established bishopric estate.

The Essex and Herts. Domesdays are therefore consistent and clear in their description of the bishop's fee: it is a purchased lordship. There remains, however, another and less certain dimension. Round assumed that the first section in the Essex Domesday, headed 'Land of the Bishop of London', contrasted totally with the fee since all its estates, other than Laindon, had 'been held at some period by his see'. For Laindon he hypothesised that the previous owner, a free woman, might have bestowed it on the church.[112] In fact if it is the Ligenadune of the ship list St Paul's may have had a pre-Conquest interest there. Otherwise, though, the assumption is unproven, and is not convincingly supported either by further knowledge of the London endowment or by comparison with Thetford, the other similarly divided episcopal entry.

The division in the Norfolk Domesday between the bishop of Thetford's land and his fee is absolutely straightforward. The heading for the twenty estates of the first section is 'Land of the bishop of Thetford pertaining to the bishopric TRE'.[113] The separately listed fee, which contains over seventy entries, covers all the post-Conquest acquisitions. Most were new purchases but, unlike London, there were other sources as well.[114] Several had been held privately TRE by the then

---

[110] Roffe draws attention to the importance of such differences, 161–2.
[111] *VCH Essex*, i, 339–40.
[112] *VCH Essex*, i, 339.
[113] *Domesday Book*, ii, 191.
[114] *Domesday Book*, ii, 193b–201b.

bishop, Aelmar (1047–70).[115] The new acquisitions included an estate annexed when the woman who held it remarried within a year of her husband's death.[116]

This is not the same division as at London. The fact that the first section there is only headed 'Land of the bishop of London' is not simply an omission but a reflection of a real difference. In the first place there were the restitutions, which had not occurred (and therefore did not have to be allocated) at Thetford. At London they were firmly placed in the 'Land' section. More surprisingly, so too were two three-hide estates at Layer Marney which the Essex Domesday states had been held by freemen before the Conquest, but which bishop William had adjudged (deratiocinavit) to the use of his church after king Edward's death by order of king William.[117] At Thetford these would unequivocally have fallen to the fee.

Layer Marney and Laindon are the only estates where a pre-Conquest tenant other than the bishop is named, but out of an overall total of sixteen there are three others for which no antecedents are given or known, and two more which we are told were held by the bishop TRE but for which we have no other indication of how or when they were acquired.[118] Even given the relative weakness of the other evidence, this is a surprisingly high percentage. One real possibility is that bishop William, like bishop Aelmar, acquired estates for himself or his see before the Conquest, but that at London these were entered with the lands not with the fee. Another interesting hypothesis raised by the Layer entry, and certainly not contradicted by such phrases as 'the fee which bishop William bought', is that the fee was indeed one specific purchase, and does not even stretch to other, perhaps earlier, post-Conquest acquisitions. But whether or not either speculation is valid, the important conclusion stands that the distinction between the lands and the fee is different at London and at Thetford. The Domesday scribes were applying a convenient new word loosely rather than precisely, and with no implication of bookland, military tenure, or anything similar.[119]

Both fees raise the interesting question of when and how private purchases became official possessions. At Thetford Dodwell thought that the transfer of bishop Aelmar's properties probably occurred at his downfall in 1070.[120] This would be in line with other evidence, such as bishop Theodred's will, both that the distinction between episcopal and personal estates existed and that a bishop often waited until his death to bequeath some of his privately acquired lands to his church.[121]

At London, though, the situation ought to have needed more immediate clarification if privately acquired estates, including Stortford, were rapidly used to meet

---

[115] E.g. Gunton, Beighton, Blofeld.

[116] Plumstead, ii, 199.

[117] *Domesday Book*, ii, 10a.

[118] In the first category are a substantial holding at Colchester, 15 acres at Slampseys and 3 hides at Ramsden Bellhouse; in the second, 8 hides at Chelmsford and 3 at Wickham.

[119] This contrasts with the recent conclusions of Roffe, or of Ann Williams in A. Williams (ed.), *Domesday Book: Studies*, London 1987, 37. The bishop's general charters, including those from the Conqueror (Gibbs, nos. 2–3), ensured the extension of all his privileges to all his estates.

[120] B. Dodwell, 'The Honour of the Bishop of Thetford/Norwich, in the late Eleventh and early Twelfth Centuries', *Norfolk Archaeology*, xxxiii, 1963, 186.

[121] See above, pp. 289–93.

military obligations. The first and only evidence we have comes in a royal writ to the new bishop whom the king nominated at Christmas 1085, confirming that he had 'given Maurice bishop of London the castle of Stortford and all the land that bishop William his predecessor held of me'.[122] St Paul's preserved no similar writ to the intervening bishop, Hugh d'Orivalle, whose decade in office is also totally ignored in Domesday, where again the link to bishop William is repeatedly stressed, but without any mention of the method of transfer. We are thus left free to choose between bequest, a royally commanded transfer such as occurred at Layer, or, speculatively, that the fee was acquired more or less with the castle on the initial understanding that both would pass to the see. If this were so it would acquire an extra dimension of both unity and military purpose, even though since it was never the sole resource for meeting the bishop's military obligations, it never equated to the barony of Stortford.

The location of the castle and the new estates acted together to shift the endowment's centre of gravity northwards, away from London and Middlesex. In this process the castle probably exercised a positive pull: the greatest concentration of new acquisitions was in the Hadham valley, close to Stortford, and since they came from a number of different owners rather than any common source this is unlikely to have been accidental.[123] The siting of the castle does not seem, however, to be the only reason. The bishop was equally assiduous in purchasing estates spread across Essex, many no more convenient for Stortford than was much of Middlesex. Yet in Middlesex no new estates were acquired.

Land there may well have been especially hard to obtain: the demand for estates within easy reach of London was probably particularly strong, and the supply unusually limited because a very high proportion of the county had survived the Conquest in ecclesiastical ownership. The shortage can probably be overstated, however, since much land which became available had originally been held by tenancies which had hardened into alienations. The bishop's own attempts to reclaim two estates in Stepney show that Middlesex was no different from other shires in this respect.[124]

Since successful bids to obtain estates, and retain them through later disputes, probably needed royal support, the success or failure of claims have to be seen as matters of royal as well as episcopal policy. In Herts. the bishop failed to retain against Geoffrey de Mandeville four hides in Thorley which had previously been held by a woman of Asgar the Staller, but it is noteworthy that he managed to keep other purchases made from the Staller's men.[125] In Essex there were other lesser losses, always to powerful names: Robert Gernon, Count Eustace, possibly Odo of Bayeux.[126] The canons too suffered similar small losses to great adver-

---

[122] Gibbs, nos. 5, 12. Loyn, 'Bishops', 227–9 suggests that it was the newness of Maurice's appointment which prevented his being a Domesday commissioner.

[123] Compare Stafford, *Unification*, 109–110.

[124] *Domesday Book*, i, 130b–c.

[125] *Domesday Book*, i, 133c–134a. For differing views of the degree of dismemberment of the Staller's (and others') holdings see P. Sawyer, '1066–1086: A Tenurial Revolution?', in P. Sawyer (ed.), *Domesday Book: A Reassessment*, London 1985, 77–8 and R. Fleming, 'Domesday Book and the tenurial revolution', *ante*, ix, 1986, 94.

[126] It is not clear whether Odo made his acquisitions before or after the bishop of London.

saries, but were successful in their probably equally forceful reclamation of several holdings within Navestock.[127]

In Middlesex, however, the bishop failed to recover two holdings of four and three and a half hides in Stepney, held in chief in 1086 by the lesser figures of Robert Fafiton and Robert fitz Roselin. If the criterion of having belonged of old to St Paul's, accepted for Warley in Essex, had been universally applied, there would of course have been a number of restitutions, but even on more limited grounds the bishop's case was reasonable. The TRE holders had had right of sale, but this was a grey area and one of the two, Sired, had not only been a canon of St Paul's, but the holder of another two and a half hides within Stepney also with right of sale, which by 1086 were restored to the bishop's overlordship.[128] The tenancies which the bishop created on his Middlesex estates were also different, and suggest a similar contrast in the pressures on him and in his ability to resist them. To appreciate this, though, it is necessary first to consider all the tenancies within the context of the new military obligations.

The placing of the post-Conquest obligation on the bishop alone rather than jointly with his chapter must have been felt with particular immediacy at St Paul's because of the pre-existing separation of the estates, and since the bishopric was not generously endowed additional obligations could have presented an acute problem. The relationship of the size of the endowment and the military obligation is, however, a variant of the problem of the chicken and the egg. We do not know when between 1066 and 1075 bishop William acquired his new estates, his castle, or his military obligation, finally fixed at twenty with an enfeoffment of thirty-three and a third. The new estates must have formed part of the equation, but whether to enhance the obligation or as a *sine qua non* is impossible to know.[129]

Not only the early separation of the estates, but also the absence of any discernible use either of five-hide formulae or of granted-out land in the ship list, would make London an unpromising candidate for continuity in pre- and post-Conquest arrangements for meeting its military obligations. All the evidence points to a complete break.[130] The fully developed organisation of the barony of Stortford is beyond the scope of this paper: all that is attempted here is to summarise the Domesday evidence.

In 1086 the bishop's military arrangements were still not fully fixed, but the usual trends towards transferring military obligations from household to landed retainers, and the emergence of hereditary tenures were underway.[131] Comparison of Domesday with the later *carte baronum* lists and other honorial records shows that estates subinfeudated in 1086 were normally later held by knight service.[132]

[127] *Domesday Book*, ii, 12b–13b. The canons did not win the whole of Navestock: *Domesday Book*, ii, 56a; Hart, *Early Charters*, 36.

[128] *Domesday Book*, i, 130b–c, 127b.

[129] See Gillingham, 53–64 and Holt, *ante*, vi, 1984, 89–106; the latter's discussion of the London and Thetford fees seems rather vague.

[130] For a detailed contrast see Roffe, *passim*. F. M. Stenton, *The First Century of English Feudalism 1066–1166*, 2nd edn Oxford 1961, 159, stresses the probable atypicality of Worcester. For other evidence of discontinuity, Fleming, 'Domesday Book and the tenurial revolution', especially 94–5.

[131] For details see Taylor, 'Estates', chapter 2.

[132] For London the 1210 x 1212 *carte baronum* list omits the Middlesex fees but supplies tenants' names and obligations, and the location of their fees. The 1166 list omits locations but since it

The Herts. Domesday was thus accurate when, at the end of the section detailing all the holdings in Edwinstree hundred, it stated 'The bishop of London and his *milites* hold these thirty-six hides'. *Milites*, though, had no specific connection with the fee: on the one hand two fee estates, Stortford and three-hide Widford, were directly retained; conversely, a number of small estates from the 'Land' section of the Essex Domesday, as well as parts of some retained manors, were also subinfeudated by 1086 and later held by knight service.[133] The eschewal of mathematical or any other obvious formulae continued. Even allowing for the possibility of some early multiple holdings, there is no standard size, and no relationship between size and obligation.

The London *milites* covered a wide social range. The debate concerning status was notably clarified here last year by Donald Fleming, and since the London evidence fully supports his conclusions I will not repeat the arguments again.[134] Instead, I conclude by returning to the special nature of the Middlesex tenancies, which were scarce and of high status. The difference is not simply due to the absence of newly purchased estates: the few new tenancies within Stepney and Fulham were also different and suggest very strongly that the reasons for their creation were not primarily military.

The bishop's tenants at Stepney in 1086 included Ranulf Flambard, the bishop of Lisieux and William the Chamberlain, and no similar names occur on the Essex and Herts. estates. It is also only in Stepney that a number of the itemised Domesday tenancies, including these three, cannot be traced in the later sources, where the total of five military tenures shows a decline from the eight tenancies of 1086.[135] The only later military tenure at Fulham has been identified as the sole named subinfeudation there in 1086, Fulchered's five hides.[136] Apart from Fulchered's, there were only two other single holdings which reached, or even approached, five hides in 1086, and both were within Stepney, where Hugo de Berners held five and a quarter hides and the wife of Brian five.[137] All these three occur in the later sources held for the service of half a knight, which compared to the levels demanded in the same sources from the smaller estates of Essex and Herts. was an extremely lenient rate. Finally, there were no unnamed *milites* on the demesnes at either Stepney or Fulham in 1086, but the latter, uniquely among the bishop's estates, accommodated an unspecified number of *francigeni* and London burgesses.

This is perhaps an appropriate note on which to end. This survey has suggested that the history of the see of London was regularly distorted because of its association with the city. The consequences, which were most extreme for St

---

provides both names and obligations can be shown to include all three shires, and be used as a fairly firm stepping stone back to 1086: *Red Book of the Exchequer*, RS 1896, i, 186, ii, 541–2. See also *Liber Feodorum: The Book of Fees commonly called Testa de Nevill*, Record Commission 1920.

[133] E.g. Wanstead, Layer Marney, and among the directly held manors most notably Southminster.

[134] D. Fleming, 'Landholding by milites in Domesday Book: A Revision', *ante*, xiii, 1990, 83–98.

[135] E.g. for 1242–3 in *Book of Fees*, 900.

[136] P. J. Taylor, 'A knight's fee at Acton, in the manor of Fulham', *London and Middlesex Archaeological Society Trans.*, xxviii, 1977, 316–22.

[137] The de Berners fee is Barnsbury: *VCH Middlesex*, viii, 1985, 51. The wife of Brian's fee has now been identified as Clerkenwell: P. J. Taylor, 'Clerkenwell and the religious foundations of Jordan de Bricett: a re-examination', *Historical Research* (formerly *BIHR*), lxiii, 1990, 17–28.

Paul's but also affected any other great landholders within the area, have to be seen as the result of recurrent royal responses to the special circumstances created by London's economic, military and therefore political importance. It is surely time to re-examine any views ascribing those consequences which have hitherto been noticed either to nascent urban power or to royal appreciation of the ancient claims of the city over the early Middle Saxon kingdom.[138] The West Saxon kings were even less burdened than the Conqueror by avoidable antiquarian sensitivities. The abnormality, though, is real, and means that the documents of the see have to be used with particular care in constructing generalisations. One of their main values may indeed be to function as a touchstone for those based on sources from other parts of the country.

[138] Various aspects of Stenton's still influential *Norman London* need re-examination.

THE FRATERNITY OF
ROCHESTER CATHEDRAL PRIORY ABOUT 1100*

H. Tsurushima

Nobody can deny the importance of the Norman Conquest in terms of the replacement of the native ruling and landholding class. The fate of the old English nobility during the Conquest and the settlement shortly after the Battle of Hastings was truly catastrophic. But the problems to be solved are those of how the Normans settled down in England, how they established relations with English natives and in what way the amalgamation of both Normans and English into a unity had progressed during the Anglo-Norman period.

Concerning the last question, Orderic Vitalis referred to intermarriage between them very soon after the Norman Conquest.[1] Sir Frank Stenton maintained that 'the English aristocracy as a whole reached the lowest point of its fortunes in the twenty years on either side of the year 1100' and that 'by the middle of the reign of Henry I there are signs of a change in their condition. The king himself had owed much to English support at the beginning of his reign and had married a descendant of the Old English kings. There had arisen a new generation of Englishmen qualified by education to serve in war as knights. Englishmen were becoming prominent once more in local government'.[2]

It is indeed clear that intermarriage, feudal qualification and services to the king caused a rise in the social standing of Englishmen and could help to amalgamate both peoples into one, but these elements seem to me like part of the light or the surface of boiling water in the crucible. All is the effort to survive. What is a part of the shadow element which wriggles under the surface? It is death. Man must die, and death itself is not a problem historians can solve, but how to die is very much so. In the eleventh century, people on their death bed, sincerely pursued salvation of their souls and tried to enter into fraternity with monks as intercessors of prayer. In this paper, I am going to show some aspects of the Norman settlement and the formation of social connections among Norman and English families from the view-point of fraternity.

In eleventh century France, the Cluniacs called their own monastery the refuge of the penitent (*asylum poenitentium*). Not only monks or clerks but also the laity

* I should like to thank Dr Marjorie Chibnall for giving me a chance to read this article to the Battle Conference. I am indebted to Dr John Moore, Dr Laurence Keen, Dr Diana Greenway, Professsor Robert Patterson and Dr Susan Reynolds for their comments and correction of my errors. I am also specially indebted to Dr Ann Williams for reading an earlier draft of this article, for providing invaluable comments and suggestions, and for correcting errors. Without her kind help, this paper would never have come out.

[1] Orderic, ii, 256.
[2] F. M. Stenton, 'English Families and the Norman Conquest', *TRHS*, 4th ser. xxiv, 1944, 8.

wished for the intercession of prayer and asked for society and fraternity with
Cluny. In Anglo-Norman England, on the other hand, a lack of historical sources
makes it difficult for us to investigate an actual fraternity after the Norman
Conquest except for one chartulary. This is the Textus Roffensis.[3] This unusual
chartulary, the earliest for the smallest diocese of England, was compiled as two
books in the early part of twelfth century by one major hand.[4] The latter part of it,
which used to be called *privilegia aecclesiae Sancti Andreae*,[5] contains many
charters, memoranda, lists of knights, books in the library, churches and so on.
Folios 182v to 210v contain more than fifty charters and memoranda concerning
the fraternity of Rochester diocese. Most of them were transcribed from the
originals by one major hand in about the 1120s. Although some were later twelfth
century insertions,[6] they still can narrate a genuine story of about 1100 which Sir
Frank Stenton calls the lowest point of English fortune. We had better abstain
from generalising the conclusion of this paper, since the geographical limitation is
confined to Kent.

Hugh of Port was the greatest tenant-in-chief in Hampshire and an under-tenant
of Odo, bishop of Bayeux in Hampshire and Kent.[7] He came from Port-en-Bessin
near Bayeux, but before the Conquest he had been a middling tenant of Odo in
Normandy. Although he witnessed a charter of Duke William, he was probably a
local witness rather than a member of the ducal entourage.[8] He owed his further
promotion in England not only to his ability but also to his connection with Odo
and, after Odo's disgrace in 1082, King William. His family was becoming one of
the most important baronial kindreds in England. (For convenience I put the
number in square brackets in front of the document cited. The number is synchronised with the number in Table I.)

> [1] *Hugo de Port habet nostram societatem, et dedit nobis concedentibus
> filiis suis uno quoque anno.xx.solidos ad pasca videlicet pro decima de suo
> manerio quod vocatur Ærhetha, et hanc donationem posuit super altare
> Sancti Andreae ipse et uxor ejus et filii ejus per cultellum suum.*[9]

Before he became a monk of St Peter of Gloucester in 1096,[10] he entered into
the society of the monks of Rochester and gave them an annual payment of
twenty shillings as regards the tithe of the manor called *Ærhetha* or *Erde* in
Crayford with his wife's and his sons' consent.[11] Hugh, his wife and his sons
placed this gift on the altar of St Andrew with a knife. He held this manor of the

[3] Kent Archives DRc/R1(henceforward Textus Roffensis); Thomas Hearne ed. *Textus Roffensis*,
London 1720; Peter Sawyer ed. *Textus Roffensis*, pts. i and ii, *Early English Manuscripts in
Facsimile*, vols. 9 and 11, Copenhagen 1957 and 1962 (henceforward Sawyer).
[4] Sawyer, ii, 11–19.
[5] Textus Roffensis, fo. 119.
[6] Textus Roffensis, fos. 182v, 193–193v, 197–197v, 203–208. Cf. Sawyer, ii, 12.
[7] Domesday Book, i, 6, 7–7v, 8, 9, 10–10v, 11, 44v–46v.
[8] Lewis C. Loyd (C. T. Clay and D. C. Douglas eds.), *The Origins of some Anglo-Norman
Families*, Leeds 1951, 79 (henceforward Loyd).
[9] Textus Roffensis, fo. 185.
[10] D. C. Douglas ed. *The Domesday Monachorum of Christ Church Canterbury*, London 1944, 54
and n. 12.
[11] Ærhetha is the early form of the name *Erde* in Crayford; see G. Ward, 'The List of Saxon
Churches in the Textus Roffensis', *Archaeologia Cantiana* xliv, 1932, 46. Cf. Edward Hasted, *The*

Archbishop of Canterbury and owed him two knights' service in 1093–96.[12] There is no description of him in the Domesday account of Crayford, and he was probably enfeoffed in the years between 1086 and 1096. His intimations of death compelled him to give the tithe of the manor held of the Archbishop to the priory of St Andrew.

His heir was his son Henry of Port. In 1108 Henry gave the tithe of Hawley to the monks of St Andrew's.[13] This gift was related to that by King Henry I, who in 1104–08, granted the church of Sutton, with chapels at Kingsdown and Wilmington, with their tithe in corn, cattle, pannage, mills and all other things, to Gundulph, bishop of Rochester and the priory of St Andrew.[14] Hawley is a hamlet, situated in the northern extremity of the parish of Sutton, and there was a chapel there.[15] In Domesday Book the men of Axton Hundred testified that Hawley was part of Dartford, but had been taken from that manor and was held by Hugh of Port, however it remained in the king's farm of Dartford.[16] The king's grant of Sutton stimulated Henry of Port to grant his tithe at Hawley to the monks.

The king's grants of churches and their tithes to the bishop had given such impetus to many landholders, barons or knights, French or English, who had some share in the manors concerned. They followed the king's example and gave their own tithes to the church of St Andrew. In the same charter as the aforesaid, for example, Henry I granted the church of Aylesford, an old royal capital manor in Kent, with its tithe to St Andrew, so that the old and primary mother church was laid under episcopal control.[17]

In Aylesford there is a hamlet called Tottington, held in 1086 by Robert Latimer at farm of the king.[18] Soon afterwards it passed to Richard fitz Malger of Ruxley, who, with his wife and son, accepted the society of the monks of St Andrew's church by granting all tithe of his land in Tottington in Aylesford.

[2] *Ricardus, filius Malgerii de Rokesle, cum uxore et filio acceperunt societatetm monachorum aecclesiae Sancti Andreae, et ideo illis concesserunt omnem decimam suam de Totintuna terra sua aeternaliter in omnibus rebus.*[19]

Malger, Richard's father, was a lowly knight and tenant of Odo, bishop of Bayeux.[20] He seems to have followed Odo across the Channel and his future

---

History and Topographical Survey of the County of Kent, 2nd edn., 12 vols., Canterbury 1797–1801, ii, 263ff (henceforward Hasted).

[12] *The Domesday Monachorum*, 105. In 1171–2 Adam of Port owed two knights in *Erde* to the archbishop, see, H. M. Colvin, 'A list of the archbishop of Canterbury's tenants by knight-service in the reign of Henry II', *Kent Records*, xvii, Ashford 1964, 7, 30–31 (henceforward Colvin).

[13] Textus Roffensis, fo. 198v.

[14] Textus Roffensis, fo. 186v. See also fo. 177v.

[15] Textus Roffensis, fo. 222; Hasted, ii, 353–54.

[16] *Domesday Book*, i. 2v.

[17] Such gifts might result in the dissolution of the old minster system and reorganisation of local parochial church system under episcopal control in West Kent. Cf. John Blair ed. *Minsters and Parish Churches: The Local Church in Transition 950–1200*, Oxford University Committee for Archaeology, Monograph No. 17, 1988.

[18] Domesday Book, i, 7.

[19] Textus Roffensis, fo. 191.

[20] *Domesday Book*, i, 6–6v.

Table 1   The Fraternity of Rochester Cathedral Priory about 1100: Examples from the Textus Roffensis

No.	D-N	Folio	Name	Rel	Or	Date	Place Name	Parish	Lord(inclusive DB)	Ft	Mk	Donation
1	[1]	185	Hugh of Port		F	1086-1096	Erde	Erde	Anselm ABp	S		T
2	[2]	191	Richard fitz Malger of Ruxley+W+S		F	1100-1109	Tottington	Aylesford	K/Odo Bp Bayeux/Haimo the sheriff	S		T
3-01	[3]	197v	Ansgot of Rochester		F	1086-1096	Delce Great	St.Margaret	Odo bp Bayeux	S/pm		T
-02	[4]	190	Geoffrey of Delce+W+Ss	F	F	c.1100	Delce Little	St.Margaret	Son of William Thaon/Walter Tirel	S		T
-03	[4a]	194v	Geoffrey of Delce	F/M	F	c.1100	Delce Little	St.Margaret	Son of William Thaon/Walter Tirel	S	s	L
-04	[4a]	194v	Herebert of Delce	S	F	c.1100	Delce Little	St.Margaret	Son of William Thaon/Walter Tirel			C
-05	[4a]	194v	Walter Tirel	L	F	c.1100	Delce Little	St.Margaret		S		C
-06	[5]	195	Godric of Delce	M	E	c.1100	Delce Little	St.Margaret	Son of William Thaon/Walter Tirel	S		T
The Elham Group												
4-01	[6]	188	William of Aubigny	L	F	1100-1108	Elham	Elham	K	S		T
-02	[7]	188v	Roger of Elham	M	F	1100-1108	Elham	Elham	William of Aubigny	S		1/2T
-03	[8]	188v	Ealdwlf of Shuttlesfield	M	E	1100-1108	Elham+Lyminge	Elham+Lyminge	William of Aubigny	S		1/2T
-04	[9]	188v	Leofwine Scone of Bere	M	E	1100-1108	Beerforstall	Elham	William of Aubigny	S		1/2T
-05	[10]	188v-189	Baldwine on Oferland	M	?E?F	1100-1108	Oferland	?Elham	William of Aubigny	S		1/2T
-06	[11]	189	Edward on Oferland	M	E	1100-1108	Oferland	?Elham	William of Aubigny	S		1/2T
-07	[12]	189	Blackman of Bladbean	M	E	1100-1108	Bladbean	?Elham	William of Aubigny	S		1/2T
-08	[13]	189	Leofwine on Acsted	M	E	1100-1108	Exted	Elham	William of Aubigny	S		1/2T
-09	[14]	189	Wulfric se mangere	M	E	1100-1108	?Elham	?Elham	William of Aubigny	S		1/2T
-10	[15]	189	Rainald of Boyke	M	?E?F	1100-1108	Boykewood	Elham	Humphrey/William of Aubigny	S		1/2T
-11	[16]	189	Ralf of Chieresburh	M	?E?F	1100-1108	?Elham	?Elham	William of Aubigny	S		500 Eels
-12	[17]	189-189v	Herebert of Gatindene	M	?E?F	1100-1108	?Elham	?Elham	William of Aubigny	S		T or 40s

No. D-N	Folio	Name	Rel	Or	Date	Place Name	Parish	Lord(inclusive DB)	Ft	Mk	Donation
		The Chelsfield Group									
5-01 [18]	184	Ernulf I of Chelsfield+W+his Men	L1/F1	?E?F	1096-1107	Chelsfield	Chelsfield	Ernulf of Hesdin	S/F		1/2T+L+V
-02 [19]	190	Haimfrid	M1	?E?F	1096-1107	Chelsfield	Chelsfield	Ernulf I of Chelsfield	S		T
-03 [20]	184v-185	Aethelwold of Chelsfield	?M1	E	1096-1107	Chelsfield	Chelsfield	?Ernulf I of Chelsfield	S/F		T+Prop+Eq+Arma
-04 [21]	185	Wulfmaer of Chelsfield	?M1	E	1096-1107	Chelsfield	Chelsfield	Ernulf of Hesdin	S		T
-05 [22]	230v	Ernulf II of Chelsfield	L2/S1	?E?F	1143	Chelsfield	Chelsfield	Ernulf II of Chelsfield			
-05 [22]	230v	Ernulf II of Strood	M2/S2	?E?F	1143	Strood	Frindsbury	Ernulf I of Chelsfield			
-06 [23]	201v	Ernulf I of Strood	M1/F2	?E?F	1096-1107	Strood	Frindsbury		S		T
6-01 [24]	182v-183	Robert Latimer[sheriff's officer]	H/Coh	E	c.1100	Grain	Grain	Odo/Lanfranc ABp/Haimo the sheriff			T
-02 [25]	200v-201	Wife of Robert Latimer	W	E	c.1100	Hornden	Frindsbury		Ann		L
-03 [26]	189v	Geoffrey of Ros	Coh	F	c.1100	Yaldham	Wrotham	Odo/Lanfranc ABp	Ann		T
7-01 [27]	183-183v	Leofrun, widow of Siward of Hoo	K	E	c.1100	Grain	Grain	?			T+1/2T+1/3Prop
-02 [28]	183v	Wulfward of Hoo, surnamed Henry	K	E	1108-?	Grain/Coombe	Grain/Hoo	?	S/pm		L
-03 [29]	183	Aethelnoth of Hoo	K	E	1093-1108	Grain	Grain	K		S	
8 [30]	191v-192	Goldwine Grec, burgesss of Rochester		E	1114-1124	Rochester	Rochester	?		S	2B
9-01 [31]	185	Robert of St Amand[sheriff's officer]	?L	F	c.1100	Nashenden	St.Margaret	Haimo the sheriff	S		T+Ch
-02 [32]	191-191v	Eadric of Nashenden	?M	E	c.1100	Nashenden	St.Margaret	?Robert of St Amand	S/Fs		T

Abbreviation List
D(ocument)-N(umber)
Name: S(on), W(ife).
Rel(ation): Co(-)h(older), H(usband), F(ather), K(indred), L(ord), M(an), S(on), W(ife).
Or(igin): E(nglish), F(rench).
Lord: A(rch)B(isho)p, B(isho)p, K(ing).
F(ra)t(ernity): Ann(iversary), F(raternitas), F(uneral)s(ervice), S(ocietas), p(anus)m(onachicus).
M(on)K: S(on).
Donation: B(urgage), C(onfirmation), Ch(urch), Eq(uus), L(and), Prop(erty), s(hillings), T(ithe), V(illager).

promotion in England was probably owed to Odo's prosperity. He held of Odo several manors, almost all of which were located in the Sutton Lathe of Kent. His main manor was Ruxley, which was one of the lands at issue in the Pinnenden trial between Odo and Lanfranc, archbishop of Canterbury, in the 1070s.[21] As a result of this dispute, Malger became a subtenant of the archbishop. In Domesday Book and the Domesday Monachorum he held three yokes in Orpington and owed the service of one fourth of a knight.[22] After the disgrace of Odo in 1082, his choice was to live on the soil of the countryside rather than to be expelled to Normandy. He held Ruxley of Haimo the sheriff and his heirs lasted as local figures and *milites agrarii* in West Kent into the beginning of the fourteenth century.[23]

In the time of Bishop Gundulf, the church of St Andrew and the monks there received Ansgot of Rochester into their society of benefits. In return he gave them all his tithe of Great Delce. Moreover, he granted the tithe of the mill which he built after the aforesaid donation and gave a certain piece of land included within the wall of the monks, towards the south, and five acres of land near Prestfield. Ansgot was a Domesday tenant of both Odo, bishop of Bayeux and Lanfranc, archbishop of Canterbury. His eight manors held of Odo were scattered all over the west of Kent.[24] Great Delce is one of them. Although he held Farningham from Lanfranc as one of archbishop's knights in Domesday Book , he never appeared in the list of Archbishop's knights in 1093–96.[25] This suggests the strong possibility that he died in some year between 1086 and 1096. When he was on his deathbed, the monks, at his request, gave him the monastic habit and performed service for him as for a monk.

[3] *Ansgotus de Rouecestra accepit societatem beneficiorum aecclesiae Sancti Andreae et monachorum tempore Gundulfi episcopi, et dedit eidem aecclesiae et monachis totam decimam suam de Deltsa, et de molendino similiter, quod postea fecit, totam decimam, et quandam particulam terrae, quae inclusa est infra murum monachorum versus austrum, et quinque acros terrae juxta Prestefelde dedit eis, et ipsi juxta peticionem suam dederunt ei pannos monachicos in articulo mortis suae, et fecerunt servitium pro eo sicuti pro monacho.*[26]

In those days to don a monastic habit at point of death was regarded as means to salvation (*ad succurrendum*). In the Textus there are many such examples.[27]

Great Delce lay within the bounds of the parish of St Margaret whose church

---

[21] D. C. Douglas, 'Odo, Lanfranc and the Domesday survey', in *Historical Essays in honour of James Tait*, Manchester 1933, 47–57.

[22] *Domesday Book*, i, 4; *The Domesday Monachorum*, 105.

[23] H. Hall ed., *The Red Book of the Exchequer*, RS 99, 190, 472; *The Book of Fees*, pt ii, HMSO 1923, 668, 673; James Greenstreet, 'Holders of knights' fees in Kent, Anno 38 Henry III.', *Archaeologia Cantiana* xii, 1878, 210, 218, etc.; *Feudal Aids A.D. 1284–1431*, iii, HMSO, 50; Hasted, ii, 151.

[24] *Domesday Book*, i, 6–7v, 8v–9.

[25] *Domesday Book*, i, 4; *The Domesday Monachorum*, 105.

[26] Textus Roffensis, i, 197v.

[27] E.g. *Gosfridus Pitit fecit cum monachis Sancti Andreae. Quadam vice pene ad mortem infirmabatur, et ideo requisivit ab eis monachiles pannos ad succurrendum, vel tunc, vel quando obiret* (fo. 193).

was recorded in the same Textus.[28] This parish contains all the lands outside the walls of Rochester on the south side of the city. There are several manors within the boundary of this parish. Little Delce is one of them, lying on the eastern side of this parish, about half a mile southward from the Eastgate of Rochester.[29] In Domesday Book, the son of William of Thaon held it of Odo, bishop of Bayeux.[30] Thaon lies about eleven miles eastward from Bayeux, and here we can still visit a small late-eleventh-century Romanesque parish church. William of Thaon probably accompanied Odo, as one of his knights, to England, but we cannot find the name of Thaon in the Textus. Instead, Geoffrey and Herbert of Delce held it in successive generations. Geoffrey of Delce with his wife and sons accepted the society with the monks and gave the whole tithe of Delce.

[4] *Gosfridus de Deltsa cum uxore et filiis acceperunt similiter et ipsi societatem, et concesserunt totam decimam suam de Deltsa.*[31]

Little Delce had been held by a certain Godric in 1066, and subsequently Godric of Delce accepted the society with the monks in return for the tithe of his grain-rent (*annona*). It is irresistible to suppose that two Godrics were one and the same man, although it cannot be proven. Nevertheless we must pay attention to the fact that the English could enter into the same society of benefits of the monks as could the Normans.

[5] *Godricus de Deltsa accepit societatem nostram, et ideo concessit nobis singulis annis decimam de annona sua.*[32]

Geoffrey of Delce also gave thirty acres of land near Prestfield in order to make his son a monk of Rochester. His son and heir, Herbert consented to this, and Geoffrey's lord, Walter Tirel consented to and confirmed the grant. In return, Walter accepted the society with the monks. Thus both lord and man entered the same society of the priory of Rochester Cathedral.

[4a] *Gausfridus de Deltsa dedit nobis xxx. acros terrae juxta Prestafelda pro filio suo quem fecimus monachum. Quod concessit Herebertus filius ejus. Sed et Walterius Tirel dominus ipsorum concessit postea et confirmavit, quia pro ipsa concessione accepit societatem nostram, et ita post acceptam societatem posuit cultellum suum super altare Sancti Andreae.*[33]

The case of William of Aubigny provides the best example of the relationship of English and Normans in the fraternity of Rochester. William of Aubigny, surnamed *pincerna*, was chief butler to King Henry I and founder of the family of the earls of Arundel.[34] He gave all the tithe of his manor of Elham to St Andrew of Rochester by a charter attested by his knights (*milites*). In addition, he gave land of one carucate in Exted and a wood, called *Acholte*, by the same charter, both of which lie in Elham. This manor had been held by Odo, bishop of Bayeux in

[28] Textus Roffensis, fo. 220v.
[29] Hasted, iv, 168.
[30] *Domesday Book*, i, 8v.
[31] Textus Roffensis, fo. 190.
[32] Textus Roffensis, fo. 195.
[33] Textus Roffensis, fo. 194v.
[34] I. J. Sanders, *English Baronies*, Oxford 1960, 1–2, 70 (henceforward Sanders).

demesne.[35] After the forfeiture of Odo's estates, it remained in the king's hand and was granted to William of Aubigny by William II or Henry I.[36] William of Aubigny's charter to Rochester seems to have been issued shortly after the coronation of Henry I. The date is given by the appearance in the charter of Ralf, a clerk of Bishop Gundulf between 1100 and 1108. Among the knights who witnessed is Roger of Elham, who gave half the tithe of his land in Elham in order to accept the society with the monks of St Andrew.

[6] *+Ego Willelmus de Albinneio pincerna regis concedo deo et Sancto Andreae de Rouecestria, et monachis ejusdem loci, totam meam decimam de villa mea quae vocatur Ælham in omnibus rebus, scilicet de bleio, et de pasnagio, et de molendinis, et de pecudibus, et de lana, et de caseis, et unam carrucatam de terra in Achestede, et unum boscum quod vocatur Acholte, quae duo jacent in Ælham, et medietatem decimae de Biseuuitune in omnibus rebus, pro anima domini mei Willelmi regis, et Henrici regis, atque pro anima mea, et patris mei et matris meae, et uxoris meae, et fratris mei Nigelli, et nepotis mei Hunfridi, et aliorum parentum meorum vivorum atque mortuorum. Testibus militibus meis Nigello del Wast, Ansfredo capellano, Radulfo de Chieresburh, Ricardo Caneleu, Ansgoto camerario, Rogero de Ælham, Radulfo clerico episcopi Gundulfi, et Ansfredo dapifero ejus.*[37]

[7] *Rogerius de Ælham accepit societatem monachorum aecclesiae Sancti Andreae, et ideo dedit eis dimidiam decimam de terra sua in Ælham de omni re.*[38]

In the Textus Roffensis another nine men follow Roger. They are: Ealdwulf of Shuttlesfield, Leofwine Scone of Bere, Baldwin *on Oferlande*, Edward *on Oferlande*, Blakeman of Bladbean, Leofwine of Exted, Wulfric *se mangere*, Rainald of Boyke, Ralf of 'Chieresburh', *dapifer* of William of Aubigny, and Herbert of 'Gatindene'. We can see that all of them were styled men of William of Aubingy from the witness list of Herbert of 'Gatindene's charter [17]. They all entered into the society with the monks of St Andrew by their donation in a similar way to Robert of Elham.

Shuttlesfield lies in Lyminge next to Elham.[39] The name of Ealdwulf shows that he was English.[40] He entered into the society with the monks, and in return he gave half the tithe of his land in Elham and Lyminge [probably Shuttlesfield].

[8] *Ealdulf de Scaerlesfelda accepit societatem illorum, et dedit eis dimidiam decimam de terra sua in Ælham de omni re, et dimidiam decimam de terra sua in Limmingis similiter de omni re.*[41]

Leofwine Scone of Bere, an Englishman, seems to have lived in Beerforstall

---

[35] *Domesday Book*, i, 9v.
[36] It should be noted that he called William II his lord, though he was a butler of King Henry I.
[37] Textus Roffensis, fo. 188.
[38] Textus Roffensis, fo. 188v.
[39] J. K. Wallenberg, *The Place-Names of Kent*, Uppsala 1934, 436 (henceforward Wallenberg).
[40] Olof von Feilitzen, *The Pre-Conquest Personal Names of Domesday Book*, Uppsala 1937, 242 (henceforward Feilitzen).
[41] Textus Roffensis, fo. 188v.

Farm, in Elham, where John le Barbour of Bere of Elham appeared in 1313.[42] He accepted the society with the monks in return for his donation of half the tithe of his land.

[9] *Leofuuine Scone de Bere accepit similiter societatem monachorum aecclesiae Sancti Andreae, et concessit illis dimidiam decimam de terra sua in omnibus rebus.*[43]

Although I have failed to identify Oferland anywhere in Elham, Edward was an Englishman.[44] Baldwine and Edward *on Oferland* gave the half of their tithes for their participation in the monks' society.

[10] *Baldeuuinus on Oferlande dedit similiter dimidiam decimam suam de terra sua in omnibus rebus pro societate illorum.*[45]

[11] *Eaduuord on Oferlande dimidiam decimam suam dedit illis de terra sua de omni re pro societate illorum.*[46]

Blackman, another Englishman, lived in Bladbean in Elham.[47] There appear two other Englishmen. They are Leofwine and Wulfric.[48] Leofwine *on Acsted* lived in Exted, where land of one carucate was given to the monks by the aforesaid William of Aubigny.

[12] *Blakeman of Flotbeame similiter dimidiam decimam suam dedit illis de omni re pro societate illorum de terra sua.*[49]

[13] *Leofuuine on Acstede dimidiam decimam suam dedit illis de terra sua de omnibus rebus pro societate illorum.*[50]

[14] *Uulfricus se mangere pro societate illorum dedit eis similiter dimidiam decimam suam de terra sua in omnibus rebus.*[51]

Rainald of Boyke lived in Boykewood,[52] in Elham. He gave half the tithe of his land for entrance into the society with the monks. This land he held of Humfrey, *dispensator* of William of Aubigny.

[15] *Rainaldus de Boeuuike pro societate illorum quam accepit dedit eis dimidiam decimam de terra sua quam tenebat de terra Hunfredi dispensatoris Willelmi de Albini.*[53]

The two last names in the list are those of Ralf of 'Chieresburh', *dapifer* of

---

42 Feilitzen, 317; Wallenberg, 431.
43 Textus Roffensis, fo. 188v.
44 Feilitzen, 50.
45 Textus Roffensis, fos. 188v–189.
46 Textus Roffensis, fo. 189.
47 Feilitzen, 203; Wallenberg, 431.
48 Feilitzen, 423.
49 Textus Roffensis, fo. 189.
50 Textus Roffensis, fo. 189.
51 Textus Roffensis, fo. 189.
52 Wallenberg, 431.
53 Textus Roffensis, fo. 189.

William of Aubigny and Herbert of 'Gatindene' whose charter is witnessed by all the men of William of Aubigny mentioned above.

> [16] *Radulfus de Chieresburh, dapifer Willelmi de Albini, pro societate illorum, unicuique anno promisit se daturum quingentas anguillas.*[54]

> [17] *Herbertus de Gatindene, pro societate illorum quam accepit, dedit eis totam decimam suam, aut quadraginta denarios, aut valentem in anguillis. Isti omnes homines Willelmi de Albini, scilicet Rogerius, Ealdwulf, Leofuuine, Baldeuuinus, Eadword, Blakeman, Leofuuine, Wlfricus, Rainaldus, Radulfus, Herbertus, supradictas donationes aeternaliter concesserunt monachis aecclesiae Sancti Andreae, concedente et confirmante eodem Willelmo de Albinneio domino suo.*[55]

It is safe to maintain that a substantial number of William of Aubigny's men in Elham were English in origin and they composed the local eminent group; though some of the names (such as Roger of Elham, Baldwine *on Oferland*, Rainald of Boyke, Ralf of 'Chieresburh' and Herbert of 'Gatindene') do not suggest English origins. Domesday Book often fails to give us information about such local dominant figures: we only know that in Elham there were forty-one villagers (*villani*), eight bordars (*bordarii*), and eight slaves (*servi*). The names of the more important inhabitants are supplied by the Textus Roffensis, and they are very significant. But for them, Norman settlers could not have exploited the manors in England. William of Aubigny needed them, and they needed a protector under the unstable social conditions after the Norman Conquest. This is one reason why the Normans had feudal or lord-man relations with English local figures. Although it is a matter of course that the sincere quest for salvation lay behind their acceptance of the society with the monks, it should be taken into account that in prompting the gifts of their tithes, considerations of feudal solidarity might supplement religious motivation.[56] The case of Ernulf of Chelsfield will indicate a better example of the almost synchronised entrance into the fraternity with feudal solidarity.

Ernulf of Hesdin was a tenant-in-chief in eleven shires and a tenant of Odo in Buckinghamshire and elsewhere as well as in Kent.[57] He took his name from Hesdin (dép. Pas de Calais arrond, Montreuil, Canton Hesdin).[58] Although it had been said that 'despite all researches, Ernulf of Hesdin still remains one of the most mysterious personage in Domesday' (Sir Humphrey Barkley), J. H. Round strongly maintained that the bulk of his land passed to Patrick of Chaworth and Mathilda, his wife, as her dower. Round identified her as a daughter of Ernulf of Hesdin, though he confessed that there was no good reason to support his opinion.[59] I show the family pedigree in Table II. Patrick was followed by his son Patrick who was succeeded before 1153 by his son, Pain of Mundubleil.[60] In the

---

54 Textus Roffensis, fo. 189.
55 Textus Roffensis, fo. 189–189v.
56 C. Harper-Bill, 'The struggle for benefices in East Anglia', *ante* xi, 1988, 114–115.
57 *The Domesday Monachorum*, 28, n. 7; *VCH, Berks.*, i, 363; *Bucks.*, i, 230, 238.
58 Loyd, 51.
59 *VCH, Berks.*, i, 313; Cal. Docs. France, xlvii; Sanders, 125, follows Round's identification.
60 *Regesta*, ii, nos. 436, 438a, 1940; Cal. Docs. France, nos. 318, 1033, 1326, 1386.

Table II   Ernulf of Hesdin and some of his descendants

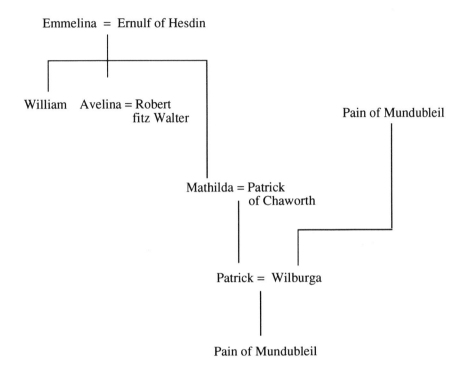

Cartae Baronum of 1166, he was responsible for twelve-and-a-half knights de *veteri* and one-third de *novo*. In this *carta* Simon of Chelsfield owed the service of five knights to Pain of Mundubleil.[61]

Chelsfield was the main manor which Ernulf of Hesdin held of Odo, Bishop of Bayeux. Domesday Book records that there were twenty villagers, four bordars, and four slaves and that now it is valued at twenty-five pounds and yet a man who holds it renders thirty-five pounds.[62] Who is this man? Before this question can be answered, we have to scrutinise the Textus Roffensis. In it a certain Ernulf of Chelsfield appears.

> [18] *Arnulfus de Cilesfelda dedit episcopo Gundulfo et monachis Sancti Andreae Rofecestrae totam medietatem totius decimae suae de Cilesfelda, annonam scilicet et agnos, et porcellos, et caseos, et vitulos, et pullos si ibi sunt equarum, et unum villicanum cum quinque acris terrae pro anima patris sui et matris suae, et pro se ipso. Et episcopus et monachi susceperunt ipsum Arnulfum cum uxore sua et homines suos quos et quot volebat in fraternitatem et in societatem totius beneficii ipsius aecclesiae, et super hoc fecerunt unum annuale missarum pro defunctis patre et matre. Et isti sunt testes hujus rei. Anscetillus archidiaconus, Radulfus prior Cadomi, Hunfridus monachus, Radulfus clericus, Simon dapifer episcopi, Atheloldus frater ejus, Wido Biset, Haimfridus dapifer Arnulfi, et alii multi.*[63]

He gave to Gundulf, bishop of Rochester, and the monks of St Andrew the moiety of his tithe of Chelsfield, that is, the grain, lambs' wool, piglets, cheese, deer-calves and foals if there be any such, and one peasant with land of five acres.[64] In return for this donation, the bishop and monks received him and his wife, and, in addition, his men, whomever and as many of them as he should like, into their fraternity and society, that is to be partakers of the benefits of their prayers. Here the last phrase shows the clear meaning of society: on account of this they say an annual mass for his deceased father and mother. Here we can see a clearer example of the Cluniac grant of confraternity to laymen in England than I have already presented.[65] The date of this agreement, in some year between 1096 and 1107, is established by the appearance of Anschitil the archdeacon of Rochester.[66]

Hasted thought that Ernulf of Hesdin and Ernulf of Chelsfield were the same person.[67] But this is not the case. In the Textus Roffensis there is a charter of 1143 addressed to Ascelin, bishop of Rochester by Ernulf of Chelsfield. He was probably the son of the previous Ernulf of Chelsfield. In this charter Ernulf (II) of

---

[61] *The Red Book of the Exchequer*, 297.

[62] *Domesday Book*, i, 6v.

[63] Textus Roffensis, fo. 184.

[64] R. E. Lennard took this donation of a villager with a land as an example of his 'peasant tithe-collector' (*EHR* 69, 1954, 587).

[65] From the point of view of phraseology, Rochester Cathedral Priory followed Cluny. This suggests a strong possibility that the fraternity of St Andrew's originated from Cluny and Bishop Gundulf introduced it via Bec; see H. E. J. Cowdrey, 'Unions and Confraternities with Cluny', *Journal of Ecclesiastical History* 16, 1965, 152–62.

[66] John le Neve (comp. by D. E. Greenway), *Fasti Ecclesiae Anglicanae 1066–1300, ii Monastic Cathedrals*, London 1971, 12, 81, 81 n. 3.

[67] Hasted, ii, 84–5.

Chelsfield, with Agnes his wife, Simon the eldest son and his heir, Elias the clerk, and Hugh a knight, his sons, confirmed the gift by Ernulf of Strood, his man, to the monks of Rochester, of land in Pennenden and in 'Godricesdune', which Ernulf of Chelsfield had held in demesne, free from the whole service, on the condition that Ernulf of Strood and his successors would perform their customary service, which he owed to Ernulf of Chelsfield from his fief.[68] The witnesses included Siward the priest, Symon, Hugh, and Elias, Ernulf's sons, Agnes his wife, Samson his brother, Richard his nephew, Adalulf his knight and other members of his household in order. The very first person on the witness list, Siward, must be the priest of Chelsfield parish church. Actually it is irresistible to assume that he was a kinsman of Ernulf of Chelsfield.[69] If so, the family of Chelsfield could be English rather than in Norman in origin. If not, the charter still informs us about the family and household of Ernulf (II) of Chelsfield in the middle of the twelfth century and for my purpose it can point towards the lineage of the family of Chelsfield, for Simon is that man who owed five knights' service to Pain of Mundubleil in 1166.[70] I show the pedigree of Chelsfield family in Table III; it shows clearly that Ernulf I of Chelsfield and Ernulf of Hesdin are different individuals.[71]

Thus it is safe to maintain that Ernulf I of Chelsfield was an under-tenant of Ernulf of Hesdin and identical with *he who holds* Chelsfield in Domesday Book. Domesday Book also records an Esbern of Chelsfield who before 1066 held the liberties of sac and soc for all his lands throughout the lathes of Sutton and Aylesford.[72] Although it cannot be proved whether or not Ernulf of Chelsfield was the successor of Esbern, it is very tempting to assume that before Odo subinfeudated Chelsfield to Ernulf of Hesdin, the family of Chelsfield had been already the local English lord of the soil, and that after Odo's subinfeudation, the two Ernulfs formed a feudal connection with each other. While for Ernulf of Hesdin the formation of patronage with a local man gave him security for collecting rent, it also enabled Ernulf of Chelsfield to survive as lord of the soil after the confusion of the Norman Conquest, despite a downgrading in the social scale. Of course there is another possible explanantion; Ernulf of Chelsfield was a follower of Ernulf of Hesdin, and after the Norman Conquest he settled himself in Chelsfield and married a sister or daughter of Esbern.

But these speculations are beyond proof. A far more important point here is

---

[68] Strood is one of the estates held by Chelsfield family. See below, n. 70.

[69] Dr Ann Williams suggested to me a possibility that he might be a brother of Ernulf I of Chelsfield. She found that the Reading Abbey Cartularies contain a charter of Ernulf II (1138 x 48) in whose witness list there appear, in the same order as the Textus Roffensis grant, Siward the priest and three sons of Ernulf, that is, Simon, Elyas, and Hugh (*Testes sunt huius conventionis et concessionis Siwardus sacerdos, et tres filii predicti Arnulfi, Simon scilicet et Helyas et Hugo, Simon de Godintona, et Willelmus filius ejus, et multi alii*); B. R. Kemp ed. *Reading Abbey Cartularies*, I, Camden Fourth Ser. xxxi, London 1986, 209. His appearance in the charter concerning Buckinghamshire shows Siward's close connection with the family of Chelsfield; he was rather more than a mere local priest in Chelsfield. For his name, see Feilitzen, 361–363.

[70] In 1198 the estates of Simon of Chelsfield, described as Chelsfield, Strood, Goddington (in Chelsfield), Faringham, Horton Kirby, Farnborough, Caldecote (in Chelsfield) and Houghton were divided by his three co-heiresses; '*Pedes Finium*', *Archaeologia Cantiana*, vol. 1, 255.

[71] The Reading Abbey Cartularies also give us the same pedigree of this family; *Reading Abbey Cartularies*, i, 209–10, 212, 214–218, 472–5.

[72] *Domesday Book*, i, 1v.

that even within the small boundary of Chelsfield, Ernulf of Chelsfield had his own retainers and consideration of such man-lord solidarity helped the entrance into the fraternity of his retainers, Normans and English alike. In the witness-list of the donation charter of Ernulf (I) of Chelsfield, Haimfrid *dapifer* of Ernulf appears. Haimfrid, as man of Ernulf of Chelsfield, transferred the tithe of his land in Chelsfield to the monks for the society of prayer he had accepted

[19] *Heimfred homo Ernulfi de Cilesfeld, pro societate quam accepit, concessit decimam de terra sua quam habebat in Cilesfeld.*[73]

In the same witness-list appear Simon dapifer of the bishop and his brother *Atheloldus* (Æthelwold). The name of Æthelwold might imply that he was an Englishman in origin.[74] This Æthelwold is also called Adelold of Chelsfield or Goddington.[75] Indeed there is other evidence that he was a man of Ernulf.[76] But more important is that the Textus Roffensis reveals that he was a local figure and knight. Æthelwold, brother of Baldwin, monk of Rochester, gave all his tithe to the monks of St Andrew. In addition on his death bed, he transferred horses and arms as well as all his property. The monks gave him their society and fraternity. The gift of horses and arms suggests that he was a knight, though he never appeared in any lists of knights.[77]

[20] *Adeloldus, frater Balduini nostri monachi, dedit nobis omnem suam decimam, etiam de mobili pecunia, et quando de hac vita migraverit omnem suam partem totius pecuniae suae, et praeter hoc suos equos et sua arma, et concessimus ei fraternitatem et societatem nostri monasterii.*[78]

Æthelwold also gave counsel to Wulfmaer, a man of Ernulf of Hesdin, when Wulfmaer transferred to the monks of St Andrew his tithe valued at ten shillings

[73] Textus Roffensis, fo. 190.
[74] Feilitzen, 188.
[75] Textus Roffensis, fo.196. In the charter of Gilbert Glanville, bishop of Rochester (1185 x 1214), Æthelwold (*Alold*)'s donation was called the tithe of Goddington, which is a manor within the parish of Chelsfield; John Thorpe ed. *Registrum Roffense*, London 1769, 47. Hasted, ii. 89. Wallenberg, 18.
[76] The aforesaid final concord (n. 70 above) also shows the tenants of Simon of Chelsfield, such as John of Goddington who owed him the service of two knights in Goddington, Strood and Farnborough. He was probably a successor of Simon of Goddington who also appeared in the aforesaid charter of Reading Abbey. This Simon must be a successor of Adelold of Chelsfield. In 1171 a Simon of Goddington owed one knight to the archbishop of Canterbury for unnamed land, though he recognised the service of half a knight. Professor Du Boulay suggests that this Simon may be the same as Simon of Chelsfield, but the two Simons cannot be identical; F. R. H. Du Boulay, *The Lordship of Canterbury*, London 1966, 346 (henceforward, Du Boulay). Colvin, however, identifies Goddington as Goddington in Chart, not Goddington in Chelsfield and suggests Simon is a descendant of Robert, son of Godbert (Colvin, 31).
[77] It also suggests that he was an English knight, for in pre-Conquest England the heriot of a lesser thegn was his arms and horse (II Cnut, 71–2; A. J. Robertson, *The Laws of the Kings of England From Edmund to Henry I*, Cambridge 1925, 211). Adelold's gift may represent a survival of old English custom. After the Norman knights conquered England, both they and English knights were recorded as *miles*, thegn, and *cniht*. The difference between them is not their social standing but the languages in which they were recorded. The word *miles* did not imply social standing but military function as a soldier; see, H. Tsurushima, 'The Concept *miles* in Eleventh and Twelfth Century England', *The Studies of English History*, 34, 1983, 1–17 (written in Japanese).
[78] Textus Roffensis, fos. 184v–185.

Table III Ernulf of Chelsfield and his descendants

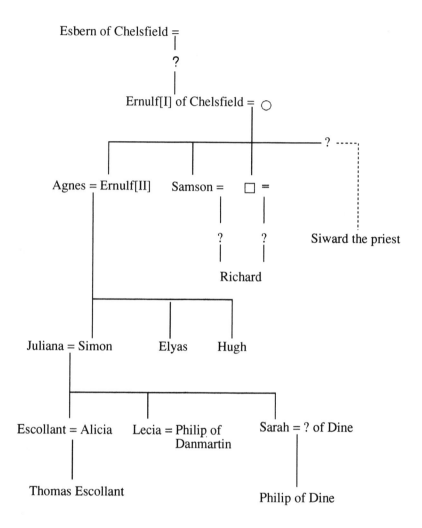

yearly. For this donation he accepted the society with the monks. Judging from his name, Wulfmaer was an Englishman.[79] He seems to be as an intermediary man between Ernulf of Hesdin, Domesday lord, and other dominant figures in Chelsfield.

[21] *Uulmerus, homo Arnulfi de Hesdinc, consilio Adeloldi fratris Balduini nostri monachi accepit nostram societatem et dedit nobis suam decimam, quae valet per annum decem solidos.*[80]

In his charter of 1143 Ernulf (II) confirmed the gift of his man, Ernulf of Strood, to Rochester.

[22] *Domno Ascelino Rofensi episcopo, et Radulfo castellano et omnibus civibus Rouecestriae, totique hundred de Scamele, Ernulfus de Chielsfelda salutem. Notum vobis sit quod ego Ernulfus et Agnes uxor mea, et Symon primogenitus et heres meus, et Helyas clericus, et Hugo miles filii mei, donationem quam Ernulfus de Strodes homo meus Sancto Andreae et monachis de Rouecestria pro filio suo in ecclesia Rofensi ad monachatum suscepto dedit, partem scilicet terrae suae, quae Pinindene vocatur, et terram illam quam in suo dominico habebat in alio loco qui vocatur Godricesdune, liberam ab omni servicio et quietam aeterno jure monachis ejsdem possidendam concessimus. Quod si praedictus Ernulfus vel aliquis heredum aut successorum ejus a solito quod michi de feudo suo debet servicio defecerit, a reliqua quam de me tenet terra exigetur, elemosina autem ab omni exactione et querela et calumnia libera permaneat. Et hanc quidem concessionem pro salute animae meae, et uxoris, et liberorum, et patris, et matris meae, bono et devoto animo feci, et signo sanctae crucis, + proprioque signavi sigillo. Cujus rei testes sunt, Syuuardus presbyter, Symon, Hugo, Elyas, filii Ernulfi, et Agnes uxor sua, Samson frater, Ricardus nepos domini, Adalulfus miles, Willelmus dapifer, Ernulfus dispensator, Haimo Brito, Ernulfus clericus, Rainaldus secretarius, Ricardus de Clouilla, Elfuuinus Catere, Rodbertus filius Bunde, Godefridus nepos Goislani, Robertus cognatus Clementis monachi, et alii multi. Anno ab incarnatione domini MCXLIII.*[81]

This Ernulf of Strood is probably a son of an earlier Ernulf [I] of Strood, who, about 1100, accepted the society with the monks, in company with Richard Bell, and both their wives. For this they gave all their tithe to the monks, for the right of burial in the church. The funeral service and burial in the cemetery of the priory is one of the important aspects of the fraternity.

[23] *Ricardus Bellus et Ernulfus de Strodes cum uxoribus suis acceperunt societatem nostram et dederunt nobis omnem decimam suam etiam de mobili pecunia et sepeliemus.*[82]

One of the greatest obstacles to research into local society is the historical fact that many English people had changed their names from English to Norman style

[79] Feilitzen, 421.
[80] Textus Roffensis, fo. 185.
[81] Textus Roffensis, fo. 230v.
[82] Textus Roffensis, fo. 201v.

after the Conquest.[83] So we cannot tell whether an individual was Norman or English from his or her name, which might have followed Norman fashion. Robert Latin or Latimer is a good example. He was a wealthy tenant of Odo, bishop of Bayeux, in Kent, particularly West Kent and is identified as Robert the Interpreter in the Domesday Monachorum.[84] He also held part of Otford manor of the Archbishop jointly with Geoffrey of Ros and shared the title of thegn (*teigni*) with Geoffrey and even Haimo the sheriff.[85] If we take into consideration that Haimo and Geoffrey appeared in the list of the knights' service of the archbishop of Canterbury, it is likely that Robert could also be regarded as a knight, in spite of his non-appearance in the list.[86] In the notification charter of Bishop Gundulf addressed to Haimo the sheriff, Robert Latimer appeared as one of the officials of the sheriff with his brother, Ælfwine the reeve of Chatham.[87] This implies that he was an Englishman.[88] Why was he named Robert? His nickname 'Interpreter' gives us the clue; he could speak both English and French, and was working as an interpreter among the officials of the sheriff during the Domesday Survey.[89] This close connection with Nomans made him change his name from English to Norman style, and moreover made it possible for him and Geoffrey of Ros to hold jointly. In the same charter of Gundulf we find the names of Geoffrey of Ros and of Ansgot of Rochester. The three of them had their main estates in West Kent,[90] and probably recognised each other as neighbours.

On his death bed, Robert Latimer gave to the church of St Andrew and the monks a marshland in the Isle of Grain, which he held of Anselm, archibishop of Canterbury for the salvation of his soul. The Archbishop consented to this donation and the monks received thirty shillings yearly from it. He died in about 1100 during the pontificate of Anselm. Indeed here there is no word of *societas* or *fraternitas*, and the former part of the document is a later insertion of the twelfth century. But still we may well assume that Robert entered into the fraternity of the monks.

---

[83] M. T. Clanchy, *England and its Rulers 1066–1272*, Oxford 1983, 56–57; H. Tsurushima, 'How did the English change their names from Saxon to continental style just after the Norman Conquest', *Shigaku* 50–1, 1991, 1–30 (written in Japanese).

[84] *Domesday Book*, i, 6v, 7, 8, 8v, 11v; *The Domesday Monachorum*, 87.

[85] Domesday Book, i, 3; *The Domesday Monachorum*, 87.

[86] *The Domesday Moanchorum*, 105.

[87] *Gundulfus, Rofensium, gracia dei, episcopus, Haimoni vicecomiti, et omnibus baronibus regis de Caert Francigenis et Anglis, salutem, et benedictionem dei, et suam quantum potest. . . . Et illos tres acros terrae, quos pro illis tribus dedi regi in cambitionem, liberavi jam ministris vicecomitis, Rodberto scilicet de Sancto Amando, et Rodberto Latimier, et Ælfuuino fratre ejus praeposito de Cetham, et Gretoni de Rouecestra de nostra dominica terra de Burchestealla, praesentibus testibus istis: Ansgoto de Rouecestra, Gosfrido Talebot, Goisfrido de Ros, Radulfo pincerna Adamae, Rodulfo clerico,et aliis multis de nostra familia et de civibus ejusdem villae* (Textus Roffensis, fos. 211v–212). After the forfeiture of Odo's lands, Robert probably became a man of Haimo the sheriff. After Robert's death, his lands passed to the Crevequer family, the descendants of Haimo; H. Tsurushima, 'On the Norman Settlement and Anglo-Saxon Knights' *The Studies in Western History*, 123, 1981, 40, n. 58 (written in Japanese).

[88] Feilitzen, 181.

[89] Another interpreter was Godric Latimer, whose predecessor was Oswy Wild the priest; A. Ballard, *An Eleventh Century Inquisition of St Augustine, Canterbury* (The British Academy Records of the Social and Economic History of England and Wales), 4, pt 2, London 1920, 30.

[90] Geoffrey of Ros (*Domesday Book*, i, 6–6v, 8); Ansgot of Rochester, see n. 24 above; Robert Latimer, see n. 84 above.

[24] *Rodbertus Latimier, imminente articulo mortis suae, dedit aecclesiae Sancti Andreae et monachis illic deo servientibus unum mariscum infra insulam de Grean pro anima sua inperpetuum. Quod donum concessit libenter archiepiscopus Anselmus, de quo tenuit illim. Et monachi habent inde singulis annis xxx^{da}.solidos.*[91]

After the death of Robert, his widow contracted with the monks of St Andrew's for a corrody. The Textus Roffensis tells us an interesting story about their agreement and about a small but significant part of the pedigree of Latimer family.[92] She held the land called Hornden in Frindsbury for her life and paid twenty shillings to the reeve of Frindsbury yearly. She affirmed that her kindred should succeed to it, but the monks claimed it should revert to them after her death. But long before her death, she gave up her claim and decided to transfer the land at issue to the monks of St Andrew for the salvation of the souls of her husband, herself and her parents. After the proccession one Sunday, she came forward in front of the altar and handed it over to them with all belonging to it to be possessed by them for ever, in the presence of monks, French, English and other people. For her donation, the monks gave her sixty shillings of which Brod the priest, her daughter's husband, robbed her in a fit of passion. They promised her besides, food and clothing so long as she should live, that is, food from the cellarer as much as for one monk and one dish of flesh four days in the week, and clothing from the chamberlain, honorable, such as became her age and person. In addition they promised to give to one man and one maid-servant such food as the rest of servants of the church had. Besides this they promised to give her twenty shillings yearly to pay their wages, cloth them, and procure other necessaries for herself. When she died, the convent agreed that they would bury her and keep her anniversary yearly. The list of witnesses follows; Robert the priest, the son of Goldwine the priest, Ordheah the priest of Hoo, Ralph clerk, Hugh clerk, *Wigetus* clerk, Goldwine Grec, his brother Edwine *fot*, Robert secretary, and Guthred the son of Dioring.

[25] *Haec conventio habita est inter monachos Roffenses et uxorem Rodberti Latimarii. Haec mulier tenebat quandam terram de Freondesberia quae vocabatur Thorniduna, et reddebat inde viginti solidos praeposito Freondesberiae per singulos annos, et debebat terram illam tenere usque ad mortem suam. Post mortem autem suam debebat esse Sancti Andreae et monachorum, non alicujus parentum illius sicut ipsa affirmabat. Diu ergo ante mortem suam placuit ei ut terram eandem redderet Sancto Andreae et monachis pro salute animae viri sui et suae et parentum suorum. Veniens itaque die dominica quadam post processionem ante altare Sancti Andreae, astantibus monachis et Francis et Anglis et multis reddidit terram ipsam*

---

[91] Textus Roffensis, fo. 182v–183.

[92] Robert Latimer's parents were Æthelric the priest of Chatham and Godgifu; see Henry Wharton, *Anglia Sacra* i, London 1691, 340 and Du Boulay, 99. Æthelric had been a canon of the cathedral chapter at Rochester, which was replaced by a body of Benedictine monks soon after Gundulf's accession to the bishopric. He gave a house to the monks in order to bury his wife with honour: *Ægelricus presbyter de Cettham qui quondam canonicus aecclesiae Sancti Andreae extiterat, pro anima uxoris suae Godgyfe, et pro eo quod sepelierunt eam honorifice monachi, dedit eis unam mansam, reddentem, Xii. denarios per annum* (Textus Roffensis, 190v–191).

apostolo Sancto et monachis aeternaliter possidendam, dans cum terra omnia quae habebantur super ipsam terram. Monachi vero pro hac re magis confirmanda dederunt illi sexaginta solidos, quos postea Brodo presbyter qui ejus filiam habebat calide extorsit, et praeterea promiserunt ei quia invenirent ei victum et vestitum quam diu viveret, victum videlicet de celario quantum uni monacho, et praeter hoc unum ferculum de carne quattuor diebus in Ebdomada, vestitum vero de camera honorabilem qualem ejus aetatem et personam deceret. Uni autem ejus servienti et uni pedisequae qui ei servirent talem darent victum qualem ceteris aecclesiae servientibus. Super haec omnia darent ipsi dominae viginti solidos singulis annis quibus servientes sibi solidaret et vestiret, et caetera sibi necessaria prout vellet ipsa procuraret. Cum autem obiret, conventus eam sepeliret, et anniversarium ejus singulis annis faceret. Hujus conventionis sunt testes, Rodbertus presbyter filius Golduuini presbyteri, Ordegus presbyter de Ho, Radulfus clericus, Hugo clericus, Uuigetus clericus, Golduuinus Grecus et frater ejus Eaduuinus, Eaduuinus fot, Rodbertus secretarius, Gudredus filius Dioringi, et alii multi.[93]

By this agreement she entered into the fraternity of the monks, since the burial and anniversary mass by them are the essential part of it.[94] She and her husband, Robert Latimer, were probably buried side by side in the cemetery of the priory. Robert's co-holder in Otford, Geoffrey of Ros, was one of Odo's tenants and a Norman who came from Rots (Calvados, arr. Caen, cant. Tilly-sur-Seulles).[95] He asked for the anniversay mass for his wife by giving the tithe of Yaldham in Wrotham to the monks. I have already told how Ansgot of Rochester entered into the same society of prayer. The consciousness of sharing the same religious background of the fraternity may well have reinforced the sentiments of neighbourhood established between English and Normans one generation after the Norman Conquest.

[26] *Gosfridus de Ros dedit aeternaliter decimam suam de Ealdeham monachis Sancti Andreae pro anima uxoris suae, quae terra pertinet ad Uuroteham, et ipsi monachi facient anniversarium illius uxoris singulis annis.*[96]

A tale is told of the entrance into the fraternity of another local English figure. In the pontificate of Gundulf, an Englishwoman Lyafrun (Leofrun) gave a marshland in the Isle of Grain to the monks of St Andrew's in perpetuity for the salvation of the souls of herself and her husband, Siward of Hoo, after his death.[97] After Gundulf's death, Wulfward, surnamed Henry, of Hoo claimed that this land should belong to him because of ties of blood.[98] But such an evil design caused

---

[93] Textus Roffensis, fo. 200v–201.
[94] The case of Ingelburg, widow of Herulf sutor is a good example: *Ingelburgis quae fuit uxor Herulfi sutoris dedit mansam suam monachis Sancti Andreae quatinus ipsi tribuerent ei victum et vestitum de elemosinis illorum omni vita sua, et societatem concesserunt, et servitium in fine sicut pro sorore promiserunt facere* (Textus Roffensis, fo. 190v).
[95] Loyd, 86. He died before 1130 and his son, Geoffrey (II) of Ros accounted for twenty shillings for his father's land; *Pipe Roll 31 Henry I*, 64.
[96] Textus Roffensis, fo. 189v.
[97] Feilitzen, 315.
[98] Feilitzen, 425–26.

serious illness. On his death bed, he retracted his claim, consented to her donation, and therefore he required the monastic habit for the quest of the love of God
and the salvation of his soul. The monks would receive forty shillings yearly from
the land.

> [27] *Lyafrun quae fuit uxor Syuuardi de Hou dedit aecclesiae Sancti An-*
> *dreae et monachis ibidem deo servientibus post mortem ipsius viri sui*
> *Syuuardi unum mariscum infra insulam de Grean pro anima sua, et pro*
> *anima ipsius Syuuardi mariti sui aeternaliter possidendum, et hoc donum*
> *fecit in tempore Gundulfi episcopi. Post mortem vero ipsius episcopi, qui-*
> *dam Uulfuuardus cognomine Henricus de Hou calumniatus est ipsum ma-*
> *riscum, dicens suum esse debere per consanguinitatis parentelam. Sed infra*
> *calumniam illam infirmatus est ad mortem. Unde requirens monachiles*
> *pannos a monachis Sancti Andreae, et quia impetravit quod petiit, calum-*
> *niam illam pro amore dei et redemptione animae suae dimisit, et ipsum*
> *mariscum aecclesiae Sancti Andreae et monachis ejus omnino quietum*
> *clamavit in secula seculorum. De quo singulis annis habent monachi inde*
> *quadraginta solidos.*[99]

Wulfward still could not escape from the fear of death, so he accepted the
society with the monks of St Andrew's. In return for this benefit, he gave to the
priory the whole tithe of Coombe, the half of his tithe in Hoo, and third part of his
substance after his death, to which his wife and his son Robert, and his brothers
Hereward, Siward, and Edward, consented. I show the pedigree of the family in
Table V.[100]

> [28] *Wlfuuardus de Hou cognomine Henricus accepit societatem monacho-*
> *rum aecclesiae Sancti Andreae, pro qua dedit eis totam decimam suam de*
> *Cobbeham. Postea vero alia vice decimam suam de Hou dimidiam conces-*
> *sit eis, et terciam partem suae substantiae post mortem suam. Quod uxor*
> *illius et filius suus Rodbertus, et fratres sui, Hereuuardus videlicet et*
> *Siuuardus et Eaduuardus, libentissime concesserunt.*[101]

This Hoo must be the parish of St Mary, Hoo, in which the manor of Coombe
lies.[102] Wulfward de Hoo, surnamed Henry, was an English lord of this manor and
a local figure to whom Domesday Book never refers. It records only that Hoo was
held by Odo, bishop of Bayeux and only two tenants, the Normans, Adam son of
Hubert and Anschitil of Ros are named.[103] But the Textus Roffensis reveals an
Englishman still in possession in the twelfth century.

Moreover a second Englishman, holding of the king, appears as a tenant of
Hoo. Æthelnoth of Hoo is described as 'a good man of king'.[104] He also gave to
the monks of St Andrew's a marsh-land in the Isle of Grain in order to make his

---

[99] Textus Roffensis, fos. 183–183v.
[100] This family clearly shows the process of Englishmen changing their names into the Norman
style. Wulfward had a Norman surname, Henry and gave his son the Norman name of Robert,
although all his brothers had English names.
[101] Textus Roffensis, fo. 183v.
[102] Hasted, i. 23.
[103] *Domesday Book*, i, 8v.
[104] Feilitzen, 185–86.

Table IV   Robert Latimer and his family

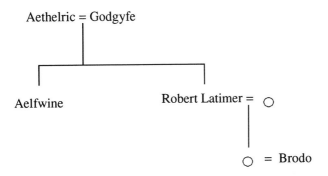

Table V   Wulfward of Hoo and his kindred

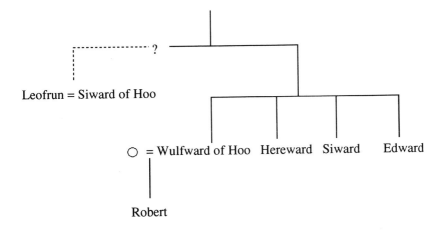

son a monk here. They received fifteen shillings yearly from it and Anselm consented to this donation.

[29] *Ægelnothus quidam probus homo regis de Hou, similiter dedit aecclesiae Sancti Andreae et monachis unum mariscum in eadem insula, pro filio suo quodam quem fecit monachum ibi. De quo marisco habent monachi xv. solidos uno quoque anno. Et hoc donum quoque concessit Anselmus archiepiscopus.*[105]

In the Textus Roffensis many people gave donations to the priory in order to make their sons,[106] brothers[107] and even themselves monks. Rochester burgesses are particularly remarkable for their frequent appearance. Goldwine surnamed Grec, for example, gave to the monks of St Andrew's two burgages, belonging to Frindsbury, and a part of the king's land adjacent to them in order to make his son a monk there. In addition to this, he gave the half of the burgage, adjacent to the cemetery of the priory, belonging to Borstall on the condition that he would continue to hold it until the monks had dismantled the houses, using the land to widen their cemetery.

[30] *Golduuinus cognomento Grecus dedit aecclesiae Sancti Andreae et monachis pro filio suo ibidem facto monacho duas hagas terrae in Rouecestra, pertinentes ad Frendesberia, et partem terrae regis quae est juxta ipsas hagas. Praeter has autem hagas dedit et dimidiam hagam juxta cimiterium appendentem ad Borchstellam, sed istam dimidiam hac conventione dedit, quod eam tenebit donec monachi alias hagas hinc et inde habeant et domos auferant ad ampliandum cimiterium suum. Et tunc sine omni mora vel contradictione tradet eam in manus monachorum, vel ipse si vixerit, vel uxor et filii ejus si mortuus fuerit. Hujus conventionis testes sunt, Heruisus archidiaconus, Radulfus clericus et Robdertus filius ejus, Golduinus presbyter, Gelduinus et Rodbertus monetarii, Gudredus filius Diringi, Stephanus filius Goduuini, Uuiet filius Goduuini, et alii multi.*[108]

Also such Rochester burgesses as Coc, Godwine son of Edith, and Goldwine the priest of Rochester gave their burgages or lands to the monks of St Andrew's in order that they might make their sons monks there.[109] Another burgess of Rochester, named Geldwine the moneyer, even made himself a monk of St

---

[105] Textus Roffensis, fo. 183.
[106] Examples include Eadmer of Darenth (fos. 183v–84), Gerald (fo. 185), William of Clovill (fo. 186). Gerald had a nephew with the English name Wulfgar (Feilitzen, 419). His son, Thurstan, was a monk of the Cathedral Priory. Wulfgar accepted the society of the monks in return for giving the tithe of his land (Textus Roffensis, fo. 189v).
[107] Haimo son of Vital (fo. 185v), Richard Brutin of Gillingham (fos. 191). This Vital was probably one of three knights depicted in the Bayeux Tapestry. He was the founder of a local knightly family, named 'De Shofford' (H. Tsurushima, 'Three knights depicted in the Bayeux Tapestry' (written in Japanese)', *History* (The University of Tohoku) 64, 1985, 54–70. A Ralf Brutin owed the service of one third of a knight to the bishop of Rochester (Textus Roffensis, fo. 217).
[108] Textus Roffensis, fos. 191v–192.
[109] Coc (fo. 192v), Godwine son of Edith (fo. 192v), Goldwine the priest of Rochester (fos. 199v–200).

Andrew's by granting to them the lands adjacent to the priory.[110] They also appear as witnesses to each others' donation charters. Goldwine Grec and Robert the priest, son of the aforesaid Goldwine the priest were two of the witnesses of Robert Latimer's wife's corrody agreement. Geldwine the moneyer was also a witness of Goldwine Grec's charter. Such a network of witnesses extended beyond the local circle of English to the Normans. In the notification charter of an agreement of Bishop Ernulf with Ralf clerk, Brod the priest,[111] a son-in-law of Robert Latimer and robber of his wife's pension, appears as a witness with Fubert of Chilham, a founder of the barony of Dover, whose father Hugh probably came from Dovres in the Bessin, north of Caen.[112]

In the notification charter of Bishop Gundulf addressed to Haimo the sheriff, Robert of St Amand appears as one of the officials of the sheriff with Robert Latimer.[113] He must be Norman. Robert of St Amand accepted the society with the monks and gave half the tithe of Nashenden to the church of St Andrew. Afterwards he gave the remaining tithe and the church of Nashenden in order to make his son a monk.

[31] *Rodbertus de Sancto Amando accepit societatem nostram et dedit Sancto Andreae medietatem decimae suae de Hescendena. Postea dedit nobis aliam medietatem cum aecclesia quae ibi est pro filio suo quem fecimus monachum.*[114]

Nashenden is a small manor in Rochester.[115] In the list of churches in the Textus Roffensis it appears as a chapelry in the parish of St. Margaret.[116] This donation suggests that the church of Nashenden was the *Eigenkirche* of Robert of St Amand.[117] He was the lord of this manor and his descendant, Thomas of Nashenden, held by the service of one knight from Daniel of Crevequer, a descendant of Haimo the sheriff in 1166.[118] This gift also affected an Englishman who lived in Nashenden. Eadric of Nashenden with his wife and two sons accepted the society with the monks on condition that when they died, the monks said the same mass for them as for monks.

[32] *Eadric de Hescendena cum uxore et duobus filiis acceperunt societatem nostram eo pacto, ut quando obierint faciemus servitium pro eis, sicuti pro fratribus, et habebimus decimas aeternaliter de terris illorum quas habent in Borcstealla, et in Freondesberia, in annona tantum.*[119]

The Textus Roffensis records that when the wife of Robert Latimer contracted with the monks for a corrody in front of the altar of St Andrew, there attended a

---

[110] Textus Roffensis, fos. 191v–192.
[111] An English name, see Feilitzen, 208.
[112] Textus Roffensis, fos. 198v–199v; Sanders. 111.
[113] Textus Roffensis, fo. 212.
[114] Textus Roffensis, fo. 185.
[115] Hasted, iv, 166–167.
[116] Textus Roffensis, fo. 220v, 222.
[117] There are two other examples of the donation of *Eigenkirchen*, both in the archbishopric of Canterbury. The aforesaid Haimo son of Vital gave the church of Stourmouth to the monks (fo. 185v), and Hugh of Newham, with his wife and son Fulk, gave the church of Norton in order to accept the society of the monks (190v).
[118] *The Red Book of the Exchequer*, 191.
[119] Textus Roffensis, fos. 191–191v.

congregation of English and French. How interesting it is to suppose that Gold-wine, surnamed Grec, and Robert the priest, Geldwine the moneyer, Robert of St Amand and Eadric of Nashenden were present at the ceremony. When people entered into the fraternity of the monks, a congregation of English and Normans must have been notified of that news. Some of them also accepted the society, and some made their sons, brothers and even themselves monks and in some cases, established feudal relationships among themselves. Such a sense of sharing the fraternity of the monks would strengthen their feelings of solidarity and neigh-bourhood.

When a layman entered into the fraternity of the monks, he could feel that he was drawn to the monastic order. As H. E. J. Cowdrey suggests, 'the bonds were vertical, in the sense that *confratres* were made partakers of the prayers and good deeds of the monks on their behalf. Their fellowship was with monks; there is no trace of horizontal bonds of any kind'.[120] But although association with the monks was personal, the initial impulse to enter into such bonds was influenced by feudal ties. The Chelsfield group described above is a good example of this. The fraternity could spread beyond the diocese of Rochester, as shown in the case of Eadmær anhænde. He was a burgess of London, and requested entrance into the fraternity of Rochester, in return for his hospitality to Bishop Gundulf, when the bishop was engaged in building the tower of London.[121] But many families, English and Normans, who entered into the fraternity of the monks of St Andrew's, and whose sons became monks of that community, were close neigh-bours and associates and knew each other well. They probably formed a large part of the congregation of the church of St Andrew. The memorandum of Goldwine surnamed Grec suggests that the priory was compelled to enlarge its cemetery.[122] This is partly because the number of monks had increased since the pontificate of Gundulf, but mainly because the priory received lay members into the fraternity with the monks and buried them in their cemetery.[123] To enter into the same fraternity, that is, to be buried in the same cemetery and to hear the funeral mass and anniversary together strengthened the sense of unity between English and Normans. The fraternity of Kentishmen, English or Norman, with

---

[120] Cowdrey, 'Unions and Confraternities', 162.

[121] *Haec est conventio inter Gundulfum episcopum et Eadmerum anhænde burgensem Londoniae. Dum idem Gundulfus ex praecepto regis Willelmi magni praeesset operi magnae turris Londoniae, et hospitatus fuisset apud ipsum Ædmerum, quadam vice ipse coepit episcopum rogare, ut concedet sibi societatem aecclesiae quam regebat videlicet Sancti Andreae. Quod ei episcopus satis libenter concessit. Et ideo concessit Sancto Andreae & fratribus ibidem deo servientibus medietatem piscariae quae vocatur Niuue Uere, quam diu viveret. Cum vero moreretur, totam eam ibidem concessit, et totam terram suam quam habebat in Lundonia. et domos tali pacto, ut ipse et uxor ejus ad Rouecestram deferrentur & ibidem sepelirentur, omnique anno eorum anniversarium observaretur. Isti sunt testes hujus rei: duo filii Brihtmari Ægeluuinus et Orgarus, Radulfus clericus episcopi, et Godefridus Grossus, et alii multi* (Textus Roffensis, fo. 210v).

[122] See above, n. 108.

[123] Before the pontification of Gundulf, the small community of five canons constituted the cathedral chapter of whom the father of Robert Latimer, Æthelric, was one. They were compelled to leave the church by Bishop Gundulf, who appointed in their place twenty-two Benedictine monks. Before his death (1108), the numbers had risen to over sixty; Textus Roffensis, fos. 172–172v.

the monks of St Andrew's consolidated horizontal bonds.[124] When in the early twelfth century, Ailnoth of Canterbury, an Englishman living in Denmark and a biographer of Saint Cnut, lamented the fate of *Anglorum gens nobilissima*,[125] a new sense of community in his native shire was being consolidated from the crucible of the Norman settlement.[126]

[124] Here it is not a particular type of horizontal tie but some kind of sympathy collectively shared by them that is emphasised. Such sympathy made it possible and much easier for them to establish particular horizontal ties of various kinds.

[125] J. Langebek ed. *Historia Sancti Canuti Regis*, in *Scriptores*, iii, 347.

[126] Some brief reference must be made to the origin of the fraternity of Rochester Cathedral Priory. There are two possible explanations: (1) that something like an Anglo-Saxon gild was transformed into a fraternity after the Norman Conquest; (2) that the fraternity was introduced by Bishop Gundulf. The latter is the more likely for several reasons. First, the earliest records of the fraternity date from Gundulf's time. Secondly the fraternity was fundamentaly concerned with personal links with the monks, in order to share with them in prayers and alms, and this differed from the drinking and dining associations of the earlier gilds. Moreover, the Textus Roffensis uses phraseology reminiscent of the fraternity of Cluny, with which Bec had close ties (see G. Rosser, 'The Anglo-Saxon Gilds', in Blair, *Minsters and Parish Churches*, 31–34; T. Sekiguch, 'Confraternity with Cluny in the High Middle Ages', *The Studies in Western History*, 105, 1977, 1–20, esp. 18 (written in Japanese); D. Knowles, *The Monastic Order in England*, 2nd edn, Cambridge 1963, 124. The influence of Bec upon Rochester has been shown by R. A. L. Smith who emphasises Gundulf's role: 'following the precedent which Lanfranc had established at Canterbury Gundulf stood in *loco abbatis* to the monks. He was *rector* and *persona* of the cathedral church and monastery. To these monks, zealous in the performance of the Divine Office, Lanfranc almost certainly sent his *Statuta* – those monastic constitutions based on the *Consuetudines ecclesiae Beccensis* which were so familiar to him and Gundulf at Bec and Caen, whence they were introduced to Christ Church, Canterbury' ('The Place of Gundulf in the Anglo-Norman Church', *EHR*, 58, 1943, 265). Thus we may well talk about the influence of Bec on the introduction of the fraternity into Rochester. Moreover taking into consideration the fact that there was no fraternity in Canterbury Cathedral Priory shortly after the Norman Conquest, we may stress Gundulf's initiative in its introduction. The documents concerned were mainly concentrated in the years when Bishop Gundulf separated the monks' property from his own and confirmed it by royal charter (J. P. Migne ed. *Vita Gundulfi, Patrologia Latina*, 159, 1854, 830). The financial demands might have urged him to the introduction, or he might have felt the need to absorb local figures into the society with the monks and especially to put *Eigenkirchen* under episcopal control, in order to reconstruct his bishopric as the old minster *parochiae* collapsed. In any case, it is to Gundulf and his personality that the fraternity of Rochester Cathedral Priory owed most.